Engraved by H.B. Hall From an Original Drawing by Thomas Nast.

Benj. F. Butler

GENERAL BUTLER IN NEW ORLEANS.

HISTORY OF THE ADMINISTRATION

OF THE

DEPARTMENT OF THE GULF

IN THE YEAR 1862:

WITH

AN ACCOUNT OF THE CAPTURE OF NEW ORLEANS, AND A SKETCH OF THE PREVIOUS CAREER OF THE GENERAL, CIVIL AND MILITARY.

By JAMES PARTON,

AUTHOR OF THE "LIFE AND TIMES OF AARON BURR," "LIFE OF ANDREW JACKSON," ETC., ETC.

NEW YORK:
MASON BROTHERS, 5 & 7 MERCER STREET.
BOSTON: MASON & HAMLIN. PHILADELPHIA: J. B. LIPPINCOTT & CO.
LONDON: D. APPLETON & CO., 16 LITTLE BRITAIN.
1864.

C. A. ALVORD, STEREOTYPER AND PRINTER.

"Whatever they call him, what care I!—
Aristocrat, Democrat, Autocrat,—one
Who can rule and dare not lie."—*Maud.*

PREFACE.

It can not be necessary to apologize for an attempt to relate the history of the most remarkable episode of the war, respecting which opinions so violently contradictory are expressed, both at home and abroad. The vindication of the country itself seems to require that a policy should, at least, be understood, which the country has accepted as just, wise, and humane, and which the enemies of the country, foreign and domestic, denounce as arbitrary, savage, and brutal.

It is, however, of the first necessity to state how this book came to be written, and from what sources its contents have been derived.

In common with the other devotees of the Union and the Flag, I had watched the proceedings of General Butler in Louisiana with interest and approval; and shared also the indignation with which they regarded the perverse misinterpretation put upon his measures by the faction which has involved the Southern States in ruin, and by their "neutral" allies abroad.

Upon the return of General Butler to the North, I wrote to him, saying that I should like to write an account of his administration of the Department of the Gulf, as well as a slighter sketch of the previous military career of a man who, wherever he had been employed, has shown an ability equal to the occasion; but that this could not be done, and ought not to be attempted, without his consent and co-operation.

To this, the general thus replied:

"I am too much flattered by your request, and will endeavor to give you every assistance in the direction you mention. My letter and order books shall be at your disposal, as well as the official and unofficial correspondence directed to me. If I can, by personal conversation, elucidate many matters wherein otherwise history might be a perversion of the truth, I will be at your service.

"One thing I beg shall be understood between us, however (as I have no doubt it would have been without this paragraph), that while I will furnish you with every possible facility to learn everything done by me in New Orleans and elsewhere, it will be upon the express condition that you shall report it in precisely the manner you may choose, without the slightest sense of obligation 'aught to extenuate' because of the source from which you derive the material of your work; and farther, that no sense of delicacy of position, in relation to myself, shall interfere with the closest investigation of every act alleged to have been done or permitted by me. I will only ask that upon all matters I may have the privilege of presenting to your mind the documentary and other evidences of the fact."

I had not the pleasure of General Butler's personal acquaintance, but our correspondence ended with my going to Lowell, where I lived for a considerable time in the general's own house, and received from him, from his staff, and from Mrs. Butler, every kind of aid they could render for the work proposed. We talked ten hours a day, and lived immersed in the multitudinous papers and letters relating to the events which have excited so much controversy. The general placed at my disposal the whole of those papers and letters, besides giving the most valuable verbal elucidations, and relating many anecdotes previously unrecorded.

Respecting the manner in which the material should be used, he did not then, and has not since, made a single suggestion of any kind. He left me perfectly free in every respect. Nor has he seen a line of the manuscript, nor asked a question about it.

Therefore, while the whole value and the greater part of the interest of this volume are due to the aid afforded by General Butler, he is not to be held responsible for anything in it except his own writings. If I have misunderstood or misinterpreted any event or person, or used the papers injudiciously, at my door let all the blame be laid, for it is wholly my fault.

And farther: I must explicitly declare, that if I have been led to form an unfavorable opinion of the conduct of any person mentioned in these pages, I did not derive that ill opinion from any thing said by him. So far as his own conduct is concerned, General Butler is one of the most candid of men; and he is particularly so with regard to any of his acts which have brought obloquy upon him, or which he may himself regret. It is foreign to his nature to conceal or qualify or justify his own conduct. But with regard to the conduct of others, and especially of his superiors in the government, he is reticent and charitable. To be plain: I have never heard him say a word respecting the persons who are supposed to have thwarted him, or to have been instrumental in his recall, which might not be repeated in their hearing without giving them offense.

I have been solicitous to preserve as much as possible of the remarkable writings of General Butler. He was always at bay in Louisiana. Assailed by consuls, "neutrals," and traitors, whose misrepresentations found their way to Washington, he was continually obliged to defend himself by relating the truth. With what point, humor, and cogency he would do this, the public do not need to be told. Of the three great writers of the war—General Butler, President Lincoln, and Mr. Wilkes, of the *Spirit of the Times*—he had the advantage of a position entirely unique in the history of warfare, and his writings are instinct both with his own originality and the originality of his position. As Mr. Richard Grant White has observed: "General Butler's orders and official correspondence at New Orleans, for hitting the nail square upon the head, and clinching it with a twist of humor, have not been surpassed by any writings of their kind. By reading them, the man weary of the grand style, or fretted with the flippancy of the familiar, may obtain real mental refreshment." These writings, too, contain the heart of the matter. If the United States is right in this great contest, the argument of those compositions is sound, and the measures which they explain were just. If the United States is in the wrong, those writings are fallacious, and those measures were unjustifiable. In word and deed General Butler is, at least, logical.

I have related, at some length, the civil and military career of General Butler previous to the capture of New Orleans. This was chiefly done, that the reader might judge whether such a man as General Butler was before he went to New Orleans was likely to do such things there as the enemies of his country say he did.

It is of the most momentous importance to the future of the United States, that whatever is written respecting this war should be written truly. Upon the class of writers it chiefly devolves to garner up, for our future warning, solace, and instruction, the experience gained by such an appalling expenditure of life and of the means of living. Let us leave all lying, all delusion, all boasting, all unworthy suppressions, to the malignants who know no better. For *us*, the TRUTH, though it blast us. We owe it to the heroic dead, who died that we might more worthily live. We owe it to the living, who are so anxious and so perplexed, through the incompleteness of their knowledge. We owe it to the inconceivable multitude of our brethren and fellow-citizens unborn.

For myself, I can say that every page of this volume has been prepared with the single object of conveying to the reader's mind a correct impression of the facts related.

My grateful acknowledgments are due to Mr. Samuel F. Glenn, advocate, of New Orleans, who relinquished, in my favor, a project he had formed of writing a volume on the same subject. He had made, indeed, some progress in the work, sufficient to render its relinquishment an act of great generosity. I told him that the record of an eye-witness would have a value of its own, not to be affected by publications of another nature; but he kindly preferred to retire from the field, and resume his professional labors in New Orleans.

NEW YORK, *October* 20, 1863.

CONTENTS.

GENERAL BUTLER IN NEW ORLEANS.

CHAPTER I.

GENERAL BUTLER BEFORE THE WAR.

HE came of fighting stock. His father's father, Captain Zephaniah Butler, of Woodbury, Connecticut, fought under General Wolfe at Quebec, and served in the continental army in the war of the revolution. A large, old-fashioned powder-horn, covered with quaint carving, done by this old soldier's own hand and jack-knife, which was slung at his side when he climbed the hights of Quebec, and the sword which he wore during the war for independence, now hang in the library of General Butler at Lowell, the relics of an honorable career. The mother of General Butler descends from the Cilleys of New Hampshire, a doughty race of Scotch-Irish origin; one of whom fought at the battle of the Boyne on the wrong side. That valiant Colonel Cilley, who at the battle of Bennington commanded a company that had never seen a cannon, and who, to quiet their apprehensions, sat astride of one while it was discharged, was an ancestor of our general. Mr. Cilley, member of congress from Maine, who was shot in a memorable duel, twenty-five years ago, was the general's cousin. Thus the tide that courses the veins of Benjamin Franklin Butler is composed, in about equal parts, of that blood which we call Anglo-Saxon, and of that strenuous fluid which gives such tenacity and audacity to the Scotch-Irish. Such a mixture affords promise of a mitigated Andrew Jackson or of a combative Benjamin Franklin.

The father of General Butler was John Butler, of Deerfield, New Hampshire; captain of dragoons during the war of 1812; a faithful soldier who served for a while under General Jackson at New

Orleans, and there conceived such love for that tough old hero, as to name his first boy Andrew Jackson. After the war, he engaged in the West India trade, sailing sometimes as supercargo, sometimes as merchant, sometimes as captain of the schooner, enjoying for several years a moderate sufficient prosperity. In politics, a democrat, of the pure Jeffersonian school; and this at a time when in New Hampshire to be a democrat was to live under a social ban. He was one of the few who gave gallant support to young Isaac Hill, of the New Hampshire Patriot, the paper which at length brought the state into democratic line. He was a friend, personal as well as political, of Isaac Hill, and shared with him the odium and the fierce joy of those early contests with powerful and arrogant federalism. A 'hearted' democrat was Captain Butler; one whose democracy was part of his religion. In Deerfield, where he lived, there were but eight democratic voters, who formed a little brotherhood, apart from their fellow townsmen, shunned by the federalists as men who would have been dangerous from their principles if they had not been despicable from their fewness. His boys, therefore, were born into the ranks of an abhorred but positive and pugnacious minority—a little spartan band, always battling, never subdued, never victorious.

In March, 1819, Captain Butler, while lying at one of the West India Islands with his vessel, died of yellow fever, leaving to the care of their mother his two boys, Benjamin being then an infant five months old. A large part of his property he had with him at the time of his death, and little of it ever found its way to his widow. She was left to rear her boys as best she could, with slender means of support. But it is in such circumstances that a New England mother shows the stuff she is made of. Capable, thrifty, diligent, devoted, Mrs. Butler made the most of her means and opportunities, and succeeded in giving to one of her boys a good country education, and helped the other on his way to college, and to a liberal profession. She lives still, to enjoy in the success of both of them, the fruit of her self-denying labors and wise management; they proud to own that to her they owe whatever renders them worthy of it, and thanking God that she is near them to dignify and share their honors and their fortune.

Of late, the world has heard a good deal of that variety of the human being called the YANKEE. Our Southern ex-brethren have bestowed much strong language upon him. Mr. Russell, of the *London Times*, has given him passing notice. Some orations have been pronounced upon him, and numberless anecdotes told of him. He has, also, as usual, had something to say upon the subject himself; for the Yankee, I regret to say, is somewhat given to boasting of the qualities and exploits of his race. The various accounts do not harmonize. If Dr. Bellows regards the Yankee as the consummate man, Jefferson Davis considers him a companion less desirable than the hyena. It is with the Yankee as with other noted personages, the more that is printed about them, the more difficult it becomes to get any knowledge of them. In these circumstances, it may be edifying to some readers to have a recent specimen of this curious and renowned people caught and examined; his growth and formation briefly narrated; his peculiarities and capabilities noted. General Butler is a Yankee. He has traits which are peculiar to himself and to his family; but in the great outlines, both of his career and of his character, he shows himself a Yankee of that type, of which his namesake, Benjamin Franklin, is the perfect and immortal example. Behold, then, in the paragraphs following, the process by which a Yankee becomes the creature we find him in these very days now passing over us.

General Butler was born at Deerfield, an agricultural town of NewHampshire, on Guy Faux day, the fifth of November, 1818.

The fatherless boy was small, sickly, tractable, averse to quarrels, and happy in having a stout elder brother to take his part. Reading and writing seem to come by nature in New England, for few of that country can recollect a time when they had not those accomplishments. The district school helped him to spelling, figures, a little geography, and the rudiments of grammar. He soon caught that passion for reading which seizes some New England boys, and sends them roaming and ravaging in their neighborhood for printed paper. His experience was like that of his father's friend, Isaac Hill, who limped the country round for books, reading almanacs, newspapers, tracts, "Law's Serious Call," the Bible, fragments of histories, and all printed things that fell in his way. The boy hunted for books as some boys hunt for birds'-nests and early apples; and, in the great scarcity of the article, read the few he had so often as to learn large portions of them by heart; devouring with special eagerness the story of the revolution, and all tales of battle and adventure. The Bible was his mother's sufficient library, and the boy pleased her by committing to memory long passages; once, the whole book of Matthew. His memory then, as always, was something wonderful. He can, at this hour, repeat more poetry, perhaps, than any other person in the country who has not made the repeating of poetry a profession. His mother, observing this gift, and considering the apparent weakness of his constitution, early conceived the desire of giving him a liberal education, cherishing also the fond hope, as New England mothers would in those days, that her boy would be drawn to enter the ministry.

One chilly morning in November, 1821, when he was in his fourth year, half a dozen sharp-eyed Boston gentlemen, Nathan Appleton being one of them, might have been seen (but were not) tramping about in the snow near the Falls of the Merrimac. There was a hamlet near by of five or six houses, and a store, but these gentlemen wandered along the banks of the river among the rocks and trees, unobserved, conversing with animation. The result of that morning's walk and talk was the city of Lowell, now a place of forty thousand inhabitants, with thirteen millions invested in cotton and woolen mills, and two hundred thousand dollars a month paid in wages to operatives. In 1828, when our young friend was ten years old, and Lowell was a thriving town of two thousand inhabitants, his mother removed thither with her boys.

It was a fortunate move for them all. The good mother was enabled to increase her income by taking a few boarders, and her book-loving son had better schools to attend, and abundant books at command. He improved these opportunities, graduating from a common school to the high school, and, at a later day, preparing for college at the academy of Exeter in his native state.

As the time approached for his entering college, the question was anxiously discussed in the family, What college? Probably one half the boys in the United States, even in those piping times of peace, had a lurking desire to enter the military academy at West Point. At present, *every* boy has such a desire, except those who prefer the naval school at Newport. Perhaps the boys are right. In those institutions the fundamental conditions of manly education are complied with in a respectable degree. There is physical training; there is science; there modern languages have their proper place; there drawing and dancing, riding and fencing are taught; there is due suppression of those rooted obstacles to all useful acquisition, Latin and Greek; there is that sweet and noble thing, so dear to ingenuous youth, DISCIPLINE; there, if anywhere, a rude cub of a boy can be transformed into that beautiful creature, the true fighting animal, but the man nowhere out of place—a Gentleman! In them, too, the education that fits a man for life proceeds simultaneously with that which prepares him for his profession—schooling and apprenticeship going hand in hand—which is the only system by which any considerable proportion of the youth of a country can ever be liberally educated. Would that venerable Harvard, venerable Yale, Amherst, Williams, Columbia, and the rest, would heed the lessons the times are teaching us, and place themselves, by a sweeping revolution, upon a footing worthy of the age, and prepare to give the education which the youth of the country are so eager to receive. If existing institutions refuse it, a hundred West Points will spring into being, and the glory of the good old colleges will depart for ever.

The boy was decided in favor of West Point. Nor was a cadetship unattainable, in the days of Jackson and Isaac Hill, to the son of Captain John Butler. But the cautious mother hesitated. She feared he would forget his religion, and disappoint her dream of seeing him in the pulpit of a Baptist church. She consulted her minister upon the subject. He agreed with her, and recommended Waterville college, in Maine, recently founded by the Baptists, with a special view to the education of young men for the ministry. It promised, also, the advantage of a manual labor department, in which the youth, by working three hours a day, could earn part of his expenses. At Waterville, moreover, there could be no danger of the student's neglecting religion, since the great object of the college was the inculcation of religion, and all the influences of the place were religious. The president himself was a clergyman, several of the professors were clergymen. Attendance at church on Sundays was compulsory, and there was even a fine of ten cents for every unexcused absence from prayers. With such safeguards, what danger could there be to the religious principles instilled into the mind of the young man from his earliest childhood? Thus argued the minister. The mother gave heed to his opinions, and the youth was consigned to Waterville.

He was a slender lad of sixteen, small of stature, health infirm, of fair complexion, and hair of reddish brown; his character conspicuously shown in the remarkable form of his head. Over his eyes an immense development of the perceptive powers, and the upper forehead retreating almost like that of a flat-head Indian. A youth of keen vision, fiery, inquisitive, fearless; nothing yet developed in him but ardent curiosity to know, and perfect memory to retain. Phrenologists would find proof of their theory in comparing the portrait of the youth with the well-rounded head of the man mature, his organs developed by a quarter of a century of intense and constant use of them. His purse was most slenderly furnished. His mother could afford him little help. A good New Hampshire uncle gave him some assistance now and then, and he worked his three hours a day in the manual labor department at chair-making, earning wages ridiculously small. He was compelled to remain in debt for a considerable part of his college expenses.

Mr. Carlyle observes that the natural history of a hawk written by a sparrow could not be flattering to the hawk. Nor could it be just. Sedate and orthodox professors are the natural prey of a lad like this, born into a minority, trained to the audacious advocacy of unpopular opinions, and accustomed to regard the powers that be in the light of objects of attack. I fear, therefore, that the college career of this student, if it should be related by his instructors, would not present him to us in a favorable light. Perhaps, there is something in the clerical character and training which, in some degree, disqualify a man for gaining an ascendency over the minds of youth. The example of Arnold may be cited against such an opinion, but Arnold was an exceptional man, in an exceptional sphere.

The professors attached to New England colleges present certain varieties of character and position:—The president, a grave and awful Doctor of Divinity, highest in place, sometimes lowest in accomplishment, owing his appointment to his ecclesiastical importance rather than to his learning; sometimes the butt of the college, often deeply loved and venerated. There is the professor renowned beyond the college walls, its advertisement and boast, not always highly valued in the class-room. There is the absorbed professor, book-worm and devotee of his subject, who knows not the name of the president of the United States, and never heard of Dickens and

Thackeray. There is the unpopular professor, a prying, meddling gentleman, keen in the scent of a furtive cigar, prompt to appear at the moment he is least expected and desired. There is the beloved professor, the students' gentle friend and father, whom to insult or annoy rouses the retributive wrath of the whole class. There is the professor of doubtful scholarship, often wrong in his dicta, the tortured victim of the knowing ones, who have explored the shallows of his mind, and know what questions he cannot answer. There is the dandy professor, deliverer of flowery orations, or of sermons trivial and showy. There is the professor who is writing a book, and gets students of the softer sort to copy for him. There is the professor who once wrote an article for the "North American Review," and gives the number containing it to his favorites. There is the foreign-born professor of immense learning, not too fond of attending morning prayers, totally unable to keep order in his class. And there is the lynx-eyed professor, whom no one attempts to cheat; and the absent-minded professor, who sits cogitating his next sermon, regardless of the written translation, or the forbidden "key."

Waterville was a young college, but it could boast most of these varieties; and to as many as there were, our young friend was occasionally an affliction. Most of them were clergymen and theologians more than they were instructors of youth; their object being to make good Baptists as well as good scholars.

But the college was of vast benefit to our young friend, as any college must have been, conducted in the interests of virtue, and attended by a hundred and seventy-five young men from the simple and industrious homes of New England; most of them eager to improve, and perfectly aware that upon themselves alone depended the success of their future career. If he was prone to undervalue some parts of the college course, he made most liberal use of the college library. He was an omnivorous reader. All the natural sciences were interesting to him, particularly chemistry; and his fondness for such studies inclined him long to choose the medical profession. No student went better prepared to the class-room of the professor of natural philosophy.

Seduced by his example, there arose a party in the college opposed to the regular course of studies, advocates of an unregulated *browse* among the books of the library, each student to read only such subjects as interested him. There was a split in the Literary Society. Of the retiring body, after immense electioneering, young Butler was elected president, and the question was then debated with extreme earnestness for several weeks, whether the mind would fare better by confining itself to the college routine, or by reading whatever it had appetite for. I know not which party carried the day; but our friend was foremost in maintaining both by speech and example, that knowledge was knowledge, however obtained, and that the mind could get most advantage by partaking of the kind of nutriment it craved. He laid a wager with a noted plodder of the college, that he would continue for a given term his desultory reading, and yet beat him in the regular lessons of the class. The wager was won by an artifice. He did continue his desultory reading, as well as his desultory wanderings about the country, but late at night, when all the college slept, he spent some hours in vigorous *cram* for the next day's lesson. His memory was such, that he found it easier to commit to memory such lessons as "Wayland's Moral Philosophy," than to prepare them in the usual way. He astonished his plodding friend one day, by repeating thirteen pages of Wayland, without once hesitating.

He came into collision with his reverend instructors on a point of college discipline. The fine of ten cents imposed for absence from prayers, was a serious matter to a young gentleman naturally averse to getting up before daylight, and who earned not more than two or three ten cent pieces daily in the chair shop. But it was not of the fine that he complained. It was a rule of the college, that the fine should carry with it a loss of standing in class. This our student esteemed unjust, and he thought he had good reason to complain since, though, upon the whole, a good scholar, he was always on the point of expulsion from the loss of marks for his morning delinquency. He took an opportunity, at length, to protest against this apparent injustice in a highly audacious and characteristic manner. One of the professors, a distinguished theologian, preached in the college church, a sermon of the severest Calvinistic type, in the course of which he maintained propositions like these: 1. The Elect, and the Elect alone, will be saved. 2. Of the people commonly called Christians, probably not more than one in a hundred will be saved. 3. The heathen have a better chance of salvation than the inhabitants of Christian countries who neglect their opportunities. Upon these hints, the young gentleman spake. He drew up a petition to the faculty, couched in the language of profound respect, asking to be excused from further attendance at prayers and sermons, on the grounds so ably sustained in the discourse of the preceding Sunday. If, he said, the doctrine of that sermon was sound, of which he would not presume to entertain a doubt, he was only preparing for himself a future of more exquisite anguish by attending religious services. He begged to be allowed to remind the faculty, that the church in which the sermon was preached, had usually a congregation of six hundred persons, nine of whom were his revered professors and tutors; and as only one in a hundred of ordinary Christians could be saved, three even of the faculty, good men as all of them were, were inevitably damned. Could he, a mere student, and not one of the most exemplary, expect to be saved before his superiors? Far be from him a thought so presumptuous. Shakspeare himself had intimated that the lieutenant cannot expect salvation before his military superior. Nothing remained, therefore, for him but perdition. In this melancholy posture of affairs, it became him to beware of hightening his future torment by listening to the moving eloquence of the pulpit, or availing himself of any of the privileges of religion. But here he was met by the college laws, which compelled attendance at chapel and church; which imposed a pecuniary fine for non-attendance, and entailed a loss of the honors due to his scholarship. Threatened thus with damnation in the next world, bankruptcy and disgrace in this, he implored the merciful consideration of the faculty, and asked to be excused from all further attendance at prayers and at church.

This unique petition was drawn with the utmost care, and the reasoning fully elaborated. Handsomely copied, and folded into the usual form of important public documents, it was sent to the president. The faculty did not take the joke. Before the whole college in chapel assembled, the culprit standing, he was reprimanded for irreverence. It was rumored at the time, that he narrowly escaped expulsion. He had a friend or two in the faculty who, perhaps, could forgive the audacity of the petition, for the sake of its humor.

It must be owned, that the Calvinistic theology in vogue at Waterville, did not commend itself to the mind of this young man.

He was formed by nature to be an antagonist; and youth is an antagonist regardless of remote consequences. At West Point he would have battled for his hereditary tenets against all who had questioned them. At Waterville, nothing pleased him better than to measure logic with the staunchest doctor of them all. It chanced toward the close of his college course, that the worthy president of the institution delivered a course of lectures upon miracles, maintaining these two propositions: 1. If the miracles are true, the gospel is of Divine origin and authority. 2. The miracles are true, because the apostles, who must have known whether they were true or false, proved their belief in their truth by their martyrdom. At the close of each discourse, the lecturer invited the class to offer objections. Young Butler seized the opportunity with alacrity, and plied the doctor hard with the usual arguments employed by the heterodox. He did not fail to furnish himself with a catalogue of martyrs who had died in the defense, and for the sole sake of dogmas now universally conceded to be erroneous. All religions, he said, boasted their army of martyrs; and martyrdom proved nothing—not even the absolute sincerity of the martyr. And as to the apostles, Peter notoriously denied his Lord, Thomas was an avowed skeptic, James and John were slain to please the Jews, and the last we heard of Paul was, that he was living in his own hired house, commending the government of Nero. The debate continued day after day, our youth cramming diligently for each encounter, always eager for the fray. He chanced to find in the village a copy of that armory of unbelief, "Taylor's Diegesis of the New Testament;" and from this, he and his comrades secretly drew missives to let fly at the president after lecture. The doctor maintained his ground ably and manfully, little thinking that he was contending, not with a few saucy students, but with the accumulated skeptical ingenuity of centuries.

All this, I need scarcely say, was mere intellectual exercise and sport. The youth came out of college as good a Christian as he went in. Christianity, hardened down into a system of opinions, has long been an object of criticism; every young and fearless intellect, during the last century and a half, has tried itself upon it. Christianity, as a controller of action, as organized Virtue, as the benign inspirer of motives, as the tamer of the human savage, as the weekly monitor and rest, rescuer of a whole day in seven from the routine of toil, ten years of possible millennium in every unabbreviated life—who has ever quarreled with that? I suppose our student would have heartily subscribed the remark of John Adams, in one of those delightful letters of his old age to Mr. Jefferson, upon the materialistic controversy. "You and I," said the old man, "have as much authority to settle these disputes as Swift, Priestley, Dupuis, or the Pope; and if you will agree with me, we will issue our bull, and enjoin it upon all these gentlemen to be silent, until they can tell us what matter is, and what spirit is, and, *in the meantime*, to observe the commandments and the Sermon on the Mount."

His college course was done. He would have graduated with honor, if his standing as a scholar had not been lost through his delinquencies as a rebel. As it was, it was touch-and-go, whether he could be permitted to graduate at all. He was, however, assigned a low place in the graduating class, and bore off as good a piece of parchment as the best of them. He had outlived his early preference for the medical profession. In one of his last years at college, he had witnessed in court a well-contested trial, and as he marked with admiration the skillful management of the opposing counsel, and shared the keen excitement of the strife, he said to himself: "*This* is the work for me." He left college in debt, and with health impaired. He weighed but ninety-seven pounds. In all the world, there was no one to whom he could look for help, save himself alone.

Yet, in the nick of time, he found a friend who gave him just the aid he needed most. It was an uncle, captain of a fishing schooner, one of those kind and brave old sailors of Yankee land, who, for two hundred years, have roamed the northern seas in quest of something to keep the pot boiling on the rock-bound shores of Home. The good-hearted captain observed the pale visage and attenuated form of his nephew. "Come with me, lad, to the coast of Labrador, and heave a line this summer. I'll give you a bunk in the cabin, but you must do your duty before the mast, watch and watch, like a man. I'll warrant you'll come back sound enough in the fall." Thus, the ancient mariner. The young man went to the coast of Labrador; hove a line; ate the flesh and drank the oil of cod; came back, after a four months' cruise, in perfect health, and had not another sick day in twenty years. His constitution developed into the toughest, the most indefatigable compound of brain, nerve and muscle lately seen in New England. A gift of twenty thousand dollars had been a paltry boon in comparison with that bestowed upon him by this worthy uncle.

He returned to Lowell in his twentieth year, and took hold of life with a vigorous grasp. The law office which he entered as a student was that of a gentleman who spent most of his time in Boston, and from whom he received not one word of guidance or instruction; nor felt the need of one. He read law with all his might, and began almost immediately to practice a little in the police courts of Lowell, conducting suits brought by the factory girls against the mill corporations, and defending petty criminal cases; glad enough to earn an occasional two dollar fee. The presiding justice chanced to be a really learned lawyer and able man, and thus this small practice was a valuable aid to the student. Small indeed were his gains, and sore his need. One six months of his two years' probation, he taught a public school in Lowell, in order to procure decent clothing; and he taught it well, say his old pupils. What with his school, his law studies, and his occasional practice, he worked eighteen hours in the twenty-four.

At this time he joined the City Guard, a company of that Sixth regiment of Massachusetts militia, so famous in these years for its bloody march through Baltimore. Always fond of military pursuits and exercises, he has served in every grade—private, corporal, sergeant, third lieutenant, second lieutenant, first lieutenant, captain, major, lieutenant-colonel, colonel, and brigadier-general; making it a point to hold every one of these positions in due succession. For many years, the drills, parades and annual encampings of his regiment were the only recreation for which he would find leisure—much to the wonder of his professional friends, who were wont, in the old, peaceful times, to banter him severely upon what seemed to them a rather ridiculous foible. "What a fool you are," they would say, "to spend so much time in marching around town in soldier-clothes!" This young gentleman, however, was one of those who take hold of life as they find it; not disdaining the duties of a citizen of a free country, but rejoicing in them, and making them serve his purposes, as they should. There is a 'set' in Massachusetts who hold aloof from the homely, vigorous life around them, contemplating the world from library windows, and reserving all their sympathies for other and distant civilizations—to their own infinite and irreparable damage. Our young student-at-law was not, and could not be one of these. He took much of his knowledge, not diluted and corrupted by literary decoction, but at the original sources—in the street, the police court, the school-room, the political meeting, the parade ground, and grew, at least, *robust* upon that fresh, substantial fare.

A trifling incident of these early years marks at once the Yankee and the man. That every-day wonder of the modern world, a locomotive, was then first seen at Lowell. Many of us remember seeing our first locomotive, and how we comported ourselves on the interesting occasion. Our young lawyer behaved thus: In company with his friend, the engineer, he visited the wondrous engine at its own house, and spent five hours in studying it, questioning both it and its master until he understood the why and the wherefore of every part, and felt competent to navigate the machine to Boston. This small anecdote contains the essence of old New England; which is expressed, also, in one of the country exclamations: "*I want to know!*"

I thought I had a very pretty story to tell here of the manner in which our young student-at-law won the affections of the Lowell mill-girls: How one of the girls brought a suit against a wealthy corporation of mill-owners for a small sum of disputed wages, and employed Mr. B. F. Butler to prosecute her claim: How he looked about the mills of the company to find a piece of property to "attach," of "about the value" of the amount demanded: How he could not attach the real estate of the company, because that would have entailed upon him the necessity of giving a bond for an odd million or so, which neither he nor his client could do; and how the same difficulty arose when he proposed to lay the sheriff's paralyzing hand upon the looms, or even upon one of them: How he fixed, at length, upon the water-wheel of the principal mill, and placed a keeper in charge of the same, to forbid its making a single revolution until his client was satisfied: How the managers of the mill were brought to reflection by this maneuver, and hastened to compromise with the girl; and how the ingenuity and audacity of the young student called the attention of the whole community of girls to his talents, and caused him to be employed in all their little suits against the mill-owners, and so gave him an excellent start in his profession.

The story has been told and printed a thousand times, and it is to this day one of the stock anecdotes of Lowell. General Butler informs me, however, that the story is totally destitute of truth. No event at all resembling it has ever occurred in his career. Moreover, the *ruse* is a legal impossibility.

In 1840, being then twenty-two years of age, he was admitted to the bar. An early incident brought him into favor with some of the mill-owners. There was a strike among his friends and patrons, the girls; two or three thousand of whom assembled in a grove near Lowell, to talk over their grievances and organize for their redress. They invited the young lawyer to address them, and he accepted the invitation. It was a unique position for a gentleman of twenty-two, not wanting in the romantic element, to stand before an audience of three thousand young ladies, the well-instructed daughters of New England farmers and mechanics. He gave them sound advice, such as might have come from an older head. Admitting the justice of their claims, he showed the improbability of their obtaining them at a time when labor was abundant, and places in the mills were sought by more girls than could be employed. The mill-owners, he said, could, at that time, allow their mills to stand idle for a considerable period without serious loss—perhaps, even with advantage; but could the girls afford to lose any considerable part of a season's wages? Strikes were always a doubtful, often a desperate measure, and entailed suffering upon the operatives a thousand times greater than the evils for which they sought redress. The time might come when a strike would be the only course left them; but, at present, he counseled other measures. He concluded by strongly advising the girls to return to their work, and endeavor by remonstrance, and, if that failed, by appeals to the legislature, to procure a shorter day and juster compensation. The girls took his advice and returned to work.

The day's work in the mills was then thirteen hours—a literally killing period. Thirteen hours a day in a mill means this: incessant activity from five in the morning until nine in the evening the year round. It means a tired and useless Sunday. It means torpidity or death to all the nobler faculties. It means a white and bloated face, a diseased and languid body, a premature death. As much as to any other man in Massachusetts the subsequent change to eleven hours was owing to "the girl's lawyer," as we shall see in a moment.

His advice to the girls, at their mass-meeting in the grove, was well pleasing to the lords of the mill, some of whom, from this time, gave him occasional employment.

But our young friend remained a democrat—a democrat during the administration of General Jackson—a democrat in *Lowell*, supposed to be the creation of that protective tariff which a democratic majority had reduced and was reducing! It was like living at Cape Cod and voting against the fishing bounties, or in Louisiana and opposing the sugar duty. And this particular democrat was a man without secrets and without guile; positive, antagonistic and twenty-two; a friend and disciple of Isaac Hill, and one who had seen that little lame hero of democracy assaulted by the huge Upham in the streets of Exeter, with feelings *not* unutterable. In such odium were his opinions held in Lowell at that time, that he could not appear at the tavern table in court time without being tabooed or insulted. The first day of his sitting at dinner with the bar, the discussion grew so hot that the main business of the occasion was neglected, and he concluded that if he meant to take sustenance at all he must dine elsewhere. He did so for one day; but feeling that such a course looked like abandoning the field, he returned on the day following, and faced the music to the end of the session.

His audacity and quickness stood him in good stead at this period. One of his first cases being called in court, he said, in the usual way, "Let notice be given!"

"In what paper?" asked the aged clerk of the court, a strenuous whig.

"In the *Lowell Advertiser*," was the reply; the *Lowell Advertiser* being a Jackson paper, never mentioned in a Lowell court; of whose mere existence, few there present would confess a knowledge.

"The *Lowell Advertiser?*" said the clerk, with disdainful nonchalance, "I don't know such a paper."

"Pray, Mr. Clerk," said the lawyer, "do not interrupt the proceedings of the court; for if you begin to tell us what you don't know, there will be no time for anything else."

He was always prompt with a retort of this kind. So, at a later day, when he was cross-questioning a witness in not the most respectful manner, and the court interposing, reminded him that the witness was a professor in Harvard college, he instantly replied; "I am aware of it, your honor; we hung one of them the other day."

His politics were not, in reality, an obstacle to his success at the bar, though his friends feared they would be. There are two sides to every suit; and as people go to law to win, they are not likely to overlook an advocate who, besides the ordinary motives to exertion, has the stimulus of political and social antagonism. He won his way rapidly to a lucrative practice, and with sufficient rapidity, to an important, leading, conspicuous practice. He was a bold, diligent, vehement, inexhaustible opponent. He accepted the theory of his profession without limitation or reserve, conceiving it to be his duty to save or serve his client with not the slightest regard to the moral aspects of the matter in dispute. *That* is the concern of the law-maker and the court; the advocate's business, in his opinion, is simply and solely, to serve his client's interests. And if there should be lawyers at all, this is, beyond question, the correct theory of the vocation.

In some important particulars, General Butler surpassed all his contemporaries at the New England bar. His memory was such, that he could retain the whole of the testimony of the very longest trial without taking a note. His power of labor seemed unlimited. In fertility of expedient, and in the lightning quickness of his devices, to snatch victory from the jaws of defeat, his equal has seldom lived. To these gifts, add a perseverance that knew no discouragement, and never accepted defeat while one possibility of triumph remained. One who saw him much at the bar in former times, wrote of him three years ago:

"His devices and shifts to obtain an acquittal and release are absolutely endless and innumerable. He is never daunted or baffled until the sentence is passed and put into execution, and the reprieve, pardon, or commutation is refused. An indictment must be drawn with the greatest nicety, or it will not stand his criticism. A verdict of guilty is nothing to him; it is only the beginning of the case; he has fifty exceptions; a hundred motions in arrest of judgment; and after that the *habeas corpus* and personal replevin. The opposing counsel never begins to feel safe until the evidence is all in;

for he knows not what new dodges Butler may spring upon him. He is more fertile in expedients than any man who practices law among us. His expedients frequently fail, but they are generally plausible enough to bear the test of trial. And faulty and weak as they oftentimes are, Butler always has confidence in them to the last; and when one fails, he invariably tries another. If it were not that there must be an end to everything, his desperate cases would never be finished, for there would be no end to his expedients to obtain his case."

An old friend and fellow-practitioner of General Butler, Mr. J. Q. A. A. Griffin, of Charlestown, Massachusetts, favors the reader with some interesting reminiscences of the general's career at the bar:

"General Butler," he remarks, "has the power possessed by but few men, of attending to several important mental operations at the same time. An incident will show you my meaning:

"In a trial of a quite important matter, in the year 1860, I was counsel on the same side with General Butler. It was a busy season of the year for lawyers like him who always had an overflowing docket. The trial began just after his return from the nomination of Breckinridge. He was to make a report of his doings to his constituents at Lowell. The meeting was called to be held at night. Dissatisfaction existed in the party, and the General therefore must speak with care and consideration. He determined to write what he was to say. But the court began early and sat late. He took his seat in court, and while the adverse party examined their witnesses in chief, he wrote out his speech, apparently absorbed therein. But he cross-examined each witness at great length, with wonderful thoroughness and acuteness, evincing a perfect knowledge, not only of what the witness had said in substance, but when needful, of the phrases in which he had uttered it. At noon, over our dinner, he read over what he had written and made such corrections as were needful, which were quite as few, I thought, as would have been found if the speech had been written in the quiet of his study. In the afternoon he went through the same routine, and at night made his speech. This is but an instance. Amid confusion of transactions, where other men became indecisive, he always saw his way clear. Whatever his occupations, however intently his mind was employed, it was always safe to interrupt him by suggestions or inquiries about the matter in hand, or anything else, for he could answer on the instant, clearly and without the slightest confusion, or distraction of his purpose.

"Unexampled success attended his professional efforts, so characterized by shrewdness and zeal. When the war summoned him from these toils, he had a larger practice than any other man in the state. I have no doubt, he tried four times more causes, at least, than any other lawyer, during the ten years preceding the war. The same qualities which make him efficient in the war, made him efficient as a lawyer. Fertile in resources and stratagem; earnest and zealous to an extraordinary degree; certain of the integrity of his client's cause, and not inclined to criticise or inquire whether it was strictly 'constitutional' or not, but defending the whole line with a boldness and energy that generally carried court and jury alike. His ingenuity is exhaustless. If he makes a mistake in speech or action, it has no sinister effect, for the reason that he will himself discover and correct the error, before any 'barren spectator' has seized upon it.

"He is faithful and tenacious to the last degree. There is no possibility of treachery in his conduct. 'He would not betray the devil to his fellow.' Every other prominent Massachusetts democrat, when it became profitable to do so, condemned a previous coalition that had been entered into between them and the free-soilers after they had taken and consumed its fruits. General Butler's political interests strongly urged him to the same dishonor. But he never hesitated an instant, and uniformly justified the coalition, and openly defended it in every presence and to the most unwilling ears. In his personal relations the same traits are observable. He is quite too ready, I have sometimes thought, to *forgive* (he never forgets) injuries, but his memory never fails as to his friends.

"'The basis of Napoleon's character,' says Gourgand, 'was a pleasant humor.' 'And a man who jests,' continues Victor Hugo, 'at important junctures, is on familiar terms with events.'

"A pleasant humor and a lively wit, and their constant exercise, are the possession and the habit of General Butler. Everybody has his anecdote of him. Let me refer to one anecdote of him in this respect, and that shall suffice for the hundreds that I might recall.

"The general was a member of our house of representatives

one year, when his party was in a hopeless and impotent minority, except on such occasions as he contrived to make it efficient by tactics and stratagems of a technical, parliamentary character. The speaker was a whig, and a thorough partisan. The whigs were well drilled and had a leader on the floor of very great capacity, Mr. Lord, of Salem. During one angry debate, General Butler attempted to strangle an obnoxious proposal of the majority by tactics. Accordingly he precipitated upon the chair divers questions of order and regularity of proceeding, one after the other. These were debated by Mr. Lord and himself, and then decided by the speaker uniformly according to the notions advanced by Mr. Lord. The general bore this for some time without special complaint, contenting himself with raising new questions. At length, however, he called special attention to the fact that he had been overruled so many times by the chair, within such a space of time, and that, as often, not only had the speaker adopted the result of Mr. Lord's suggestions, but generally had accepted the same words in which to announce it; and, said he, 'Mr. speaker, I cannot complain of these rulings. They doubtless seem to the speaker to be just. I perceive an anxiety on your part to be just to the minority and to me, by whom at this moment they are represented, for, like Saul, on the road to Damascus, your constant anxiety seems to be, LORD, what wilt *thou* have me to do?'

"No man in America can remember facts, important and unimportant, like General Butler. Whatever enters his mind remains there for ever. And his knowledge, as I have said, is available the instant it is needed, without confusion or tumult of thought. The testimony delivered through days of dreary trials, without minutes or memoranda of any kind, he could recall in fresher and more accurate phrases, remembering always the substance, and generally all the important expressions, with far more precision than the other counsel and the court could gather it from their 'writing books,' wherein they had endeavored to record it. Practice for a long series of years had so disciplined his mind in this respect that I think it quite impossible for him to forget. And as he has mingled constantly with every business and interest of humanity since he was admitted to the bar, he has become possessed of a marvelous extent and variety of knowledge respecting the affairs of mankind."

These passages, written by men conversant with the bar of

Massachusetts, and who knew him before he had become known to the nation, are better for our purpose than the observations of later friends. They illustrate the main position, that General Butler used *all* the means known to the law to get his cases, leaving the *whole* responsibility of maintaining justice to those who made and those who administered the laws.

One example of what a writer styles General Butler's legerdemain. A man in Boston, of respectable connections and some wealth, being afflicted with a mania for stealing, was, at length, brought to trial on four indictments; and a host of lawyers were assembled, engaged in the case, expecting a long and sharp contest. It was hot summer weather; the judge was old and indolent; the officers of the court were weary of the session, and anxious to adjourn. General Butler was counsel for the prisoner. It is a law in Massachusetts, that the repetition of a crime by the same offender, within a certain period, shall entail a severer punishment than the first offense. A third repetition, involves more severity, and a fourth, still more. According to this law, the prisoner, if convicted on all four indictments, would be liable to imprisonment in the penitentiary, for the term of sixty years. As the court was assembling, General Butler remonstrated with the counsel for the prosecution, upon the rigor of their proposed proceedings. Surely, one indictment would answer the ends of justice; why condemn the man to imprisonment for life for what was, evidently, more a disease than a crime? They agreed, at length, to quash three of the indictments, on condition that the prisoner should plead guilty to the one which charged the theft of the greatest amount. The prisoner was arraigned.

"Are you guilty, or not guilty?"

"Say guilty, sir," said General Butler, from his place in the bar, in his most commanding tone.

The man cast a helpless, bewildered look at his counsel, and said nothing.

"Say guilty, sir," repeated the General, looking into the prisoner's eyes.

The man, without a will, was compelled to obey, by the very constitution of his infirm mind.

"Guilty," he faltered, and sunk down into his seat, crushed with a sense of shame.

"Now, gentlemen," said the counsel for the prisoner, "have I, or have I not, performed my part of the compact?"

"You have."

"Then perform yours."

This was done. A *Nol. Pros.* was duly entered upon the three indictments. The counsel for the prosecution immediately moved for sentence.

General Butler then rose, with the other indictment in his hand, and pointed out a flaw in it, manifest and fatal. The error consisted in designating the place where the crime was committed.

"Your honor perceives," said the general, "that this court has no jurisdiction in the matter. I move that the prisoner be discharged from custody."

Ten minutes from that time, the astounded man was walking out of the court-room free.

The flaw in the indictment, General Butler discovered the moment after the compact was made. If he had gone to the prisoner, and spent five minutes in inducing him to consent to the arrangement, the sharp opposing counsel, long accustomed to his tactics, would have suspected a ruse, and eagerly scanned the indictment. He relied, therefore, solely on the power which a man, with a will, has over a man who has none, and so merely commanded the plea of guilty. The court, it is said, not unwilling to escape a long trial, laughed at the maneuver, and complimented the successful lawyer upon the excellent "discipline" which he maintained among his clients.

This was a case of legal "legerdemain." Many of General Butler's triumphs, however, were won after long and perfectly contested struggles, which fully and legitimately tested his strength as a lawyer. Perhaps, as a set-off to the case just related, I should give one of the other description.

A son of one of the general's most valued friends made a voyage to China as a sailor before the mast, and returned with his constitution ruined through the scurvy, his captain having neglected to supply the ship with the well-known antidotes to that disease, lime juice and fresh vegetables. A suit for damages was instituted on the part of the crew against the captain. General Butler was retained to conduct the cause of the sailors, and Mr. Rufus Choate defended the captain. The trial lasted nineteen working days.

General Butler's leading positions were: 1. That the captain was bound to procure fresh vegetables if he could; and, 2. That he could. In establishing these two points, he displayed an amount of learning, ingenuity and tact, seldom equaled at the bar. The whole of sanitary science and the whole of sanitary law, the narratives of all navigators and the usages of all navies, reports of parliamentary commissions and the diaries of philanthropical investigators, ancient log-books and new treatises of maritime law; the testimony of mariners and the opinions of physicians, all were made tributary to his cause. He exhibited to the jury a large map of the world, and, taking the log of the ship in his hand, he read its daily entries, and as he did so, marked on the map the ship's course, showing plainly to eye of the jury, that on four different occasions, while the crew were rotting with the scurvy, the ship passed within a few hours' sail of islands, renowned in all those seas for the abundance, the excellence, and the cheapness of their vegetables. Mr. Choate contested every point with all his skill and eloquence. The end of the daily session was only the beginning of General Butler's day's work; for there were new points to be investigated, other facts to be discovered, more witnesses to be hunted up. He rummaged libraries, he pored over encyclopedias and gazetteers, he ferreted out old sailors, and went into court every morning with a mass of new material, and followed by a train of old doctors or old salts to support a position shaken the day before. In the course of the trial, he had on the witness-stand nearly every eminent physician in Boston, and nearly every sea-captain and ship-owner. Justice and General Butler triumphed. The jury gave damages to the amount of three thousand dollars; an award which to-day protects American sailors on every sea.

Such energy and talent as this, could not fail of liberal reward. After ten years of practice at Lowell, with frequent employment in Boston courts, General Butler opened an office in Boston, and thenceforward, in conjunction with a partner in each city, carried on two distinct establishments. For many years he was punctual at the depot in Lowell at seven in the morning, summer and winter; at Boston soon after eight; in court at Boston from half past nine till near five in the afternoon; back to Lowell, and to dinner at half past six; at his office in Lowell from half past seven till midnight, or later. When the war broke out, he had the most lucrative practice in New England—worth, at a moderate estimate, eighteen thousand dollars a year. At the moment of his leaving for the scene of war, the list of cases in which he was retained numbered five hundred. Happily married at an early age to a lady, in whom are united the accomplishments which please, and the qualities that inspire esteem, blessed with three affectionate children, he enjoyed at his beautiful home, on the lofty banks of the tumbling Merrimac, a most enviable domestic felicity. At the age of forty, though he had lived liberally, he was in a condition to retire from business if he had so chosen.

Such particulars, in an ordinary sketch of a living man, would, perhaps, be out of place. In the present instance they constitute part of the case. I hold this opinion: that no man is fit to be entrusted with public affairs who has not successfully managed his own. And this other opinion: the fact that a man *has* conducted his own affairs with honorable success is a reason for believing that his management of public affairs has been just and wise.

Mr. Griffin well remarks that a lawyer in great practice as an advocate has peculiar opportunities of acquiring peculiar knowledge. That famous scurvy case, for example, made him acquainted with the entire range of sanitary science. A great bank case opens all the mysteries of finance; a bridge case the whole art of bridge building; a railroad case the law and usages of all railroads. A few years ago when General Butler served as one of the examiners at West Point, he put a world of questions to the graduating class upon subjects connected with the military art, indicating unexpected specialities of knowledge in the questioner. "But how did you know anything about that?" his companions would ask. "Oh, I once had a case which obliged me to look into it." This answer was made so often that it became the jocular custom of the committee, when any knotty point arose in conversation, to ask General Butler whether he had not had a *case* involving it. The knowingness and direct manner of this Massachusetts lawyer left such an impression upon the mind of one of the class, (the lamented General George G. Strong,) that he sought service under him in the war five years after. This curious speciality of information, particularly his intimate knowledge of ships, banks, railroads, sanitary science, and engineering, was of the utmost value to him and to the country at a later day.

And now a few words upon the political career of General Butler in Massachusetts. Despite his enormous and incessant labors at the bar, he was a busy and eager politician. From his twentieth year he was wont to stump the neighboring towns at election time, and from the year 1844, never failed to attend the national conventions of his party. Upon all the questions, both of state and national politics, which have agitated Massachusetts during the last twenty years, his record is clear and ineffaceable. Right or wrong, there is not the slightest difficulty in knowing where he has stood or stands. He has, in perfection, what the French call "the courage of opinion;" which a man could not fail to have who has passed his whole life in a minority, generally a hopeless minority, but a minority always active, incisive, and inspired with the audacity which comes of having nothing to lose. I need not remind any American reader that during the last twenty-five years the democratic party in Massachusetts has seldom had even a plausible hope of carrying an election. If ever it has enjoyed a partial triumph, it has been through the operation of causes which disturbed the main issue, and enabled the party to combine with factions temporarily severed from a majority otherwise invincible.

The politics of an American citizen, for many years past, have been divided into two parts: 1. His position on the questions affected by slavery. 2. His position on questions not affected by slavery. Let us first glance at General Butler's course on the class of subjects last named.

As a state politician, then, the record of which lies before me in a heap of pamphlets, reports, speeches, and proceedings of deliberative bodies, I find his course to have been soundly democratic, a champion of fair play and equal rights. In that great struggle which resulted in the passage of the eleven-hour law, he was a candidate for the legislature, on the "ten-hour ticket," and fought the battle with all the vigor and tact which belonged to him. A few days before the election, as he was seated in his office at Lowell, a deputation of workingmen came to him, excited and alarmed, with the news, that a notice had been posted in the mills, to the effect, that any man who voted the Butler ten-hour ticket would be discharged.

"Get out a hand-bill," said the general, "announcing that I will address the workingmen to-morrow evening."

The hall was so crammed with people that the speaker had to be passed in over the heads of the multitude. He began his speech with unwonted calmness, amid such breathless silence as falls upon an assembly when the question in debate concerns their dearest interests—their honor, and their livelihood. He began by saying that he was no revolutionist. How could he be in Lowell, where were invested the earnings of his laborious life, and where the value of all property depended upon the peaceful labors of the men before him? Nor would he believe that the notice posted in the mills was authorized. Some underling had doubtless done it to propitiate distant masters, misjudging them, misjudging the workingmen of Lowell. The owners of the mills were men too wise, too just, or, at least, too prudent, to authorize a measure which absolutely extinguished government; which, at once, invited, justified, and necessitated anarchy. For tyranny less monstrous than this, men of Massachusetts had cast off their allegiance to the king of Great Britain, and plunged into the bloody chaos of revolution; and the directors of the Lowell mills must know that the sons stood ready, at any moment, to do as their sires had done before them. But this he would say: If it should prove that the notice *was* authorized; if men should be deprived of the means of earning their bread for having voted as their consciences directed, then, WOE TO LOWELL! "The place that knows it shall know it no more for ever. To my own house, I, with this hand, will first apply the torch. I ask but this: give me time to get out my wife and children. All I have in the world I consecrate to the flames!"

Those who have heard General Butler speak can form an idea of the tremendous force with which he would utter words like these. He is a man capable of infinite wrath, and, on this occasion, he was stirred to the depths of his being. The audience were so powerfully moved, that a cry arose for the burning of the town that very night, and there was even the beginning of a movement toward the doors. But the speaker instantly relapsed into the tone and line of remark with which he had begun the speech, and concluded with a solemn appeal to every voter present to vote as his judgment and conscience directed, with a total disregard to personal consequences.

The next morning the notice was no more seen. The election passed peacefully away, and the ten-hour ticket was elected. Two priceless hours were thus rescued from the day of toil, and added to those which rest and civilize.

The possibility of high civilization to the whole community—the mere possibility—depends upon these two things: an evening of leisure, and a Sunday without exhaustion. These two, well improved during a whole lifetime, will put any one of fair capacity in possession of the best results of civilization, social, moral, intellectual, esthetic. And this is the meaning and aim of democracy—to secure to all honest people a fair chance to acquire a share of those things, which give to life its value, its dignity, and its joy. Justly, therefore, may we class measures which tend to give the laborer a free evening as democratic.

In the legislature, to which General Butler was twice elected, once to the assembly, and once to the senate, he led the opposition to the old banking system, and advocated that which gives perfect security to the New York bill-holder, and which is often styled the New York system, recently adopted as a national measure. He had the courage, too, to report a bill for compensating the proprietors of the Ursuline convent of Charlestown, destroyed, twenty years ago, by a mob, and standing now a blackened ruin, reproaching the commonwealth of Massachusetts. It is said, that he would have succeeded in getting his bill passed, had not an intervening Sunday given the Calvinistic clergy an opportunity to bring their artillery to bear upon it. He represented Lowell in the convention to revise the constitution of Massachusetts, a few years ago, and took a leading part in its proceedings. With these exceptions, though he has run for office a hundred times, he has figured only in the forlorn hope of the minority, climbing toward the breach in every contest, with as much zeal as though he expected to reach the citadel.

"But why so long in the minority? why could he and Massachusetts never get into accord?" This leads us to consider his position in national politics.

Gentlemen of General Butler's way of thinking upon the one national question of the last twenty years have been styled "pro-slavery democrats." This expression, as applied to General Butler, is calumnious. I can find no utterance of his which justifies it; but on the contrary, in his speeches, there is an evidently purposed avoidance of expressions that could be construed into an approbation of slavery. The nearest approach to anything like an apology for the "institution" which appears in his speeches, is the expression of an opinion, that sudden abolition would be ruin to the master, and a doubtful good to the slave. On the other hand, there is no word in condemnation of slavery. There is even an assumption that with the moral and philanthropic aspects of slavery, we of the north had nothing to do. He avowed the opinion, that we were bound to stand by the compromises of the constitution, not in the letter merely, but in the spirit, and that the spirit of those compromises bound the government to give slavery a chance in the territories.

I have been curious to inquire of Hunker Democrats in Massachusetts how this subject presented itself to their minds in former years, so as to lead them to an opinion violently opposed to the moral feeling of the communities in which they lived. This is the more puzzling, from the fact that many of the ablest of them had not the slightest expectation or desire of political position, but maintained their ground for half a lifetime from the purest conviction. I have read to some of these gentlemen the conversation, published a year or two since, between Commodore Stuart and Mr. Calhoun in 1812, of which the following is the material portion:

Mr. Calhoun: "I admit your conclusion in respect to us Southrons. That we are essentially aristocratic, I cannot deny, but we can and do yield much to democracy. This is our sectional policy; we are, from necessity, thrown upon, and solemnly wedded to that party, however it may occasionally clash with our feelings for the conservation of our interests. It is through our affiliation with that party in the middle and western states that we hold power; but when we cease thus to control this nation, through a disjointed democracy, or any material obstacle in that party which shall tend to throw us out of that rule and control, we shall then resort to the dissolution of the Union. The compromises in the constitution, under the circumstances, were sufficient for our fathers, but under the altered condition of our country from that period, leave to the South no resource but dissolution; for no amendments to the constitution can be reached through a convention of the people under their three-fourths rule."

Commodore Stuart (laughing incredulously), "Well, Mr. Calhoun, ere such can take place, you and I will have been so long *non est*, that we can now laugh at its possibility, and leave it with complacency to our children's children, who will then have the watch on deck."

Here was the southern programme frankly disclosed just fifty years ago. I have, also, pointed out the constantly aggressive policy of the southern leaders; their arrogance, their ceaseless and violent agitation of the slavery question; absolutely *forcing it* upon the northern mind, and constantly supplying the abolitionists of the north with new arguments and new motives. Now, the puzzling question is this: How could men of spirit and discernment, having no political aspirations, submit so long to be *used* by these people for their purposes, and those purposes bad?

Perhaps, I can now throw a little light upon this subject.

Even in the errors of honest men there is something of nobleness. The basis of General Butler's interest in politics, and that of his hunker friends was, and is an entire and fond belief in the principles upon which this government was founded, and an intense desire that the great Experiment should gloriously succeed. Among educated Americans, there are two kinds of men, namely, democrats and snobs. The gentlemen, of whom I speak, are democrats. In the very strength of their attachment to democratic principles, is to be found the cause of their ignoring the claims upon our consideration of the four million black laborers, who earn an important part of the country's revenue. They thought that any question of *their* rights was petty in comparison with the mighty stake of mankind in the union of these states, and the triumph of democratic institutions. The only danger to the Union, as they thought, arose from the agitation of questions respecting slavery, and they strove with all their might to avert or defer it.

Again: The leading democrats of the North were personally acquainted with the leaders of the South, and knew that they were prepared to fight for slavery. Republicans were incredulous on this point, down to the time of the bombardment of Fort Sumter. They were accustomed to laugh at Mr. Buchanan's terrors as those of a weak and timorous old man, and to despise the threats of the southern fire-eaters as the vaporings of demagogues and braggadocios. Democrats knew better. They were perfectly aware that the South was, at all times, ready to take up arms the moment it should feel really alarmed for the safety of the thing they call their 'institution.' As Mr. Choate, one day, was about to make a 'union saving' speech, his partner and son-in-law, Major Bell, said to him:

"Don't you think the people are getting tired of this sort of thing?"

"Yes," said Mr. Choate, "they are perfectly sick of it. They don't believe the Union in danger. But if they knew the South as I know it, they would be more frightened than I am."

Such men as Mr. Choate saw the open abyss, and could see beyond it—*nothing!* The spell of the Union once broken, what could come but chaos? This terror of an *immeasurable* danger; this dread of a convulsion which, having occurred, no man could foresee any probable end of any kind; this look-out upon a sea of difficulty, of which nothing could be known except that it was tempest-tossed, and full of all perils; it was this that made so many honest patriots shut their eyes, on principle, to the moral aspects of slavery questions, and impelled them to concede, and concede, and concede to the slave power. And thus it was, that the very love of freedom worked to the support of slavery.

At the same time, democrats, though they had some external familiarity with slaveholders, knew nothing about slavery. They did not wish to know anything about it. They would not know anything about it. They shut their ears, on principle, to the cry of the slave, the pleading of the abolitionist, and the arguments of the statesmen who strove to keep the giant evil from spreading. How easily the human mind excludes from itself unwelcome knowledge, is known to all who have observed the workings of their own minds.

Besides: If the South used the democratic party, the democratic party used the South. Each was absolutely dependent upon the other for any constitutional success.

And yet again: Democrats, looking at the subject through southern eyes, were compelled to consider questions respecting slavery in a practical manner—as questions affecting the power, the property, the existence of their friends and others. Men of the other party contemplated the subject more in the spirit of a moral essayist; it did not threaten business or firesides; it was something abstract and remote. One party propounded moral truths and philanthropic sentiments; the other had always the question uppermost in their minds: "Well, what is to be *done* about it?"

I do not suppose that the fear of impending danger was consciously present in the mind of General Butler in those years; but it doubtless had its influence. A ruling motive with him was a keen sense of the sacredness of compacts. Add to this a strong, hereditary party spirit, and some willful pleasure in acting with a minority. In his speeches on the slavery question there is candor, force and truth; and their argument is unanswerable, if it be granted that slavery can have any rights whatever not expressly granted by the letter of the constitution. There is nothing in them of base subserviency, nothing of insincerity, nothing uncertain, no vote-catching vagueness.

When the wretched Brooks had committed the assault upon Charles Sumner in the senate chamber, there were men of Massachusetts who, surpassing the craven baseness of Brooks himself gave him a supper, and stooped even to sit at the table and help him to eat it. General Butler, blazing with divine wrath, publicly denounced the act in Washington in such terms as became a man, and called upon Mr. Sumner to express his horror and his sympathy. He saw with his own eyes, and felt with his own hands, that the wounds could only have been given while the senator was bending low over his desk, absorbed and helpless.

When John Brown, the sublime madman, or else the one sane man in a nation mad, had done the deed for which unborn pilgrims will come from afar, to look upon the sod that covers his bones, General Butler spoke at a meeting held in Lowell, to reassure the alarmed people of the South. This speech very fairly represents his habit of thought upon the vexed subject before the war. He spoke in strong reprobation of northern abolitionists, and southern fire-eaters, as men equally guilty of inflaming and misleading their fellow-citizens; so that, at length, it had come to pass, that neither section understood the other. "The mistake," said he, "is mutual. We look at the South through the medium of the abolitionist orators—a very distorted picture. The South see us only as rampant abolitionists, ready to make a foray upon their rights and property."

"It is," he continued, "the province of such meetings as this, which are now being holden throughout the North, to correct on our part this picture of ourselves to our southern brethern, to convince them of the truth, as we believe and know it—that by far the largest portion of the North are true in heart and spirit in their devotion to the Union, and in their determination to carry out the only principles by which its full benefit can be enjoyed in the fair, just and honest fulfillment of every constitutional requirement, both in spirit and in letter, with each state, and to the whole country.

"And let us not be taunted with 'truckling to the South,' or seeking to curry favor by so doing. It is not so; and it is neither correct nor manly so to state it. Let us fairly appreciate the difference of our position. These questions, which to us locally are of so little practical consequence as hardly to call our attention, are to them the very foundations of society—ominous of rapine, murder, and all the horrors of a servile war, in their practical application.

"And because the discussions of the question about negro emancipation do not disquiet us here, we should be blind indeed not to see the wide difference of such discussions to them, if the results are reduced to practice. Then may we not, ought we not, who are so little, as to ourselves, practically interested in this matter, take the first step, if need be, toward allaying their excitement on this subject?

"We claim to be in proportion of fifteen millions of freemen to six millions. Can it fairly be said to be 'truckling,' to hold out to them the hand of amity upon a cause of real or supposed grievances? It would not be so thought amongst belligerent foreign countries. We are the stronger, as we consider ourselves. To make overtures of peace to the weaker ought to be considered our part among friendly states.

"Therefore, I began by saying: 'It is well for us to be gathered here.' Let us proclaim to all men, that the Union, first and foremost of all the good gifts of God, must and shall be preserved. That it is a duty we recognize and will fulfill, to grant to every part of the country its rights as guaranteed by the constitution, and due by the compact. That we will, and every part of the country shall, respect those institutions of every other part of the country, with which they and we have nothing to do, save to let them alone, whether they are palatable to us or not.

"We have the right to form our own domestic institutions as we please, to our own liking, and not to any other community's liking, and will exercise that right, and under the constitution, must be protected in that right. Every other state has the same right to please herself in her own institutions, and is not obliged to please us in her selection of them; and as in duty, and of right bound to do, we will protect her in that right, whether we like them or not.

"Thus doing our duty, and claiming our rights, and granting those of others, as every man will do, who is a just man, and not a thief—must not the union be perpetual? Let no man mistake upon the matter. This Union, this republic, the great experiment of equal rights, this power of self-government by the people, this great instrument of civilization, the banding together of the intellectual and political power of those races which are to civilize the world by their energy of action, is not to fail, and human progress be set back a thousand years, because of the difference of opinion as to the supposed rights and interests of a few negroes.

"As well might the peasant expect the Almighty to stay the thunder storm, which, by its beneficent action, clears the atmosphere of a nation from pestilence, lest the lightning bolt should in its flash kill his cow. This Union is strong enough to take care of itself, to protect each and every part from foreign aggression or internal dissension, to keep everybody in it that is desirable to have in it, to take in everybody that ought to be in it, and to keep out everybody that is not wanted in it.

"It is not like a family, because its members must never separate and divide the homestead. It is not like a partnership, because it contains no elements or period of dissolution. It is not like a confederation, because it contains no clause or means by which one or more of its members can withdraw. It is either organization or chaos. It is possible that it may crumble into atoms. It cannot be split in fragments. A despotism may be erected upon its ruins, but little, snarling, imbecile republics can never be made from its pieces.

"'It is well, then, to be gathered here.' To pledge each other and the South, that we are true to each other and to them. To assure them that we and we alone speak the true voice of the North. That threats of disunion will never terrify us into being just to her and ourselves. That the North shall and will be just to her, because she respects herself as well as the South. To assure her that we appreciate her difficulties, and sympathize with our southern brethren, because we understand the great questions which agitate them. To us here they so little enter into our affairs as to hardly call the attention of any of us who have anything to do, save to annoy our neighbors. Yet to them they are questions of order or anarchy, life or death.

"'It is well, then, to be gathered here.' Again to pledge ourselves to each other, that whenever occasion demands, we will march as one man to protect our beloved country from all dismemberment, and to bury the traitor who shall by overt act attempt it, whether he be a member of the Hartford convention, aggrieved because of a commercial question, or a South Carolinian, aggrieved because of a tariff question, or an abolition incendiary who seeks civil war and bloodshed at Harper's Ferry.

"That to us no 'star in our glorious banner differeth from another star in glory,' but all must and shall shine on together in one constellation, to bless the world with its benign radiance for ever."

Such were the sentiments of General Butler, in February of the year for ever memorable to Americans—1860.

CHAPTER II.

IN THE CHARLESTON CONVENTION.

General Butler was elected a delegate to the democratic convention, held at Charleston, in April, 1860.

He went to Charleston with two strong convictions on his mind. One was, that concessions to the South had gone as far as the northern democracy could ever be induced to sustain. The other was, that the fair nomination of Mr. Douglas, by a national democratic convention was impossible.

When the convention had been organized, by the elections of Mr. Cushing, of Massachusetts, to the chair, a committee was appointed of one member from each state, for the purpose of constructing that most perplexing piece of political joinery, a Platform. In this committee, General Butler represented the state of Massachusetts.

The committee met. May we not say, that in the room which it occupied began the contention which now desolates large portions of the southern country. What transpired in the committee room has been related, with exactness and brevity, by General Butler himself.

"As a member of the committee," he says,* "I felt that I had but one course to pursue,and I held that with unwavering tenacity of purpose. It was to obtain the affirmation of these democratic principles, laid down at Cincinnati, with which we had outrode the storm of sectionalism in 1856. * * * *

"With these views, I proposed, in committee, the following resolution:

"'*Resolved*, That we, the democracy of the Union, in convention assembled, hereby declare our affirmance of the democratic resolutions unanimously adopted and declared as a platform of principles at Cincinnati, in the year 1856, without addition or alteration; be-

* Speech at Lowell, May 15, 1860.

lieving that democratic principles are unchangeable in their nature, when applied to the same subject-matter.'

"After a long and animated discussion, this was rejected by a vote of seventeen states to sixteen; young Oregon giving the casting vote against the Cincinnati platform, to which and the democracy she owed her existence as a sovereign state.

"There was but one additional resolution which, it was proposed, should be added, and that is as follows:

"'*Resolved*, That it is the duty of the United States to extend its protection alike over all its citizens, whether native or naturalized.'

"This was to meet the case of the contradictory interpretations of the rights of foreign-born citizens, when abroad, made by the State Department. To this I had pledged myself, when the case arose. It is but just to add, that to this resolution, no opposition was made. The propositions of a majority of the committee were then brought forward, and by the same majority of one, were passed through the committee. They provided, in substance, for a slave code for the territories, *and upon the high seas.*

"Upon these two propositions, the committee divided; sixteen free states one way, and fifteen slave states, with Oregon and California, the other; and the difference was apparently irreconcilable. Without impugning the motives, or too closely criticising the course of any member of the committee, I saw, or thought I saw, that this disagreement was rather about men than principles. It seemed to me, that gentlemen of the extreme South were making demands which they did not consider it vital to be passed, *lest a man should be nominated distasteful to them*, and men from the North were willing to make concessions not desired by the South, and which would not be justified, either by democratic principles or their northern constituencies, in order to the success of their favorite candidate.

"Subsequent events showed the correctness of this opinion, because, after the minority and majority of the committee had separated, sixteen to seventeen, and each had retired to make up its report, and when the sixteen northern states had nothing to do save to report the Cincinnati platform, pure and simple, then it was that three gentlemen came into the room where the minority of the committee were in consultation, and announced themselves as a subcommittee of a caucus of the friends of Judge Douglas, charged with a resolution which his friends desired to be reported to the convention, in order, as the chairman said, 'to help the southern friends of Judge Douglas.' One member of the committee on resolutions (General Butler) immediately raised a point of order. He said that the committee of the convention of the whole democracy, could not act under the dictation of a caucus of anybody's friends; that his self-respect would forbid—that the report of the minority of the committee would lose all moral power, if they adopted such a resolution thus presented. The point of order of that member of the committee was overruled, and the caucus resolution was received and adopted in the minority report, almost in the words in which it was presented and passed in the caucus, as follows:

"'*Resolved*, That all questions in regard to the rights of property in states or territories, arising under the constitution of the United States, are judicial in their character; and the democratic party is pledged to abide by, and faithfully carry out such determination of these questions, as has been, or may be made by the Supreme Court of the United States.'

"This resolution was insisted upon by the committee, as then constituted, because it would give aid and ground to stand upon at home to the southern friends of Judge Douglas. Not advocated on principle, not claimed for the North, but a concession to the South, which, as the sequel showed, the South neither desired, would adopt or accept. A piece of expediency, which your delegate would 'neither adhere to nor carry out.'

"To him it seemed quite immaterial whether a slave-code was made by congress or the decision of the courts. He had seen some of the most obnoxious laws made by judicial decisions, both in England and in this country. Indeed, a congressional slave-code were preferable to one made by a court, because the former could be defined, and if unjust, could be repealed, while the latter might be indefinite, shifting to meet the exigency of the case, and only limited by the partnership, or restrained by the consciences of judges holding office by a life-tenure, even if they were appointed like the midnight judges 'of John Adams,' in the last hour of an expiring administration, upon which the people set the seal of reprobation."

So the committee could not agree. General Butler adhered to his proposal of the Cincinnati platform; the majority adhered to their demand for a slave-code for the territories and protection to the slave trade; the minority adhered to the resolution framed by Mr. Douglas, which left all questions relating to slavery in the territories to the decision of the Supreme Court. On returning to the convention, therefore, the committee furnished three reports, one from the majority, one from the minority, and one from General Butler; all agreeing in recommending the Cincinnati platform as a basis; all differing as to the nature of the additional "planks."

The majority report proposed four additional resolutions respecting slavery:

"1. *Resolved*, That the democracy of the United States hold these cardinal principles on the subject of slavery in the territories: First, That congress has no power to abolish slavery in the territories. Second, That the territorial legislature has no power to abolish slavery in any territory, nor to prohibit the introduction of slaves therein, nor any power to exclude slavery therefrom, nor any power to destroy or impair the right of property in slaves by any legislation whatever.

"2. *Resolved*, That the enactments of state legislatures to defeat the faithful execution of the fugitive slave law, are hostile in character, subversive of the constitution, and revolutionary in their effect.

"3. *Resolved*, That it is the duty of the federal government to protect, when necessary, the rights of persons, and property on the high seas, in the territories, or wherever else its constitutional authority extends. (Designed to protect the reopened slave trade.)

"4. *Resolved*, That the national democracy earnestly recommend the acquisition of the Island of Cuba at the earliest practicable period."

The minority report, introduced by Mr. Payne of Ohio, also presented the Cincinnati platform, with sundry additions, of which the following are the important ones:

"1. *Resolved*, That all questions in regard to the rights of property in states or territories, arising under the constitution of the United States, are judicial in their character; and the democratic party is pledged to abide by and faithfully carry out such determination of these questions as has been or may be made by the Supreme Court of the United States.

"2. *Resolved*, That the democratic party are in favor of the acquisition of the Island of Cuba, on such terms as shall be honorable to ourselves, and just to Spain.

"3. *Resolved*, That the enactments of state legislatures to defeat the faithful execution of the fugitive slave law, are hostile in character, subversive of the constitution, and revolutionary in their effect."

General Butler reported the two resolutions given in his narrative.

Such were the three reports. The first was supposed to express the sentiments of the party who afterward selected Mr. Breckinridge as their candidate. The second was the Douglas platform. The third conveyed the sense of northern democrats, who were aware that the Cincinnati platform conceded all to the South, that the North could concede. Mr. Douglas perfectly understood that, and he invented the device of the Supreme Court, to delay or confuse the issue. Each of the reports was explained and advocated at much length; the first by Mr. Avery of North Carolina, the chairman of the committee; the second by Mr. Payne of Ohio. Toward the close of the day, General Butler obtained the floor, and spoke in support of his views to a house crowded and excited beyond description, amid interruptions more entertaining to the audience than helpful to the speaker. His speech was ingenious and amusing, particularly that part of it which aimed to deprive the Douglas men of capital borrowed from the Supreme Court. Some of the personal hits produced prodigious effect.

He began by asking members around him why, if the Cincinnati platform was so defective, they had given it such enthusiastic indorsement in 1856. "I am told that it may be subjected to two interpretations. Will any man here attempt to make a platform that will not be subject to two or more interpretations? Why, sir, when Omniscience sends us the Divine law for our guidance through life and our hope in death, for 2,000 years almost bands of men have been engaged in different interpretations of that Divine law, and they have sealed their honesty of purpose with blood—they have burned their fellow creatures at the stake as an evidence of the sincerity of their faith." (Laughter.)

Adverting to the resolution which was evidently designed to throw the protection of the national flag over the slave trade, he humorously affected to be ignorant of its real purpose. "Our *carping opponents*," said he, "will see in it what I am sure southern gentlemen do not mean—the reopening of the African slave trade, and it will be so construed that no man can get rid of the interpretation. It will be proclaimed from every stump, flaunted from every pulpit, thundered from every lyceum in the North, until we, your friends—and in no boasting spirit I say, without us you are powerless—the last refuge of the constitutional rights of the South within the Union are stricken down powerless for ever; so that without farther modification it would be impossible for me to adopt the majority report."

He proceeded to show the utter nothingness of the minority resolution, referring questions in dispute to the Supreme Court: "Now, men of the North, suppose that the Supreme Court should decide upon questions of property arising in the states—and I hope that there is no danger of their so deciding—that slavery exists in Massachusetts, and that it was forced upon us by the constitution of the United States—are you ready to carry out that decision? You might have to submit to that, but would you not move at once for an alteration of that state constitution to prevent such decision taking effect, and adopt such other remedies as your good judgment might devise? You, men of the South, suppose you were foolishly to go apart from us, and Mr. Seward were to be elected president. There sit to-day upon the bench of the Supreme Court nine judges, eight of whom are seventy years old, three of them so debilitated that they may never take their seats again. What happens? Without any act of congress, Mr. Seward being president of the United States, that court is reorganized, and it decides that slavery nowhere exists by natural law, and that man can hold no property in man. What are you to do then? Are you to abide by the decision?"

Here, Mr. Reverdy Johnson, of Maryland, made a remark implying that it became the representative of a state which never gave a democratic majority to be modest in offering advice to a democratic convention. The retort was ready:

"You may taunt me with the fact that I am speaking for poor old Massachusetts, that has never given a democratic vote since the days of Jefferson. She did give a democratic vote *then*. By that vote the South acquired the rich inheritance of Louisiana, and I see here from the gulf states men who but for that vote I never would have had the pleasure of meeting, except as subjects of Napoleon III. Then do not taunt me with speaking for a state that can not give an electoral vote. I feel mortified enough about it. I do not like to be taunted with it; I do not think it quite kind in my friend from Maryland to make the remark he did. I would have thought it more unkind if my friend from Mississippi had said anything of the kind, but I thought it especially unkind in my friend from Maryland, because he violated the well-known maxim in my country, that the "pot should never call the kettle black." (Laughter.)

Mr. Johnson: "While Maryland obeys the laws of the Union, as she has ever done and does now, she considers herself equal to all other states; but when she refuses to acknowledge even the force of the constitution, and the laws made in pursuance thereof, she will then be more modest in the expression of her opinions."

General Butler: "Comparisons are odious, but I say that any man in Massachusetts can walk up to the polls and vote for anybody on earth without having his head broken by a cudgel." (Great laughter.)

Mr. Johnson attempted to reply, but General Butler would not yield the floor.

"Very well, then," said the Marylander, "have it so."

The speaker continued: "I will say this to the gentleman, that everything that the democratic party could do in his state has been nobly done to protect men in their rights. Will he give old Massachusetts the same credit, that everything the democracy of Massachusetts could do to stand by the constitution and the Union, the rights of his state and my own, has been done without fear, favor, affection, or hope of reward? (Applause.) Therefore, I say again, that I do not like to be told that this platform is only represented by states which are sure to give electoral votes for the democratic candidate. Let me call the attention of the gentleman from Maryland to the fact, that by the vote from his state the house of representatives got a black republican organization. (Applause.) And my gallant friends from Tennessee—are your skirts quite clear? And how stands Kentucky—the dark and bloody battle-ground? She has five to five in the house of representatives, is a cipher there, and if they do not take care, will be a cipher in the electoral vote. And how stands the old state of North Carolina. Four and four in the house of representatives. These states I have enumerated were never reliable democratic states, and, therefore, I have ventured to say, that I have a good right to speak here for the

3

gallant states of the North, who have sometimes given, and always want to give, democratic votes."

General Butler concluded by advising the convention to adopt his report, and then "nominate some firm, trustworthy, out-and-out, hard working democrat for president, and go home and elect him."

The convention, after debates that threatened to be endless, followed this advice in part. They adopted the report of General Butler, with non-essential alterations, by a vote of 230 to 40.

Then came the tug of war. The platform completed, it remained to select a man to stand upon it.

"The whole discussion of the platform," says General Butler, in the narrative quoted above, "led me to the belief that the difference was about *men*, not principles; and the unfortunate and unjustifiable secession of eight of the southern states by their delegates, in whole or in part, justifies the statement. When they went out of the convention, we had adopted no principles but those to which every seceding state, and many of the seceding delegates, had been pledged only four years since. There was in this, therefore, no disruption, no *casus belli*, no justification for so serious a step as the dismemberment of the democratic party, and endangering the harmony and safety of the Union.

"What then was feared by the seceding states? Evidently, that the majority of the convention, composed of northern delegates, would force the nomination of Judge Douglas, who had given an *interpretation* to that platform to which the southern democracy would not, and, as their delegates claimed, could not agree. They said, 'You, of the North, have the platform; and if you will put a man upon it that has given an interpretation hostile to the South, then we can not sustain ourselves at home, if we would,' and the more ardent of the southern men added, 'we would not, if we could.'

"That there was this fear of his nomination, was made certain by the act of Tennessee, Virginia, Maryland, North Carolina and Kentucky, who remained in the convention, but by their delegates insisted, that if a resolution was not passed, requiring two-thirds of the whole electoral college to make a nomination, they, too, would withdraw from the convention; and thereby the convention must have been dissolved, as California and Oregon would have gone with them, leaving only a minority of the states in number, with a loss of every democratic state. The passage of this resolution made the nomination of Judge Douglas simply impossible; and, although New York cast her thirty-five votes steadily for him afterward, yet she voted for this rule which would render her vote for Douglas useless, as it was evident to all that more than one-third the convention was unalterably opposed to his nomination.

"I believe there was a *majority* opposed to him in fact. Grant that he received upon one ballot a bare majority of the whole vote. But how was that majority made up? Simply, by the *unit* rule, which stifled minorities in northern states, under instructions. In New York, there were fifteen votes opposed to Judge Douglas, from first to last, yet these thirty-five votes were cast for him on every ballot. In Ohio six votes, in Indiana five votes, and Minnesota two votes were opposed to him, yet by that rule cast for him, so that the majority was more apparent than real. The southern states generally acting without direct instructions, by a cunningly devised resolution of the committee on organization, were for the most part voting separately, so that all of Judge Douglas's strength in the southern delegations, substantially appeared.

Now, with the South opposed to Judge Douglas, even to the disruption of the party; with every democratic free state voting against him; with two-thirds of the great state of Pennsylvania firmly against him; with one-half, nearly, of New York hostile; New Jersey divided, and the only state in New England where the democracy can have much hope, Connecticut, nearly equally balanced, what was it the part of wisdom for your delegate to do? Should he, coming from a state where there was no hope of a democratic electoral vote, persistently endeavor to force upon the democratic states a candidate distasteful to them, as shown by those votes, insomuch that they were ready to sunder all political ties, rather than submit to his nomination? Were his preferences and yours for a given man to be insisted on at all hazards? He thought not then; he thinks not still. * * * * * *

"We must accept facts as we find them. A truth is a truth, however unpalatable. No man can act wisely who disregards facts and truths in shaping his course, whether in political or other actions. '*I would*,' must always wait upon '*I ought*.' For these reasons before stated, I found Judge Douglas's nomination an impossibility, without a disruption of the party and throwing away all chance of success.

"You may say this is a great misfortune. Be it so. It is a fact upon which you and I, fellow-democrats, must judge and act. I found a very large majority of the democratic states unalterably opposed to him. ''Tis true 'tis a pity, and pity 'tis, 'tis true.' I found him in a bitter feud with a democratic administration, and without caring to inquire which is to blame for it, such conflict is not a help to democratic votes in a closely contested election, especially when the democracy desire to carry the state of Pennsylvania, where, to say the least, the administration has both prestige and power.

"I found also that Judge Douglas was in opposition to almost the entire democratic majority of the senate of the United States. No matter who is right or who is wrong, this is not a pleasant position for the candidate of the democratic party. I found him opposed by a very large majority of the democratic members of the house of representatives. It is doubtless all wrong that this should be so, yet so it is. I have heard that the 'sweetest wine makes the sourest vinegar,' but I never heard of vinegar sour enough to make sweet wine. Cold apathy and violent opposition are not the prolific parents of votes. I found, worse than all for a democratic candidate for the presidency, that the clerk of the republican house of representatives was openly quoted as saying that the influential paper, controlled by him, would either support Douglas or Seward, thus making himself, apparently, an unpleasant connecting link between them.

"With these facts before me, and impressing upon me the conviction that the nomination of Judge Douglas could not be made with any hope of safety to the democratic party, what was I to do? I will tell you what I did do, and I am afraid it is not what I ought to have done. Yielding to your preferences, I voted seven times for Judge Douglas, although my judgment told me that my votes were worse than useless, as they gave him an appearance of strength in the convention which I felt he had not in the democratic party. If this was an error it was your fault.

"I then looked round to throw my vote where, at least, it would not mislead anybody. I saw a statesman of national fame and reputation, who had led his regiment to victory at Buena Vista, a democrat with whom I disagreed in some things, but with whom I could act in most. Loving his country first, his section next, but just to all—so that through his endeavors in the senate of the United States, Massachusetts obtained from the general government her just dues, deferred for forty years, of hundreds of thousands of dollars, a feat which none of her agents had ever been able to accomplish. Besides, his friends were not pressing his name before the convention, so that he was not a partisan in the personal strife there going on. I thought such a man deserved, at least, the poor compliment of a vote from Massachusetts, and therefore I threw my vote for Jefferson Davis, of Mississippi; and I claim, at least, that that vote was guided by intelligence.

"Through a series of fifty-seven ballotings, the voting did not materially change. Afterward, almost by common consent, an adjournment was carried, and we are to go to Baltimore, on the 18th of June next, to finish our work."

General Butler went to Baltimore. All possibility of uniting the party was there prevented by the immovable resolve of the friends of Mr. Douglas to force his nomination. The convention was again divided, and General Butler went out with the delegates who had a determination equally fixed to defeat the nomination of Mr. Douglas. The Douglas men nominated their chief for the presidency. They selected, as a candidate for the second office, Herschell Johnson, of Georgia, an avowed disunionist, and an open advocate of the slave trade, who, at a public meeting in industrial Philadelphia, had permitted himself to say, that he thought "it was the best plan for capital to own its labor." The retiring body nominated for the presidency, Mr. Breckinridge, of Kentucky, and Mr. Lane, of Oregon, for the vice-presidency. These candidates received from General Butler an energetic, an unwavering support—the only kind of support he ever gave to anything.

Let us see how the four parties stood in the contest of that year.

The Cincinnati platform of 1856 said: Let the people in each territory decide, when they form a constitution, whether they will come into the Union as a slave state or as a free state.

But the delay in the admission of Kansas, gave intense interest to the question, whether slavery could exist in a territory before its admission.

This was the issue in 1860.

The republican platform said: No, it can not exist. Freedom is the normal condition of all territory. Slavery can exist only by local law. There is no authority anywhere competent to legalize slavery in a territory of the United States. The Supreme Court can not do it. Congress can not do it. The territorial legislature can not do it.

The Douglas platform said: We do not know whether slavery can exist in a territory or not. There is a difference of opinion among us upon the subject. The Supreme Court must decide, and its decision shall be final and binding.

The Breckinridge platform said: Slavery lawfully exists in a territory the moment a slave-owner enters it with his slaves. The United States is bound to maintain his right to hold slaves in a territory. But when the people of the territory frame a state constitution, they are to decide whether to enter the Union as a slave or as a free state. If as a slave state, they are to be admitted without question. If as a free state, the slave owners must retire or emancipate.

The Bell and Everett party, declining to construct a platform, expressed no opinion upon the question at issue.

Thus, of the four parties in the field, two only had the courage to look the state of things in the face, and to avow a positive conviction, namely, the republicans and the Breckinridge men. These two, alone, made platforms upon which an honest voter could intelligently stand. The other parties shirked the issue, and meant to shirk it. The most pitiable spectacle ever afforded in the politics of the United States, was the stump wrigglings of Mr. Douglas during the campaign, when he taxed all his great ingenuity to seem to say something that should win votes in one section, without losing votes in the other. Tragical as the end was to him, all men felt that his disappointment was just, though they would have gladly seen him recover from the shock, take the bitter lesson to heart, and join with his old allies in saving the country.

Before leaving Baltimore, the leaders of the Breckinridge party came to an explicit understanding upon two important points.

First, the northern men received from Mr. Breckinridge and his southern supporters, not merely the strongest possible declarations of devotion to the Union and the Constitution, but a particular disavowal and repudiation of the cry then heard all over the South, that in case of the success of the republican party, the South would secede. There is no doubt in the minds of the well-informed, that Mr. Breckinridge was sincere in these professions, and it is known that he adhered to the Union, in his heart, down to the time when war became evidently inevitable. There is reason, too, to believe that he has since bitterly regretted having abandoned the cause of his country.

Secondly, the Breckinridge leaders at Baltimore arranged their programme of future operations. They were aware of the certainty of their defeat. In all probability, the republicans would come into power. That party (as the Breckinridge democrats supposed) being unused to govern, and inheriting immense and unexampled difficulties, would break down, would quarrel among themselves, would become ridiculous or offensive, and so prepare the way for the triumphant return of the democracy to power in 1865. Mr. Douglas, too, they thought, would destroy himself, as a political power, by having wantonly broken up his party. The democrats, then, would adhere to their young and popular candidate, and elect him; if not in 1864, then in 1868.

Having concluded these arrangements, they separated, to meet in Washington after the election, and renew the compact, or else to change it to meet any unexpected issue of the campaign.

On his return to Lowell, General Butler found himself the most unpopular man in Massachusetts. Not that Massachusetts approved the course or the character of Mr. Douglas. Not that Massachusetts was incapable of appreciating a bold and honest man, who stood in opposition to her cherished sentiments. It was because she saw one of her public men acting in conjunction with the party which seemed to her identified with that which threatened a disruption to the country if it should be fairly beaten in an election. The platform of that party was profoundly odious to her. It appeared to her, not merely erroneous, but immoral and monstrous, and she could not but feel that the northern supporters of it were guilty of a kind of subserviency that bordered upon baseness. She did not understand the series of events which would have compelled Mr. Douglas, if he had been elected, to go to unimagined lengths in quieting the apprehensions of the South. She could not, in that time of intense excitement, pause to consider, that if General Butler's course was wrong, it was, at least, disinterested and unequivocal.

He was hooted in the streets of Lowell, and a public meeting, at which he was to give an account of his stewardship, was broken up by a mob.

A second meeting was called. General Butler then obtained a hearing, and justified his course in a speech of extraordinary force and cogency. He characterized the Douglas ticket as "two-faced," designed to win both sections, by deceiving both. "Hurrah for Johnson! he goes for intervention. Hurrah for Douglas! he goes for non-intervention unless the Supreme Court tells him to go the other way. Hurrah for Johnson! he goes against popular sovereignty. Hurrah for Douglas! he goes for popular sovereignty if the Supreme Court will let him! Hurrah for Johnson! he is for disunion! Hurrah for Douglas! he is for the Union."

He met the charge brought against Mr. Breckinridge of sympathy with southern disunionists. "In a speech, but a day or two since at Frankfort, in the presence of his life-long friends and political opponents, who could have gainsayed the declaration if it were not true, Mr. Breckinridge proudly said:—'I am an American and a Kentuckian, who never did an act nor cherished a thought that was not full of devotion to the constitution and the Union.' Proud words, proudly spoken, and incapable of contradiction. Yet we, who support this gallant and conservative leader, are called disunionists, and charged with being untrue to democracy. By whom is this charge made? By Pierre Soulé, an avowed disunionist, in Louisiana; by John Forsyth and the 'Atlanta Confederacy,' in Georgia, which maintains the duty of the South to leave the Union if Lincoln is elected; and yet these same men are the foremost of the southern supporters of Douglas; by Gaulding, of Georgia, who is now stumping the state for Douglas, making the same speech that he made in the convention at Baltimore, where he argued that non-intervention meant that congress had no power to prevent the exportation of negroes from Africa, and that the slave trade was the true popular sovereignty in full expansion.

"Would you believe it, fellow-citizens, this speech was applauded in the Douglas convention, and that too, by a delegate from Massachusetts, ay, and from Middlesex county.

"When I left that convention, I declared that I would no longer sit where the African slave trade, made piracy and felony by the laws of my country, was openly advocated and applauded. Yet such, at the South, are the supporters of Douglas."

General Butler was the Breckinridge candidate for the governorship of Massachusetts. He had been a candidate for the same office a few years before, and had received the full support of his party, about 50,000 votes. On this occasion only 6,000 of his fellow-citizens cast their votes for him; the whole number of voters being more than 170,000.

CHAPTER III.

MASSACHUSETTS READY.

PERHAPS the commonest mistake made in commenting upon human actions, is to overrate the understanding, and underrate the moral worth of the actor. We flatter ourselves that we are very great and very bad beings; the humiliating truth seems to be, that we are rather good and extremely little. Mr. Dickens has a character in one of his novels, who was fond of giving out that he was born in a ditch, and struggled up from that lowly estate to the position of a man whose check was good for any number of thousands of pounds; but it came out at last, that he was born of "poor but respectable parents," who had given him the rudiments of education in the most ordinary and common-place way. The blustering fool could not face the homely, creditable truth of his origin, and so invented the flattering lie, that he was the castaway offspring of a stroller. A vanity of this kind is common to the race. We do not, as a general thing, purposely deceive ourselves, but it appears to be universally taken for granted, that man is a tremendous creature, capable of seeing the end from the beginning, and accustomed to form plans which contemplate and cause the actual issue. This delusion, I suppose, is nourished, by our constantly viewing the results of human ingenuity in vast accumulation. We omit to consider, that it took all the lifetime of man to build the Great Eastern, and that a new suit of Sunday clothes is the result of the severe cogitation and laboriously gathered knowledge of all the ingenious tailors that ever lived, to say nothing of the inventive weavers, curriers, and shoemakers.

Hence, when a great thing has occurred, like this rebellion of the slave power against the power which alone could protect it, we are apt to imagine that it was all deliberately and deeply planned beforehand. The final history of the war, when it comes to be written, many years hence, will probably disclose that there was not much actual planning. The event was of the nature of a conflagration. There had been, indeed, for thirty years, a most diligent collection of combustible matter. Every oratorial demagogue had wildly tossed his bundle of painted sticks upon the heap, and such men as Calhoun had burrowed through the mass, and inserted some solid-looking timbers of false doctrine; and the necessities of despotism had built a wall around it, so that the fire-apparatus of outside civilization could not be brought to bear. In such circumstances, there is no great need of plan, when mere destruction is the object. A few long heads, like John Slidell, with the aid of a few madmen in Charleston, were competent to apply the requisite number of matches, and blow upon the incipient flames. It will probably appear, that those who have since been most conspicuous in controlling the movement, were men who hung back from inaugurating it; men who would have preferred to remain in the Union, and who were as much "carried away" by the rush of events, as the planters of North Carolina, Georgia, and Louisiana, are known to have been.

In December, 1860, Mr. Lincoln having been elected, and congress met, General Butler went to Washington, according to the agreement at Baltimore, in June, to confer with democratic leaders upon the future course of the party. South Carolina had gone through the form of seceding from the Union, and her three commissioners were at the capital, to present to the president the ordinance of secession, and negotiate the terms of separation. Regarding themselves in the light of ambassadors, and expecting a long negotiation, they had taken a house, which served as the headquarters of the malcontents. Excitement and apprehension pervaded all circles. General Butler, in visiting his southern friends, found that most of them considered secession a fact accomplished, nothing remaining but to arrange the details. Mr. Breckinridge, however, still steadfast to his pledges, indignant, sorrowful, was using his influence to bring about a convention of the border states, which should stand between the two hostile bodies, and compel both to make the concessions supposed to be necessary for the preservation of the Union. By day and night, he strove to stem the torrent of disaffection, and bring the men of the South to reason. He strove in vain. The movement which he endeavored to effect was defeated by Virginians, particularly by Mason and Hunter. Finding his plan impossible, he went about Washington, pale and haggard, the picture of despair, and sought relief, it is said, where despairing southern men are too apt to seek it, in the whisky bottle.

"What does all this mean?" asked General Butler, of an old southern democrat, a few hours after his arrival in Washington.

"It means simply what it appears to mean. The Union is dead. The experiment is finished. The attempt of two communities, having no interest in common, abhorring one another, to make believe that they are one nation, has ceased for ever. We shall establish a sound, homogeneous government, with no discordant elements. We shall have room for our northern friends. Come with us."

"Have you counted the cost? Do you really think you can break up this Union? Do *you* think so yourself?"

"I do."

"You are prepared, then, for civil war? You mean to bring this thing to the issue of arms?"

"Oh, there will be no war. The North won't fight."

"The North will fight."

"The North won't fight."

"The North *will* fight."

"The North *can't* fight. We have friends enough at the North to prevent it."

"You have friends at the North as long as you remain true to the constitution. But let me tell you, that the moment it is seen that you mean to break up the country, the North is a unit against you. I can answer, at least, for Massachusetts. She is good for ten thousand men to march, at once, against armed secession."

"Massachusetts is not such a fool. If your state should send ten thousand men to preserve the Union against southern secession, she will have to fight twice ten thousand of her own citizens at home who will oppose the policy."

"No, sir; when we come from Massachusetts we shall not leave a single traitor behind, unless he is hanging on a tree."

"Well, we shall see."

"You *will* see. I know something of the North, and a good deal about New England, where I was born and have lived forty-two years. We are pretty quiet there now because we don't believe that you mean to carry out your threats. We have heard the same story at every election these twenty years. Our people don't yet believe you are in earnest. But let me tell you this: As sure as you attempt to break up this Union, the North will resist the attempt to its last man and its last dollar. You are as certain to fail as that there is a God in Heaven. One thing you *may* do: you may ruin the southern states, and extinguish your institution of slavery. From the moment the first gun is fired upon the American flag, your slaves will not be worth five years' purchase. But as to breaking up the country, it can not be done. God and nature, and the blood of your fathers and mine have made it one; and one country it must remain."

And so the war of words went on. The general visited his old acquaintances, the South Carolina commissioners, and with them he had similar conversations; the substance of all being this:

Secessionists: "The North won't fight."

General Butler: "The North will fight."

Secessionists: "If the North fights, its laborers will starve and overturn the government."

General Butler: "If the South fights, there is an end of slavery."

Secessionists: "Do you mean to say that you yourself would fight in such a cause?"

General Butler: "I would; and, by the grace of God, I will."

The general sat at the table, once more, of Jefferson Davis, for whom he had voted in the Charleston convention. Mr. Davis, at that time, appeared still to wish for a compromise and the preservation of the Union. But he is a politician. He gave in to the sentiment, that he owed allegiance, first, to the state of Mississippi; secondly, to the United States; which is the same as saying that he owed no allegiance to the United States at all. So, if a majority of the legislature of Mississippi should pronounce for secession, he was bound to abandon that which, for fifty years, he had been proud to call his "country."

In times like those, every man of originating mind has his scheme. If in the multitude of counselors there were safety, no country had been safer than this country was in December, 1860, when Mr. Buchanan was assailed and confounded with advice from all quarters, near and remote, from friends and foes. General Butler, too, had an idea. As a leading member of the party in power, he was entitled to be listened to, and he was listened to. Mr. Black, the legal adviser of the government, had given it as his opinion, that the proceedings of South Carolina were legally definable as a "riot," which the force of the United States could not be lawfully used in suppressing.

General Butler said to the attorney-general:—"You say that the government can not use its army and navy to coerce South Carolina *in* South Carolina. Very well. I do not agree with you; but let the proposition be granted. Now, secession is either a right, or it is treason. If it is a right, the sooner we know it the better. If it is treason, then the presenting of the ordinance of secession is an overt act of treason. These men are coming to the White House to present the ordinance to the president. Admit them. Let them present the ordinance. Let the president say to them:—'Gentlemen, you go hence in the custody of a marshal of the United States, as prisoners of state, charged with treason against your country.' Summon a grand jury, here in Washington. Indict the commissioners. If any of your officers are backward in acting, you have the appointing power; replace them with men who feel as men should, at a time like this. Try the commissioners before the Supreme Court, with all the imposing forms and stately ceremonial which marked the trial of Aaron Burr. I have some reputation at home as a criminal lawyer, and will stay here and help the district attorney through the trial without fee or reward. If they are convicted, execute the sentence. If they are acquitted, you will have done something toward leaving a clear path for the incoming administration. Time will have been gained; but the great advantage will be, that both sides will pause to watch this high and dignified proceeding; the passions of men will cool; the great points at issue will become clear to all parties; the mind of the country will be active while passion and prejudice are allayed. Meanwhile, if you can not use your army and navy in Charleston harbor, you can certainly employ them in keeping order here."

This was General Butler's contribution to the grand sum total of advice with which the administration was favored. Mr. Black seemed inclined to recommend the measure. Mr. Buchanan was of opinion, that it would cause a fearful agitation, and probably inflame the South to the point of beginning hostilities forthwith. Besides, these men claimed to be ambassadors; and though we could not admit the claim, still they had voluntarily placed themselves in our power, and seemed to have a kind of right to be, at least, warned away, before we could honorably treat them as criminals or enemies. In vain General Butler urged that his object was simply to get their position defined by a competent tribunal; to ascertain whether they were, in reality, ambassadors or traitors. His scheme was that of a bold and steadfast patriot, prepared to go all lengths for his country. It could not but be rejected by Mr. Buchanan.

General Butler frankly told the commissioners the advice he had given.

"Why, you would'nt hang us, would you?" said Mr. Orr.

"Oh, no," replied the General; "not unless you were found guilty."

Then came the electric news of Major Anderson's "change of base" from Fort Moultrie to Fort Sumter; one of those trivial events which generally occur at times like those to decide the question of peace or war. The future historian will probably tell us, that there was never a moment after that event when a peaceful solution of the controversy was possible. He will probably show that it was the skillful use of that incident, at a critical moment, which enabled the secessionists of Georgia, frustrated till then, to commit that great state to the support of South Carolina; and Georgia is the empire state of the cotton South, whose defection involved that of all the cotton states, as if by a law of nature.

The president of the United States had allowed himself to promise the South Carolina commissioners that no military movement should occur in Charleston harbor during the negotiation at Washington. They promptly demanded the return of Major Anderson to Fort Moultrie. Floyd supported their demand. Mr. Buchanan consented. Then the commissioners, finding the president so pliant, demanded the total withdrawal of the troops from South Carolina, and Floyd supported them in that modest demand also. While the president stood hesitating upon the brink of this new infamy, the enormous frauds in Floyd's department came to light, and his

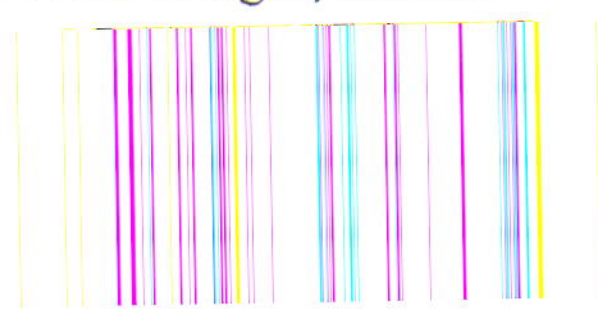

influence was at an end. The question of withdrawal being proposed to the cabinet, it was negatived, and the virtuous Floyd relieved his colleagues by resigning. Mr. Holt succeeded him; the government stiffened; the commissioners went home; and General Butler, certain now that war was impending, prepared to depart.

He had one last, long interview with the southern leaders, at which the whole subject was gone over. For three hours he reasoned with them, demonstrating the folly of their course, and warning them of final and disastrous failure. The conversation was friendly, though warm and earnest on both sides. Again he was invited to join them, and was offered a share in their enterprise, and a place in that "sound and homogeneous government" which they meant to establish. He left them no room to doubt that he took sides with his country, and that all he had, and all he was, should be freely risked in that country's cause. Late at night they separated to know one another no more except as mortal foes.

The next morning, General Butler went to Senator Wilson, of Massachusetts, an old acquaintance, though long a political opponent, and told him that the southern leaders meant war, and urged him to join in advising the governor of their state to prepare the militia of Massachusetts for taking the field.

At that time, and for some time longer, the southern men were divided among themselves respecting the best mode of beginning hostilities. The bolder spirits were for seizing Washington, preventing the inauguration of Mr. Lincoln, and placing Breckinridge, if he would consent, or some other popular man if he would not, in the presidential mansion, who should issue a proclamation to the whole country, and endeavor to rally to his support a sufficient number of northern democrats to distract and paralyze the loyal states. That more prudent counsels prevailed was not from any sense of the turpitude of such treason, but from a conviction that if anything *could* rouse the North to armed resistance, it would be the seizure of the capital. Nothing short of that, thought the secessionists, would induce a money-making, pusillanimous people to leave their shops and their counting-houses, to save their country from being broken to pieces and brought to naught. The dream of these traitors was to destroy their country without fighting; and so the scheme of a *coup d'état* was discarded. But General Butler left Washington believing that the bolder course was the one which would be adopted. He believed this the more readily, because it was the course which he would have advised, had he, too, been a traitor. One thing, however, he considered absolutely certain: there was going to be a war between Loyalty and Treason; between the Slave Power and the Power which had so long protected and fostered it.

He found the North anxious, but still incredulous. He went to Governor Andrew, and gave him a full relation of what he had heard and seen at Washington, and advised him to get the militia of the state in readiness to move at a day's notice. He suggested that all the men should be quietly withdrawn from the militia force who were either unable or unwilling to leave the state for the defense of the capital, and their places supplied with men who could and would. The governor, though he could scarcely yet believe that war was impending, adopted the suggestion. About one-half the men resigned their places in the militia; the vacancies were quickly filled; and many of the companies, during the winter months, drilled every evening in the week, except Sundays. General Butler further advised that two thousand overcoats be made, as the men were already provided with nearly every requisite for marching, except those indispensable garments, which could not be extemporized. To this suggestion there was sturdy opposition, since it involved the expenditure of twenty thousand dollars, and that for an exigency which Massachusetts did not believe was likely to occur. One gentleman, high in office, said that General Butler made the proposal in the interest of the moths of Boston, which alone would get any good of the overcoats. Others insinuated that he only wanted a good contract for the Middlesex Woolen Mills, in which he was a large shareholder. The worthy and patriotic governor, however, strongly recommended the measure, and the overcoats were begun. The last stitches in the last hundred of them were performed while the men stood drawn up on the common waiting to strap them to their knapsacks before getting into the cars for Washington.

Having thus assisted in preparing Massachusetts to march, General Butler resumed his practice at the bar, vibrating between Boston and Lowell as of old, not without much inward chafing at the humiliating spectacle which the country presented during those dreary, shameful months. One incident cheered the gloom. One word was uttered at Washington which spoke the heart of the country. One man in the cabinet felt as patriots feel when the flag of their country is threatened with dishonor. One order was given which did not disgrace the government from which it issued. "IF ANY ONE ATTEMPTS TO HAUL DOWN THE AMERICAN FLAG SHOOT HIM ON THE SPOT!" "When I read it," wrote General Butler to General Dix long after, "my heart bounded with joy. It was the first bold stroke in favor of the Union under the past administration." He had the pleasure of sending to General Dix, from New Orleans, the identical flag which was the object of the order, and the confederate flag which was hoisted in its place; as well as of recommending for promotion the sailor, David Ritchie, who contrived to snatch both flags from the cutter when traitors abandoned and burnt her as Captain Farragut's fleet drew near.

The fifteenth of April arrived. Fort Sumter had fallen. The president's proclamation calling for troops was issued. In the morning came a telegram to Governor Andrew from Senator Wilson, asking that twenty companies of Massachusetts militia be instantly dispatched to defend the seat of government. A few hours after, the formal requisition arrived from the secretary of war calling for two full regiments. At quarter before five that afternoon, General Butler was in court at Boston trying a cause. To him came Colonel Edward F. Jones, of the Sixth regiment, bearing an order from Governor Andrew, directing him to muster his command forthwith in Boston common, in readiness to proceed to Washington. This regiment was one of General Butler's brigade, its headquarters being Lowell, twenty-five miles distant, and the companies scattered over forty miles of country. The general endorsed the order, and at five Colonel Jones was on the Lowell train. There was a good deal of swift riding done that night in the region round about Lowell; and at eleven o'clock on the day following, there was Colonel Jones with his regiment on Boston common. Not less prompt were the Third and Eighth regiments, for they began to arrive in Boston as early as nine, each company welcomed at the dépôt by applauding thousands. The Sixth regiment, it was determined, should go first, and the governor deemed it best to strengthen it with two additional companies. "It was nine o'clock, on the evening of the 16th," reports Adjutant-General Schouler, "before your excellency decided to attach the commands of Captains Sampson and Dike to the Sixth regiment. A messenger was dispatched to Stoneham, with orders for Captain Dike. He reported to me at eight o'clock the next morning, that he found Captain Dike at his house in Stoneham, at two o'clock in the morning, and placed your excellency's orders in his hands; that he read them, and said: 'Tell the adjutant-general that I shall be at the state house with my full company by eleven o'clock to-day.' True to his word, he reported at the time, and that afternoon, attached to the Sixth, the company left for Washington. Two days afterward, on the 19th of April, during that gallant march through Baltimore, which is now a matter of history, Captain Dike was shot down while leading his company through the mob. Several of his command were killed and wounded, and he received a wound in the leg, which will render him a cripple for life."

The general, too, was going. During the night following the 15th of April, he had been at work with Colonel Jones getting the Sixth together. On the morning of the 16th, he was in the cars, as usual, going to Boston, and with him rode Mr. James G. Carney, of Lowell, president of the Bank of Redemption, in Boston.

"The governor will want money," said the general. "Can not the Bank of Redemption offer a temporary loan of fifty thousand dollars to help off the troops?"

It can, and shall, was the reply, in substance, of the president; and in the course of the morning, a note offering the loan was in the governor's hands.

General Butler went not to court that morning. As yet, no brigadier had been ordered into service, but there was one brigadier who was on fire to serve; one who, from the first summons, had been resolved to go, and to stay to the end of the fight, whether he went as private or as lieutenant-general. Farewell the learned plea, and the big fees that swell the lawyers' bank account! Farewell the spirit-stirring speech, the solemn bench, and all the pomp and circumstance of glorious law! General Butler's occupation was about to be changed. He telegraphed to Mr. Wilson, asking him to remind Mr. Cameron, that a brigade required a brigadier; and back from Washington came an order calling for a brigade of four full regiments, to be commanded by a brigadier-general.

That point gained, the next was to induce Governor Andrew to select the particular brigadier whom General Butler had in his mind when he dispatched the telegram to Mr. Wilson. There were two whose commissions were of older date than his own; General Adams and General Pierce; the former sick, the latter desiring the appointment. General Pierce had the advantage of being a political ally of the governor. On the other hand, General Butler had suggested the measures which enabled the troops to take the field, had got the loan of fifty thousand dollars, had procured the order for a brigadier. He was, moreover, Benjamin F. Butler, a gentleman not unknown in Boston, though long veiled from the general view by a set of obstinately held unpopular political opinions. These considerations, aided, perhaps, by a little wire-pulling, prevailed; and in the morning of the 17th, at ten o'clock, he received the order to take command of the troops.

All that day he worked as few men can work. There were a thousand things to do; but there were a thousand willing hearts and hands to help. The Sixth regiment was off in the afternoon, addressed before it moved by Governor Andrew and General Butler. Two regiments were embarked on board a steamer for Fortress Monroe, then defended by two companies of regular artillery—a tempting prize for the rebels. Late at night, the General went home to bid farewell to his family, and prepare for his final departure. The next morning, back again to Boston, accompanied by his brother, Colonel Andrew Jackson Butler, who chanced to be on a visit to his ancient home, after eleven years' residence in California; where, with Broderick and Hooker, he had already done battle against the slave power, the lamented Broderick having died in his arms. He served now as a volunteer aid to the General, and rendered good service on the eventful march. At Boston, General Butler stopped at his accustomed barber-shop. While he was under the artist's hands, a soldier of the departed Sixth regiment came in sorrowful, begging to be excused from duty; saying that he had left his wife and three children crying.

"I am not the man for you to come to, sir," said the General, "for I have just done the same," and straightway sent for a policeman to arrest him as a deserter.

A hurried visit to the steamer bound for Fortress Monroe. All was in readiness there. Then to the Eighth regiment, in the Common, which he was to conduct to Washington, by way of Baltimore; no intimation of the impending catastrophe to the Sixth having yet been received. The Eighth marched to the cars, and rolled away from the dépôt, followed by the benedictions of assembled Boston; saluted at every station on the way by excited multitudes. At Springfield, where there was a brief delay to procure from the armory the means of repairing muskets, the regiment was joined by a valuable company, under Captain Henry S. Briggs. Thence, to New York. The Broadway march of the regiment; their breakfast at the Metropolitan and Astor; their push through the crowd to Jersey City; the tumultuous welcome in New Jersey; the continuous roar of cheers across the state; the arrival at Philadelphia in the afternoon of the memorable nineteenth of April, who can have forgotten?

Fearful news met the general and the regiment at the dépôt. The Sixth regiment, in its march through Baltimore that afternoon, had been attacked by the mob, and there had been a conflict, in which men on both sides had fallen! So much was fact; but, as inevitably happens at such a time, the news came with appalling exaggerations, which could not be corrected; for soon the telegraph ceased working, the last report being that the bridges at the Maryland end of the railroad were burning, and that Washington, threatened with a hostile army, was isolated and defenseless. Never, since the days when "General Benjamin Franklin" led a little army of Philadelphians against the Indians after Braddock's defeat, the Indians ravaging and scalping within sixty miles of the city, and expected soon to appear on the banks of the Schuylkill, had Philadelphia been so deeply moved with mingled anger and apprehension. The first blood shed in a war sends a thrill of rage and horror through all hearts, and *this* blood shed in Baltimore streets, was that of the countrymen, the neighbors, the relatives of these newly arrived troops. A thousand wild rumors filled the air, and nothing was too terrible to be believed. He was the great man of the group, who had the most incredible story to tell; and each listener went his way to relate the tale with additions derived from his own frenzied imagination.

General Butler's orders directed him to march to Washington by way of Baltimore. That having become impossible, the day being far spent, his men fatigued, and the New York Seventh coming, he marched his regiment to the vacant Girard House for a night's rest, where hospitable, generous Philadelphia gave them bountiful entertainment. The regiment slept the sleep that tired soldiers know.

For General Butler there was neither sleep nor rest that night, nor for his fraternal aid-de-camp. There was telegraphing to the governor of Massachusetts; there were consultations with Commodore Dupont, commandant of the Navy Yard; there were interviews with Mr. Felton, president of the Philadelphia and Baltimore railroad, a son of Massachusetts, full of patriotic zeal, and prompt with needful advice and help; there was poring over maps and gazetteers. Meanwhile, Colonel A. J. Butler was out in the streets, buying pickaxes, shovels, tinware, provisions, and all that was necessary to enable the troops to take the field, to subsist on army rations, to repair bridges and railroads, and to throw up breastworks. All Maryland was supposed to be in arms; but the general was going through Maryland.

Before the evening was far advanced, he had determined upon a plan of operations, and summoned his officers to make them acquainted with it—not to shun responsibility by asking their opinion, nor to waste precious time in discussion. They found upon his table thirteen revolvers. He explained his design, pointed out its probable and its possible dangers, and said that, as some might censure it as rash and reckless, he was resolved to take the sole responsibility himself. Taking up one of the revolvers, he invited every officer who was willing to accompany him to signify it by accepting a pistol. The pistols were all instantly appropriated. The officers departed, and the general then, in great haste, and amid ceaseless interruptions, sketched a memorandum of his plan, to be sent to the governor of Massachusetts *after* his departure, that his friends might know, if he should be swallowed up in the maelstrom of secession, what he had intended to do. Many sentences of this paper betray the circumstances in which they were written.

"My proposition is to join with Colonel Lefferts of the Seventh regiment of New York. I propose to take the fifteen hundred troops to Annapolis, arriving there to-morrow about four o'clock, and occupy the capital of Maryland, and thus call the state to account for the death of Massachusetts men, my friends and neighbors. If Colonel Lefferts thinks it more in accordance with the tenor of his instructions to wait rather than go through Baltimore, I *still propose to march with this regiment.* I propose to occupy the town, and hold it open as a means of communication. I have then but to advance by a forced march of thirty miles to reach the capital, in accordance with the orders I at first received, but which subsequent events in my judgment vary in their execution, believing from the telegraphs that there will be others in great numbers to aid me. Being accompanied by officers of more experience, who will be able to direct the affair, I think it will be accomplished. We have no light batteries; I have therefore telegraphed to Governor Andrew to have the Boston Light Battery put on shipboard at once, to-night, to help me in marching on Washington. In pursuance of this plan, I have detailed Captains Devereux and Briggs, with their commands, to hold the boat at Havre de Grace.

"Eleven, A. M. *Colonel Lefferts has refused to march with me.* I go alone at three o'clock, P. M., to execute this imperfectly written plan. If I succeed, success will justify me. If I fail, purity of intention will excuse want of judgment or rashness."

The plan was a little changed in the morning, when the rumor prevailed that the ferry-boat at Havre de Grace had been seized and barricaded by a large force of rebels. The two companies were not sent forward. It was determined that the regiment should go in a body, seize the boat and use it for transporting the troops to Annapolis.

"I may have to sink or burn your boat," said the general to Mr. Felton.

"Do so," replied the president, and immediately wrote an order authorizing its destruction, if necessary.

It had been the design of General Butler, as we have seen, to leave Philadelphia in the morning train; but he delayed his departure in the hope that Colonel Lefferts might be induced to share in the expedition. The Seventh had arrived at sunrise, and General Butler made known his plan to Colonel Lefferts, and invited his co-operation. That officer, suddenly intrusted with the lives (but the honor also) of nearly a thousand of the flower of the young men of New York, was overburdened with a sense of responsibility, and felt it to be his duty to consult his officers. The consultation was long, and, I believe, not harmonious, and the result was, that the Seventh embarked in the afternoon in a steamboat at Philadelphia, with the design of going to Washington by the Potomac river, leaving to the men of Massachusetts the honor and the danger of opening a path through Maryland. It is impossible for a New Yorker, looking at it in the light of *subsequent* events, not to regret, and keenly regret, the refusal of officers of the favorite New York regiment to join General Butler in his bold and wise movement. But they had not the light of subsequent events to aid them in their deliberations, and they, doubtless, thought that their first duty was to hasten to the protection of Washington, and avoid the risk of detention by the way. It happened on this occasion, as in so many others, that the bold course was also the prudent and successful one. The Seventh was obliged, after all, to take General Butler's road to Washington.

At eleven in the morning of the twentieth of April, the Eighth Massachusetts regiment moved slowly away from the dépôt in Broad street toward Havre de Grace, where the Susquehannah river empties into the Chesapeake Bay—forty miles from Philadelphia, sixty-four from Annapolis. General Butler went through each car explaining the plan of attack, and giving the requisite orders. His design was to halt the train one mile from Havre de Grace, advance his two best drilled companies as skirmishers, follow quickly with the regiment, rush upon the barricades and carry them at the point of the bayonet, pour headlong into the ferry-boat, drive out the rebels, get up steam and start for Annapolis.

Having assigned to each company its place in the line, and given all due explanation to each captain, the general took a seat and instantly fell asleep.

And now, the bustle being over, upon all those worthy men fell that seriousness, that solemnity, which comes to those who value their lives, and whose lives are valuable to others far away, but who are about, for the first time, to incur mortal peril for a cause which they feel to be greater and dearer than life. Goethe tells us that valor can neither be learned nor forgotten. I do not believe it. Certainly, the *first* peril does, in some degree, appall the firmest heart, especially when that peril is quietly approached on the easy seat of a railway car during a two hours' ride. Scarcely a word was spoken. Many of the men sat erect, grasping their muskets firmly, and looking anxiously out of the windows.

One man blenched, and one only. The general was startled from his sleep by the cry of, "Man overboard!" The train was stopped. A soldier was seen running across the fields as though pursued by a mad dog. Mad Panic had seized him, and he had jumped from a car, incurring ten times the danger from which he strove to escape. The general started a group of country people in pursuit, offering them the lawful thirty dollars if they brought the deserter to Havre de Grace in time. The train moved again; the incident broke the spell, and the cars were filled with laughter. The man was brought in. His sergeant's stripe was torn from his arm, and he was glad to compound his punishment by serving the regiment in the capacity of a menial.

At the appointed place, the train was stopped, the regiment was formed, and marched toward the ferry-boat, skirmishers in advance. It mustered thirteen officers and seven hundred and eleven men.*

* EIGHTH REGIMENT OF MASSACHUSETTS INFANTRY.

FIELD AND STAFF.

Colonel	Timothy Munroe, Lynn.	
Afterwards	Edward W. Hinks, Lynn.	
Lieutenant-Colonel	Andrew Elwell, Gloucester.	
Major	Ben. Perley Poore, Newburyport.	
Adjutant	George Creasey, Newburyport.	
Quartermaster	E. Alfred Ingalls, Lynn.	
Paymaster	Roland G. Usher, Lynn.	
Surgeon	Bowman B. Breed, Lynn.	
Assistant-Surgeon	Warren Tapley, Lynn.	
Chaplain	Gilbert Haven, Malden.	
Sergeant-Major	John Goodwin, jr., Marblehead.	
Quartermaster-Sergeant	Horace E. Monroe, Lynn.	
Drum-Major	Samuel Roads, Marblehead.	
Total, Field and Staff		13

COMPANIES AND COMMANDERS.

A,—Newburyport	Captain Albert W. Bartlett, Newburyport	80
B,—Marblehead	Captain Richard Philips, Marblehead	58
C,—Marblehead	Captain Knott V. Martin, Marblehead	63
D,—Lynn	Captain George T. Newhall, Lynn	69
E,—Beverly	Captain Francis E. Porter, Beverly	72
F,—Lynn	Captain James Hudson, jr., Lynn	89
G,—Gloucester	Captain Addison Center, Gloucester	66
H,—Marblehead	Captain Francis Boardman, Marblehead	52
J,—Salem	Captain Arthur F. Devereux, Salem	72
K,—Pittsfield	Captain Henry S. Briggs, Pittsfield Captain Henry H. Richardson, Pittsfield	77
Total, Officers and Men		711

—*Report of Adjutant-General Schouler, for* 1861.

CHAPTER IV.

ANNAPOLIS.

It was a false alarm. There was not an armed enemy at Havre de Grace. The ferry-boat Maryland lay at her moorings in the peaceful possession of her crew; and nothing remained but to get up steam, put on board a supply of coal, water and provisions, embark the troops, and start for Annapolis.

Whether the captain and crew were loyal or treasonable—whether they were likely to steer the boat to Annapolis or to Baltimore, or run her ashore on some traitorous coast, were questions much discussed among officers and men. The captain professed the most ardent loyalty, and General Butler was more inclined to trust him than some of his officers were. There were men on board, however, who knew the way to Annapolis, and were abundantly capable of navigating any craft on any sea. It was resolved, therefore, to permit the captain to command the steamer, but to keep a sharp lookout ahead, and an unobserved scrutiny of the engine-room. Upon the first indication of treachery, captain and engineers should find themselves in an open boat upon the Chesapeake, or stowed away in the hold, their places supplied with seafaring Marbleheaders. Never before, I presume, had such a variously skilled body of men gone to war as the Massachusetts Eighth. It was not merely that all trades and professions had their representatives among them, but some of the companies had almost a majority of college-bred men. Major Winthrop did not so much exaggerate when he said, that if the word were given, "Poets to the front!" or "Painters present arms!" or "Sculptors charge bayonets!" a baker's dozen out of every company would respond. Navigating a steamboat was the simplest of all tasks to many of them.

At six in the evening they were off, packed as close as negroes in the steerage of a slave ship. Darkness closed in upon them, and the men lay down to sleep, each with his musket in his hands. The general, in walking from one part of the boat to another, stumbled over and trod upon many a growling sleeper. He was too anxious upon the still unsettled point of the captain's fidelity to sleep; so he went prowling about among the prostrate men, exchanging notes with those who had an eye upon the compass, and with those who were observing the movements of the engineers. There were moments when suspicion was strong in some minds; but captain and engineers did their duty, and at midnight the boat was off the ancient city of Annapolis.

They had, naturally enough, expected to come upon a town wrapped in midnight slumber. There was no telegraphic or other communication with the North; how could Annapolis, then, know that they were coming? It certainly could not; yet the whole town was evidently awake and astir. Rockets shot up into the sky. Swiftly moving lights were seen on shore, and all the houses in sight were lighted up. The buildings of the Naval Academy were lighted. There was every appearance of a town in extreme commotion. It had been General Butler's intention to land quietly while the city slept, and astonish the dozing inhabitants in the morning with a brilliantly executed reveille. Noting these signs of disturbance, he cast anchor, and determined to delay his landing till daylight.

Colonel Andrew Jackson Butler volunteered to go on shore alone, and endeavor to ascertain the cause of the commotion. He was almost the only man in the party who wore plain clothes. The general consenting, a boat was brought round to the gangway, and Colonel Butler stepped into it. As he did so, he handed his revolver to a friend, saying, that he had no intention of fighting a town full of people, and if he was taken prisoner, he preferred that his pistol should fight, during the war, on the Union side. The brother in command assured him, that if any harm came to him in Annapolis, it would be extremely bad for Annapolis. The gallant colonel settled himself to his work, and glided away into the darkness.

The sound of oars was again heard, and a boat was descried approaching the steamer. A voice from the boat said:

"What steamer is that?"

The steamer was as silent as though it were filled with dead men.

"What steamer is that?" repeated the voice.

No answer. The boat seemed to be making off.

"Come on board," thundered General Butler.

No reply from the boat.

"Come on board, or I'll fire into you," said the general.

The boat approached, and came alongside. It was rowed by four men, and in the stern sat an officer in the uniform of a lieutenant of the United States navy. The officer stepped on board, and was conducted by General Butler to his cabin, where, the door being closed, a curious colloquy ensued.

"Who are you?" asked the lieutenant.

"Who are *you?*" said the general.

He replied that he was Lieutenant Matthews, attached to the Naval Academy, and was sent by Captain Blake, commandant of the post, and chief of the Naval Academy, who directed him to say that they must not land. He had, also, an order from Governor Hicks to the same effect. The United States quartermaster, too, had requested him to add from Lieutenant General Scott, that there were no means of transportation at Annapolis.

General Butler was still uncommunicative. Both gentlemen were in a distrustful state of mind.

The truth was that Captain Blake had been, for forty-eight hours, in momentary expectation of an irruption of "plug uglies" from Baltimore, either by sea or land. He was surrounded by a population stolidly hostile to the United States. The school-ship Constitution, which lay at the academy wharf, was aground, and weakly manned. He had her guns shotted, and was prepared to fight her to the last man; but she was an alluring prize to traitors, and he was in dread of an overpowering force. "Large parties of secessionists," as the officers of the ship afterward testified, "were round the ship every day, noting her assailable points. The militia of the county were drilled in sight of the ship in the day time; during the night signals were exchanged along the banks and across the river, but the character of the preparation, and the danger to the town in case of an attack, as one of the batteries of the ship was pointed directly upon it, deterred them from carrying out their plans. During this time the Constitution had a crew of about twenty-five men, and seventy-six of the youngest class of midshipmen, on board. The ship drawing more water than there was on the bar, the secessionists thought she would be in their power whenever they would be in sufficient force to take her." In these circumstances, Captain

Blake, a native of Massachusetts, who had grown gray in his country's service, as loyal and steadfast a heart as ever beat, was tortured with anxiety for the safety of the trust which his country had committed to him. Upon seeing the steamer, he had concluded that here, at last, were the Baltimore ruffians, come to seize his ship, and lay waste the academy. Secessionists in the town were prepared to sympathize, if not to aid in the fell business. All Annapolis, for one reason or another, was in an agony of desire to know who and what these portentous midnight voyagers were. Captain Blake, his ship all ready to open fire, had sent the lieutenant to make certain that the new-comers were enemies, before beginning the congenial work of blowing them out of the water.

General Butler and the lieutenant continued for some time to question one another, without either of them arriving at a satisfactory conclusion as to the loyalty of the other. The general, at length, announced his name, and declared his intention of marching by way of Annapolis to the relief of Washington. The lieutenant informed him that the rails were torn up, the cars removed, and the people unanimous against the marching of any more troops over the soil of Maryland. The general intimated that the men of his command could dispense with rails, cars, and the consent of the people. They were bound to the city of Washington, and expected to make their port. Meanwhile, he would send an officer with him on shore, to confer with the governor of the state, and the authorities of the city.

Captain P. Haggerty, aid-de-camp, was dispatched upon this errand. He was conveyed to the town, where he was soon conducted to the presence of the governor and the mayor, to whom he gave the requisite explanations, and declared General Butler's intention to land. Those dignitaries finding it necessary to confer together, Captain Haggerty was shown into an adjoining room, where he was discovered an hour or two later, fast asleep on a lounge. Lieutenant Matthews was charged by the governor with two short notes to General Butler, one from himself, and another from the aforesaid quartermaster. The document signed by the governor, read as follows:

"I would most earnestly advise, that you do not land your men at Annapolis. The excitement is very great, and I think it prudent that you should take your men elsewhere. I have telegraphed to the secretary of war against your landing your men here."

This was addressed to the "Commander of the Volunteer troops on Board the Steamer." The quartermaster, left Captain Morris J. Miller, wrote thus:

"Having been intrusted by General Scott with the arragnements for transporting your regiments hence to Washington, and it being impracticable to procure cars, I recommend, that the troops remain on board the steamer until further orders can be received from General Scott."

This appears to have been a mere freak of the captain's imagination, since no troops were expected at Annapolis by General Scott.

Captain Haggerty returned on board "the steamer," and the notes were delivered to the general commanding.

What had befallen Colonel Butler, meanwhile? Upon leaving the steamer, he rowed toward the most prominent object in view, and soon found himself alongside of what proved to be a wharf of the Naval Academy. He had no sooner fastened his boat, and stepped ashore, than he was seized by a sentinel, who asked him what he wanted.

"I want to see the commander of the post."

To Captain Blake he was, accordingly, taken. Colonel Butler is a tall, fully developed, imposing man, devoid of the slightest resemblance to the ideal "Plug Ugly." Captain Blake, venerable with years and faithful service on many seas, in many lands, was not a person likely to be mistaken for a rebel. Yet these two gentlemen eyed one another with intense distrust. The navy had not then been sifted of all its traitors; and upon the mind of Captain Blake, the apprehension of violent men from Baltimore had been working for painful days and nights. He received the stranger with reticent civility, and invited him to be seated. Probing questions were asked by both, eliciting vague replies, or none. These two men were Yankees, and each was resolved that the other should declare himself first. After long fencing and "beating about the bush," Colonel Butler expressed himself thus:

"Captain Blake, we may as well end this now as at any other time. They are Yankee troops on board that boat, and if I don't get back pretty soon, they will open fire upon you."

The worthy Captain drew a long breath of relief. Full explanations on both sides followed, and Captain Blake said he would visit General Butler at daybreak. Colonel Butler returned on board the Maryland.

The general was soon ready with replies to the notes of Governor Hicks and Captain Miller.

To the governor: "I had the honor to receive your note by the hands of Lieutenant Matthews of the United States Naval School at Annapolis. I am sorry that your excellency should advise against my landing here. I am not provisioned for a long voyage. Finding the ordinary means of communication cut off by the burning of railroad bridges by a mob, I have been obliged to make this detour, and hope that your excellency will see, from the very necessity of the case, that there is no cause of excitement in the mind of any good citizen because of our being driven here by an extraordinary casualty. I should, at once, obey, however, an order from the secretary of war."

To Captain Miller: "I am grieved to hear that it is impracticable for you to procure cars for the carriage of myself and command to Washington, D. C. Cars are not indispensable to our progress. I am not instructed that you were to arrange for the transporting of my command; if so, you would surely have been instructed as to our destination. We are accustomed to much longer journeys on foot in pursuance of our ordinary avocations. I can see no objection, however, to our remaining where we are until such time as orders may be received from General Scott. But without further explanation from yourself, or greater inconveniences than you suggest, I see no reason why I should make such delay. Hoping for the opportunity of an immediate personal interview, I remain, etc."

Captain Blake came off to the steamer at dawn of day, and soon found himself at home among his countrymen.

"Can you help me off with the Constitution? Will your orders permit you?"

"I have got no orders," replied the general. "I am making war on my own hook. But we can't be wrong in saving the Constitution. That is, certainly, what we came to do."

How the regiment now went to work with a will to save the Constitution; how the Maryland moved up along side, and put on board the Salem Zouaves for a guard, and a hundred Marbleheaders for sailors; how they tugged, and tramped, and lightened, and heaved, and tugged, and tugged again; how groups of sulky secesh stood scowling around, muttering execrations; how the old frigate was started from her bed of mud at length, amid such cheers as Annapolis had never heard before, and has not heard since Captain Blake bursting into tears of joy after the long strain upon his nerves; these things have been told, and have not been forgotten.

But the ship was not yet safe, though she was moving slowly toward safety. General Butler had now been positively assured that the captain of his ferry-boat was a traitor at heart, and would like nothing better than to run both steamer and frigate on a mud bank. He doubted the statement, which indeed was false. The man was half paralyzed with terror, and was thinking of nothing but how to get safely out of the hands of these terrible men. Nevertheless, the general deemed it best to make a remark or two by way of fortifying his virtuous resolutions, and neutralizing any hints he may have received from people on the shore. The engine-room he knew was conducted in the interest of the United States. for he had given it in charge to four of his own soldiers. He had no man in his command who happened to be personally acquainted with the shallows of the river Severn.

"Captain," said he, "have you faith in my word?"

"Yes," said the captain.

"I am told that you mean to run us aground. I think not. If you do, as God lives, and you live, I'll blow your brains out."

The poor captain, upon hearing these words, evinced symptoms of terror so remarkable, as to convince General Butler that if any mishap befell the vessels, it would not be owing to any disaffection on the part of the gentleman in the pilot-house.

All seemed to be going well. The general dozed in his chair. He woke to find the Maryland fast in the mud. Believing the captain's protestations, and the navigation being really difficult, he did not molest his brains, which were already sufficiently discomposed, but ordered him into confinement. The frigate was still afloat, and was, soon after, towed to a safe distance by a tug. The Eighth Massachusetts could boast that it had rendered an important service. But there the regiment was upon a bank of mud; provisions nearly consumed; water casks dry; and the sun doing its duty. There was nothing to be done but wait for the rising of the tide, and, in the mean time, to replenish the water casks from the shore.

The men were tired and hungry, black with coal dust, and tormented with thirst, but still cheerful, and even merry; and in the twilight of the Sunday evening, the strains of religious hymns rose from groups who, on the Sunday before, sang them in the choirs of village churches at home. The officers, as they champed their biscuit, and cut their pork with pocket knives, laughingly alluded to the superb breakfast given them on the morning of their departure from Philadelphia by Paran Stephens at the Continental. Mr. Stephens, a son of Massachusetts, had employed all the resources of his house in giving his countrymen a parting meal. The sudden plunge from luxury brought to the perfection of one of the fine arts, to army rations, scant in quantity, ill-cooked, and a short allowance of warm water, was the constant theme of jocular comparison on board the Maryland. It was a well-worn joke, to call for delicate and ludicrously impossible dishes, which were remembered as figuring in the Continental's bill of fare; the demand being gravely answered by the allowance of a biscuit, an inch of salt pork, and a tin cup half full of water.

General Butler improved the opportunity of going on shore. He met Governor Hicks and the mayor of Annapolis, who again urged him not to think of landing. All Maryland, they said, was on the point of rushing to arms; the railroad was impassable, and guarded by armed men; terrible things could not fail to happen, if the troops attempted to reach Washington.

"I *must* land," said the general; "my men are hungry. I could not even leave without getting a supply of provisions."

They declared that no one in Annapolis would sell him anything. To which the general replied, that he hoped better things of the people of Annapolis; but, in any case, a regiment of hungry soldiers were not limited to the single method of procuring supplies usually practiced in time of peace. There *were* modes of getting food other than the simple plan of purchase. Go to Washington he must and should, with or without the assistance of the people of Annapolis. The governor still refused his consent, and, the next day, put his refusal into writing; "protesting against the movement, which, in the excited condition of the people of this state, I can not but consider an unwise step on the part of the government. But," he added, "I must earnestly urge upon you, that there shall be no halt made by the troops in this city." No halt? Seven hundred and twenty-four famishing men, with a march of thirty miles before them, were expected to pass by a city abounding in provisions, and not halt! Great is Buncombe!

Another night was passed on board the Maryland. The dawn of Monday morning brought with it a strange apparition—a steamer approaching from the sea, crammed with troops, their arms soon glittering in the rays of the rising sun. Who could they be? They cheered the stars and stripes waving from the mast of the rescued Constitution; so they were not enemies, at least.

The steamer proved to be the Boston, with the New York Seventh on board, thirty-six hours from Philadelphia. They had steamed toward the mouth of the Potomac, but, on speaking the light-ships, were repeatedly told that the secessionists had stationed batteries of artillery on the banks of the river, for the purpose of preventing the ascent of troops. There was no truth in the story, but it seemed probable enough at that mad time; and, therefore, Colonel Lefferts, after the usual consultation, deemed it most prudent to change his course, and try General Butler's road to the capital; the regiment by no means relishing the change. The two regiments exchanged vigorous volleys of cheers, and preparations were soon made for getting the Maryland afloat.

General Butler, counting now upon Colonel Lefferts's hearty co-operation, issued to his own troops a cheering order of the day:—

"At five o'clock A. M. the troops will be called by companies to be drilled in the manual of arms, especially in loading at will and firing by file in the use of the bayonet, and these specialties will be observed in all subsequent drills in the manual; such drills will continue until 7 o'clock; then all the arms may be stacked upon the upper deck, great care being taken to instruct the men as to the mode of stacking their arms, so that a firm stack, not easily overturned, shall be made. Being obliged to drill at times with the weapons loaded, great damage may be done by the overturning of the stack and the discharge of a piece. This is important. Indeed, an accident has already occurred in the regiment from this cause, and although slight in its consequences, yet it warns us to increased diligence in this regard.

"The purpose which could only be hinted at in the orders of yesterday has been accomplished. The frigate Constitution has lain for a long time at this port substantially at the mercy of the armed mob which sometimes paralyzes the otherwise loyal state of Maryland. Deeds of daring, successful contests, and glorious victories had rendered Old Ironsides so conspicuous in the naval history of the country, that she was fitly chosen as the school

4*

in which to train the future officers of the navy to like heroic acts. It was given to Massachusetts and Essex County first to man her; it was reserved to Massachusetts to have the honor to retain her for the service of the Union and the laws. This is a sufficient triumph of right—a sufficient triumph for us. By this the blood of our friends shed by the Baltimore mob is in so far avenged. The Eighth regiment may hereafter cheer lustily upon all proper occasions, but never without orders. The old 'Constitution,' by their efforts, aided untiringly by the United States officers having her in charge, is now safely 'possessed, occupied, and enjoyed' by the government of the United States, and is safe from all her enemies.

"We have been joined by the Seventh regiment of New York, and together we propose peaceably, quietly, and civilly, unless opposed by some mob or other disorderly persons, to march to Washington in obedience to the requisition of the President of the United States; and if opposed, we shall march steadily forward. My next order, I hardly know how to express. I cannot assume that any of the citizen soldiery of Massachusetts or New York could, under any circumstances whatever, commit any outrages upon private property in a loyal and friendly state; but fearing that some improper person may have, by stealth, introduced himself among us, I deem it proper to state that any unauthorized interference with private property will be most signally punished, and full reparation therefor be made to the injured party, to the full extent of my power and ability. In so doing I but carry out the orders of the War Department. I should have done so without those orders.

"Colonel Monroe will cause these orders to be read at the head of each company before we march. Colonel Lefferts's command not having been originally included in this order, he will be furnished with a copy for his instruction."

The Maryland could not be floated. The men threw overboard coal and crates, and all heavy articles that could be spared. The Boston tugged her strongest. The Eighth ran in masses from side to side, and from end to end. After many hours of strenuous exertion, the men suffering extremely from thirst and hunger, the general himself not tasting a drop of liquid for twelve hours, the attempt was given up, and it was resolved that the Boston should land the Seventh at the grounds of the Naval Academy, and then convey to the same place the Massachusetts Eighth.

Desirous not to seem wanting in courtesy to a sovereign state, General Butler now sent to Governor Hicks, a formal written request for permission to land. The answer being delayed and his men almost fainting for water, he then dispatched a respectful note announcing his intention to land forthwith. It was to these notes that Governor Hicks sent the reply, already quoted, protesting against the landing, and urging that no halt be made at Annapolis.

In the course of the afternoon, both regiments were safely landed at the academy grounds, and the Seventh hastened to share all they had of provender and drink with their new friends. The men of the two regiments fraternized immediately and completely; nothing occurred, during the laborious days and nights that followed, to disturb, for an instant, the perfect harmony that reigned between them. The only contest was, which should do most to help, and cheer, and relieve the other.

I regret to be obliged to state that this pleasant state of affairs did not extend at all times, to the powers controlling the two regiments. An obstacle, little expected, now arose in General Butler's path.

From the moment when the Seventh had entered the grounds of the naval school, systematic attempts appear to have been made to alarm Colonel Lefferts for the safety of his command. Messengers came in with reports that the academy was surrounded with rebel troops; and even the loyal middies could testify, that during that very day, a force of Maryland militia had been drilling in the town itself. True, this force consisted of only one company of infantry and one of cavalry; but probably the exact truth was not known to Colonel Lefferts's informants. Certain it is, that he was made to believe that formidable bodies of armed men only waited the issue of the regiments from the gates of the walled inclosure in which they were, to give them battle, if, indeed, the inclosure itself was safe from attack. Accordingly he posted strong guards at the gates, and ordered that no soldier should be allowed to pass out. Nor were his apprehensions allayed when a Tribune reporter, who, accompanied by two friends, had strolled all over the town unmolested, brought back word that no enemy was in sight, and that the storekeepers of Annapolis were perfectly civil and willing to sell their goods to Union soldiers. Colonel Lefferts was assured that the hostile troops were purposely keeping out of sight, to fall upon the regiment where it could fight only at a fatal disadvantage.

Consequently, he determined not to march with General Butler. He placed his refusal in writing, in the following words:—

"ANNAPOLIS ACADEMY, MONDAY NIGHT, *April 22d*, 1861.

"General B. F. BUTLER, Commanding Massachusetts Volunteers.

"SIR:—Upon consultation with my officers, I do not deem it proper, under the circumstances, to co-operate in the proposed march by railroad, laying track as we go along—particularly in view of a large force hourly expected, and with so little ammunition as we possess. I must be governed by my officers in a matter of so much importance. I have directed this to be handed to you upon your return from the transport ship.

"I am, sir, yours respectfully, MARSHALL LEFFERTS."

It *was* handed to the general on his return from the transport ship. He sought an interview with Colonel Lefferts, and endeavored to change his resolve. Vain were arguments; vain remonstrance; vain the biting taunt. Colonel Lefferts still refused to go. General Butler then said he would go alone, he and his regiment, and proceeded forthwith to prepare for their departure. He instantly ordered two companies of the Massachusetts Eighth to march out of the walled grounds of the academy, and seize the railroad dépôt and storehouse. With the two companies, he marched himself to the dépôt, and took possession of it without opposition. At the storehouse, one man opposed them, the keeper in charge.

"What is inside this building?" asked the general.

"Nothing," replied the man.

"Give me the key."

"I hav'nt got it."

"Where is it?"

"I don't know."

"Boys, can you force those gates?"

The boys expressed an abundant willingness to try.

"Try, then."

They tried. The gates yielded, and flew open.

A small, rusty, damaged locomotive was found to be the "nothing," which the building held.

"Does any one here know anything about this machine?"

Charles Homans, a private of company E, eyed the engine for a moment, and said:

"Our shop made that engine, general. I guess I can put her in order and run her."

"Go to work, and do it."

Charles Homans picked out a man or two to help, and began, at once, to obey the order.

Leaving a strong guard at the dépôt, the general viewed the track, and ascertained that the rails had, indeed, been torn up, and thrown aside, or carelessly hidden. Returning to the regiment, he ordered a muster of men accustomed to track-laying; who, with the dawn of the next day, should begin to repair the road.

At sunset that evening, the Seventh regiment, to the delight of a concourse of midshipmen and other spectators, performed a brilliant evening parade, to the music of a full band.

Two members of this regiment (many more than two, but two especially), preferred the work that General Butler was doing, and implored him to give them an humble share in it. One of them was Schuyler Hamilton, grandson of one of the men whose names he bore, and great-grandson of the other; since distinguished in the war, and now General Hamilton. The other was Theodore Winthrop. General Butler found a place on his staff for Schuyler Hamilton, who rendered services of the utmost value; he was wise in counsel, valiant and prompt to execute. To Winthrop the general said:

"Serve out your time in your regiment. Then come to me, wherever I am, and I will find something for you to do."

Happily, a change came over the minds of the officers of the Seventh the next morning. As late as three o'clock at night, Colonel Lefferts was still resolved to remain at Annapolis; for, at that hour, he sent off a messenger, in an open boat, for New York, bearing dispatches asking for reinforcements and supplies. He informed the messenger that he had certain information of the presence of four rebel regiments at the Junction, where the grand attack was to be made upon the passing troops. But when the day dawned, and the cheering sun rose, and it became clear that the Massachusetts men at the dépôt had not been massacred, and were certainly going to attempt the march, then the officers of the Seventh came into General Butler's scheme, and agreed to join their brethren of Massachusetts. From that time forward, there was no hanging back. Both regiments worked vigorously in concert—Winthrop foremost among the foremost, all ardor, energy and merriment. Campaigning was an old story to him, who had roamed the world over in quest of adventure; and few men, of the thousands who were then rushing to the war, felt the greatness and the holiness of the cause as he felt it. Before leaving home, he had solemnly given his life to it, and, in so doing, tasted, for the first time, perhaps, a joy that satisfied him.

It would be unfair to censure Colonel Lefferts for his excessive prudence. He really believed the stories told him of the resistance he was to meet on the way. Granting that those tales were true, his course was, perhaps, correct. The general had one great advantage over him in the nature of his professional training. General Butler is one of the most vigorous and skillful cross-questioners in New England. In other words, he had spent twenty years of his life in detecting the true from the plausible; in dragging up half-drowned Truth, by her dripping locks, from the bottom of her well. Such practice gives a man at last a kind of intuitive power of detecting falsehood; he acquires a habit of balancing probabilities, he scents a lie from afar. Doubtless, he believed their march might be opposed at some favorable point; but, probably, he had too a tolerable certainty that slow, indolent, divided Maryland, could not, or would not, on such short notice, assemble a force on the line of railroad, capable of stopping a Massachusetts regiment bound to Washington on a legitimate errand. He had had, at Havre de Grace, a striking instance of the difference between truth and rumor, and his whole life had been full of such experiences. Colonel Lefferts, as a New York merchant, had passed his life among people who generally speak the truth, and keep their word. He was unprepared to believe that a dozen people could come to him, all telling substantially the same story, many of them believing what they told, and yet all uttering falsehoods.

Tuesday was a busy day of preparation for the march. Rails were hunted up and laid. Parties were pushed out in many directions but found no armed enemies. Lieutenant-Colonel Hinks, with two companies of the Massachusetts Eighth, advanced along the railroad three miles and a half, without meeting the slightest appearance of opposition. Soldiers strolled about the town, and discovered that the grimmest secessionist was not unwilling to exchange such commodities as he had for coin of the United States. Negroes gave furtive signs of good will, and produced baskets of cakes for sale. Madame Rumor was extremely diligent; there were bodies of cavalry here, and batteries of artillery there, and gangs of Plug-Uglies coming from terrible Baltimore. The soldiers worked away, unmolested by anything more formidable than vague threats of coming vengeance.

General Butler received and wrote divers brief epistles in the course of the day. Early in the morning he took the liberty of inquiring of the master of transportation, whether the rails of the road had been taken up "for the purpose of hindering the transportation of the United States militia under my charge to Washington. An immediate and explicit answer is desired." An immediate and explicit answer was returned, that the rails *had* been removed for the purpose mentioned; a mob having threatened to destroy the road if any troops of the United States should pass over it to Washington. The master of transportation desired to know by what authority General Butler had taken possession of the property of the railroad company. The general replied:

"I will answer your inquiry with the same explicitness that you did mine. My authority is the order of the government. My justification, the necessity for transportation. Your reparation, the pledge of the faith of the government."

He also informed the gentleman that a list of the property seized, and a receipt therefor, had been given to the person found in charge.

A startling rumor prevailed in the morning that the negroes in the vicinity of Annapolis were about to rise against their masters, and do something in the St. Domingo style—as per general expectation. The commanding general thought it proper to address to Governor Hicks the letter which became rather famous in those days:

"I did myself the honor, in my communication of yesterday, wherein I asked permission to land on the soil of Maryland, to inform you that the portion of the militia under my command were armed only against the disturbers of the peace of the state of Maryland and of the United States.

"I have understood within the last hour that some apprehension is entertained of an insurrection of the negro population of this neighborhood. I am anxious to convince all classes of persons that the forces under my command are not here in any way to interfere, or countenance an interference, with the laws of the state. I, therefore, am ready to co-operate with your excellency in suppressing most promptly and efficiently any insurrection against the laws of the state of Maryland. I beg, therefore, that you announce publicly, that any portion of the forces under my command is at your excellency's disposal, to act immediately for the preservation of the peace of this community."

The governor gave immediate pub icity to this letter, and it is said to have had a remarkable effect in quieting the apprehensions of the people. Many who had fled from their homes returned to them, and gave aid and comfort to the troops. The governor, however, was still in a protesting humor. His next communication to the general was the following:

"Having, by virtue of the powers vested in me by the constitution of Maryland, summoned the legislature of the state to assemble on Friday, the 26th instant, and Annapolis being the place in which, according to law, it must assemble; and having been credibly informed that you have taken military possession of the Annapolis and Elk Ridge railroad, I deem it my duty to protest against this step; because, without at present assigning any other reason, I am informed that such occupation of said road will prevent the members of the legislature from reaching this city."

To which General Butler replied:

"You are correctly informed that I have taken possession of the Annapolis and Elk Ridge railroad. It might have escaped your notice, but at the official meeting which was had, between your excellency and the mayor of Annapolis and the committee of the government and myself, as to the landing of my troops, it was expressly stated, as the reason why I should not land, that my troops could not pass the railroad, because the company had taken up the rails, and they were private property. It is difficult to see how it can be, that if my troops could not pass over the railroad one way, the members of the legislature could pass the other way. I have taken possession for the purpose of preventing the execution of the threats of the mob, as officially represented to me by the master of transportation of the railroad in this city, 'that if my troops passed over the railroad, the railroad should be destroyed.'

"If the government of the state had taken possession of the road in any emergency, I should have long hesitated before entering upon it; but as I had the honor to inform your excellency in regard to another insurrection against the laws of Maryland, I am here armed to maintain those laws, if your excellency desires, and the peace of the United States against all disorderly persons whatsoever. I am endeavoring to save and not to destroy; to obtain means of transportation, so that I can vacate the capital prior to the sitting of the legislature, and not be under the painful necessity of incumbering your beautiful city while the legislature is in session."

All was in readiness for the start before the men slept that night. The engine had been tried, and found sufficient. A few platform cars had been discovered. The general in command, issued the order for the march, in which he endeavored to provide for all probable events:

"The detachment of the Eighth, under command of Lieutenant-Colonel Hinks, which has already pushed forward and occupied the railroad three and one-half miles, will remain at its advance until joined by two companies of the New York Seventh, which will take the train now in our possession, and push forward as far as the track is left uninjured by the mob. These companies will then leave the cars, and, throwing out proper skirmishers, carefully scour the country along the line of the road, while the working party of the Eighth is repairing the track; taking care, however, not to advance so fast as not to be in reach of the main body, in case of an attack. The train of cars will return, and take up the advanced detachment of the Eighth now holding possession of the dépôt. These will again go forward as far as can be done with safety, on account of the state of the track, when they will leave the train, assist the party repairing it, and push forward as rapidly as possible, taking care that the track is put in order for the passage of the train. In the mean time, the train will return to the dépôt, and taking on board such a portion of the baggage as may be proper, will again go forward. The remaining portions of the Massachusetts and New York regiments will put themselves on the march, and consolidate the two regiments as rapidly as possible." Minute directions follow respecting the supply of provisions, the halt of two hours in the middle of the day, the sacredness of private property, and the measures to be used, if the troops were attacked.

Early the next morning, the troops were in motion. It was a bright, warm spring day, the sun gleaming along the line of bayonets, the groves vocal with birds, the air fragrant with blossoms. The engine driven by Charles Homans,—a soldier with fixed bayonet on each side of him,—came and went panting through the line of marching troops. As the sun climbed toward the zenith, the morning breeze died away, and the air in the deeper cuttings became suffocatingly warm. The working parties, more used to such a temperature, plied the sledge and the crowbar unflaggingly, but the daintier New Yorkers reeled under their heavy knapsacks, and were glad, at length, to leave them to the charge of Homans. With all their toil, the regiments could only advance at the rate of a mile an hour, for the farther they went, the more complete was the destruction of the road. Bridges had to be repaired, as well as rails replaced. A shower in the afternoon gave all parties a welcome drenching, and left the atmosphere cool and bracing; but when night closed in, and the moon rose, they were still many miles from the junction.

"O Gottschalk!" exclaims Winthrop, "what a poetic night march we then began to play, with our heels and toes on the railroad track!"

"It was full-moonlight and the night inexpressibly sweet and serene. The air was cool, and vivified by the gust and shower of the afternoon. Fresh spring was in every breath. Our fellows had forgotten that this morning they were hot and disgusted. Every one hugged his rifle as if it were the arm of the Girl of his Heart, and stepped out gayly for the promenade. Tired or foot-sore men, or even lazy ones, could mount upon the two freight-cars we were using for artillery-wagons. There were stout arms enough to tow the whole.

"It was an original kind of march. I suppose a battery of howitzers never before found itself mounted upon cars, ready to open fire at once, and bang away into the offing with shrapnel or into the bushes with canister. Our line extended a half-mile along the track. It was beautiful to stand on the bank above a cutting and watch the files strike from the shadow of a wood into a broad flame of moonlight, every rifle sparkling up alert as it came forward. A beautiful sight to see the barrels writing themselves upon the dimness, each a silver flash.

"By-and-by, 'Halt!' came, repeated along from the front, company after company. 'Halt! a rail gone.'

"From this time on we were constantly interrupted. Not a half-mile passed without a rail up. Bonnell was always at the front laying track, and I am proud to say that he accepted me as aid-de-camp. Other fellows, unknown to me in the dark, gave hearty help. The Seventh showed that it could do something else than drill.

"At one spot, on a high embankment over standing water, the rail was gone, sunk probably. Here we tried our rails, brought from the turn-out. They were too short. We supplemented with a length of plank from our stores. We rolled our cars carefully over. They passed safe. But Homans shook his head. He could not venture a locomotive on that frail stuff. So we lost the society of the 'J. H. Nicholson.' Next day the Massachusetts commander called for some one to dive in the pool for the lost rail. Plump into the water went a little wiry chap and grappled the rail. 'When I come up,' says the brave fellow afterward to me, 'our officer out with a twenty-dollar gold piece and wanted me to take it. 'That a'n't what I come for,' says I. 'Take it,' says he, 'and share with the others.' 'That a'n't what they come for,' says I. But I took a big cold,' the diver continued, 'and I'm condemned hoarse yit,'—which was the fact.

"Farther on we found a whole length of track torn up, on both sides, sleepers and all, and the same thing repeated with alternations of breaks of single rails. Our howitzer-ropes came into play to hoist and haul. We were not going to be stopped."

In the afternoon of the day following, the Seventh marched by the White House, and saluted the President of the United States. Not an armed foe had been seen by them on the way.

It had been General Butler's intention to accompany the troops to Washington; but before they had started the steamer Baltic arrived, loaded with troops from New York, giving abundant employment to the general and his extemporized staff. Before they had been disposed of, other vessels arrived, and, on the day following, came an order from General Scott, directing General Butler to remain at Annapolis, hold the town and the road, and superintend the passage of the troops. Before the week ended, the "department of Annapolis," embracing the country lying twenty miles on each side of the railroad, was created, and Brigadier-General Butler placed in command; with ample powers, extending even to the suspension of habeas corpus, and the bombardment of Annapolis, if such extreme measures should be necessary for the maintenance of the supremacy of the United States.

During the next ten days, General Butler's unequaled talent for the dispatch of business, and his unequaled powers of endurance, were taxed to the uttermost. Troops arrived, thousands in a day. The harbor was filled with transports. Every traveler from North or South was personally examined, and his passport indorsed by the general in command. Spies were arrested. The legislature of Maryland was closely watched, and no secret was made of General Butler's intention to arrest the entire majority if an ordinance of secession was passed. It was not known to that body, I presume, that one of their officers had consigned to General Butler's custody the Great Seal of the Common wealth, without which no act of theirs could acquire the validity of law. Such was the fact, however. In the total inexperience of commanding officers, every detail of the disembarkation, of the encampments, of the supply, and of the march, required the supervision of the general. From daylight until midnight he labored, keeping chaos at bay. One night as the clock was striking twelve, when the general, after herculean toils, had cleared his office of the last bewildered applicant for advice or orders, and he was about to trudge wearily to bed, an anxious-looking correspondent of a newspaper came in.

"General," said he, "where am I to sleep to-night?"

This was, really, too much.

"Sir," said the tired commander of the Department of Annapolis, "I have done to-day about everything that a man ever did in this world. But I am not going to turn chambermaid, by Jove!"

And, so saying, he escaped from the room.

We need not linger at Annapolis. General Butler's services there were duly appreciated by the president, the lieutenant-general, Governor Andrew, and the country. One act alone of his elicited any sign of disapproval; it was his offer of the troops of Massachusetts to the governor of Maryland, to aid in suppressing an insurrection of the slaves. It is proper that we should place on convenient record here his reasons for that step, with the letter of Governor Andrew, which called them forth.

GOVERNOR ANDREW TO GENERAL BUTLER.

COMMONWEALTH OF MASSACHUSETTS,
EXECUTIVE DEPARTMENT,
COUNCIL CHAMBER, BOSTON, *April* 25, 1861.

GENERAL: I have received, through Mayor Ames, a dispatch transmitted from Perryville, detailing the proceedings at Annapolis from the time of your arrival off that port until the hour when Major Ames left you to return to Philadelphia. I wish to repeat the assurance of my entire satisfaction with the action you have taken, with a single exception. If I rightly understood the telegraphic dispatch, I think that your action in tendering to Governor Hicks the assistance of our Massachusetts troops to suppress a threatened servile insurrection among the hostile people of Maryland was unnecessary. I hope that the fuller dispatches, which are on their way from you, may show reasons why I should modify my opinion concerning that particular instance; but, in general, I think that the matter of servile insurrection among a community in arms against the Federal Union, is no longer to be regarded by our troops in a political, but solely in a military point of view, and is to be contemplated as one of the inherent weaknesses of the enemy, from the disastrous operations of which we are under no obligation of a military character to guard them, in order that they may be enabled to improve the security which our arms would afford, so as to prosecute with more energy their traitorous attacks upon the Federal government and capital. The mode in which such outbreaks are to be considered, should depend entirely upon the loyalty or disloyalty of the community in which they occur, and in the vicinity of Annapolis, I can, on this occasion, perceive no reason of military policy, why a force summoned to the defense of the Federal government, at this moment of all others, should be offered to be diverted from its immediate duty, to help rebels, who stand with arms in their hands, obstructing its progress toward the city of Washington. I entertain no doubt that whenever we shall have an opportunity to interchange our views personally on this subject, we shall arrive at entire concordance of opinion. Yours faithfully,

JOHN A. ANDREW.

GENERAL BUTLER TO GOVERNOR ANDREW.

DEPARTMENT OF ANNAPOLIS,
HEAD-QUARTERS, ANNAPOLIS, *May* 9, 1861.

To His Excellency JOHN A. ANDREW, Governor and Commander-in-Chief:

SIR:—I have delayed replying to your excellency's dispatch of the 25th April, in my other dispatches, because as it involved only disapprobation of an act done, couched in the kindest language, I supposed the interest of the country could not suffer in the delay; and incessant labor up to the present moment, has prevented me giving full consideration to the topic. Temporary illness, which forbids bodily activity, gives me now a moment's pause.

The telegraph, with more than usual accuracy, had rightly informed your excellency that I had offered the services of the Massachusetts troops under my command to aid the authorities of Maryland in suppressing a threatened slave insurrection. Fortunately for us, all the rumor of such an outbreak was without substantial foundation. Assuming, as your excellency does, in your dispatch, that I was carrying on military operations in an enemy's country, when a war *à l'outrance* was to be waged, my act might be a matter of discussion. And in that view, acting in the light of the Baltimore murders, and the apparent hostile position of Maryland, your excellency might, without mature reflection, have come to the conclusion of disapprobation expressed in your dispatch. But the facts, especially as now aided by their results, will entirely justify my act, and reinstate me in your excellency's good opinion.

True, I landed on the soil of Maryland against the formal protest of its governor and of the corporate authorities of Annapolis, but without any armed opposition on their part, and expecting opposition only from insurgents assembled in riotous contempt of the laws of the state. Before, by letter, and at the time of landing, by personal interview, I had informed Governor Hicks that soldiers of the Union, under my command, were armed only against the insurgents and disturbers of the peace of Maryland and of the United States. I received from Governor Hicks assurances of the loyalty of the state to the Union—assurances which subsequent events have fully justified. The mayor of Annapolis also informed me that the city authorities would in no wise oppose me, but that I was in great danger from the excited and riotous mobs of Baltimore pouring down upon me, and in numbers beyond the control of the police. I assured both the governor and the mayor that I had no fear of a Baltimore or other mob, and that, supported by the authorities of the state and city, I should repress all hostile demonstrations against the laws of Maryland and the United States, and that I would protect both myself and the city of Annapolis from any disorderly persons whatsoever. On the morning following my landing I was informed that the city of Annapolis and environs were in danger from an insurrection of the slave population, in defiance of the laws of the state. What was I to do? I had promised to put down a white mob and to preserve and enforce the laws against that. Ought I to allow a black one any preference in a breach of the laws? I understood that I was armed against all infractions of the laws, whether by white or black, and upon that understanding I acted, certainly with promptness and efficiency. And your excellency's shadow of disapprobation, arising from a misunderstanding of the facts, has caused all the regret I have for that action. The question seemed to me to be neither military nor political, and was not to be so treated. It was simply a question of good faith and honesty of purpose. The benign effect of my course was instantly seen. The good but timid people of Annapolis who had fled from their houses at our approach, immediately returned; business resumed its accustomed channels; quiet and order prevailed in the city; confidence took the place of distrust, friendship of enmity, brotherly kindness of sectional hate, and I believe to-day there is no city in the Union more loyal than the city of Annapolis. I think, therefore, I may safely point to the results for my justification. The vote of the neighboring county of Washington, a few days since, for its delegate to the legislature, wherein 4,000 out of 5,000 votes were thrown for a delegate favorable to the Union, is among the many happy fruits of firmness of purpose, efficiency of action, and integrity of mission. I believe, indeed, that it will not require a personal interchange of views, as suggested in your dispatch, to bring our minds in accordance; a simple statement of the facts will suffice.

But I am to act hereafter, it may be, in an enemy's country, among a servile population, when the question may arise, as it has not yet arisen, as well in a moral and Christian, as in a political and military point of view, What shall I do? Will your excellency bear with me a moment while this question is discussed?

I appreciate fully your excellency's suggestion as to the inherent weakness of the rebels, arising from the preponderance of their servile population. The question, then, is, In what manner shall we take advantage of that weakness? By allowing, and, of course, arming, that population to rise upon the defenseless women and children of the country, carrying rapine, arson and murder—all the horrors of San Domingo, a million times magnified—among those whom we hope to reunite with us as brethren, many of whom are already so, and all who are worth preserving, will be, when this horrible madness shall have passed away or be threshed out of them? Would your excellency advise the troops under my command to make war in person upon the defenseless women and children of any part of the Union, accompanied with brutalities too horrible to be named? You will say, "God forbid!" If we may not do so in person, shall we arm others so to do, over whom we can have no restraint, exercise no control, and who, when once they have tasted blood, may turn the very arms we put in their hands against ourselves, as a part of the oppressing white race? The reading of history so familiar to your excellency, will tell you the bitterest cause of complaint which our fathers had against Great Britain in the war of the Revolution, was the arming by the British ministry of the red man with the tomahawk and the scalping-knife against the women and children of the colonies, so that the phrase, "May we not use all the means which God and nature have put in our power to subjugate the colonies?" has passed into a legend of infamy against the leader of that ministry who used it in parliament. Shall history teach us in vain? Could we justify ourselves to ourselves, although with arms in our hands, amid the savage wildness of camp and field, we may have blunted many of the finer moral sensibilities, in letting loose four millions of worse than savages upon the homes and hearths of the South? Can we be justified to the Christian community of Massachusetts? Would such a course be consonant with the teachings of our holy religion? I have a very decided opinion upon the subject, and if any one desires, as I know your excellency does not, this unhappy contest to be prosecuted in that manner, some instrument other than myself must be found to carry it on. I may not discuss the political bearings of this topic. When I went from under the shadow of my roof-tree, I left all politics behind me, to be resumed only when every part of the Union is loyal to the flag, and the potency of the government through the ballot-box is established.

Passing the moral and Christian view, let us examine the subject as a military question. Is not that state already subjugated which requires the bayonets of those armed in opposition to its rulers, to preserve it from the horrors of a servile war? As the least experienced of military men, I would have no doubt of the entire subjugation of a state brought to that condition. When, therefore—unless I am better advised—any community in the United States, who have met me in honorable warfare, or even in the prosecution of a rebellious war in an honorable manner, shall call upon me for protection against the nameless horrors of a servile insurrection, they shall have it, and from the moment that call is obeyed, I have no doubt we shall be friends and not enemies.

The possibility that dishonorable means of defense are to be taken by the rebels against the government, I do not now contemplate. If, as has been done in a single instance, my men are to be attacked by poison, or as in another, stricken down by the assassin's knife, and thus murdered, the community using such weapons may be required to be taught that it holds within its own border a more potent means for deadly purposes and indiscriminate slaughter than any which it can administer to us.

Trusting that these views may meet your excellency's approval, I have the honor to be, very respectfully, your obedient servant,

BENJ. F. BUTLER.

We all remember how universal the expectation was, at the beginning of the war, that the negroes would everywhere embrace the opportunity to rise upon their masters, and commit frightful outrages. That expectation grew out of our general ignorance of the character and feelings of the southern negro; and none of us were so ignorant upon these points as hunker democrats. If they had some acquaintance with slaveholders, they knew nothing about slavery, because they *would* know nothing. It is a propensity of the human mind, to put away from itself unwelcome truths. American democrats, I repeat, know nothing of American slavery. It was pleasant and convenient for them to think, that Mr. Wendell Phillips, Mr. Garrison, Mrs. Stowe, and Mr. Sumner, were persons of a fanatical cast of character, whose calm and very moderate exhibitions of slavery were totally beneath consideration—distorted, exaggerated, incredible. It was with the most sincere *astonishment*, that General Butler and his hunker staff discovered, when they stood face to face with slavery, and were obliged to administer the law of it, and tried to do justice to the black man as well as to the white, that the worst delineations of slavery ever presented to the public fell far short of the unimaginable truth.* They were ready to confess their ignorance of that of which they had been hearing and reading all their lives, and that this 'patriarchal institution,' for which some of them had pleaded or apologized, was simply the most hellish thing that ever was in this world.

Nevertheless, there has never been the slightest danger of an insurrection of the slaves. The real victim of slavery is the white man, not the black. Whatever little good there is in the system, the black man has had; while most of the evil has fallen to the white man's share. Under slavery, the black man has deeply suffered and slowly improved; the white man has ignobly enjoyed and rapidly degenerated. Three or four, or five generations of servitude have extirpated whatever of warlike and rebellious energy the negro may have once possessed; and, of late years, the Christian religion, in a rude and tropical form—much feeling and little knowledge—has exerted a still more subduing influence upon them. Some more or less correct version of the story of the Cross has become familiar to them all, as well as the sentiments of the Sermon on the Mount. To no people, of all the suffering sons of men, has that wondrous tale come home with such power as to these sad and docile children of Africa. Are not they, too, men of sorrow? Are not they, too, acquainted with grief? Have not they, too, to suffer and be silent?—revenge impossible, forgiveness divinely commanded?

Insurrection! If a Springfield musket and a Sheffield bowie-knife were this day placed in every negro hut in the South, and every master gone to the war, the negroes might use those weapons, but it would be to defend, not to molest, their masters' wives

* "On reading Mrs. Stowe's book, 'Uncle Tom's Cabin,' I thought it to be an overdrawn, highly-wrought picture of southern life; but I have seen with my own eyes, and heard with my own ears, many things which go beyond her book, as much as her book does beyond an ordinary school-girl's novel."—*Speech of General Butler at the Fifth Avenue Hotel, New York, on his return from New Orleans, January* 8, 1863.

and children. There is many a negro in the southern states who does actually stand in the same *kind* of moral relation to his master as that which Jesus Christ bore to the Jews, when he said, "Father, forgive them, for they know not what they do." And not *moral* relation only; for the negro often has a clear mental perception of the fact stated. He sometimes stands above his master, at a hight which the master can neither see nor believe in.

CHAPTER V.

BALTIMORE.

When war breaks out in a country after a long peace, it is natural that the people should look for guidance first to men who won distinction in the wars of the past. The history of wars shows us that this is generally an error, fruitful of disaster. It gave us Washington, it is true; but Washington was but forty-four years of age when he left Philadelphia to take command of the armies of the revolution; and he had passed the twenty years which had elapsed since Braddock's defeat, not in the routine of a military office, but in hunting the fox, and in managing a great estate, which involved the control of some hundreds of human beings. The almost sovereign lord of a little principality, he spent half his days in the saddle, and was constantly engaged in pursuits somewhat akin to those of a commander of armies. Neither his mind nor his blood could stagnate, roaming those extensive fields and forests, foreseeing, calculating, providing, governing. But the rule usually holds good, that a war develops its own hero; the heroes of the past not proving adequate to the new emergency.

At the beginning of this rebellion, there was an officer at the seat of government who had been a general in the service of the United States for forty-nine years. Two generations had been accustomed to regard him as the ablest of American soldiers; and for a long series of years, he had been highest in place, as well as highest in the confidence of the public. The reputation of a living person has in it a principle of growth. If a man has done something which so enters into the history of his nation, that children necessarily become familiar with his name at school, he may sit still for thirty years, and yet find his reputation growing; until, by the death of cotemporaries, it becomes, perhaps, unique and overshadowing. The haze of antiquity gathers round it, veiling and yet magnifying the basis of fact upon which it rests. And if, perchance, the ancient hero, emerging from the vast, dim halo of his name, presents himself to view, in his old age, at the head of a conquering army, thundering at the gates of an enemy's capital, vague reverence is changed to conscious enthusiasm, and no one doubts that here, indeed, is the "first captain of the age." When the war began, therefore, and rumors of an impending attack upon the capital alarmed the country, the name of Winfield Scott appeared sufficient to allay apprehension. It seemed of itself a tower of strength; it was a rallying point for the gathering forces of the country; it gave assurance to millions of minds that the resources of the nation, so lavishly offered, would be employed with intelligence and success. If there was a moment when some men feared that the mania of secession might seize even him, the fear was quickly dispelled, when he was seen renewing his oath of allegiance, and responding in unequivocal language to the cheers of arriving regiments. There he was, the center of attraction, conspicuous among the conspicuous, apparently rolling up the whirlwind, and elaborating the storm that was supposed to be about to sweep over the rebellious states resistless.

Fatal delusion!

General Scott was seventy-five years of age. An old wound partly disabled him. A recent accident had shaken him severely. He could not mount a horse. He could not walk a mile. The motion of a carriage soon fatigued him. His vast form was itself a heavy burden. He required a great deal of sleep. He moved, thought, and acted slowly. Accustomed for fifty years to the pettiest details of a small, widely scattered army, he was now suddenly called upon to organize many armies, and direct their movements against enemies in the field. A task more difficult than ever Napoleon or Wellington performed, was laid upon a man who, in his best days, would have been signally unequal to it; for he had not been gifted by nature with that genius for command which alone could have formed invincible armies out of masses of loosely organized men, having nothing that belongs to soldiers except arms and a willingness to use them for the restoration of their country. He was a man of exact, formal, unpliant mind. Accustomed long to the first place—accustomed also to that extravagant adulation which we used to bestow upon conspicuous persons, he was less likely to suspect his infinite insufficiency.

This was well known, however, to every thinking man familiar with Washington. Mr. Lincoln was not familiar with Washington. He, too, had been accustomed to survey General Scott from a great distance, and he took for granted the correctness of the popular estimate, which pronounced him the first captain of the age! Mr. Cameron, the secretary of war, was totally ignorant of the first rudiments of the military art; and he had, too, a painful sense of his ignorance, which he frequently expressed. Hence, the military resources of the country were laid, as it were, humbly at the feet of General Scott, for him to use or misuse according to his good pleasure.

Baltimore was the ruling topic in those days. Baltimore, still severed from all its railroad connections with the North, and still under control of the secession minority. One of the last reporters who made his way through the city, two or three days after the attack of the mob upon the Sixth Massachusetts, gave a striking narrative of his adventures, which kept alive the impression that Baltimore had gone over, as one man, to the side of the rebels, and meant to resist to the death the passage of Union troops.

"In the streets," he wrote, "of the lower part of the city, there were immense crowds, warm discussions, and the high pitch of excitement which discussion engenders. The mob—for Baltimore street was one vast mob—was surging to and fro, uncertain in what way to move, and apparently without any special purpose. Many had small secession cards pinned on their coat collars, and not a few were armed with guns, pistols and knives, of which they made the most display.

"I found the greatest crowd surging around the telegraph office, waiting anxiously, of course, for news. The most inquiry was as to the whereabouts of the New York troops—the most frequent topic, the probable results of an attempt on the part of the Seventh regiment to force a passage through Baltimore. All agreed that the force could never go through—all agreed that it would make the attempt if ordered to do so, and none seemed to entertain a doubt that it would leave a winrow of the dead bodies of those who assailed it in the streets through which it might attempt to pass.

"I found the police force entirely in sympathy with the secessionists and indisposed to act against the mob. Marshal Kane and the commissioners do not make any concealment of their proclivities for the Southern Confederacy. Mayor Brown, upon whom I called, seemed to be disposed to do his duty—providing he knew what it was, and could do it safely. He was in a high state of exsitement when I mentioned my name and purpose. He manifested a disposition to be civil, and to give me information, but was evidently afraid that I was a Northern aggressor, with whom it was indiscreet for him to be in too close communication. Seeing his condition, I left him and went out in the crowd to gather public opinion again."

Wild rumors were afloat. "At one time government had backed down—then it was going ahead; Virginia was coming—Virginia was not coming. The New Yorkers, Pennsylvanians, the Massachusetts men and the Rhode Islanders, were at one time marching one hundred abreast over the state, looking neither to the right nor the left—at another, no 'd—d Yankee' would dare thus to pollute the sacred soil of Maryland. One told that Fort McHenry had been blown up, another that it was going to 'shell' the city, a third that it was only garrisoned by a handful, while a fourth was positive that at least a force double the full war allotment was within its walls. There was some talk that the fort would be attacked, but the opinion that there was a full garrison, having generally obtained, the attacking part of the programme was postponed. Though large crowds remained in the streets until morning, no unusual events transpired. Curiosity to see what was going on appeared to be the prevailing motive with those who were tramping about. * * *

"About eight o'clock the next morning, the streets began again to be crowded. The bar-rooms and public resorts were closed, so that the incentive to precipitate action might not be too readily accessible. Nevertheless, there was much excitement, and among the crowds this morning, there were many men from the country, who carried shot and duck guns, and old-fashioned horse-pistols, such as the 'Maryland' line might have carried from the first to the present war. The best weapons appeared to be in the hands of young men—boys of eighteen, with the physique and dress and style of deportment, cultivated by the 'Hook Boys' and 'Dead Rabbits' of New York, as villainous looking compounds of reckless rascality as were ever produced in any community.

"About ten o'clock, a cry was raised that 3,000 Pennsylvania troops were at the Calvert street dépôt of the Pennsylvania railroad, and were about to take up their line of march through the city. With a portion of the crowd, I made my way to the dépôt to find it by far the most quiet place in the city. There it was said that the 3,000 were at Pikesville, about fifteen miles from the city, and were going to fight their way around the city. The crowd did not seem disposed to interfere with a movement that required a preliminary tramp of fifteen miles through a heavy sand. But the city authorities, however, rapidly organized and armed some three or four companies and sent them toward Pikesville. Ten of the Adams express wagons passed up Baltimore, loaded with armed men. In one or two there were a number of mattresses, as if wounded men were anticipated. A company of cavalry also started for Pikesville, I supposed to sustain the infantry that had been expressed.

"All through the day, the accessions from the country were coming in. Sometimes a squad of infantry, sometimes a troop of horse, and once a small park of artillery. It was nothing extraordinary to see a 'solitary horseman' riding in from the counties, with shotgun, powder-horn and flask. Some came with provender lashed to the saddle, prepared to picket out for the night. Boys came with their fathers, accoutered apparently with the war sword and holster-pistols that had done service a century ago. There were strange contrasts between the stern, solemn bearing of the father, and the buoyant, excited, enthusiastic expressions of the boy's face. I had frequent talks with these people, and could not but be impressed with their devotion and patriotism; for, mistaken as they were, they were none the less actuated by the most unselfish spirit of loyalty. They hardly knew, any of them, for what they had so suddenly come to Baltimore. They had a vague idea only, that Maryland had been invaded, and that it was the solemn duty of her sons to protect their soil from the encroachments of an invading force."*

* *N. Y. Daily Times*, April 24th, 1861.

Upon reading such letters as this, a great cry arose in the North for the re-opening of the path to Washington through Baltimore, even if it should involve the destruction of the rebellious city. The proceedings of General Butler at Annapolis, and the departure from Baltimore of the leading spirits of the mob to join the rebel army in Virginia, quieted the city, and gave the Union men some chance to make their influence felt. But this change was not immediately understood at Washington, and General Scott was meditating a great strategic scheme for the conquest of the city.

His plan, as officially communicated on the 29th of April, to General Butler, General Patterson, and others who were to co-operate, were as follows: "I suppose," wrote the lieutenant-general, "that a column from this place (Washington) of three thousand men, another from York of three thousand men, a third from Perryville, or Elkton, by land or water, or both, of three thousand men, and a fourth from Annapolis, by water, of three thousand men, might suffice. But it may be, and many persons think it *probable*, that Baltimore, before we can get ready, will re-open the communication through that city, and beyond, each way, for troops, army supplies, and travelers, voluntarily. When can we be ready for the movement on Baltimore on this side? Colonel Mansfield has satisfied me that we want, at least, ten thousand additional troops here to give security to the capital; and, as yet, we have less than ten thousand, including some very indifferent militia from the district. With that addition, we will be able, I think, to make the detachment for Baltimore."

A day or two after the receipt of this letter, General Butler went to Washington to confer with the general-in-chief. He conversed with him fully upon the state of affairs. One suggestion offered on this occasion, by General Butler, has peculiar interest in view of subsequent events. He was of opinion, with Shakspeare, that the place to fight the wolf is not at your own front door, but nearer its own den. Manassas Junction he suggested, not Arlington Heights, was the place where Washington should first be defended; and he offered to march thither with two thousand men, destroy the railroad connections with the South, and fortify the position. As there were then no rebel troops at the Junction, this could have been done without loss or delay. General Scott negatived the proposal. The Committee on the Conduct of the War have since characterized the omission to seize Manassas Junction at this time, as "the great error of that campaign." "The position at Manassas," add the Committee, "controlled the railroad communication in all that section of country. The forces which were opposed to us at the battle of Bull Run were mostly collected and brought to Manassas during the months of June and July. The three months' men could have made the place easily defensible against any force the enemy could have brought against it; and it is not at all probable that the rebel forces would have advanced beyond the line of the Rappahannock had Manassas been occupied by our troops."

General Butler strongly urged his scheme of seizing Manassas, both in conversation and in writing, to various influential persons. General Scott's veto was decisive.

The reduction of Baltimore was, however, the chief topic of discussion between General Butler and the commander-in-chief. General Scott was still of opinion that some time must elapse before troops could be spared for the attempt; but he consented to General Butler's taking a regiment or two, and holding the Relay House, a station nine miles from Baltimore. Before leaving on this expedition, he asked General Scott what were the powers of a general commanding a department. The reply was, that, except as limited by specific orders and by military law, his powers were absolute; he could do whatever he thought best. Upon receiving this information, General Butler privately consulted an officer of engineers, who ascertained for him, by reference to authoritative maps, that the city of Baltimore was within the Department of Annapolis, as defined in the order creating it.

Saturday afternoon, May 4th, the Eighth New York, the Sixth Massachusetts, and Cook's battery of artillery received the welcome order to be ready to march by two o'clock the next morning. General Butler had given a solemn promise to the Sixth, his own home regiment, which he had joined before his beard was grown, that they should, one day, if his advice was taken, march again through Baltimore. His selection of the regiment on this occasion was the beginning of the fulfillment of that promise. At daylight on Sunday morning, a train of thirty cars glided from the dépôt at Washington; from which, two hours later, the regiments issued at the Relay House, where they seized the dépôt and swarmed over the adjoining hills, reconnoitering.

No enemy was discovered; there was no formidable enemy at that time any where near Washington, *and there had not been;* but every man they met had something terrible to tell them of rebel dragoons hovering near. Cannons were planted on the heights. Camps were formed, and scouting parties sent out. Officers were detailed to go through all passing trains and seize articles contraband of war—such as weapons, powder, and intrenching tools. The general wrote to Washington to know if he might not arrest certain prominent traitors who lived near—members of the Carroll family and others. He concluded his first dispatch with these words: "I find the people here exceedingly friendly, and I have no doubt that with my present force I could march through Baltimore. I am the more convinced of this because I learn that, for several days, many of the armed secessionists have left for Harper's Ferry, or have gone forth plundering the country. I trust my acts will meet your approbation, whatever you may think of my suggestions."

General Butler remained a week at the Relay House. Large numbers of friendly people from Baltimore drove out to his camp, and, with them, some who were not friendly. He became perfectly well informed of the condition of the city. General Scott wrote approvingly of his acts, and authorized him to use his discretion in arresting the disaffected, and in seizing contraband articles. He also informed him that he need not remain at the Relay House "longer than he deemed his presence there of importance." He did not.

Incidents occurred in camp at the Relay House, which created, at the time, a general sensation. A man from Baltimore, lounging about among the New York soldiers, said to some of them, that the Baltimore mob was right in attacking the Massachusetts regiment, and would give them a still warmer reception on their return. Two officers at once arrested the man. In general orders of the next morning, General Butler thanked the officers for doing so, and consigned the culprit to prison at Annapolis. In the same order, the general alluded to other events in a characteristic manner.

"Two incidents of the gravest character marked the progress of yesterday. Charles Leonard, private, Company G, Eighth regiment of New York, was accidentally killed instantaneously by the discharge of a musket from which he was drawing the charge. He was buried with all the honors, amidst the gloom and sorrow of every United States soldier at this post, and the tender sympathies of many of the loyal inhabitants in our neighborhood. * * * The first offering of New York of the life of one of her sons upon the country's altar, his blood mingling on the soil of Maryland with that of the Massachusetts men murdered at Baltimore, will form a new bond of union between us and all loyal states, so that without need of further incentive to our duty, we are spurred on by the example of the life and death of Leonard.

"The other matter to which the general desires to call the attention of the troops is this: Wishing to establish the most friendly relations between you and this neighborhood, the general invited all venders of supplies to visit our camp, and replenish our somewhat scanty commissariat. But, to his disgust and horror, he finds well-authenticated evidence that a private in the Sixth regiment has been poisoned, by means of strychnine administered in the food brought into the camp by one of these peddlers. I am happy to be informed that the man is now out of danger. This act will, of course, render it necessary for me to cut off all purchases from unauthorized persons.

"Are our few insane enemies among the loyal men of Maryland prepared to wage war upon us in this manner? Do they know the terrible lesson of warfare they are teaching us? Can it be that they realize the fact, that we can put an agent, with a word, into every household, armed with this terrible weapon? In view of the terrible consequences of this mode of warfare, if accepted by us from their teaching, with every sentiment of devotional prayer, may we not exclaim, 'Father, forgive them; they know not what they do!' Certain it is, that any such other attempt, reasonably authenticated as to the persons committing it, will be followed by the swiftest, surest, and most condign punishment."

Such events as this could not but confirm the impression upon the minds of the troops, that they were posted in an enemy's country. The vigilance of some of the officers was carried to a troublesome extreme. One rainy night, the whole body of the troops, seventeen hundred in number, were called to arms four times by false alarms. On the last occasion, the general in command addressed a peculiar reproof to the officer whose inexperience had given the troops so many needless drenchings. This gentleman being a tailor by trade, the general roared out:

"In God's name, Colonel ———, where are the other eight?"

General Butler managed the case of this over-zealous, but wofully ignorant officer with good-natured tact. He opened a way for his quiet transfer to a clerkship in a custom-house, where he served his country well.

On the 13th of May, General Butler arrived at the conclusion that his presence at the Relay House was no longer necessary. Early in the morning, he telegraphed to General Scott, among other things, that Baltimore was in the department of Annapolis. An answer came back from Colonel Schuyler Hamilton, then on the staff of the lieutenant-general, which certainly could not be construed as forbidding the movement contemplated.

"General Scott desires me to invite your attention to certain guilty parties in Baltimore, namely, those connected with the guns and military cloths seized by your troops (at the Relay House), as well as the baker who furnished supplies of bread for Harper's Ferry. It is probable that you will find them, on inquiry, proper subjects for seizure and examination. He acknowledges your telegram of this morning, and is happy to find that Baltimore is within your department."

Later in the day, arrived a second dispatch from Colonel Hamilton:—

"General Scott desires me to inform you that he has received information, believed to be reliable, that several tons of gunpowder, designed for those unlawfully combined against the government, are stored in a church in Baltimore, in the neighborhood of Calhoun street, between Baltimore and Fayette streets. He invites your attention to the subject."

It is said that General Scott, who required much sleep, and who was oppressed with a multiplicity of business, did not always scrutinize very closely the dispatches sent in his name, when they were supposed to relate to matters of mere detail. It may be that the meaning and tendency of these dispatches escaped his attention. Colonel Hamilton, who had enjoyed the opportunity at Annapolis of becoming acquainted with the quality of the Massachusetts brigadier, was, certainly, not inclined to place any obstacles in his way.

At four o'clock in the afternoon of May 13th, the rebel spies at the Relay House felt sure, that at length, they were about to have something important to communicate to their employers at Baltimore. Two trains of cars stood upon the track, both headed toward Harper's Ferry, both loaded with troops. One was a short train, with a force of fifty men on board. The other was of immense length. It contained the whole of the Sixth Massachusetts, some companies of the New York Eighth, and two pieces of artillery, in all nine hundred men. The general's white horse, horses for the staff and artillery were on the train. When everything was in readiness, word was brought to the general that two fast Baltimore trotters were harnessed in a stable near by, which were to convey the tidings of the movement to Baltimore the moment the trains had started.

"Let them go," said the general.

The two trains moved slowly toward Harper's Ferry. The fast nags, at the same moment, were put on the road to Baltimore. General Butler secretly resolved to give them plenty of time to reach the city. Except himself and a few members of his staff, every man in the train was ignorant of his real design.

Two miles from the Relay House, both trains halted a while. Then the smaller train kept on its way. It was bound to Frederick, where the troops were ordered to seize the millionaire, Ross Winans, and the machine then figuring ominously in the newspapers, or Winans's steam gun; a useless rattle-trap, as it proved. Winans was a thorough-going traitor, and one who, from his prodigious wealth (fifteen millions, it was thought), could give his fellow traitors abundant aid and very solid comfort. Already, he had manufactured five thousand pikes for the use of the Baltimore mob against the forces summoned by his country to defend its capital. An arch-traitor, and an old; gray hairs did what they could to "make his folly venerable." If ever treason was committed, he had committed it; for he had not even the empty excuse of the passage of an ordinance of secession by the legislature of his state. General Butler will interpret his orders with exact literalness, if this hoary-headed traitor falls into his hands, while he remains in command of the department of Annapolis, including the city of Baltimore.

About six o'clock in the evening, the long train, with its nine hundred men, the artillery and the horses, backed slowly past the Relay House again, and continued backing until it reached the dépôt at Baltimore.

A thunder-storm of singular character, extraordinary both for its violence and its extent, hung over the city, black as midnight. It was nearly dark when the train arrived. No rain had yet fallen; but the whole city was soon enveloped in rushing clouds of dust. Flashes of lightning, vivid, incessant—peals of thunder, loud and continuous, gave warning of the coming deluge. The dépôt was nearly deserted, and scarcely any one was in the streets. By the time the troops were formed, it had become dark, except when the flashes of lightning illumined the scene, as if with a thousand Drummond lamps. This continuous change, from a blinding glare of light to darkness the most complete, was so bewildering, that if the general had not had a guide familiar with the city, he could scarcely have advanced from the dépôt. This guide was Mr. Robert Hare, of Philadelphia, son of the celebrated chemist, who, after rendering valuable services to the general elsewhere, had joined him at the Relay House, and now volunteered to pilot him to Federal Hill.

The word was given, and the troops silently emerged from the dépôt; the general, Mr. Hare, and the staff in the advance. The orders were, for no man to speak a needless word; no drums to beat; and if a shot was fired from a house, halt, arrest every inmate, and destroy the house, leaving not one brick upon another.

When the line had cleared the dépôt, the storm burst. Such torrents of rain! Such a ceaseless blaze of lightning! Such crashes and volleys of thunder! At one moment the long line of bayonets, the ranks of firm white faces, the burnished cannon, the horses and their riders, the signs upon the houses, and every minutest object, would flash out of the gloom with a distinctness inconceivable. The next, a pall of blackest darkness would drop upon the scene. Not a countenance appeared in any window; for, so incessant was the thunder, that the tramp of horses, the tread of the men, the rumble of the cannon, were not heard; or if heard for a moment, not distinguished from the multitudinous noises of the storm. As the general and his staff gained the summit of Federal Hill, which rises abruptly from the midst of the town, and turned to look back upon the troops winding up the steep ascent, a flash of unequaled brilliancy gave such startling splendor to the scene, that an exclamation of wonder and delight broke from every lip. The troops were formed upon the summit, the cannon were planted, and Baltimore was their own.

Except a shanty or two, used in peaceful times as a lager-beer garden, there was no shelter on the hill. The men had to stand still in the pouring rain, with what patience they could. When the storm abated, scouts were sent out, who ferreted out a wood-yard, from which thirty cords of wood were brought; and soon the top of the hill presented a cheerful scene and picturesque; arms stacked and groups of steaming soldiers standing around fifty blazing fires, each man revolving irregularly on his axis, trying to get himself and his blanket dry.

General Butler established his head-quarters in the German shanty. An officer, who had been scouting, came to him there in considerable excitement, and said:

"I am informed, general, that this hill is mined, and that we are all to be blown up."

"Get a lantern," replied the general, "and you and I will walk round the base of the hill, and see."

They found, indeed, deep cavities in the side of the hill, but these proved to be places whence sand had been dug for building. After a thorough examination, the general said:

"I don't think we shall be blown up; but if we are, there is one comfort, it will dry us all."

Returning to his shanty, General Butler, still as wet as water could make him, set about preparing his proclamation.

At half-past eight in the morning, he received a note from the mayor, which showed how completely his movements had been concealed by the storm. The note had been written during the previous evening.

"I have just been informed," wrote the mayor, "that you have arrived at the Camden Station with a large body of troops under your command. As the sudden arrival of a force will create much surprise in the community, I beg to be informed whether you propose that it shall remain at the Camden Station, so that the police may be notified, and proper precautions may be taken to prevent any disturbance of the peace."

The mayor had not long to wait for information. An extra *Clip-*

per of the morning, containing General Butler's proclamation, advised all Baltimore of his intentions. That document read as follows:

"PROCLAMATION.

"DEPARTMENT OF ANNAPOLIS,
"FEDERAL HILL, BALTIMORE, *May* 14, 1861.

"A detachment of the forces of the Federal government, under my command, have occupied the city of Baltimore for the purpose, among other things, of enforcing respect and obedience to the laws, as well of the state, if requested thereto by the civil authorities, as of the United States laws, which are being violated within its limits by some malignant and traitorous men; and in order to testify the acceptance by the Federal government, of the fact that the city and all the well-intentioned portion of its inhabitants are loyal to the Union and the Constitution, and are to be so regarded and treated by all. To the end, therefore, that all misunderstanding of the purpose of the government may be prevented, and to set at rest all unfounded, false, and seditious rumors; to relieve all apprehensions, if any are felt, by the well-disposed portion of the community, and to make it thoroughly understood by all traitors, their aiders and abettors, that rebellious acts must cease; I hereby, by the authority vested in me, as commander of the department of Annapolis, of which Baltimore forms a part, do now command and make known that no loyal and well-disposed citizen will be disturbed in his lawful occupation or business; that private property will not be interfered with by the men under my command, or allowed to be interfered with by others, except in so far as it may be used to afford aid and comfort to those in rebellion against the government whether here or elsewhere, all of which property, munitions of war, and that fitted to aid and support the rebellion, will be seized and held subject to confiscation, and, therefore, all manufacturers of arms and munitions of war are hereby requested to report to me forthwith, so that the lawfulness of their occupation may be known and understood, and all misconstruction of their doings may be avoided. No transportation from the city to the rebels of articles fitted to aid and support troops in the field will be permitted; and the fact of such transportation, after the publication of this proclamation, will be taken and received as proof of illegal intention on the part of the consignors, and will render the goods liable to seizure and confiscation.

"The government being now ready to receive all such stores and supplies, arrangements will be made to contract for them immediately to the owners; and manufacturers of such articles of equipment and clothing, and munitions of war and provisions, are desired to keep themselves in communication with the commissary-general, in order that their workshops may be employed for loyal purposes, and the artisans of the city resume and carry on their profitable occupations.

"The acting assistant-quartermaster and commissary of subsistence of the United States here stationed, has been instructed to proceed and furnish, at fair prices, 40,000 rations for the use of the army of the United States; and further supplies will be drawn from the city to the full extent of its capacity, if the patriotic and loyal men choose so to furnish supplies.

"All assemblages, except the ordinary police, of armed bodies of men, other than those regularly organized and commissioned by the state of Maryland, and acting under the orders of the governor thereof, for drill and other purposes, are forbidden within the department.

"All officers of the militia of Maryland, having command within the limits of the department, are requested to report through their officers forthwith to the general in command, so that he may be able to know and distinguish the regularly commissioned and loyal troops of Maryland, from armed bodies who may claim to be such.

"The ordinary operations of the corporate government of the city of Baltimore, and of the civil authorities, will not be interfered with; but on the contrary, will be aided by all the power of the commanding general, upon proper call being made; and all such authorities are cordially invited to co-operate with the general in command, to carry out the purposes set forth in the proclamation, so that the city of Baltimore may be shown to the country to be what she is in fact, patriotic and loyal to the Union, the Constitution, and the laws.

"No flag, banner, ensign or device of the so-called Confederate States, or any of them, will be permitted to be raised or shown in this department; and the exhibition of either of them by evil disposed persons will be deemed, and taken to be, evidence of a design to afford aid and comfort to the enemies of the country. To make it the more apparent that the government of the United States far more relies upon the loyalty, patriotism, and zeal of the good citizens of Baltimore and vicinity, than upon any exhibition of force calculated to intimidate them into that obedience to the laws which the government doubts not will be paid from inherent respect and love of order, the commanding general has brought to the city with him, of the many thousand troops in the immediate neighborhood, which might be at once concentrated here, scarcely more than an ordinary guard; and until it fails him, he will continue to rely upon that loyalty and patriotism of the citizens of Maryland, which have never yet been found wanting to the government in time of need. The general in command desires to greet and treat in this part of his department all the citizens thereof as friends and brothers, having a common purpose, a common loyalty, and a common country. Any infractions of the laws by the troops under his command, or any disorderly, unsoldierlike conduct, or any interference with private property, he desires to have immediately reported to him, and pledges himself that if any soldier so far forgets himself as to break those laws that he has sworn to defend and enforce, he shall be most rigorously punished.

"The general believes that if the suggestions and requests contained in this proclamation are faithfully carried out by the co-operation of all good and Union-loving citizens, and peace, and quiet, and certainty of future peace and quiet are thus restored, business will resume its accustomed channels, trade take the place of dullness and inactivity, efficient labor displace idleness, and Baltimore will be in fact, what she is entitled to be, in the front rank of the commercial cities of the nation.

"Given at Baltimore the day and year herein first above written.

"BENJ. F. BUTLER,

"*Brigadier-general commanding department of Annapolis.*"

Not the slightest disturbance of the peace occurred. The suggestions and requests of the general were observed. There was plenty of private growling, and some small, furtive exhibitions of disgust, but nothing that could be called opposition. Contraband gunpowder, pikes, arms and provisions were seized. The Union flag was hoisted upon buildings belonging to the United States, and the flag of treason nowhere appeared. The camp equipage of the troops was brought in, and camps were formed upon the hill. Early in the afternoon, General Butler and his staff mounted their horses, and rode leisurely through the streets to the Gilmore house, where they dismounted, and strolled into the dining-room and dined; after which they remounted, and enjoyed a longer ride in the streets, meeting no molestation, exciting much muttered remark. General Butler does not mount a horse quite in the style of a London guardsman. In mounting before the Gilmore house, across a wide gutter, he had some little difficulty in bestriding his horse, which, a passing traitor observing, gave rise to the report, promptly conveyed to Washington, that the general was drunk that day, in the streets of Baltimore. Such a misfortune is it to have short legs, with a gutter and a horse to get over. From that time, the soldiers, in twos and threes, walked freely about the city, exhilarated, now and then, by a little half-suppressed vituperation from men, and a ludicrous display of petulance on the part of lovely woman. Often they were stopped in the streets by Union men, who shook them warmly by the hand, and thanked them for coming to their deliverance.

There is a limit to the endurance of man. General Butler performed that day, one of his day's work. At night, exhausted to an extreme, for he had not lain down in forty hours, and racked with headache, he ventured to go to bed; leaving orders, however, that he was to be instantly notified if anything extraordinary occurred. It perversely happened that many extraordinary things did occur that night. Some important seizures were made; some valuable information was brought in; many plausible rumors gained a hearing; and, consequently, the general was disturbed about every half hour during the night. He rose in the morning unrefreshed, feverish, almost sick. His feelings may be imagined, when, at half-past eight, he received the following dispatch from the lieutenant-general, dated May 14th:

"Sir,—Your hazardous occupation of Baltimore was made without my knowledge, and, of course, without my approbation. It is a God-send, that it was without conflict of arms. It is, also, reported, that you have sent a detachment to Frederick; but this is impossible. Not a word have I received from you as to either movement. Let me hear from you."

This epistle was not precisely what General Butler thought was due to an officer who, with nine hundred men, had done what General Scott was preparing to do with twelve thousand. It was a damper. It looked like a rebuke for doing his duty too well. The sick general took it much to heart; not for his own sake merely; he could not but augur ill of the conduct of the war if a neat and triumphant little audacity, like his march into Baltimore, was to be rewarded with an immediate snub from head-quarters. Being only a militia brigadier, he did not clearly see how a war was to be carried on without incurring some slight risk, now and then, of a conflict of arms.

But there was little time for meditation. There were duties to be done. For one item, he had Ross Winans a prisoner in Fort McHenry; his pikes and steam-gun being also in safe custody, with other evidence of his treason. He was preparing to try Mr. Winans by court-martial, and telegraphed to Mr. Cameron, asking him not to interfere, at least, not to release him, until General Butler could go to Washington and explain the turpitude of his guilt. It was, and is, the general's opinion, that the summary execution of a traitor worth fifteen millions, would have been an exhibition of moral strength on the part of the government, such as the times required. His guilt was beyond question. If there is, or can be, such a crime as treason against the United States, this man had committed it, not in language only, but in overt acts, numerous and aggravated. Mr. Seward, I need scarcely say, took a different view of the matter. Winans was released. Why his pikes and his steam-gun were not returned to him, does not appear. A few months after, it was found necessary to place him again in confinement.

Nothing would appease General Scott short of the recall of General Butler from Baltimore, and the withdrawal of the troops from Federal Hill. General Butler was recalled, and General Cadwallader ruled in his stead. The troops were temporarily removed, and General Butler returned to Washington.

That the president did not concur with the rebuke of General Scott, was shown by his immediately offering General Butler a commission as major-general, and the command of Fortress Monroe. That the secretary of war did not concur with it, I infer from a passage of one of his letters from St. Petersburgh. "I always said," wrote Mr. Cameron, "that if you had been left at Baltimore, the rebellion would have been of short duration;" a remark, the full significance of which may, one day, become apparent to the American people. I believe I may say, without improperly using the papers before me, that more than one member of the cabinet held the opinion, that General Butler's recall from Baltimore was solely due to his frustration of the sublime strategic scheme of taking the city by the simultaneous advance of four columns of three thousand men each.

The people made known their opinion of General Butler's conduct in all the usual ways. On the evening of his arrival in Washington, he was serenaded, and most abundantly cheered. His little speech on this occasion was a great hit. The remarkable feature of it was, that it expressed, without exaggeration, as without suppression, his habitual feeling respecting the war into which the nation was groping its way. He talked to the crowd just as he had often talked, and talks to a knot of private friends:

"FELLOW-CITIZENS:—Your cheers for the old commonwealth of Massachusetts are rightly bestowed. Foremost in the ranks of those who fought for tho liberty of the country in the revolution were the men of Massachusetts. It is a historical fact, to which I take pride in now referring, that in the revolution, Massachusetts sent more men south of Mason and Dixon's line to fight for the cause of the country, than all the southern colonies put together; and in this second war, if war must come, to proclaim the Declaration of Independence anew, and as a necessary consequence, establish the Union and the constitution, Massachusetts will give, if necessary, every man in her borders, ay, and woman! [Cheers.] I trust I may be excused for speaking thus of Massachusetts; but I am confident there are many within the sound of my voice whose hearts beat with proud memories of the old commonwealth. There is this difference, I will say, between our southern brothers and ourselves, that while we love our state with the true love of a son, we love the Union and the country with an equal devotion. [Loud and prolonged applause.] We place no 'state rights' before, above, or beyond the Union. [Cheers.] To us our country is first, because it is our country [three cheers], and our state is next and second, because she is a part of our country and our state. [Renewed applause.] Our oath of allegiance to our country, and our oath of allegiance to our state, are interwreathed harmoniously, and never come in conflict nor clash. He who does his duty to the Union, does his duty to the state; and he who does his duty to the state does his duty to the Union—'one inseparable, now and for ever.' [Renewed applause.] As I look upon this demonstration of yours, I believe it to be prompted by a love of the common cause, and our common country—a country so great and good, a government so kind, so beneficent, that the hand from which we have only felt kindness is now for the first time raised in chastisement. [Applause.] Many things in a man's life may be worse than death. So, to a government there may be many things, such as dishonor and disintegration, worse than the shedding of blood. [Cheers.] Our fathers purchased our liberty and country for us at an immense cost of treasure and blood, and by the bright heavens above us, we will not part with them without first paying the original debt, and the interest to this date! [Loud cheers.] We have in our veins the same blood as they shed; we have the same power of endurance, the same love of liberty and law. We will hold as a brother him who stands by the Union; we will hold as an enemy him who would strike from its constellation a single star. [Applause.] But, I hear some one say, 'Shall we carry on this fratricidal war? Shall we shed our brothers' blood, and meet in arms our brothers in the South?' I would say, 'As our fathers did not hesitate to strike the mother country in the defense of our rights, so we should not hesitate to meet the brother as they did the mother.' If this unholy, this fratricidal war, is forced upon us, I say, ' Woe, woe to them who have made the necessity. Our hands are clean, our hearts are pure; but the Union must be preserved [intense cheering. When silence was restored, he continued] at all hazard of money, and, if need be, of every life this side the arctic regions. [Cheers.] If the 25,000 northern soldiers who are here, are cut off, in six weeks 50,000 will take their place; and if they die by fever, pestilence, or the sword, a quarter of a million will take their place, till our army of the reserve will be women with their broomsticks, to drive every enemy into the gulf. [Cheers and laughter.] I have neither fear nor doubt of the issue. I feel only horror and dismay for those who have made the war. God help them! we are here for our rights, for our country, for our flag. Our faces are set south, and there shall be no footstep backward. [Immense applause.] He is mistaken who supposes we can be intimidated by threats or cajoled by compromise. The day of compromise is past.

"The government must be sustained [cheers]; and when it is sustained, we shall give everybody in the Union their rights under the constitution, as we always have, and everybody outside of the Union the steel of the Union, till they shall come under the Union. [Cheers, and cries of 'good, go on.'] It is impossible for me to go on speech making; but if you will go home to your beds, and the government will let me, I will go south fighting for the Union, and you will follow me."*

A different scene awaited him the next morning in the office of the lieutenant-general, respecting which it is best to say little. He bore the lecture for half an hour without replying. But General Butler's patience under unworthy treatment is capable of being exhausted. It was exhausted on this occasion. Indeed, the spectacle of cumbrous inefficiency which the head-quarters of the army then presented, and continued long to present, was such as to grieve and alarm every man acquainted with it, who had also an adequate knowledge of the formidable task to which the country had addressed itself. I am not ashamed to relate, that General Butler, on reaching his apartment, was so deeply moved by what had passed, and by the inferences he could but draw by what had passed, that he burst into hysteric sobs, which he found himself, for some minutes, unable to repress. And, what was worse, he had serious thoughts of declining the proffered promotion, and going home to resume his practice at the bar. Not that his zeal had flagged in the cause; but it seemed doubtful whether, in the circumstances, a man of enterprise and energy would be allowed to do anything of moment to promote the cause.

* *N. Y. Daily Times.*

CHAPTER VI.

FORTRESS MONROE.

The president had no lecture to bestow upon General Butler; but, on the contrary, compliment and congratulation. He urged him to accept the command of Fortress Monroe, and use the same energy in retaking Norfolk as he had displayed at Annapolis and Baltimore. After a day's consideration, the general said he was willing enough to accept the proffered promotion and the command of the fortress, if he could have the means of being useful there. As a base for active operations, Fortress Monroe was good; he only objected to it as a convenient tomb for a troublesome militia general. Could he have four Massachusetts regiments, two batteries of field artillery, and the other requisites for a successful advance? Not that Massachusetts troops were better than others, only he knew them better, and they him. Yes, he could have them, and should, and whatever else he needed for effective action. An active, energetic campaign was precisely the thing desired and expected of him, and nothing should be wanting on the part of the government to render such a campaign possible. This being understood, he joyfully accepted the commission and the command. General Butler's commission as major-general dates from May 16th, two days after his thunderous march into Baltimore. He is now, therefore, *in reality*, the senior major-general in the service of the United States. On that day, General McClellan and General Banks were still in the pay of their respective railroad companies; General Dix was at home; General Fremont was in Europe, attending to his private affairs.

May 20th, General Butler received orders from General Scott for his guidance at the scene of his future labors:

"You will proceed," wrote the lieutenant-general, "to Fortress Monroe and assume the command of that post, when Colonel Dimmick will limit his command to the regular troops composing a part of its garrison, but will, by himself and his officers, give such aid in the instruction of the volunteers as you may direct.

"Besides the present garrison of Fortress Monroe, consisting of such companies of regular artillery, portions of two Massachusetts regiments of volunteers, and a regiment of Vermont volunteers, nine additional regiments of volunteers from New York may soon be expected there. Only a small portion, if any, of these can be conveniently quartered or encamped in the fort, the greater part, if not the whole area of which will be necessary for exercises on the ground. The nine additional regiments must, therefore, be encamped in the best positions outside of and as near the fort as may be. For this purpose it is hoped that a pine forest north of the fort, near the bay, may be found to furnish the necessary ground and shade for some three thousand men, though somewhat distant from drinking and cooking water. This, as well as feed, it may be necessary to bring to the camp on wheels. The quartermaster's department has been instructed to furnish the necessary vehicles, casks, and draft animals. The war garrison of Fortress Monroe, against a formidable army, provided with an adequate siege train, is about 2,500 men. You will soon have there, inside and out, near three times that number. Assuming 1,500 as a garrison adequate to resist any probable attack in the next six months, or, at least, for many days or weeks, you will consider the remainder of the force, under your command, disposable for aggressive purposes and employ it accordingly.

"In respect to more distant operations, you may expect specific instructions at a later date. In the mean time, I will direct your attention to the following objects: 1st. Not to let the enemy erect batteries to annoy Fortress Monroe; 2d. To capture any batteries the enemy may have within a half day's march of you, and which may be reached by land; 3d. The same in respect to the enemy's batteries, at or about Craney Island, though requiring water craft; and 4th. To menace and to recapture the navy yard at Gosport, in order to complete its destruction, with its contents, except what it may be practicable to bring away in safety. It is expected that you put yourself into free communication with the commander of the U. S. naval forces in Hampton Roads, and invite his cordial co-operation with you in all operations, in whole or in part, by water, and no doubt he will have received corresponding instructions from the Navy Department.

"Boldness in execution is nearly always necessary; but in planning and fitting out expeditions or detachments, great circumspection is a virtue. In important cases, where time clearly permits, be sure to submit your plans and ask instructions from higher authority.

"Communicate with me often and fully on all matters important to the service."

May 22d, at eight o'clock in the morning, the guns of the fortress saluted General Butler as the commander of the post; and as soon as the ceremonies of his arrival were over, he proceeded to look about him, to learn what it was that had fallen to his share. In the course of the day, he made great progress in the pursuit of knowledge.

Fortress Monroe is a sixty-five acre field, with a low, massive stone wall around it; big, black guns peering through and over the top of the wall; and a mile and a half of canal wound round its base. Inside, are long barracks, hospitals, a little chapel, trees, avenues of trees, gardens, parade-grounds, green lawns, gravel walks; and, in the midst, surrounded by trees and garden, a solid, broad, slate-peaked mansion, the residence of the commander of the post. Old Point Comfort, broadening at the extremity, so as to form a peninsula, seems made to be the site of a fort, and such it must remain as long as man wages war. Whoever holds it, and knows how to use it, is master of Virginia and North Carolina; for it either commands or threatens, and can be used so as to control their navigable rivers, their harbors, and their railroad connections with the South. The Southern Confederacy, so called, must have it, or retire to the Gulf. Without it, the Confederacy is nothing; and the place can only be taken by a naval power superior to that of the United States, or by treachery. If it had been built with a prophetic view to the events of the last three years, the site could not have been better selected for the purposes of the United States. That it has not been used with all the effect it might have been, was not the fault of the new commandant, as shall soon be demonstrated.

The country around it, on the main land, is level; the soil, as Winthrop describes it, a fine fertile loam, easily running to dust as the English air does to fog; the woods dense and beautiful; the roads, miserable cart tracks; the cattle "scallawags," the people ditto; the farm houses dilapidated and mean; such dens as a northern drayman would have disdained, and a hod-carrier only occupied on compulsion. A country settled for two hundred and thirty years, but not as pleasant, nor as commodious, nor as populated, nor as civilized, as a county of Minnesota only surveyed ten years ago. But many of the people, though of incredibly contracted intelligence, were kind and hospitable, and, as events have shown, brave and enduring. If life seemed stagnant in that region, there was in it a latent energy and force, which poor Winthrop did not suspect, but which, however misdirected, he would have been among the first to recognize. Life stagnant is not so fatal as life wasted of its raw material.

This huge fort was one of the hinges of the stable-door which was shut after the horse had been stolen, in the war of 1812. It had never been used for warlike purposes, and had been, usually, garrisoned by a company or two, or three, of regular troops, who paraded and drilled in its wide expanses with listless punctuality, and fished in the surrounding waters, or strolled about the adjacent village. Colonel Dimmick was the commandant of the post when the war broke out; a faithful, noble-minded officer, who, with his one man to eight yards of rampart, kept Virginia from clutching the prize. Two or three thousand volunteers had since made their way to the fortress, and were encamped on its grounds.

General Butler soon discovered that of the many things necessary for the defense of the post, he had a sufficiency of one only, namely, men. There was not one horse belonging to the garrison; nor one cart nor wagon. Provision barrels had to be rolled from the landing to the fort, three-quarters of a mile. There was no well or spring within the walls of the fortress; but cisterns only, filled with rain-water, which had given out the summer before when there were but four hundred men at the post. Of ammunition, he had but five thousand rounds, less than a round and a half per man of the kind suited to the greater number of the muskets brought by the volunteers. The fort was getting over-crowded with troops, and more were hourly expected; he would have nine more regiments in a few days. Room must be found for the new comers outside the walls. He found, too, that he had, in his vicinity, an active, numerous, increasing enemy, who were busy fortifying points of land opposite or near the fort; points essential for his purposes. The garrison was, in effect, penned up in the peninsula; a rebel picket a mile distant; a rebel flag waving from Hampton Bridge in sight of the fortress; rebel forces preparing to hem in the fortress on every side, as they had done Sumter; rumor, as usual, magnifying their numbers tenfold. Colonel Dimmick had been able to seize and hold the actual property of the government; no more.

Water being the most immediate necessity, General Butler directed his attention, first of all, to securing a more trustworthy supply. Can the artesian well be speedily finished, which was begun long ago, and then suspended? It could, thought Colonel de Russy, of the engineers, who, at once, at the general's request, consulted a contractor on the subject. There was a spring a mile from the fortress, which furnished 700 gallons a day. Can the water be conducted to the fortress by a temporary pipe? It can, reported the colonel of engineers; and the general ordered it done. Meanwhile, water from Baltimore, at two cents a gallon. To-morrow, Colonel Phelps, with his Vermonters, shall cross to Hampton, reconnoiter the country, and see if there is good camping ground in that direction; for the pine forest suggested by General Scott was reported by Colonel de Russy to be unhealthy as well as waterless. In a day or two, Commodore Stringham, urged thereto by General Butler, would have shelled out the rising battery at Sewall's Point, if he had not been suddenly ordered away to the blockade of Charleston harbor. Already the general had an eye upon Newport News, eleven miles to the south, directly upon one of the roads he meant to take by and by, when the promised means of offensive warfare arrived. Word was brought that the enemy had an eye upon it, too; and General Butler determined to be there before them. That rolling of barrels from the landing would never do; on this first day, the general ordered surveys and estimates for a railroad between the wharf and the fortress. The men were eating hard biscuit: he directed the construction of a new bake-house, that they might have bread.

The next day, as every one remembers, Colonel Phelps made his reconnoissance in Hampton and its vicinity—not without a show of opposition. Upon approaching the bridge over Hampton Creek, Colonel Phelps perceived that the rebels had set fire to the bridge. Rushing forward at the double-quick, the men tore off the burning planks and quickly extinguished the fire; then marching into the village, completed their reconnoissance, and performed some evolutions for the edification of the inhabitants. Colonel Phelps met there several of his old West Point comrades, whom he warned of the inevitable failure of their bad cause, and advised them to abandon it in time. The general himself was soon on the ground, and took a ride of seven miles in the enemy's country that afternoon, still eager in the pursuit of knowledge.

One noticeable thing was reported by the troops on their return. It was, that the negroes, to a man, were the trusting, enthusiastic friends of the Union soldiers. They were all glee and welcome; and Colonel Phelps and his men were the last people in the world to be backward in responding to their salutations. No one knew better than he that in every worthy black man and woman in the South the Union could find a helping friend if it would. By whatever free-masonry it was brought about, the negroes received the impression, that day, that those Vermonters and themselves were on the same side.

This Colonel Phelps is one of the remarkable figures of the war. A tall, loose-jointed, stout-hearted, benignant man of fifty, the soul of honesty and goodness. It had been his fortune, before his retirement from the army, to be stationed for many years in the South. For the last thirty years, if any one had desired to test, with the utmost possible severity, a New Englander's manhood and intelligence, the way to do it was to make him an officer of the United States army, and station him in a slave state. If there was any lurking atom of baseness in him, slavery would be sure to find it out, and work upon it to the corruption of the entire man. If there was even defective intelligence or weakness of will, as surely as he continued to live there, he would, at last, be found to have yielded to the seducing influence, and to have lost his moral sense: first enduring, then tolerating, defending, applauding, participating. For slavery is of such a nature, that it must either debauch or violently repel the man who is obliged to live long in the hourly contemplation of it. There can be no medium or moderation. No man can hate slavery a little, or like it a little. It must either spoil or madden him if he lives with it long enough. Colonel Phelps stood the test; but, at the same time, the long dwelling upon wrongs which he could do nothing to redress, the long contemplation of suffering which he could not stir to relieve, impaired, in some degree, the healthiness, the balance of his mind. He seemed, at times, a man of one idea. With such tenderness as his, such quickness and depth of moral feeling, it is a wonder he did not go raving mad. When the war began, he was at home upon his farm, a man of wealth for rural Vermont; and now he was at Fortress Monroe, commanding a regiment of three months' militia; a very model of a noble, brave, modest, and righteous warrior, full in the belief that the longed-for time of deliverance had come. It was a strange coming together, this of the Massachusetts democrat and the Vermont abolitionist—both armed in the same cause. General Butler felt all the worth of his new friend, and they worked together with abundant harmony and good-will.

Colonel Phelps's reconnoissance led to the selection of a spot between Hampton and the fort for an encampment. The next day, General Butler went in person to Newport News, and, on the fifth day after taking command of the post, had a competent force at that vital point, intrenching and fortifying. Meanwhile, in extensive dispatches to head-quarters, he had made known to General Scott his situation and his wants. He asked for horses, vehicles, ammunition, field-artillery, and a small force of cavalry. Also (for attacks upon the enemy's shore batteries), he asked for fifty surf-boats, "of such construction as the lieutenant-general caused to be prepared for the landing at Vera Cruz, the efficiency and adaptedness of which has passed into history." He asked for the completion of the artesian well, and the construction of the short railroad. He justified the occupation of Newport News, on the ground that it lay close to the obvious highway, by water, to Richmond, upon which already General Butler had cast a general's eye.

On the evening of the second day after his arrival at the post, the event occurred which will for ever connect the name of General Butler with the history of the abolition of slavery in America. Colonel Phelps's visit to Hampton had thrown the white inhabitants into such alarm that most of them prepared for flight, and many left their homes that night, never to see them again. In the confusion three negroes escaped, and, making their way across the bridges, gave themselves up to a Union picket, saying that their master, Colonel Mallory, was about to remove them to North Carolina to work upon rebel fortifications there, far away from their wives and children, who were to be left in Hampton. They were brought to the fortress, and the circumstance was reported to the general in the morning. He questioned each of them separately, and the truth of their story became manifest. He needed laborers. He was aware that the rebel batteries that were rising around him were the work chiefly of slaves, without whose assistance they could not have been erected in time to give him trouble. He wished to keep these men. The garrison wished them kept. The country would have deplored or resented the sending of them away. If they had been Colonel Mallory's horses, or Colonel Mallory's spades, or Colonel Mallory's percussion caps, he would have seized them and used them, without hesitation. Why not property more valuable for the purposes of the rebellion than any other?

He pronounced the electric words, "These men are CONTRABAND OF WAR; set them at work."

"An epigram," as Winthrop remarks, "abolished slavery in the United States." The word took; for it gave the country an excuse for doing what it was longing to do. Every one remembers how relieved the "conservative" portion of the people felt, when they found that the slaves could be used on the side of the Union, without giving Kentucky a new argument against it, Kentucky, at that moment, controlling the policy of the administration. "The South," said Wendell Phillips, in a recent speech, "fought to sustain slavery, and the North fought not to have it hurt. But Butler pronounced that magic word, 'contraband,' and summoned the negro into the arena. It was a poor word. I do not know that it is sound law; but Lord Chatham said, '*nullus liber homo*' is coarse Latin, but it is worth all the classics. Contraband is a bad word, and may be bad law, but it is worth all the Constitution; for in a moment of critical emergency it summoned the saving elements into the national arena, and it showed the government how far the sound fiber of the nation extended."

By the time the three negroes were comfortably at work upon the new bake-house, General Butler received the following brief epistle, signed, "J. B. Carey, major-acting, Virginia volunteers:"

"Be pleased to designate some time and place when it will be agreeable to you to accord me a personal interview."

The general complied with the request. In the afternoon two groups of horsemen might have been seen approaching one another on the Hampton road, a mile from the fort. One of these consisted of General Butler and two of his staff, Major Fay and Captain Haggerty; the other, of Major Carey and two or three friends. Major Carey and General Butler were old political allies, having acted in concert both at Charleston and at Baltimore—hard-shell democrats both. After an exchange of courteous salutations, and the introduction of companions, the conference began. The conversation was, as nearly as can be recalled, in these words:

Major Carey: "I have sought this interview, sir, for the purpose of ascertaining upon what principles you intend to conduct the war in this neighborhood."

The general bowed his willingness to give the information desired.

Major Carey: "I ask, first, whether a passage through the blockading fleet will be allowed to the families of citizens of Virginia, who may desire to go north or south to a place of safety."

General Butler: "The presence of the families of belligerents is always the best hostage for their good behavior. One of the objects of the blockade is to prevent the admission of supplies of provisions into Virginia, while she continues in an attitude hostile to the government. Reducing the number of consumers would necessarily tend to the postponement of the object in view. Besides, the passage of vessels through the blockade would involve an amount of labor, in the way of surveillance, to prevent abuse, which it would be impossible to perform. I am under the necessity, therefore, of refusing the privilege."

Major Carey: "Will the passage of families desiring to go north be permitted?"

General Butler: "With the exception of an interruption at Baltimore, which has now been disposed of, the travel of peaceable citizens through the North has not been hindered; and as to the internal line through Virginia, your friends have, for the present, entire control of it. The authorities at Washington can judge better than I upon this point, and travelers can well go that way in reaching the North."

Major Carey: "I am informed that three negroes, belonging to Colonel Mallory, have escaped within your lines. I am Colonel Mallory's agent, and have charge of his property. What do you intend to do with regard to those negroes?"

General Butler: "I propose to retain them."

Major Carey: "Do you mean, then, to set aside your constitutional obligations?"

General Butler: "I mean to abide by the decision of Virginia, as expressed in her ordinance of secession, passed the day before yesterday. I am under no constitutional obligations to a foreign country, which Virginia now claims to be."

Major Carey: "But you say, we *can't* secede, and so you can not consistently detain the negroes."

General Butler: "But you say, you *have* seceded, and so you can not consistently claim them. I shall detain the negroes as contraband of war. You are using them upon your batteries. It is merely a question whether they shall be used for or against the government. Nevertheless, though I greatly need the labor which has providentially fallen into my hands, if Colonel Mallory will come into the fort and take the oath of allegiance to the United States, he shall have his negroes, and I will endeavor to hire them from him."

Major Carey: "Colonel Mallory is absent."

The interview here terminated, and each party, with polite farewell, went its way.

This was on Friday, May 24. On Sunday morning, eight more negroes came in, and were received. On Monday morning, forty-seven more, of all ages; men, women, and children; several whole families among them. In thé afternoon, twelve men, good field hands, arrived. And they continued to come in daily, in tens, twenties, thirties, till the number of contrabands in the various camps numbered more than nine hundred. A commissioner of negro affairs was appointed, who taught, fed, and governed them; who reported, after several weeks' experience, that they worked well and cheerfully, required no urging, and perfectly comprehended him when he told them that they were as much entitled to freedom as himself. They were gentle, docile, careful and efficient laborers; their demeanor dignified, their conversation always decent.

General Butler's correspondence with the government on this subject is not forgotten; but it is proper that it should be repeated here. He merely related his interview with Major Carey in his first letter to General Scott, and asked for instructions. In his second dispatch, dated May 27th, he referred to the subject again.

"Since I wrote my last," he observed, "the question in regard to slave property is becoming one of very serious magnitude. The inhabitants of Virginia are using their negroes in the batteries, and are preparing to send their women and children south. The escapes from them are very numerous, and a squad has come in this morning, and my pickets are bringing their women and children.

Of course these can not be dealt with upon the theory on which I designed to treat the services of able-bodied men and women who might come within my lines, and of which I gave you a detailed account in my last dispatch.

"I am in the utmost doubt what to do with this species of property. Up to this time I have had come within my lines men and women, with their children, entire families, each family belonging to the same owner. I have, therefore, determined to employ, as I can do very profitably, the able-bodied persons in the party, issuing proper food for the support of all, and charging against their services the expense of care and sustenance of the non-laborers, keeping a strict and accurate account as well of the services as of the expenditures, having the worth of the services, and the cost of the expenditure determined by a board of survey hereafter to be detailed. I know of no other manner in which to dispose of this subject, and the questions connected therewith. As a matter of property, to the insurgents it will be of very great moment, the number that I now have amounting, as I am informed, to what in good times would be of the value of $60,000.

"Twelve of these negroes, I am informed, have escaped from the erection of the batteries on Sewall's Point, which fired on my expedition as it passed by out of range. As a means of offense, therefore, in the enemy's hands, these negroes, when able-bodied, are of great importance. Without them the batteries could not have been erected, at least for many weeks. As a military question, it would seem to be a measure of necessity, and deprives their master of their services.

"How can this be done? As a political question, and a question of humanity, can I receive the services of a father and a mother, and not take the children? Of the humanitarian aspect I have no doubt; of the political one I have no right to judge. I therefore submit all this to your better judgment; and, as these questions have a political aspect, I have ventured, and I trust I am not wrong in so doing, to duplicate the parts of my dispatch relating to this subject, and forward them to the secretary of war."

The secretary replied, May 30th: "Your action in respect to the negroes who came within your lines, from the service of the rebels, is approved. The department is sensible of the embarrassments, which must surround officers conducting military operations in a state, by the laws of which slavery is sanctioned. The government can not recognize the rejection by any state of its federal obligation; resting upon itself, among these federal obligations, however, no one can be more important than that of suppressing and dispersing any combination of the former for the purpose of overthrowing its whole constitutional authority. While, therefore, you will permit no interference, by persons under your command, with the relations of persons held to service under the laws of any state, you will on the other hand, so long as any state within which your military operations are conducted, remain under the control of such armed combinations, refrain from surrendering to alleged masters any persons who come within your lines. You will employ such persons in the services to which they will be best adapted, keeping an account of the labor by them performed, of the value of it, and the expenses of their maintenance. The question of their final disposition will be reserved for future determination."

So the matter rested for two months, at the expiration of which events revived the question. Meanwhile, General Butler was observant of the conduct and the character of the negroes, and had divers reflections upon the tendency of the patriarchal institution. The negroes accepted readily enough their new name of Contrabands, without being able to get any one to answer intelligibly their frequent question, why the white folks called them so.

Many strange scenes occurred in connection with this flight of the negroes to "Freedom Fort," as they styled it; for one of which, perhaps, space may be spared here. It gives us a glimpse into one of those ancient Virginia homes suddenly desolated by the war. Major Winthrop, I should premise, had now arrived at the fortress. He came just in time to take the place of military secretary to the general commanding, which had been vacant only a day or two, and was now a happy member of the general's family, winning his rapid way to all hearts. I mention him here because his comrades remember how intensely amused he was at the interview about to be described. If he had lived a few days longer than he did, he would probably have told it himself, in his brief, bright, graphic manner. The office of the general at head-quarters was the place where the scene occurred.

Enter, an elderly, grave, church-warden looking gentleman, apparently oppressed with care or grief. He was recognized as a respectable farmer of the neighborhood, the owner, so called, of thirty or forty negroes, and a farm-house in the dilapidated style of architecture, which might be named the Virginian Order. Advancing to the table, he announced his name and business. He said he had come to ask the officer commanding the post for the return of one of his negroes—only one; and he proceeded to relate the circumstances upon which he based his modest request. But he told his tale in a manner so measured and woful, revealing such a curious ignorance of any other world than the little circle of ideas and persons in which he had moved all his life, with such *naive* and comic simplicity, that the hearers found it impossible to take a serious view of his really lamentable situation. He proceeded in something like these words:—

"I have always treated my negroes kindly. I supposed they loved me. Last Sunday, I went to church. When I returned from church, and entered into my house, I called Mary to take off my coat and hang it up. But Mary did not come. And again I called Mary in a louder voice, but I received no answer. Then I went into the room to find Mary, but I found her not. There was no one in the room. I went into the kitchen. There was no one in the kitchen. I went into the garden. There was no one in the garden. I went to the negro quarters. There was no one at the negro quarters. All my negroes had departed, sir, while I was at the house of God. Then I went back again into my house. And soon there came to me James, who has been my body-servant for many years. And I said to James:

"'James, what has happened?'

"And James said, 'All the people have gone to the fort.'

"'While I was gone to the house of God, James?'

"And James said, 'Yes, master; they're all gone.'

"And I said to James, 'Why didn't you go too, James?'

"And James said, 'Master, I'll never leave you.'

"'Well James,' said I, 'as there's nobody to cook, see if you can get me some cold victuals and some whisky.'

"So James got me some cold victuals, and I ate them with a heavy heart. And when I had eaten, I said to James:

"'James, it is of no use for us to stay here. Let us go to your mistress.'

"His mistress, sir, had gone away from her home, eleven miles, fleeing from the dangers of the war.

"'And, so, James,' said I, 'harness the best horse to the cart, and put into the cart our best bed, and some bacon, and some corn meal, and, James, some whisky, and we will go unto your mistress.'

"And James did even as I told him, and some few necessaries besides. And we started. It was a heavy load for the horse. I trudged along on foot, and James led the horse. It was late at night, sir, when we arrived, and I said to James:

"'James, it is of no use to unload the cart to-night. Put the horse into the barn, and unload the cart in the morning.'

"And James said, 'Yes, master.'

"I met my wife, sir; I embraced her, and went to bed; and, notwithstanding my troubles, I slept soundly. The next morning, *James was gone!* Then I came here, and the first thing I saw, when I got here, was James peddling cabbages to your men out of that very cart."

Up to this point, the listeners had managed to keep their countenances under tolerable control. But the climax to the story was drawled out in a manner so lugubriously comic, that neither the general nor the staff could longer conceal their laughter. The poor old gentleman, unconscious of any but the serious aspects of his case, gave them one sad, reproachful look, and left the fort without uttering another word. He had fallen upon evil times.

General Butler, meanwhile, had been studying the country around him with a true general's eye. His dispatches to head-quarters teem with evidence that, inexperienced as he was in the business of waging war, he comprehended the advantages and opportunities of his position. The uppermost thought in his mind was, that the way to Richmond was by the James river—not through the mazes of Manassas and the wilderness beyond him. Hear him:

May 27, the fourth day of his command: "The advantages of Newport News are these: There are two springs of very pure water there. The bluff is a fine, healthy situation. It has two good, commodious wharves, to which steamers of any draft of water may come up at all stages of the tide. It is as near any point of operation as Fortress Monroe, where we are obliged to lighten all vessels of draft over ten feet, and have but one wharf.

The News, upon which I propose to have a water battery of four eight-inch guns, commands the ship channel of James river, and a force there is a perpetual menace to Richmond. My next point of operation, I propose, shall be Pig Point battery, which is exactly opposite the News, commanding Nansemond river. Once in command of that battery, which I believe can easily be turned, I can then advance along the Nansemond and easily take Suffolk, and there either hold or destroy the railroad connection both between Richmond and Norfolk, and between Norfolk and the South. With a perfect blockade of Elizabeth river, and taking and holding Suffolk, and perhaps York, Norfolk will be so perfectly hemmed in, that starvation will cause the surrender, without risking an attack on the strongly fortified intrenchments around Norfolk, with great loss, and perhaps defeat. If this plan of operations does not meet the approbation of the lieutenant-general, I would be glad of his instructions specifically. If it is desirable to move on Richmond, James and York rivers, both thus held, would seem to be the most eligible routes. I have no co-operation, substantially, by the navy, the only vessels now here being the Cumberland and the Harriet Lane; the former too unwieldy to get near shore to use her battery; the other so light in her battery as not to be able to cope with a single battery of the rebels. I have great need of surf-boats for sea-coast and river advances, and beg leave to suggest the matter again to you."

June 4—eight days later. "I have here, altogether, about six thousand effective men. I am, as yet, without transportation or surf-boats, which I must have, in order to make a movement. * * I am preparing myself, however, to be able to land, by causing one regiment, at least, to be drilled in embarking in and landing from boats. I have also sent up to the mouth of the Susquehannah, to charter or purchase ten of a kind of boat which, I am informed by a gentleman connected with the squadron, will be the best possible, excepting regularly constructed surf-boats, for the purpose of landing troops."

June 6. "The intrenchments at Newport News will have been completed by the time this report reaches you, and the place is really very strong. A battery of four eight-inch columbiads will command the channel of the river upon one side, but still leaves open the channel on the Nansemond side. On that side, as you will perceive, is Pig Point, upon which the rebels have erected batteries, which they are striving now to finish, mounting seven guns, thirty-twos and forty-fours. If we were in possession of Pig Point, the James and Nansemond would be both under our control, and the services of our blockading vessels might be dispensed with, which are now required to prevent water communication between Richmond and Williamsburgh, and between Norfolk and Suffolk. My proposition is, therefore, to make a combined land and naval attack upon Pig Point, and endeavor to carry the batteries, both by turning them, and by direct attack upon the naval force. If we succeed, then to intrench ourselves there with what speed we may, and re-establish the battery. But, at the same time, to push on, with the same flotilla of boats with which we landed, up the Nansemond, which is navigable for boats, and, I believe, light-draught steamers, to Suffolk, a distance of twelve miles. When once there, the commanding general's familiarity with the country" (his native region), "or a glance at the map, will show that we are in possession of all the railroad communication between Richmond, Petersburgh and Norfolk, and also of the great shore line connecting Virginia with North Carolina, *via* Weldon, by which the guns taken at the navy yard will be sent south, whenever operations in that direction demand.

"By going eight and a half miles further by the Jericho Canal, we enter Drummond Lake, a sheet of water some six miles by four. From this lake the feeders of the Dismal Swamp Canal may be cut, and that means of transport cut off. Once at Suffolk, with three lines of the enemy's communication cut off, Norfolk must fall with her own weight. Starvation, to be brought on simply by gathering up the provisions of Princess Anne County, will make her batteries and the theft of the navy yard guns substantially valueless, and will save many lives which would be otherwise spent in their reduction.

"I am not insensible to the disadvantages and difficulties of the project, the advantages of which I may have painted with too much *couleur de rose*.

"I do not recognize as among the most formidable the reduction of Pig Point battery, as there is plenty of depth of water within point-blank range, to float the Cumberland; but the battery once reduced, there must be a pretty active march on Suffolk to prevent troublesome fortifications there, which I believe have not yet been undertaken.

"If I am right in the importance which I attach to this position, then I must expect all the force of the rebels, both from Norfolk and Richmond, brought thither by railroad, to be precipitated upon me, and be prepared to meet it in the open field. Could they do otherwise? Norfolk would be hemmed in. Am I able to withstand such an attack, between two forces which may act in conjunction, with the necessary drafts from my forces to keep open the line of communication by the Nansemond with Newport News, which would then be the right flank of my base of operations? All these questions, much more readily comprehended by the general-in-chief than by myself, with the thousand suggestions that will at once present themselves to his mind, are most respectfully submitted.

"May I ask for full and explicit instructions upon the matter?"

This was the scheme. It meant, Begin the war HERE. Strike at Richmond from *this* point. Sever Virginia from the South, by darting *hence* upon her railroad centers. Make war where your navy can co-operate. *Use* the means which God and nature have given you, and which Colonel Dimmick preserved. DON'T sit there in Washington, puttering upon forts and defenses, listening anxiously to the roar from the North, "On to Richmond;" but give the enemy something to do elsewhere, far away from your capital and your sacred things, yet made near to *you* by your command of the sea.

General Butler's plans might not have been completely successful; but if they had been adopted we should have had no Bull Run; and, perhaps, no Merrimac—the true cause of the failure of the peninsular campaign. Other disasters we might have suffered, but surely nothing so bad as Bull Run and the Merrimac, the most costly calamities that ever befell a country.

The reply to General Butler's eager dispatches present to us a curious study. The reader must make what he can of it. Date, June 10th:

"Sir,—Your letters of the 1st and 6th instant are received. The general-in-chief desires me to say in reply, that he highly commends your zeal and activity, which oblige the enemy to strengthen his camps and posts in your vicinity, and hold him constantly on the alert. The principal value of your movement upon Suffolk is, that it would be the easiest route to the Gosport Navy Yard, and the objects (including many ships of war) which our people on the former occasion left undestroyed. The possession of Norfolk in itself is of no importance whilst we blockade Hampton Roads; but the destruction of the railroads leading from that city, as far as you may find it practicable, would be a valuable coercive measure. The naval commander should aid you in the collection of boats, and the secretary of war has said that he would cause some eighty horses to be bought and shipped to you for a light battery."

These were the "full and explicit instructions" for which General Butler had written. He must have been puzzled to decide whether the letter was designed to sanction or discourage his enterprise. Nor was it easy to see what the naval commander could do in the way of providing the requisite number of boats. If, however, the words of the commander-in-chief were equivocal, his conduct was not. No horses were sent, nor battery of field artillery, nor vehicles, nor cavalry, nor boats. No objection to the railroad, the artesian well, the bake-house, the intrenched camps; but whatever was needful for an advance beyond half a day's march was withheld. Such was the scarcity of horses that the troops were constantly seen drawing wagon loads of supplies. A reporter writes: "A picture in the drama of the camp has this moment passed my quarters. It is a gang of the Massachusetts boys hauling a huge military wagon, loaded. They have struck up 'The Red, White and Blue.' They believe in it, and consequently render it with true patriotic inspiration. They pause and give three rousing cheers; and now they dash off like firemen, which they are, shouting and thundering along at a pace that makes the drowsy horses they pass prick up their ears." To supply the most pressing occasions, General Butler had nine horses of his own brought from Lowell, and these were all he had for the public service for more than two months. Another reporter writes, June 28th: "Among the passengers on board the steamer to the fortress was Colonel Butler, brother of the general, who went to Washington last week to get orders for the purchase of horses, without which not a single step can be made in advance, simply because the forces here are entirely destitute of the means of transportation. He got orders and succeeded in buying one hundred and thirty-five very good horses, mainly in Baltimore, whereupon the government immediately sent up and took one hundred of them for the artillery service at Washington. This was pretty sharp practice, and gives rise to comment on the inability of the authorities at the capital to see anything but Washington worthy of a moment's thought in connection with the present war."

The state of things certainly gave rise to comment, as the replies of official persons in Washington to General Butler's solicitations, abundantly show. One gentleman, who was necessarily acquainted with all that was going on at the seat of government, expressed himself with remarkable freedom in a letter to our general.

June 8th, "I received your letter and dispatch, and, contrary to your orders, I read both to the president, under the seal of confidence, however. I have told him that —— would never let you have any troops to make any great blow, and I read the dispatch to show that I understood my man. He intended to treat you as he did ——, and as he has always treated those whom he knew would be effective if he gave them the means, retaining everything in his own power and under his own immediate control, so as to monopolize all the reputation to be made.

"I have been a little afraid lest you might attempt more than your means justified, under the impression that you would otherwise disappoint the country. But I am pleased to see that you have not made this mistake. You must work on patiently till you feel yourself able to do the work you attempt, and not play into your enemies' hands, or those of the miserable do-nothings here, by attempting more than in your cool judgment the force you have can effect. You will gradually get the means, and then you may make an effective blow. Unfortunately, indeed, the difficulties increase as your force increases, if not more rapidly. We have forty thousand men, I believe, and provisions and transportation enough to take them to Richmond any day, and yet our lines do not extend five miles into Virginia, where there are not, in my opinion, men enough to oppose the march of half the number to Richmond. Old —— is at —— with 20,000 men, and is moving as cautiously toward the Potomac as if the banks were commanded by an army of Bonaparte's best legions, instead of a mob, composed for the most part of men who only wait for an opportunity to desert a flag they detest. This war will last for ever if *something* does not happen to unseat old ——. —— in the West, with 60,000 men under canvas, has not made a movement except let a few regiments march up the Baltimore and Ohio railroad, at the urgent solicitations of the people. So we go. Congress will probably catch us without our having performed any service worthy of the great force we have under pay."

"I grumble this way all the time, and to every body, in the hope that I may contribute to push on the column. I am very much in hopes we shall be pushed into action by the indignation of the people, if not by our own sense of what is due to the cause we have taken in hand."

CHAPTER VII.

GREAT BETHEL.

When this letter reached the fortress, General Butler was immersed in the last details of a movement, the result of which was to show him, and show the country, that sitting in an office arranging a masterly plan of action is one thing, and the successful execution of the same is another. His correspondent read the answer to his letter in the newspapers; first with exultation, then with bewilderment, lastly with dismay. For the news of Great Bethel came to us as so much of the news of the war has come; first, in enormous flattering lies; secondly, in exaggerated contradictory rumors of disaster; finally, and gradually, in a dim resemblance to the truth.

"Severe engagement near Fortress Monroe—Two hours' fight at Big Bethel—Terrible mistake of the Seventh and Third regiments—Masked batteries of Rifled Cannon open on our troops—Twenty-five killed, and one hundred wounded—Withdrawal from the Field—Renewal of the Battle by General Butler—The Rebel Batteries Captured, and One Thousand Prisoners taken."

Thus was the disaster first Heralded. Then came news, that our unfortunate regiments had been hurled upon a battery armed with thirty pieces of rifled cannon, protected in front by an impassable creek, from which, after standing "a terrific fire" for an hour and a half, they had recoiled, with a loss, variously stated, from twenty-five to a hundred. Other accounts assured us that our men were on the point of taking the battery, when an order came from some unknown source to retire.

The whole truth about Great Bethel does not appear to have been anywhere published. Mr. Pollard's rebel account is a little nearer the truth than any other which I have seen; though, of course, it is distorted by the insanity of hatred common to all our "Southern brethren."* Our "Southern brethren" excel in the business of hating through constant practice. Mr. Pollard would have been a man of honor and truth if he had been reared five degrees north of Richmond. As it is, he only escapes being one, when certain imaginary beings, whom he names *Yankees*, are the theme of his vigorous pen.

The affair of Great Bethel happened thus:

The forced inaction of General Butler had the effect of making the enemy bolder in approaching his lines. They would send parties from Yorktown, who would come down within sight of the Union pickets near Hampton, and seize both Union men and negroes, conscripting the former, using the latter on their batteries. Major Winthrop, always on the alert, learned from a contraband, George Scott by name, that the rebels had established themselves at two points between Yorktown and the fort, where they had thrown up intrenchments, and whence they nightly issued, seizing and plundering. George Scott described the localities with perfect correctness, and Winthrop himself, accompanied by George repeatedly reconnoitered the road leading to them. On one point only was the negro guide mistaken: he thought the rebels were two thousand in number; whereas, when he saw them, five hundred was about their force. They had eleven or twelve hundred men in the two Bethels on the day of the action, but not more than five hundred took part in it; the rest having arrived, on a run, from Yorktown while the "battle" was proceeding, and, before they had recovered breath, it was over.

Major Winthrop reported to General Butler, who resolved to attempt the capture of the two posts. His orders restricted him to advances of half a day's march. Great Bethel being nine miles distant, might be considered within the limit.

* "First year of the war." New York Edition. p. 77.

Now, all was excitement and activity at head-quarters—no one so happy as Winthrop, who threw himself, heart and soul, into the affair. The first rough plan of the expedition, drawn up in his own hand, lies before me; brief, hasty, colloquial, interlined; resembling the first sketch of an "article" or a story; such as, doubtless, he had often dashed upon paper at Staten Island.

PLAN OF ATTACK BY TWO DETACHMENTS UPON LITTLE BETHEL AND BIG BETHEL.

A regiment or battalion to march from Newport News, and a regiment to march from Camp Hamilton—*Duryea's*. Each will be supported by sufficient reserves under arms in camp, and with advanced guards out on the road of march.

Duryea to push out two pickets at 10 P. M.; one two and a half miles beyond Hampton, on the county road, but not so far as to alarm the enemy. This is important. Second picket half as far as the first. Both pickets to keep as much out of sight as possible. No one whatever to be allowed to pass out through their lines. Persons to be allowed to pass inward toward Hampton—unless it appears that they intend to go roundabout and dodge through to the front.

At 12, midnight, Colonel Duryea will march his regiment, with fifteen rounds cartridges, on the county road towards Little Bethel. Scows will be provided to ferry them across Hampton Creek. March to be rapid; *but not hurried.*

A howitzer with canister and shrapnel to go.

A wagon with planks and material to repair the Newmarket Bridge.

Duryea to have the 200 rifles. He will pick the men to whom to intrust them.

Rocket to be thrown up from Newport News. Notify Commodore Pendergrast of this to prevent general alarm.

Newport News movement to be made somewhat later, as the distance is less.

If we find the enemy and surprise them, men will fire one volley, if desirable; *not reload*, and go ahead with the bayonet.

As the attack is to be by night, or dusk of morning, and in two detachments, our people should have some token, say a white rag (or dirty white rag) on the left arm.

Perhaps the detachments who are to do the job should be smaller than a regiment 300 or 500, as the right and left of the attack would be more easily handled.

If we bag the Little Bethel men, push on to Big Bethel, and similarly bag them. Burn both the Bethels, or blow up if brick.

To protect our rear in case we take the field-pieces, and the enemy should march his main body (if he has any) to recover them, it would be well to have a squad of competent artillerists, regular or other, to handle the captured guns on the retirement of our main body. Also spikes to spike them, if retaken.

George Scott to have a shooting-iron.

Perhaps Duryea's men would be awkward with a new arm in a night or early dawn attack, where there will be little marksman duty to perform. Most of the work will be done with the bayonet, and they are already handy with the old ones.

"George Scott to have a shooting-iron!" So, the first suggestion of arming a black man in this war came from Theodore Winthrop. George Scott *had* a shooting-iron.

This plan, the joint production of the general and his secretary, was substantially adopted, and orders in accordance therewith were issued.

The command of the expedition was given to Brigadier-General E. W. Pierce, of Massachusetts, a brave and good man, totally without military experience except upon parade-grounds on training days. General Butler, as we have before said, was his junior in the militia of Massachusetts, and had been selected by Governor Andrew to command the first brigade which left the state, over the head of General Pierce, who desired to go. It was by way of atonement to General Pierce for having taken the place which belonged by seniority to him, that General Butler assigned him to the command. The motive was honorable to his feelings as a man. On Boston Common the act would have been highly becoming and quite unobjectionable. But, alas! the theater of action was not Boston Common.

General Butler has an eye for the man he wants. This was the first time, and the last time, in his military career, that he has selected an officer for an independent command, for any other reason but a conviction that he was the best man at hand for the duty to be done. General Pierce was a brave and good man; reputed then to be such; since proved to be such; but he was not the best man at hand for the duty to be done. Out of a good citizen you can make a good soldier in four months; but a good officer is a creature slowly produced. Seven years in peace, one year in war, may do it, but he *must* have served an apprenticeship, before he is fit to be in-

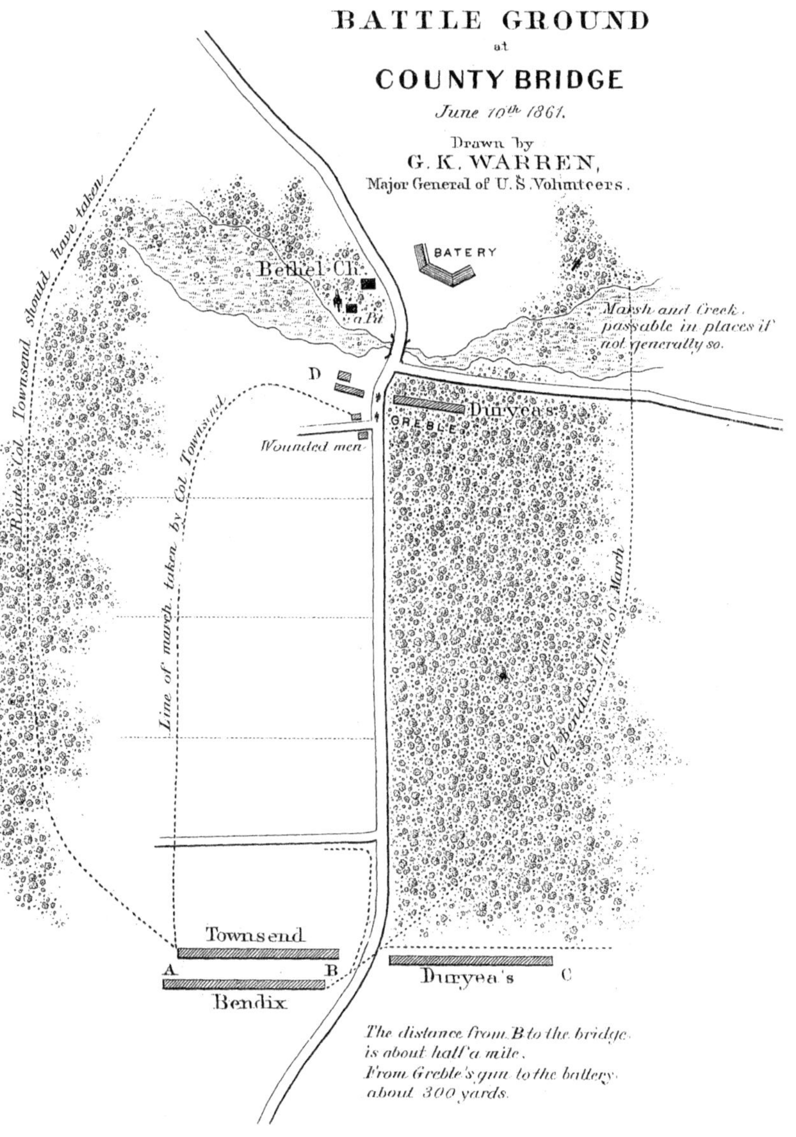
Sketch of
BATTLE GROUND
at
COUNTY BRIDGE
June 10th 1861.
Drawn by
G. K. WARREN,
Major General of U. S. Volunteers.
BATERY
Bethel Ch.
a Pit
Marsh and Creek, passable in places if not generally so.
D
Duryea's
GREBLE
Wounded men
Route Col. Townsend should have taken
Line of march taken by Col. Townsend
Col. Bendix's Line of March
Townsend
A
B
Bendix
Duryea's
C
The distance from B to the bridge is about half a mile.
From Greble's gun to the battery about 300 yards.

trusted with the lives of men and the honor of a country. The day before Bethel, General Butler had the brains of a general, the courage of a general, the toughness of a general, the technical knowledge of a general; but to fit him for independent command, he still needed some such harsh and bitter experience as now awaited him. The day after Bethel, he had made a prodigious stride in his military education, for he is a man who can take a hint. The whole secret of war was revealed in the flash and thunder, the disaster and shame, of that sorry skirmish.

All went well until near the dawn of day, June 10th, when the forces were to form their junction near Little Bethel. There Colonel Bendix's regiment saw approaching over the crest of a low hill what seemed, in the magnifying dusk, a body of cavalry. It was Colonel Townsend's regiment which they saw. Knowing that General Butler had no cavalry, Colonel Bendix concluded, of course, that they were a body of mounted rebels. The fatal order was given to fire, and ten of Colonel Townsend's men fell; two killed and eight wounded. The fire was returned in a desultory manner, without loss to the regiment of Colonel Bendix. Of the confusion that followed, the double-quick counter-marching, the alarm to friends and foes, I need not speak. The dawn of day revealed the error, and then the question arose, whether to advance or to return to the fortress. A surprise was no longer possible, and the inhabitants of the country concurred in stating the force of the enemy at four or five thousand, with formidable artillery. Colonel Duryea had already captured the picket at Little Bethel. The enemy, therefore, fully warned, must be concentrated at Great Bethel. Major Winthrop and Lieutenant Butler, both of the commanding general's staff, united in most earnestly advising an advance, and General Pierce gave no reluctant assent. He had sent back for re-enforcements which were soon on the march to join him.

At half past nine, he had arrived within a mile of the enemy, with two regiments and four pieces of cannon of small caliber, one of which was the gun of Lieutenant Greble of the regular artillery. Two other regiments were approaching. The ground may be roughly described thus: An oblong piece of open country, surrounded on three sides by woods, General Pierce entering at the end where there was no wood. The enemy's position was near the upper end, but behind a strip of wood which concealed it. It was, in some slight degree, protected in front by a creek twelve feet wide and three deep. Their battery consisted of *four* pieces of field artillery, one of which becoming disabled through the disarrangement of the trigger-apparatus, was useless. The earthworks, hastily thrown up in front of the guns, added scarcely any strength to the position, for they were less than three feet high on the outside. A boy ten years old could have leaped over them; a boy ten years old could have waded the creek. The breastworks were, in fact, so low that the wheels of the enemy's guns were embedded in the earth, in order to get the carriages low enough to be protected. These facts I learn from a Union officer of high rank, who afterward became familiar with the ground. Behind these trivial works were five hundred rebel troops, who were re-enforced while the action was going on with six hundred more from Yorktown, thoroughly *blown* with running. This was the real strength of the enemy, whom General Pierce firmly believed to consist of four or five thousand troops strongly posted, and well supplied with artillery.

General Pierce and his command then stood, at half-past nine, on the high road leading from Hampton to Yorktown, a mile from the enemy, whose battery commanded the road. That battery was so placed that it could have been approached within fifty yards without the attacking party leaving the woods. Nor was there any serious obstacle to turning it either on the right or on the left. This not being immediately perceived, Colonel Duryea and Lieutenant Greble marched along the high road into the enemy's fire, and soon the cannon balls began to play over their heads, falling far to the rear. The men gave three cheers and kept on their way. Soon, however, the enemy fired better, and some men were struck; not many, for the total loss of Colonel Duryea's regiment that day was four killed, and twelve wounded. To these troops, in their inexperience, it seemed that work of this kind could not be down in the programme. They also received the impression that the enemy's three pieces of cannon were thirty at least, and that, upon the whole, this was not the right road to the battery. So they sidled off into the woods, and there remained waiting for some one to tell them what to do next. Greble kept on to a point three hundred yards from the enemy, where he planted his gun, and maintained a steady and effective fire upon them for an hour and a half.

I say effective. It did not kill a rebel; but it had the effect of keeping them within their works, and giving them the idea that they were attacked.

After Colonel Duryea had retired to the woods, there was a long pause in the operations, during which a good plan was matured for turning the enemy's battery, and getting in behind it. It was agreed that Colonel Townsend should keep well away to the left, near the wood, or through the wood, and go on to the Yorktown road beyond the battery; then turn down upon it, and dash in. Colonel Duryea and Colonel Bendix were to march through the woods on the right, and penetrate to the same road below the battery, and then rush in upon it simultaneously with Colonel Townsend. It was an excellent and most feasible scheme, certain of success if executed with merely tolerable vigor and resolution. Colonel Duryea again advanced, this time through the woods. He went as far as the creek, and concluding it to be impassable by his "Zouaves," retired a second time, with some trifling loss; Lieutenant-Colonel Warren, and a few brave men remaining long enough to bring away the body and the gun of poor Greble, shot by the enemy's last discharge. Meanwhile Colonel Townsend was making his way far on the other side of the road. He was going straight to victory; Major Winthrop among the foremost, full of ardor and confidence, and the men in good heart. In five minutes more he would have gained a position on the Yorktown road beyond the battery, from which they could have marched upon the enemy, as in an open field. Then occurred a fatal mistake. In the haste of the start, two companies of the regiment had marched on the other side of a stone fence; and, anxious to get forward, were coming up to the front at some distance from the main body in the open field. Colonel Townsend seeing these troops, supposed that they were a body of the enemy coming out to attack him in flank. He ordered a halt, and then returned to the point of departure to meet this imaginary foe. Winthrop, as is supposed, did not hear the order to retire. With a few troops he still pressed on, and when they halted, still advanced, and reached a spot thirty yards from the enemy's battery. With one companion, private John M. Jones of Vermont, he sprang upon a log to get a view of the position, which he alone that day clearly saw. A ball pierced his brain. He almost instantly breathed his last. His body being left on the field fell into the hands of the foe. In their opinion, he was the only man in the Union force who displayed "even an approximation to courage," and they gave his remains the honorable burial due to the body of a hero, and returned his watch and other effects to his commanding officer.

General Pierce, with the advice of all the colonels present, now gave the order to return to camp; and so the "battle" of Great Bethel ended. Some of the companies retired in tolerable order. But there was a great deal of panic and precipitation, though the pursuit was late and languid. The noble Chaplain Winslow and the brave Lieutenant-Colonel G. K. Warren,* with a few other firm men, remained behind; and, all exhausted as they were, drew the wounded in wagons nine miles, from the scene of the action to the nearest camp.

Lieutenant-Colonel Warren reports:

"I remained on the ground about an hour after all the force had left. As Colonel Carr retired, Captain Wilson, of his regiment, carried off the gun at which Lieutenant Greble had been killed, but left the limber behind. I withdrew this along with Lieutenant Greble's body, assisted by Lieutenant Duncan and twelve men of the N. Y. First, and sent it on to join the piece. I remained with Chaplain Winslow, and a few men of the N. Y. Third, Fifth, and Seventh, getting the wounded together, whom we put into carts and wagons, and drew off by hand. There were three or four mortally wounded and several dead, whom we had to leave from inability to carry them. I sent several messengers to get assistance; and as we moved slowly, finding no one, I pushed ahead as fast as I could go on foot (having given the animal I rode to a wounded man). I overtook none but the worn-out stragglers till I came up to Captain Kapff, of the N. Y. Seventh, who with seven or eight men stopped, as also did Captain McNutt of the Second, detailed by Colonel Carr. They both rendered essential service in checking the advance of the enemy's horsemen, who finally came on and pursued up to New Market Bridge.

"The noble conduct of Chaplain Winslow, and the generous-hearted men who remained behind to help the wounded, deserves the highest praise; and the toilsome task which they accomplished

* Since brigadier-general and chief of staff to General Meade—distinguished on many fields, particularly at the battles in Pennsylvania in June, 1863.

of dragging the rude vehicles, filled with their helpless comrades, over a weary road of nine miles in their exhausted condition, with the prospect of an attack every minute, bespeak a goodness of heart and a bravery never excelled. Besides the wounded and dead left behind, there were a number of canteens and haversacks, and a few muskets and bayonets, all of which I think was caused by a misunderstanding. Our regiment did not think we were going back more than a few hundred yards to rest a little, out of fire, and then make another attack. There was no pursuing force, or the least excuse for precipitancy. No shots were fired at the little party who carried away the limber of Lieutenant Greble's gun, and the long while which elapsed without any one appearing in front of the enemy's lines, would indicate that he was very weak in numbers, or perhaps had begun to retire. The force which the enemy brought into action was not, I think, greater than 500 men. His great advantage over us was artillery protected from our fire. I still am of the opinion that the position, as we found it, was not difficult to take with experienced troops, and could have been turned on our left. The trees protected our approach, and sheltered us from their battery till we were quite close, and the march in front was practicable for footmen. We labored under great disadvantage in want of experience in firing, and in the exhaustion of our men from want of sleep, long marching, and hunger.

"The enemy had a rifled gun or two, shooting bolts of about the caliber of four-pounders, and eight inches long, with soft metal base; some of them were hollow, with a Boarman fuse at the point, and all did not burst. Some of their twelve-pounder shells also failed to explode. There were probably three to five guns sheltered by a breastwork, and one or two that were moved around to different points.

"The breastwork was placed so that the guns enfiladed the little bridge. The gun placed to sweep the long reach of road before you came to the bridge was driven away by Lieutenant Greble's fire, which prevented our loss from being far greater than it was. The skill and bravery displayed by Lieutenant Greble could not have been surpassed; and the fortune which protected him from the enemy's fire only deserted him at the last moment. The discharge which killed him was one of the last made by the enemy's guns. His own guns were never silenced by the enemy's fire, and the occasional pauses were to husband his ammunition."

The Union loss in killed and permanently disabled was twenty-five. The rebel loss, one man killed and three wounded. A few hours after the action, Great Bethel was evacuated. If General Pierce had withdrawn his men out of fire, and caused them to sit down and eat their dinner, it is highly probable the enemy would have retreated; for they were greatly outnumbered, and were perfectly aware that one regiment of steady and experienced troops, led by a man who knew his business, could have taken them all prisoners in twenty minutes. For the most part, our men, I am assured, behaved as well as could have been expected. All they wanted was commanders who knew what was the right thing to do, and who would go forward and show them how to do it. One well-compacted, well-sustained rush from any point of approach, and the battery had been theirs.

CHAPTER VIII.

CONSEQUENCES OF GREAT BETHEL.

GREAT BETHEL was a trifling skirmish; but, occurring just when it did, it was a calamity. It was the first shock of arms between the belligerents, and gave the key-note to at least the overture of the war—the first campaign. Splendid fighting has since been done, and a great deal of it. There has, also, been much bad fighting, many ill-concerted movements, much misconduct on the part of officers, some shameful flights and panics. It does not appear certain that we have yet learned to comply with all the fundamental conditions of successful war. We still seem capable, occasionally, of starting back in affright from phantoms, instead of marching forward and preventing phantoms from becoming realities. We all know what allowances were to be made for these Bethel regiments. We knew how they had left their counting-rooms and shops for a long frolic at soldiering, with officers who were, perhaps, *more* ignorant of their new profession than if they had never shone on parade, or distinguished themselves in the drill room. There is a kind of knowledge which deludes more than total ignorance, since it seems to conceal our ignorance from ourselves and from others.

It was rather surprising than otherwise that the first fighting of the war was done as well as it was done, since all the influences of our education and business had long tended to abate that exuberance of spirit, that confidence in our strength, which makes men mighty to dare and to overcome. The training which diminishes a man's fighting power is not culture, but effeminacy.

But if we had not learned the true secret of successful warfare, we are learning it; we shall learn it. Much creditable fighting has been done by the Union armies. But, contending as we are with a desperate foe, our armies must acquire the *coherency* which is only obtained by supplying them with officers whose superiority of knowledge will command the confidence of the men in critical moments. For many a year to come, perhaps, the *élite* of the young men of America will have to be bred to arms as a profession.

The day after Bethel was a sad one at Fortress Monroe. Lieutenant Greble's father was on his way to visit his son, and arrived only to take back his remains to his family, followed by the sorrow of the whole command. The fate of Winthrop was not yet known; he was reported only among the "missing." Before leaving head-quarters he had borrowed a gun of the general, saying, gayly, "I may want to take a pop at them." In the course of the morning, this gun was brought in, with such information as led to the conclusion that he must have fallen; perhaps, thrown his life purposely away. During his short residence at head-quarters he had endeared himself to all hearts; to none more than to the general and Mrs. Butler. He was mourned as a brother by those who had known him but sixteen days.

As Mr. Curtis beautifully says in his fine sketch of his friend's career, "Theodore Winthrop's life, like a fire long smoldering, suddenly blazed up into a clear bright flame, and vanished. Descended from John Winthrop and Jonathan Edwards, numbering among his ancestors seven presidents of Yale College, of which he was himself a distinguished graduate, with fine gifts, powerful friends, good opportunities, he lived thirty-three years without finding work that could absorb and content him, unless it were literature, and for that he seemed to lack the something—bodily stamina, confidence in his powers, force of ambition or pressure of necessity—which could convert his longing into a career. His desk was full of manuscripts, since rightly valued; but his name was unknown to the public till he wrote the story of the march of the Seventh regiment. It was not force of vitality that he wanted. He had been everywhere, seen everything; walked over Scotland, Italy, Switzerland; ridden over our western plains and deserts. A short, slight, most active figure. "Often," says Mr. Curtis, "after writing for a few hours in the morning, he stepped out of doors, and, from pure love of the fun, leaped and turned summersets upon the grass, before going up to town. In walking about Staten Island, he constantly stopped by the roadside fences, and, grasping the highest rail, swung himself swiftly and neatly over and back again, resuming the walk and the talk without delay." Overwork at school and college had robbed him of that unchecked growth without which there can be no sustained fullness of endeavor. Unlearning what he had learned amiss, learning essential things of which the schools had given him no hint, chasing the world over after health—so passed the years of his maturity.

To the mother of his dead comrade, General Butler addressed the following letter:

"Head-quarters Department of Virginia,
"*June 13th*, 1861.

"My Dear Madam:—The newspapers have anticipated me in the sorrowful intelligence which I have to communicate. Your son Theodore is no more. He fell mortally wounded from a rifle shot, at County Bridge. I have conversed with private John M. Jones, of the Northfield company in the Vermont regiment, who stood beside Major Winthrop when he fell, and supported him in his arms.

"Your son's death was in a few moments, without apparent anguish. After Major Winthrop had delivered the order with which he was charged, to the commander of the regiment, he took his rifle, and while his guide held his horse in the woods in the rear, with too daring bravery, went to the front; while there, stepping upon a log to get a full view of the force, he received the fatal shot. His friend, Colonel Wardrop, of Massachusetts, had loaned him a sword for the occasion, on which his name was marked in full, so that he was taken by the enemy for the colonel himself.

"Major Winthrop had advanced so close to the parapet, that it was not thought expedient by those in command to send forward any party to bring off the body, and thus endanger the lives of others in the attempt to secure his remains, as the rebels remorselessly fired upon all the small parties that went forward for the purpose of bringing off their wounded comrades.

"Had your gallant son been alive, I doubt not he would have advised this course in regard to another. I have assurances from the officer in command of the rebel forces at County Bridge, that Major Winthrop received at their hand a respectful and decent burial.

"His personal effects found upon him, will be given up to my flag of truce, with the exception of his watch, which has been sent to Yorktown, and which I am assured will be returned through me to yourself.

"I have given thus particularly these sad details, because I know and have experienced the fond inquiries of a mother's heart respecting her son's acts.

"My dear madam! although a stranger, my tears will flow with yours in grief for the loss of your brave and too gallant son, my true friend and brother.

"I had not known him long, but his soldierly qualities, his daring courage, his true-hearted friendship, his genuine sympathies, his cultivated mind, his high moral tone, all combined to so win me to him, that he had twined himself about my heart with the cords of a brother's love.

"The very expedition which resulted so unfortunately for him, made him all the more dear to me. Partly suggested by himself, he entered into the necessary preparations for it with such alacrity, cool judgment, and careful foresight, in all the details that might render it successful, as gave great promise of future usefulness in his chosen profession. When, in answer to his request to be permitted to go with it, I suggested to him that my correspondence was very heavy, and he would be needed at home, he playfully replied: 'O general, we will all work extra hours, and make that up when we get back. The affair can't go on without me, you know.' The last words I heard him say before his good-night, when we parted, were, 'If anything happens, I have given my mother's address to Mr. Green.' His last thoughts were with his mother; his last acts were for his country and her cause.

"I have used the words 'unfortunate expedition for him!' Nay, not so; too fortunate thus to die doing his duty, his whole duty, to his country, as a hero, and a patriot. Unfortunate to us only who are left to mourn the loss to ourselves and our country.

"Permit me, madam, in the poor degree I may, to take such a place in your heart that we may mingle our griefs, as we already do our love and admiration for him who has only gone before us to that better world where, through the 'merits of Him who suffered for us,' we shall all meet together.

"Most sincerely and affectionately,

"Yours, BENJ. F. BUTLER."

It may not be improper to add to this just and affecting tribute, a note addressed by the sister of the deceased officer to Mrs. Butler:

"STATEN ISLAND, *June 10th*, 1861.

"DEAR MRS. BUTLER:—I can not let this opportunity pass without expressing my gratitude to you, and General Butler, for your great kindness to my dear brother, and for your tenderness to us in our grief. It is a great comfort to us to know that we have your sympathy; to know that you valued Theodore, and appreciated him. We must always feel a warm friendship for you and yours, with whom he spent the last weeks of his life, the most eventful, the most useful, and the happiest, perhaps, he had ever spent. You know in some degree what we have lost, and I trust we shall one day meet as friends, and talk of things of the deepest interest to us, and which I am sure are not without interest to you. It does make us stronger to bear our sorrow, when we think of the cause for which our dear brother died; a cause long dear to us all, and now far dearer than ever. I trust our country will be nobler and worthier than ever of our love, after this dark hour of trial is past. May she not have, like Rachel, to weep for many more of her children. Yet truth and freedom can not be too dearly bought, by blood and tears.

"It is a great satisfaction to us to know from Theodore's letters, that some of the last acts of his life were kindnesses to an oppressed race, a race he never forgot, as a part of the Nation whose battle he fought.

"My mother and sisters join with me in affectionate remembrances, and in the hope of expressing in person at some future time our heartfelt gratitude, our interest and friendship for you as well as General Butler, whose career we watch with warm interest and admiration. Yours affectionately,

"LAURA W. JOHNSON."

I must not leave this melancholy subject without mentioning the noble, and, I believe, unique atonement made by General Pierce for whatever errors he may have committed at Great Bethel. He served out his term of three months in such extreme sorrow as almost to threaten his reason. He then enlisted as a private in a three years regiment, and served for some time in that honorable lowliness. Appointed, at length, to the command of a regiment, he served with distinction through the campaign of the peninsula, where, in one of the battles, he was severely wounded.

General Butler, as we all remember, did not escape the censures of the press on this occasion. He was frequently favored with comments like the following:

"Men can not be required to stand in front of a rampart, thirty feet from the muzzles of mounted guns, loaded with grape, and canister, and musket-balls, doing nothing. When they are commanded to march through fire, and reach the ditch, they must be provided with the means to cross it, or jump into it, and sticking their bayonets into the slope of the scarp, form with them ladders by means of which the more active can mount the parapet. But before men are sent into a position—recollecting that every ditch will be swept by a flank fire—they must not only be instructed in their duties, but supported by a steady fire upon the enemy. Advantage must be taken of darkness or the weather; false assaults must be made in conjunction with the true one, and so supported, too, that the false attack may, if circumstances favor it, be followed up and made the real one."

Indeed, the great calamity of Bethel was, that it concealed from the country for a time the merit of the man who, more than most, was able to give it the service it needed. The country wanted a man who could not be scared by phantoms, and whose energy and talents could keep phantoms from growing into grim realities. The man was at hand, but imperfectly recognized. A complete success at Great Bethel, added to the fame of Baltimore and Annapolis, would have given General Butler a position before the country which could not have been disregarded. The failure there nearly cost him a rejection by the senate. He was saved by two votes only, and that bare majority he owed to the friendly exertions of that Colonel Baker whose life was squandered at Ball's Bluff. Colonel Baker had served with his regiment at Fortress Monroe.

An interesting correspondence between General Butler and Colonel Magruder, shows us that the question of the exchange of prisoners was not regarded as a difficult one, at that stage of the war, by either of those officers. Colonel Magruder had been an acquaintance of General Butler in happier times. They had last met, I believe, at a ball at Newport:

COLONEL MAGRUDER TO GENERAL BUTLER.

"HEAD-QUARTERS, YORKTOWN, VIRGINIA, *June* 12th, 1861.

"MAJOR-GENERAL B. F. BUTLER, Commanding Fortress Monroe, &c.

"SIR:—Our people had orders to bring any communications intended for the commander of the forces at 'County Bridge' or Bethel to this place, and by a particular route—hence the delay.

"I understood from Captain Davies, the bearer of the flag, that you have four prisoners, to wit: One trooper and three citizens; Messrs. Carter, Whiting, Lively and Mariam, the latter three being citizens of Virginia, in your possession; and you state that you are desirous to exchange them for a corresponding number of federal troops, who are prisoners with me. I accept your offer, so far as the trooper, who was a vidette, in question, and will send to-morrow, at four o'clock in the afternoon, if it will suit your convenience, a federal soldier in exchange for him. With respect to the wounded, my first care was to have them attended to. Medical advice and careful nursing have been provided, and your dead I had buried on the field of battle, and this was done in sight of the conflagration which was devastating the homes of our citizens.

"The citizens in your possession are men who doubtless defended their homes against a foe who, to their certain knowledge, had, with or without the authority of the federal government, destroyed the private property of their neighbors, breaking up even the pianos of the ladies, and committing depredations, numberless and of every description. The federal prisoners, if agreeable to you, will be sent to or near Hampton, by a sergeant, who will receive the vidette (Carter) who was captured by your troops. I do not think a more formal proceeding necessary, you having but one prisoner, and he not taken in battle.

"If my proposition to deliver one federal prisoner at or near Hampton in charge of a sergeant, to be exchanged for private Carter, the captured vidette, be accepted, please inform me or the officer in command at Bethel church, and it shall be done.

"It is scarcely necessary to say that the gentlemen who bear your flag have been received with every courtesy by our citizens, as well as ourselves. I have the honor to be,

"Very respectfully, your obedient servant,

"J BANKHEAD MAGRUDER, *Colonel Commanding.*"

GENERAL BUTLER TO COLONEL MAGRUDER.

HEAD-QUARTERS DEPARTMENT OF VIRGINIA,
FORTRESS MONROE, *June 13th*, 1861.

"COLONEL J. B. MAGRUDER, Commanding Forces at Yorktown.

"SIR:—Your favor of June 12, by Captain Davies, with a flag of truce, was this morning received. I desire first to thank you for the courtesy shown to the flag and its messengers. I will accept the exchange for private Carter. The two citizens, Whiting and Lively, were taken with arms in their hands, one of which was discharged from the house of Whiting upon the column of our troops when all resistance was useless, and when his attack was simply assassination, and when no offense had been committed against him. The house from which this shot was fired, and a building which formed a part of your outpost are the only conflagrations caused by the troops under my command. And the light of these had ceased hours before your men ventured out from under their earthworks and ditches, to do us the courtesy of burying our dead, for which act you have my sincere thanks.

"After our troops returned from the field—hours after—a building was burned which had furnished our wounded some shelter, and from which we had removed them, but not by our men. For your kind treatment of any wounded you may have, please accept my assurance of deep obligation, with the certainty that at any and every opportunity such courtesy and kindness will be reciprocated. I am sorry that an officer so distinguished in the service of the United States as yourself could for a moment suppose that the wanton destruction of private property would in any way be authorized or tolerated by the federal government and its officers, many of whom are your late associates. Even now, while your letter is being answered, and this is on its way to you, a most ignominious and severe punishment, in the presence of all the troops, is being inflicted upon men who had enlisted in the service of the United States—not soldiers—for plundering private property. All private property which would not, by the strictest construction, be considered contraband of war, as means of feeding and aiding the enemy, which has been brought within my lines or in any way has come in the possession of my troops and discovered, with the strictest examination has been taken account of and collected together to be given to those peaceable citizens who have come forward to make claim for it. A board of survey has been organized, and has already reported indemnity for the property of peaceable citizens necessarily destroyed. In order to convince you that no wrong has been done to private property by any one in authority in the service of the United States, I do myself the honor to inclose a copy of a general order from this department, which will sufficiently explain itself. And the most active measures have been taken rigidly to enforce it, and to punish violations thereof. That there have been too many sporadic acts of wrong to private property committed by bad men under my command, I admit and most sincerely regret, and believe they will in the future be substantially prevented; and I mean they shall be repaired in favor of all loyal citizens so far as lies in my power.

"You have done me the honor to inform me that vidette Carter is not a prisoner taken in battle. That is quite true. He was asleep on his post, and informs me that his three companions left in such haste that they neglected to wake him up. And they being mounted and my men on foot, the race was a difficult one. If it is not the intention of your authorities to treat the citizens of Virginia taken in actual conflict with the United States, as soldiers, in what light shall they be considered? Please inform me in what light you regard them. If not soldiers, must they not be assassins?

"A sergeant of Captain Davies's command will be charged to meet your sergeant at four o'clock, at the village of Hampton, for the purpose of exchange of private Carter.

"I need not call your attention to the fact that there will be unauthorized acts of violence committed by those who are not sufficiently under restraint of their commanding officers. My men complain that the ambulance having the wounded was fired into by your cavalry. And I am informed that if you have any prisoners, they were taken while engaged in pious duty to their wounded comrades, and not in battle. It has not occurred to my mind that either firing into the ambulance or capturing persons in charge of the wounded men was an act either authorized, recognized, or sanctioned by any gentleman in command of the forces in Virginia. Before this unhappy strife, I had not been so accustomed to regard the acts of my late associate citizens of the United States, and I have seen nothing in the course of this contest in the acts of those in authority, to lead me to a different conclusion.

"I have the honor to be, most respectfully, your obedient servant,

"BENJ. F. BUTLER,

"*Major-General Commanding United States Forces.*"

General Butler learned the lesson first taught by the failure at Great Bethel, since repeated on so many disastrous fields. That lesson was, the utter insufficiency of the volunteer system as then organized, and the absolute necessity of officers morally and professionally superior to the men under their command. The southern social system, at least, leads to the selection of officers to whom the men are accustomed to look up. Our officers, on the contrary, must have a *real* superiority, both of knowledge and of character, in order to bind a regiment into coherency and force. General Butler had under his command captains, majors and colonels who owed their election chiefly to their ability to bestow unlimited drinks. There were drunkards and thieves among them; to say nothing of those who, from mere ignorance and natural inefficiency, could maintain over their men no degree whatever of moral or military ascendancy. The general saw the evil. In a letter to the secretary of war, June 26th, he pointed out the partial remedy which was afterward adopted.

"I desire," he wrote, "to trouble you upon a subject of the last importance to the organization of our volunteer regiments. Many of the volunteers, both two and three years men, have chosen their own company officers, and in some cases their field officers, and they have been appointed without any proper military examination before a proper board, according to the plan of organization of the volunteers. There should be some means by which these officers can be sifted out. The efficiency and usefulness of the regiment depend upon it. To give you an illustration: In one regiment I have had seven applications for resignation, and seventeen applications for leave of absence; some on the most frivolous pretexts, by every grade of officers under the colonel. I have yielded to many of these applications, and more readily than I should otherwise have done, because I was convinced that their absence was of benefit rather than harm. Still, this absence is a virtual fraud upon the United States. It seems as if there must be some method other than a court-martial of ridding the service of these officers, when there are so many competent men ready, willing, and eager to serve their country. Ignorance and incompetency are not crimes to be tried by court martial, while they are great misfortunes to an officer. As at present the whole matter of the organization is informal, without direct authority of law in its details, may not the matter be reached by having a board appointed at any given post, composed of three or five, to whom the competency, efficiency, and propriety of conduct of a given officer might be submitted? And that upon the report of that board, approved by the commander and the department, the officer be dropped without the disgrace attending the sentence of a court-martial?"

Meanwhile, the general labored most earnestly to raise the standard of discipline in the regiments. The difficulty was great, amounting, at times, to impossibility. At one time there were thirty-eight vacancies among the officers of the New York regiments alone. The men, accustomed to active industry, and now compelled to endure the monotony of a camp, sought excitement in drink. It was, for some weeks, a puzzle at head-quarters where the soldiers obtained such abundant supplies of the means of intoxication. "We used," said General Butler, in his testimony before the war committee, "to send a picket guard up a mile and a half from Fortress Monroe. The men would leave perfectly sober, yet every night when they came back we would have trouble with them on account of their being drunk. Where they got their liquor from we could not tell. Night after night, we instituted a rigorous examination, but it was always the same. The men were examined over and over again; their canteens were inspected, and yet we could find no liquor about them. At last it was observed that they seemed to hold their guns up very straight, and, upon examination being made, it was found that every gun-barrel was filled with whisky; and it was not always the soldiers who did this."

Further investigation disclosed facts still more distressing. An eye-witness reports:

"General Butler ascertained that what was professedly the sutler's store of one of the regiments, was but a groggery. This he visited, and stove the heads of some half dozen barrels, and spilled all the liquor of every sort to be found. He found a book, in which the account with a single regiment was kept, which disclosed a state of things truly startling. Scarcely an officer of the regiment but had an open account, footing up for the single month amounts ranging from $10 to $1,000. The items charged, and the space of time within which the liquor was obtained, and, of course, consumed, was truly astonishing, and proved the depth of demoralization to which the officers, and, I fear, consequently, the entire regiment, had become reduced. I purposely suppress a narrative of the scenes of debauchery and violence in the camp at Newport News, where the regiment has lately been removed, a few evenings since, resulting in the shooting, if not the death, of a soldier, fired on by an officer while both were intoxicated.

"General Butler having possessed himself of the book in question, went to Newport News yesterday afternoon, having previously summoned all the commissioned officers of the regiment to meet him alone on the boat on his arrival. They came as summoned. General Butler told them frankly and pointedly what was the object of the meeting; exhibited to them the evidence that was in his hands of the astonishing amounts of liquor which they as officers had purchased; pointed them to the consequences as seen in the demoralized condition of the regiments; the late scenes of violence, the waste of money, the injustice of such conduct toward New York, after she had been to the expense of giving them a liberal outfit, and, with a princely liberality, was supporting so many of the families of soldiers and others; and, more than all, the deplorable consequences that must ensue to the cause from such indulgence. General Butler said there must and should be a stop put to it. He said he himself was not a total-abstinence man, but he pledged to the officers he addressed his word of honor as an officer and a man that, so long as he remained in this department, intoxicating drinks should be banished from his quarters, and that he would not use them except when medicinally prescribed; and he wanted the officers present to give him their pledge that henceforth this should be the rule of their conduct. As he had determined to tell no man to go, where he could not say come, so, in this matter, he required no officer to do that which he would not first do himself. General Butler enforced his views and the grounds of the determination he had formed feelingly and forcibly, and the affirmative response was unanimous, with only one exception, he being a captain, whose resignation Colonel Phelps announced was then in his hands, and which General Butler instantly accepted.

"This interview over, General Butler directed Captain Davis, the provost-marshal, and his deputy, W. H. Wiegel, to proceed to search every place known to sell liquor, or suspected of being engaged in the traffic, and to destroy the same. Within one hour between twenty and thirty barrels of whisky, brandy, and other concoctions were emptied on the ground, amid the cheers of the soldiers. The proceeding elicited the warmest approbation of the whole camp, and especially of the men, who, as patrons of the sutlers, had been swindled by them. The sutlers themselves, and all others guilty of having contributed to demoralize the troops, were taken into custody and brought to the fortress, and will be sent hence."

General Butler's order on the subject of intoxicating drinks is too characteristic to be omitted.

"HEAD-QUARTERS, DEPARTMENT VIRGINIA,
"FORT MONROE, VA., *August* 2, 1861.

'GENERAL ORDER, No. 22.—The general commanding was informed on the first day of the month, from the books of an unlicensed liquor dealer near this post, and by the effect on the officers and soldiers under his command, that the use of intoxicating liquors prevailed to an alarming extent among the officers of his command. He had already taken measures to prevent its use among the men, but had presumed that officers and gentlemen might be trusted; but he finds that as a rule, in some regiments, that assumption is ill-founded, while there are many honorable exceptions to this unhappy state of facts; yet, for the good of all, some stringent measures upon the subject are necessary.

"Hereafter, all packages brought into this department for any officer of whatever grade, will be subjected to the most rigid inspection; and all spirituous and intoxicating liquors therein will be taken and turned over to the use of the medical department. Any officer who desires may be present at the inspection of his own packages.

"No sale of intoxicating liquor will be allowed in this department, and any citizen selling will be immediately sent out.

"If any officer finds the use of intoxicating liquor necessary for his health, or the health of any of his men, a written application to the medical director will be answered; and the general is confident that there is a sufficient store for all necessary purposes.

"The medical director will keep a record of all such applications, the name of the applicant, date of application, amount and kind of liquor delivered, to be open at all times for public inspection.

"In view of the alarming increase in the use of this deleterious article, the general earnestly exhorts all officers and soldiers to use their utmost exertions, both of influence and example, to prevent the wasting effects of this scourge of all armies.

"The general commanding does not desire to conceal the fact that he has been accustomed to the use of wine and liquors in his own quarters, and to furnish them to his friends; but as he desires never to ask either officers or men to undergo any privation which he will not share with them, he will not exempt himself from the operation of this order, but will not use it in his own quarters, as he would discourage its use in the quarters of any other officer. Amid the many sacrifices of time, property, health and life, which the officers and soldiers of his command are making in the service of their country, the general commanding feels confident that this, so slight, but so necessary a sacrifice of a luxury, and pandering to appetite, will be borne most cheerfully, now that its evil is seen and appreciated.

"This order will be published by reading it at the head of every battalion, at their several evening parades.

"By command of

"MAJOR-GENERAL BUTLER.

"T. J. HAINES, *A. A. A. General.*"

The whisky at Fortress Monroe inspired one piece of wit, which amused the command. This was the time when it was customary to "administer the oath" to arrested secessionists, and set them at liberty. A scouting party having brought in a rattlesnake, the question arose what should be done with it. A drunken soldier hiccoughed out: "d—n him, swear him in and let him go."*

With equal vigor, General Butler made war upon a practice which no commanding officer has ever been able entirely to suppress, that of plundering abandoned houses. The possession of a chair, a table, a piece of carpet, an old kettle, or even a piece of plank, adds so much to the comfort of men in camp, that the temptation to help themselves to such articles is sometimes irresistible. If any man could have prevented plundering, Wellington was that individual; but he could not, though he possessed and used the power to hang offenders on the spot. Subsequent investigation proved

* It also gave rise to the following correspondence:

"ASTORIA, N. Y., *July* 26, 1861.

"General B. F. BUTLER—SIR: You are aware of the interest felt by the loyal people of this country in their army. Men and women are ready to do all in their power to sustain and encourage the noble men who have gone forth to defend our country. This very day many of the ladies of this village have been seen hard at work making up garments and other things for hospital use. Our ladies here sent a large quantity of articles to Fort Monroe, and have others ready to send. I doubt not in other places thousands have been similarly employed. This being the case, we feel that everything affecting the character of our army concerns us. A lady in the village has received a letter from a soldier under your command, *a reliable man*, who says, *one of the officers has been drunk a week. An army in which such conduct is tolerated, is of course demoralized.* I felt it my duty as a citizen to inform you of the impression made by such a statement on all who hear it. Our cause is hopeless if such men are to hold office in our army, or if such conduct does not receive condign punishment. Most respectfully yours,

"B. F. STEAD, *Pastor of the Presbyterian church, Astoria, L. I.*"

"HEAD-QUARTERS, DEPARTMENT OF VIRGINIA, *July* 29, 1861.

"MY DEAR SIR: Your note received. I am pained by its contents. '*A reliable man* says that an officer has been drunk for a week.'

"I did not appoint this officer. I do not know who he is. I have no means of knowing unless the '*reliable man*' will complain of him to me. I do not 'tolerate' such conduct. Why did the people of his county, who must have known that officer's habits, allow him to be commissioned? Why did this reliable man vote for him?

"I have established a scrutiny over the packages sent to the men to have them cleared of liquor given by misguiding friends: and have taken away to be turned over to hospital as many as one hundred and five packages of liquor a day from one express company.

"I have assumed that the officers chosen and commissioned by the state of New York could be trusted to receive unopened packages from their friends. If in your judgment they can not be so trusted, please apply to the governor, and upon his suggestion I will have the stores and boxes sent to New York officers seized and searched.

"No spirituous liquors are permitted to be sold within the lines in my department; and every barrel of whisky not under the charge of an officer, when there is reason to believe sales have been made, has been stove and contents spilled, and the seller sent out of the lines. I have no power to discharge a drunken or incompetent officer. I can only call a court-martial when charges are preferred. If I prefer charges I can not call a court. I assure you, sir, a court-martial is as unwieldy a machine for investigating a certain class of offenses as a council of ministers would be. I have appeared before both tribunals as advocate, and know how difficult it is to convict in either.

"But, sir, have the charges made, and the reliable man sent as a witness, and I will have the officer punished if possible. Thanking you for the interest you take in the case,

"I am, most respectfully yours, BENJAMIN F. BUTLER."

that our troops around Fortress Monroe plundered little, considering their opportunities and their temptation. But that little was disgraceful enough, and gave rise to much clamor. All that any man could have done to prevent and punish offenses of this nature was done by the commanding general.* No man abhorred plundering more than Colonel Phelps; but he could not quite prevent it. Coming in to dinner one day, he saw upon the table a porcelain dish filled with green peas. He stood for a moment with eyes fixed upon the suspicious vessel, wrath gathering in his face.

"Take that dish away," said he, in a tone of fierce command for so gentle a man.

The alarmed contraband prepared to obey, but ventured to ask what he should do with the peas.

"Put them into a wash-basin, if you can't find anything better. But take that dish away, and never let me see it again."

The dish was removed, and Colonel Phelps ordered it to be taken to the hospital for the use of the sick.

One truth became very clear to General Butler while he held command in Virginia. It was, that men enlisted for short terms can not, as a rule, be relied upon for effective service. When the time of the three months men was half expired, all other feelings seemed to be merged in the longing for release. Like boys at school before the holidays, they would cut notches in a stick and erase one every day; and, as the time of return home drew nearer,

* The following order on this subject was issued during the first week of General Butler's command:—

"HEAD-QUARTERS, DEPARTMENT OF VIRGINIA, *May* 26, 1861.

"The general in command of this department has learned with pain that there are instances of depredation on private property, by some persons who have smuggled themselves among the soldiers under his command. This must not and shall not be. The rights of private property and of peaceable citizens must be respected. When the exigencies of the service require that private property be taken for public use, it must be done by proper officers, giving suitable vouchers therefor. It is made the special duty of every officer in command of any post of troops on detached service, or in camp, to exercise the utmost vigilance in this behalf, to cause all offenders in the matter of this order to be sent to head-quarters for punishment, and such measure of justice will then be meted out to them as is due to thieves and plunderers.

"If any corps shall share or aid in receiving such plundered property or offenders, such corps shall be dealt with in its organization in such a manner as to check such practices.

"This order will be promulgated by being three times read with distinctness to each battalion at evening parade.

"Any citizen at peace with the United States, despoiled in his person or property by any of the troops in this department, will confer a favor by promptly reporting the outrage to the nearest officer.

"By order of

"BENJ. F. BUTLER, *Major-General Commanding.*"

they would cut half a notch away at noon. It appeared that short-term troops are efficient for not more than half their time of enlistment; after that, their hearts are at home, not in their duty. The general was of opinion, that an army, if possible, should be enlisted not for any definite term, but for the war; thus supplying the men with a most powerful motive for efficient action; the homeward path lying through victory over the enemy.

CHAPTER IX.

RECALL FROM VIRGINIA.

The visitors attracted to the fortress severely taxed the time and hospitality of the general in command and of the gracious lady who presided at his table. Senators, representatives, governors, editors, officers, private persons, crowded that table to the number of thirty a day. Some enterprising individuals even projected grand excursions to the fortress, threatening it with steamboat loads of pleasure seekers. An order was issued to prevent such an untimely irruption, and requiring a special permit to land.

Mr. Russell of the London *Times* has given us an amusing record of his visit to the fortress. General Butler went the rounds with him.

"The day," he reports, "was excessively hot, and many of the soldiers were lying down in the shade of arbors formed of branches from the neighboring pine wood, but most of them got up when they heard the general was coming round. A sentry walked up and down at the end of the street, and as the general came up to him he called out 'Halt.' The man stood still. 'I just want to show you, sir, what scoundrels our government has to deal with. This man belongs to a regiment which has had new clothing recently served out to it. Look what it is made of.' So saying the general stuck his fore-finger into the breast of the man's coat, and with a rapid scratch of his nail tore open the cloth as if it was of blotting paper. 'Shoddy, sir. Nothing but shoddy. I wish I had these contractors in the trenches here, and if hard work would not make honest men of them, they'd have enough of it to be examples for the rest of their fellows.'

"In the course of our rounds we were joined by Colonel Phelps, who was formerly in the United States army, and saw service in Mexico, but retired because he did not approve of the manner in which promotions were made, and who only took command of a Massachusetts regiment because he believed he might be instrumental in striking a shrewd blow or two in this great battle of Armageddon—a tall, saturnine, gloomy, angry-eyed, sallow man, soldier-like too, and one who places old John Brown on a level with the great martyrs of the Christian world. * * *

"'Yes, I know them well. I've seen them in the field. I've sat with them at meals. I've traveled through their country. These Southern slaveholders are a false, licentious, godless people. Either we, who obey the laws and fear God, or they, who know no God except their own will and pleasure, and know no law except their passions, must rule on this continent: and I believe that Heaven will help its own in the conflict they have provoked. I grant you they are brave enough, and desperate too, but, surely justice, truth and religion, will strengthen a man's arm to strike down those who have only brute force and a bad cause to support them.' * *

"In the afternoon the boat returned to Fortress Monroe, and the general invited me to dinner, where I had the pleasure of meeting Mrs. Butler, his staff, and a couple of regimental officers from the neighboring camp. As it was still early, General Butler proposed a ride to visit the interesting village of Hampton, which lies some six or seven miles outside the fort, and forms his advance post. A powerful charger, with a tremendous Mexican saddle, fine housings, blue and gold-embroidered saddle-cloth, was brought to the door for your humble servant, and the general mounted another, which did equal credit to his taste in horseflesh; but I own I felt rather uneasy on seeing that he wore a pair of large brass spurs, strapped over white jean brodequins. He took with him his aide-de-camp and a couple of orderlies. In the precincts of the fort outside, a population of contraband negroes has been collected, whom the general employs in various works about the place, military and civil; but I failed to ascertain that the original scheme of a debit and credit account between the value of their labor and the cost of their maintenance had been successfully carried out. The general was proud of them, and they seemed proud of themselves, saluting him with a ludicrous mixture of awe and familiarity as he rode past. 'How-do, Massa Butler? How-do, general?' accompanied by absurd bows and scrapes. 'Just to think,' said the general, 'that every one of these fellows represents some 1,000 dollars at least out of the pockets of the chivalry yonder.' 'Nasty, idle, dirty beasts,' says one of the staff, *sotto voce*, 'I wish to Heaven they were all at the bottom of the Chesapeake. The general insists on it that they do work, but they are far more trouble than they are worth.'

"The road towards Hampton traverses a sandy spit, which, however, is more fertile than would be supposed from the soil under the horses' hoofs, though it is not in the least degree interesting. A broad creek or river interposed between us and the town, the bridge over which had been destroyed. Workmen were busy repairing it, but all the planks had not yet been laid down or nailed, and in some places the open space between the upright rafters allowed us to see the dark waters flowing beneath. The aide said, 'I don't think, general, it is safe to cross;' but his chief did not mind him until his horse very nearly crashed through a plank, and only regained its footing with unbroken legs by marvelous dexterity; whereupon we dismounted, and, leaving the horses to be carried over in the ferry-boat, completed the rest of the transit, not without difficulty. * * * * * *

"Most of the shops were closed; in some the shutters were still down, and the goods remained displayed in the windows. 'I have allowed no plundering,' said the general; 'and if I find a fellow trying to do it, I will hang him as sure as my name is Butler. See here,' and as he spoke he walked into a large woolen-draper's shop where bales of cloth were still lying on the shelves, and many articles, such as are found in a large general store in a country town, were disposed on the floor or counters; 'they shall not accuse the men under my command of being robbers.' The boast, however, was not so well justified in a visit to another house occupied by some soldiers. 'Well,' said the general, with a smile, 'I dare say you know enough of camps to have found out that chairs and tables are irresistible; the men will take them off to their tents, though they may have to leave them next morning.'

"Having inspected the works—as far I could judge, too extended, and badly traced—which I say with all deference to the able young engineer who accompanied us to point out the various objects of interest—the general returned to the bridge, where we remounted, and made a tour of the camps of the force intended to defend Hampton, falling back on Fortress Monroe in case of necessity. Whilst he was riding *ventre à terre*, which seems to be his favorite pace, his horse stumbled in the dusty road, and in his effort to keep his seat the general broke his stirrup-leather, and the ponderous brass stirrup fell to the ground; but, albeit a lawyer, he neither lost his seat nor his *sang froid*, and calling out to his orderly "to pick up his toe-plate," the jean slippers were closely pressed, spurs and all, to the sides of his steed, and away we went once more through dust and heat so great that I was by no means sorry when he pulled up outside a pretty villa, standing in a garden, which was occupied by Colonel Max Weber, of the German Turner regiment, once the property of General Tyler. * *

"The shades of evening were now falling, and as I had been up before five o'clock in the morning, I was not sorry when General Butler said, 'Now we will go home to tea, or you will detain the steamer.' He had arranged before I started that the vessel, which, in ordinary course, would have returned to Baltimore at eight o'clock, should remain till he sent down word to the captain to go.

"We scampered back to the fort, and judging from the challenges and vigilance of the sentries, and inlying pickets, I am not quite so satisfied that the enemy could have surprised the place. At the tea-table there were no additions to the general's family; he therefore spoke without any reserve. Going over the map, he explained his views in reference to future operations, and showed cause, with more military acumen than I could have expected from a gentleman of the long robe, why he believed Fortress Monroe was the true base of operations against Richmond. * * *

"But whilst the general and I are engaged over our maps and mint juleps,* time flies, and at last I perceive by the clock that it is time to go. An aide is sent to stop the boat, but he returns ere I leave with the news that 'She is gone.' Whereupon the general sends for the quartermaster, Talmadge, who is out in the camps, and only arrives in time to receive a severe 'wigging.' It so happened that I had important papers to send off by the next mail

* This visit occurred before the promulgation of the liquor order.

from New York, and the only chance of being able to do so depended on my being in Baltimore next day. General Butler acted with kindness and promptitude in the matter. 'I promised you should go by the steamer, but the captain has gone off without orders to leave, for which he shall answer when I see him. Meantime it is my business to keep my promise. Captain Talmadge, you will at once go down and give orders to the most suitable transport steamer or chartered vessel available, to get up steam at once, and come up to the wharf for Mr. Russell.' "

A steamer was prepared, the general's promise was kept, and Mr. Russell reached Washington in time to witness the final preparations for the advance upon Richmond, by way of Manassas.

The battle that ensued ended General Butler's hopes of being useful at Fortress Monroe. It was on the very day of the battle of Bull Run that he first received the means of moving a battery of field artillery, and of completing his preparations for sweeping clear of armed rebels the Virginia tip of the peninsula, of which Maryland forms the greater part. Colonel Baker was to command the expedition. Two days after the retreat came a telegram from General Scott: "Send to this place without fail, in three days, four regiments and a half of long-term volunteers, including Baker's regiment and a half." The troops were sent, and the expedition was necessarily abandoned.

The news of the great defeat created at the fortress a degree of consternation almost amounting to panic; for, at once, the rumor spread that the victorious enemy were about to descend upon the fortress, and overwhelm it. General Butler was not alarmed at this new phantom. One of the first cheering voices that reached the administration was his. A few hours after reading the news, he wrote to his friend, the postmaster-general:

"We have heard the sad news from Manassas, but are neither dismayed nor disheartened. It will have the same good effect upon the army in general that Big Bethel has had in my division, to teach us wherein we are weak and they are strong, and how to apply the remedy to our deficiences. Let not the administration be disheartened or discouraged. Let no compromises be made, or wavering be felt. God helping, we will go through to ultimate assured success. But let us have no more of the silk glove in carrying on this war. Let these men be considered, what they have made themselves, 'our enemies,' and let their property of all kinds, whenever it can be useful to us, be taken on the land where they have it, as they take ours upon the sea where we have it. There seems to me now but one of two ways, either to make an advance from this place with a sufficient force, or else, leaving a simple garrison here, to send six thousand men that might be spared on the other line; or, still another, to make a descent upon the southern coast. I am ready and desirous to move forward in either."

In another part of this letter he strongly recommends Colonel Phelps for promotion: "Although some of the regular officers will, when applied to, say that he is not in his right mind—the only evidence I have seen of it, is a deep religious enthusiasm upon the subject of slavery, which, in my judgment, does not unfit him to fight the battles of the North. As I never had seen him until he came here, as he differs with me in politics, I have no interest in the recommendation, save a deliberate judgment for the good of the cause after two months of trial." He had soon after the pleasure of handing to Colonel Phelps the shoulder straps of a brigadier-general.

"I am as much obliged to you, general," said he, "as though you had done me a favor."

The withdrawal of so large a number of his best troops, compelled the evacuation of Hampton. He was even advised, and that, too, by a member of the cabinet, as well as by many officers high in rank at the post, to abandon Newport News; but he would not let go his hold upon a point so important to the future movement which he had advised. The evacuation of Hampton was the event which called forth his well-known letter to the secretary of war upon the disposition of the contrabands.

GENERAL BUTLER TO MR. CAMERON.

"HEAD-QUARTERS, DEPARTMENT OF VIRGINIA,
"FORTRESS MONROE, *July* 30, 1861.

"HON. SIMON CAMERON, Secretary of War:

"SIR:—By an order received on the morning of the 26th July from Major-General Dix, by a telegraphic order from Lieutenant-General Scott, I was commanded to forward, of the troops of this department, four regiments and a half, including Colonel Baker's California regiment, to Washington, *viâ* Baltimore. This order reached me at 2 o'clock A. M., by special boat from Baltimore. Believing that it emanated because of some pressing exigency for the defense of Washington, I issued my orders before daybreak for the embarkation of the troops, sending those who were among the very best regiments I had. In the course of the following day they were all embarked for Baltimore, with the exception of some four hundred, for whom I had not transportation, although I had all the transport force in the hands of the quartermaster here to aid the bay line of steamers, which, by the same order from the lieutenant-general, was directed to furnish transportation. Up to, and at the time of the order, I had been preparing for an advance movement, by which I hoped to cripple the resources of the enemy at Yorktown, and especially by seizing a large quantity of negroes who were being pressed into their service in building the intrenchments there. I had five days previously been enabled to mount, for the first time, the first company of light artillery, which I had been empowered to raise, and they had but a single rifled cannon, an iron six-pounder. Of course, everything must and did yield to the supposed exigency and the orders. This ordering away the troops from this department, while it weakened the posts at Newport News, necessitated the withdrawal of the troops from Hampton, where I was then throwing up intrenched works to enable me to hold the town with a small force, while I advanced up the York or James River. In the village of Hampton there were a large number of negroes, composed in a great measure of women and children of the men who had fled thither within my lines for protection, who had escaped from marauding parties of rebels who had been gathering up able-bodied blacks to aid them in constructing their batteries on the James and York Rivers. I had employed the men in Hampton in throwing up intrenchments, and they were working zealously and efficiently at that duty, saving our soldiers from that labor under the gleam of the mid-day sun. The women were earning substantially their own subsistence in washing, marketing, and taking care of the clothes of the soldiers, and rations were being served out to the men who worked for the support of the children. But by the evacuation of Hampton, rendered necessary by the withdrawal of troops, leaving me scarcely five thousand men outside the fort, including the force at Newport News, all these black people were obliged to break up their homes at Hampton, fleeing across the creek within my lines for protection and support. Indeed, it was a most distressing sight to see these poor creatures, who had trusted to the protection of the arms of the United States, and who aided the troops of the United States in their enterprise, to be thus obliged to flee from their homes, and the homes of their masters who had deserted them, and become fugitives from fear of the return of the rebel soldiery, who had threatened to shoot the men who had wrought for us, and to carry off the women who had served us, to a worse than Egyptian bondage. I have, therefore, now within the peninsula, this side of Hampton Creek, nine hundred negroes, three hundred of whom are able-bodied men, thirty of whom are men substantially past hard labor, one hundred and seventy-five women, two hundred and twenty-five children under the age of ten years, and one hundred and seventy between ten and eighteen years, and many more coming in. The questions which this state of facts present are very embarrassing.

"*First.* What shall be done with them? and, *Second.* What is their state and condition?

"Upon these questions I desire the instructions of the department.

"The first question, however, may perhaps be answered by considering the last. Are these men, women, and children slaves? Are they free? Is their condition that of men, women, and children, or of property, or is it a mixed relation? What their *status* was under the constitution and laws, we all know. What has been the effect of a rebellion and a state of war upon that *status?* When I adopted the theory of treating the able-bodied negro fit to work in the trenches as property liable to be used in aid of rebellion, and so contraband of war, that condition of things was in so far met, as I then and still believe, on a legal and constitutional basis. But now a new series of questions arise. Passing by women, the children, certainly, can not be treated on that basis; if property, they must be considered the incumbrance rather than the auxiliary of an army, and, of course, in no possible legal relation could be treated as contraband. Are they property? If they were so, they have been left by their masters and owners, deserted, thrown away, abandoned, like the wrecked vessel upon the ocean. Their former possessors and owners have causelessly, traitorously, rebelliously, and, to carry out the figure, practically abandoned them to be swallowed up by the winter storm of starvation. If property, do they not become the property of the salvors? But we, their salvors, do not need and will not hold such property, and will assume no such ownership: has not, therefore, all proprietary relation ceased? Have they not become, thereupon, men, women, and children? No longer under ownership of any kind, the fearful relicts of fugitive masters, have they not by their masters' acts, and the state of war, assumed the condition, which we hold to be the normal one, of those made in God's image? Is not every constitutional, legal, and moral requirement, as well to the runaway master as their relinquished slaves, thus answered? I confess that my own mind is compelled by this reasoning to look upon them as men and women. If not free born, yet free, manumitted, sent forth from the hand that held them never to be reclaimed.

Of course, if this reasoning, thus imperfectly set forth, is correct, my duty as a humane man is very plain. I should take the same care of these men, women, and children, houseless, homeless, and unprovided for, as I would of the same number of men, women, and children, who, for their attachment to the Union, had been driven or allowed to flee from the Confederate

States. I should have no doubt on this question, had I not seen it stated that an order had been issued by General McDowell in his department, substantially forbidding all fugitive slaves from coming within his lines, or being harbored there. Is that order to be enforced in all military departments? If so, who are to be considered fugitive slaves? Is a slave to be considered fugitive whose master runs away and leaves him? Is it forbidden to the troops to aid or harbor within their lines the negro children who are found therein, or is the soldier, when his march has destroyed their means of subsistence, to allow them to starve because he has driven off the rebel masters? Now, shall the commander of a regiment or battalion sit in judgment upon the question, whether any given black man has fled from his master, or his master fled from him? Indeed, how are the free born to be distinguished? Is one any more or less a fugitive slave because he has labored upon the rebel intrenchments? If he has so labored, if I understand it, he is to be harbored. By the reception of which are the rebels most to be distressed, by taking those who have wrought all their rebel masters desired, masked their battery, or those who have refused to labor and left the battery unmasked?

"I have very decided opinions upon the subject of this order. It does not become me to criticise it, and I write in no spirit of criticism, but simply to explain the full difficulties that surround the enforcing it. If the enforcement of that order becomes the policy of the government, I, as a soldier, shall be bound to enforce it steadfastly, if not cheerfully. But if left to my own discretion, as you may have gathered from my reasoning, I should take a widely different course from that which it indicates.

"In a loyal state, I would put down a servile insurrection. In a state of rebellion I would confiscate that which was used to oppose my arms, and take all that property which constituted the wealth of that state, and furnished the means by which the war is prosecuted, beside being the cause of the war; and if, in so doing, it should be objected that human beings were brought to the free enjoyment of life, liberty, and the pursuit of happiness, such objection might not require much consideration.

"Pardon me for addressing the secretary of war directly upon this question, as it involves some political considerations as well as propriety of military action. I am, sir, your obedient servant,

"BENJAMIN F. BUTLER."

MR. CAMERON TO GENERAL BUTLER.

"WASHINGTON, *August* 8, 1861.

"GENERAL:—The important question of the proper disposition to be made of fugitives from service in the states in insurrection against the federal government, to which you have again directed my attention, in your letter of July 30, has received my most attentive consideration. It is the desire of the president that all existing rights in all the states be fully respected and maintained. The war now prosecuted on the part of the federal government is a war for the Union, for the preservation of all the constitutional rights of the states and the citizens of the states in the Union; hence no question can arise as to fugitives from service within the states and territories in which the authority of the Union is fully acknowledged. The ordinary forms of judicial proceedings must be respected by the military and civil authorities alike for the enforcement of legal forms. But in the states wholly or in part under insurrectionary control, where the laws of the United States are so far opposed and resisted that they can not be effectually enforced, it is obvious that the rights dependent upon the execution of these laws must temporarily fail; and it is equally obvious that the rights dependent on the laws of the states within which military operations are conducted must necessarily be subordinate to the military exigencies created by the insurrection, if not wholly forfeited by the treasonable conduct of the parties claiming them. To this the general rule of the right to service forms an exception. The act of Congress approved August 6, 1861, declares if persons held to service shall be employed in hostility to the United States, the right to their services shall be discharged therefrom. It follows of necessity that no claim can be recognized by the military authority of the Union to the services of such persons when fugitives.

"A more difficult question is presented in respect to persons escaping from the service of loyal masters. It is quite apparent that the laws of the state under which only the services of such fugitives can be claimed must needs be wholly or almost wholly superseded, as to the remedies, by the insurrection and the military measures necessitated by it; and it is equally apparent that the substitution of military for judicial measures for the enforcement of such claims must be attended by great inconvenience, embarrassments, and injuries. Under these circumstances, it seems quite clear that the substantial rights of loyal masters are still best protected by receiving such fugitives, as well as fugitives from disloyal masters, into the service of the United States and employing them under such organizations and in such occupations as circumstances may suggest or require. Of course a record should be kept showing the names and descriptions of the fugitives, the names and characters, as loyal or disloyal, of the masters, and such facts as may be necessary to a correct understanding of the circumstances of each case.

"After tranquillity shall have been restored upon the return of peace, congress will doubtless properly provide for all the persons thus received into the service of the Union, and for a just compensation to loyal masters. In this way only, it would seem, can the duty and safety of the government and just rights of all be fully reconciled and harmonized. You will therefore consider yourself instructed to govern your future action in respect to fugitives from service by the premises herein stated, and will report from time to time, and at least twice in each month, your action in the premises to this department. You will, however, neither authorize nor permit any interference by the troops under your command with the servants of peaceable citizens in a house or field, nor will you in any manner encourage such servants to leave the lawful service of their masters, nor will you, except in cases where the public good may seem to require it, prevent the voluntary return of any fugitive to the service from which he may have escaped. I am, very respectfully, your obedient servant,

"SIMON CAMERON, *Secretary of War*."

Mr. Cameron handled the topic gingerly. The administration had not yet taken off its gloves.

General Butler's letter pleased most the party most opposed to the one with which he had been all his life identified. We find Mr. Lewis Tappan writing to him applaudingly, and the general replying in a friendly spirit. He wrote to Mr. Tappan, August 10th:

"I have the honor to acknowledge the many kind expressions of approbation of my acts. I have endeavored to do my duty, following the best light I have, and the event must be in the hands of Him who ordereth all things well. I am of opinion, that it would not be profitable to the negroes to be sent north. There is plenty of waste land for them here, and they can be better and more cheaply cared for here than amid the rigor of our northern winter.

"They are at present, in my judgment, earning the subsistence furnished them by the United States, and if any benevolent individual desires to show active sympathy in their behalf, I would recommend that the committee you suggest, furnish a number of suits of substantial cheap clothing fit for winter service, for the women and children. Shoes are especially desirable. I will see that such clothing is distributed among them according to their necessities. The clothing for the men will soon be worn out, and as you are aware, we have no supply. Many of them are now dressed in the cast-off clothing and uniforms of the soldiers.

"This is all the particular aid, I think, we are in a situation to receive for them at this time.

"To send them north, amid the stagnation of business, and at a season when all agricultural operations, except harvesting, are about to be suspended, to fill our towns with a new influx of people, where labor is not wanted, while here in Virginia there is land enough cultivated, and houses enough deserted, amid scenes to which they are attached, where they may live, would in my judgment, be unwise.

"If the war continues, they will be safe here. If the war ends, the wisdom and the care of the government will be exerted for their protection here or elsewhere. This part of the state is but little more cultivated than in the days of Powhattan; and it would seem hardly prudent to take away from it a class of mostly agricultural laborers, who are fitted to the soil.

"The most of them would not desire to go north, if they can be assured (as I can assure them) of their safety at the south. I shall continue to receive and protect all the negroes, especially women and children, who come to me, as well for reasons of humanity as for strategical policy, of which it is not now best to speak."

The southern people, it is worth remarking, had already shown their sense of General Butler's services to his country. They knew their enemy. It has been their cue to compliment some of the generals conspicuous in the service of the United States; but for *him*, who first established the rule of employing the courtesies which mitigate the horrors of war, they have had only vituperation. They were right in their instinctive perceptions, for he was also the first to recognize them as enemies incurable, whose destruction as a power was essential to the restoration of the country. Few readers can have forgotten the biography of General Butler which circulated in southern newspapers in these months. It ran thus:

"He is the son of a negro barber, who, early in the century, did business on Poydras street, in New Orleans. The son, in early manhood, emigrated to Liberia, where an indisposition for labor and some talent turned his attention to the bar, to prepare for which he repaired to Massachusetts. Having mastered his profession, he acquired a fondness for theological studies, and became an active local preacher, the course of his labors early leading him to New York, where he attracted the notice of Mr. Jacob Barker, then in the zenith of his fame as financier, and who, discovering the peculiar abilities in that direction of the young mulatto, sent him to northern New York to manage a banking institution. There he divided his time between the counting-house and the court-room, the prayer-meeting and the printing-office," etc.

This, with a variety of comments, was the southern response to Annapolis and Baltimore.

The North seemed slower to recognize his services. After the withdrawal of the four regiments, he found himself in a false position at Fortress Monroe, incapable of acting, yet expected by the country to act. His embarrassment was not diminished by discovering that the intention to remove his troops was known and published before the battle of Bull Run, and that they were still detained at Baltimore inactive.

"As soon," he wrote to Colonel Baker, "as I began to look like activity, my troops are all taken away. And almost my only friend and counselor, on whose advice I could rely, is taken away by name. * * * * What ought I to do under these circumstances? I ought not to stay here and be thus abused. Tell me as a true friend, as I know you are, what ought to be done in justice to myself. To resign, when the country needs service, is unpatriotic. To hold office which government believes me unfit for, is humiliating. To remain here disgraced and thwarted by every subordinate who is sustained by the head of the department, is unbearable."

The government resolved his doubts. A day or two after the reply to General Butler's contraband letter had been dispatched, he was removed from the command of the department, and General Wool appointed in his stead. Whether the two acts had any connection, or whether the removal was a compliance with the suggestions of a leading newspaper, has not been disclosed. "General Wool," commented the New York *Times*, "is assigned the command of Fortress Monroe. So far, so good. The nation was deeply dissatisfied, not to say indignant, at the fact that one of the bravest, as well as one of the most skillful and experienced of American generals, was persistently kept in quiet retreat at Troy, N. Y., while political brigadiers were fretting away the spirit of the army by awkward blunderings upon masked batteries." There had, indeed, been much clamor of this kind, and worse. One gallant colonel, removed from his command for drunkenness, had caused letters to be published, accusing General Butler of disloyalty. Other officers, who had left the service for the service's good, were not silent, and one or two reporters, who had been ordered away from the post, still had the use of their pens. Nor had the public the means of understanding the causes of General Butler's inactivity. They saw the most important military post in the possession of the United States, apparently well supplied with troops, contributing nothing to the military strength of the country. The blame was naturally laid at the door of the general commanding it.

On the eighteenth of August, General Butler gracefully resigned the command of the department to his successor. In his farewell order he said: "The general takes leave of the command of the officers and soldiers of this department with the kindest feelings toward all, and with the hope that in active service upon the field, they may soon signalize their bravery and gallant conduct, as they have shown their patriotism by fortitude under the fatigues of camp duty. No personal feeling of regret intrudes itself at the change in the command of the department, by which our cause acquires the services in the field of the veteran general commanding, in whose abilities, experience and devotion to the flag, the whole country places the most implicit reliance, and under whose guidance and command all of us, and none more than your late commander, are proud to serve."

He had been in command of the department of Virginia two months and twenty-seven days.

CHAPTER X.

HATTERAS.

The order which relieved General Butler from command in Virginia assigned him to no other duty. He was simply ordered to resign his command to General Wool. Whether he was to remain at the fortress, or repair to head-quarters, or go home, was left to conjecture. What should he do? Where should he go? Friends unanimously advised: 'Go home. The government plainly intimates that it does not want you.' The game is lost; throw up your hand. "No," said he, "whatever I do, I can't go home. That were the end of my military career, and I am in for the war." It ended in his asking General Wool for something to do; and General Wool, who could not but see what efficient service he had rendered at the post, and heartily acknowledged it, gave him the command of the volunteer troops outside the fortress.* So he vacated the mansion within the walls, and served where he had been wont to rule.

A week after, the expedition to reduce the forts at Hatteras Inlet was on the point of sailing. It was a scheme of the general's own. A Union prisoner being detained at the inlet, had brought the requisite information to the fortress many weeks before. He said, that through that gap in the long sand-island which runs along the coast of North Carolina, numberless blockade runners found access to the main land. His report being duly conveyed to head-quarters, a joint expedition, military and naval, was ordered to take the forts, destroy them, block up the inlet with sunken stone, and return to Fortress Monroe. Preparations for this expedition were at full tide when General Butler was superseded. Nine hundred troops were detailed to accompany it; a small corps for a major-general. General Butler volunteered to command them, and General Wool accepted his offer; kind friends whispering, "*infra dig.*"

He went. Every one remembers the details of that first cheering success after the summer of our discontent. It seemed to break the spell of disaster, and gave encouragement to the country, dispro portioned to the magnitude of the achievement. General Butler enjoyed a share of the *eclat*, which restored much of the public favor lost at Great Bethel.

Two points of the general's conduct on this occasion, we may notice before passing on to more stirring scenes. The reader has not forgotten, that the rebel commander first offered to surrender, provided the garrison were allowed to retire, and that General But-

* "HEAD-QUARTERS, DEPARTMENT OF VIRGINIA,
"FORTRESS MONROE, VIRGINIA, *August* 21, 1861.

"SPECIAL ORDERS, No. 9.

"Major-General B. F. Butler is, hereby placed in command of the volunteer forces in this department, exclusive of those at Fort Monroe. His present command at Camps Butler and Hamilton will include the First, Second, Seventh, Ninth, and Twentieth regiments, the battalion of Massachusetts volunteers, the Union Coast Guard, and the Mounted Rifles.

"C. C. CHURCHILL, *Acting Assistant Adjutant-General.*

"By command of Major-General WOOL."

ler refused the terms, demanding unconditional surrender. "The Adelaide," he reports, "on carrying in the troops, at the moment my terms of capitulation were under consideration by the enemy, had grounded upon the bar. * * At the same time, the Harriet Lane, in attempting to enter the bar had grounded, and remained fast; both were under the guns of the fort. By these accidents, a valuable ship of war, and a transport steamer, with a large portion of my troops, were within the power of the enemy. I had demanded the strongest terms, which he was considering. He might refuse, and seeing our disadvantage, renew the action. But I determined to abate not a tittle of what I considered to be due to the dignity of the government; nor even to give an official title to the officer in command of the rebels. Besides, my tug was in the inlet, and, at least, I could carry on the engagement with my two rifled six-pounders, well supplied with Sawyer's shell." It was an anxious moment, but his terms were accepted, and the victory was complete.

One of the guns of the Minnesota was worked during the action by contrabands from Fortress Monroe. The danger was slight, for the enemy's balls fell short. But it was observed and freely acknowledged on all hands, that no gun in the fleet was more steadily served than theirs, and no men more composed than they when danger was supposed to be imminent. In action and out of action their conduct was everything that could be desired.

The other matter which demands a word of explanation, relates to General Butler's sudden return from Hatteras, which elicited sundry satirical remarks at the time. He had been ordered not to hold but to destroy the port. But on surveying the position, he was so much impressed with the importance of retaining it, that he resolved to go instantly to Washington and explain his views to the government. He did so, and the government determined to hold the place. Nor was haste unnecessary, since supplies had been brought for only five days. The troops must have been immediately withdrawn or immediately provisioned.

And now again he was without a command. The government did not know what to do with him, and he did not know what to do with himself. Recruiting was generally at a stand still, and there were no troops in the field that had not their full allowance of major generals. West Point influence was in the ascendant, as surely it ought to be in time of war; and this lawyer in epaulets seemed to be rather in the way than otherwise.

CHAPTER XI.

RECRUITING FOR SPECIAL SERVICE.

General Butler now recalled the attention of the government to his scheme for expelling rebel forces from the Virginia peninsula, which had been suspended by the sudden transfer of Colonel Baker and his command from Fortress Monroe. He obtained authority from the war department to recruit troops in Massachusetts for this purpose. Recruiting seemed to be proceeding somewhat languidly in the state, although her quota was yet far from full; and it was supposed, that General Butler could strike a vein of hunker democrats which would yield good results. Not that hunker democrats had been backward in enlisting; but it was thought that many of them who still hesitated would rally to the standard of one who had so often led them in the mimic war of elections. On going home, however, he found that General Sherman was before him in special recruiting, and that to him Governor Andrew had promised the first regiments that should be completed. He hastened back to Washington. He had been engaged to speak in Faneuil Hall, but left a note of excuse, ending with these words: "That I go for a vigorous prosecution of the war is best shown by the fact that I am gone." At Washington, a change of programme. He penned an order, dated Sept. 10th, enlarging his sphere of operations to all New England, which the secretary of war signed:—

"Major-General B. F. Butler is hereby authorized to raise, organize, arm, uniform, and equip a volunteer force for the war, in the New England states; not exceeding six (6) regiments of the maximum standard, of such arms, and in such proportions, and in such manner as he may judge expedient; and for this purpose his orders and requisitions on the quartermaster, ordnance, and other staff departments of the army, are to be obeyed and answered: provided the cost of such recruitment, armament, and equipment does not exceed, in the aggregate, that of like troops, now or hereafter raised, for the service of the United States."

To make assurance doubly sure, he asked the additional sanction of the president's signature. The cautious president, always punctiliously respectful to state authority, first procured by telegraph the assent of all the governors of New England, and then signed the order.

It was upon General Butler's return to New England to raise these troops, that the collision occurred between himself and the governor of Massachusetts, which caused so much perplexity to all the parties concerned. Without wishing to revive the ill feeling of a controversy between gentlemen equally devoted to the common cause, it appears, nevertheless, unavoidable to explain the point of collision. At first, I was inclined to think that General Butler, in the impetuosity of his desire to take the field, had given the governor just cause of offense. Upon a review of the whole case, as published in divers pamphlets, official and unofficial, it appears clearly enough, that Governor Andrew was justified in taking offense; but it is equally clear that no offense was intended by General Butler; and that, hurried as he was, he employed reasonable means to come to a friendly understanding with the governor. The case, as I understand it, illustrates the old Spanish maxim, that when two honest men differ, both are in the right.

Perhaps, there was already a slight soreness in the governor's mind owing to the publication by General Butler of the correspondence relating to the offer of Massachusetts troops to Governor Hicks, for the suppression of an insurrection of the slaves. General Butler published these letters, because the Boston correspondent of the *Tribune* had informed the public that Governor Andrew disapproved the offer of the troops for such a purpose. The act was also freely commented upon in the newspapers. A question arose as to the source of the correspondent's information. General Butler emphatically exonerated the governor, but intimated that, perhaps, some clerk or copyist had betrayed his trust. The private secretary of the governor, who alone had charge of the governor's papers, conceived that this intimation was pointed at him, and resented it accordingly. A private secretary, posted as he is close to the ear of his chief, can not but have considerable influence over him. A private secretary has sometimes been a governor's governor, a general's general, a prime minister's prime minister. Private secretaries have ruled empires. It is, at least, not desirable to have the ill-will of a private secretary if you wish to stand well with his chief. You might almost as well slight the king's mistress, and then ask a favor of the king. I do not suppose that the worthy and patriotic governor of Massachusetts was unduly influenced by his secretary. But he is a human being, and his secretary felt aggrieved at General Butler.

The true cause of the difficulty was the chaos that reigned in the war department at Washington. Mr. Cameron was a faithful and most laborious minister; but probably no man ever existed capable of really *doing* the work suddenly accumulated upon the secretary of war by the stupendous scale upon which the military operations of the government were undertaken. We did not embrace the war as the settled business of the country for years, but as if preparing for two or three enormous raids into an enemy's country. Hurry, confusion, incoherence, marked all our first proceedings. Mr. Cameron did what he could; but much remained undone; much was done amiss; much was necessarily left to subordinates. There was no time for deliberation; everything had to be decided on the instant. In such circumstances, a man must have the memory of a Butler to avoid giving contradictory orders. It should be also noted, that General Butler is one of those gentlemen who can say No, with delightful promptness and unmistakable emphasis, but *to* whom it is difficult to say No; and both the president and the secretary of war were disposed to comply with the desires of a man whose talents and energy they appreciated.

General Sherman, as we have said, was already in Massachusetts recruiting for Port Royal. Another gentleman had also received authority from the war department to raise a regiment in Massachusetts. The governor objecting to this special recruiting, remonstrated, and the secretary promised, August 28, that no more such authorizations should be issued. The president, also, September 6th, spoke of "the impossibility of relying upon the states to respond promptly to regular requisitions for troops, if their recruiting system should be harassed by the competition of individuals engaged in recruiting under independent permissions; but he said such independent permissions as had hitherto been issued, had been extorted by the pressure of certain persons, who, if they had been refused, would have accused the government of rejecting the services of so many thousands of imaginary men; a pressure, of the persistency of which, no person not subjected to it could conceive. He said that perhaps he had been in error in granting such independent permissions at all, even under this pressure."

Hence, before sanctioning General Butler's scheme of raising six regiments in New England, the president procured by telegraph the consent of all the governors.

Now, the point of collision between Governor Andrew and General Butler was this: The governor desired to fill the regiments already begun before any others were started; the general was anxious to open his vein of hunkers at once, and avail himself immediately of his personal popularity. He thought he could enlist men who would not join regiments already begun; and he was right; for more than a thousand men enlisted under his banner as soon as it was set up.

When General Butler presented himself at the State House, September 14th, armed with authority to raise six regiments in New England, Governor Andrew received him with all his wonted cordiality, and promised hearty co-operation. He requested, however, that he would announce no new regiments till General Sherman's were filled, which would require another week. The general consented and went to Maine, where his efforts, promptly seconded by the governor of that State, were immediately successful. He returned to Boston, to find that Governor Andrew had caused a formal order to be published, which forbade new recruiting until regiments already begun were completed. Two of these incomplete regiments he had, indeed, assigned to General Butler, one of which existed only in skeleton. General Butler fearing delay, and desiring himself to have a voice in selecting the officers who were to accompany him, hit upon an expedient to remove the unexpected obstacle. He flew to Washington, and to General Scott. Result, the following order:

"The six New England States will temporarily constitute a separate military department, to be called the Department of New England. Head-quarters, Boston. Major-General B. F. Butler, United

States Volunteer Service, while engaged in recruiting his division will command."

Next he went to Mr. Cameron, who signed an order giving half a month's pay in advance to all troops enlisted by General Butler for special service.

Surely, thought the general, all is right *now*. Returning to New England, he again set to work, published his new powers, advertised for recruits, opened offices, established camps. His activity was wonderful. One day we see him addressing a legislature; the next conferring with a governor; anon, haranguing the troops, then, consulting with officers; now in Vermont, to-morrow in Maine, the next day in New Hampshire. Men flocked in. In a month he would have been ready to march but for one powerful opposing influence, which emanated from the state house at Boston. Governor Andrew, wedded to his own system, puzzled and indignant at the contradictory orders from Washington, would not sanction the proceedings of General Butler, but opposed them by all the means he could command. Endless perplexity and recrimination followed; the governor, by telegraph and by letter, remonstrating with the department of war; Mr. Cameron standing in torment between two fires, vainly endeavoring to quiet the governor by real applause and apparent concession; the Massachusetts senators mediating; the president putting in a conciliatory word now and then; General Butler keeping steadily to his object of getting the six regiments ready in the shortest possible time, pausing a moment to dictate a hurried reply to voluminous remonstrance, then rushing away to a remote camp, always under a full head of steam.

While the unhappy difference was still capable of adjustment, General Butler asked an interview with the governor, thinking that a few minutes' frank conversation could hardly fail to bring them to friendly co-operation. Unhappily, Governor Andrew, being exceedingly pressed by business, declined the interview, naming no time when he could accord one. The tongue is an unruly member; but the pen, too, is a mischievous implement; it is a tongue free from the restraints imposed by the presence of the person addressed. One of General Butler's letters, couched in most respectful language, gave extreme offense to the governor, through an error of the copyist. It was written in the third person, and the governor was designated by the words "His Excellency," which occurred fourteen times. The person who made the copy sent to the governor, with perverse uniformity, placed inverted commas before and after those words, as if to intimate that the author of the letter used them reluctantly, and only in obedience to a custom. It looked like an intentional and elaborate affront, and served to embitter the controversy. When, at length, the general was made acquainted with the mishap, he was not in a humor to give a complete explanation; nor, indeed, is it a custom with him to get out of a scrape by casting blame upon a subordinate.*

Time did not heal the breach. The governor refused to issue commissions to the officers recommended by General Butler. Many offensive things were said and done on both sides, and the quarrel soon escaped from the state house into the newspapers; from newspapers into pamphlets. Let us draw a veil over these painful scenes. A quarrel is divided into two parts. Part first embraces all that is said and done while both parties keep their temper: part second, all that is said and done after one or both of the parties loses it. The first part may be interesting, and even important; the second is sound and fury, signifying nothing. Governor Andrew felt that General Butler was interfering with his prerogative. General Butler, intent on the work in hand, was exasperated at the obstacles thrown in his way by Governor Andrew. General Butler, who had had bitter experience of subaltern incompetency, was anxious to secure commissions to men in whom he could confide. Governor Andrew naturally desired to give commissions to men in whose fitness he could himself believe. General Butler's friends were chiefly of the hunker persuasion; Governor Andrew was better acquainted with gentlemen of his own party. Both were honest and zealous servants of their country. Long may both of them live to serve and honor it.

The six thousand troops were raised. But the delay in Massachusetts deprived General Butler of the execution of his peninsula scheme, which fell to the lot of General Dix, who well performed it in November. So General Butler went to Washington to learn what he was to do with his troops, now that he had them.

For many months the government had been silently preparing for the recovery of the southern strongholds, which had been seized at

* This explanation of the much-discussed quotation points, I derived from a confidential member of General Butler's staff, the late General Strong.

the outbreak of the war, while the last administration was holding parley with treason at the capital. Commodore Porter was busy at the Brooklyn Navy Yard with his fleet of bomb-boats. The navy had been otherwise strengthened, though the day of iron-clads had not yet dawned in Hampton Roads. Immense provision had been ordered of the cumbrous material used in sieges. But, as yet, preparations only had been made; the points first to be attempted had not been selected; the chief attention of the government being still directed to the increase and organization of the army of the Potomac, held at bay by the phantom of two hundred thousand rebels, and endless imaginary masked batteries at Manassas. The arrival of General Butler at Washington recalled the consideration of the government to more distant enterprises.

Mobile was then the favorite object, both at the head-quarters of the army and at the navy department; and General Butler was directed to report upon the best rendezvous for an expedition against Mobile. Maps, charts, gazetteers, encyclopedias, and sea captains were zealously overhauled. In a day or two, the general was ready with his report, which named Ship Island as the proper rendezvous for operations against any point upon the gulf coast. Ship Island it should be then. To New England the general quickly returned, and started a regiment or two for the rendezvous under General Phelps, whose services he had especially asked. Then to Washington once more, where he found that Mobile was not in high favor with the ruling member of the cabinet, who thought Texas a more immediately important object. It was natural that he should so regard it, as he was compelled by his office to look at the war in the light shed from foreign correspondence. General Butler was now ordered to prepare a paper upon Texas, and the best mode of reannexing it. Nothing loath, he rushed again at the maps and gazetteers, collaring stray Galvestonians by the way. An elaborate paper upon Texas was the prompt result of his labors, a production justly complimented by General McClellan for its lucid completeness. Texas was in the ascendant. Texas should be re-annexed; the French kept out; the German cotton planters delivered; the rebels quelled; the blockading squadron released. Homeward sped the general to get more of his troops on the way. The Constitution, which had conveyed General Phelps to Ship Island and returned, was again loaded with troops. Two thousand men were embarked, and the ship was on the point of sailing, when a telegram from Washington arrived of singular brevity:—

"DON'T SAIL. DISEMBARK."

No explanation followed; nor did General Butler wait long for one. The next day he was in Washington, in quest of elucidation. The explanation was simple. Mason and Slidell were in Fort Warren; England had demanded their surrender; war with England was possible, not improbable. If war were the issue, the Constitution would be required, not to convey troops to Ship Island, but to bring back those already there.

Nothing remained for General Butler but to return home, and wait till the question was decided. He went, but not till he had avowed his entire conviction that justice and policy united in demanding that the rebel emissaries should be retained. He thought that New England alone, drained as she was of men, would follow him to Canada, that winter, with fifty thousand troops, and seize the commanding points before the April sun had let in the English navy. The country, he thought, was not half awake—had not put forth half its strength. He felt that in *such* a quarrel, America would do as Greece had done when Xerxes led his myriads against her—every man a soldier, and every soldier a hero. He did not despair of seeing, first the border states, and then the gulf states, fired with the old animosity, and joining against the hereditary foe. Knowing what England had done in the way of violating the flag of neutrals, he regarded her conduct in this affair as the very sublime of impudence. He boiled with indignation whenever he thought of it, and he thought of little else during those memorable weeks.

Fortunately, as most of us think, other counsels prevailed at Washington, and a blow was struck at the rebellion, by the surrender of the men, of more effect than the winning of a great battle. The restoration of the Union will itself avenge the wrong, and cut deeper into the power that has misled England than the loss of many Canadas.

The dispute with the governor continued. It was a question whether the troops raised by him in Massachusetts, in opposition to the governor, would be entitled to the aid granted by the legislature to the families of volunteers. The following letter touches upon this subject:

"CAMP SEWARD, PITTSFIELD, *Tuesday*, *Jan.* 7, 1862.

"Lieut. Col. WHELDEN, Commanding Western Bay State Regiment:

"COLONEL:—I have been much gratified with the appearance, discipline and proficiency of your regiment, as evidenced by the inspection of to-day. Of the order, quiet, and soldierly conduct of the camp, the commanding general cannot speak in too much praise.

"Notwithstanding the difficulties of season, opposition and misrepresentation, the progress made would be creditable if no such obstacles had existed.

"In the matter of the so-called state aid to the families of the volunteers under your command, I wish to repeat here, most distinctly, the declaration heretofore made to you. I will personally, and from my private means, guarantee to the family of each soldier the aid which ought to be furnished to him by his town, to the same extent and amount that the state would be bound to afford to other enlisted men, from and after this date, if the same is not paid by the commonwealth to them as to other Massachusetts soldiers; and all soldiers enlisting in your regiment may do so upon the strength of this guarantee.

"I have no doubt upon this subject whatever. The commonwealth will not permit her soldiers to suffer or be unjustly dealt with, under whosesoever banner they may enlist.

"The only question that will be asked will be, Are these men in the service of their country, shedding their blood in defense of its constitution and laws? If so, they stand upon an equality with every other man who is fighting for his country, and will be treated by the state with the same equal justice, whatever may be the wounded pride or overweening vanity of any man or set of men.

"I love and revere the justice, the character, the equity, the fame and name of our glorious old commonwealth too much to doubt of this for a moment, and will at any time peril whatever I may have of private fortune, upon the faith engendered by that love and reverence.

"Accept for yourself, personally, and for your officers, my most earnest thanks for the energetic services which you have rendered in the recruitment of your excellent regiment.

"Most truly your friend,

"BENJ. F. BUTLER,

"*Major-General Commanding.*"

General Butler was, indeed, most ably seconded by the officers whom he had selected to accompany him.

Captain Paul R. George, of Lowell, a retired officer of the army, distinguished in the Mexican war, afterward successful in business, was his quartermaster. To the remarkable talents and long experience of Captain George, the country owed it, that the expedition was fitted out with unrivaled completeness and economy, affording another proof that a man who conducts his own affairs wisely, can serve the public with the same energetic tact. Captain George forsook ease and luxury to aid General Butler, and labored for many weeks in the details of the equipment with admirable assiduity and skill. A cabal caused his rejection by the senate before the last detachment sailed, and the general was thus deprived of assistance upon which he had relied, and which he needed then more than ever.

General Butler was most fortunate, too, in his chief of staff, Major George C. Strong, a graduate of West Point; one of those cadets who had marked and liked the ways of the Massachusetts lawyer, when he served as an examiner of the military academy. He met the general in Washington—being a lieutenant then upon the staff of the commander-in-chief, and gladly left all to follow his fortunes. His West Point comrades marveled that an officer so clearly in the way of promotion, high in the confidence of the chief of the army, should choose to serve under a general not trained to arms in the highlands of the Hudson river. But there are people who know a man when they see one. West Point, however, is right in pluming itself upon its graduates, for no one can deny that most of the good soldiering done in this war, on either side, has been done under West Point men. How well General Strong appreciated the merits of the military academy, we may now all see in his pleasant little book, "Cadet Life at West Point," the authorship of which he modestly concealed during his lifetime. But he was not a West Point bigot.

Happy, too, was General Butler in the aid of Lieutenant Weitzel, chief engineer to the expedition, who graduated second in his class at West Point; afterward long employed in completing the forts below New Orleans, acquiring perfect familiarity with the adjacent country. He, too, reflected honor upon the military academy, as he has recently done upon the country, by his splendid conduct at Port Hudson. General Butler, in common with his whole command, held the character and talents of Lieutenant Weitzel in the profoundest esteem.

One of the volunteer aids stands boldly out from the group surrounding the general, Major J. M. Bell, of Boston, a distinguished member of the bar of New England, son-in-law and partner of the late Rufus Choate. Major Bell, who had, I believe, retired from practice, asked his old hunker chieftain, if there was any work for him to do in the new, mysterious enterprise. General Butler hailed the offer with gladness, well knowing the worth and capacity of him who made it. Major Bell found unexpected work in the southern country, which forced him to furbish his legal weapons, and keep them exceedingly bright.

Colonel Andrew Jackson Butler, as chief commissary, lent a powerful and a dexterous hand to the equipment of the expedition, till he, too, was rejected by the senate. Captain Peter Haggerty, whom we saw going ashore at Annapolis, was still by the general's side, as aide-de-camp. Lieutenant J. B. Kinsman, another Boston lawyer, joined at the last moment, for a six weeks' cruise, but served to the end. We shall meet those gentlemen again, and their comrades on the general's staff. It is here only requisite to note, that if the expedition was fitted out with extraordinary dispatch and thoroughness, it was because General Butler, himself a mighty achiever, knows how to pick out from the mass of indifferent men the individuals who have it in them to achieve. This is the supreme, the all-including talent of a commander. A little of that talent, the United States, three years ago, might have paid one thousand mil lions of dollars for, and yet saved money by the operation.

Mason and Slidell were given up. The troops sailed for Fortress Monroe. General Butler, early in January, 1862, went to Washington to conclude the last arrangements, intending to join his command in Hampton Roads. At the war department mere confusion reigned, for this was the time when Mr. Cameron was going out, and Mr. Stanton coming in. Nothing could be done; the troops remained at Fortress Monroe; the general was lost to finite view in the mazes of Washington.

We catch a brief glimpse of him, however, testifying before the committee on the conduct of the war. No reader can have forgotten that the great question then agitating the country was, why General McClellan, with his army of two hundred thousand men, had remained inactive for so many months, permitting the blockade of the Potomac, and allowing the superb weather of November and December to pass unimproved into the mud and cold of January. The established opinion at head-quarters was, that the rebel army before Washington numbered about two hundred and forty thousand men. Upon this point General Butler, from much study of the various sources of information, had arrived at an opinion which differed from the one in vogue, and this he communicated to the committee; and not the opinion only, but the grounds of the opinion. He presented an argument on the subject, having thoroughly got up the case as he had been wont to do for gentlemen of the jury. Subjecting General Beauregard's report of the two actions near Manassas to a minute analysis, he showed that the rebel army at the battle of Bull Run numbered 36,600 men. He cross-examined those reports, counting first by regiments, secondly by brigades, and found the results of both calculations the same. He then computed the quotas of the various rebel states, and concluded that the entire Confederate force on the day of the battle of Bull Run was about 54,000. He next considered the increase to the rebel armies since the battle of Bull Run. We, with our greatly superior means of transportation, with our greater population, and the command of the ocean, had been able, by the most strenuous exertions, to assemble an army before Washington of little more than 200,000. Could the rebels have got together half that number in the same time? It was not probable, it was scarcely possible. Then the extent of country held by the rebel army was known, and forbade the supposition entertained at head-quarters. Upon the whole, he concluded that the armies menacing Washington consisted of about 70,000 men; which proved to be within 5,000 of the truth.

This opinion was vigorously pooh-poohed in the higher circles of the army, but leading members of the committee were evidently convinced by it. One officer of high rank, a frequenter of the office of the general-in-chief, was good enough to say, when General Butler had finally departed, that he hoped they had now found a hole big enough to bury that Yankee general in.

During the delay caused by the change in the department of war, an almost incredible incident occurred, which strikingly illustrates the confusion sometimes arising from having three centers of military authority—the president, the secretary of war, and the commander-in-chief. By mere accident General Butler heard one day that his troops had been sent, two weeks before, from Fortress

Monroe to Port Royal. "What!" he exclaimed, "have I been played with all this time?" He discovered, upon inquiry, that such an order had indeed been issued. He procured an interview with Mr. Stanton, gave him a history of his proceedings, and asked an explanation of the order. Mr. Stanton knew nothing about it; Mr. Cameron knew nothing about it; General McClellan knew nothing about it. Nevertheless, the order in question had really been sent. Mr. Stanton readily agreed to countermand the order, provided the troops had not already departed. The general hurried to the telegraph office, where, under a rapid fire of messages, a still more wonderful fact was disclosed. The mysterious order had been received in Baltimore by one of General Dix's aids, who had put it into his pocket, *forgotten it, and carried it about with him two weeks!* From the depths of his pocket it was finally brought to light. The troops were still at the fortress.

Mr. Stanton soon made himself felt in the dispatch of business. General Butler obtained an ample hearing, and the threads of his enterprise were again taken up. One day (about January 10th), toward the close of a long conference between the general and the secretary, Mr. Stanton suddenly asked:

"Why can't New Orleans be taken?"

The question thrilled General Butler to the marrow.

"IT CAN!" he replied.

This was the first time New Orleans had been mentioned in General Butler's hearing, but by no means the first time he had thought of it. The secretary told him to prepare a programme; and for the third time the general dashed at the charts and books. General McClellan, too, was requested to present an opinion upon the feasibility of the enterprise. He reported that the capture of New Orleans would require an army of 50,000 men, and no such number could be spared. Even Texas, he thought, should be given up for the present.

But now General Butler, fired with the splendor and daring of the new project, exerted all the forces of his nature to win for it the consent of the government. He talked New Orleans to every member of the cabinet. In a protracted interview with the president, he argued, he urged, he entreated, he convinced. Nobly were his efforts seconded by Mr. Fox, the assistant secretary of the navy, a native of Lowell, a schoolmate of General Butler's. His whole heart was in the scheme. The president spoke, at length, the decisive word, and the general almost reeled from the White House in the intoxication of his relief and joy. One difficulty still remained, and that was the tight clutch of General McClellan upon the troops. At Ship Island there were 2,000 men; on ship-board 2,200; ready in New England, 8,500; total, 12,700. General Butler demanded a total of 15,000. As the general-in-chief would not hear of sparing men from Washington, three of the Baltimore regiments were assigned to the expedition; and these were the only ones in General Butler's division which could be called drilled. Not one of his regiments had been in action.

About January 23d, the last impediment was removed, and General Butler went home, for the last time, to superintend the embarkation of the rest of the New England troops. The troops detained so long at Fortress Monroe, were hurried on board the Constitution, and started for Ship Island. Other transports were rapidly procured; other regiments dispatched. A month later, General Butler was again in Washington to receive the final orders; the huge steamship Mississippi, loaded with his last troops, lying in Hampton Roads, waiting only for his coming to put to sea. It may interest some readers to know, that the total cost of raising the troops and starting them on their voyage, was about a million and a half of dollars.

It was not without apprehensions that General Butler approached the capital on this occasion—there had been so many changes of programme. But all the departments smiled propitiously, and the final arrangements were soon completed. A professional spy, who had practiced his vocation in Virginia too long for him to venture again within the enemy's lines with much chance of getting out again, was on his way to New Orleans, having agreed to meet the general at Ship Island with a full account of the state of affairs in the crescent city. A thousand dollars, if he succeeds. The department of the gulf was created, and General Butler formally placed in command of the same. The following were the orders of the commander-in-chief:

"HEAD-QUARTERS OF THE ARMY,
"*February* 23*d*, 1862.

"Major-General B. F. Butler, United States Army:

"General:—You are assigned to the command of the land forces destined to co-operate with the navy in the attack upon New Orleans. You will use every means to keep the destination a profound secret, even from your staff officers, with the exception of your chief of staff, and Lieutenant Wietzel, of the engineers.

"The force at your disposal will consist of the first thirteen regiments named in your memorandum handed to me in person, the Twenty-first Indiana, Fourth Wisconsin, and Sixth Michigan (old and good regiments from Baltimore)—these three regiments will await your orders at Fort Monroe. Two companies of the Twenty-first Indiana are well drilled at heavy artillery. The cavalry force already *en route* for Ship Island, will be sufficient for your purposes. After full consultation with officers well acquainted with the country in which it is proposed to operate, I have arrived at the conclusion that three light batteries fully equipped and one without horses, will be all that will be necessary.

"This will make your force about 14,400 infantry, 275 cavalry, 580 artillery, total 15,255 men.

"The commanding general of the department of Key West is authorized to loan you, temporarily, two regiments; Fort Pickens can probably give you another, which will bring your force to nearly 18,000. The object of your expedition is one of vital importance—the capture of New Orleans. The route selected is up the Mississippi river, and the first obstacle to be encountered, perhaps the only one, is in the resistance offered by Forts St. Philip and Jackson. It is expected that the navy can reduce the works; in that case, you will, after their capture, leave a sufficient garrison in them to render them perfectly secure; and it is recommended that on the upward passage a few heavy guns and some troops be left at the pilot station, at the forks of the river, to cover a retreat in the case of a disaster, the troops and guns will of course be removed as soon as the forts are captured.

"Should the navy fail to reduce the works, you will land your forces and siege train, and endeavor to breach the works, silence their fire, and carry them by assault.

"The next resistance will be near the English Bend, where there are some earthen batteries; here it may be necessary for you to land your troops, to co-operate with the naval attack, although it is more than probable that the navy, unassisted, can accomplish the result. If these works are taken, the city of New Orleans necessarily falls.

"In that event it will probably be best to occupy Algiers with the mass of your troops, also the eastern bank of the river above the city—it may be necessary to place some troops *in* the city to preserve order; though if there appears sufficient Union sentiment to control the city, it may be best for purposes of discipline to keep your men out of the city.

"After obtaining possession of New Orleans, it will be necessary to reduce all the works guarding its approaches from the east, and particularly to gain the Manchac Pass.

"Baton Rouge, Berwick Bay, and Fort Livingston will next claim your attention.

"A feint on Galveston may facilitate the objects we have in view. I need not call your attention to the necessity of gaining possession of all the rolling stock you can, on the different railways, and of obtaining control of the roads themselves. The occupation of Baton Rouge, by a combined naval and land force, should be accomplished as soon as possible after you have gained New Orleans; then endeavor to open your communication with the northern column of the Mississippi, always bearing in mind the necessity of occupying Jackson, Mississippi, as soon as you can safely do so, either after or before you have effected the junction. Allow nothing to divert you from obtaining full possession of *all* the approaches to New Orleans. When that object is accomplished to its fullest extent, it will be necessary to make a combined attack on Mobile, in order to gain possession of the harbor and works, as well as to control the railway terminus at the city. In regard to this, I will send more detailed instructions, as the operations of the northern column develop themselves. I may simply state that the general objects of the expedition are *first*, the reduction of New Orleans and all its approaches, then Mobile, and all its defenses, then Pensacola, Galveston, etc. It is probable that by the time New Orleans is reduced, it will be in the power of the government to re-enforce the land forces sufficiently to accomplish all these objects; in the mean time you will please give all the assistance in your power to the army and navy commanders in your vicinity, never losing sight of the fact that the great object to be achieved is the capture and firm retention of New Orleans.

"Very respectfully, your obedient servant,

"GEORGE B. MCCLELLAN,

"*Major-General Commanding, &c., &c.*"

February 24th was General Butler's last day in Washington.

"Good-by, Mr. President. We shall take New Orleans, or you'll never see me again."

Mr. Stanton: "The man that takes New Orleans is made a lieutenant-general."

February 25th, at nine in the evening, the steamship Mississippi sailed from Hampton Roads, with General Butler and his staff, and fourteen hundred troops on board. Mrs. Butler, the brave and kind companion of her general in all his campaigns hitherto, was still at his side on the quarter-deck of the Mississippi. Except himself, Major Strong, and Lieutenant Wietzel, no man in the ship, and no man on the island to which they were bound, knew the object of the expedition. Articles and maps had appeared in the *Herald*, calculated to lead the enemy to suppose that New Orleans, if attacked at all, would be attacked from above, not from the gulf. The northern public were completely in the dark; no one even guessed New Orleans.

CHAPTER XII.

SHIP ISLAND.

Ship Island is a long wave of whitest, finest sand, that glistens in the sun, and drifts before the wind like New England snow. It is one of four islands that stretch along ten or twelve miles from the gulf coast, forming Mississippi sound. It was to one of these sand islands that the British troops repaired after their failure before New Orleans in 1815, where they lived for several weeks, amusing themselves with fishing and play-acting. Ship Island, seven miles long and three quarters of a mile wide, containing two square miles of land—the best of the four for a rendezvous—is sixty-five miles from New Orleans, ninety-five from the mouths of the Mississippi, fifty from Mobile bay, ten from the nearest point of the state of Mississippi, of which the island is a part. It lies so low among the white, tumbling waves, that, when covered with tents, it looked like a camp floating upon the sea. Land and water are menacingly blended there. Numberless porpoises, attracted by the refuse of the camps, floundered all around the shore, which was lined with a living fringe of sea-gulls, flapping, plunging, diving, and screaming. The waves and the wind seemed to heave and toss the sand as easily as they did the water. In great storms the island changes its form; large portions are severed, others submerged; new bays and inlets appear. On landing, the voyager does not so much feel that he has come on shore as that he has got down over the ship's side to the shifting bottom of the sea, raised for a moment by the mighty swell of waters, threatening again to sink and disappear. *Terra firma*, it is not.

It was observed that the first aspect of this island struck death to the hopes of arriving troops. They faintly strove to cheer their spirits with jocular allusions to the garden of Eden and to Coney Island; and one of General Phelps's men, on looking over the ship's side upon the desolate scene of his future home, raised a doleful laugh by exclaiming, in the language of Watts:

"Lord, what a wretched land is this,
Which yields us no supplies!"

Appearances, however, were deceptive. The wretched land was found to yield abundant supplies of commodities and conveniences, most essential to soldiers. At the western end there is a really superior harbor, safe in all winds, admitting the largest vessels. At the eastern extremity groves of pine and stunted oak have succeeded in establishing themselves, and afford plenty of wood. For fresh water, it is only necessary to sink a barrel three feet; it immediately fills with rain water, pure from the natural filter of the sand. Oysters of excellent quality can be had by wading for them; fish abound; and the woods, strange to relate. furnished the means of raccoon-hunting. The climate, too, in the winter months, is more enjoyable than Newport in midsummer, and the bathing not inferior. Nevertheless, it must be owned, that with all these advantages, Ship Island was never regarded by the troops with high favor; they never recovered from the first shock of disappointment.

Before the arrival of General Phelps, in December, 1861, the island had been the theater of many events. The breaking out of the rebellion found workmen, in the service of the United States, building a fort for the defense of the harbor. They soon abandoned the place, and the rebels immediately landed, burned the houses, damaged the fort, destroyed the lantern of the light-house, and retired. Then the blockading squadron appeared, captured many prizes, and nearly stopped the coasting trade between Mobile and New Orleans. But the coast being clear for a few days, a rebel force again landed, and proceeded to repair the damage they had done, mounting heavy guns upon the fort, and erecting extensive works, Commodore McKean unable to reach them with the guns of the Massachusetts. In September, alarmed by rumors of a coming expedition, the rebels again abandoned the island; but, in so doing, were so much accelerated by the vigilant McKean, that, though they took their guns with them, they left the fort standing, and the commodore captured a vessel laden with timber, hewn and cut for the defensive works. From September to December, Commodore McKean, with a hundred and seventy sailors and marines, under Lieutenant McKean Buchanan, had held the harbor, and labored to remount the fort, and complete the works begun by the enemy; darting out occasionally, and pouncing upon venturesome schooners from Mobile, or blockade-runners from Nassau. Five or six prizes were there when General Phelps hove in sight, and two light-draft steamers among them, invaluable for landing troops.

During the next three months the island presented a busy scene. The huge steamer Constitution landed her little army of troops, sailed, and returned with more; General Phelps and Commodore McKean striving, meanwhile, to complete the defenses, and to prepare in all ways for coming events, whatever those events might be; neither of them knowing the designs of the government. General Phelps, a strict disciplinarian, assiduously drilled and reviewed the troops. He signalized his brief tenure of command by issuing his well-remembered proclamation, which must be pronounced the most unexpected piece of composition which the war has elicited. A reporter records, that during the last days of the voyage of the Constitution, General Phelps was observed to spend more time than usual in the solitude of his cabin. "He did not come so promptly as the rest of the officers to the table, and when he did appear, seemed more occupied with his own thoughts than with the current of conversation. The cause of this temporary reticence was explained on the day following our arrival at Ship Island. Observing that he was more than usually busy about some interesting matter, your correspondent, in the exercise of that watchfulness which is requisite in the reporter, but, at the same time, with that diffidence not always characteristic of the profession, seized a favorable moment for putting himself *en rapport* with the commander, and ascertained that he was about to issue a very important paper, defining the *animus* of the expedition to the people of the country. General Phelps explained that he regarded the occasion as a peculiarly fitting one for setting forth, in a frank and at the same time a tolerant spirit, the sentiments which would govern his conduct in prosecuting the war against rebellion in the southwest. The document was copied in a plain hand, and on the evening of our arrival in Ship Island Roads, it was read aloud in the presence of the passengers and officers, who were convened in the steamer's saloon. On the following morning, other copies were made, one of which was read to the officers on board the United States steamer Massachusetts, in the hearing of several secession prisoners who had been taken on board of the rebel steamers and other prizes in port."*

The document, it should be observed, was addressed to the loyal people of the southwest, not to the enemies of the United States.

PROCLAMATION.

"Head-quarters Middlesex Brigade, Ship Island,
"Mississippi, *Dec.* 4, 1861.

"To the loyal citizens of the Southwest:

"Without any desire of my own, but contrary to my private inclinations, I again find myself among you as a military officer of the government. A proper respect for my fellow-countrymen renders it not out of place that I should make known to you the motives and principles by which my command will be governed.

"We believe that every state that has been admitted as a slave state into the Union, since the adoption of the constitution, has been so admitted in direct violation of that constitution.

"We believe that the slave states which existed, as such, at the adoption of our constitution, are, by becoming parties to that compact, under the highest obligations of honor and morality to abolish slavery.

"It is our conviction that monopolies are as destructive, as competition is conservative, of the principles and vitalities of republican government; that slave labor is a monopoly which excludes free labor and competition; that slaves are kept in comparative idleness and ease in a fertile half of our arable national territory, while free white laborers, constantly augmenting in numbers from Europe, are confined to the other half, and are often distressed by want; that the free labor of the North has more need of expansion into the southern states, from which it is virtually excluded, than slavery had into Texas in 1846; that free labor is essential to free institutions; that these institutions are naturally better adapted and more conge-

* Correspondence of the *N. Y. Daily Times*, December 17, 1861.

nial to the Anglo-Saxon race, than are the despotic tendencies of slavery; and, finally, that the dominant political principle of this North American continent, so long as the Caucasian race continues to flow in upon us from Europe, must needs be that of free institutions and free government. Any obstructions to the progress of that form of government in the United States must inevitably be attended with discord and war.

"Slavery, from the condition of a universally recognized social and moral evil, has become at length a political institution, demanding political recognition. It demands rights to the exclusion and annihilation of those rights which are insured to us by the constitution; and we must choose between them which we will have, for we can not have both. The constitution was made for freemen, not for slaves. Slavery, as a social evil, might for a time be tolerated and endured; but as a political institution it becomes imperious and exacting, controlling, like a dread necessity, all whom circumstances have compelled to live under its sway, hampering their action and thus impeding our national progress. As a political institution it could exist as a co-ordinate part only of two forms of governments, viz: the despotic and the free; and it could exist under a free government only where public sentiment, in the most unrestricted exercise of a robust freedom, leading to extravagance and licentiousness, had swayed the thoughts and habits of the people beyond the bounds and limits of their own moderate constitutional provisions. It could exist under a free government only where the people in a period of unreasoning extravagance had permitted popular clamor to overcome public reason, and had attempted the impossibility of setting up permanently, as a political institution, a social evil which is opposed to moral law.

"By reverting to the history of the past, we find that one of the most destructive wars on record, that of the French Revolution, was originated by the attempt to give political character to an institution which was not susceptible of political character. The church, by being endowed with political power, with its convents, its schools, its immense landed wealth, its associations, secret and open, became the ruling power of the state, and thus occasioned a war of more strife and bloodshed, probably, than any other war which has desolated the earth.

"Slavery is still less susceptible of political character than was the church. It is as fit at this moment for the lumber-room of the past, as was in 1793 the monastery, the landed wealth, the exclusive privilege, etc., of the Catholic Church in France. It behooves us to consider, as a self-governing people, bred, and reared and practiced in the habits of self-government, whether we can not, whether we *ought* not to revolutionize slavery out of existence, without the necessity of a conflict of arms like that of the French Revolution.

"Indeed, we feel assured, that the moment slavery is abolished, from that moment our southern brethren, every ten of whom have probably seven relatives in the north, would begin to emerge from a hateful delirium. From that moment, relieved from imaginary terrors, their days become happy, and their nights peaceable and free from alarm: the aggregate amount of labor, under the new stimulus of fair competition, becomes greater day by day; property rises in value, invigorating influences succeed to stagnation, degeneracy and decay; and union, harmony and peace, to which we have so long been strangers, become restored, and bind us again in the bonds of friendship and amity, as when we first began our national career, under our glorious government of 1789.

"Why do the leaders of the rebellion seek to change the form of your ancient government? Is it because the growth of the African element of your population has come at length to render the change necessary? Will you permit the free government under which you have thus far lived, and which is so well suited for the development of true manhood, to be altered to a narrow and belittling despotism, in order to adapt it to the necessities of ignorant slaves, and the requirements of their proud and aristocratic owners? Will the laboring men of the south bend their necks to the same yoke that is suited to the slave? We think not. We may safely answer that the time has not yet arrived when our southern brethren, for the mere sake of keeping Africans in slavery, will abandon their long cherished free institutions, and enslave themselves.

"It is the conviction of my command, as a part of the national forces of the United States, that labor—manual labor—is inherently noble; that it cannot be systematically degraded by any nation without ruining its peace, happiness and power; that free labor is the granite basis on which free institutions must rest; that it is the right, the capital, the inheritance, the hope of the poor man everywhere; that it is especially the right of five millions of our fellow-countrymen in the slave states, as well as of the four millions of Africans there, and all our efforts, therefore, however small or great, whether directed against the interference of governments from abroad, or against rebellious combinations at home, shall be for free labor. Our motto and our standard shall be, here and everywhere, and on all occasions, FREE LABOR AND WORKINGMEN'S RIGHTS. It is on this basis, and this basis alone, that our munificent government, the asylum of the nations, can be perpetuated and preserved.

"J. W. PHELPS,
"*Brigadier-General of Volunteers Commanding.*"

It is a proof of the very great respect entertained for the good general, that the issue of such a proclamation, in the name of the troops, provoked little more than a feeling of astonishment. There was, it is true, some foolish talk of resigning commissions;

and one naval commander relieved his mind by tearing a copy in pieces and throwing it overboard.

"What," asked General Phelps, on hearing of these adverse opinions, "did these officers come down here for? Was it to sacrifice their ease, to waste their time, and perhaps to lay down their lives in a war, simply that a few persons may hold slaves? I did not come for any such purpose. I came to fight, and if anybody is afraid, they had better go home. These people, among whom we have come, do not ask any favors of us, and I ask none of them. I did not come here to steal, but to tell them just what I mean to do."

He declared, further, that his principles were anti-slavery, and he desired the country to know it. He did not, however, wish to harm his countrymen of the South, but believing as he did that slavery was the cause of the war, and all other troubles of any moment that have ever arisen among the American people, he had a right to say so, and could not see the propriety of longer apologizing for such a baneful institution. "And as for those officers," continued he, "who are so fearful that the Union army may do some harm to the rebels, they had better come forward and let us know which side they are on."

A copy, it appears, was taken to the Mississippi shore, and handed to some one found there. It was extensively used in Secessia as fuel for firing the southern heart. In due time, we are told, it was translated for the warning of the people of Cuba, who were invited to compute what would be the value of their slaves if the United States, known to be covetous of Cuba, should succeed in restoring its power by the destruction of slavery in the southern states. General Butler, in common with the whole country, read the proclamation of his brigadier with much surprise, but was far from joining in the hue and cry against it. In transmitting General Phelps's report to head-quarters, he merely remarked: "I need hardly say that the issuing of any proclamation, upon such occasion, was neither suggested nor authorized by me, and most certainly not such an one. With that exception, I commend the report, and ask attention to its clear and business-like statements."

General Phelps, with his quaint and kindly ways, and his efficiency as a commanding officer, soon lived down the clamor excited by his proclamation. The rigor of his rule was alleviated by his humorous mode of settling difficulties and administering reproof. Two bottles of illicit champagne-cider were brought to his tent one day, and the question occurred what was to be done with the property—value three dollars.

"Orderly," said the general, "strike those bottles together, and see which is the hardest; that is the way to dispose of liquor taken from drunken soldiers."

On another occasion, he called a captain from the line of his regiment, and addressed him thus:

"Captain ——, I find that you are exceedingly attentive to *everything*."

The general paused here for a moment, and the captain waited to hear the conclusion of the compliment. But the general completed the sentence in an unexpected manner; "except your duty," said he. The captain retired to his place amid the titter of the regiment.

December, January, and February passed slowly and drearily by. The island was covered with troops; the fleet augmented in the harbor. The troops being inconveniently crowded, General Phelps sent over a party to the main land to see if there was room and safety there for a portion of his command. A sudden shower of canister from a battery near the wharf of Mississippi City was interpreted to mean that, though there might be room enough, there was not safety. The troops, therefore, were obliged to remain cooped and huddled together on the small part of the island that afforded tolerable camping ground. The monotony of their lives, in these forlorn and restricted circumstances, told upon the spirits of the men. The resigning fever broke out among the officers, and "carried off" several victims. At the end of February, when the last transports arrived, General Phelps learned that the next arrival would be that of General Butler himself, who might be daily expected, and then active operations would begin. But the days passed on, and no general came. Two large steamers were lying in the harbor, at a daily expense to the government of three thousand dollars. Now, General Phelps is one of those gentlemen who take the true view of the public money, regarding it as the *most* sacred of all money, to be expended with the thoughtful economy with which an honest guardian expends the slender portion of a girl bequeathed to his care by a dying friend. Still unacquainted with the plans of the government, hearing, too, that General Butler had been lost at sea, the costly presence of those steamers distressed his righteous soul; and, at length, he ordered them home. So there were ten thousand men, on a strip of sand, on a hostile coast, with no great supply of provisions, destitute of any adequate means either of getting away or of getting supplies. A deep despondency settled upon the troops as the month of March wore on, and they vainly scanned the horizon for a smoky harbinger of their expected commander. Fears for his safety received melancholy confirmation, when a vessel arrived, bringing Brigadier-General Williams from Hatteras Inlet, for whom the Mississippi was to have called on her way. For a month, General Phelps waited for General Butler in painful suspense.

The rumors of disaster to the Mississippi were far from groundless. In getting to Ship Island, General Butler had almost as many adventures as Jason in search of the golden fleece. To him, and to his staff, who had already encountered so many obstacles in Massachusetts and at Washington, it seemed now as if gods and men were contending against their expedition. But they were animated with desperate resolution, feeling that only some signal achievement could vindicate their enterprise, and enable them to show themselves again in Massachusetts without shame. The general had assumed so much of the responsibility of the expedition, had borne it along on his own shoulders through so many difficulties, against so much opposition or lukewarm support, that he felt there were two alternatives for him, glorious success or a glorious death. Nor did he suppose for a moment, that the brunt of the affair would fall upon the wooden ships of the navy. He expected powerful aid from the navy, but he took it for granted, that the closing and decisive encounter would be with the Confederate army on the swamps and bayous of the Delta, defended by works supposed by the enemy to be impregnable. Storming parties, scaling ladders, siege guns, headlong assaults into the imminent, deadly breach—these were the means by which he supposed the work was to be finally done, and this was evidently the impression of the secretary of war when he spoke of the reward which would be due to the man who should take New Orleans.

February 25th, at nine in the evening, the Mississippi steamed from Hampton Roads, and bore away for Hatteras and General

Williams. The weather was fine, and the night passed pleasantly. The morning broke beautifully upon a tranquil sea, and the superb ship bowled along before a fair wind. Landsmen began to fear that they should complete the voyage without having experienced what is so delightful to read about in Byron—a storm at sea. But, in the afternoon—a change, and such a change. The horizon thickened and drew in; the wind rose; and when, at six o'clock, they were eight miles off Hatteras Inlet, there was no getting in that night. The ship made for the open sea, and in so doing, ran within a few feet of perdition, in the form of a shoal, over which the waves broke into foam. The ship escaped, but not the captain's reputation. The general's faith in his captain was not entire before this ominous occurrence, but from that moment it was gone, and he left the deck no more while the danger lasted. The gale increased as the night came on, until at midnight it blew half a hurricane. The vessel being short-handed, there was a rummaging among the sleeping and sea-sick troops for sailors; numbers of whom responded to the call, who rendered good service during the night—their general awake, ubiquitous. It lulled toward morning; and by noon, the wind had ceased. The ship was then so far from Hatteras, that it was determined to give up General Williams, and make straight for the gulf. "All felt relieved," remarks Major Bell in his itinerary, "and such as had desired to see a storm at sea, had had their wildest wish fully realized, and were satisfied."

Again, the magnificent ship went prosperously on her way. The sea-sick struggled on deck; the disheartened were reassured; and those who had lost confidence in the captain had had their faith in the general renewed. The night was serene; the morning fine. At seven, the ship was off Cape Fear, going at great speed, wind and steam co-operating; land in sight; men in high spirits over their coffee and biscuit. At half-past eight, when the general and his staff were at breakfast in the cabin, they heard and felt that most terrible of all sounds known to seafaring men, the harsh grating of the ship's keel upon a shoal. Every one started to his feet, and hurried to the deck. The sky was clear, the land was five miles distant, a light-house was in sight. The vessel ground upon the rocks, but still moved. Her course was altered and altered again; all points of the compass were tried; but still she touched.

Boats were lowered, and soundings were taken in all directions, without a practicable channel being discovered. The captain, amazed and confounded, gave the fatal order to let go the bow anchor; and the ship, with three sails set, drove upon the fluke, which pierced the forward compartment, and the water poured in in a torrent that baffled the utmost exertions of men and pumps. Benjamin Franklin, dead in Christ church burial-ground at Philadelphia, saved the ship from filling; for it was he who first learned from the Chinese, and suggested to the occidental world, the expedient of building ships with water-tight compartments. In an hour from the first shock, the good steamer Mississippi was hard and fast upon Frying Pan Shoals, one compartment filled to the water line, and the forward berths all afloat. There was no help in the captain; he was in such a maze that he could not ascertain from his books even the state of the tide, whether it was rising or falling, a question upon which the safety of the ship depended.

The general, in effect, took command of the ship. Major Bell and Captain R. S. Davis, both volunteer aids, were ordered to look into the captain's library for the hour of the next high tide. They reported falling water; high tide at 8 P. M. Signals of distress were hoisted, guns were fired, efforts were still made to get the ship afloat. Horsemen were descried on the shore, and fears were entertained that some Confederate vessel, lurking on the coast, might come out and make an easy capture of a defenseless transport. Amid the manifold perils of the situation, the troops behaved with admirable composure, and perfect order was maintained without effort on the part of the officers. It could scarcely have been otherwise, for the men saw, during that long and anxious day, Mrs. Butler, with her attendant, tranquilly hemming streamers on the quarter-deck, she not suspecting the essential aid she was rendering the officers in command. The men confessed the next day, that nothing cheered them so much while they were in peril, as the sight of Mrs. Butler sitting there, in the sight of them all, calmly plying her needle. And the danger was indeed most imminent. An ordinary squall would have broken up the ship; it would have taken days to land the men in the ship's boats; and they were upon a hostile shore. The strain was severest upon the nerves of those who were most familiar with a coast noted for the suddenness and violence of its gales. One man's hair turned white; one went mad.

Toward noon, a steamer hove in sight; reviving hope in some, quickening the fears of others. She approached cautiously, as if doubtful of the character of the grounded ship. The Union flag was made out flying from her mast-head, but still she hung off in the distance suspiciously. General Butler sent Major Bell on board, who discovered that she was the gun-boat Mount Vernon, Commander O. S. Glisson, of the United States navy, blockading Wilmington. Captain Glisson, who had, indeed, doubted the character of the Mississippi, came on board, and placed his vessel at the service of General Butler. The sea was still smooth, but tokens of change being manifest, it was deemed best to transfer Mrs. Butler and her maid to the Mount Vernon. A hawser was attached to the Mississippi, and the gun-boat made many fruitless attempts to drag her from the shoals. Three hundred men were put on board the Mount Vernon; shells were thrown overboard; the troops ran in masses from bow to stern, and from stern to bow; the engine worked at full speed; but still she would not budge. As the tide rose, the wind and waves rose also; it became difficult to transfer the troops; and, soon, the huge ship began to roll and strike the rocks alarmingly. The sun went down, and twilight was deepening into darkness, the wind still increasing. But soon after seven, to the inexpressible relief of all on board, she moved forward a few feet, and then surged ahead into deeper water, and was afloat. The Mount Vernon went slowly on to show the way, the Mississippi following; the lead continuing for a whole hour to show but six inches of water under her keel. The vessel hung down heavily by the head, the forward compartment being filled, and no one had a sense of safety until, at midnight, both vessels came to anchor in the Cape Fear river. "All behaved wonderfully well," Major Bell records. "The resources of the general seemed inexhaustible; his seeming calmness and his clear judgment, in view of the responsibility which the ignorance of the captain left upon him, were wonderful."

The next morning, after a survey of the damaged vessel, it was decided to go on to Port Royal for repairs, trusting to the settled appearance of the weather; the Mount Vernon to accompany. Mrs. Butler and the troops returned to the Mississippi, except one gentleman, the chaplain of a regiment, who resigned his commission, and stuck to the vessel that had a competent captain and no hole in her bottom. General Butler was ingenious in expedients to check the tendency to resign, which is apt to manifest itself in certain circumstances; but he placed no obstacle in the way of the chaplain's escape. The vessels put to sea in the afternoon. The next day was Sunday, and prayers were said on the deck of the Mississippi. The most profound solemnity prevailed in the dense throng of soldiers, who literally watched and prayed; prayed to Heaven and watched the weather. In the afternoon they were cheered with the sight of the great fleet blockading Charleston, one of the vessels of which took the place of the Mount Vernon. At sunset, on the second of March, the Mississippi and her new consort, the Matanzas, anchored off Hilton Head.

As no adequate transportation for the troops could be had at Port Royal, nothing remained but to attempt to repair the Mississippi, and this, too, in the absence of a dry dock or other facilities for handling so large a vessel. The ship was taken to Seabrook Landing, on Shell Creek, seven miles from Hilton Head, and the men and stores were removed. The naval officers on the station, Captain Boggs, Captain Renshaw, Captain Boutelle, and others, conferred with the general, and lent all possible aid to the work in hand. Plan after plan was proposed, discussed, rejected. Men and pumps strove in vain to clear the compartment of water. Twice the leak was plugged from the inside, and twice the water burst through again, and destroyed in an hour the work of two days and nights. It can be truly averred, that General Butler's indomitable resolution and inexhaustible ingenuity were the cause of the final success; for long after every one else had despaired, he persisted, and still suggested new expedients. A sail was at length, with inconceivable difficulty, and after many disheartening failures, drawn over the leak; the pumps gained upon the water, and as the head of the vessel rose, the work became more feasible. When the water had fallen below the leak, a few hours of vigorous exertion sufficed to stop it, and the naval gentlemen pronounced the vessel fit for sea.

The troops were re-embarked, and the luckless Mississippi started for the mouth of the harbor. The captain, disregarding the advice of the naval officers, who were familiar with the soundings, ran her aground upon a bed of shells, and there she stuck as fast as upon Frying Pan Shoals. "It now became painfully evident," remarks

Major Bell, "that if we ever hoped to get the Mississippi to Ship Island *by water*, we must have a new captain." General Butler yielded to the universal desire, and to his own sense of the necessity of the case; he ordered a board of inquiry, which reporting the captain incompetent, he deposed him and placed him under arrest in his state-room. "I am grieved," he wrote to the captain, "to be obliged to this action, for our personal relations have been of the kindest character, and I know yourself will believe that only the sternest sense of duty would compel me to it."

Acting-master Sturgis, of the Mount Vernon, took the vacant place. Under his skillful direction, the ship was once more floated, but not till the men had been again landed, and all the tugs in port had done their utmost. March 13th, under a salute of fifteen guns from the flag-ship, the Mississippi put to sea, still accompanied by the Matanzas with part of the troops on board.

No more disasters. Seven days of prosperous sailing brought them in sight of Ship Island, a long camp floating flat upon the gulf. Dismal scene! A gale was blowing as the ship steamed into the harbor, and huge waves were seen rolling up, apparently among the tents, and no man could tell which was water and which was land. For two days and more, the gale continued, and the men, unable to land, looked out upon the island dolefully. It seemed a sorry port to come to after *such* a voyage. A gloom that some men who were not easily dismayed could scarcely endure, much less conceal, fell upon every heart. I have heard General Butler say, that when he saw what Ship Island was, and learned that General Phelps had sent away the transports, and thought of the many chances there were of the failure of supplies, and how absolutely dependent they all were upon external and distant resources, his heart, for the first time during the war, died within him, and it required all the resolution and fortitude he could command to maintain a decent show of cheerfulness. He was somewhat debilitated too, at this time, by a return of the disease contracted some years before, at the National Hotel in Washington.

On the twenty-fifth of March, just thirty days from Hampton Roads, the troops were landed. There being no house on the island, a shanty of charred boards, eighteen feet square, was erected for the residence of Mrs. Butler, furniture for which was opportunely procured from a captured vessel. A vast old-fashioned French bedstead half filled the little cabin.

A closer acquaintance with the island did not raise the spirits of the troops. The heat was intense. Innumerable were the flies. The general discomfit was extreme; and to add to the gloom, phantoms were not wanting. As the belief gained ground that New Orleans was the object of the expedition, rumors of the immense preparations of the enemy to defend the city obtained currency; the river was lined with batteries for a hundred miles; "rams" of fearful magnitude and power had been constructed; an army of fifty thousand men were in the field. And soon after General Butler's arrival, the news reached the island, with enormous exaggerations, of the foray of the Merrimac among the fleet in Hampton Roads. Were the iron-clads of New Orleans likely to be less formidable? Had we any Monitors to meet them? If the Wellington heroes under Pakenham could not take the city when it was defended by only four thousand militia, badly armed, what was the prospect now, when all the appliances of modern science had been employed, and the place was defended by forts, columbiads, cables, a whole fleet of Merrimacs, and a large army?*

* New Orleans newspapers were brought over from Biloxi in considerable numbers. Such paragraphs as the following were found in them: "The Mississippi is fortified so as to be impassable for any hostile fleet or flotilla. Forts Jackson and St. Philip are armed with one hundred and seventy heavy guns (sixty-three pounders, rifled by Barkley Britton, and received from England). The navigation of the river is stopped by a dam of about a quarter of a mile from the above forts. No flotilla on earth would force that dam in less than two hours, during which it would be within short and cross range of one hundred and seventy guns of the heaviest caliber, many of which would be served with red-hot shot, numerous furnaces for which have been erected in every fort and battery.

"In a day or two we shall have ready two iron-cased floating batteries. The plates are four and a half inches thick, of the best hammered iron, received from England and France. Each iron-cased battery will mount twenty sixty-eight pounders, placed so as to skim the water, and striking the enemy's hull between wind and water. We have an abundant supply of incendiary shells, cupola furnaces for molten iron, congreve rockets and fire-ships.

"Between New Orleans and the forts there is a constant succession of earthworks. At the Plain of Chalmette, near Janin's property, there are redoubts, armed with rifled cannon, which have been found to be effective at five miles range. A ditch thirty feet wide and twenty deep extends from the Mississippi to La Cipriore.

"In Forts St. Philip and Jackson, there are three thousand men, of whom a goodly portion are experienced artillery-men, and gunners who have served in the navy.

"At New Orleans itself we have thirty-two thousand infantry, and as many more quartered in the immediate neighborhood. In discipline and drill they are far superior to the Yankees. We have two very able and active generals, who possess our entire confidence, General Mansfield Lovell, and Brigadier-General Ruggles. For commodore, we have old Hollins, a Nelson in his way."—*New Orleans Picayune, April 5th*, 1862.

It happened, however, that the men in command of the joint expedition were peculiarly insensible to phantoms. General Butler was at once immersed in the details of preparation, and rose superior to the prevailing depression. Captain Farragut—the immortal Farragut—who had arrived within a few days, and taken command of the fleet, had all an old sailor's contempt for everything that bore the name of ram. From the first, he regarded the naval part of the enemy's preparations as unworthy of serious consideration. Give *him* wooden ships. He would answer for the rams and iron-clads—floating caldrons to boil sailors in. *He* was for fighting on deck, not in the bottom of a tea-kettle. Wooden ships were good enough for Nelson, Perry, Lawrence, Decatur; and they were good enough for him. The rebels were heartily welcome to their rams and floating batteries, their railroad-ironed steamboats, and their fire-rafts of pine knots.

A few hours after General Butler had landed his troops, he was in consultation with Captain Farragut—Captain Bailey of the navy being also present, as well as Major Strong and Lieutenant Wietzel. The plan of operations then adopted was the one which was substantially carried out, and which resulted in the capture of the city.

I. Captain Porter, with his fleet of twenty-one bomb-schooners, should anchor below the two forts, Jackson and St. Philip, and continue to fire upon them until they were reduced, or until his ammunition was nearly exhausted. During the bombardment, Captain Farragut's fleet should remain out of fire, as a reserve, just below the bomb-vessels. The army, or so much of it as transportation could be found for, should remain at the mouth of the river, awaiting the issue of the bombardment. If Captain Porter succeeded in reducing the forts, the army would ascend the river and garrison them. It would then be apparent, probably, what the next movement should be.

II. If the bombardment did not reduce or silence the forts, then Captain Farragut, with his fleet of steamers, would attempt to run by them. If he succeeded, he proposed to clear the river of the enemy's fleet, cut off the forts from supplies, and push on at least far enough to reconnoiter the next obstruction.

III. Captain Farragut having passed the forts, General Butler would at once take the troops round to the rear of Fort St. Philip, land them in the swamps there, and attempt to carry the fort by assault. The enemy had made no preparations to resist an attack from that quarter, supposing the swamps impassable. But Lieutenant Wietzel, while completing the fort, had been for two years in the habit of duck-shooting all over those swamps, and knew every bay and bayou of them. He assured General Butler that the landing of troops there would be difficult, but not impossible; and hence this part of the scheme. Both in the formation of the plan and in its execution the local knowledge and pre-eminent professional skill of Lieutenant Wietzel were of the utmost value. Few men contributed more to the reduction of the city than he. There are few more valuable officers in the service than General Wietzel, as the country well knows.

IV. The forts being reduced, the land and naval force would advance toward the city in the manner that should then seem best.

This was the plan. The next question was: When could they be ready to begin? Captain Farragut said he would sail at once for the mouths of the river, and thought he could be ready to move thence toward the forts in seven days. General Butler engaged to have six thousand men embarked and prepared in seven days. He would fill all the steamers he had, and take the remainder of the force in tow in sailing vessels. These arrangements concluded, Captain Farragut and the fleet departed, and General Butler set to work to do a month's work in seven days and nights.

He did it. He labored night and day. Having no quartermaster, no priceless Captain George, who was consigned to Lowell because a senator wanted his place for a relative, General Butler was seen on the wharf, blending the quartermaster with the major-general, not disdaining the duty of the stevedore, when the stevedore's duty became the vital one. A hundred Massachusetts carpenters were detailed to make scaling ladders; a hundred boatmen to help to man the thirty boats which were to nose their devious way through the reeds, creeks, pools and sharks in the rear of Fort St. Philip. The troops were formed into three brigades; the first under General Phelps, the second under General Williams, the third under Colonel Shepley, of the Twelfth Maine. The staff was announced.* A court-martial was organized, to bring up arrears of discipline, and a board to examine the new officers. A blast issued from head-quarters against intoxicating drinks, "the curse of the army." "Forbidden," added the general, "by every regulation, prohibited by official authority, condemned by experience, it still clings to the soldier, although more deadly, in this climate, than the rifle. All sales, therefore, within this department, will be punished by instant expulsion of the party offending, if a civilian, or by court-martial, if an officer or soldier. All intoxicating liquors kept for sale or to be used as a beverage, will be seized and destroyed, or confiscated to hospital uses."

On the sixth day, seven regiments and two batteries of artillery were embarked, ready to sail as soon as the word should come from Captain Farragut. But high winds and low tides were placing unexpected obstacles in the way of the fleet, the larger vessels of which were many days in getting over the bar. General Butler was obliged to disembark his troops, and await the tardy lightering of the ships into the river. A tedious fortnight passed before the fleet was ready, the general vibrating between the island and the mouths of the river.

A romantic incident occurred during this interval, which led to a variety of curious adventures. A mischance of war tossed upon the sand-beach of Ship Island, a beautiful little girl, three years of

* "HEAD-QUARTERS, DEPARTMENT OF THE GULF, SHIP ISLAND, *March* 20, 1862.

"GENERAL ORDERS, No. 1.

"Pursuant to General Order No. 20, of February 23, 1862, from the head-quarters of the army, Major-General B. F. Butler, U. S. Volunteers, assumes command of this department.

His staff is announced as follows:

Major George C. Strong, A. A. General, Ordnance Officer and Chief of Staff.
Captain Jonas H. French, A. D. C. and Acting Inspector-General.
Captain Peter Haggerty, Aide-de-Camp.
First Lieutenant W. H. Wiegel, A. D. C.
First Lieutenant J. W. Cushing, Thirty-first Mass. Volunteers, Acting Chief Quartermaster.
First Lieutenant J. E. Easterbrook, Thirtieth Mass. Volunteers, Acting Chief Commissary.
Captain George A. Kensel, Chief of Artillery.
First Lieutenant Godfrey Wietzel, Chief Engineer.
First Lieutenant J. C. Palfrey, Assistant Engineer.
First Lieutenant C. N. Turnbull, Chief of Topographical Engineers.
Surgeon Thomas H. Bache, Medical Director.
Major J. M. Bell, Volunteer Aide-de-Camp.
Captain R. S. Davis, Volunteer Aide-de-Camp.
First Lieutenant J. B. Kinsman, "
Second Lieutenant H. C. Clarke, "

"By command of MAJOR-GENERAL BUTLER.

"GEORGE C. STRONG, *A. A. G.*"

age, the child of a New Orleans physician, a rebel of noted bitterness. She was voyaging in Mississippi Sound with her parents and nurse, when the vessel being chased by a gun-boat, foundered, and all hands took to the boats. The little creature was a pet with the sailors; she was among them in the forecastle, when the vessel went down, and they took her with them into the boat, while the parents and the nurse hurried into another boat with the captain and mate. The boats were soon separated in the gale, and the one containing the child was picked up by a cruiser, and brought to Ship Island. The arrival of the child among the troops, so many of whom had left children or little sisters at home, excited a degree of interest difficult to conceive. She was taken to Mrs. Butler's shanty, her clothes all wet and torn, and there she was provided with such clothing as could be hastily made, and otherwise provided for with the tenderest care. But Ship Island, in such circumstances, was no fit place for her. She could tell her name, and seemed to have a lively sense of having a grandfather in New Orleans, whose name she also knew. The general determined to send her as far on her way to this grandfather as he could. Whether her parents had survived the storm no one knew.

A sloop was manned, and Major Strong was directed to convey her, under a flag of truce, to Biloxi, the nearest point of the opposite shore, and place her in the custody of a magistrate, with money to pay her expenses to New Orleans. Major Strong performed this congenial duty. He found at Biloxi a probate of wills, who was also a justice of the peace, to whom he committed the child, and gave him a sum of money in gold, sufficient to defray the cost of her transportation to the city. In the dusk of the evening, the tide having fallen, the sloop started to return, but grounded on the bar, a few hundred yards from the shore. Nothing remained but to wait six hours for the rising of the tide. Soon after dark, a boat came off with four men, one of whom Major Strong recognized as a person who had conversed with him in a friendly manner on shore. This gentleman warned him that he would be attacked by a large force in the course of the evening, and advised him to surrender. Scarcely believing that men could be found base enough to assail a flag of truce on such an errand as his, Major Strong nevertheless thought it best to send a boat to the nearest cruiser for assistance. He had seven men with him. Five of these he sent away in the boat, under Captain Conant, leaving three men and eight muskets in the sloop. Major Strong was one of those soldiers who knew nothing about surrendering; it formed no part of his calculations; he had not studied the subject, and did not admit it as a branch of the art military. He barricaded the deck of the sloop, put his eight muskets into position, and extended a stout log of wood over the side to play the part of a howitzer. His two men were ordered below, having been first instructed in their role. One of the men, Macdonald by name, had brought his violin with him, and kept up a lively performance in the cabin, of national airs and dancing tunes.

About nine o'clock two large boats, filled with armed men, were seen approaching from the shore. Voices called out:

"Surrender! Surrender!"

Major Strong replied: "I am here under a flag of truce, performing an errand of mercy to one of your citizens. If you attempt to violate the laws of this sacred mission, I will blow you with this howitzer," laying his hand on the log, "so deep into ——, that your commander will find it difficult to produce you at taps."

"We'll see about that," returned a voice.

The boats hauled off as if to consider the matter. They soon approached again, one on each side.

"Keep those boats on the same side of the sloop," shouted the Major, "or I'll sink both of you."

The order was obeyed. The boats came together, and lay off at hailing distance.

"Don't come any nearer," cried Major Strong. "If you have anything to say to me, send one man."

A man came wading, and halted a few yards from the vessel.

"How many men have you got there?" asked Major Strong.

"Forty," replied the man. "How many have you?"

"Well, not many, but enough to defend this vessel."

The major was aware that anything like a boast of his numbers would confirm the opinion of the magnanimous foe, that he was in reality defenseless.

While this colloquy was going on, the two men in the hold were performing an important part. They contrived to make a great deal of noise, and Macdonald continued his fiddling, Major Strong frequently calling out:

"Keep quiet down there, men." "No, don't come on deck yet." "All heads below, I say." "Major Jones, look to your men there forward, and keep those heads below the hatches." "Stop that fiddling, Macdonald; there'll be time enough to dance by and by."

The wading hero returned to the boats, which lingered a while, and then, firing a volley at the sloop, rapidly disappeared, and were no more seen. A gun-boat soon came to the rescue of the party, and the facts were duly reported to the general in the morning.

The boiling indignation excited in all minds by the dastardly conduct of the Biloxi savages may be imagined. The general instantly determined to give them a lesson in good manners. At half-past two that very afternoon, two gun-boats, the Jackson and New London, and the transport Lewis, with Colonel Cahill's Ninth Connecticut, and Captain Everett's battery on board, sailed for Biloxi, for the purpose of conveying that lesson to their benighted minds. Major Strong commanded the expedition, attended by Captain Jonas H. French, Lieutenant Turnbull, Captain Conant, Lieutenant Kinsman, Captain Davis, Captain John Clark, and Lieutenant Biddle.

Soon after four o'clock, the armed steamers anchored off Biloxi, and the transport Lewis made fast to the wharf. The inhabitants lined the beach, and one wild son of Mississippi stood on the wharf, rifle in hand, defying the troops to come on shore. The men were marshaled on the wharf. Major Strong placed himself at their head, and gave the word to advance. The wild son of Mississippi retired. In a few minutes Biloxi was surrounded and pervaded by Union troops, the people looking sullenly and silently on. Biloxi was a watering place in other times; the Mississippi cotton-planters' Long Branch, now half deserted, dilapidated and forlorn. Major Strong found ample quarters in the building which had served as a summer hotel. Two prisoners were brought in; one, the valorous Mississippian just mentioned; the other, a four-footed ass.

"What do you bring that creature here for?" asked the commander of the force.

"Isn't he a Saypoy secessionist?" replied the Irishman who had brought him in.

"Let him run," said the major.

"Very well, sir," said the witty O'Dowd, as he obeyed the

order. "I think myself we had better not touch the privates till we catch the commander."

By the time the surrounding country had been well reconnoitered, night closed in, and further proceedings were deferred till the morrow. The troops slept in and around the town. Not a Biloxian was molested, not a house was plundered or disfigured, not a hen-roost disturbed, not a garden despoiled. An Irish officer asked a group, where the blackguards were who had fired into the boat that brought home the infernal secessionist's darlin' shipwrecked daughter; but as he elicited no response, the subject was dropped for the night. Indeed, the sad, despairing expression of every face, the evident poverty of the people, the many abandoned houses, and the utter desolation of the scene, seemed to disarm the resentment of the troops, and a feeling of pity for the "poor devils" arose in its stead. The manner in which the caught Mississippian devoured his rations, led the men to infer that provisions were not abundant in Biloxi; which was found to be true, not of Biloxi only, but of all that coast for hundreds of miles. The people were intense and vigilant devotees of secession, however. The spy who had been engaged by General Butler at Washington, six weeks before, had accomplished his mission so far as to visit New Orleans, and had come to Biloxi, designing to steal over to Ship Island. But he was there suspected, closely watched, and finally arrested. He was then in prison at New Orleans. Not a scrap of paper was found upon him, but he was still detained on suspicion.

At dawn the next morning, Captain Clark and Lieutenant Kinsman led a boat chase after a schooner laden with molasses; but wind proving a better resource than oars, the schooner escaped. As the day advanced, the citizens of Biloxi presented themselves at Major Strong's head-quarters, all avowing themselves secessionists, none of them justifying the attack on the sloop. The major's orders were to procure a written apology from the mayor, and from the commander of the Confederate forces, if any such there were. The mayor, however, kept out of the way; and it was not till his daughter had been politely conducted to head-quarters as a hostage for his appearance, that he could be found. He gave the written apology required, alleging that the party who fired upon the sloop were a mob which he had no force to control. At sunset, with the band playing and colors flying, Major Strong re-embarked the troops, and the fleet steamed westward for Pass Christian, where a regiment of the enemy was posted, and which the general's orders authorized him to visit. At ten in the evening, the steamers anchored off the pass, and the troops slept on board.

Danger was approaching them while they slept. The thunder of cannon woke them as the day was dawning; and before the troops had rubbed their eyes open, crash came a ten-inch shot through the transport, perforating the steam-pipe, passing through the cabin-lights, and out through the smoke-stack. In an instant, a second shot struck her, which carried away the cook's galley and part of the wheel-house. Three of the enemy's gun-boats, their lights all out, had stolen from Lake Borgne upon our little squadron, and this was their morning salutation. A sharp action ensued. It was twenty minutes before the Lewis could get steam enough to move, during which she received three more shots, and escaped three. But at length she both moved and acted. Fortunately, she had been provided with two rifled cannon, which were used with so much effect as to materially aid in the repulse of the enemy. The two gun-boats plied the foe with shot and shell for more than an hour before they thought proper to seek safety in the shallows of Lake Borgne. Strange to relate, but one man of the Union force was wounded, and he slightly—Captain Conant, of the Thirty-First Massachusetts.

Major Strong executed his purpose. He landed his troops, and took possession of the town, a sea-side summer resort, frequented by the people of New Orleans. He dashed upon the camp of the Confederate regiment, three miles distant, and reached it so quickly after the flight of the enemy as to find in the colonel's tent an unfinished dispatch, and the pen with which he was writing it still wet with ink. The dispatch was designed to inform General Lovell, commanding at New Orleans, of the descent upon Biloxi and Pass Christian, and announced the colonel's "desire" to attack the Union troops "toward evening." The camp was destroyed; the public stores in the town were also seized, part of them carried away, and the rest burnt.

At Pass Christian, the Union officers had their first taste of the quality and humor of the ladies of the south-west.

"A portion of the women," writes an officer, "stood their ground;

Mrs. and Miss Lee were of this number. Mrs. Lee and her husband keep a hotel, which is known as 'Lee's boarding house.' It is a snug inn. But Mrs. Lee is a tartar. She told Major Strong, that 'Mr. Lee, although he kept a hotel, was of one of the first families of Virginia.'

"'I dare say,' replied the Major; 'there is nothing incompatible with great qualities in the business he pursues!'

"While this parley was going on, Miss Lee pushed herself through the front door. She pouted as she passed over the portico, pulling as she went an unwilling hood over her handsome face, then somewhat disfigured by a frown.

"After the miniature sea and land fights, the officers met again at Lee's boarding house. Bread and butter, and poor claret, were the substance of the repast; Mrs. Lee and her fire-emitting daughter insisting upon occupying chairs at the table, while Mr. Lee waited upon the guests and drew the corks. The display of appetite was good. I think every man ate the worth of the gold dollar which he gave Mrs. Lee, who carefully folded away the hateful Lincoln coin in the corner of her dirty apron. It struck me as queer to see this 'first lady' in clothes which soap could have improved."

Miss Lee could not be appeased. She continued to pout and frown, and to say rude things to the officers in reply to their polite banter, when silence or witty retort would have been in better accord with the lofty claims of her family.

The squadron returned to Ship Island without farther adventure. General Butler marked his sense of the excellent conduct of the troops in a general order:

"Of their bravery in the field," he said, "he felt assured; but another quality, more trying to the soldier, claims his admiration. After having been for months subjected to the privations necessarily incident to camp life upon this island, these well-disciplined soldiers, although for many hours in full possession of two rebel villages, filled with what to them were most desirable luxuries, abstaining from the least unauthorized interference with private property, and all molestation of peaceable citizens. This behavior is worthy of all praise. It robs war of half its horrors—it teaches our enemies how much they have been misinformed by their designing leaders, as to the character of our soldiers and the intention of our government—it gives them a lesson and an example in humanity and civilized warfare much needed, however little it may be followed. The general commanding commends the action of the men of this expedition to every soldier in this department. Let it be imitated by all in the towns and cities we occupy, a living witness that the United States soldier fights only for the Union, the constitution, and the enforcement of the laws."

Readers will care to know, that the child, the unconscious cause of these proceedings, was restored to her parents. Her father was seeking her at Fort Pickens, under a flag of truce, while Major Strong was conveying her to Biloxi. Her mother, some weeks later, induced the gentleman to call upon General Butler at New Orleans, and thank him for his goodness to their offspring.

April 15th, the welcome word came from Captain Farragut, that all his fleet were over the bar, and reloaded, and that he hoped, the next day, to move up the river to the vicinity of the forts. He had made all possible haste; but the dense, continuous fogs, and the extraordinary lowness of the water had retarded every movement. On the 17th, General Butler was at the mouths of the river with his six thousand troops ready to co-operate. If the fleet had been delayed a few days longer, General Butler would have taken Pensacola, which he learned had been left almost defenseless. The naval commander vetoed the scheme, not anticipating further delay in operating against the forts.

CHAPTER XIII.

REDUCTION OF THE FORTS.

The distance from the mouths of the Mississippi to New Orleans is one hundred and five miles. The two forts are situated at a bend in the river, seventy-five miles below the city, and thirty from the place where the river breaks into the passes or mouths. Fort Jackson, on the western bank, is hidden from the view of the ascending voyager by a strip of dense woods, which extends along the bank to a point eight miles below it; but Fort St. Philip, on the eastern shore, lies plainly in sight, because it is placed in the upper part of the bend, and the ground in front is covered only by a thick growth of reeds. These forts do not look very formidable to the unprofessional eye. They do not stand boldly out of the water, presenting great masses of fine masonry, like those to which we are accustomed in northern seaports. Fort Jackson is but twenty-five feet high, and St. Philip nineteen; and as the ditches and outer works are neatly sodded, the passing traveler sees little more than extensive slopes of green, close-shaven grass, and a low red-brick wall, with many guns mounted on it, and several piercing it.

But these forts, lying low in the bend of a river half a mile wide and running four miles an hour, presented an obstacle to an ascending foe such as, I believe, no fleet had ever been able to overcome. *One* poor fort at that bend, half finished and half manned, had kept a British fleet at bay, in 1815, for nine days; the English vainly using the same thirteen-inch bombs which were to be employed in 1862. General Jackson's "Tom Overton," who commanded Fort St. Philip on that occasion, was uncle of Thomas Overton Moore, governor of Louisiana under Jefferson Davis. It was not till the eighth day that Overton could get one bomb in position capable of throwing a shell among the enemy, but that one sent them flying down the river—two bomb vessels, one brig, one sloop and one schooner. A thousand heavy shells had fallen about the fort, without impairing its defensive power.* But now there were two forts in the bend, constructed by professional engineers, at a cost of a million and a quarter of dollars. Fort Jackson, a five-sided work, of immense strength, mounted seventy-four guns, fourteen of which were under cover; and below it was a supplementary battery mounting six. Fort St. Philip was of inferior strength, mounting forty guns; but it was protected by distance, being a few hundred yards higher up the river, and had a strong battery on each side of it on the river bank. The unmilitary reader does not take the comfort which uncle Toby found in such words as bastion, glacis, scarp, counterscarp, fosse, covered-way, curtain, casemate and barbette. We are informed, however, that the forts had all these things and more. I have often looked out those words in the dictionary, and find the sum total of their meaning to be, that the forts, with their outer works, pointed one hundred and

* Parton's Life of Jackson, ii., 239.

twenty-eight heavy guns upon the river; that fourteen of those guns could be worked under cover, and that the batteries were protected by ditches wide and deep, by walls of immense strength, by bulwarks of earth and sods, and by enfilading howitzers. All had been done for them which the skill of Beauregard and Weitzel could accomplish, working with leisurely deliberation, and aided by the treasury of the United States. What they had left undone, the zeal of the Confederates had supplied during many months of preparation.

They were garrisoned, as it appears, by fifteen hundred men, commanded by General J. K. Duncan, a recreant Pennsylvanian, educated at West Point. The commander of St. Philip was Colonel Higgins, once an officer of the army of the United States. A large proportion of the garrisons were men of northern birth, who had been consigned to the forts because their devotion to the Confederate cause was considered questionable. But experience shows that it is a matter of little consequence by what process men are got together within the brick walls of a fort or the wooden walls of a ship, provided they are ably, justly, and firmly commanded. "An English seventy-four," says Carlyle, "is one of the impossiblest entities. A press-gang knocks men down in the streets of sea-towns, and drags them on board. If the ship were to be stranded, I have heard they would nearly all run ashore and desert." Nevertheless, while the ship remains at sea, they usually do all that the various occasions demand. Duncan had a motley, ill-clad, discontented, and rather turbulent garrison, but they stood manfully to the guns as long as standing to the guns could avail.

The weakness of the forts was the kind of guns with which they were armed. "All of them," says Lieutenant Weitzel, "were the old, smooth-bore guns picked up at the different works around the city, with the exception of about six ten-inch columbiads, and two one hundred pound rifled guns of their own manufacture, a formidable kind of gun." He is of the opinion that if the forts had been provided with a full complement of the best modern artillery, they could not have been reduced or passed by wooden ships.

It was not, however, upon the forts that the enemy wholly relied. Across the river, from a point just below Fort Jackson, a cable was stretched, upon which the enemy had expended prodigious labor. They had first supported it by heavy logs thirty feet long attached to seven large anchors. But this cable caught the floating trees and timber which, in a few weeks, formed a heaped-up, Red-river raft, extending half a mile above the cable. The chain broke at length, and the whole structure, cable, logs, anchor, buoys, and trees, were swept down by the current toward the gulf. A lighter cable was then procured from the stores at Pensacola. Seven or eight schooners, dismasted and filled with logs, were strongly anchored in a row across the river, and the chain was laid across each of them and securely fastened round the capstan. At the end of the cable, on the shore opposite Fort Jackson, a mud battery was built to drive off parties attempting to sever the barrier. Under this cable the floating timber freely passed; and there was an ingenious contrivance near the fort, by which the vessels of the foe were quickly admitted and the aperture quickly closed.

This cable, because of its signal failure as a means of defense, has been too lightly regarded. It might have been a formidable obstacle. Our naval officers think that if it had been placed just above St. Philip, instead of just below Fort Jackson, it could scarcely have been cut; because, in that case, the party attempting it would have had to run the gauntlet of a hundred guns against a rapid current, remain under the fire of most of them during the operation, and then descend two miles under the same fire before reaching the fleet. Placed where it was, however, there was reason to hope that a party could steal silently upon it in the darkness of a foggy night, and work upon it for a considerable time before being discovered; and even if discovered, the night fire of heavy guns might be borne long enough to effect the object; particularly as the supporting hulks would afford cover for the boats. The cable was not ill-planned, but wrongly placed.

Another error appears to have been committed by the enemy, in not cutting away more of the woods below Fort Jackson. They removed enough to enable them to bring their guns to bear upon the channel of the river, but left enough for Captain Porter to string his bomb-schooners behind along the western shore, around the bend, completely out of sight. He had no need to *see* his object, for his bombs were purposely set to throw the shells high into the air and down upon the forts like falling meteors; but their guns were designed to be sighted and aimed at a visible mark. The forts were stationary, and their exact position was known; the schooners were movable, and could only be hit by chance, unless they could be seen.

Besides the forts and the cable, the enemy had a fleet of fourteen or fifteen gun-boats, several of which were iron-clad. No one has thought it worth while to draw up a descriptive catalogue of these vessels, and none of them ventured far below the cable after Captain Farragut had got his fleet into the river. The sudden collapse and total destruction of most of them in the haze and darkness of an April morning, deprived our men of an opportunity of studying their construction. The greater number were probably river steamboats, strengthened and armed. "The celebrated ram Manassas" resembled the Merrimac in appearance, but was not a Merrimac in power or strength. One real Merrimac dashing down headlong among our wooden ships, might have given them some damaging blows—might have driven them out of the river; but the builders of "the celebrated ram Manassas" had not a steam frigate to serve as the basis of their structure, and they knew her too well to trust her among Captain Farragut's steamers. There was also a huge thing called the Louisiana, built upon the hull of a dry dock, propelled by four engines, and armed with sixteen heavy guns. This ponderous engine of war was a main reliance of the enemy, but it was not finished in time to join in the fray. Fire-rafts and long river-scows filled with pine knots had been prepared in considerable numbers for the entertainment of the attacking fleet.

In the swamps, a mile and a half from Fort Jackson, two hundred "sharp-shooters" were stationed, whose chief employment was to scout along the banks of the river and overhear conversation in the fleet. It may have been these men who conveyed to General Duncan the most prompt and accurate information of every movement of our ships, and every scheme of movement. Such information we *know* that he had. The camp of the scouting sharp-shooters was not undisturbed during the operations, and many of them deserted; but, probably, enough remained to catch the talk of the sailors plying their bombs a few yards from the shore.

The confidence of the enemy in their ability to defend the forts against any possible force—against "the navies of the world"—was complete. It was long before General Duncan and Colonel Higgins believed that the fleet would do more than reconnoiter the position, or, perhaps, transfer the blockading station to the head of the passes. This of itself would have been an advantage worth considerable outlay. But their position they firmly believed was impregnable; and, perhaps, it was impregnable. Certain it is that the forts were never taken.

For the reduction of these forts, thus defended and supported, there was then in the Mississippi the most powerful expedition that had ever sailed under the flag of the United States. The strength and composition of the army we have seen; it consisted of fifteen thousand troops, most of them men of New England, fully provided with the means of offensive war, and led by a general endowed by nature with the ability to command, and trained by education to assume responsibilities and invent expedients. The fleet consisted of forty-seven armed vessels, of which eight were large and powerful sloops of war propelled by steam; seventeen were steam gun-boats, most of them new, and all heavily armed; two were sailing vessels, ranking as sloops of war; and twenty-one were mortar schooners, each provided with a bomb capable of throwing a shell weighing two hundred and fifteen pounds to a distance of three miles. The steam sloops carried from nine to twenty-eight guns each; the gun-boats five or six guns each. The whole number of guns and mortars was about three hundred and ten; many of the heaviest caliber, and of the newest construction.

The fleet had been provided with everything which naval men could suggest as likely to increase its efficiency. We have heard a great deal concerning the imaginary somnolence of the heads of the navy department. I suppose this has been because the navy department has been conducted with such consummate energy and tact, and with a wonderful uniformity of triumph. We can not praise enough our generals who have failed, nor censure with too much severity a department which has known little but success. Both in fitting out this expedition and in selecting the men to command it, the department displayed a foresight and ability that proved sufficient in the day of trial. There were only two mishaps: a delay in the arrival of the medical stores, and a scant supply of coal, owing to the month's detention in getting the ships over the bar. But General Butler, through the wise abundance provided by Captain George, was able to lend Captain Farragut a competent supply of surgeons' stores and a thousand tons of coal.

The men in chief command of the fleet had spent their lives in the navy. Of the sixty-three years that Captain Farragut had lived, he had been fifty-two an officer in the navy of the United States. He was a boy midshipman as far back as the war of 1812, not undistinguished then in at least one bloody sea-fight. Though advanced in years, his heart was young, his frame light and active, his face and bearing those of a man of middle age. "He was the youngest man in the fleet," says General Butler; alert in climbing to the mast-head, quick in getting into his boat, capable of long-continued, severe exertion.* A modest, quiet man, doing his duty with the minimum of show and fuss, using simple words, preferring simple topics. Above all, he has a firm, brave, honest heart, that can not be dismayed by phantoms, and knows no fear, except the noble dread, lest in any way, through fault of his, the fleet intrusted to his care should disappoint the reasonable expectations of the country. The language of eulogy is so lavishly employed in these times, that it has acquired an opprobrious quality. But these things are literally true of this valiant and noble Tennessean. The country knows what he has done; but his modest worth, his utter sincerity, his entire and single-eyed devotion to his duty; of these there will be much to tell, when the final record is made up. It is pleasing to notice in the papers relating to the expedition, how perfect was the accord between the commander of the fleet, and the commander of the army. Whatever either could do, during their long connection, to forward the plans, or enhance the glory of the other, was done with generous promptitude and fullness.

The month of delay at the mouth of the river had been well spent. Assistant-engineer Hoyt, of the Richmond, conceived the happy idea of protecting the boiler and engine of his ship by an extemporized armor of chain-cable, hung down from the gun-deck to below the water-line, and fastened by an ingenious system of bolts and cordage. The engineers of the Brooklyn, Pensacola and Iroquois employed the same contrivance, which was supposed to be equivalent to a four-inch plating of iron. The boilers of other vessels were protected by an interior structure of sand-bags, layers

* Tennesseans are young at seventy. Tennessee, that central garden-land of the country, combining the advantages of North and South, and better adapted for all human purposes than any other region on the continent, is singularly favorable to longevity. It abounds in wonderful old men. Have we not seen this very summer, MAJOR WILLIAM B. LEWIS, of Nashville (staunch and true to the Union, of course), walking the streets of New York ten hours a day, and carrying his eighty years with the gayety and ease of a young man?

of cable, bales of bagging, and logs. Howitzers were placed in the tops of all the sloops, protected by plates of boiler iron, or thick screens of cordage. Some of the vessels had small anchors at their yard-arms, to drop down upon the enemy's gun-boats and fire-rafts, and grapple them. Strong nettings of cordage were drawn under the rigging, to prevent the cannon-balls, which might be stopped aloft, from dropping on deck. All the bomb-schooners, and several of the gun-boats and sloops received a coat of mud-colored paint. Last of all, to the masts of the greater number of the bomb-vessels were fastened large branches of trees, which, mingling with the tree-tops of the sheltering forest, would still more completely conceal them from the enemy. A few of these vessels, which were designed to be stationed in full view of Fort St. Philip, were covered with a coating of the reeds which grew on the marshy level in front of the fort. All hands, under the direction of the engineers, labored incessantly to increase the offensive and defensive power of the fleet; and it was to this month's preliminary work that the success of the expedition was chiefly owing. Not one precaution too many was taken; every expedient was justified by its manifest utility in the hour of trial. The absence of the chain-plating from the sides of the flag-ship proved the value of that mode of protection; for, at a critical moment, the want of it nearly lost the ship.

Meanwhile, the gentlemen of the coast-survey, under Mr. F. H. Gerdes, specially detailed by Professor Bache for the purpose, were busy in preparing a chart for the guidance of Captain Porter in stationing his bomb-vessels. This was an indispensable preliminary, since nearly every bomb was expected to be discharged upon a computed aim. The map was completed in five days, but not without difficulty and danger. "Frequently," says Mr. Gerdes, "the members of the party were compelled to mount their instruments on the chimney-tops of dilapidated houses. In other places boats were run under overhanging trees on the shore, in which signal-flags were hoisted, and the angles measured below with sextants. It was very satisfactory, however, that the last measurement determined (leading to the flag-staff on St. Philip) agreed almost identically with the location given by the coast-survey several years ago. It seemed to be a regular occupation of the garrison in the fort, to destroy, during the night-time, the marks and signals which were left daily by the party; and for this reason, Mr. Gerdes caused numbered posts to be set in the river banks, and screened with grass and reeds so that they could not be found by the enemy in the dark. From these marks, which were separately determined, he was enabled to furnish to Captain Porter the distances and bearings from almost any point on the river to the forts, and by the resulting data the commander selected the positions for his mortar-vessels. * * * Twice Captain Porter ordered some of the vessels to change their positions when he found localities that would answer better; the coast-survey party furnished the new data required. From the schooners, which were fastened to the trees on the river-side, none of the works of the enemy were visible, but the exact station of each vessel, and its distance and bearings from the forts, had been ascertained from the chart. The mortars were accordingly charged and pointed, and the fuses regulated. Thus the bombardment was conducted entirely upon theoretical principles, and as such, with its results, presents perhaps a new feature in naval warfare."*

The position of the enemy had been repeatedly reconnoitered. As early as March 28th, Captain Bell, in the gun-boat Kennebec, had run up near enough to inspect the cable, and to discover the out-lying batteries, and to draw a thundering fire from both forts. On the 6th of April, Captain Farragut himself had a peep at them, Captain Bell showing the way. "About noon," says one who accompanied, "we came in sight of the two forts, which could be seen through the glass to be thronged with rebel officers watching our movements. As we came within range, a white puff of smoke floated upward from Fort Jackson, and a hundred-pound rifled shell screeched through the air, striking the water and exploding only about a hundred yards in advance of us. Flag-Officer Farragut and Flag-Captain Bell had meanwhile gone aloft, where they sat in the cross-trees taking observations. There was another white puff of smoke, and another monster shot came screeching toward us. This passed perhaps fifty feet over the heads of the gentlemen aloft, and struck the water two-thirds across the river. 'Back her,' from aloft, and we drift down the river two or three ships' lengths, and only just in time, a third furious shell striking and bursting in the water just at the point we had a moment before

* *Continental Monthly*, May, 1863.

left. A low murmur of applause at this remarkably excellent gunnery is drawn from our men as we steam slowly up again. Another shot falls short, another bursts prematurely (this one from a forty-two-pound smooth-bore), when 'whiz-z-z-z,' with a fearful sound, a hundred pound shell passes low down, between our smoke-stack and mainmast, the wind of its swift passage actually rocking one of the ship's boats hanging on the side."*

A third reconnoissance was more cheering, since it revealed the enemy employed in repairing the cable damaged by the rush of a sudden rise of the river. The sailors of the fleet held the cable in much contempt.

The last day of preparation is usually the busiest. It was the 17th of April. The fleet had all reached the vicinity of the forts on the evening previous, and the dawn of the 17th found the vessels anchored in a tempting huddle four miles below Fort Jackson. The rebels began the fight. As the sun was rising, a flat-boat piled with wood saturated with tar and turpentine, was fired by them and cut adrift. A fresh wind was blowing up the river, and the descent of this magnificent bonfire was slow. Nevertheless, it came, at length, roaring and blazing by, causing a sudden slipping of cables and a general anxiety to get out of the way. As it was supposed to contain something of the torpedo kind, the Mississippi fired a few shells into it, without effect. A boat from the Iroquois soon tackled the monster, and, fixing three grappling-irons in the leeward end, towed it ashore, where it burned itself harmlessly away. The work of preparation then proceeded. The dressing of the masts of the mortar-boats was completed, and they looked as if prepared for a festival instead of a bombardment. In the afternoon, some of the mortars were towed into position and fired a few experimental shells, fragments of which were exhibited the next day at New Orleans. Preparations were made by Captain Porter for the proper reception of fire-rafts, in case the enemy should again employ them. All the boats of the mortar-fleet were ordered to be provided with axes, ropes, and grappling-hooks; and early in the evening, the boats were reviewed, furnishing a pretty spectacle to the rest of the fleet; nay, a pair of spectacles.

"The boats pulled round the Harriet Lane, the flag-ship of Captain Porter, in single line, each officer in charge being questioned

* Correspondence of *New York Herald*, May, 1862.

as he passed, by Commodore Porter, as follows: 'Fire buckets? axes? rope?' A responsive 'Ay, ay, sir,' and the commodore directed—'Pull around the Mississippi and return to your vessels.' The Mississippi being a quarter of a mile ahead, the men gave way sturdily, in order to beat the rival boats. There were not less than one hundred and fifty boats under review, many of them ten-oared, and the whole scene reminded me more of a grand regatta than of anything else.

"An hour after the review, the men had an opportunity to test, in a practical manner, their means for destroying fire-rafts, and they proved to be an admirable success. A turgid column of black smoke, arising from resinous wood, was seen approaching us from the vicinity of the forts. Signal lights were made, the varied colors of which produced a beautiful effect upon the foliage of the river bank, and rendered the darkness intenser by contrast when they disappeared; instantly a hundred boats shot out toward the raft, which now was blazing fiercely and casting a wide zone of light upon the water. Two or three of the gun-boats then got under way and steamed boldly toward the unknown thing of terror. One of them, the Westfield, Captain Renshaw, gallantly opens her steam-valves, and dashes furiously upon it, making sparks fly and timbers crash with the force of her blow. Then a stream of water from her hose plays upon the blazing mass. Now the small boats lay alongside, coming up helter-skelter, and actively employing their men. We see everything distinctly in the broad glare—men, oars, boats, buckets and ropes. The scene looks phantom-like, supernatural; intensely interesting, inextricably confused. But finally the object is nobly accomplished. The raft, yet fiercely burning, is taken out of range of the anchored vessels and towed ashore, where it is slowly consumed. As the boats return they are cheered by the fleet, and the scene changes to one of darkness and repose, broken occasionally by the gruff hail of a seaman when a boat, sent on business from one vessel to another, passes through the fleet."*

The next morning the bombardment began. At daylight, each of the small steamers attached to the mortar-fleet took four of the schooners in tow, and drew them slowly up the river, the bright green foliage waving above their masts. Fourteen of them were

* Correspondence of the *New York Daily Times*, May 8, 1862.

ranged in line, close together, along the western shore, behind the forest; the one in advance being a mile and three-quarters below Fort Jackson. Six were stationed near the eastern bank, in full view of both forts, two miles and three-quarters from St. Philip. The orders were to concentrate the fire upon Fort Jackson, the nearest to both divisions; since if that were reduced, St. Philip must necessarily yield. At nine, before all the mortar-vessels were in position, Fort Jackson began the conflict, the balls plunging into the water a hundred yards too short. The gun-boat Owasco, which had steamed up ahead of the schooners, was the first to reply. In a few minutes, however, the deep thunder of the first bomb struck into the overture, and a huge black ball, two hundred and fifteen pounds of iron and gunpowder, whirled aloft, a mile into the air, with the "roar of ten thousand humming-tops," and curved with majestic slowness down into the swamp near the fort, exploding with a dull, heavy sound. The mortar men were in no haste. For the first half hour, they fired very slowly, while Captain Porter was observing the effect of the fire and giving new directions respecting the elevations, the length of fuse, and the weight of the charge of powder. The calculations were made with such nicety that the changes in the weight of the charge were made by single ounces, when the whole charge was nearly twenty pounds. The enemy, too, fired slowly and badly during the first half-hour. By ten o'clock, however, both sides had ceased to experiment, and had begun to work.

The scene at this time was in the highest degree exciting and picturesque. The rigging of the Union fleet, just below the mortar-vessels, was filled with spectators, from rail to mast-head, who watched with breathless eagerness the rise and descent of every shell, and burst into the heartiest cheers when a good shot was made. Four or five of the gun-boats were moving about in the middle of the river, between the two divisions of mortars, keeping up a vigorous fire upon the nearer batteries. Both forts were firing steadily and well, their shots splashing water over the mortar-vessels on the eastern side, and throwing up the soft soil of the bank high over the masts of those on the western. It is wonderful how many splendid shots may be made at a distant object without one hitting it. The balls fell all around the mortar-boats all day, and only two of them were struck, and they not seriously

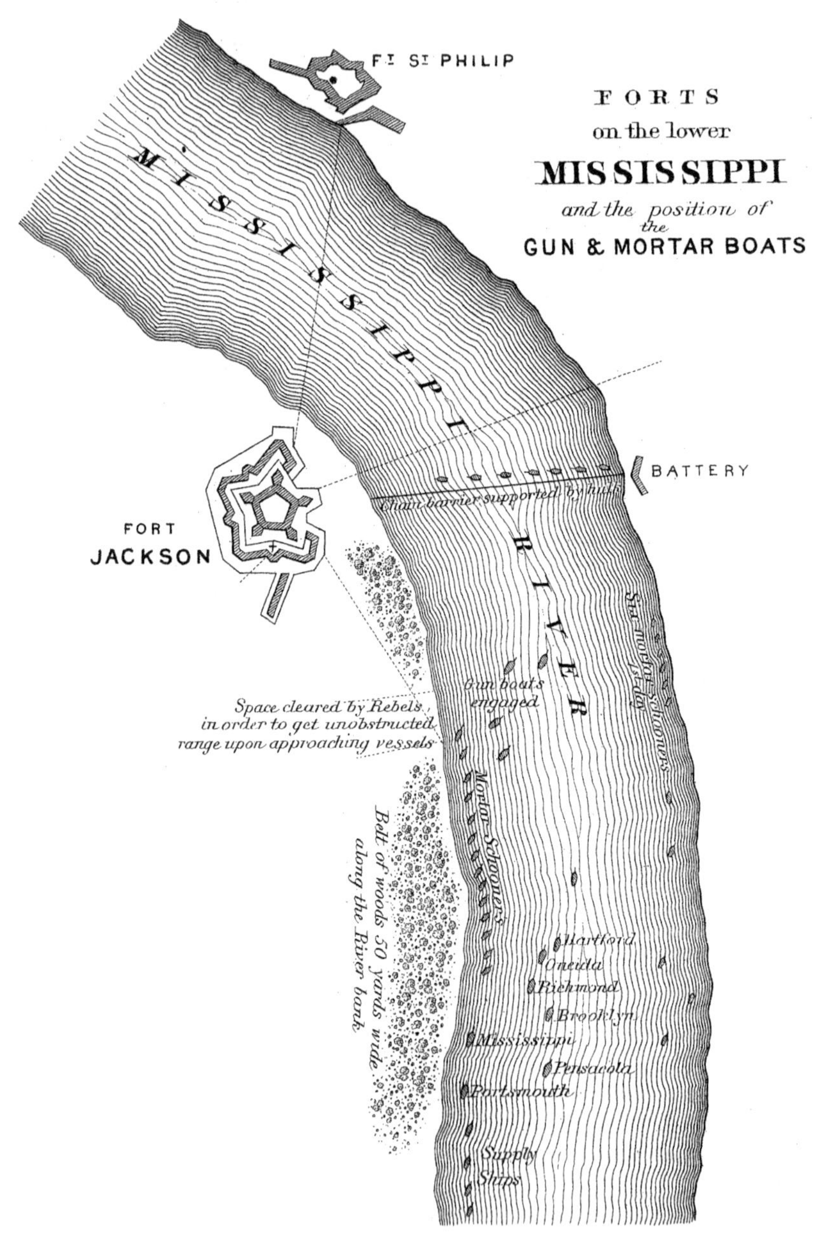
FT ST PHILIP
FORTS
on the lower
MISSISSIPPI
and the position of the
GUN & MORTAR BOATS
MISSISSIPPI
RIVER
BATTERY
Chain barrier supported by
FORT
JACKSON
Six mortar schooners
1st day
Gun boats
engaged
Space cleared by Rebels
in order to get unobstructed
range upon approaching vessels
Mortar Schooners
Belt of woods 50 yards wide
along the River bank
Hartford
Oneida
Richmond
Brooklyn
Mississippi
Pensacola
Portsmouth
Supply
Ships

injured. Not a man was hurt in the mortar-fleet the first day, except those who were sickened by the tremendous concussion which followed every discharge. The men stood on tip-toe and with open mouths to lessen the effect of the stunning sound. But men can get used to anything. They came, at length, to be able to sleep upon the deck of the mortar-boats, while the bombs were going off at the rate or two in a minute. It was exhausting work handling those huge globes of iron; and the men, too tired to go below, would lie down along the forecastle, fall instantly asleep, and never stir till they were called to duty again.

Men can bear what no other creatures can. As the firing grew hotter, the very bees in the woods could not endure it, but came in swarms over the river, and buzzed about the ears of the men in the rigging of the fleet. It was too much even for the fish in the river; large quantities of dead fish floated past, killed by the close thunder of the guns. Those who looked over the side at this new wonder did not see any of those sealed bottles of news go bobbing by, which the Union men in the forts afterward said they had sent down the river.

When the fire had lasted an hour and a half, the scene was enlivened by a new feature. "Over the woods, beyond the forts," says a highly competent witness, "we can count seven or eight moving columns of smoke, which indicate that the rebel steamers are passing about, probably plotting some mischief against us. Soon one, and then another, and afterward a third, appear in view, steering toward the forts. Before reaching them, however, the steamers dash to cover again, and we see that three huge burning rafts have been set adrift. The swift current sweeps them toward us; below they are a brilliant blaze, and rising from the flames is a spiral, funnel-shaped cloud of grayish black smoke, so dense as to shut from sight the fort and all else in that direction. Nearer and nearer these seemingly formidable rafts approach, but they occasion very little anxiety. We know how to dispose of them. The sailors from the large ships are called out of the rigging, which they have been permitted to occupy as interested spectators of the battle, and in a short time boats have the rafts in tow, and they are landed on the river bank to burn away. We all confess to an admiration of these pyrotechnic displays. They add vastly to the picturesqueness of our surroundings, and are perfectly harmless.

The brave fellows on the schooners did not relax their fire during this exciting interlude."*

The day wore on. Noon came and passed. The charm of novelty subsided. At four, General Butler's little steamer, Saxon, arrived, with the news that the general and his troops were below, and ready, and that the Monitor had sunk the Merrimac. Captain Farragut telegraphed the tidings to the fleet. It had a wonderfully inspiriting effect.

An hour later, the fleet was further cheered by witnessing an indication that the fire had not been ineffectual. Flames were seen bursting from Fort Jackson, and the fire of its guns slackened. It soon became evident that the citadel and the wooden barracks within the fort were on fire, as the barracks of Fort Sumter had been when it was defended by Major Anderson. Both forts ceased firing, and all the evening, till two o'clock the next morning, a magnificent conflagration illumined the scene. At half-past six, Captain Porter gave the signal to cease firing, and the night passed in silence. After dark, he withdrew the six schooners from their exposed situation on the eastern shore, and stationed them in the line upon the western side of the river. This appears to have been an excess of caution, for the most effective shots made during the bombardment came from that division, and none of the vessels had been disabled. It is not improbable that the bombardment might have silenced the fort, if that division had been doubled instead of removed. Its transfer to the shelter of the forest on the western shore, was a great relief to the enemy.

The next morning disappointed those who had indulged hopes from the burning of the wooden barracks. Fort Jackson was prompt and vigorous in responding to the fire of the mortars. At half-past eleven, a rifle-ball crushed completely through one of the bomb-schooners, and sunk her in twenty minutes, but harming no man. The Oneida, Captain Lee, was twice hit in the afternoon, as she was steaming about in advance; two gun-carriages were knocked to pieces, and nine men wounded. The fort, too, suffered so much, that its fire sensibly slackened long before the day closed. One shell bursting in the levee had flooded the interior of the fort with water. Another broke into the officers' mess-room while they were at dinner, and the ugly thing lay smoking on the ground between

* *New York Times*, May 8th, 1862.

them and the only door. They sprang away from it into the farthest corner of the apartment, and remained clutched together in awful suspense for half a minute, when the fuse went out without exploding the shell. Often, when a shell sank twenty feet into the miry delta near the walls, and exploding there, threw a whole eruption of black mud into the air, the fort seemed to shake to its foundations, and to threaten the total submersion of the garrison deep in the black bowels of the earth. The men, however, were surprisingly cool after the first day. They discovered that the bombs were terrible chiefly to the nerves and the imagination; they could see them coming and get out of the way; and beyond dismounting a gun now and then, the shells did no essential harm—no harm which impaired the defensive power of the fort. The soft earth of the delta is easily stirred and shaken; but of all known substances it offers to cannon-balls the most completely baffling resistance. The fire of the fort often slackened and occasionally ceased; but it was only to repair damages, which, however serious they may have seemed, were, in reality, not considerable.

General Butler and his staff arrived in the afternoon, and had hospitable welcome on board the flag-ship Hartford. He found that the faith of the naval men in the efficiency of the bombs had ebbed away under the monotony of the ineffectual fire of two days. The cable was looming up, as the ruling topic of conversation. The cable must be cut; how shall we cut the cable? After dark the general and some members of his staff went up the river in a small boat, to take a look at this inconvenient barrier. They satisfied an enlightened curiosity without molestation from the enemy; but on returning were fired upon by one of the mortar-boats, and narrowly escaped being hit. The cable did not strike these Yankees as being an obstacle absolutely insurmountable.

All night, at long intervals, the mortars played upon the fort, each of the three divisions taking the duty in turn. A deserter, a Dan Rice circus performer from Pennsylvania, made his way through the swamps from Fort Jackson to the fleet, lighted and guided by the fire of the mortars, often floundering in mire up to his arm-pits. He could only tell that the fort was well battered by the bombs. He escaped in the confusion caused by the explosion of a shell in alarming proximity to the magazine.

The third day of the bombardment presented no new incident to the outside spectator. The mortar-men were beginning to grumble at the inaction of the statelier vessels of the fleet, and the officers commanding those vessels were arriving at the conclusion, that the work of reducing the fort would, after all, devolve upon them. A council of captains was held in the cabin of the Hartford. The prevailing opinion was, that the mortar experiment should be fully tried, and then the running-by attempted. Captain Farragut issued, in the course of the day, the following order:

"The flag-officer, having heard all the opinions expressed by the different commanders, is of the opinion that whatever is to be done will have to be done quickly, or we will again be reduced to a blockading squadron, without the means of carrying on the bombardment, as we have nearly expended all the shells and fuses and material for making cartridges. He has always entertained the same opinions which are expressed by Commodore Porter—that is, that there are three modes of attack, and the question is, which is the one to be adopted? His own opinion is that a combination of two should be made, viz.: The forts should be run, and when a force is once above the forts to protect the troops, they should be landed at quarantine from the gulf side, by bringing them through the bayou; and then our forces should move up the river, mutually aiding each other, as it can be done to advantage.

"When, in the opinion of the flag-officer, the propitious time has arrived, the signal will be made to weigh and advance to the conflict. If, in his opinion, at the time of arriving at the respective positions of the different divisions of the fleet, we have the advantage, he will make the signal for 'close action,' and abide the result, conquer or to be conquered, drop anchor or keep under weigh as, in his opinion, is best. Unless the signal above mentioned is made, it will be understood that the first order of sailing will be formed after leaving Fort St. Philip, and we will proceed up the river in accordance with the original opinion expressed."

But first, the cable must be cut. It was resolved to attempt it that very evening. Petards had been brought from the north for the purpose of blowing up the hulks which supported it, and Mr. Kroehl, the inventor of the contrivance, was on board the fleet to superintend the operation. The plan was to throw a petard on board one of the hulks, and discharge it by an electric spark sent along a wire from a gun-boat. Captain Bell was detached to conduct the daring and difficult enterprise. Two of the gun-boats, the Pinola and the Itasca, were placed under his command, and they were to be supported by the Iroquois, the Kennebec and the Winona.

The night was fortunately dark; but the current, under the influence of the recent freshet, ran with unwonted velocity, and a gale was blowing down the river. At ten, the Pinola and the Itasca started on their errand, watched as they passed into the darkness beyond the flag-ship, with an interest which no language can describe. The success of the expedition, the fate of New Orleans, was felt to depend upon that night's work. When the two vessels had gone beyond the line of mortar-schooners, Captain Porter opened a fire upon the forts, so heavy, so continuous, that the previous bombardment seemed mere play in comparison with it. At some moments, eight shells were in the air at once, eight globes of fire, curving magnificently over the black outline of the forest. Amid this hurly-burly, the Pinola ran up toward the cable, near the western shore, almost under the guns of the fort, and approached one of the hulks. Mr. Kroehl was ready with his petard, and threw it successfully on board. But as the engine had been stopped at the same moment, the wind and current instantly carried the vessel down the stream, and the coil of wire on deck ran out like the cord of a harpoon when the whale has been struck. Before the operator could discharge the spark, the wire snapped, and the attempt was a failure; the Pinola whirling away down the river at a prodigious rate. Such was the force of the gale and the current, and such the darkness of the night, that it was half an hour before the vessel was again under command with her bow toward the cable.

The Itasca, meanwhile, under Captain Caldwell, had tackled the next schooner, one near the middle of the river. The Itasca had no petard; she trusted to dexterous hands and cold steel. Steaming up close to the hulk, men sprang on board, lashed the gun-boat securely to her side, and then proceeded, in a groping way, to study the arrangement of the cable. A rocket shot into the air. They were discovered. Both forts opened fire; but, protected by the darkness and the smoke, the gallant men of the Itasca worked in perfect security, not a shot coming near enough to discompose them. Half an hour sufficed. The cable was severed with sledge and chisel; the anchors of the hulks were slipped; and instantly, gun-boat and hulk, borne away by wind and tide, swung round to the eastern shore, and grounded in the mud, under the fire of both forts. Luckily the hulk had the inside berth; still, the Itasca was hard and fast by the forefoot. By this time, however, the Pinola was at her post once more, and came to the assistance of her consort. For an hour or more she tugged to get her afloat; parted two five-inch hawsers without moving her; but started her at last with one of eleven inches; when both vessels came down in triumph without a scratch.

The success of the enterprise was complete; for after the removal of the central hulk, the current caused the one on each side of the aperture to swing away, so as to make an opening wide enough to admit several large ships abreast. A boat's crew of the Itasca's men pulled up two nights after into the opening, sounded the channel, and found no obstruction whatever to the ascent of the fleet. Well done, Itasca!

The last cheers died away. The bombardment subsided to its usual nightly average, and the forts were silent. The moon rose. At two o'clock a fire-raft of immense extent came down before the north wind and rushing current, blazing, roaring, cracking, and rolling aloft the densest volumes of smoke. It passed by the mortar-fleet, and whirled past the flag-ship, only fifty feet from her side, scorching the men on deck, grazed the Scioto, and went on its way toward the lower divisions of the fleet. But the mortar-men grappled the monster in time, towed it on shore, and put out the fire. There was little sleep in the fleet that night. The sleepy but indomitable reporter of the *Herald* was obliged to fall back upon the reflection, that, if the expedition was successful, it would be a fine thing to talk about for the rest of his mortal life. Meanwhile, the work was rather wearing to a reporter, dozing within a few yards of a bombarding fleet, and having to tumble up every few minutes to witness spectacles that had ceased to be interesting. Let us gratefully note that the gentlemen of the press, connected with the fleet and the army, served the public with signal fidelity. It is no joke to prepare, during such a week as this, in such circumstances as theirs, a mass of manuscript equivalent to a hundred pages of foolscap, abounding in passages highly pictorial, and the whole executed with an evident desire to tell the truth. Would that these brave and laborious public servants were more justly rewarded.

The fourth day of the bombardment passed without incident. Nearly four thousand shells had been fired, and still the forts replied with no perceptible diminution of vigor. It was a costly business, this bombardment; each shell costing the government not far from fifty dollars. In the evening the enemy appeared to be making some attempts to repair the cable, but the fire of the gun-boats in advance kept them from effecting their purpose. Another fire-raft at night paled its ineffectual fire under the dexterous handling of the mortar-men.

The fifth day dawned—April 22d. Captain Farragut had intended that this should be the last of the bombardment; but it chanced that two of the gun-boats had been so much injured as to require the assistance of all the carpenters in the fleet. He determined, therefore, to wait another day. The morning of the twenty-fourth, between midnight and daylight, if wind and weather were not too perverse, was the designated time. The conduct of the enemy showed, what their officers afterward asserted, that they were aware of this determination before sunrise on the morning of the 23d.

The sixth day, the forts were silent. Not one gun was fired by them from morning till night. The bombardment was languidly continued. Green-horns said Fort Jackson had been evacuated. Others thought the enemy were drawing a new cable across the river above St. Philip. Men at the mast-head of the flag-ship reported twelve steamers above the forts, with steam up, moving about briskly. Occasionally one of these came down to the old cable, as if to reconnoiter, drew the fire of a gun-boat, and away up the river again. No inference could be drawn from the absence of a flag from Fort Jackson, for it had hoisted no flag after the first day. Evidently the rebels were there—were active; but what they were doing could only be guessed.

We now knew that they were collecting their strength for the final struggle, in perfect confidence of victory. The general commanding in New Orleans wrote that day to General Duncan: "Say to your officers and men that their heroic fortitude in enduring one of the most terrific bombardments ever known, and the courage which they have evinced will surely enable them to crush the enemy whenever he dares come from under cover. Their gallant conduct attracts the admiration of all, and will be recorded in history as splendid examples for patriots and soldiers. Anxious but confident families and friends are watching them with firm reliance, based on their gallant exhibition thus far made of indomitable courage and great military skill. The enemy will try your powers of endurance, but we believe with no better success than already experienced."

Duncan reported: "Heavy and continued bombardment all night, and still progressing. No further casualties, except two men slightly wounded. God is certainly protecting us. We are still cheerful, and have an abiding faith in our ultimate success. We are making repairs as best we can. Our barbette guns are still in working order. Most of them have been disabled at times. The health of the troops continues good. Twenty-five thousand thirteen-inch shells have been fired by the enemy, one thousand of which fell in the fort. They must soon exhaust themselves; if not, we can stand as long as they can."

Not twenty-five thousand shells: five thousand. *Not* a thousand inside the fort: only three hundred. The recreant must have purposely exaggerated. He could not but have known better. The whole number of shells thrown was five thousand five hundred and thirty-two; and when Duncan wrote, the grand, final, volcanic eruption of shells had not taken place.

At sunset, on the evening of the 23d, Captain Farragut had completed his arrangements for running by. The fleet was in five divisions. The mortar-boats were to retain the position they had held during the bombardment, and cover the attack with the most rapid fire of which they were capable. The six small steamers attached to the mortar-fleet—the Harriet Lane, Westfield, Owasca, Clifton, Miami and Jackson, the last named towing the Portsmouth—were to engage the water-battery below Fort Jackson, but not attempt to pass the forts. Captain Farragut, with the three largest ships, the Hartford, Richmond and Brooklyn, were to advance upon Fort Jackson. Captain Bailey, second in command, with the Cayuga, Pensacola, Mississippi, Oneida, Varuna, Katahdin, Kineo, and Wissahickon, were to proceed along the eastern bank, and close with Fort St. Philip. Captain Bell, commanding the third division, which consisted of the Scioto, Iroquois, Pinola, Winona, Itasca, and Kennebec, was to advance in the middle of the river, and push on to the attack of the enemy's fleet above the forts. As night drew on, these divisions lay in their proper order, ready for the signal.

The norther had died away. The night was still, and a very light southerly breeze spread a haze over the river. The occasional discharge of the bombs, like minute-guns over the dead, seemed but to deepen the hush and awfulness of the hour. The men went early to their hammocks, and the officers conversed in the low tone of men on the eve of battle. Lieutenant Weitzel continued to impart to them the benefit of his local and professional knowledge. He advised them to run in as close as possible to the forts. The tendency of all men in battle, he said, was to fire too high, and the gunners of the forts had been for a week firing as high as the guns could be elevated. Besides, they would naturally expect the ships to keep at a distance, and would aim for the middle of the river. The ships, too, would certainly fire over those low forts, unless the officers took particular precautions to keep the guns depressed. General Butler, Lieutenant Weitzel, and the rest of the staff, went on board the Saxon, leaving the naval officers to their repose. The general ordered steam to be kept up upon the little steamer, that he might be in instant readiness to join the army at the head of the passes, if the fleet should pass the forts.

Men sleep the night before their execution, but not the night before their trial. There was not much sleeping achieved in the fleet, though the stillness of death pervaded the ships. "For myself," said a reporter, "I could not think of sleep, because of my anxiety for the success of the momentous undertaking which was soon to commence. I passed the slow hours in gazing at the dark outlines of the vessels. A death-like stillness hung over every ship, unrelieved by the faintest glimmer of lamp-light. There were no warm colors in the picture, and its cold, dreary aspect, was suggestive of any but pleasant thoughts."*

At eleven, a signal from the Itasca announced that all was clear at the cable. Note, however, that the hulks, all but the one removed by the Itasca, were still in the river. The opening was

* *Times.*

wide, but, in the darkness of the night, the hulks might prove troublesome, especially as the smoke of the ascending ships' guns would roll over them. It was just the night for smoke to settle down, and, mingling with the fog, hang in an impenetrable mass over the river; for the breeze was of the lightest, and the atmosphere was heavy. In every respect, the night was favorable for an enterprise which darkness alone could render possible. The moon would peep over the horizon at three; but, by the time she had risen above the forest, it was hoped that her light would be welcome.

At one, all hands were called. Hammocks were stowed. The last preparations were made. The low hiss of steam was heard at the boilers. At two o'clock, the signal to weigh anchor ascended to the peak of the flag-ship. "I had the honor," says the *Herald* correspondent, "to hoist the signal with my own hands." He did himself the honor also to run by with the ship—he and the artist of *Harper's Weekly*—gallant fellows both.

Captain Farragut's division, close in to the western bank, was ready to move at half-past two; but Captain Bailey, on the eastern shore, with a more numerous division, was a little slower, and had some distance to go before getting abreast of Captain Farragut. At half-past three, the moon slanting a beam upon the swift river, the night still hazy, the ships began their simultaneous and silent advance. During the first few minutes, the very mortars held their breath. In the distance, away up near the forts, fires could be seen, perhaps to light the ships to their destruction. The fleet advanced against the stream not faster than four miles an hour. The distance from the starting-place to a point above the forts beyond the reach of their guns, was about five miles—two miles to the forts, one mile under their guns, two miles to perfect safety.

The mortars spoke. Everything had been prepared for the rapidest fire possible; and the men surpassed all their previous exertions. Never less than five of those tremendous shells were in the air at the same moment; often seven or eight; sometimes, as many as eleven. The thunder, the roar, the crash, the smoke, the glowing bombs circling over the woods on the western bank—this was the mighty prelude to the opening scene.

The fleet advanced in the appointed three lines, one ship close behind the other. Captain Bailey, on the eastern side, caught the first fire. His Cayuga had just passed through the opening in the cable, when both forts discovered him, and opened upon him with every available gun. The balls flew around the ship; but the firing was much too high, and he was seldom hulled. As yet, the Cayuga was silent, and the rebel gunners, as they afterward said, could see nothing whatever; they averred that they aimed no gun that morning at an object, except when the flash of Union guns gave them a momentary delusive target. Captain Bailey's division steamed on three-quarters of a mile under this fire, without firing a shot in reply, guided on the way by the flashes of St. Philip. Running in, at length, close under the fort, he gave them broadsides of grape and canister as he passed. The Pensacola, the Mississippi, the Varūna and the rest of the division followed close behind, each delivering broadsides of small shot, and keeping steadily on in the wake of the Cayuga. All of the division passed the forts with little material damage, except the sailing Portsmouth, which could only get up near enough to fire one broadside, and then, losing her tow, became unmanageable and drifted away down the river.

The middle division, under Captain Bell, was less fortunate, because it *was* the middle division. Half of Captain Bell's ships, the Scioto, the Iroquois, and the Pinola, went handsomely by, under the most tremendous fire; but the gallant Itasca, when directly opposite St. Philip, received a cataract of shot, one of which pierced her boiler, and she dropped helpless down the river. The Winona recoiled from the same annihilating fire, and retired. The Kennebec was caught in the cable, and when disentangled, lost her way in the stygian blackness of the smoke, and returned to her anchorage unharmed.

Captain Farragut, meanwhile, was having, to use his own language, "a rough time of it." The Hartford advanced to within a mile and a quarter of Fort Jackson before receiving the attentions of the foe—Captain Farragut, in the fore-rigging, peering into the night with his glass—all silent below and aloft. Then the fort opened upon the ship a fire that was better aimed than that which had saluted Captain Bailey. The ship was repeatedly struck. Captain Farragut, anticipating the situation, had taken the precaution to mount two guns upon the forecastle, with which he now replied to the fire of the enemy, still steaming directly for the fort. At the distance of half a mile, says the captain, "we sheered off and gave them such a fire as they never dreamed of in their philosophy." Broadsides of grape and canister drove every man in the fort under cover; but the casemate guns were in full play, and the Hartford was well peppered. The Richmond quickly followed, and deluged the fort with grape and canister. The Brooklyn, the last ship of this division, had the ill luck to be caught by one of the cable hulks, and so lagged behind. How nobly she redeemed herself, let Captain Craven relate:

"I extricated my ship from the rafts, her head was turned up stream, and a few minutes thereafter she was fully butted by the celebrated ram Manassas. She came butting into our starboard gangway, first firing from her trap-door when within about ten feet of the ship, directly toward our smoke-stack—her shot entering about five feet above the water-line, and lodging in the sand-bags which protected our steam-drum. I had discovered this queer-looking gentleman while forcing my way over the barricade lying close in to the bank, and when he made his appearance the second time, I was so close to him that he had not an opportunity to get up his full speed, and his efforts to damage me were completely frustrated, our chain-armor proving a perfect protection to our sides. He soon slid off and disappeared in the darkness.

"A few minutes thereafter, being all this while under a raking fire from Fort Jackson, I was attacked by a large rebel steamer. Our port broadside, at the short distance of only fifty or sixty yards, completely finished him, setting him on fire almost instantaneously.

"Still groping my way in the dark, or under the black cloud of smoke from the fire-raft, I suddenly found myself abreast of St. Philip, and so close that the leadsman in the starboard chains gave the soundings 'thirteen feet, sir.' As we could bring all our guns to bear for a few brief moments, we poured in grape and canister, and I had the satisfaction of completely silencing that work before I left it, my men in the tops witnessing, in the flashes of their bursting shrapnel, the enemy running like sheep for more comfortable quarters."

Quartermaster James Beck, he adds, stood by the wheel seven hours after receiving a severe contusion, and would not leave his post till positively ordered.

Most of the ships had run by, and Captain Farragut, having escaped Fort Jackson, was advancing toward the other fort, when a new enemy appeared—the fleet of rebel gun-boats, lying in order of battle just above St. Philip. Captain Bailey, still leading the advance in the Cayuga, was in the very midst of them before he was aware of their presence; in the midst of them, and so far as he could see, he was alone. It was a moment of anxiety. The rebel steamers ran at him, full tilt; but by skillful steering he contrived to avoid their blows, and pouring eleven-inch solid shot into them, reduced three to surrender before the other ships of his division came up. "The Varuna and Oneida came dashing in," says Captain Bailey, "and soon made a finish of them;" but not until the Varuna had gone down in glory to the bottom of the river, firing as she sank.

"After passing the batteries with the Varuna," says Captain Boggs, "finding my vessel amid a nest of rebel steamers, I started ahead, delivering her fire, both starboard and port, at every one that she passed. The first vessel on her starboard beam that received her fire appeared to be crowded with troops. Her boiler was exploded, and she drifted to the shore. In like manner three other vessels, one of them a gun-boat, were driven ashore in flames, and afterward blew up. * * * The Varuna was attacked by the Morgan, iron-clad about the bow, commanded by Beverly Kennon, an ex-naval officer. This vessel raked us along the port gangway, killing four and wounding nine of the crew, butting the Varuna on the quarter and again on the starboard side. I managed to get three eight-inch shells into her abaft her armor, as also several shot from the after rifled gun, when she dropped out of action partially disabled.

"While still engaged with her, another rebel steamer, iron-clad, with a prow under water, struck us in the port gangway, doing considerable damage. Our shot glanced from her bow. She backed off for another blow, and struck again in the same place, crushing in the side; but, by going ahead fast, the concussion drew her bow around, and I was able with the port guns to give her, while close alongside, five eight-inch shells abaft her armor. This settled her, and drove her ashore in flames.

"Finding the Varuna sinking, I ran her into the bank, let go the anchor, and tied up to the trees.

"During all this time our guns were actively at work crippling the Morgan, which was making feeble efforts to get up steam. The fire was kept up until the water was over the gun-truck, when I turned my attention to getting the wounded and crew out of the vessel. The Oneida, Captain Lee, seeing the condition of the Varuna, had rushed to her assistance, but I waved her on, and the Morgan surrendered to her, the vessel being in flames. I have since learned that over fifty of her crew were killed and wounded, and she was set on fire by her commander, who burnt his wounded with his vessel."

Thus, six of the enemy's fleet fell under the Varuna's fire before she sank, with colors flying, to the river's bed.

While Captain Farragut was still battling with the forts, pouring broadsides into St. Philip, and receiving the fire of both, a huge fire-raft suddenly blazed up before him, revealing the ram Manassas pushing the raft upon the Hartford. In attempting to steer clear of the raft, the Hartford ran upon the bank, when the raft came crashing alongside. "In a moment," says Captain Farragut, "the ship was one blaze all along the port side, half-way up to the main and mizzen tops. But, thanks to the good organization of the fire department by Lieutenant Thornton, the flames were extinguished and at the same time we backed off and got clear of the raft. But all this time we were pouring the shells into the forts, and they into us, and every now and then a rebel steamer would get under our fire and receive our salutation of a broadside. At length the fire slackened, the smoke cleared off, and we saw to our surprise that we were above the forts, and here and there a rebel gun-boat on fire. As we came up with them, trying to make their escape, they were fired into and riddled, so that they ran them on shore; and all who could made their escape to the shore. The Mississippi and the Manassas made a set at each other at full speed, and when they were within forty yards, the ram dodged the Mississippi and ran on shore, when the latter poured her broadside into her, knocked away her smoke-stack, and then sent men on board of her; but she was deserted and riddled, and after a while she drifted down the stream full of water. She was the last of the eleven we destroyed."

In the hurly-burly, Captain Farragut was struck by the wind of a passing shot, as he sat in the fore-rigging. Our friend of the

Herald mentions that a shot, at the same time, knocked his cabin to pieces, shattered his effects, and nearly carried off the toilfully prepared manuscript of the bombardment.

The scene when the fire caught the flag-ship, which was the crowning moment of the battle, is wholly beyond the imagination to conceive; much more beyond the power of words to describe. I shall not attempt the impossible. The mere noise was an experience unique to the oldest officers:—Twenty mortars, a hundred and forty-two guns in the fleet, a hundred and twenty on the forts; the crash of splinters, the explosions of boilers and magazines; the shouts, the cries, the shrieks of scalded and drowning men. Add to this the belching flashes of the guns, the blazing raft, the burning steamboats, the river full of fire. The confined space in which the action was fought is to be also considered; and, confined as it was, each ship was fighting its own battle, ignorant of nearly all that passed beyond its own guns. "The river," says Captain Farragut, "was too narrow for more than two or three vessels to act to advantage, but all were so anxious, that my greatest fear was that we would fire into each other, and Captain Wainwright and myself were hollowing ourselves hoarse at the men not to fire into our ships." The time, too, was wonderfully short. The forts were passed, and the enemy's fleet destroyed in an hour and a half after the ships had left their anchorage.

The Cayuga had been struck forty-two times in the melee, to the great damage of masts and rigging. But Captain Bailey, keeping on up the river, descried, in the gray light of the dawn, a camp upon the shore at the quarantine station, five miles above the forts, the rebel soldiers in full flight. The flight was promptly arrested, and the officers surrendered the position. The fleet came up, ship after ship, each received with cheers, each responding with cheers, as she dropped her anchor in line along the shore. The dead, thirty in number, were buried. The wounded, of whom there were a hundred and nineteen, were duly cared for. Repairs were made, and the rigging was spliced; for Captain Farragut was going on in quest of other batteries that still blocked the way. Captain Boggs, hailed by his generous comrades the hero of the morning, being without a ship, undertook to convey a dispatch round to General Butler in an open boat through a tortuous bayou. Two gun-boats were detailed to remain at the quarantine station and co-operate with the troops in the contemplated landing behind Fort St. Philip. At eleven in the morning, Captain Farragut gave the signal, and the fleet stood up the river—so slight was the damage received in the action. Except the Itasca and the Varuna, no vessel had received sufficient injury to seriously impair her effective force—an escape that was wholly due to the darkness of the night. In daylight no wooden ship could have passed those forts; nor could ironclads, if the forts had mounted such guns as the rebels now have at Charleston.

Of those who witnessed the scenes of this memorable morning, none looked on with an interest so absorbing and profound as General Butler and a group of his staff officers—Major Strong, Major Bell, Lieutenant Weitzel, and Lieutenant Kinsman. They were on board the Saxon, which followed closely in the rear of Captain Bailey's division, until the shells from the forts, splashing in the water before and behind the little vessel, warned the general that he had gone far enough. "We forgot," says Major Bell, "that Porter's twenty mortar-boats were vomiting from beside us a horrid discharge of shell; we forgot that we were within the range of the enemy's and our own guns, and that the shells of both were falling about us—such was the fascination which lured us on behind the advancing ships." The Saxon had eight hundred barrels of powder on board—a fact of which her captain was painfully conscious. He was a happy man when the general gave the word to drop a little astern. From a point just below the reach of the guns, the party on the forecastle of the Saxon saw the fleet vanish into the bend, and heard the tremendous uproar of the fire. "Combine," says Major Bell, "all you have ever heard of thunder, and add to it all you have ever seen of lightning, and you have, perhaps, a conception of the scene." They could not tell what was happening, nor who was winning. Still more puzzled were they when the fleet seemed to have passed the forts, and the cannonade, which had slackened, broke out again with more fury than before. Then the forts were illumined with fire. Is it a burning ship? "No," said Lieutenant Weitzel, "it is too low for that." Portions of the burning raft, steamboats burning and hissing came by, the river at times covered with fire. The vessels that failed to get past drifted down, but could give little information of what had been achieved.

The cannonade subsided at length, and the fiery masses disappeared from the river. It was the time of sunrise, but a pall of smoke hung over land and water. It was darker than midnight. A breeze sprang up, and rolled the smoke from the river. Startling change! In three minutes the sun of a bright April morning shone upon the scene. There lay the forts, with the flag of secession waving from both flag-staffs, hoisted to denote that they were still unsubdued. But, away up the river, beyond the forts, could be seen the top-masts of the fleet, dressed in the stars and stripes! Captain Porter's fleet of steamers were coming rapidly down the river, propelled by a report that the "celebrated ram Manassas" was after them. "And sure enough," says Captain Porter, "there she was, apparently steaming along shore, ready to pounce upon the apparently defenseless mortar-vessels. Two of our steamers and some of the mortar-vessels opened fire on her, but I soon discovered that the Manassas could harm no one again, and I ordered the vessels to save their shot. She was beginning to emit some smoke from her ports or holes, and was discovered to be on fire and sinking. Her pipes were all twisted and riddled with shot, and her hull was also well cut up. She had evidently been used up by the squadron as they passed along. I tried to save her, as a curiosity, by getting a hawser around her and securing her to the bank; but just after doing so she faintly exploded, her only gun went off, and emitting flames through her bow port, like some huge animal, she gave a plunge and disappeared under the water. Next came a steamer on fire, which appeared to be a vessel of war belonging to the rebels; and after her two others, all burning and floating down the stream."

This looked like victory. But was it a victory? The rebel flags waved defiance still; and it soon appeared that three of the enemy's gun-boats had escaped destruction, one of which was the ponderous armed dry-dock, named the Louisiana. True, she was a phantom—a useless, lumbering, unmanageable hulk. But this was not suspected. She was supposed to be a steam battery of sixteen Merrimac power, capable of crushing a poor little row of mortar boats with one graze of her iron-clad sides.

About seven in the morning, Captain Porter sent a gun-boat toward the forts, with a flag of truce, to demand their surrender. Five cannon-balls from one of them (the color of the flag not having been discerned), gave an intimation of the answer that might be expected. The gun-boat retired, followed soon by a rebel officer with apologies, who also brought a reply to the summons: No surrender, the forts will never surrender. The rebel gun-boats hovered about above the cable, drawing renewal of fire from the mortar-vessels. But the Louisiana! Word was brought by a gun-boat, which had given the rebel messenger a friendly tow up the stream, that Fort Jackson was transferring heavy guns to the monster, which, it was thought, would soon be down among the residue of the fleet. Captain Porter ordered the mortar-vessels to weigh anchor and hasten down the stream. Towed by the steamers belonging to them, they abandoned the vicinity of the forts, leaving the enemy to repose, and proceeded to the head of the passes. Two killed, six wounded, one vessel sunk, four or five slightly injured, were the losses the mortar-fleet had sustained during the bombardment.

General Butler, perceiving now that the time had come for the army to play its part, borrowed a light-draft steamer from Captain Porter, and hastened down the river to join his troops.

During the next three days the forts were not molested and fired not a gun. Dismounted guns were replaced, some repairs were made, and the garrisons rested from their labors; their numbers little diminished by the week's fire, the forts as strong in defensive power as when the bombardment began. Captain Porter in his first report remarked: "These forts can hold out still for some time, and I would suggest that the Monitor and Mystic, if they can be spared, be sent here without a moment's delay, to settle the question." There was still a chance then, for General Butler and his impatient troops, who had been lying a week at the passes, hearing, when the wind blew down the river, the distant thunder of the bombardment.

Up anchor, all the transport steamers! The sailing vessels in tow to remain in the river under General Phelps. General Williams to command the troops on board the steamers.

Sable Island, twelve miles in the rear of St. Philip, was the rendezvous. Twenty-four hours were lost by the grounding of the borrowed Miami, an ex-ferry-boat, drawing seven feet and a half. Captain Boggs reached the general with a dispatch from Captain Farragut, having been twenty-six hours in an open boat. "We had a hot time of it," wrote the flag-officer: "but after being on fire and run at by the ram, and attacked by forts and rebel steamers, we succeeded in getting through, taking all their gun-boats and the ram to boot." He added that he should "push on" to New Orleans, leaving the forts to the tender mercies of the general.*

On the 26th of April, the Twenty-sixth Massachusetts under Colonel Jones, the same Colonel Jones that led the Sixth Massachusetts through Baltimore on the 19th of April, 1861, was crowded on board the Miami, with companies of the Fourth Wisconsin and Twenty-first Indiana. Cautiously the little steamer felt her way in those shallows; but when the fort was still six miles distant, she grounded again. The thirty boats were manned and filled with troops. Guided by Lieutenant Weitzel, and by Captain Everett of the Sixth Massachusetts battery, who had been out reconnoitering there during the bombardment, the boats pulled for the swampy shore. The bayous empty into the gulf at that point with such a rush of cross-currents, that, at times, it was all the boats could do to hold their own. Four miles and a half of fierce rowing brought them into Mannel's canal, which, running like a mill-race, forbade farther progress by rowing. Soldiers sprang into the water—a line of soldiers clutching the side of each boat; and floundering thus breast-deep in water and mire, and phantom sharks, drew the boats by main force a mile and a half, to a landing place five miles above St. Philip. By this laborious process two hundred of the troops were landed from the Miami in the course of the day, meeting no

* Captain Boggs brought a characteristic note to Captain Porter also:

"DEAR PORTER: We had a rough time of it, as Boggs will tell you, but, thank God, the number of killed and wounded was very small, considering. This ship had two killed and eight wounded. We destroyed the ram in a single combat between her and the old Mississippi, but the ram backed out when she saw the Mississippi coming at him so rampantly, and he dodged her, and ran on shore, whereupon Smith put two or three broadsides through him, and knocked him all to pieces. The ram pushed a fire-raft on to me, and in trying to avoid it, I ran the ship on shore. He again pushed the fire-raft on me, and got the ship on fire all along one side. I thought it was all up with us, but we put it out, and got off again, proceeding up the river, fighting our way. We have destroyed all but two of the gun-boats, and these will have to surrender with the forts. I intend to follow up my success and push for New Orleans, and then come down and attend to the forts, so you hold them in *statu quo* until I come back. I think if you send a flag of truce, and demand their surrender they will yield, for their intercourse with the city is cut off. We have cut the wires above the quarantine, and are now going ahead. I took three hundred or four hundred prisoners at quarantine. They surrendered, and I paroled them not to take up arms again. I could not stop to take care of them. If the general will come up to the bayou and land a few men, or as many as he pleases, he will find two of our gun-boats there to protect him from gun-boats that are at the forts. I wish to get to the English Turn, where they say they have not placed a battery yet, but have two above, nearer New Orleans. They will not be idle, and neither will I. You supported us most nobly. Very truly yours,

"D. G. FARRAGUT."

opposition. Lieutenant Weitzel stationed part of them on the western bank, part on the eastern. Captain Porter had, meanwhile, placed some of his mortar-schooners in the bay behind Fort Jackson; and thus, on the morning of the 27th, the forts were invested on every side—up the river, down the river, and in the rear.

That night came the thrilling news that Captain Farragut's fleet was at an anchor before New Orleans. General Butler, perceiving the absolute necessity of light-draft steamers for landing his heavy guns and ammunition, desiring also to confer with Captain Farragut, left General Williams to continue the landing of the troops—a work of days—and went up to the city, accompanied by Captain Boggs.

The same night, a picket of Union men on the western bank had a peculiar and joyful experience. A body of rebel troops, two hundred and fifty in number, came out of Fort Jackson, and gave themselves up. They said they had fought as long as fighting was of any use; but, seeing the forts surrounded, they had resolved not to be sacrificed upon a point of honor, and therefore had mutinied, spiked the up-river guns, and broken away. The forts were still defensible, however, and could have given the troops a tough piece of work. But, the next morning, the officers deemed it best to surrender. Captain Porter, who chanced to be present in the river, and had the means of reaching the forts by water, negotiated the surrender, granting conditions more favorable than were necessary. The officers were allowed to retain their side-arms and private property, and both officers and men were released on parole. While the negotiations were proceeding in the cabin of the Harriet Lane, the huge Louisiana was set on fire by her officers, and set adrift down the river. She blew up only just in time not to destroy the Union fleet, toward which she was drifting. The explosion was regarded by the army as a commentatory note of exclamation upon the favorable terms conceded to the garrison. Captain Porter justly placed in close confinement the officers who had done the dastardly act.

The joy, the curiosity with which the troops entered the forts and scanned the result of the long fire upon them, may be imagined. St. Philip, beyond one or two slight abrasures, was absolutely uninjured. Respecting the damage done to Fort Jackson, different opinions have been published. It is important for our instruction in the art of war that the truth upon this point should be known and established. The testimony of Lieutenant Weitzel will settle the question in the mind of every officer of the regular army. In a report to General Butler, dated May 5th, 1862, Lieutenant Weitzel says:

"The navy passed the works, but did not reduce them. Fort St. Philip stands, with one or two slight exceptions, to-day without a scratch. Fort Jackson was subjected to a torrent of thirteen-inch and eleven-inch shells during a hundred and forty-four hours. To an inexperienced eye it seems as if this work were badly cut up. *It is as strong to-day as when the first shell was fired at it.* The rebels did not bomb-proof the citadel; consequently the roof and furring caught fire. This fire, with subsequent shells, ruined the walls so much that I am tearing it down and removing the debris to the outside of the work. Three shot-furnaces and three cisterns were destroyed. At several points the breast-hight walls were knocked down. One angle of the magazine on the north side of the postern was knocked off. Several shells went through the flank casemate arches (which were not covered with earth), and a few through the other casemate arches (where two or more struck in the same place). At several points in the casemates, the thirteen-inch shell would penetrate through the earth over the arches, be stopped by the latter, then explode, and loosen a patch of brick work in the souffoir of the arch about three feet in diameter and three-quarters of a brick deep, at its greatest depth.

"To resist an assault, and even regular approaches, it is as strong to-day as ever it was. I conducted a land force, after the navy had passed up the river by the way of the gulf, through a bayou and canal which were familiar to me, to a point on the river about five miles above the works, and in plain sight of the rebels, but out of range. The garrison of Fort Jackson seeing themselves completely surrounded, became demoralized, three hundred mutinied and deserted in a body, and were taken by a picket which I had posted as soon as I landed on the west bank of the river, from Cyprien's canal to Allen's store. The commanding officer the next day surrendered both works. He had provisions in them for four months, and ammunition in abundance.

"They had about eighty heavy guns mounted, in all, at Fort Jackson, and about forty at Fort St. Philip. All of them were the old guns picked up at the different works around the city, with the exception of about six ten-inch columbiads, and two one-hundred-pounder rifled guns (the latter of their own manufacture and quito a formidable gun). They had done nothing to the lower battery at Fort Jackson in the way of building the breast-heights and laying the platforms. Nearly all the platforms are at the works. They had only six guns in the lower battery at Fort Jackson, only fourteen guns in casemate at the same fort (all smooth bore). They had seventeen guns in the upper battery and eighteen in the lower battery at Fort St. Philip (all the old guns), and only five in the main work.

"The fleet suffered most from the two batteries at Fort St. Philip. They being so low the fleet fired over them, and they in their turn repeatedly hulled the vessels.

"The fire on both sides, as a general thing, was too high. The fleet followed the advice I gave them, to run in right close, and a great many of the officers have already thanked me for my advice. I was with the fleet during the bombardment, giving the flag-officer and others the benefit of my knowledge of the works, and during the engagement was on board the armed transport Saxon, in the bend of the river just opposite Fort Jackson, and had a good view of the engagement.

"In conclusion I beg leave to say, that you have every reason to be proud of the works; and had they had their full armament (the new one), with the proper amount of shell-guns, that fleet would never have passed them. The chain was removed two nights before the attack, without any loss. It was a grand humbug."

If the splendid daring of Captain Farragut and the fleet deprived General Butler of his lieutenant-generalship, it is but just to him and the army to declare, that it was the prompt and unexpected landing of the troops in the rear of St. Philip that caused the mutiny which led to the surrender. Fighting wins the laurel, and justly wins it, for fighting is the true and final test of soldierly merit: but a maneuver which accomplishes results without fighting—that also merits recognition.

CHAPTER XIV.

THE PANIC IN NEW ORLEANS.

NEW ORLEANS did not rush headlong into secession in the Charleston manner. The doctrine, that if Mr. Lincoln was elected the nation must be broken up, was not popular there during the canvass of 1860; it was, on the contrary, scouted by the ablest newspapers, and the influential men. In 1856, the city had given a majority of its votes to Mr. Fillmore; in 1860, Bell and Everett were the favorite candidates. Bell, 5,215; Douglas, 2,996; Breckinridge, 2,646; Lincoln, 0. The fact was manifest to all reflecting men, that the two states which derived from the Union the greatest sum-total of direct pecuniary benefit were Massachusetts and Louisiana.

The great sugar interest, the Creole sugar-planters, who held the best of the cultivated parts of the state, stood by the Union last of all. Thomas J. Durant, an eminent lawyer of New Orleans, one of the half dozen men of position who have never deserted the cause of their country, says, in a letter to General Butler:

"The protection and favor which were enjoyed by these men under the government of the United States, and the benefit they derived from their possession of the home market for their product, to the utter exclusion of all foreign competition, was thoroughly understood by them. They are men retaining all the peculiarities of a French ancestry: not apt in what is called business, yet fond of gain; generous, high-spirited, and averse to the active strife of commerce as well as of politics. They never concerned themselves too eagerly in the contests of party, and no equal body of men in the South looked upon secession with so much reluctance, or were so unwilling to be dragged into it, as the sugar-planters of Louisiana. It is true, they at last yielded to the moral epidemic which overspread the South; and when the young men, under the excitement of martial enthusiasm and a mistaken view of the interests of their section, went to the war, their feelings became, to a certain extent, enlisted on the side of the Confederacy. But no prominent officer in the Confederate army has come from the ranks of the sugar-planters of Louisiana of French descent, and, indeed, only one from the sugar-planters at all—Brigadier-General Richard Taylor, son of the late president of the United States."

The first gun fired in a war, carries conviction to wavering minds. Every man in the world either is a secessionist, or could become one, who holds slaves, or who could hold slaves, with an easy conscience, or who can contemplate the fact with indifference that slaves are held. In this great controversy, the United States has not one hearty and perfectly trustworthy adherent on earth, who is not *now* an abolitionist. Its actual and possible enemies are all who do not detest slavery, whether they be called secessionists, copperheads, or Englishmen.

So the "moral epidemic" spread in New Orleans, and it became nearly unanimous for secession. If the majority for secession was small in the city, it sufficed to make secession master. Union men were banished by law; Union sentiments suppressed by violence. I know not whether the horrid tale of the New England schoolmistress stripped naked in Lafayette Square, and tarred and feathered amid the jeers of the mob, is true or false. I presume it is false; but the fact remains, that neither man nor woman could utter a syllable for the Union in New Orleans in the hearing of the public, and live. A very few persons of pre-eminent standing in the city, like the noble Durant, and a few old men, who could not give up their country and the flag they had fought under in the days of their youth, were tolerated even with ostentation—so firm in the saddle did secession feel itself.

Even the foreign consuls were devoted secessionists; all except Señor Ruiz, the Mexican consul. Reichard, the consul of Prussia, raised a battalion in the city, and led it to Virginia, where he rose to the rank of brigadier-general, having left in New Orleans, as acting-consul, Mr. Kruttsmidt, his partner, who had married a daughter of the rebel secretary of war. The other consuls, connected with secession by ties of business or matrimony, or both, were among the most zealous adherents of the Confederate cause. This is an important fact, when we consider that two-thirds of the business men were of foreign birth, and a vast proportion of the whole population were of French, Spanish, and German descent.

The double blockade—blockade above and blockade below—struck death to the commerce of New Orleans, a city created and sustained by commerce alone. How wonderful was that commerce! The crescent bend of the river upon which the city stands, a waving line seven miles in extent, used to display the commercial activity of the place to striking advantage. Cotton ships, eight or ten deep; a forest of masts, denser than any but a tropical forest; steamboats in bewildering numbers, miles of them, puffing and hissing, arriving, departing, and threatening to depart, with great clangor of bells and scream of whistles; cotton-bales piled high along the levee, as far as the eye could reach; acres and acres covered with hogsheads of sugar; endless flotillas of flat-boats, market-boats, and timber-rafts; gangs of negroes at work upon every part of the levee, with loud chorus and outcry; and a constant crowd of clerks, merchants, sailors, and bandanna-crowned negro women selling coffee, cakes, and fruit. It was a spectacle without parallel on the globe, because the whole scene of the city's industry was presented in one view.

What a change was wrought by the mere announcement of the blockade! The cotton ships disappeared; the steamboats were laid away in convenient bayous, or departed up the river to return no more. The cotton mountains vanished; the sugar acres were cleared. The cheerful song of the negroes was seldom heard, and grass grew on the vacant levee. The commerce of the city was dead; and the forces hitherto expended in peaceful and victorious industry, were wholly given to waging war upon the power which had called that industry into being, defended it against the invader, protected and nourished it for sixty years, guiltless of wrong. The young men enlisted in the army, compelling the reluctant stevedores, impressing with violence the foreign born. At the Exchange, books were opened for the equipment of privateers. For the first six months there was much running of the blockade, one vessel in three escaping, and the profit of the third paying for the two lost. Hollins was busy in getting ready a paltry fleet of armed vessels for the destruction of the blockaders, and there was rare hammering upon rams and iron-clad steamboats. Seventeen hundred families meanwhile were daily supplied at the "free market." Look into one wholesale grocery store through the following advertisement:

"We give notice to our friends generally, that we have been

compelled to discontinue the grocery business, particularly for the reason that we have now no goods for sale, except a little L. F. salt. Persons ordering goods of us must send the cash to fill the order, unless they have money to their credit. Four of our partners and six of our clerks are in the army, and having sold out our stock of goods on credit, we have no money to buy more to be disposed of that way."

A word or two upon the "Thugs" of New Orleans, the party controlling municipal affairs for some years past. New Yorkers are in a position to understand this matter with very little explanation, since the local politics of New Orleans and of New York present the same essential features, the same dire results of the fell principle of universal suffrage. Martin Van Buren predicted it all forty-two years ago, when opposing the admission to the polls of every man out of prison who was twenty-one years of age. He said then, what we now know to be true, that universal suffrage, in large commercial cities, would make those cities a dead weight upon the politics of the states to which they belong; would repel from local politics the men who ought to control them; would consign the cities to the tender mercies of the Dexterous Spoiler,* who could only be dethroned by bloody revolution. Is it not so? Who is master of certain great cities *but* Dexterous Spoiler, supported by the dollars of Head Jew?

It *must* be so under universal suffrage. Here we have, say, ten thousand ignorant voters; ignorant, many of them, of the very language of the country; ignorant, most of them, of the art of reading it. These ten thousand are thirsty men, hangers-on of our six or seven thousand groggeries, the keepers of which are as completely the minions and servants of Dexterous as though they were in his pay. New Yorkers know *why* this is so. Here, then, are sixteen or seventeen thousand votes to begin with, as capital-stock and basis of political business. Add to these five thousand of those lazy, thoughtless men in the carpeted spheres of life, who can *never* be induced to vote at all; some even pluming themselves upon the fact. So there are twenty thousand votes or more, which Dexterous can, in all cases, and in all weathers, count upon with absolute certainty. Then there are sundry other thousands who can only be got to the polls by moving heaven and earth; which is an ex-

* See Mr. Van Buren's argument in Parton's Life of Jackson, iii., 129.

pensive process, involving unlimited Roman candles and endless hirings of the Cooper Institute. The majority of these, in most elections, allow themselves to remain in the scale that weighs down struggling Decency. In a word, our Dexterous Spoiler, by his possession of the ten thousand votes which a justly restricted suffrage would exclude, controls the politics of the city. Probably, the mere exclusion of all voters who can not read would render the politics of cities manageable in the interests of Decency. In the absence of *all* restriction, the Spoiler *must* bear sway.

As in New York, so in New Orleans; only worse. The curse of universal suffrage in New York is mitigated by several circumstances, which have hitherto sufficed to keep anarchy at bay. First, it is still true in New York, that when the issue is distinct and sole between Decency and Spoliation, and there has been the due moving of heaven and earth, the party of Decency can always secure a small majority of the whole number of votes. Secondly, one evening, about fifteen years ago, New York rowdyism fell, weltering in blood, in Astor Place, before the fire of the Seventh regiment. It has known three days of resurrection since, owing to a combination of causes never likely to be again combined. Third, New York has had the supreme happiness of rescuing its police from all control of the Spoiler. The police department has been taken out of politics, and has daily improved ever since, until now there is no better police in the world, and no city where the reign of order is more unbroken—where life and property are more secure. Again: the alliance between the Spoiler and the Banker compels the Spoiler to stop short of attempting the manifestly anarchic. The Spoiler, too, has his moneys and his usances, and values the same.

What New York *would* have been without its small, safe majority on the side of Decency, without the Astor Place riot, and without the timidity of Wall street, *that* New Orleans was, for many years before the rebellion; with all evil tendencies accelerated and aggravated by the presence of slavery. New Orleans was the metropolis of the cotton kingdom, the receptacle of its wealth and of its refuse, the theater of its display and the pool of its abominations.

Now, the peculiarity of the cotton kingdom—that which chiefly distinguishes it from the other kingdoms of the earth, is this: In other kingdoms wickedness is committed, but is admitted to *be* wickedness; it is reprobated and warred upon; it hides itself, and is ashamed. But the cotton kingdom distinctly, and in the hearing of the whole world, adopted wickedness as its portion and specialty. It did not say, Evil be thou our Good; but our Evil is not evil; it is good, beneficent, and even Divine. In the case of Cain versus Abel, the cotton kingdom, with the utmost possible clearness and decision, supported Cain. If the "difficulty" between the brothers had occurred in the rotunda of the St. Charles hotel, Public Opinion would have clapped Cain on the back, and called him a high-spirited, chivalrous young fellow, a worthy son of one of our first families. It was the unwritten law of New Orleans, that if one man said to another man an offensive word, the proper penalty was instant assassination; which was precisely the principle upon which Cain acted. In New Orleans, every man carried about his person the means of executing this law with certainty and dispatch.

Doctor McCormick, of the United States army, medical director at New Orleans during General Butler's administration, familiar with the city in former years, related to me the following anecdote:—

Time—about ten years before secession. Place—the Charity Hospital at New Orleans, in charge of Doctor McCormick. A friend from the North visited the doctor at the hospital, and went the rounds with him one morning. Among the patients were four men wounded in affrays during the previous evening and night; two mortally, whose wounds the doctor dressed. The morning tour completed, the friends were leaving the building, when they met a man coming in who had been just stabbed in the eye, in a street quarrel. The doctor dressed his wound, and again the friends turned to go. Before reaching the front-door, they met a man with four balls in his chest, received in an affray. His wounds were dressed, and the gentlemen then succeeded in making their escape.

"Doctor," exclaimed the visitor, aghast, "is this common?"

"Not to this extent," replied the doctor, "not six a day. But two or three a day is common: that is about the daily average during the season."

"Well," said his friend, "this is no place for me. I meant to stay a week; but I leave New Orleans to-night."

Duels, too. Miss Martineau's "fifteen duels on one Sunday morning" was probably no exaggeration. Doctor McCormick declared, that he has himself witnessed six in one day from a window of the United States barracks. He has seen men in mortal combat while driving along a road near the city with his wife; seen them fighting as he passed; seen the dead body of one of them as he returned.

"What could the fools find to fight about?" asks the incredulous northern reader. Hear a very competent witness:

"Young men meet around the festive board. The wine-cup passes freely." The climate favors drinking; men can drink three times the quantity of wine that a northern head can bear. "Conversation becomes a confusion of unmeaning words. One declares that General Lopez was a patriot and martyr to the cause of freedom and the world, and another that he was an adventurer, and in bowing his neck to the garrote, only paid the penalty of his rashness. One avers that Isabella Catholica, mother to the baby prince of the Asturias, is another Semiramis—worse only—having had Christian baptism. Another, with equal warmth, contends that this same queen-mother, patroness of all the bull-fights, and queen of the Antilles, is a wedded Vestal, more chaste than the icicle which hangs on Diana's temples, purer than Alpine snows. One cries, 'God save Spain's royal mistress;' and another swears that an anointed Amazon, who rides a-straddle through the streets, shall have no vivas from him. A slap in the face! The rising of the sun sees them on the battle-field, arrayed all in white. Under the spreading oaks of Gentilly, they crush the daisies beneath their feet, and brush the dew from the lilies that brightly blossom there. Is there none to whisper peace? None. There is a click of the swift trigger, and a hiss of the leaden death; a spring into the air; a yell, a groan, a gurgling of the purple life-current; and it is done! What now? Chains and a prison for the slayer? Neither; but honor and laudation for him who has had the bravery to kill."*

"Honor and laudation," says our narrator, await the murderer. Even so. Let me relate one of Dr. McCormick's duel anecdotes; he having witnessed the scenes he described, and assisted at them as attending surgeon. The events occurred near New Orleans—the parties well known there, all of them being men of wealth and great note in the cotton kingdom. Time, 1841.

* *New Orleans Delta*, June 3d, 1863.

The principals were Colonel Augustus Alston, a graduate of West Point, and Colonel Lee Reed; planters, both; chief men of their county; politicians, of course. Long-standing, bitter feud between the families, aggravated by political aspirations and disappointments; the whole county sympathizing with one or the other —eagerly, wildly sympathizing. The quarrel relieved the tedium of idleness; served instead of morning paper to the men, supplied the want of new novels to the women. At length, one of the Alston party, on slight pretext, challenged Reed, which challenge Reed refused to accept; no man but Alston for *his* pistol. Another Alstonian challenge, and yet another, he declined. Then Alston himself sent a challenge—Alston, the best shot in a state whose citizens cultivated the deadly art with the zeal of saints toiling after perfection. This challenge Lee instantly accepted. Weapon, the rifle, hair-trigger, ounce ball. Men to stand at twenty paces, back to back; to wheel at the word One; to fire as soon as they pleased after the word; the second to continue counting as far as five; after which, no firing.

Lee was a slow, portly man—a good shot if he could fire in his own way without this preliminary wheeling. He regarded himself as a dead man; he felt that he had no chance whatever of his life on such terms, not one in a thousand. He bought a coffin and a shroud, and arranged all his affairs for immediate death. The day before the duel, his second, a captain in the army, took him out of town and gave him a long drill in the wheel-and-fire exercise. The pupil was inapt—could not get the knack of wheeling. If he wheeled quickly, his aim was bad; if he wheeled slowly, there was no need of his aiming at all, for his antagonist was as ready with heel as with trigger, from old training at West Point. "Lee," said the captain, "you *must* wheel quicker or you've no chance." Stimulated with this remark, Lee wheeled with velocity, and fired with such success as to bring down a neighbor riding along the road.

Lee sent his coffin and shroud to the field. Mrs. Alston accompanied her husband. "I have come," she said, "to see Lee Reed shot."

The men were placed, and the second counted *one*. In swiftly wheeling, the light cape of Alston's coat touched the hair-trigger, and his ball whistled over Reed's head, who stood amazed, with rifle half presented. The word *two*, recalled him to himself; he fired; and Alston fell pierced through the heart. Mrs. Alston flew to her fallen husband, and found the ball which had slain him. In the sight and hearing of all the witnesses of the duel, her dead husband bleeding at her feet, she lifted up the ball, and with loud voice and fierce dramatic gesture, swore that that ball should kill Lee Reed.

Now, observe the conduct of the "chivalry" upon this occasion. Note the Public Opinion of that community. Were they touched by Lee's magnificent courage? Were they moved to gentler thoughts by Alston's just but lamentable end? The Montagues and Capulets were reconciled over dead Juliet and Romeo:

> "O brother Montague, give me thy hand;
> This is my daughter's jointure; for no more
> Can I demand."

Not so, the chivalry of the South. In the afternoon, ten of the Alston party, headed by Willis Alston, brother of the deceased, drew themselves up, rifle in hand, bowie-knife and pistol in belt, before the hotel in which the adherents of Reed were assembled congratulating their chief. They sent in a messenger challenging ten of the Lee party to come forth and fight them in the public square. Much parleying ensued, which ended in the refusal of the Lees to accept the invitation.

A few days after, Lee was seated at the table of the hotel, in the public dining-room, at which also sat men, ladies and children—a large number—Dr. McCormick among them. Willis Alston entered, took his stand opposite Lee, drew a pistol, and shot him through the liver. The wound was not mortal. After some months of confinement, Lee was well again, and went about as usual, the bloody-minded Alston still loose among the people. They met at length in the streets of the town, and Alston shot him again, inflicting this time a mortal wound.

Then, there was a hideous farce of a trial. Every man in the court-room, except two, was armed to the teeth. Those two were the judge, and the principal witness, Doctor McCormick. The jurymen all had a rifle at their side in the jury-box—twelve men, twelve rifles. The prisoner had two enormous horse-pistols protruding from his vest. The spectators were all armed; the Lees to prevent a rescue in case of conviction, the Alstons to protect their man in case of acquittal. The counsel for the accused admitted that their client had shot the deceased, but contended that the wound then inflicted was not the cause of his death. Doctor McCormick was called, and took the stand amid the deepest silence, the prisoner glaring at him like the wild beast he was.

"Is it your belief that the deceased came to his death from the wound inflicted by the prisoner at the bar?"

"I have no belief on the subject," replied the witness. "It is not a matter of belief, but of fact. I *know* he did."

That night, the trial not yet concluded, the prisoner deemed it best to escape from prison. He went to Texas; met on a road there an old enemy, whom he shot dead in his saddle; and on reaching the next town, boasted of his exploit to the murdered man's friends and neighbors. Thirty of them seized him, tied him to a tree, and shot him, all the thirty firing at once, to divide the responsibility among them. And so the brute's career was fitly ended.

Nor can we pity the murdered Reed, brave as he was; for he, too, was a man of blood. They tell of an early duel of his so incredibly savage, that, in comparison with it, General Jackson's little affair with Charles Dickinson seems the play of boys. Picture it. Two men standing sixty feet apart, back to back, each armed with two revolvers and a bowie knife. They are to wheel at the word, approach one another firing, fire as fast as they choose, advance as rapidly as they choose. Pistols failing, then the grapple and the knife. As it was arranged, so it was done. Lee fired his last charge, but his antagonist was still erect. The men were within six feet of one another, when Lee, bleeding fast from several wounds, collected his remaining strength, and threw his pistol, with desperate force in his antagonist's face, and felled him with the blow. Lee staggered forward, and fell upon him. Drawing his knife, he was seen feeling for the heart of his enemy, and having found it, he placed the point of the knife over it and tried to drive it home. He could not. Then holding the knife with one hand he tried to raise himself with the other, so as to fall upon the knife, and kill his adversary by mere gravitation. This amazing spectacle was too much even for the seconds in a southern duel, one of whom seized the man by the feet and drew him off. It was found that his antagonist was dead where he lay; but Lee recovered to figure in another of these savage conflicts, and to die by violence in the streets.

We may ask, with Dr. McCormick's friend, "Were such things common in the 'cotton kingdom?'" The doctor's answer will suffice: "Not to this extent;" but scenes like these were common; and the spirits, the habits, the cast of character, which gave rise to them, were all but universal. What, then, must New Orleans have been, the chief city of that kingdom, with a police subject to the city government, the city government controlled by "Thugs," and the "Thugs" managed by the Spoiler, in alliance with the money-changer?

We return to the morning of April 24th, on which the Union fleet ran past the forts.

Never before were the people of New Orleans so confident of a victorious defense, as when they read in the newspapers of that morning the brief report of General Duncan, touching the twenty-five thousand ineffectual shells. Always the city had implicitly relied on its defenses; but, after six days of vain bombardment, the confidence of the people was such that news from below had ceased to be very interesting, and every one went about his business as though nothing unusual was going on.

At half-past nine in the morning, late risers still dawdling over their coffee and *Delta*, the bell of one of the churches, which had been designated as the alarm bell, struck the concerted signal of alarm—twelve strokes four times repeated. It was the well-known summons for all armed bodies to assemble at their head-quarters. There was a wild rush to the newspaper bulletin-boards.

"IT IS REPORTED THAT TWO OF THE ENEMY'S GUN-BOATS HAVE SUCCEEDED IN PASSING THE FORTS."

This was all that came over the wires before Captain Farragut cut them; but it was enough to give New Orleans a dismal premonition of the coming catastrophe. The troops flew to their respective rendezvous. The city was filled with rumors. The whole population was in the streets all day. The bulletin-boards were besieged, but nothing more could be extracted from them. There were but twenty-eight hundred Confederate troops in the city; and General Lovell, their commander, had gone down to the forts the day before, and was now galloping back along the levee like a man riding a steeple-chase. The militia, however, were numerous; conspicuous among them the European Brigade, composed of French, English and Spanish battalions. A fine regiment of free colored men was on duty also. But, in the absence of the general, and the uncertainty of the intelligence, nothing was done or could be done, but assemble and wait, and increase the general alarm by the spectacle of masses of troops.

The newspapers of the afternoon could add nothing to the intelligence of the morning. But, at half-past two, General Lovell arrived, bringing news that the Union fleet had passed the forts, destroyed the Confederate gun-boats, and was approaching the city. Then the panic set in. Stores were hastily closed, and many were abandoned without closing. People left their houses forgetting to shut the front-door, and ran about the streets without apparent object. There was a fearful beating of drums, and a running together of soldiers. Women were seen bonnetless, with pistol in each hand, crying: "Burn the city. Never mind us. Burn the city." Officers rode about impressing carts and drays to remove the cotton from store-houses to the levee for burning. Four millions of specie were carted from the banks to the railroad stations, and sent out of the city. The consulates were filled with people, bringing their valuables to be stored under the protection of foreign flags. Traitor Twiggs made haste to fly, leaving his swords to the care of a young lady—the swords voted him by Congress and legislature for services in Mexico. Other conspicuous traitors followed his prudent example. The authorities, Confederate and municipal, were at their wit's end. Shall the troops remain and defend the city, or join the army of Beauregard at Corinth? It was concluded to join Beauregard; at least to get out of the city, beyond the guns of the fleet, and so save the city from bombardment. Some thousands of the militia, it appears, left with the twenty-eight hundred Confederate troops, choking the avenues of escape with multitudinous vehicles. Other thousands remained, doffing their uniforms, exchanging garments even with negroes, and returned to their homes. The regiment of free colored men would not leave the city—a fact which was remembered, some months later, to their advantage.

At such a time could the Thugs be inactive? To keep them in check, to save the city from conflagration and plunder, the mayor called upon the European brigade, and placed the city under their charge. They accepted the duty, repressed the tumult, and prevented the destruction of the town, threatened alike by frenzied women and spoliating rowdies.

So passed the afternoon of Thursday, April 24th. I indicate only the leading features of the scene. The reader must imagine the rest, if he can. Only those who have seen a large city suddenly driven mad with apprehension and rage, can form an adequate conception of the confusion, the hurry, the bewilderment, the terror, the fury, that prevailed. Such denunciations of Duncan, of the governor of the state, of the general in command! Such maledictions upon the Yankees! Such a strife between those who wished New Orleans to be another Moscow, and those who pleaded for the homes of fifty thousand women and children! Such a hunting down of the few Union men and women, who dared to display their exultation! Such a threatening of instant lamp-post, or swifter pistol bullet, to any who should so much as look at a Yankee without a scowl! Woe, woe, to the man who should give them the slightest semblance of aid or sympathy! Hail, yellow fever! once the dreaded scourge of New Orleans; more welcome now than the breezes of October after a summer of desolation! Come, Destroyer; come, and blast these hated foes of a sublime southern chivalry! Come, though we also perish!

During the evening of Thursday, before it was known whether the batteries at Chalmette could retard the upward progress of the fleet, the famous burning of cotton and ships began: fifteen thousand bales of cotton on the levee; twelve or fifteen cotton ships, in the river; fifteen or twenty river steamboats; an unfinished ram of great magnitude; the dry-docks; vast heaps of coal; vaster stores of steamboat wood; miles of steamboat wood; ship timber; board-yards; whatever was supposed to be of use to Yankees; all was set on fire, and the heavens were black with smoke. Hogsheads of sugar and barrels of molasses were stove in by hundreds. Parts of the levee ran molasses. Thousands of negroes and poor white people were carrying off the sugar in aprons, pails, and baskets. And, as if this were not enough, the valiant governor of Louisiana fled away up the river in the swiftest steamboat he could find, spreading alarm as he went, and issuing proclamations, calling on the planters to burn every bale of cotton in the state which the ruthless invaders could reach.

"If," said he, "you are resolved to be free; if you are worthy of the heroic blood that has come down to you through hallowed generations; if you have fixed your undimmed eyes upon the brightness that is spread out before you and your children, and are determined to shake away for ever all political association with the venal hordes that now gather like a pestilence about your fair country; now, my fellow-citizens, is the time to strike." He meant strike a *light;* for he continues thus: "One sparkling, living torch of fire, for one hour, in manly action upon each other's plantation, and the eternal seal of southern independence is fired and fixed in the great heart of the world."

This sublime effusion had its effect, supported as it was by the presence of the Union fleet in the sacred river. Hence, as we are officially informed, two hundred and fifty thousand bales of cotton were consumed, during the next few days, in a region already impoverished by the war. Not a pound of this cotton was in danger of seizure; it was safer after the fall of the city than before.

About twelve o'clock, the fleet hove in sight of assembled New Orleans. The seven miles of crescent levee were one living fringe of human beings, who looked upon the coming ships with inexpressible sorrow, shame, and anger. Again the cry arose, burn the city; a cry that might have been obeyed but for the known presence and determination of the European brigade. The people were given over to a strong delusion, the result of two generations of De Bow falsehood and Calhoun heresy. That fleet, if they had but known it, was Deliverance, not Subjugation; it was to end, not begin, the reign of terror and of wrong. The time will come when New Orleans will know this; when the anniversary of this day will be celebrated with thankfulness and joy, and statues of Farragut and Butler will adorn the public places of the city. But before that time comes, what years of wise and heroic labor! The fleet drew near and cast anchor in the stream, the crowd looking on, some in sullen silence, many uttering yells of execration, a few secretly rejoicing, all deeply moved.

CHAPTER XV.

NEW ORLEANS WILL NOT SURRENDER.

CAPTAIN FARRAGUT's fleet emerged from the hurly-burly of the fight on the morning of the 24th, into a beautiful and tranquil scene. Soon after leaving quarantine, the sugar plantations, with their villas girdled with pleasant verandas, and surrounded with trees, each with its village of negro huts near by, appeared on both sides of the river. The canes were a foot high, and of the brightest April green, rendered more vivid by the background of forest a mile from the river. Except that a white flag or rag was hung from many of the houses, and, in some instances, a torn and faded American flag, a relic of better times, there was little to remind the voyagers that they were in an enemy's country. Here and there a white man was seen waving a Union flag; and occasionally a gesture of defiance or contempt was discerned. The negroes who were working in the fields in great numbers—in gangs of fifty, a hundred, two hundred—these alone gave an unmistakable welcome to the ships. They would come running down to the levee in crowds, hoe in hand, and toss their battered old hats into the air, and shout, sing and caper in their wild picturesque fashion. Other gangs, held under stronger control, kept on their work without so much as looking at the passing vessels, unless it might be that one or two of them, watching their chance, would wave a hand or hat, and straight to hoe again.

None of those batteries with which the river was said to be "lined," were discovered. At three o'clock the ships were off Point la Hache, which had been reported to be impassably fortified. No guns were there. On the contrary, on a plantation near by thirty plows were going, and two hundred negroes came to the shore in the highest glee, to greet the ships. "Hurrah for Abraham," cried one. At eight o'clock in the evening, at a point eighteen miles below the city, the fleet came to anchor for the night. The city was not more than half that distance in a straight line, and consequently, the prodigious volumes of smoke from the burning cotton were

12

plainly seen, exciting endless speculation in the minds of officers and crew. Perhaps another Moscow. Who knows? Nothing is too mad for secesh; secession itself being madness.

At midnight, an alarm! Three large fires ahead, concluded to be fire-rafts. Up anchor, all! The vessels cruised cautiously about in the river for an hour or two; Captain Farragut not caring to venture higher in an unexplored river, said to be lined with batteries. The fires proved to be stationary; and when the fleet passed them the next morning, they were discovered to be three large cotton ships burning—their blockade-running ended thus for ever.

At Chalmette, Jackson's old battle-ground, now but three miles below the city, the river really was "lined" with batteries; *i. e.*, there was a battery on each side of the river, each mounting eight or ten old guns. The signal to engage them was made the moment they came in sight. The leading ships were twenty minutes under fire before they could return it; but then a few broadsides of shell and grape drove the unsheltered foe from the works, with the loss of one man in the fleet knocked overboard by the wind of a ball, and our *Herald* friend hit with a splinter, but not harmed. "It was what I call," says Captain Farragut, "one of the little elegancies of the profession—a dash and a victory."

Round the bend at noon, into full view of the vast sweep of the Crescent City. What a scene! Fires along the shore farther than the eye could reach; the river full of burning vessels; the levee lined with madmen, whose yells and defiant gestures showed plainly enough what kind of welcome awaited the new-comers. A faint cheer for the Union, it is said, rose from one part of the levee, answered by a volley of pistol-shots from the by-standers. As the fleet dropped anchor in the stream, a thunder-storm of tropical violence burst over the city, which dissolved large masses of the crowd, and probably reduced, in some degree, the frenzy of those who remained.

The banks, the stores, all places of business were closed in the city. The mayor, by formal proclamation, had now invested the European Brigade, under General Juge, "with the duty of watching over the public tranquillity; patrols of whom should be treated with respect, and obeyed." General Juge and his command saved the city from plunder and anarchy—probably from universal conflagration. Night and day they patrolled the city; and the general, by personal entreaty and public proclamation, induced some of the butchers and grocers to open their shops. A fear of starvation was added to the other horrors of the time; for the country people feared to approach the city, and the markets were alarmingly bare of provisions. And then the Confederate currency—would that be of any value under the rule of the United States? "It is as good now as it ever has been," said the mayor, in one of his half-dozen proclamations, "and there is no reason to reject it;" but "those who hold Confederate currency, and wish to part with it, may have it exchanged for city bills, by applying to the Committee of Public Safety." Another proclamation called upon those who had carried off sugar from the levee to bring it back; another promised a free market and abundant provisions on Monday; another desired the provision dealers to re-open their stores; another urged the people to be calm, and trust the authorities with their welfare and their honor.

At one o'clock, the fleet was anchored. The rain was falling in torrents, but the crowd near the Custom-House was still dense and fierce, the rain having melted away the softer elements. A boat put off from the flag-ship—man-of-war's boat, trim and tidy, crew in fresh tarpaulins and clean shirts, no flag of truce flying. In the stern sat three officers, Captain Bailey, second in command of the fleet, Lieutenant Perkins, his companion in the errand upon which he was sent, and Acting-Master Morton in charge of the boat. Just after the boat put off, a huge thing of a ram Mississippi, pierced for twenty guns, a kind of monster Merrimac, or fortified Noah's Ark, came floating down the river past the fleet, wrapped in flames. At another time the spectacle would have been duly honored by the fleet, but at that moment every eye was upon Captain Bailey's boat, nearing the crowd on the levee.

We all remember the greeting bestowed upon this officer. It was by no means that which a conquered city usually confers upon the conqueror. Deafening cheers for "Jeff. Davis and the South;" thundering groans for "Lincoln and his fleet;" sudden hustling and collaring of two or three men who dared cheer for the "old flag." Captain Bailey and Lieutenant Perkins, however, stepped on shore, and announced their desire to see the mayor of the city. A few respectable persons in the crowd had the courage to offer to conduct them to the City Hall, under whose escort the officers started on their perilous journey, followed and surrounded by a yelling, infuriated multitude, regardless of the pouring rain. "No violence," says a *Delta* reporter, "was offered to the officers, though certain persons who were suspected of favoring their flag and cause were set upon with great fury, and roughly handled. On arriving at the City Hall, it required the intervention of several citizens to prevent violence being offered to the rash embassadors of an execrated dynasty and government."

Mayor Monroe is a gentleman of slight form and short stature; he was not equal to the exceedingly perplexing situation in which he found himself. Supported, however, by the presence of several of the "city fathers," as he styled them, and aided by the talents of Mr. Soulé, he performed his part in the curious interview with tolerable dignity. While the colloquy proceeded, the City Hall was surrounded by an ever growing crowd, whose cheers for Jeff. Davis and groans for "Abe Lincoln" served as loud accompaniment to the mild discord within the building. Captain Bailey and his companion were duly presented to the mayor, and courteous salutations were exchanged between them.

"I have been sent," said the captain, "by Captain Farragut, commanding the United States fleet, to demand the surrender of the city, and the elevation of the flag of the United States over the Custom-House, the Mint, the Post-Office, and the City Hall."

"I am not," replied the mayor, "the military commander of the city. I have no authority to surrender it, and would not do so if I had. There is a military commander now in the city. I will send for him to receive and reply to your demand."

A messenger was accordingly dispatched for General Lovell, who, though he had sent off his troops, remained in the town, a train waiting with steam up to convey him and his staff to camp.

Polite conversation ensued between the officers and the gentlemen in the office of the mayor, with fitful yell accompaniment from the outside crowd. The officers praised with warm sincerity the stout defense made by the forts, and the headlong valor with which the rebel fleet had hurled itself against the Union ships. Captain Bailey regretted the wholesale destruction of property in the city, and said that Captain Farragut deplored it no less than himself. To this the mayor replied, not with the courtesy of his monitor, Mr. Soulé, that the property being their own, the destruction of it did not concern outsiders. Captain Bailey remarked that it looked to him like biting off your nose to spite your face. The mayor intimated that he took a different view of the subject.

Cheers from the mob announced the arrival of General Lovell, who soon entered the office. The officers were presented to him.

"I am General Lovell," said he, "of the army of the Confederate States, commanding this department."

Whereupon he shook hands with the Union officers. Captain Bailey repeated the demand with which he had been charged, adding that he was instructed by Captain Farragut to say, that he had come to protect private property and personal rights, and had no design to interfere with any private rights, and especially not with negro property.

General Lovell replied that he would not surrender the city, nor allow it to be surrendered; that he was overpowered on the water by a superior squadron, but that he intended to fight on land as long as he could muster a soldier; he had marched all of his armed men out of the city; had evacuated it; and if they desired to shell the town, destroying women and children, they could do so. It was to avoid this that he had marched his troops beyond the city limits, but a large number even of the women of the city had begged him to remain and defend the city even against shelling. He did not think he would be justified in doing so. He would therefore retire and leave the city authorities to pursue what course they should think proper.

Captain Bailey said, that nothing was farther from Captain Farragut's thoughts than to shell a defenseless town filled with women and children. On the contrary, he had no hostile intentions toward New Orleans, and regretted extremely the destruction of property that had already occurred.

"It was done by my authority sir," interrupted General Lovell. He might have added that his own cotton was the first to be fired.

It was then concluded that the Union officers should return to the fleet, and the mayor would lay the matter before the common council, and report the result to Captain Farragut. Captain Bailey requested protection during their return to the levee, the crowd being evidently in no mood to allow their peaceful departure. The general detailed two of his officers to accompany them, and went himself to harangue the multitude. Mr. Soulé also addressed the people, counseling moderation and dignity. The naval officers meanwhile were conducted to the rear of the building, where a carriage was procured for them, and they were driven rapidly to their boat. The crew were infinitely relieved by their arrival, for during the long period of their absence, the crowd had assailed them with every epithet of abuse, to which the only possible reply was silence. The officers stepped on board, and were soon alongside of the flag-ship, the parting yell of the mob still ringing in their ears. At the same time General Lovell was making his way to the cars, and was seen in New Orleans no more.

Captain Farragut was a little amused and very much puzzled at the singular position in which he found himself. There was nothing further to be done, however, until he heard from the mayor. All hands were tired out. New Orleans, too, was exhausted with the excitement of the last three days. So, both the fleet and the city enjoyed a night more tranquil than either had known for some time. "The city was as peaceful and quiet as a country hamlet—much quieter than in ordinary times," said the *Picayune* the next morning.

April 26th, Saturday, at half-past six, a boat from shore reached the flag-ship, containing the mayor's secretary and chief of police, bearers of a message from the mayor. The mayor said the common council would meet at ten that morning, the result of whose deliberations should be promptly submitted to Captain Farragut. The captain, not relishing the delay, still less the events of yesterday, sent a letter to the mayor recapitulating those events, and again stating his determination to respect private rights. "I, therefore, demand of you," said the flag-officer, "as its representative, the unqualified surrender of the city, and that the emblem of the sovereignty of the United States be hoisted over the City Hall, Mint and Custom-House, by meridian this day, and all flags and other emblems of sovereignty other than that of the United States be removed from all the public buildings by that hour. I particularly request that you shall exercise your authority to quell disturbances, restore order, and call upon all the good people of New Orleans to return at once to their avocations; and I particularly demand that no person shall be molested in person or property for sentiments of loyalty to their government. I shall speedily and severely punish any person or persons who shall commit such outrages as were witnessed yesterday, of armed men firing upon helpless women and children for giving expression to their pleasure at witnessing the 'old flag.'"

This demand of Captain Farragut, that the enemy should *themselves* hoist the Union flag, gave the mayor, aided by Mr. Soulé, an opportunity to make an advantageous reply.

The common council met in the course of the morning. Besides relating the interview with Captain Bailey, the mayor favored the council with his opinion upon the same. "My own opinion is," said he, "that as a civil magistrate, possessed of no military power, I am incompetent to perform a military act, such as the surrender of the city to a hostile force; that it would be proper to say, in reply to a demand of that character, that we are without military protection, that the troops have withdrawn from the city, that we are consequently incapable of making any resistance, and that, therefore, we can offer no obstruction to the occupation of the Mint, the Custom-House and the Post-Office; that these are the property of the Confederate government; that we have no control over them; and that all acts involving a transfer of property must be performed by the invading force—by the enemy themselves; that we yield to physical force alone, and that we maintain our allegiance to the Confederate government. Beyond this, a due respect for our dignity, our rights, and the flag of our country, does not, I think, permit us to go."

Upon receiving this message, the common council unanimously adopted the following resolutions:

"*Whereas*, the common council of the city of New Orleans, having been advised by the military authorities that the city is indefensible, declare that no resistance will be made to the forces of the United States;

"*Resolved*, That the sentiments expressed in the message of his honor the mayor to the common council, are in perfect accordance with the sentiments entertained by the entire population of this metropolis; and that the mayor be respectfully requested to act in the spirit manifested by the message."

While waiting for the deliberations of the council, Captain Farragut went up the river, seven miles, to Carrollton, where batteries had been erected to defend the city from an attack from above. He found them deserted, the guns spiked, and the gun-carriages burning.

April 27th, Sunday.—An eventful day; to one unhappy man, a fatal day. The early morning brought the mayor's reply to Captain Farragut: "I am no military man, and possess no authority beyond that of executing the municipal laws of the city of New Orleans. It would be presumptuous in me to attempt to lead an army to the field, if I had one at command; and I know still less how to surrender an undefended place, held, as this is, at the mercy of your gunners and your mortars. To surrender such a place were an idle and unmeaning ceremony. The city is yours by the power of brutal force, not by my choice or the consent of its inhabitants. It is for you to determine what will be the fate that awaits us here. As to hoisting any flag not of our own adoption and allegiance, let me say to you that the man lives not in our midst whose hand and heart would not be paralyzed at the mere thought of such an act; nor could I find in my entire constituency so desperate and wretched a renegade as would dare to profane with his hand the sacred emblem of our aspirations." With more of similar purport. The substance of the mayor's meaning seemed to be: "Come on shore and hoist what flags you please. Don't ask *us* to do your flag-raising." A rather good reply—in the substance of it. Slightly impudent, perhaps; but men who are talking from behind a bulwark of fifty thousand women and children, *can* be impudent if they please.

The commander of the fleet refused to confer farther with the mayor; but, with regard to the flag-hoisting, determined to take him at his word. Captain Morris, of the Pensacola, the ship that lay off the Mint, was ordered to send a party ashore, and hoist the flag of the United States upon that edifice. At eight in the morning, the stars and stripes floated over it once more. The officer commanding the party warned the by-standers that the guns of the Pensacola would certainly open fire upon the building if any one should be seen molesting the flag. Without leaving a guard to protect it, he returned to his ship, and the howitzers in the maintop of the Pensacola, loaded with grape, were aimed at the flagstaff, and the guard ordered to fire the moment any one should attempt to haul down the flag. I think it was an error to leave the flag unprotected. A company of marines could have kept the mob at bay; would have prevented the shameful scenes that followed.

At eleven o'clock, the crews of all the ships were assembled on deck for prayers: "to render thanks," as the order ran, "to Almighty God for His great goodness and mercy in permitting us to pass through the events of the last two days with so little loss of life and blood." As the clouds threatened rain, the gunner of the Pensacola, just before taking his place for the ceremony, removed from the guns the "wafers" by which they are discharged. One look-out man was left in the main-top, who held the strings of the howitzers in his hand, and kept a sharp eye upon the flag-staff of the Mint. The solemn service proceeded for twenty minutes, with such emotions on the part of those brave men as may be imagined, not related.

A discharge from the howitzers overhead, startled the crew from their devotions! They rushed to quarters. Every eye sought the flag-staff of the Mint. Four men were seen on the roof of the building, who tore down the flag, hurried away with it, and disappeared. Without orders, by an impulse of the moment, the cords of the guns all along the broadside were snatched at by eager hands. Nothing but the chance removal of the wafers saved the city from a fearful scene of destruction and slaughter. The exasperation of the fleet at this audacious act, was such that, at the moment, an order to shell the town would have seemed a natural and proper one.

New Orleans hailed it with vociferous acclamations. "The names of the party," said the *Picayune* of the next morning, "that distinguished themselves by gallantly tearing down the flag that had been surreptitiously hoisted, we learn, are W. B. Mumford, who cut it loose from the flag-staff amid the shower of grape, Lieutenant N. Holmes, Sergeant Burns and James Reed. They deserve great credit for their patriotic act. New Orleans, in this hour of adversity, by the calm dignity she displays in the presence of the enemy, by the proof she gives of her unflinching determination to sustain to the uttermost the righteous cause for which she has done so much and made such great sacrifices, by her serene endurance undismayed of the evil which afflicts her, and her abiding confidence in the not distant coming of better and brighter days—of speedy deliverance from the enemy's toils—is showing a bright example to her sister cities, and proving herself, in all respects, worthy of the proud position she has achieved. We glory in being a citizen of this great metropolis."

"Calm dignity!" quotha? The four men having secured their prize, trailed it in the mud of the streets amid the yells of the mob; mounted with it upon a furniture car and paraded it about the city with fife and drum; tore it, at last, into shreds, and distributed the pieces among the crowd. Such was the calm dignity of New Orleans. Such the valor of ruffians protected by a rampart of fifty thousand women and children.

Captain Farragut was equally indignant and embarrassed. Seldom has a naval commander found himself in a position so beset with contradictions—defied and insulted by a town that lay at his mercy. A few hours after these events, General Butler arrived to share the exasperation of the fleet and join in the counsels of its chief. He advised the captain to threaten the city with bombardment, and to order away the women and children. Captain Farragut, in part, adopted the measure, and sent a communication to the mayor warning him of the peril which the city incurred by such scenes as those of Sunday morning. He informed him of the danger of drawing from the fleet a destructive fire, by the spontaneous action of the men. "The election is with you," he concluded, "but it becomes my duty to notify you to remove the women and children from the city within forty-eight hours, *if I have rightly understood your determination*." The authorities of the city chose to interpret this note as a formal announcement of a bombardment at the expiration of the specified period. So, at least, they represented it to Captain De Clouet, commanding a French man of war which had just arrived before the city. That officer thought it his duty to demand a longer time for the removal of the women and children. "Sent by my government," he wrote to Captain Farragut, "to protect the persons and property of its citizens, who are here to the number of thirty thousand, I regret to learn at this moment that you have accorded a delay of forty-eight hours for the evacuation of the city by the women and children. I venture to observe to you that this short delay is ridiculous; and, in the name of my government, I oppose it. If it is your resolution to bombard the city, do it; but I wish to state that you will have to account for the barbarous act to the power which I represent. In any event, I demand sixty days for the evacuation."

Captain Farragut and General Butler had visited Captain De Clouet on his arrival, and had received from him polite congratulations upon the success of the expedition. It was no fault of his that Captain Farragut's notification was so egregiously misunderstood.

General Butler meanwhile perceiving that light-draft steamers were not to be had, and that nothing effectual could be done without landing a force in the city, hastened down the river to attempt the reduction of the forts with such means as he could command. Before leaving, however, he had the satisfaction of receiving the spy, engaged at Washington many weeks before, who had escaped in the confusion, and brought full details of the condition of the city. Mr. Summers, too, once recorder of New Orleans, fled on board one of the ships from the violence of a mob in whose hearing he had declared his attachment to the Union. A lady, also, came off, and delivered a paper of intelligence and congratulation.

On his way down the river, General Butler met the glad tidings of the surrender of the forts, and had the pleasure, on the 28th, of walking over them with Captain Porter among the joyful troops. Colonel Jones, of the Twenty-sixth Massachusetts, was appointed to command the garrison, and Lieutenant Weitzel began forthwith to put the forts in repair. All the rest of the troops were ordered up the river with the utmost speed. General Phelps was already at the forts, and the transports from Sable Island were making their way under General Williams to the mouth of the river.

The news of the surrender of the forts, which reached the fleet on Monday, relieved Captain Farragut from embarrassment. He could now afford to wait, if New Orleans could, though the fleet still beheld with impatience the flauntings of the rebel flags. General Duncan, that day, harangued the crowd upon the levee, declaring, "with tears in his eyes," that nothing but the mutiny of part of his command could have induced him to surrender. But for that, he could and would have held out for months. "He cried like a child," says one report. The tone of the authorities appeared to be somewhat lowered by the news. They dared not formally disclaim the exploit of Mumford and his comrades; but Captain Farragut was privately assured that the removal of the flag from the Mint was the unauthorized act of a few individuals. On the 29th, Captain Bell, with a hundred marines, landed on the levee, marched into the city, hauled down the Confederate flag from the Mint and Custom-House, and hoisted in its stead the flag of the United States. Captain Bell locked the Custom-House and took the keys to his ship. These flags remained, though the marines were withdrawn before evening.

The work of the European Brigade was approaching a conclusion. The portion of it called the British Guard, composed of unnaturalized Englishmen—unnatural Englishmen, rather—voted at their armory, a day or two after, to send their weapons, accouterments and uniforms to General Beauregard's army, as a slight token of their affection for the Confederate States. Some of these "neutral" gentlemen had occasion to regret this step before the month of May was ended.

There was a general coming up the river, who had the peculiarity of feeling toward the rebellion that the rebel leaders felt toward the government they had betrayed. He *hated* it. He meant to do his part toward putting it down by the strong hand, not conciliating it by insincere palaver. The reader is requested to bear in mind this peculiarity, for it is the key to the understanding of General Butler's administration. Consider always that his attachment to the Union and the flag was of the same intense and uncompromising nature, as the devotion of South Carolinians to the cause of the Confederacy. His was indeed a nobler devotion, but in mere warmth and entireness, it resembled the zeal of secessionists. He meant well to the people of Louisiana; he did well by them; but it was his immovable resolve that the ruling power in Louisiana henceforth should be the UNITED STATES, which had bought, defended, protected, and enriched it. Think what secessionists would have done in New Orleans, if it had remained true to the Union, and fallen into their hands in the second year of the war. *That* General Butler did; only, with exactest justice, with ideal purity; employing all right methods of conciliation; rigorous only to secure the main object—the absolute, the unquestioned supremacy of the United States.

CHAPTER XVI.

LANDING IN NEW ORLEANS.

THE troops had a joyful trip up the river among the verdant sugar-fields, welcomed, as the fleet had been, by capering negroes. The transport Mississippi, with her old complement of fourteen hundred men, and Mrs. Butler on the quarter-deck, hove in sight of the forts at sunset on the last day of April. The forts were covered all over with blue-coated soldiers, who paused in their investitures to cheer the arriving vessels, and, especially, the Lady who had borne them company in so many perils. It was an animated and glorious scene, illumined by the setting sun; one of those intoxicating moments which repay soldiers for months of fatigue and waiting. The general came on board, and, at midnight, the transport steamers started for the city. At noon on the 1st of May, the Mississippi lay alongside the levee at New Orleans.

A crowd rapidly gathered; but it was by no means as turbulent or noisy as that which had howled at Captain Bailey five days before. There were women among them, many of whom appeared to be nurses carrying children. Mulatto women with baskets of cakes and oranges were also seen. Voices were frequently heard calling for "Picayune Butler," who was requested to "show himself," and "come ashore." The general, who is fond of a joke, requested Major Strong to ascertain if any of the bands could play the lively melody to which the mob had called his attention. Unluckily, none of the bandmasters possessed the music; so the general was obliged to forego his joke, and fall back upon Yankee Doodle and the Star Spangled Banner. Others of the crowd cried: "You'll never see home again." "Yellow Jack will have you before long." "Halloo, epaulets, lend us a picayune." With divers other remarks of a chafing nature, alternating with maledictions.

General Butler waited upon Captain Farragut, and heard a narrative of recent events. The general announced his determination to land forthwith, and Captain Farragut notified the mayor of this resolve; adding that he should hold no farther correspondence with the authorities of New Orleans, but gladly yielded the situation to the commander of the army. Returning to the Mississippi, General Butler directed the immediate disembarkation of the troops,* and the operation began about four o'clock in the afternoon. A company of the Thirty-first Massachusetts landed on the extensive platform raised above the levee for the convenient loading of cotton, and, forming a line, slowly pressed back the crowd, at the point of the bayonet, until space enough was obtained for the regiments to form. When the Thirty-first had all landed, they marched down the cotton platform to the levee, and along the levee to De Lord street, where they halted. The Fourth Wisconsin was then disembarked, after which the procession was formed in the order following:

First, as pioneer and guide, marched Lieutenant Henry Weigel, of Baltimore, aid to the general, who was familiar with the streets of the city, and now rose from a sick bed to claim the fulfillment of General Butler's promise that he, and he only, should guide the troops to the Custom-House.

Next, the drum-corps of the Thirty-first Massachusetts. Behind these, General Butler and his staff on foot, no horses having yet been landed, a file of the Thirty-first marching on each side of them. Then Captain Everett's battery of artillery, with whom marched Captain Kensel, chief of artillery to the expedition. The Thirty-first followed, under Colonel O. P. Gooding. Next, General Williams and his staff, preceded by the fine band of the Fourth Wisconsin, and followed by that regiment under Colonel Paine. The same orders were given as on the march into Baltimore: silence; no notice to be taken of mere words; if a shot were fired from a house, halt, arrest inmates, destroy house; if fired upon from the crowd, arrest the man if possible, but not fire into the crowd

* "HEAD-QUARTERS DEPARTMENT OF THE GULF,
"NEW ORLEANS, *May* 1, 1862.

"GENERAL ORDER NO. 15.

"I. In anticipation of the immediate disembarkation of the troops of this command amid the temptations and inducements of a large city, all plundering of public or private property, by any person or persons, is hereby forbidden, under the severest penalties.

"II. No officer or soldier will absent himself from his station without arms or alone, under any pretext whatever.

"III. The commanders of regiments and companies will be held responsible for the strict execution of these orders, and that the offenders are brought to punishment.

"By command of MAJOR-GENERAL BUTLER.

"GEO. C. STRONG, *A. A. General.*"

unless absolutely necessary for self-defense, and then not without orders.

At five the procession moved, to the music of the Star Spangled Banner. The crowd surged along the pavements on each side of the troops, struggling chiefly to get a sight of the general; crying out: "Where is the d—d rascal?" "There he goes, G—d d—n him!" "I see the d—d old villain!" To which were added such outcries, as "Shiloh," "Bull Run," "Hurrah for Beauregard;" "Go home, you d—d Yankees." From some windows, a mild hiss was bestowed upon the troops, who marched steadily on, looking neither to the right hand nor to the left. The general, not having a musical ear, was observed to be chiefly anxious upon the point of keeping step to the music—a feat that had never become easy to him, often as he had attempted it in the streets of Lowell. And so they marched; along the levee to Poydras street; Poydras street to St. Charles street; past the famous hotel, closed and deserted now, though alive with five hundred inmates three days before; along St. Charles street to Canal street and the Custom-House—that vast, unfinished, roofless structure, upon which the United States had expended so many millions, one Beauregard being engineer.

The troops surrounded the edifice; Captain Kensel posted his artillery, so as to command the adjacent streets; and the general ordered the Thirty-first to enter and occupy the building. But Captain Bell had locked the door and put the key into his pocket. The door was forced, therefore, and by six o'clock, the Thirty-first was lodged in the second story, making preparations for the evening meal. Strong guards were posted at all needful points. The general and his staff then returned to the levee, and went on board the Mississippi for the night. The Twelfth Connecticut, Colonel Deming, bivouacked upon the levee near the ship, happy to lie down once more under the stars, after being so long huddled in a transport ship. The evening was warm and serene, and the city was again as still as a country hamlet. General Phelps came on shore at twilight, and walked about the city unattended and unmolested. Nay, he reported that the people whom he had spoken to, answered his inquiries with politeness, despite his uniform. "You didn't mention your name; did you, General?" asked an officer. "No," replied he, laughing; "no one asked it."

That evening, General Butler having put the finishing touches to his proclamation, sent two officers of his staff to the office of the *True Delta*, to get it printed as a hand-bill. He forbore to demand its insertion in the paper, unwilling to bring upon any one establishment the odium that its insertion could not but excite. In all ways, he was for trying the *suaviter in modo*, before resorting to the *fortiter in re*. The officers reached the office at ten, after the proprietor and editors had gone home. The foreman in charge replied, that in the absence of the proprietor, the document could not be printed. The officers returned to the ship, reported, and received farther orders. At eight the next morning, the same officers were again at the office of the *True Delta*, where they found the chief proprietor, and repeated their request.

No; the *True Delta* office could not think of printing General Butler's proclamation.

The officers quietly intimated that, in that case, they would be under the painful necessity of seizing the office, and using the materials therein for the purpose of printing it. The proprietor objected. He said that the selection of his establishment for the printing of such a manuscript, was invidious and unjust; it looked as if the design was to make him and his colleagues obnoxious and loathsome to their fellow-citizens. "I can not resist," said he, "the seizure of the office, but, under no circumstances, shall it be used for the purpose designated, with my approval or consent."

The officers bowed and retired. After two hours' absence, they returned with a file of soldiers, armed and equipped, who drew up before the building. Half a dozen of them entered the printing-office, where they laid aside their weapons of war, and took up the peaceful implements of their trade. The proclamation was soon in type, and a few copies printed; enough for the general's immediate purpose. The proprietor himself testified, in the paper of the next day, that the troops effected their purpose and retired, "without offering any offense in language or behavior, or manifesting the least desire to interfere with the regular business of the office, or to injure or derange its property." It would have been better if he could have refrained from other comment. But he did not. He added: "As this first step of the commander of the federal troops in possession of this city is indicative of a determination, on his part, to subject us to a supervision utterly subversive of the character of fearless patriotism which the *True Delta* has ever maintained, we will promise this much, and we will perform it, namely, to suspend our publication, even if our last crust be sacrificed by the act, rather than molt one feather of that independence which, in presence of every discouragement and danger, we have ever made our honest boast. We have no favors to ask; we have never asked or desired any from any party; and we are prepared to stand or fall with the fortunes of our adopted Louisiana."

General Butler ordered the suspension of the *True Delta* until farther orders. The proprietors, however, yielded to the inevitable, promised compliance with the general's requisitions, and obtained, on the next day, permission to resume the publication of the paper. It was not, however, till the 6th of May, that the proclamation appeared in its columns. The other newspapers took the hint, and exhibited, in their comments upon passing events, a blending of the politic with the audacious that was ingenious and amusing, but not always ingenious enough, as General Butler occasionally reminded them. Editing a secession newspaper in New Orleans during the next eight months, was an affair which could be described as "ticklish;" rather more so, than conducting a journal in the New Orleans interest, under the nose of Louis Bonaparte.

The second day of the occupation of the city was crowded with events of the highest interest.

The landing of the troops was resumed with the dawn. Colonel Deming encamped his fine regiment in Lafayette Square in front of the City Hall. Other regiments were posted in convenient localities. Troops were landed in Algiers on the opposite bank of the river, and the railroad terminating there was seized, with its cars and buildings. General Phelps went up the river several miles in the Saxon to reconnoiter, and select a site for a camp above the city. Captain Everett was busy extracting the spikes from the cannon lying about the Custom-House, and preparing to mount some of them in it and upon it. He cast an inquiring and interested eye upon the eight hundred bells—church bells, school bells, plantation bells, hand bells, cow bells—which had been sent to New Orleans upon General Beauregard's requisition; some of which now call the children of New England to school; others, factory girls to their labor; others, rural congregations to church; for they were all sold at auction, sent to the North, and distributed over the country.

The quartermaster to the expedition had a world of trouble with the draymen of the city, whom he needed for transporting the tents and baggage. Not one of them dared, not many of them wished, to serve him. He was obliged to compel their assistance at the point of the pistol. Everything seized for the use of the troops, on this day and on all days, was either paid for when taken, or a receipt given therefor which was equivalent to gold. The behavior of the troops was *faultless*. No resident of New Orleans was harmed or insulted. None complained of harm or insult. A stranger would have supposed, from the quiet demeanor of the troops and the arrogant air of the people, that the soldiers were prisoners in an enemy's town, not conquerors in a captured one. For the most part, the troops held no intercourse whatever with the inhabitants. It was, indeed, perilous in the extreme, for a resident of the city to speak to an old friend, if that friend wore the uniform of the United States. Major Bell mentions that he met several old acquaintances about the city, but they either gave him the cut direct, or else bestowed a hurried, furtive salutation, and passed rapidly on. Another officer reports that on accosting an acquaintance, the gentleman said, in an anxious undertone, "Don't speak to me, or I shall have my head blown off."

A gentleman connected with the expedition, but not in uniform,* tells me that he strolled into a market that morning, and bought a cup of coffee, for which he gave a gold dollar, and received in change nineteen dirty car-tickets, part of the established currency of the city.

Quarters were required for the commanding general and his staff. What could they be but the St. Charles hotel, vacated five days before by General Lovell? Major Strong, Colonel French, and Major Bell, accompanied by Mr. Glenn, formerly a resident of New Orleans, were dispatched, early in the morning, to make the preliminary arrangements. They found the building closed. Going round to the ladies' entrance they gained admission to the famous rotunda—bar-room and slavemart, scene of countless "difficulties" and chivalric assassinations. There they met a son of one of the proprietors, to whom they stated their wishes. He replied, that both the proprietors were absent; and as to his giving up the hotel to General Butler, his head would be shot off before he could reach the next corner if he should do it. He declared that waiters would

* Mr. Samuel F. Glenn, afterward clerk of the provost-court.

not dare to wait upon them, nor cooks to cook for them, nor porters to carry for them. Moreover, there were no provisions to be had in the market; he did not see what could be got for them beyond army rations. These objections were offered by the young gentleman with the utmost politeness of manner. Major Strong observed, with equal suavity, that he need give himself no concern with regard to giving up the hotel. In the name of General Butler, they would venture to *take* it. And as to the lack of provisions, they were used to army rations, had found them sufficient, and could make them do for an indefinite period. With regard to waiters and cooks, the army of occupation were chiefly men of the Yankee persuasion, who were accustomed to wait on themselves, and could do a little of everything, from cooking upward. The young gentleman had nothing farthèr to offer, and so the St. Charles became the head-quarters of the army. The general arrived in the course of the morning, and established his office in one of the ladies' parlors. Mrs. Butler still remained on board the Mississippi.

The three officers and Mr. Glenn next proceeded to the City Hall, in search of the mayor. They found that public functionary, after some delay. They informed him, with all possible courtesy, that General Butler, commanding the department of the Gulf, had established his head-quarters at the St. Charles hotel, where he would be happy to confer with the mayor and council of New Orleans, at two o'clock on that day. The reply of the mayor was to the effect, that his place of business was at the City Hall, where any gentleman who had business with him could see him during office hours. Colonel French politely intimated that that was not an answer likely to satisfy the commanding general, and expressed a hope that the mayor, on reflection, would not complicate a state of affairs, already embarrassing enough, by raising questions of etiquette. General Butler was well disposed toward New Orleans and its authorities; he merely desired to come to a clear understanding with them as to the future government of the city. The officers retired. The mayor, upon reflection, concluded to wait upon the general. At two o'clock, accompanied by Mr. Soulé and a considerable party of friends, highly respectable gentlemen of the city, he sat face to face with General Butler in the ladies' parlor of the St. Charles.

The interview was destined to be interrupted and abortive. The seizure of the St. Charles hotel appeared to have rekindled the passions of the populace, who surrounded the building in a dense mass, filling all the open space adjacent. A cannon was posted at each of the corners of the building; a regiment surrounded it; and the brave General Williams was in command. But it seemed as if the quiet demeanor of the troops, since the landing of the evening before, had been misinterpreted by the mob, who grew fiercer, louder and bolder, as the day wore on. The mayor and his party had not been long in the presence of General Butler, when an aide-de-camp rushed in and said:

"General Williams orders me to say, that he fears he will not be able to control the mob."

General Butler, in his serenest manner, replied:

"Give my compliments to General Williams, and tell him, if he finds he can not control the mob, to open upon them with artillery."

The mayor and his friends sprang to their feet in consternation.

"Don't do that, general!" exclaimed the mayor.

"Why not, gentlemen?" said the general. "The mob must be controlled. We can't have a disturbance in the street."

"Shall I go out and speak to the people?" asked the mayor.

"Anything you please, gentlemen," replied General Butler. "I only insist that order be maintained in the public streets."

The mayor and other gentlemen addressed the crowd; and, as their remarks were enforced by the rumor of General Butler's order, there was a temporary lull in the storm. The crowd remained, however; vast, fierce and sullen.

The interview having been resumed, the mayor was proceeding to descant, in the high-flown rhetoric of the South, upon General Butler's former advocacy of the rights of the southern states. The South had looked upon him as its special friend and champion, etc.

"Stop, sir," said the general. "Let me set you right on that point at once. I was always a friend of southern rights, but an enemy of southern wrongs."

The conversation was going on in an amicable strain, when another aid entered the apartment, Lieutenant Kinsman, of General Butler's staff, who requested a word with the general.

This officer had been sent to the fleet that morning in search of telegraphic operators. On board the Mississippi (the man-of-war, not the transport steamer), he was accosted by Judge Summers, who had sought refuge on board the ship, as we have before related. The unhappy judge, who was anxious to get to the city, requested Lieutenant Kinsman to take him on shore, and give him adequate protection against the mob, who, he said, would tear him limb from limb, if they should catch him alone. The lieutenant, who had left the city perfectly quiet, was disposed to make light of the danger; but said he could go on shore with him if he chose, and he would endeavor to get him safe to the St. Charles. On reaching the levee, Lieutenant Kinsman impressed a hack into his service, and the two passengers were started for the hotel. Unluckily, the ex-recorder is a man of gigantic stature—six feet five, and of corresponding magnitude; a man of such pronounced peculiarity of appearance, that even if he had never sat on the bench and thus become familiar to the eyes of scoundrels, he must have been known by sight to all who frequented the streets of the city. He was instantly recognized. A crowd gathered round the carriage, hooting, yelling, cursing; new hundreds rushing in from every street; for all the men in the city were idle and abroad. Several times the carriage came to a stand; but Lieutenant Kinsman, pistol in hand, ordered the driver to go on, and kept him to his work, until they reached the troops guarding the hotel, where both succeeded in alighting and entering the building unharmed.

Judge Summers was thoroughly unnerved, as most men would have been in the same circumstances. A mob is of all wild beasts the most cowardly, the most easily managed by a man that is unscarable by phantoms. The mob that attacked the *Tribune* office, last July, was scattered by the *report* of one pistol. I saw it done. Never have I seen the square in front of the building so bare of people as it was in ten seconds after that solitary pistol was fired. But a mob is, at the same time, the most terrific thing to look at, especially if its vulgar and savage eye is fixed upon *you*, that can be imagined. Mr. Summers felt unsafe, even in the hotel. "Give me some protection," said he; "they'll tear me all to pieces if they get in here;" and it looked, at the time, as if the mob would get in.

Hence it was, that Lieutenant Kinsman interrupted the general, and asked a word with him.

General Butler came out, and heard the lieutenant's report.

The ex-recorder said there was no place in the St. Charles where he could be safe.

"Well, then," said the general, "there's the Custom-House over yonder; that will hold you. You can go there, if you choose."

"But how can I get there? The mob will tear me to pieces."

The general reflected a moment. Then said, assuming all the "major-general commanding:"

"We may as well settle this question now as at any other time. Lieutenant Kinsman, take this man over to the Custom-House. Take what force you require. If any one molests or threatens you, arrest him. If a rescue is attempted, fire."

Having said this, he returned to the conference with the mayor, and Lieutenant Kinsman proceeded to obey the order. He conducted Mr. Summers to a side door, which he opened, and disclosed to the view of his charge a compact mass of infuriated men, held at bay by a company of fifty soldiers.

"Don't attempt it," said the judge, recoiling from the sight.

"I must," returned the lieutenant. "The general's orders were positive. I have no choice but to obey."

The company of soldiers were soon drawn up in two lines, four feet apart, two men closing the front and two the rear of the column. In the open space were Lieutenant Kinsman and Mr. Summers.

"Forward, march!" The column started. The crowd recognizing the giant judge, yelled and boiled around the slowly pushing column. The active men of the mob were not those within reach of the soldiers. The nearest men prudently held their peace and watched their chance. Consequently, no arrests were made until the column had gone half way to the Custom-House. At that point stood an omnibus with one man in it, who was urging on the mob, by voice and gesture, with the violence of frenzy.

"Halt! Bring out that man!"

Two soldiers sprang into the omnibus, collared the lunatic, drew him out, and placed him between the lines, where he continued to yell and gesticulate in the most frantic manner.

"Stop your noise!" thundered the lieutenant.

"I won't," said the man; "my tongue is my own."

"Sergeant ———, lower your bayonet. If a sound comes out of that man's mouth, run him through!"

The man was silent.

"Forward—march!" The column pushed on again, but very slowly. After going some distance, the lieutenant perceived that one man, who had been particularly vociferous, was within clutching distance.

"Halt—bring in that man," pointing him out.

The man was seized and placed in the column. He continued to shout, but a lowered bayonet brought him to his senses also. The column pushed on again, and lodged the judge and the two prisoners safely in the impregnable Custom-House, the citadel of New Orleans. The company marched back, in the same order, through a crowd "as silent as a funeral," to use the lieutenant's own language.

This scene was witnessed from the windows of the St. Charles by General Butler and his staff, and by the mayor and his friends, the conference being suspended by common consent. The general informs me, that the firmness of Lieutenant Kinsman on this occasion, aided by the soldierly steadiness of the troops, and the perfect coolness of their officers, contributed most essentially to the subjugation of the mob of New Orleans. It was never so rampant again. The company was Captain Paige's of the Thirty-first Massachusetts.

The reader perceives how it fared with the conference. The afternoon wore away amid these interruptions, and it was finally agreed to postpone farther conversation till the evening, when all matters in dispute should be thoroughly discussed. By that time too, copies of the Proclamation would be ready from the *True Delta* office. So the mayor and his friends departed.

In the dusk of the evening, a carriage having been with difficulty procured, General Butler, with a single orderly on the box, drove to the levee, a distance of three-quarters of a mile, and went on board the transport Mississippi. Mrs. Butler and her maid had passed an anxious day there, ignorant of what was passing in the city. "Get ready to go on shore," said the general. The trunks were locked and strapped, and transferred to the carriage. Mrs. Butler and her attendant took their places, the general followed them, and the party was driven to the hotel without molestation or outcry.

There was a curious tea-party that evening in the vast dining-room of the St. Charles, where hundreds of people had been wont to consume luxurious fare. At one end of one of the tables sat the little company, lost in the magnitude of the room—the general, Mrs. Butler, and two or three members of the staff. The fare was neither sumptuous nor abundant, and the solitary waiter was not at his ease, for he was doing an act that was death by the mob law of New Orleans. The general entertained the company by reading choice extracts from the anonymous letters which he had received in the course of the day. "We'll get the better of you yet, old cock-eye," remarked one of his nameless correspondents. Another requested him to wait a month or two, and see what Yellow Jack would do for him. Another warned him to look out for poison in his food. Both the General and Mrs. Butler received many epistles of this nature during the first few weeks, as well as some of a highly eulogistic tenor. Occasionally the general would reply to one of the abusive letters in the manner following:

"Madame: I have received the letter in which you remark upon my conduct in New Orleans, which I regret does not meet your approbation. It may interest you to know that others view it in a very different light, and I, therefore, beg to inclose for your perusal a letter received this day, in which my administration is commented upon in a strain different from that in which you have done me the honor to review it. I am, madame," etc.

As the frugal repast in the St. Charles was drawing to a close, a band on the balcony in front of the building, in full view of the crowd, struck up the Star Spangled Banner, filling the void immensity of the dining-room with a deafening noise. The band continued to play during the evening, the crowd standing silent and sullen.

Our business, however, lies this evening in the ladies' parlor. It is a spacious, lofty and elegant apartment. On one side, in a large semi-circle, sat the representatives of New Orleans, the mayor, the common council, other magnates, and Mr. Pierre Soulé, spokesman and orator of the occasion. Mr. Soulé had long been the special favorite of the Creole population; popular, also, with all his fellow-citizens; a kind of pet, or ladies' delight among them; renowned, too, at the bar. New Yorkers may call him, if they please, the James T. Brady of New Orleans. In appearance, he is not unlike Napoleon Bonaparte—about the stature, complexion, and general style of Napoleon; only with an eye of marvelous brilliancy, and hair worn very long, black as night. A melodious, fluent, graceful, courteous man, formed to take captive the hearts of listening men and women. Of an independent turn of mind, too; not too tractable in the courts; not one of those who made haste to sever the ties that had bound them to their country. He appears to have accepted secession as a fact accomplished, rather than helped to make it such. In conventions and elsewhere, General Butler had often met him before to-day, and their intercourse had always been amicable.

On the opposite side of the room, also in a semi-circle, sat General Butler and his staff, in full uniform, brushed for the occasion. Readers are familiar with those annihilating caricatures, which are called photographs of General Butler. In truth, the general has an imposing presence. Not tall, but of well-developed form, and fine, massive head; not graceful in movement, but of firm, solid aspect; self-possessed; not silver-tongued, not fluent, like Mr. Soulé; on the contrary, he is slow of speech, often hesitates and labors, can not at once bring down the sledge-hammer squarely on the anvil; but down it comes at last with a ring that is remembered. It is only in the heat and tempest of contention, that he acquires the perfect use of his parts of speech. A lady who may, for anything I know, have been peeping into the room this evening from some coigne of vantage, compares the two combatants on this occasion to Richard and Saladin, as described by Scott in the Talisman; where Saladin, all alertness and grace, cuts the silk with gleaming, swiftest cimeter, and burly Richard, with ponderous broad-sword, which only he could wield, severs the bar of iron.

General Butler opened the conversation by saying that the object for which he had requested the attendance of the mayor and council, was to explain to them the principles upon which he intended to govern the department to which he had been assigned, and to learn from them how far they were disposed to co-operate with him. He added that he had prepared a proclamation to the people of New Orleans, which expressed his intentions; and which he would now read. After reading it he would be happy to listen to any remarks from gentlemen representing the people of the city. He then read the proclamation as follows:

PROCLAMATION OF GENERAL BUTLER.

"HEAD-QUARTERS, DEPARTMENT OF THE GULF,
"NEW ORLEANS, *May* 1, 1862.

"The city of New Orleans and its environs, with all its interior and exterior defenses, having surrendered to the combined naval and land forces of the United States, and being now in the occupation of the forces of the United States, who have come to restore order, maintain public tranquillity, and enforce peace and quiet, under the laws and constitution of the United States, the major-general commanding hereby proclaims the object and purposes of the government of the United States in thus taking possession of New Orleans and the state of Louisiana, and the rules and regulations by which the laws of the United States will be for the present, and during the state of war, enforced and maintained, for the plain guidance of all good citizens of the United States, as well as others who may have heretofore been in rebellion against their authority.

"Thrice before has the city of New Orleans been rescued from the hands of a foreign government, and still more calamitous domestic insurrection,* by the money and arms of the United States. It has of late been under the military control of the rebel forces, and at each time, in the judgment of the commanders of the military forces holding it, it has been found necessary to preserve order and maintain quiet by an administration of martial law. Even during the interim from its evacuation by the rebel soldiers and its actual possession by the soldiers of the United States, the civil authorities have found it necessary to call for the intervention of an armed body known as the European Legion, to preserve the public tranquillity. The commanding general, therefore, will cause the city to be guarded, until the restoration of the United States authority and his further orders, by martial law.

"All persons in arms against the United States are required to surrender themselves, with their arms, equipments, and munitions of war. The body known as the European Legion, not being understood to be in arms against the United States, but organized to protect the lives and property of the citizens, are invited to still co-operate with the forces of the United States to that end, and, so acting, will not be included in the terms of this order, but will report to these head-quarters.

"All ensigns, flags, devices, tending to uphold any authority whatever, save the flags of the United States and those of foreign consulates, must not be exhibited, but suppressed. The American ensign, the emblem of

*1st, by purchase in 1803. 2d, by General Wilkinson in 1807, when the city was supposed to be threatened by Aaron Burr. 3d, by General Jackson in 1814.

the United States, must be treated with the utmost deference and respect by all persons, under pain of severe punishment.

"All persons well disposed towards the government of the United States, who shall renew the oath of allegiance, will receive a safeguard of protection to their persons and property from the army of the United States, and the violation of such safeguard will be punishable with death. All persons still holding allegiance to the Confederate States, will be deemed rebels against the government of the United States, and regarded and treated as enemies thereof. All foreigners, not naturalized and claiming allegiance to their respective governments, and not having made oath of allegiance to the government of the Confederate States, will be protected in their persons and property, as heretofore, under the laws of the United States. All persons who may have heretofore given adherence to the supposed government of the Confederate States, or been in their service, who shall lay down or deliver up their arms, return to peaceful occupations, and preserve quiet and order, holding no farther correspondence nor giving aid and comfort to enemies of the United States, will not be disturbed in their persons or property, except so far under the orders of the commanding general as the exigencies of the public service may render necessary.

"Keepers of all public property, whether state, national, or confederate, such as collections of art, libraries and museums, as well as all public buildings, all munitions of war and armed vessels, will at once make full returns thereof to these head-quarters. All manufacturers of arms and munitions of war will report to these head-quarters their kind and places of business. All the rights of property, of whatever kind, will be held inviolate, subject only to the laws of the United States. All the inhabitants are enjoined to pursue their usual avocations. All shops and places of amusement are to be kept open in the accustomed manner, and services are to be held in the churches and religious houses, as in times of profound peace.

"Keepers of all public houses and drinking saloons are to report their names and numbers to the office of the provost-marshal, and they will then receive a license, and be held responsible for all disorders and disturbances arising in their respective places.

"Sufficient force will be kept in the city to preserve order and maintain the laws. The killing of American soldiers by any disorderly person or mob, is simply assassination and murder, and not war, and will be so regarded and punished. The owner of any house in which such murder shall be committed will be held responsible therefor, and the house be liable to be destroyed by the military authority. All disorders, disturbances of the peace, and crimes of an aggravated nature, interfering with the forces or laws of the United States, will be referred to a military court for trial and punishment. Other misdemeanors will be subject to the municipal authority, if it desires to act.

"Civil causes between party and party will be referred to the ordinary tribunals.

"The levy and collection of taxes, save those imposed by the laws of the United States, are suppressed, except those for keeping in repair and lighting the streets, and for sanitary purposes. These are to be collected in the usual manner.

"The circulation of Confederate bonds, evidences of debt (except notes in the similitude of bank-notes) issued by the Confederate States, or scrip, or any trade in the same, is forbidden. It has been represented to the commanding general by the civil authorities that these Confederate notes, in the form of bank-notes, in a great measure, are the only substitutes for money which the people have been allowed to have, and that great distress would ensue among the poorer classes if the circulation of such notes should be suppressed. Such circulation, therefore, will be permitted so long as any one will be inconsiderate enough to receive them, until farther orders.

"No publication of newspapers, pamphlets, or hand-bills, giving accounts of the movements of the soldiers of the United States within this department, reflecting in any way upon the United States, intended in any way to influence the public mind against the United States, will be permitted, and all articles on war news, editorial comments, or correspondence making comments upon the movements of the armies of the United States, must be submitted to the examination of an officer, who will be detailed for that purpose from these head-quarters. The transmission of all communications by telegraph will be under the charge of an officer detailed from these head-quarters.

"The armies of the United States came here not to destroy, but to restore order out of chaos, to uphold the government and the laws in the place of the 'passage' of men. To this end, therefore, the efforts of all well disposed are invited, to have every species of disorder quelled.

"If any soldier of the United States should so far forget his duty or his flag as to commit outrage upon any person or property, the commanding general requests his name to be instantly reported to the provost guard, so that he may be punished and his wrongful act redressed. The municipal authority, so far as the police of the city and environs are concerned, is to extend as before indicated, until suspended.

"All assemblages of persons in the streets, either by day or night, tend to disaster, and are forbidden. The various companies composing the Fire Department of New Orleans will be permitted to retain their organizations, and are to report to the provost-marshal, so that they may be known, and not interfered with in their duties.

"And, finally, it may be sufficient to add, without farther enumeration, that all the requirements of martial law will be imposed so long as, in the judgment of the United States authorities, it may be necessary; and while it is desired by these authorities to exercise this government mildly, and after the usages of the past, it must not be supposed that it will not be rigorously and firmly administered as the occasion calls for it."

"By command of MAJOR-GENERAL BUTLER.

"GEO. B. STRONG, *A. A. G.*, *Chief of Staff.*"

"The sum and substance of the whole," said General Butler, "is this: I wish to leave the municipal authority in the full exercise of its accustomed functions. I do not desire to interfere with the collection of taxes, the government of the police, the lighting and cleaning of the streets, the sanitary laws, or the administration of justice. I desire only to govern the military forces of the department, and to take cognizance only of offenses committed by or against them. Representing here the United States, it is my wish to confine myself solely to the business of sustaining the government of the United States against its enemies."

Mr. Soulé replied. He said, that his first concern was for the tranquillity of the city, which, he felt sure, could not be maintained so long as the federal troops remained within its limits. He therefore urged and implored General Butler to remove the troops to the outskirts of the town, where the hourly sight of them would not irritate a sensitive and high-spirited people. "I know the feelings of the people so well," said he, "that I am sure your soldiers can have no peace while they remain in our midst." The Proclamation, he added, would give great offense. The people would never submit. They were not conquered, and could not be expected to behave as a conquered people. "Withdraw your troops, general, and leave the city government to manage its own affairs. If the troops remain, there will certainly be trouble."

This absurd line of remark—absurd as a reply to the general's proposals—fired the commander of the department of the gulf. He spoke, however, in a measured though decisive manner.

"I did not expect," said he, "to hear from Mr. Soulé a threat on *this* occasion. I have been long accustomed to hear threats from southern gentlemen in political conventions; but let me assure gentlemen present, that the time for tactics of that nature has passed never to return. New Orleans *is* a conquered city. If not, why are we here? How did we get here? Have you opened your arms and bid us welcome? Are we here by your consent?

Would you or would you not, expel us if you could? New Orleans has been conquered by the forces of the United States, and by the laws of all nations, lies subject to the will of the conquerors. Nevertheless, I have proposed to leave the municipal government to the free exercise of all its powers, and I am answered by a threat."

Mr. Soulé disclaimed the intention to threaten the troops. He had desired merely to state what, in his opinion, would be the consequences of their remaining.

"Gladly," continued General Butler, "will I take every man of the army out of New Orleans the very day, the very hour it is demonstrated to me that the city government can protect me from insult or danger, if I choose to ride alone from one end of the city to the other, or accompanied by one gentleman of my staff. Your inability to govern the insulting, irreligious, unwashed mob in your midst has been clearly proved by the insults of your rowdies toward my officers and men this very afternoon, and by the fact that General Lovell was obliged to proclaim martial law while his army occupied your city, to protect the law abiding citizens from the rowdies. I do not proclaim martial law against the respectable citizens of this place, but against the same class that obliged General Wilkinson, General Jackson, and General Lovell to declare it. I have means of knowing more about your city than you think, and I am aware that at this hour there is an organization here established for the purpose of assassinating my men by detail; but I warn you that if a shot is fired from any house, that house will never again cover a mortal's head; and if I can discover the perpetrator of the deed, the place that now knows him shall know him no more for ever. I have the power to suppress this unruly element in your midst, and I mean so to use it, that in a very short period, I shall be able to ride through the entire city, free from insult and danger, or else this metropolis of the South shall be a desert, from the Plains of Chalmette to the outskirts of Carrollton."

Mr. Soulé, in reply, delivered an oration, the beauty and grace of which were admired by all who heard it. I regret that we have no report of his speech. It was, in part, a defense and eulogy of New Orleans, and, in part, a secession speech of the usual tenor, illumined by the rhetoric of an accomplished speaker. He said that New Orleans contained a smaller proportion of the mob element than any other city of equal size, and that the proclamation of martial law by General Lovell was aimed, not at the mob, but at the Union men and "traitors" in their midst.

The conversation then turned to a topic of immense moment to the people of the city, the supply of provisions. The general said he had determined to issue permits to dealers and others, which should protect them in bringing in provisions from a certain distance beyond his lines. The awful situation of the poor of the city should have his immediate attention; in the mean time, the Confederate currency in their hands should be allowed to circulate, since many of them had nothing else of the nature of money.

After much farther discussion, the general being immovable, the mayor announced, that the functions of the city government would be at once suspended, and the general could do with the city as seemed to him good.

A member of the council promptly interposed, saying, that a matter of so much importance should not be disposed of until it had been considered and acted upon by the common council. The mayor assented. General Butler offered no objection. It was finally agreed that the council should confer upon the subject the next morning, and make known the result of their deliberations to the general in the course of the day. The gentlemen then withdrew: the crowd in the streets gradually dispersed, and the city enjoyed a tranquil night.

The next morning, the Proclamation was published; *i. e.*, hand-bills, containing it, were freely given to all who would take one. Two important appointments were also announced: Major Joseph W. Bell, to be provost-judge, and Colonel Jonas H. French, to be provost-marshal. Colonel French notified the people, by hand-bill, that he "assumed the position of provost-marshal, for the purpose of carrying out such of the provisions of the Proclamation of the general commanding within this department, as were not left to municipal action. * * * Particularly does he call attention to the prohibition against assemblages of persons in the streets; the sale of liquor to soldiers; the necessity for a license on the part of keepers of public houses, coffee-houses, and drinking saloons; to the posting of placards about the streets, giving information concerning the action or movements of rebel troops, and the publishing in the newspapers of notices or resolutions laudatory of the enemies of the United States. "The soldiers of this command are subject, upon the part of some low-minded persons, to insult. This must stop. Repetition will lead to instant arrest and punishment. In the performance of his duties the undersigned will, in no degree, trench upon the regularly established police of the city, but will confine himself simply to the performance of such acts as were to be assumed by the military authorities of the United States; and, in such action, he hopes to meet with the ready co-operation of all who have the welfare of the city at heart."

At noon, the foreign consuls waited upon General Butler, accompanied by General Juge, commanding the European Brigade. The interview was in the highest degree amicable and courteous. General Butler explained to the consuls the line of conduct he had marked out for himself, and related the leading points of his proposal to the mayor and council, whose reply he was then awaiting. He also assured the consuls, that nothing should be wanting on his part, to facilitate the discharge of their public duties. His most earnest desire, he said, was to confine his attention to his military duty, and leave all public functionaries, domestic and foreign, to the unrestrained discharge of their vocations. He warmly thanked General Juge for his eminent services during the last week, expressed regret that he had disbanded his men, hoped he would reorganize them, and aid him in maintaining order. The gentlemen retired, apparently well pleased with what they had heard. They all shook hands with the general at parting.

A delegation from the common council next appeared, who informed the general that his proposal of the evening before was accepted. The city government should go on as usual; but they requested that the troops should be withdrawn from the vicinity of the City Hall, that the authorities might not seem to be acting under military dictation. This request was granted: the troops were withdrawn.

The general went farther. He sent a considerable body of troops under General Phelps to Carrollton, where a permanent camp was formed. A brigade under General Williams soon went up the river with Captain Farragut, to take possession of and hold Baton Rouge. Other troops were posted in the various forts upon the lakes abandoned by the enemy. Others were at Algiers. The camps in the squares of the city were broken up. When all the troops were posted, there remained in the city, during the first few weeks, two hundred and fifty men: and these men lodged in the Custom-House, and served merely as a provost-guard. Mr. Soulé, therefore, had his desire, or nearly so, for the general was fully resolved to omit no fair means of conciliating the people, and winning them back to their allegiance.

Thus, by the end of the third day, the city was tranquil, and there seemed a prospect of the two sets of authorities going on peacefully together, each keeping to its own department; General Butler governing the army, and extending the area of conquest; the mayor and council ruling the city, aided, if necessary, by General Juge and his brigade. This was the theory upon which General Butler began his memorable administration. This was the offer which he sincerely made to the people and government of the city. We shall discover, in time, whose fault it was that the theory proved so signally untenable.

The comments of the press of New Orleans upon the new order of things, were far more favorable to General Butler than could have been expected. The *True Delta* frankly admitted the truth of that part of the Proclamation which gave to the European Brigade the credit of having preserved the city. "For seven years past," said the *True Delta*, of May 6th, "the world knows that this city, in all its departments—judicial, legislative and executive—has been at the absolute disposal of the most godless, brutal, ignorant and ruthless ruffianism the world has ever heard of since the days of the great Roman conspirator. By means of a secret organization emanating from that fecund source of every political infamy, New England, and named Know Nothingism or 'Sammyism'—from the boasted exclusive devotion of the fraternity to the United States—our city, from being the abode of decency, of liberality, generosity and justice, has become a perfect hell; the temples of justice are sanctuaries for crime; the ministers of the laws, the nominees of blood-stained, vulgar, ribald caballers; licensed murderers shed innocent blood on the most public thoroughfares with impunity; witnesses of the most atrocious crimes are either spirited away, bought off, or intimidated from testifying; perjured associates are retained to prove alibis, and ready bail is always procurable for the immediate use of those whom it is not immediately prudent to enlarge otherwise. The electoral system is a farce and a fraud; the knife, the slung-shot, the brass knuckles determining, while the sham is being enacted, who shall occupy and administer the offices of the municipality and the commonwealth. Can our condition then surprise any man? Is it, either, a fair ground for reproach to the well-disposed, kind-hearted and intelligent fixed population of New Orleans, that institutions and offices designed for the safety of their persons, the security of their property, and maintenance of their fair repute and unsullied honor, should by a band of conspirators, in possession by force and fraud of the electoral machinery, be diverted from their legitimate uses and made engines of the most insupportable oppression? We accept the reproach in the Proclamation, as every Louisianian alive to the honor and fair fame of his state and chief city must accept it, with bowed heads and brows abashed."

The *Bee* of May 8th said: "The mayor and municipal authorities have been allowed to retain their power and privileges in everything unconnected with military affairs. The federal soldiers do not seem to interfere with the private property of the citizens, and have done nothing that we are aware of to provoke difficulty. The usual nightly reports of arrests for vagrancy, assaults, wounding and killing have unquestionably been diminished. The city is as tranquil and peaceable as in the most quiet times."

CHAPTER XVII.

FEEDING AND EMPLOYING THE POOR.

New Orleans was in danger of starving. It contained a population of, perhaps, one hundred and fifty thousand, for whom there was in the city about thirty days' supply of provisions, held at prices beyond the means of all but the rich. A barrel of flour could not be bought for sixty dollars; the markets were empty, the provision stores closed. The trade with Mobile, which had formerly whitened the lakes and the sound with sails, was cut off. The Texas drovers had ceased to bring in cattle, and no steamboats from the Red River country were running. The lake coasts were desolate and half deserted, because the trade with New Orleans had ceased, and because the locusts of secession had devoured their substance.

New Orleans was thus a starving city in the midst of an impoverished country. The river planters, who had been wont to send marketing to the city, now feared to trust their sloops, their produce and their slaves, within the lines of an army which they had been taught to believe was bent on plunder only. A large proportion of the men of New Orleans were away with the Confederate armies, at Shiloh, in Virginia, and elsewhere, having left wives and children, mistresses and their offspring, to the public charge. The city taxes were a million dollars in arrears; and the city government, it was soon discovered, was expending its energies and its ingenuity upon a business more congenial than that of providing for the poor, namely, that of frustrating and exasperating the commander of the Union army. In a word, fifty thousand human beings in New Orleans saw before them a prospect, not of want, not of a long struggle with adversity, but of starvation; and that immediate—to-morrow or the next day; and General Butler, wielding the power and resources of the United States, alone could save them.

To this task he addressed himself; it necessarily had the precedence of all other work during the first few days. If we confine ourselves to this topic for a short time, so as to show in one view all that General Butler did for the poor of New Orleans, the reader will please bear in mind, that the commanding general was by no means able to confine *his* attention to it. *He* had everything to do at once. The business of the city was dead; he strove to revive it. Confidence in the honest intentions of the Union authorities did not exist; he endeavored to call it into being. The currency was deranged; it was his duty to rectify it. The secessionists were audaciously diligent; he had to circumvent and repress them. The yellow fever season was at hand; he was resolved to ward it off. The city government was obstructive and hostile; it was his business to frustrate their endeavors. The negro problem loomed up, vast and portentous; he had to act upon it without delay. The banks were in disorder; their affairs demanded his attention. The consulates were so many centers of hostile operations; he had to penetrate their mysteries. His army was considerable, his field of operation immense; he could not neglect the chief business of his mission. All these affairs claimed his immediate attention, and had it. But though a thousand events may occur simultaneously, it is not convenient to relate them simultaneously. We shall have sometimes to disregard the order of time, and pursue one subject or class of subjects to the end.

General Butler's first measures for the supply of the city were taken upon the suggestion of the city magnates. The following orders were promulgated on the third day of the occupation of the city:

I.

"The commanding general of this department has been informed that there is now at Mobile a stock of flour purchased by the city of New Orleans for the subsistence of its citizens. The suffering condition of the poor of this city, for the want of this flour, appeals to the humanity of those having authority on either side. For the purpose of the safe transmission of this flour to this city, the commanding general orders and directs that a safe conduct be afforded to a steamboat, to be laden with the same to this place. This safe conduct shall extend to the entire protection of the boat in coming, reasonable delay to discharge, and return to Mobile.

"The boat will take no passengers, save the owners and keepers of the flour, and will be subject to the strict inspection of the harbor-master detailed from these head-quarters, to whom its master will report its arrival. The faith of the city is pledged for the faithful performance of the requirements of this order on the part of the agent of the city authorities, who will be allowed to pass each way with the boat, giving no intelligence or aid to the Confederates."

II.

"The president, directors, &c., of the Opelousas railroad are authorized and required to run their cars over their road for the purpose of bringing to the city of New Orleans all materials for provisions, marketing, and supplies of food which may be offered in order to supply the wants of the city. No passengers other than those having the care of such supplies, as owners and keepers, are to be permitted to come into the city, and none other are to leave the city. All other supplies are prohibited transport over the road either way, except cotton and sugar, which may be safely brought over the road, and will be purchased at their fair market value by the United States in specie. The transmission of live stock is especially enjoined. An agent of the city government will be allowed to pass over the road either way, stopping at all points, on the faith of a pledge of such government that he transmits no intelligence and affords no aid to the Confederates. The officer commanding the post having the terminus of such road within his pickets, will cause a thorough inspection of the cars and boats for the purpose of farthering this order, and will offer no farther hindrance so long as this order is in good faith complied with."

III.

"The commanding general of the Department of the Gulf has been informed that live stock, flour, and provisions, purchased for subsistence of the inhabitants of the city of New Orleans, are now at the junction of the Red and Mississippi rivers. The suffering condition of the poor of the city, for want of these supplies, appeals to the humanity of those having authority on either side. For the purpose, therefore, of the safe transmission of these supplies to the city, the commanding general orders and directs that a safe conduct be afforded for two steamers, to be laden with provisions, cattle, and supplies of food, either alive or slaughtered, each day, if so many choose to come. This safe conduct shall extend to their entire protection by the forces of the United States during their coming, reasonable delay for discharge, not exceeding six days, unless in case of accident to their machinery, and in returning to or near the junction of the Red and Mississippi rivers.

"And safe conduct is farther granted to boats, laden as before stated, with provisions for New Orleans from any point above the junction of such rivers, if at any time during which these supplies are needed the forces of the United States should be at or above such junction.

"These boats will take no passengers save the owners or keepers of the freight aforesaid, and will be subject to strict inspection by the harbor-master detailed from these head-quarters, to whom they will report their arrival.

"The faith of the city is pledged for the faithful execution of the requirements of this order on the part of the agent of the city authorities, who will be allowed to pass with the boats either way, he giving no intelligence or aid to the Confederates."

For the immediate relief of the poor, General Butler gave from his own resources a thousand dollars, half in money, half in provisions. His brother, Colonel A. J. Butler, who found himself, by the action of the senate, without employment in New Orleans, and having both capital and credit at command, embarked in the business of bringing cattle from Texas, to the great advantage of the city and his own considerable profit. The quartermaster's chest being empty, General Butler placed all the money of his own, which he could raise, at his disposal. Provisions soon began to arrive, but not in the requisite quantities. At the end of a month, flour had fallen to twenty-four dollars a barrel; but nearly nineteen hundred families were daily fed at the public expense, and thousands more barely contrived to subsist.

It immediately appeared that every one of the passes and permits issued by the general, in accordance with the orders just given, was abused, to the aid and comfort of secession. It was discovered that provisions were secretly sent out of the city to feed General Lovell's troops. It was ascertained that Charles Heidsieck, one of the champagne Heidsiecks, had come from Mobile in the provision steamboat, disguised as a bar-keeper, and conveyed letters to and from that city; an offense which consigned him speedily to Fort Jackson. Nor did the city government stir in the business of providing for the poor; not a dollar was voted, not a relieving act was passed. The city was reeking, too, with the accumulated filth of many weeks, the removal of which would have afforded employment to many hungry men; but it was suffered to remain, inviting the yellow fever.

General Butler, on the 9th of May, reminded the mayor and council of the compact between himself and the city authorities made five days before. "I desire," said he, "to call your attention to the sanitary condition of your streets. Having assumed, by the choice of your fellow-citizens and the permission of the United States authorities, the care of the city of New Orleans in this behalf, that trust must be faithfully administered. Resolutions and inaction will not do. Active, energetic measures, fully and promptly executed, are imperatively demanded by the exigencies of the occasion. The present suspension of labor furnishes ample supplies of hungry men, who can be profitably employed to this end. A tithe of the labor and effort spent upon the streets and public squares, which was uselessly and inanely wasted upon idle fortifications, like that about the United States Mint, will place the city in a condition to insure the health of its inhabitants. It will not do to shift the responsibility from yourselves to the street commissioners, from thence to the contractor, and thence to the sub-contractors, and through all the grades of civic idleness and neglect of duty. Three days since I called the attention of Mr. Mayor to this subject, and nothing has been done."

The mayor boldly replied that three hundred extra men had been set to work upon the streets. No such force could be discovered by the optics of Union officers. Steps may have been taken toward the employment of men, and even "extra men," in cleaning the city; but it is certain that, up to the ninth of May, no street-cleaners were actually at work. The weather was extremely hot, and the need of purification was manifest and pressing.

On the same day, General Butler issued one of his startling general orders, the terms and tone of which were doubtless influenced by the mayor's audacious reply, as well as by the abuse of the passes which admitted food to a starving city.

"NEW ORLEANS, *May* 9, 1862.

"The deplorable state of destitution and hunger of the mechanics and working classes of this city has been brought to the knowledge of the commanding general.

"He has yielded to every suggestion made by the city government, and ordered every method of furnishing food to the people of New Orleans that government desired. No relief by those officials has yet been afforded. This hunger does not pinch the wealthy and influential, the leaders of the rebellion, who have gotten up this war, and are now endeavoring to prosecute it, without regard to the starving poor, the workingman, his wife and child. Unmindful of their suffering fellow-citizens at home, they have caused or suffered provisions to be carried out of the city for Confederate service since the occupation by the United States forces.

"Lafayette Square, their home of affluence, was made the dépôt of stores and munitions of war for the rebel armies, and not of provisions for their poor neighbors. Striking hands with the vile, the gambler, the idler, and the ruffian, they have destroyed the sugar and cotton which might have been exchanged for food for the industrious and good, and regrated the price of that which is left, by discrediting the very currency they had furnished, while they eloped with the specie; as well that stolen from the United States, as from the banks, the property of the good people of New Orleans, thus leaving them to ruin and starvation.

"Fugitives from justice many of them, and others, their associates, staying because too puerile and insignificant to be objects of punishment by the clement government of the United States.

"They have betrayed their country:

"They have been false to every trust:

"They have shown themselves incapable of defending the state they had seized upon, although they have forced every poor man's child into their service as soldiers for that purpose, while they made their sons and nephews officers:

"They can not protect those whom they have ruined, but have left them to the mercies and assassinations of a chronic mob:

"They will not feed those whom they are starving:

"Mostly without property themselves, they have plundered, stolen, and destroyed the means of those who had property, leaving children penniless and old age hopeless.

"MEN OF LOUISIANA, WORKINGMEN, PROPERTY-HOLDERS, MERCHANTS, AND CITIZENS OF THE UNITED STATES, of whatever nation you may have had birth, how long will you uphold these flagrant wrongs, and, by inaction, suffer yourselves to be made the serfs of these leaders?

"The United States have sent land and naval forces here to fight and subdue rebellious armies in array against her authority. We find, substantially, only fugitive masses, runaway property-burners, a whisky-drinking mob, and starving citizens with their wives and children. It is our duty to call back the first, to punish the second, root out the third, feed and protect the last.

"Ready only for war, we had not prepared ourselves to feed the hungry and relieve the distressed with provisions. But to the extent possible, within the power of the commanding general, it shall be done.

"He has captured a quantity of beef and sugar intended for the rebels in the field. A thousand barrels of these stores will be distributed among the deserving poor of this city, from whom the rebels had plundered it; even although some of the food will go to supply the craving wants of the wives and children of those now herding at 'Camp Moore' and elsewhere, in arms against the United States.

"Captain John Clark, acting chief commissary of subsistence, will be charged with the execution of this order, and will give public notice of the place and manner of distribution, which will be arranged, as far as possible, so that the unworthy and dissolute will not share its benefits."

Another measure of relief was adopted when the arrival of stores from New York had delivered the army itself from the danger of scarcity. The chief commissary was authorized to "sell to families for consumption, in small quantities, until farther orders, flour and salt meats, viz.: pork, beef, ham, and bacon, from the stores of the army, at seven and a half cents per pound for flour and ten cents for meats. City bank-notes, gold, silver, or treasury notes to be taken in payment."

The city government still neglecting the streets, General Butler conceived the idea of combining the relief of the poor with the purification of the city. There was nothing upon which he was more resolved than the disappointment of rebel hopes with regard to the yellow fever. He understood the yellow fever, knew the secret of its visitations, felt himself equal to a successful contest with it. June fourth (the mayor of the city being then in a state of suppression at Fort Jackson, for acts yet to be related), the general sketched his plan in the following letter to General Shepley and the common council:

New Orleans, *June* 4, 1862.

"To the Military Commandant and City Council of New Orleans:

"General Shepley and Gentlemen:—Painful necessity compels some action in relation to the unemployed and starving poor of New Orleans. Men willing to labor can not get work by which to support themselves and families, and are suffering for food.

"Because of the sins of their betrayers, a worse than the primal curse seems to have fallen upon them. 'In the sweat of thy face shalt thou eat bread until thou return unto the ground.'

"The condition of the streets of the city calls for the promptest action for a greater cleanliness and more perfect sanitary preparations.

"To relieve, as far as I may be able to do, both difficulties, I propose to the city government, as follows:

"1. The city shall employ upon the streets, squares, and unoccupied lands in the city, a force of men, with proper implements, and under competent direction, to the number of two thousand, for at least thirty working days, in putting those places in such condition as, with blessing of Providence, shall insure the health as well of the citizens as of the troops.

"The necessities of military operations will detain in the city a larger number of those who commonly leave it during the summer, especially women and children, than are usually resident here during the hot months. Their health must be cared for by you; I will care for my troops. The miasma which sickens the one will harm the other. The epidemic so earnestly prayed for by the wicked will hardly sweep away the strong man, although he may be armed, and leave the weaker woman and child untouched.

"2. That each man of this force be paid by the city from its revenues fifty cents per day, and a larger sum for skilled labor, for each day's labor of ten hours, toward the support of their families, and that in the selection of laborers, men with families dependent upon them be preferred.

"3. That the United States shall issue to each laborer so employed, for each day's work, a full ration for a soldier, containing over fifty ounces of wholesome food, which, with economy, will support a man and a woman.

"This issue will be fully equal in value, at the present prices of food, to the sum paid by the city.

"4. That proper muster-rolls be prepared of these laborers, and details so arranged, that only those that labor, with their families, shall be fed from this source.

"5. No paroled soldier or person who has served in the Confederate forces shall be employed, unless he takes the oath of allegiance to the United States.

"I shall be glad to arrange the details of this proposal through the aid of Colonel Shafer, of the quartermaster department, and Colonel Turner, of the subsistence department, as soon as it has been acted on by you."

General Shepley communicated this letter to the council, who readily adopted the plan, and appointed a gentleman to superintend their share in it. On the part of the United States, General Shepley named Colonel T. B. Thorpe, the well-known author of the "Bee Hunter," who had received the appointment of city surveyor. The entire management of the two thousand laborers fell to Colonel Thorpe, as his colleague refused to take the oath of allegiance to the United States, which General Butler made a *sine quâ non.* No man could have done the work better. He waged incessant and most successful war upon nuisances. He tore away shanties, filled up hollows, purged the canals, cleaned the streets, repaired the levee, and kept the city in such perfect cleanliness as extorted praise from the bitterest foes of his country and his chief. In gangs of twenty-five, each under an overseer, the street-sweepers pervaded the city.

"It was a reflecting sight," says an eye-witness, "to behold these men on the highways and by-ways, with their shovels and brooms; and it was still more gratifying to notice and to feel the happy effects of their work. The street cleaning commenced, the colonel then undertook the distribution of the food to the families of the laborers, and this was a task of no ordinary magnitude. A thousand half-starved women, made impatient by days of starvation, brought in contact and left to struggle at the entrance of some ill-arranged establishment, for their food and rights, was a formidable subject of contemplation; so the colonel organized a distributing department, and so well managed his plans that the food is being given out with all the quietness of a popular grocery. To secure the object of the charity, he had tickets printed that made the delivery of the food to the women only; in this way it was carried into the family, consumed by the helpless, and not sold by the unprincipled for rum. The moment Colonel Thorpe's name appeared in the papers, he was flooded with letters calling his attention to nuisances, the people acting voluntarily as street inspectors. By a judicious distribution of labor, in a few days the change became a subject of comment, some of the most furious secessionists admitting 'that the federals could clean the streets, if they couldn't do anything else.'"*

Colonel Thorpe's labors were permanently beneficial to the city in many ways. The freaks of the Mississippi river constantly create new land within the city limits. This land, which is called *batture* (shoal), requires the labor of man before it is completely rescued from the domains of the river. It is computed that Colonel Thorpe's skillfully directed exertions upon the batture added to the city a quantity of land worth a million of dollars.

And this leads us to the most remarkable of all the circumstances attending General Butler's relief of the poor of New Orleans. He not only made it profitable to the city, but he managed it so as not to add one dollar to the expenditures of his own government. At a time when thirty-five thousand persons were supported by the public funds, he could still boast, and with literal truth, that it cost the United States nothing. "You are the cheapest general we have employed," said Mr. Chase, when acknowledging the *return* of twenty-five thousand dollars in gold, which had been sent to General Butler's commissary.

The following general order explains the secret:

"NEW ORLEANS, *August* 4, 1862.

"It appears that the need of relief to the destitute poor of the city requires more extended measures and greater outlay than have yet been made.

"It becomes a question, in justice, upon whom should this burden fall.

"Clearly upon those who have brought this great calamity upon their fellow-citizens.

"It should not be borne by taxation of the whole municipality, because the middling and working men have never been heard at the ballot-box, unawed by threats and unmenaced by 'Thugs' and paid assassins of conspirators against peace and good order. Besides, more than the vote that was claimed for secession have taken the oath of allegiance to the United States.

"The United States government does its share when it protects, defends, and preserves the people in the enjoyment of law, order, and calm quiet.

"Those who have brought upon the city this stagnation of business, this

* Correspondent of *New York Times*, July 21, 1862.

desolation of the hearth-stone, this starvation of the poor and helpless, should, as far as they may be able, relieve these distresses.

"There are two classes whom it would seem peculiarly fit should at first contribute to this end. First, those individuals and corporations who have aided the rebellion with their means: and second, those who have endeavored to destroy the commercial prosperity of the city, upon which the welfare of its inhabitants depend.

"It is brought to the knowledge of the commanding general that a subscription of twelve hundred and fifty thousand dollars was made by the corporate bodies, business firms, and persons whose names are set forth in schedule 'A' annexed to this order, and that sum placed in the hands of an illegal body known as the 'Committee of Public Safety,' for the treasonable purpose of defending the city against the government of the United States, under whose humane rule the city of New Orleans had enjoyed such unexampled prosperity, that her warehouses were filled with trade of all nations who came to share her freedom, to take part in the benefits of her commercial superiority, and thus she was made the representative mart of the world.

"The stupidity and wastefulness with which this immense sum was spent was only equaled by the folly which led to its being raised at all. The subscribers to this fund, by this very act, betray their treasonable designs and their ability to pay at least a much smaller tax for the relief of their destitute and starving neighbors.

"Schedule 'B' is a list of cotton brokers, who, claiming to control that great interest in New Orleans, to which she is so much indebted for her wealth, published in the newspapers, in October, 1861, a manifesto deliberately advising the planters not to bring their produce to the city, a measure which brought ruin at the same time upon the producer and the city.

"This act sufficiently testifies the malignity of these traitors, as well to the government as their neighbors, and it is to be regretted that their ability to relieve their fellow-citizens is not equal to their facilities for injuring them.

"In taxing both these classes to relieve the suffering poor of New Orleans, yea, even though the needy be the starving wives and children of those in arms at Richmond and elsewhere against the United States, it will be impossible to make a mistake save in having the assessment too easy and the burden too light.

"It is therefore ORDERED—

"1st. That the sums in schedules annexed, marked 'A' and 'B,' set against the names of the several persons, business firms and corporations herein described, be and hereby are assessed upon each respectively.

"2d. That said sums be paid to Lieutenant David C. G. Field, financial clerk, at his office in the Custom-House, on or before Monday, the 11th instant, or that the property of the delinquent be forthwith seized and sold at public auction, to pay the amount, with all necessary charges and expenses, or the party imprisoned till paid.

"3d. The money raised by this assessment to be a fund for the purpose of providing employment and food for the deserving poor people of New Orleans."

The promised schedules followed. The first contained ninety-five names, arranged thus:

SCHEDULE A.

List of subscribers to the Million and a Quarter Loan, placed in the hands of the Committee of Public Safety, for the defense of New Orleans against the United States, and expended by them some $38,000.

	Sums subscribed to aid treason against the United States.	Sums assessed to relieve the poor by the United States.
Abat, Generes & Co.	$210,000	$52,500
Jonathan Montgomery	40,000	10,000
Thos. Sloo, President Sun Insurance Co.	50,000	12,500
C. C. Gaines	2,000	500
C. C. Gaines & Co.	3,000	750

The sum yielded by this schedule was $312,716.25. The second schedule, which contained ninety-four names, began thus:

SCHEDULE B.

List of Cotton Brokers of New Orleans who published in the *Crescent*, in October last, a card advising planters not to send produce to New Orleans, in order to induce foreign intervention in behalf of the rebellion.

	Sums assessed to relieve the starving poor by the United States.
Hewitt, Norton & Co.	$500
West & Villerie	250
S. E. Belknap	100
Brander, Chambliss & Co.	500
Lewis & Oglesby	100

The amount of this assessment was $29,200. General Order, No. 55, placed at the disposal of General Butler, for the support of the poor of the city, the sum of $341,916.25.

To complete our knowledge of this unique transaction, the following brief documents are requisite:

"NEW ORLEANS, *August 7th*, 1862.

"SPECIAL ORDER, No. 247.

"J. C. Ricks, D. K. Carroll and A. D. Kelley, having been absent from the city at the time of drawing up the original card, 'advising planters not to send produce to New Orleans,' but on their return, having deemed it advisable to issue a card, placing themselves in the same position, are hereby taxed in the sum of $500.00 each, in accordance with General Order No. 55."

"NEW ORLEANS, *August 6th*, 1862.

"SPECIAL ORDER, No. 244.

"The city surveyor and street commissioner are authorized to employ not less than one thousand men (including those now employed), to work on the streets, wharves and canals. In the selection of these laborers, married men will have the preference. These men to be paid out of the employment and relief fund raised by General Order No. 55.

"While this force was paid by taxation of the property of the city, the commanding general felt authorized to employ it only in the most economical manner, but it now being employed at the expense of their rebellious neighbors, the commanding general proposes that they shall be paid the same sum that was paid them by the same party for work on the fortifications, to wit: one dollar and a half for each day's labor.

"The rations, heretofore a gift to these laborers by the United States, will now be discontinued.

"The order to take effect from and after the first Monday in August, 1862."

The effect produced by a measure so boldly just, upon the minds of the ruling class of New Orleans, can scarcely be imagined. It was the more stunning from the fact, that after three months' experience of General Butler's government, his orders were known to be the irreversible fiat of irresistible power. Every man who saw his name on either catalogue, was perfectly aware that the sum annexed thereto must be paid on or before the designated day. Protest he might, but pay he must. Money first; argument afterward. The loyal *Delta*, conducted then by two officers of General Butler's army, Captain John Clark, formerly of the *Boston Courier*, and Lieutenant-Colonel E. M. Brown, of the Eighth Vermont, discoursed humorously upon the agitation in the fashionable quarter on the day the order was promulgated:

"For the first time these many months, the *habitués de la grande Rue* (Carondelet), woke from their lethargy. Sleek old gentlemen, whose stomachs are distended with turtle, and who sport ivory-headed canes, and wear on their noses two-eyed glasses rimmed with gold, came out from their umbrageous seclusions in Prytania street, Coliseum Place, and other rural portions of the Garden District, to condole with each other upon the once more animated flags. At an early hour knots of these aldermanic looking gentry, with white vests and stiffened shirt collars, had collected in the vicinity of Colonel Baxter's corner, for the purpose of discussing the merits of Order No. 55, which was destined to disturb the equilibrium of many a cash balance, and to cause unwilling fingers to dive into the depths of plethoric pockets, long undisturbed by the prying digits of their sumptuous owners. It was interesting to contemplate the sorrowful visages of this funereal crowd. Some of them had been taxed hundreds, and some to the tune of thousands; but all alike bore the solemn aspect of unresisting muttons led silently to the slaughter. They had made their money easily, to be sure, but parting with it was like pulling teeth. Some of these men are worth a million or two; a few perhaps as much as ten millions in real estate, stocks, bonds, and expectations; and others again are known as *poor men*, tolerably well to do, worth from three to five hundred thousand apiece. For these latter to be taxed as high as a hundred dollars out of the little savings which they had laid up by means of two and a half per cent. advance on cotton crops, and two and a half per cent. commissions, and yet other per centages for brokerage, and stealage, seemed rather hard, at least to them."

The *Delta*, however, assured the gentlemen, and with perfect truth, that lamentations would not do. "The poor must be employed and fed, and you must disgorge. It will never do to have it said, that while you lie back on cushioned divans, tasting turtle, and sipping the wine cup, dressed in fine linen, and rolling in lordly carriages—that gaunt hunger stalked in the once busy streets, and poverty flouted its rags for the want of the privilege to work."

There was but one court of appeal in New Orleans, open to a distressed secessionist—the consulate of the country of which he could claim to be a citizen. The consuls lent a sympathizing ear to all complaints, and willingly forwarded them to their ministers at Washington; who, in turn, laid them before the secretary of state, The protest of some of the "neutrals" in New Orleans gave Gen eral Butler the opportunity to vindicate the justice of Order No. 55, and he performed the task with a master's hand. The following letter will be found to contain important and interesting history, some curious geography, and much unanswerable argument:

"HEAD-QUARTERS, DEPARTMENT OF THE GULF,
"NEW ORLEANS, *October*, 1862.

"Hon. E. M. STANTON, Secretary of War:

"SIR:—I have the honor to report the facts and circumstances of my General Order No. 55, in answer to the complaints of the Prussian and French legations, as to the enforcement of that order upon certain inhabitants of New Orleans, claimed to be the subjects of these respective governments.

"Before discussing the speciality and personal relations of the several complainants, it will be necessary, in a general way, to give an account of the state of things which I found had existed, and was then existing at New Orleans upon its capture by the federal troops, to show the status of the several classes upon which General Order No. 55 takes effect.

"In October, 1861, about the time Mason and Slidell left the city upon their mission to Europe, to obtain the intervention of foreign powers, great hopes were entertained by the rebels, that the European governments would be induced to interfere from want of a supply of cotton. This supply was being had, to a degree, through the agency of the small vessels shooting out by the numerous bayous, lagoons and creeks, with which the southern part of Louisiana is penetrated. They eluded the blockade, and conveyed very considerable amounts of cotton to Havana and other foreign ports, where arms and munitions of war were largely imported through the same channels in exchange. Indeed, as I have before had the honor to inform the department of state, it was made a condition of the very passes given by Governor Moore, that a quantity of arms and powder should be returned in proportion to the cotton shipped.

"The very high prices of the outward as well as the inward cargoes, made these ventures profitable, although but one in three got through with safety.

"Nor does the fact, that so considerable quantities of cotton escaped the blockading force at all impugn the efficiency of the blockading squadron, when it is taken into consideration, that without using either of the principal water communications with the city through the 'Rigolets" or the 'Passes' at the Delta of the river, there are at least *fifty-three* distinct outlets to the gulf from New Orleans by water communication, by light-draught vessels. Of course, not a pound of the cotton that went through these channels found its way north, unless it was purchased at a foreign port. To prevent even this supply of the European manufactures became an object of the greatest interest to the rebels; and prior to October, 1861, all the principal cotton factors of New Orleans, to the number of about a hundred, united in an address, signed with their names, to the planters, advising them not to send their cotton to New Orleans, for the avowed reason that if it was sent, the cotton would find its way to foreign ports, and furnish the interest 'of Europe and the United States with the product of which they are most in need, * * * * and thus contribute to the maintenance of that quasi neutrality, which European nations have thought proper to avow.'

"'This address proving ineffectual to maintain the policy we had determined upon, and which not only received the sanction of public opinion here, but which has been so promptly and cheerfully followed by the planters and factors of the other states of the Confederacy,' the same cotton factors made a petition to Governor Moore and General Twiggs, to 'devise means to prevent any shipment of cotton to New Orleans whatever.'

"For answer to this petition, Governor Moore issued a proclamation forbidding the bringing of cotton within the limits of the city, under the penalties therein prescribed.

"This action was concurred in by General Twiggs, then in command of the Confederate forces, and enforced by newspaper articles, published in the leading journals.

"This was one of the series of offensive measures which were undertaken by the mercantile community of New Orleans, of which a large portion were foreigners, and of which the complainant of Order No. 55 formed a part, in aid of the rebellion.

"The only cotton allowed to be shipped during the autumn and winter of 1861 and '62, was by permits of Governor Moore, granted upon the express condition, that at least one-half in value should be returned in arms and munitions of war. In this traffic, almost the entire mercantile houses of New Orleans were engaged. Joint-stock companies were formed, shares issued, vessels bought, cargoes shipped, arms returned, immense profits realized; and the speculation and trading energy of the whole community was turned in this direction. It will be borne in mind that quite two-thirds of the trading community were foreign born, and now claim exemption from all duties as citizens, and exemption from liabilities for all their acts, because of being 'foreign neutrals.'

"When the expedition which I had the high honor to be intrusted to command, landed at Ship Island, and seemed to threaten New Orleans, the most energetic efforts were made by the state and Confederate authorities for the defense of the city. Nearly the entire foreign population of the city enrolled itself in companies, battalions, and brigades, representing different nationalities.

"They were armed, uniformed, and equipped, drilled and maneuvered and reported for service to the Confederate generals. Many of the foreign officers took the oath of allegiance to the Confederate States. The brigadier-general in command of the European Brigade, Paul Juge, *Fils*, a naturalized citizen of the United States, but born in France, renounced his citizenship, and applied to the French government to be restored to his former citizenship as a native of France, at the very time he held the command of this foreign legion.

"The Prussian consul, now General Reichard, of the Confederate army, of whom we shall have more to say in the course of this report, raised a battalion of his countrymen, and went to Virginia, where he has been promoted for his gallantry in the rebel service, leaving his commercial partner, Mr. Kruttschnidt, now acting Prussian consul, who has married the sister of the rebel secretary of war, to embarrass as much as possible the United States officers here, by subscriptions to 'city defense funds,' and groundless complaints to the Prussian minister.

"I have thus endeavored to give a faithful and exact account of the state of the foreign population of New Orleans, on the fifteenth day of February, 1862.

"In October, 1861, the city had voted to erect a battery out of this 'defense fund.' On the 19th of February, 1862, the city council, by vote, published and commented upon in the newspapers, placed in the hands of the Confederate General Lovell, fifty thousand dollars, to be expended by him in the defenses of the city.

"It will, therefore, clearly appear that all the inhabitants of the city knew that the city council were raising and expending large sums for war purposes.

"On the 20th of the same February, the city council raised an extraordinary 'Committee of Public Safety,' from the body of the inhabitants at large, consisting of sixty members, for the 'purpose of co-operating with the Confederate and state authorities in devising means for the defense of the city and its approaches.'

"On the 27th of the same February, the city council adopted a series of resolutions:—

"1st. Recommending the issue of one million dollars of city bonds, for the purpose of purchasing arms and munitions of war, and to provide for the successful defense of the city and its approaches.

"2d. To appropriate twenty-five thousand dollars for the purpose of uniforming and equipping soldiers mustered into the service of the country.

"3d. Pledging the council to support the families of all soldiers who shall volunteer for the war.

"On the 3d of March, 1862, the city council authorized the mayor to issue the bonds of the city for a million of dollars; and provided that the chairman of the finance committee might 'pay over the said bonds to the

Committee of Public Safety, appointed by the common council of the city of New Orleans, as per resolution, No. 8,930, approved 20th of February, 1862, in such sums as they may require for the purchase of arms and munitions of war, provisions, or to provide any means for the successful defense of the city and its approaches.'

"And, at the same time, authorized the chairman of the finance committee 'to pay over $25,000 to troops mustered into the state service, who should go to the fight at Columbus or elsewhere, under General Beauregard.'

"It was to this fund, in the hands of this extraordinary committee, so published with its objects and purposes, that the complainants subscribed their money, and now claim exemption upon the ground of neutrality, and want of knowledge of the purposes of the fund.

"It will be remembered that all the steps of the raising of the committee to dispose of this fund were published, and were matters of great public notoriety. The fact that the bonds were in the hands of such an extraordinary committee, should have put every prudent person on his guard.

"All the leading secessionists of the city were subscribers to the same fund.

"Will it be pretended for a moment that these persons—bankers, merchants, brokers, who are making this complaint, did not *know* what this fund was, and its purposes, to which they were subscribing by thousands of dollars?

"Did Mr. Rochereau for instance, who had taken an oath to support the Confederate States, a banker, and then a colonel commanding a body of troops in the service of the Confederates, never hear for what purpose the city was raising a million and a quarter in bonds?

"Take the Prussian consul, who complains for himself and the Mrs. Vogel whom he represents, as an example. Did *he* know about this fund? He, a trader, a Jew famed for a bargain, who had married the sister of the rebel secretary of war, the partner of General Reichard, late Prussian consul, then in command in the Confederate army, who subscribed for himself, his partner and Mrs. Vogel, the wife of his former partner, thirty thousand dollars—did *he* not know what he was doing, when he bought these bonds of this 'Committee of Public Safety?'

"On the contrary, it was done to aid the rebellion to which he was bound by his sympathies, his social relations, his business connections and marriage ties. But it is said that this subscription is made to the fund for the sake of the investment. It will appear, however, by a careful examination, that Mr. Kruttschnidt collected for his principal a note, secured by mortgage, in anticipation of its being due, in order to purchase twenty-five thousand dollars of this loan. Without, however, descending into particulars, is the profitableness of the investment to be permitted to be alleged as a sufficient apology for aiding the rebellion by money and arms? If so, all their army contractors, principally Jews, should be held blameless, for they have made immense fortunes by the war. Indeed, I suppose another Jew—one Judas—thought his investment in the thirty pieces of silver was a profitable one, until the penalty of treachery reached him.

"When I took possession of New Orleans, I found the city nearly on the verge of starvation, but thirty days' provision in it, and the poor utterly without the means of procuring what food there was to be had.

"I endeavored to aid the city government in the work of feeding the poor; but I soon found that the very distribution of food was a means faithlessly used to encourage the rebellion. I was obliged, therefore, to take the whole matter into my own hands. It became a subject of alarming importance and gravity. It became necessary to provide from some source the funds to procure the food. They could not be raised by city taxation, in the ordinary form. These taxes were in arrears to more than a million of dollars. Besides, it would be unjust to tax the loyal citizens and honestly neutral foreigner, to provide for a state of things brought about by the rebels and disloyal foreigners related to them by ties of blood, marriage, and social relation, who had conspired and labored together to overthrow the authority of the United States, and establish the very result which was to be met.

"Farther, in order to have a contribution effective, it must be upon those who have wealth to answer it.

"There seemed to me no such fit subjects for such taxation as the cotton brokers who had brought the distress upon the city, by thus paralyzing commerce, and the subscribers to this loan, who had money to invest for purposes of war, so advertised and known as above described.

"With these convictions, I issued General Order No. 55, which will explain itself, and have raised nearly the amount of the tax therein set forth.

"But for what purpose? Not a dollar has gone in any way to the use of the United States. I am now employing one thousand poor laborers, as matter of charity, upon the streets and wharves of the city, from this fund. I am distributing food to preserve from starvation nine thousand seven hundred and seven families, containing 'thirty-two thousand four hundred and fifty souls' daily, and this done at an expense of seventy thousand dollars per month. I am sustaining, at an expense of two thousand dollars per month, five asylums for widows and orphans. I am aiding the Charity hospital to the extent of five thousand dollars per month.

"Before their excellencies, the French and Prussian ministers, complain of my exactions upon foreigners at New Orleans, I desire they would look at the documents, and consider for a few moments the facts and figures set forth in the returns and in this report. They will find that out of ten thousand four hundred and ninety families who have been fed from the fund, with the raising of which they find fault, *less than one-tenth* (one thousand and ten) are Americans; nine thousand four hundred and eighty are foreigners. Of the thirty-two thousand souls, but three thousand are natives. Besides, the charity at the asylums and hospitals distributed in about the same proportions as to foreign and native born; so that of an expenditure of near eighty thousand dollars per month, to employ and feed the starving poor of New Orleans, seventy-two thousand goes to the foreigners, whose compatriots loudly complain, and offensively thrust forward their neutrality, whenever they are called upon to aid their suffering countrymen.

"I should need no extraordinary taxation to feed the poor of New Orleans, if the bellies of the foreigners were as actively with the rebels, as are the heads of those who claim exemption, thus far, from this taxation, made and used for purposes above set forth, upon the ground of their neutrality; among whom I find Rochereau & Co., the senior partner of which firm took an oath of allegiance to support the constitution of the Confederate States.

"I find also the house of Reichard & Co., the senior partner of which, General Reichard, is in the rebel army. I find the junior partner, Mr. Kruttschnidt, the brother-in-law of Benjamin, the rebel secretary of war, using all the funds in his hands to purchase arms, and collecting the securities of his correspondent before they are due, to get funds to loan to the rebel authorities, and now acting Prussian consul here, doing quite as effective service to the rebels as his partner in the field. I find Mme. Vogel, late partner in the same house of Reichard & Co., now absent, whose funds are managed by that house. I find M. Paçsher & Co., bankers, whose clerks and employés formed a part of the French legion, organized to fight the United States, and who contributed largely to arm and equip that corps. And a Mr. Lewis, whose antecedents I have not had time to investigate.

"And these are fair specimens of the *neutrality* of the foreigners, for whom the government is called upon to interfere, to prevent their paying anything toward the Relief Fund for their starving countrymen.

"If the representatives of the foreign governments will feed their own starving people, over whom the only protection they extend, so far as I see, is to tax them all, poor and rich, a dollar and a half each for certificates of nationality, I will release the foreigners from all the exactions, fines, and imposts whatever. I have the honor to be your obedient servant,

"BENJAMIN F. BUTLER,
"*Major-General Commanding.*"

There is the whole case, written out, as all of General Butler's dispatches were, late at night, after twelve or fifteen hours of intense exertion. After such a reaper there is scanty gleaning.

Let me add, however, that among the documents relating to the expedition may be found many little notes, written in an educated, feminine hand, conveying to General Butler the thanks of "Sister Emily," "Mother Alphonso," and other Catholic ladies, for the assistance afforded by him to the orphans, the widows, and the sick under their charge; "whose prayers," they add, "will daily ascend to Heaven in his behalf." During the latter half of his administration, the charities of New Orleans were almost wholly sustained from the funds wrung from "neutral" foes by Order No. 55. The great Charity hospital received, as we have seen, five thousand a month. To the orphans of St. Elizabeth, when the public funds ran low, the general gave five hundred dollars of his own money, besides ordering rations from the public stores at his own charge, and causing the Confederate notes held by the asylum to be disposed of to the best advantage. A commission was appointed, after a time, to inquire into the condition and needs of all the asylums, hospital and charity schools in the city, and to report the amount of aid proper to be allowed to each. The report of the commission shows, that the rations granted them by General Butler were all that enabled them to continue their ministrations to the helpless and the ignorant, the widow, the orphan, and the sick.

I may afford space for a letter addressed by the commanding general to the Superior of the Sisters of Charity, upon the occasion of the accidental injury of their edifice during the bombardment of Donaldsonville. It is not precisely the kind of utterance which we should naturally expect from a "Beast."

"HEAD-QUARTERS, DEPARTMENT OF THE GULF,
"NEW ORLEANS, *September* 2d, 1862.

"MADAME: I had no information until the reception of your note, that so sad a result to the sisters of your command had happened from the bombardment of Donaldsonville.

"I am very, very sorry that Rear-Admiral Farragut was unaware that he was injuring your establishment by his shells. Any injury must have been entirely accidental. The destruction of that town became a necessity. The inhabitants harbored a gang of cowardly guerillas, who committed every atrocity; amongst others, that of firing upon an unarmed boat crowded with women and children, going up the coast, returning to their homes, many of them having been at school at New Orleans.

"It is impossible to allow such acts; and I am only sorry that the righteous punishment meted out to them in this instance, as indeed in all others, fell quite as heavily upon the innocent and unoffending as upon the guilty.

"No one can appreciate more fully than myself the holy, self-sacrificing labors of the sisters of charity. To them our soldiers are daily indebted for the kindest offices. Sisters of all mankind, they know no nation, no kindred, neither war nor peace. Their all-pervading charity is like the boundless love of 'Him who died for all,' whose servants they are, and whose pure teachings their love illustrates.

"I repeat the expression of my grief, that any harm should have befallen your society of sisters; and I cheerfully repair it, as far as I may, in the manner you suggest, by filling the order you have sent to the city for provisions and medicines.

"Your sisters in the city will also farther testify to you, that my officers and soldiers have never failed to do to them all in their power to aid them in their usefulness, and to lighten the burden of their labors.

"With sentiments of the highest respect, believe me, your friend,

"BENJAMIN F. BUTLER.

"SANTA MARIA CLARA,

"*Superior and Sister of Charity.*"

The relief afforded by Order No. 55, liberal as it was, did but alleviate the distresses of the poor. The whole land was stricken. The frequent marching of armed bodies swept the country of the scanty produce of a soil deserted by the ablest of its proprietors. In the city, life was just endurable; beyond the Union lines, most of the people were hungry, half naked, and without medicine.

"The condition of the people here," wrote General Butler to General Halleck, September 1st, "is a very alarming one. They literally come down to starvation. Not only in the city, but in the country; planters who, in peaceful times, would have spent the summer at Saratoga, are now on their plantations, essentially without food. Hundreds weekly, by stealth, are coming across the lake to the city, reporting starvation on the lake shore. I am distributing, in various ways, about fifty thousand dollars per month in food, and more is needed. This is to the whites. My commissary is issuing rations to the amount of nearly double the amount required by the troops. This is to the blacks.

"They are now coming in by hundreds—say thousands—almost daily. Many of the plantations are deserted along the "coast," which, in this country's phrase, means the river, from the city to Natchez. Crops of sugar-cane are left standing, to waste, which would make millions of dollars worth of sugar."

Such were some of the fruits of this most disastrous and most beneficent of all wars. Such were some of the difficulties with which the commander of the Department of the Gulf had to contend during the whole period of his administration. Clothed with powers more than imperial, such were some of the uses to which those powers were devoted.

The government sustained Order No. 55. In December, the money derived from it having been exhausted, the measure was repeated.

"New Orleans, *December* 9, 1862.

"Under General Order No. 55, current series, from these head-quarters, an assessment was made upon certain parties who had aided the rebellion, 'to be appropriated to the relief of the starving poor of New Orleans.' "

"The calls upon the fund raised under that order have been frequent and urgent, and it is now exhausted.

"But the poor of this city have the same, or increased necessities for relief as then, and their calls must be heard; and it is both fit and proper that the parties responsible for the present state of affairs should have the burden of their support.

"Therefore, the parties named in Schedules A and B, of General Order No. 55, as hereunto annexed, are assessed in like sums, and for the same purpose, and will make payment to D. C. G. Field, financial clerk, at his office, at these head-quarters, on or before Monday, December 15, 1862."

CHAPTER XVIII.

THE WOMAN ORDER.

It concerns the people of the United States to know that secession, regarded as a spiritual malady, is incurable. Every one knows this who, by serving on "the frontiers of the rebellion," has been brought in contact with its leaders. General Rosecrans knows it. General Grant knows it. General Burnside knows it. General Butler knows it. True, a large number of Southern men who have been touched with the epidemic, have recovered or are recovering. But the hundred and fifty thousand men who own the slaves of the South, who own the best of the lands, who have always controlled its politics and swayed its drawing-rooms, in whom the disease is hereditary or original, whom it possesses and pervades, like the leprosy or the scrofula, or, rather, like the falseness of the Stuarts and the imbecility of the Bourbons—these men will remain, as long as they draw the breath of life, enemies of all the good meaning which is summed up in the words, United States. It is from studying the characters of these people that we moderns may learn why it was that the great Cromwell and his heroes called the adherents of the mean and cruel Stuarts by the name of "Malignants." They may be rendered innoxious by destroying their power, *i. e.*, by abolishing slavery, which *is* their power; but, as to converting them from the error of their minds, that is not possible.

General Butler was aware of this from the beginning of the rebellion, and his experience in New Orleans was daily confirmation of his belief. Hence, his attitude toward the ruling class was warlike, and he strove in all ways to isolate that class, and bring the majority of the people to see who it was that had brought all this needless ruin upon their state; and thus to array the majority against the few. Throwing the whole weight of his power against the oligarchy, he endeavored to save and conciliate the *people*, whom it was the secret design of the leaders to degrade and disfranchise. He was in New Orleans as a general wielding the power of his government, and as a democrat representing its principles.

The first month of his administration was signalized by several warlike acts and utterances, aimed at the Spirit of Secession; some of which excited a clamor throughout the whole secession world, on both continents, echoes of which are still occasionally heard.

The following requires no explanation:

"New Orleans, *May* 13, 1862.

"It having come to the knowledge of the commanding general that Friday next is proposed to be observed as a day of fasting and prayer, in obedience to some supposed proclamation of one Jefferson Davis, in the several churches of this city, it is ordered that no such observance be had.

"'Churches and religious houses are to be kept open as in time of profound peace,' but no religious exercises are to be had upon the supposed authority above mentioned."

This was General Order No. 27. The one next issued, the famous Order No. 28, which relates to the conduct of some of the women of New Orleans, can not be dismissed quite so summarily.

One might have expected to find among the women of the South many abolitionists of the most "radical" description. As upon the white race the blighting curse of slavery chiefly falls, so the women of that race suffer the consequences of the system which are the most degrading and the most painful. It leads their husbands astray, debauches their brothers and their sons, enervates and coarsens their daughters. The wastefulness of the institution, its bungling stupidity, the heavy and needless burdens it imposes upon housekeepers, would come home, we should think, to the minds of all women not wholly incapable of reflection. I am able to state, that here and there, in the South, even in the cotton states, there are ladies who feel all the enormity, and comprehend the immense stupidity of slavery. I have heard them avow their abhorrence of it. One in particular, I remember, on the borders of South Carolina itself, a mother, glancing covertly at her languid son, and saying in the low tone of despair:

"You cannot tell *me* anything about slavery. We women know what it is, if the men do not."

But it is the law of nature that the men and women of a community shall be morally equal. If all the women were made, by miracle, perfectly good, and all the men perfectly bad, in one generation the moral equality would be restored—the men vastly improved, the women reduced to the average of human worth. Consequently, we find the women of the South as much corrupted by slavery as the men, and not less zealous than the men in this insolent attempt to rend their country in pieces. In truth, they are more zealous, since women are naturally more vehement and enthusiastic than men. The women of New Orleans, too, all had husbands, sons, brothers, lovers or friends, in the Confederate army. To blame the women of a community for adhering, with their whole souls, to a cause for which their husbands, brothers, sons and lovers are fighting, would be to arraign the laws of nature. But then there is a choice of methods by which that adherence may be manifested.

When General Butler was passing through Baltimore, on his way to New Orleans, he observed the mode in which the Union soldiers stationed there were accustomed to behave when passing by ladies who wore the secession flag on their bosoms. The ladies, on approaching a soldier, would suddenly throw aside their cloaks or shawls to display the badge of treason. The soldier would retort by lifting the tail of his coat, to show the rebel flag doing duty, apparently, as a large patch on the seat of his trousers. The general noted the circumstance well. It occurred to him then that, perhaps, a more decent way could be contrived to shame the heroines of secession out of their silly tricks.

The women of New Orleans by no means confined themselves to the display of minute rebel flags on their persons. They were insolently and vulgarly demonstrative. They would leave the sidewalk, on the approach of Union officers, and walk around them into the middle of the street, with up-turned noses and insulting words. On passing privates, they would make a great ostentation of drawing away their dresses, as if from the touch of pollution. Secession colors were conspicuously worn upon the bonnets. If a Union officer entered a street car, all the ladies in it would frequently leave the vehicle, with every expression of disgust; even in church the same spirit was exhibited—ladies leaving the pews entered by a Union officer. The female teachers of the public schools kept their pupils singing rebel songs, and advised the girls to make manifest their contempt for the soldiers of the Union. Parties of ladies upon the balconies of houses, would turn their backs when soldiers were passing by; while one of them would run in to the piano, and thump out the Bonny Blue Flag, with the energy that lovely woman knows how to throw into a performance of that kind. One woman, a very fine lady, too, swept away her skirts, on one occasion, with so much violence as to lose her balance, and she fell into the gutter. The two officers whose proximity had excited her ire, approached to offer their assistance. She spurned them from her, saying, that she would rather lie in the gutter than be helped out by Yankees. She afterward related the circumstance to a Union officer, and owned that she had in reality felt grateful to the officers for their politeness, and added that Order No. 28 served the women right. The climax of these absurdities was reached when a beast of a woman spat in the faces of two officers, who were walking peacefully along the street.

It was this last event which determined General Butler to take public notice of the conduct of the women. At first their exhibitions and affectations of spleen merely amused the objects of them; who were accustomed to relate them to their comrades as the jokes of the day. And, so far, no officers or soldiers had done or said anything in the way of retort. No man in New Orleans had been wronged, no woman had been treated with disrespect by the soldiers of the United States. These things were done while General Butler was feeding the poor of the city by thousands; while he was working night and day to start and restore the business of the city; while he was defending the people against the frauds of great capitalists; while he was maintaining such order in New Orleans as it had never known before; while he was maturing measures designed solely for the benefit of the city; while he was testifying in every way, by word and deed, his heartfelt desire to exert all the great powers intrusted to him for the good of New Orleans and Louisiana.

It can not be denied that both officers and men became, at length, very sensitive to these annoyances. Complaints to the general were frequent. Colonels of regiments requested to be informed what orders they should give their men on the subject, and the younger staff officers often asked the general to save them from indignities which they could neither resent nor endure. Why, indeed, *should* he permit his brave and virtuous New England soldiers to be insulted by these silly, vulgar creatures, spoiled by contact with slavery? And how long could he trust the forbearance of the troops? These questions he had already considered, but the extreme difficulty of acting in such an affair with dignity and effect, had given him pause. But when the report of the spitting was brought to him, he determined to put a stop to such outrages before they provoked retaliation.

It has been said, that the false construction put upon General Order No. 28, by the enemies of the United States, was due to the carelessness with which it was composed. Mr. Seward, in his conversation on the subject with the English chargé, "regretted that, in the haste of composition, a phraseology which could be mistaken or perverted had been used." The secretary of state was never more mistaken. The order was penned with the utmost care and deliberation, and all its probable consequences discussed. The problem was, how to put an end to the insulting behavior of the women *without* being obliged to resort to arrests. So far, New Orleans had been kept down by the mere show and presence of force; it was highly desirable, for reasons of humanity as well as policy, that this should continue to be the case. If the order had said: Any woman who insults a Union soldier shall be arrested, committed to the calaboose and fined,—there would have been women who would have courted the distinction of arrest, to the great peril of the public tranquillity. If anything at all could have roused the populace to resist the troops, surely it would have been the arrest of a well-dressed women, for so popular an act as insulting a soldier of the United States.

It was with the intent to accomplish the object without disturbance, that General Butler worded the order as we find it. The order was framed upon the model of one which he had read long ago in an ancient London chronicle.

"HEAD-QUARTERS, DEPARTMENT OF THE GULF,
"NEW ORLEANS, *May* 15, 1862.

"GENERAL ORDER No. 28:

"As the officers and soldiers of the United States have been subject to repeated insults from the women (calling themselves ladies) of New Orleans, in return for the most scrupulous non-interference and courtesy on our part, it is ordered that hereafter when any female shall, by word, gesture, or movement, insult or show contempt for any officer or soldier of the United States, she shall be regarded and held liable to be treated as a woman of the town plying her avocation."

"By command of MAJOR-GENERAL BUTLER.

"GEO. C. STRONG, *A. A. G., Chief of Staff.*"

That is, she shall be held liable, according to the law of New Orleans, to be arrested, detained over night in the calaboose, brought before a magistrate in the morning, and fined five dollars.

When the order had been written, and was about to be consigned to irrevocable print, a leading member of the staff (Major Strong) said to General Butler:

"After all, general, is it not possible that some of the troops may misunderstand the order? It would be a great scandal if only *one* man should act upon it in the wrong way."

"Let us, then," replied the general, "have *one* case of aggression on our side. I shall know how to deal with that case, so that it will never be repeated. So far, all the aggression has been against us. Here we are, conquerors in a conquered city; we have respected every right, tried every means of conciliation, complied with every reasonable desire; and yet we can not walk the streets without being outraged and spit upon by green girls. I do not fear the troops; but if aggression must be, let it not be all against *us*."

General Butler was, of course, perfectly aware, as we are, that if he had expressly *commanded* his troops to outrage and ravish every woman who insulted them, those men of New England and the West would not have thought of obeying him. If one miscreant among them had attempted it, the public opinion of his regiment would have crushed him. Every one who knows the men of that army feels how *impossible* it was that any of them should practically misinterpret an order of which the proper and innocent meaning was so palpable.

The order was published. Its success was immediate and perfect. Not that the women did not still continue, with the ingenuity of the sex, to manifest their repugnance to the troops. They did so. The piano still greeted the passing officer with rebel airs. The fair countenances of the ladies were still averted, and their skirts gently held aside. Still the balconies presented a view of the "back hair" of beauty. If the dear creatures did not leave the car when an officer entered it, they stirred not to give him room to sit down, and would not see his polite offer to hand their ticket to the driver. (No conductors in the street cars of New Orleans.) It was a fashion to affect sickness at the stomach on such occasions; which led the *Delta* to remark, that the ladies should remember that but for the presence of the Union forces *some* of the squeamish stomachs would have nothing in them. But the outrageous demonstrations ceased. No more insulting words were uttered; and all the affectations of disgust were such as could be easily and properly borne by officers and men. Gradually even these were discontinued.

I need not add, that in no instance was the order misunderstood on the part of the troops. No man in the whole world misunderstood it who was not glad of any pretext for reviling the sacred cause for which the United States has been called to contend. So far from causing the women of New Orleans to be wronged or molested, it was that which saved them from the only danger of molestation to which they were exposed. It threw around them the protection of law, not tore it away; and such was the completeness of its success, that not one arrest under Order No. 28 has ever been made.

General Butler was not long in discovering that the order was to be made the occasion of a prodigious hue and cry against his administration. The puppet mayor of New Orleans was the first to lift his little voice against it; which led to important consequences.

It had already become apparent to the general and to the officers aiding him, that two powers so hostile as the city government of New Orleans and the commander of the Department of the Gulf could not co-operate—could not long exist together. The mayor and common council had violated their compact with the general in every particular. They had agreed to clean the streets, and had not done it. They had engaged to enroll two hundred and fifty of the property-holders of the town to assist in keeping the peace, that General Butler might safely withdraw his troops. The two hundred and fifty proved to be men of the "Thug" species—the hangers-on of the City Hall. The European Brigade was to be retained in service; the mayor disbanded it. Provisions had been sent out of the starving city to the hungry camp of General Lovell. Confederate notes, which had fallen to thirty cents, were redeemed by the city government at par, thus taxing the city one hundred cents to give thirty to the favorites of the mayor and council; for the redemption was not public and universal, but special and private. The tone and style of the city government, too, were a perpetual reiteration of the assertion, so dear to the deluded people of the city, that New Orleans had not been conquered—only overcome by "brute force." Nothing but the general's extreme desire to give the arrangement of May 4th so fair a trial that the whole world would hold him guiltless in dissolving it, prevented his seizing upon the government of the city on the ninth of May.

The following letter from General Butler to the mayor and council, will serve to show the state of feeling between them:

"HEAD-QUARTERS, DEPARTMENT OF THE GULF,
NEW ORLEANS, *May* 16, 1862.

"To the Mayor and Gentlemen of the City Council of New Orleans:

"In the report of your official action, published in the *Bee* of the 16th instant, I find the following extracted resolutions, with the action of part of your body thereon, viz:

"'The following preamble and resolution, offered by Mr. Stith, were read twice and adopted. The rules being suspended, were, on motion, sent to the assistant board.

"'YEAS—Messrs. De Labarre, Forestall, Huckins, Rodin, and Stith—5.

"'*Whereas*, it has come to the knowledge of this council that, for the first time in the history of this city, a large fleet of the navy of France is about to visit New Orleans—of which fleet the Catinet, now in our port, is the pioneer—this council, bearing in grateful remembrance the many ties of amity and good feeling which unite the people of this city with those of France, to whose paternal protection New Orleans owes its foundation and early prosperity, and to whom it is especially grateful for the jealousy with which, in the cession of the state, it guaranteed all the rights of property, person, and religious freedom of its citizens—

"'*Be it resolved*, That the freedom and hospitalities of the city of New Orleans be tendered through the commander of the Catinet to the French naval fleet during its sojourn in our port; and that a committee of five of this council be appointed, with the mayor, to make such tender and such other arrangements as may be necessary to give effect to the same.

"'Messrs. Stith and Forestall were appointed on the committee mentioned in the foregoing resolution.'

"This action is an insult, as well to the United States, as to the friendly and powerful nation toward whose officers it is directed. The offer of the freedom of a captured city by the captives would merit letters-patent for its novelty, were there not doubts of its usefulness as an invention. The tender of its hospitalities by a government to which police duties and sanitary regulations only are intrusted, is simply an invitation to the calaboose or the hospital. The United States authorities are the only ones here capable of dealing with amicable or unamicable nations, and will see to it that such acts of courtesy or assistance are extended to any armed vessel of the emperor of France as shall testify the national, traditional, and hereditary feelings of grateful remembrance with which the United States government and people appreciate the early aid of France, and her many acts of friendly regard, shown upon so many national and fitting occasions.

"The action of the city council in this behalf must be revised.

"Respectfully,

"B. F. BUTLER, *Major-General Commanding*."

Such being the temper of the parties, an explosion was to be expected upon the first occasion. Order No. 28 was the spark which blew up the city government.

On the day on which the order appeared in the newspapers, the mayor sent to General Butler the following letter, which was written for him by his secretary, Mr. Duncan, formerly of the *Delta:*

"STATE OF LOUISIANA, MAYORALTY OF NEW ORLEANS,
"*May* 16, 1862.

"Major-General BENJAMIN F. BUTLER, Commanding United States Forces.

"SIR:—Your General Order, No. 28, of date 15th inst., which reads as follows, is of a character so extraordinary and astonishing that I can not, holding the office of chief magistrate of this city, chargeable with its peace and dignity, suffer it to be promulgated in our presence without protesting against the threat it contains, which has already aroused the passions of our people, and must exasperate them to a degree beyond control. Your officers and soldiers are permitted, by the terms of this order, to place any construction they may please upon the conduct of our wives and daughters, and, upon such construction, to offer them atrocious insults. The peace of the city and the safety of your officers and soldiers from harm or insult have, I affirm, been successfully secured to an extent enabling them to move through our streets almost unnoticed, according to the understanding and agreement entered into between yourself and the city authorities. I did not, however, anticipate a war upon women and children, who, so far as I am aware, have only manifested their displeasure at the occupation of their city by those whom they believe to be their enemies, and I will never undertake to be responsible for the peace of New Orleans while such an edict, which infuriates our citizens, remains in force. To give a license to the officers and soldiers of your command to commit outrages, such as are indicated in your order, upon defenseless women is, in my judgment, a reproach to the civilization, not to say to the Christianity, of the age, in whose name I make this protest. I am, sir, your obedient servant,

"JOHN T. MONROE, *Mayor.*"

To this General Butler replied with promptness and brevity, and sent his reply by the hands of the provost-marshal:

"HEAD-QUARTERS, DEPARTMENT OF THE GULF,
"NEW ORLEANS, *May* 16, 1862.

"John T. Monroe, late mayor of the city of New Orleans, is relieved from all responsibility for the peace of the city, and is suspended from the exercise of any official functions, and committed to Fort Jackson until farther orders.
B. F. BUTLER, *Major-General Commanding.*"

The mayor, however, was indulged with an interview with the commanding general. He remonstrated against the order for his imprisonment. The general told him, in reply, that if he could no longer control the "aroused passions of the people of New Orleans," it was highly necessary that he should not only be relieved from any further responsibility for the tranquillity of the city, but be sent himself to a place of safety: which Fort Jackson was. The letter, added the general, was an insult which no officer, representing the majesty of the United States in a captured city, ought to submit to. The mayor, whose courage always oozed away in the presence of General Butler, declared that he had had no intention to insult the general: he had only intended to vindicate the honor of the virtuous ladies of New Orleans.

"No vindication is necessary," said General Butler, "because the order does not contemplate or allude to virtuous women." None such, he believed, could have meant to insult his officers or men by word, look, or gesture, and the order was aimed only at those who had.

Finding the mayor pliant and reasonable, as he always was in the absence of his supporters, General Butler expounded the order to him at great length, and with perfect courtesy. The mayor then declared that he was *perfectly satisfied*, and asked to be allowed to withdraw his offensive letter. General Butler, knowing well the necessity, in all dealings with puppets, of having something to show in writing, wrote the following words at the end of the mayor's letter:

"GENERAL BUTLER:—This communication having been sent under a mistake of fact, and being improper in language, I desire to apologize for the same, and to withdraw it."

This the mayor signed, and the general relieved him from arrest. The mayor then departed, and the general hoped he had done with Order No. 28.

It was very far, however, from the intention of the gentlemen who had the mayor of New Orleans in charge, to forego their opportunity of firing the southern heart. In the evening of the same 16th of May, General Butler received the following note:

"MAYORALTY OF NEW ORLEANS,
"CITY HALL, *May* 16, 1862.

"Major-General BUTLER:

"SIR:—Having misunderstood you yesterday in relation to your General Order No. 28, I wish to withdraw the indorsement I made on the letter addressed to you yesterday. Please deliver the letter to my secretary, Mr. Duncan, who will hand you this note. Your obedient servant,

"JOHN T. MONROE."

General Butler immediately replied in the following terms:

"HEAD-QUARTERS, DEPARTMENT OF THE GULF,
"NEW ORLEANS, *May* 16, 1862.

"SIR:—There can be, there has been, no room for the misunderstanding of General Order No. 28.

"No lady will take any notice of a strange gentleman, and *a fortiori* of a stranger, in such form as to attract attention. Common women do.

"Therefore, whatever woman, lady or mistress, gentle or simple, who, by gesture, look or word, insults, shows contempt for, thus attracting to herself the notice of my officers or soldiers, will be deemed to act as becomes her vocation of common woman, and will be liable to be treated accordingly. This was most fully explained to you at my office.

"I shall not, as I have not, abated a single word of that order; it was well considered. If obeyed, it will protect the true and modest woman from all possible insult. The others will take care of themselves.

"You can publish your letter, if you publish this note, and your apology.

"Respectfully, BENJAMIN F. BUTLER,
"*Major-General Commanding.*

"JOHN T. MONROE, *Mayor of New Orleans.*"

To this the mayor replied by sending to the general a copy of his first letter. General Butler summoned him again to head-quarters; he came accompanied by his secretary, Duncan. In the presence of the general his courage failed him again, and he declared that he did not wish to send the offensive letter if he could publish what the general had said to him yesterday, that Order No. 28 did not refer to *all* the ladies of New Orleans. With even an excess of patience, the general replied, that to prevent all possibility of misunderstanding he would put in writing at the bottom of a copy of the order a statement in accordance with the mayor's desires, which he would be at liberty to publish. So he wrote:

"You may say that this order refers to those women who have shown contempt for and insulted my soldiers, by words, gestures, and movements, in their presence. B. F. BUTLER."

Duncan asked the insertion of the word "only" after "women." The general assented to this also; when the mayor and his secretary retired, taking the documents with them. Again General Butler indulged the hope that the affair was satisfactorily adjusted.

Far from it. The next morning, which was Sunday, the mayor and a large party of his friends presented themselves at the private parlor of the general. The mayor said that he had come for the purpose of withdrawing his apology. General Butler replied that Sunday was not a business day with him, but if the Mayor desired to withdraw his apology, and would place himself, on Monday morning, in the chair in which he had sat when he signed it, he should have a full opportunity to do so. The general added, that he would be glad to see him the next morning, and as many friends as he chose to bring with him.

Meanwhile, information had been brought to head-quarters of a conspiracy among the paroled rebel prisoners in New Orleans, to procure arms and force their way beyond the Union lines and join General Lovell. Six of them had been arrested. The conspirators, it appeared, had called themselves the Monroe Guard, after the mayor, from whom they expected substantial aid—had probably received substantial aid already. The general was resolved to make short work with the mayor at their next interview.

On Monday morning the mayor presented himself at head-quarters, accompanied by his chief of police, a lieutenant of police, his private secretary, one of the city judges, and several others of his special backers; seven or eight persons in all. General Butler did not wait for the attack of this imposing force, but opened upon them as soon as they were in position. He made a clear and forcible statement of the many ways in which the city government had failed to observe the compact of May 4th. He told them that while he had been employing all the resources of his mind and of his position to keep the poor of the city from starving, the whole power and means of the city authorities had been expended in supporting the Confederate cause—by sending provisions to Lovell's camp, by contributing money for the maintenance of Confederate agents in the city, and by placing every obstacle in the way of the purification of the streets. He announced the discovery of the conspiracy among the paroled prisoners, the sentence of six of them to death; and discoursed upon the significance of the naming of the corps after the mayor. All this conflict of authority and of moral influence must cease, and cease at once. He had resolved to have no more of "this weathercock business."

After a long interview, he brought the matter to a very simple and direct issue. He saw before him the men who had inspired and upheld the mayor in his unnatural and unwilling contumacy. To each of them he addressed a question, the answer to which would fix his political position and indicate his future course:

"Judge Kennedy, do you sanction the mayor's letter in its substance and effect?"

Answer: "I sustain no insulting expression in this letter. The construction which the letter puts upon the order is the construction put upon it in this city generally. If I had been in the mayor's place, I should have claimed a modification, or an announcement of its intended construction."

General Butler: "Do you not believe the letter insulting? Do you aid and abet the mayor ? Do you sustain the mayor in reiterating the letter?"

Kennedy: "I can not answer. I will answer neither yes nor no, for the simple reason that it will not cover the position I take. I would not, in any communication with General Butler, use insulting language myself."

The question was then proposed to the other gentlemen in turn.

Chief of Police: "I do sustain the mayor."

Lieutenant of Police: "I have not given the letter a thought. I have never read the letter before."

Mr. Harris: The same answer.

Mr. Whann: "I do not sustain or repudiate the letter, as I know nothing about it."

Mr. Pettigrew: "I sustain the mayor."

Mr. Duncan confessed to having "assisted in the composition of the letter."

General Butler then ordered the committal to Fort Jackson of the *late* mayor, the chief of police, Judge Kennedy and Mr. Duncan. The others were dismissed. The mayor, finally wished to know if his apology would be considered withdrawn. General Butler assured him that when the letter and the apology were published, the withdrawal of the apology should be distinctly stated.

The mayor was afterward removed to Fort Pickens. The offer was always open to him to take the oath and return home. Some of his friends, it is said, prevailed upon him, at length, to return home on that hard condition; and General Butler consenting, his wife went to Fort Pickens after him. The officer who accompanied her chanced to hand the mayor a newspaper which contained a positive announcement that France had recognized the Confederacy. The worthy mayor instantly changed his mind, refused to take the oath, and permitted a faithful spouse to depart without him.

The mayor being deposed, the executive part of the city govern ment was at once suspended, and the business of governing New Orleans devolved upon the military commandant, General G. F. Shepley, of Maine. The woman order, however, merely hastened an event which the expiration of the mayor's term of office would have effected in a few days; for General Butler had already determined that no man should again be elected to office in New Orleans who had not taken the oath of allegiance to his country's government.

The day after the scene just related, General Shepley issued the following

"NOTICE.

"HEAD-QUARTERS, MILITARY COMMANDANT OF NEW ORLEANS,
"CUSTOM-HOUSE, *May* 20, 1862.

"In the absence of the late mayor of New Orleans, by order of Major-General B. F. Butler, commanding the Department of the Gulf, the military commandant of New Orleans will, for the present, and until such time as the citizens of New Orleans shall elect a loyal citizen of New Orleans and of the United States as mayor of the city, discharge the functions which have hitherto appertained to that office.

"He assures the peaceable citizens of New Orleans, that he will afford the most ample protection to their persons and property, and their honor.

"No officer or soldier of the United States army will be permitted to insult or annoy any peaceable citizen, or in any way to invade his personal rights, or rights of property.

"No citizen will be permitted to insult or interfere with any officer or soldier in the discharge of his duty.

"No person hereafter will denounce or threaten with personal violence any citizen of the United States for the expression of Union and loyal sentiments. The punishment for these offenses will be speedy and effectual.

"The functions of the chief of police wil. be exercised by Captain Jonas H. French, provost-marshal, to whom all police-officers will report immediately. He is intrusted with the duty of organizing the police force of the city, and will continue in office those found to be trustworthy, honest, and loyal.

"The several recorders are hereby suspended from the discharge of the functions of their offices, and Major Joseph M. Bell, provost judge, will hear and determine all complaints for the violation of the peace and good order of the city, of its ordinances or of the laws of the United States.

"The laws and general ordinances of the city of New Orleans, excepting such as may be inconsistent with the constitution and laws of the United States, or with any general order issued by the commanding general of this department, or with this order, are hereby continued in force.

"All contracts and engagements heretofore legally entered in by the city of New Orleans, or under the authority thereof, subject to the limitations of the foregoing paragraph, shall be held inviolate, and faithfully carried out.

"It is expected, and will be required, that all contractors shall continue to perform the duties and obligations resting upon them by contracts now in force, and all such parties will be held to rigid accountability.

"The military commandant desires the co-operation of all good citizens to enable him to carry out the duties assumed.

"He invites, and will speedily ask, the aid of a number of citizens of respectability and character, to aid in the department of the city finances, as well as in what pertains to the health, lighting, paving, cleansing, drainage, wharves, levees, and generally, all municipal affairs not excepted from civil control by the proclamation of the commanding general, or by this order; and in the mean time, all officers now charged with such functions, are retained in their respective employments until farther orders.

"In all questions of the construction and interpretation of the laws pertaining to the city and its government, and of the ordinances thereof, the military commandant will seek the guidance of a professional man of known probity and intelligence.

"The military commandant will be most happy to receive from any citizen of New Orleans written or oral suggestions, touching the welfare and good government thereof.

"In conclusion, the military commandant assures the entire population of the city, that the restoration of the authority of the United States is the re-establishment of peace, order and morality; safety to life, liberty and property under the law, and a guarantee of the future prosperity and glory of the crescent city, under the protection of the American government and constitution.

"To promote these ends, his own most strenuous efforts will be unceasingly devoted, and to their consummation, he earnestly invites the co-operation of his fellow-citizens of New Orleans.

"G. F. SHEPLEY, *Military Commandant of New Orleans.*

"EDWIN ILSLEY, *A. A. A. G.*"

General Shepley proceeded with vigor to organize the government. Colonel French advertised for five hundred policemen. Judicious appointments were made in every department, and the municipal revolution was accomplished without disturbance. Among General Shepley's first orders we notice the following:

"GENERAL ORDERS.

"OFFICE MILITARY COMMANDANT OF NEW ORLEANS,
"CITY HALL, *May* 28, 1862.

"Hereafter in the churches in the city of New Orleans, prayers will not be offered up for the destruction of the Union or constitution of the United States, for the success of rebel armies, for the Confederate States, so called, or any officers of the same, civil or military, in their official capacity.

"While protection will be afforded to all churches, religious houses, and establishments, and religious 'services are to be held as in times of profound peace,' this protection will not be allowed to be perverted to the upholding of treason or advocacy of it in any form.

"Where thus perverted, it will be withdrawn.

"G. F. SHEPLEY, *Military Commandant.*"

This order was complied with only in the letter. Thenceforward, in reaching that part of the service where prayers were accustomed to be offered for Jefferson Davis, the minister would say: "Let us now spend a few moments in silent prayer."

After suppressing the city government, it seemed to General Butler unjust and unwise to permit that potent instigator and director of treason, Mr. Pierre Soulé, to remain in the city. It was he who had assisted in the composition of the mayor's insolent letter to Captain Farragut. It was he who had countenanced, perhaps caused, the burning of the cotton. It was he who was the moral support of the contumacy of secession in New Orleans. Upon him secession chiefly relied to give it voice and effect. General Butler was clearly of opinion that to render New Orleans a dead thing to secession, it was indispensable to send away a man so powerful to nourish hostility to the Union. Captain Conant accomplished the arrest with his usual tact, and Mr. Soulé, after ample time to arrange his private business, was consigned to Fort Warren, in Boston harbor. General Butler, some time afterward, requested the government to release the prisoner on his parole not to return to New Orleans, nor commit or advise any act hostile to the United States, which was done.

Few men have had a more varied career than Pierre Soulé. A native of France—a Paris lawyer—a Paris journalist—a fugitive to the West Indies—an emigrant to New Orleans—a lawyer there of brilliant position—a senator of the United States—a minister to Madrid, where he wounded the French embassador in a duel—a member of the Ostend Cuba-coveting conference—a lawyer again in New Orleans—a Unionist—a rebel—a prisoner of state.

Before taking leave of the woman order and its consequences, it is proper to notice the use made of it by the enemies of the United States. The screech which arose from all parts of Secessia furnishes another proof that this rebellion, which was begun in falsehood, has been sustained by falsehood alone. I will give here a few of the rebel comments.

The following "appeal" appeared in most of the southern papers:

"AN APPEAL TO EVERY SOUTHERN SOLDIER.—We turn to you in mute agony! Behold our wrongs! Fathers! husbands! brothers! sons! we know these bitter, burning wrongs will be fully avenged—*never* did southern women appeal in vain for protection from insult! But, for the sake of your sisters throughout the south, with tears we implore you not to surrender your cities, 'in consideration of the defenseless women and children!' Do not leave your women to the mercy of this merciless foe! Would it not have been better for New Orleans to have been laid in ruins, and we buried up beneath the mass, than that we should be subjected to these untold sufferings? Is life so precious a boon that, for the preservation of it, *no* sacrifice is too great? Ah, no! ah, no! Rather let us die with you, oh, our fathers! Rather, like Virginius, plunge your own swords into our breasts, saying, 'This is all we can give our daughters.'

"THE DAUGHTERS OF NEW ORLEANS.

"NEW ORLEANS, *May* 24, 1862."

The governor of Louisiana discoursed upon the inviting topic in an address to the people.

"History records instances of cities sacked, and inhuman atrocities committed upon the women of a conquered town, but in no instance, in modern times, at least, without the brutal ravishers suffering condign punishment from the hands of their own commanders. It was reserved for a federal general to invite his soldiers to the perpetration of outrages, at the mention of which the blood recoils in horror—to quicken the impulse of their sensual instincts by the suggestion of transparent excuses for their gratification, and to add to an infamy already well merited these crowning titles of a panderer to lust and a desecrator of virtue.

"Organize, then, quickly and efficiently. If your enemy attempt to proceed into the interior, let his pathway be marked by his blood. It is your homes that you have to defend. It is the jewel of your hearths, the chastity of your women, you have to guard. Let that thought animate your breasts, nerve your arms, quicken your energies, and inspire your resolution. Strike home to the heart of your foe the blow that rids your country of his presence. If needs be, let his blood moisten your own grave. It will rise up before your children as a perpetual memento of a race whom it will teach to hate now and evermore."

A fair and indignant Georgian wrote to one of the newspapers of Savannah:

"*Editor of the Republican*—Seeing your spirited notice in this morning's paper, of the offer of a noble Mississippian to give a reward of $10,000 for the infamous Butler's head, can you not suggest, through your valuable journal, the propriety of every woman in our Confederacy contributing her mite to triple the sum, for a consummation dear to the insulted honor of our countrywomen, one and all?

"Respectfully, A SAVANNAH WOMAN.

"SAVANNAH, *June* 10, 1862."

Mr. Paul H. Hayne, a very worthy young gentleman and poet of Charleston, was "carried away" by the tide of feeling, and achieved a poem that is only ludicrous when we consider the real character of the event which called it forth.

BUTLER'S PROCLAMATION.

BY PAUL H. HAYNE.

"It is ordered that hereafter, when any female shall, by word, gesture, or movement, insult or show contempt for any officer or soldier of the United States, *she shall be regarded and held liable to be treated as a woman of the town plying her avocation*."—*Butler's Order at New Orleans.*"

"AY! drop the treacherous mask! throw by
The cloak which veiled thine instincts fell;
Stand forth, thou base, incarnate Lie,
Stamped with the signet brand of hell;
At last we view thee as thou art,
A trickster with a demon's heart.

* * * * * * *

"O soldiers, husbands, brothers, sires!
Think that each stalwart blow ye give
Shall quench the rage of lustful fires,
And bid your glorious women live
Pure from a wrong whose tainted breath
Were fouler than the foulest death.

* * * * * * *

"Yes! but there's *one who shall not die*
In battle harness! One for whom
Lurks in the darkness silently
Another and a sterner doom!
A warrior's end should crown the brave—
For *him*, swift cord! and felon grave!

"As loathsome, charnel vapors melt,
Swept by invisible winds to naught,
So, may this fiend of lust and guilt
Die like nightmare's hideous thought!
Naught left to mark the mother's name,
Save—immortality of shame!"

It pleased the English friends of the Confederacy, to place upon Order No. 28, the same preposterous construction. For them, however, there was this excuse: they had read "Napier's History of the Peninsular War." They knew how savages in red coats had been wont to conduct themselves in captured cities, and naturally concluded that patriots in blue would follow their example. But it is difficult to believe in the sincerity of noble lords and members of the house of commons, when *they* adopted and echoed back the rebel screech. We hesitate to think that men intrusted with the government of a great country can be so easily taken in.

Lord Palmerston.—"I am quite prepared to say, that I think no man could have read the proclamation to which our attention has been drawn, without a feeling of the deepest indignation—(cheers from both sides of the house)—a proclamation to which I do not scruple to attach the epithet infamous. (Renewed cheering.) Sir, an Englishman must blush to think that such an act has been committed by one belonging to the Anglo-Saxon race. (Cheers.) If it had come from some barbarous race that was not within the pale of civilization, one might have regretted it, but might not have been surprised; but that such an order should have been promulgated by a soldier—(cheers)—by one who had raised himself to the rank of general, is a subject undoubtedly of not less astonishment than pain. (Cheers.) Sir, I can not bring myself to believe but that the government of the United States, whenever they had notice of this order, must, of their own accord, have stamped it with their censure and condemnation."

Punch, too, whose laugh was always humane and just, till the slaveholders of the southern states rose in arms against all that Englishmen used to hold dear, had his little song on the subject:

"Haynau's lash tore woman's back,
When she riz his dander.
Bütler, by his edict black,
Stumps that famed commander.
Wreaking upon maid and dame
Savagery subtler:
None but Nena Sahib name
Along with General Butler.
Yankee doodle, doodle doo,
Yankee doodle dandy;
Butler is a rare Yahoo,
As brave as Sepoy Pandy."

These perverse and ridiculous passages may serve as encouragement to public men who are called to act in novel and difficult circumstances. They show the emptiness and harmlessness of partisan clamor when it is aimed against a measure which is wise, humane and right. General Butler could not have been quite indifferent to vituperation like this—no man could have been. He took no public notice of it at the time, having more important affairs upon his hands; but, among his private letters, there is one which briefly vindicates the order.

"I am as jealous," he wrote, "of the good opinion of my friends as I am careless of the slanders of my enemies, and your kind expressions with regard to Order No. 28 lead me to say a word to you on the subject.

"That it could ever have been so misconceived as it has been by some portions of the northern press, is wonderful, and would lead me to exclaim, with the Jew, 'Oh! Father Abraham, what these Christians are, whose own hard dealings teach them suspect the thoughts of others!'

"What was the state of things to which the woman order applied?

"We were two thousand five hundred men, in a city seven miles long by two to four wide, of a hundred and fifty thousand inhabitants, all hostile, bitter, defiant, explosive; standing literally on a magazine, a spark only needed for destruction. The devil had entered the hearts of the women of this town (you know seven of them chose Mary Magdalene for a residence) to stir up strife in every way possible. Every opprobrious epithet, every insulting gesture, was made by these be-jeweled, crinolined and laced creatures, calling themselves ladies, toward my soldiers and officers, from the windows of houses and in the streets. How long do you suppose our flesh and blood could have stood this without retort? That would have led to disturbances and riot, from which we must have cleared the streets with artillery—and then a howl that we had murdered these fine women. I had arrested the men who had hurrahed for Beauregard. Could I arrest the women? No. What was to be done? No order could be made save one which would execute itself. With anxious care, I thought I had hit upon this: 'Women who insult my soldiers are to be regarded and treated as common women, plying their vocation.'

"Pray, how do you treat a common woman plying her vocation in the streets? You pass her by unheeded. She can not insult you. As a gentleman, you can and will take no notice of her. If she speaks, her words are not opprobrious. It is only when she becomes a continuous and positive nuisance, that you call a watchman and give her in charge to him.

"But some of the northern editors seem to think that whenever one meets such a woman, we must stop her, talk with her, insult her, hold dalliance with her, and so from their own conduct they construed my order.

"The editor of the Boston *Courier* may so deal with common women, and out of the abundance of his heart his mouth may speak. But so do not I.

"Why, these she-adders of New Orleans themselves were at once tamed into propriety of conduct by the order, and from that day no woman has either insulted or annoyed any live soldier or officer, and of a certainty no soldier has insulted any woman.

"When I passed through Baltimore on the 23d of February last, members of my staff were insulted by the gestures of the ladies (?) there. Not so in New Orleans. * * *

"I can only say that I would issue the order again under like circumstances."

Among the women of New Orleans there were some who knew how to maintain, and even assert, their fidelity to the Confederate cause, without forgetting the courtesy due to officers of the United States who were simply doing their duty. To such General Butler and his staff were as complaisant as their duty permitted. The case of Mrs. Slocomb and her daughter Mrs. Urquhart, may be cited in illustration. These ladies applied for a pass to enable them to go to their country house, but stated with courteous frankness, that they could not take the oath of allegiance to the United States. At the beginning of the war, they said, they had desired the preservation of the Union; but now all their male friends and connections were in the Confederate army; one of them had lost a son, the other a brother, in the service; and they were now unalterably devoted to the cause, which they deemed just, noble, and holy. General Butler said to them, that he would make an exception to his rule and grant them the pass, if they would give up their spacious town house for the use of the United States during their absence, as he required such a house for his head-quarters. Mrs. Slocomb hesitated. With tears in her eyes, she said that her house was endeared to her by a thousand tender associations, and was now dearer to her than ever. She did not see how she could give it up.

The general said, that he "experienced peculiar pleasure in meeting ladies who, while they were enemies to his country, were yet so frank, so truthful and devoted, and remarked that if New Orleans had been defended by an army of such women as Mrs. Urquhart, he believed the Union army would have had considerable trouble in capturing the city. In regard to their house he assured them that, although he had the power to take it, yet without their permission it should not be occupied, nor a brick of it be molested, unless indeed, the city was ravaged by yellow fever, in which case he might be obliged to take every house suitable for hospital purposes; and he added, if I can find any other reason for making you an exception to my rule prohibiting passes to any who refuse to take the oath, I will do it."

Happily, he found such a reason. A day or two after, he wrote to the ladies: "I have the pleasure to inform you, that my necessities, which caused the request for permission to use your house during your absence this summer, have been relieved. I have taken the house of General Twiggs, late of the United States Army, for quarters. Inclined never on slight causes to use the power intrusted to me to grieve even sentiments only entitled to respect from the courage and ladylike propriety of manner in which they were avowed; it is gratifying to be enabled to yield to the appeal you made for favor and protection by the United States. Yours shall be the solitary exception to the general rule adopted, that they who ask protection must take upon themselves corresponding obligations or do an equal favor to the government. I have an aged mother at home, who, like you, might request the inviolability of hearthstone and roof tree from the presence of a stranger. For her sake you shall have the pass you ask, which is sent herewith. As I did myself the honor to say personally, you may leave the city with no fear that your house will be interfered with by any exercise of military right; but will be safe under the laws of the United States. Trusting that the inexorable logic of events will convict you of wrong toward your country, when all else has failed, I remain," etc.

Mrs. Slocomb acknowledged the favor: "Permit me to return my sincere thanks for the special permit to leave, which you have so kindly granted to myself and family, as also for the protection promised to my property. Knowing that we have no claim for any exception in our favor, this generous act calls loudly upon our grateful hearts, and hereafter, while praying earnestly for the cause we love so much, we shall never forget the liberality with which our request has been granted by one whose power here reminds us painfully that our enemies are more magnanimous than our citizens are brave."

Another instance. Mrs. Beauregard, the wife of the Confederate general, and her mother, were residing in the mansion of Slidell, the rebel emissary to France, who had lent it to them during his absence. This house being sequestered, Lieutenant Kinsman went to take possession, not knowing by whom it was occupied. Those distinguished and amiable ladies received the officer with dignity and politeness. He reported the fact of their occupation of the house to the commanding general, who immediately ordered that they should be allowed to reside in it undisturbed. There they remained, honored equally by the Union officers and by the people of the city.

CHAPTER XIX.

EXECUTION OF MUMFORD.

THE crime for which Mumford suffered death has been already related. If in the act of tearing down the flag of his country, he had fallen dead upon the roof of the Mint, from the fire of the howitzers in the main-top of the Pensacola, no one could have charged aught against those who had the honor of that flag in charge. His offense was two-fold: he insulted the flag of his country, and endangered the lives of innocent fellow-citizens by drawing the fire of the fleet. His life was justly forfeited to the United States and to New Orleans. His life, moreover, was not a valuable one; he was one of those who live by preying upon society, not by serving it. He was a professional gambler. Rather a fine-looking man, tall, black-bearded; age forty-two.

After the occupation of the city by the troops, he still appeared in the streets, bold, reckless and defiant, one of the heroes of the populace. He was seen even in front of the St. Charles hotel, relating his exploit to a circle of admirers, boasting of it, daring the Union authorities to molest him. He did this once too often. He was arrested and tried by a military commission, who condemned him to death, and General Butler approved the sentence, and ordered its execution.

SPECIAL ORDER NO. 10.

"NEW ORLEANS, *June* 5, 1862.

"William B. Mumford, a citizen of New Orleans, having been convicted before the military commission of treason and an overt act thereof, in tearing down the United States flag from a public building of the United States, for the purpose of inciting other evil-minded persons to farther resistance to the laws and arms of the United States, after said flag was placed there by Commodore Farragut, of the United States navy,

"It is ordered that he be executed, according to the sentence of the said military commission, on Saturday, June 7th instant, between the hours of 8 A. M. and 12 M., under the direction of the provost-marshal of the district of New Orleans; and for so doing, this shall be his sufficient warrant."

During his trial and after his condemnation, he showed neither fear nor contrition; evidently expected a commutation of his sentence, not believing that General Butler would dare execute it. His friends, the Thugs and gamblers of the city, openly defied the general; resolved, in council assembled, *not* to petition for his pardon; bound themselves to assassinate General Butler if Mumford were hanged. These things were duly reported to the general by his detective police, and were a common topic of conversation in the city. It was the almost universal belief that the condemned man would be brought to the gallows and there reprieved—according to the cruel blank-cartridge mode of weak governments.

While the friends of Mumford were thus building up a wall between him and the chance of pardon, the case was further complicated by the arrest and condemnation of the six paroled prisoners, part of the Monroe Guard, who had conspired to break away to the rebel camp. Their sentence also, the general approved:

GENERAL ORDER No. 36.

"NEW ORLEANS, *May* 31, 1862.

"Abraham McLane, Daniel Doyle, Edward C. Smith, Patrick Kane, George L. Williams, and Wm. Stanley, all enlisted men in the forces of the supposed Confederate States, captured at the surrender of Forts St. Philip and Jackson, have violated their parole of honor, under which they, as prisoners of war, were permitted to return to their homes, instead of being confined in prison, as have the unfortunates of the United States soldiers, who, falling into the hands of the rebel chiefs, have languished for months in the closest durance.

"Warned by their officers that they must not do this thing, they deliberately organized themselves in military array—chose themselves and comrades officers, relying, as they averred, upon promises of prominent citizens of New Orleans for a supply of arms and equipments. They named themselves the Monroe Life Guard, in honor of the late mayor of New Orleans.

"They conspired together, and arranged the manner in which they might force the pickets of the United States, and thus join the enemy at Corinth.

"Tried before an impartial military commission—fully heard in their defense—these facts appeared beyond doubt or contradiction, and they were convicted.

"There is no known pledge more sacred—there is no military offense whose punishment is better defined or more deserved. To this crime but one punishment has ever been assigned by any nation—Death.

"This sentence has been approved by the commanding general. To the end that all others may take warning—that solemn obligations may be preserved—that war may not lose all honorable ties—that clemency may not be abused, and that justice be done:

"It is ordered that Abraham McLane, Daniel Doyle, Edward C. Smith, Patrick Kane, George L. Williams, and William Stanley be shot to death, under the direction of the provost-marshal, immediately after reveille, on Wednesday, the 4th day of June next; and for so doing, this shall be the provost-marshal's sufficient warrant."

Here were seven men under sentence of death at the same time—seven human lives hanging upon the word of one man. General Butler is not a person of the philanthropical or humanitarian cast of character; which is compatible with strange hardness of heart toward individuals. Nor is he unaware of the frightful cruelty to society of pardoning men justly condemned. He is abundantly capable of preferring the good of the many to the convenience of one, and turning a deaf ear to the entreaties of a criminal, when, on the other hand, stands a wronged community asking protection, or an outraged country demanding justice upon its mortal foes. The fluid that courses his veins is blood, not milk and water. Nevertheless, he has the feelings that belong to a human being, and these seven forfeited lives hang heavy upon his heart.

In the case of Mumford he had no misgivings. He was able to endure the harrowing spectacle of the man's wife and three children falling upon their knees before him, begging the life of husband and father, and yet keep firmly to a just resolve. He was able to resist the tears and entreaties of his own tender-hearted wife, whose judgment he respected, to whose judgment he often deferred. Far more easily was he able to defy and scorn the threatenings of an impious clan of gamblers and ruffians. Mumford must die. That was the deliberate and changeless fiat of his best judgment.

Nor was he easily induced to alter his determination with regard to the six paroled prisoners. The events of the war had constantly deepened in his mind a sense of the general cruelty of pardons. He could not but think that the Union armies would not have lost a hundred thousand men by desertion, if, from the beginning, the just penalty of death had been inexorably inflicted; no, nor one thousand; perhaps not one hundred. He had imbibed a *horror* of all those loose, irresolute, chicken-hearted modes of proceeding, which have cost the country such incalculable suffering and blood. It is instinctive in such a man to know that, in this world, the kindest, as well as the wisest of all things, is the rigid observance of just law, the exact and prompt infliction of just penalty. So, between his sense of what was due to those six men, and his anxious consideration of extenuating circumstances, he lived many distracted days and nights. He could neither eat nor sleep.

The pressure upon him was intense, as it always is upon men whose word can save lives. Every body pleaded for them. His own officers besieged his ears for pardon. The officers of the condemned besought it. Union men of the city implored it. And at night, when the world was shut out, there was still a voice to repeat the arguments of the day. The six prisoners were poor, simple, ignorant souls. One of them had said, when arraigned before the commission, that he did not understand anything about this paroling.

"Paroling," said he, "is for officers and gentlemen: we are not gentlemen."

It is probable that this remark saved the lives of them all, for it suggested the line of argument and the kind of consideration which, probably, had most to do with changing the general's resolve. "We are not gentlemen,"—an admission which no northern prisoner would be likely to make. At the south those words really have a meaning; the poor people there *feel* a difference of rank between themselves and the lords of the plantation, and recognize a lower grade of personal obligation. A gentleman must keep his word; we poor people may get away if we can.

The earnest petition of those stanch Unionists, Mr. J. A. Rosier and Mr. T. J. Durant, had great weight with the general also.

"These men," wrote they, "are justly liable to the condign punishment which the military law metes out to so grave and heinous an offense. But a powerful government never diminishes its strength by acts of clemency and mercy. No doubt, General, these men were partly driven by want, partly deluded, and have long been so; superior minds have heretofore given them false impressions, and they have been acting under such views as have at last brought them to the threshold of the grave. Unknown to us, even from report, prior to their trial and condemnation, we see in them only men and brethren who have erred and are in danger. General, the event has just shown that these men are unable to resist the force of the government, or elude its vigilance and the fidelity of its officers. They are subdued and powerless. Their case excites our commiseration, and that of hundreds of others. We ask you to have mercy upon them. At the present moment the government needs no excessive rigor to enforce obedience or command respect. Pardon their offense. The act will restore them to sobriety of reason and to useful employment. It will fill them with gratitude to you and to the powerful government you represent. It will demonstrate the mildness of its authority, and convince our fellow-citizens that mercy and clemency, no less than force and strength, are essential attributes of the power you represent. General, receive this prayer for life, in the spirit which dictates it—an earnest and heartfelt desire to promote reconciliation and peace."

To this letter, which was received the day before the one named for the execution, General Butler replied:

"Your communication has received, as it deserved, most serious consideration. The representations of gentlemen of your known probity, intelligence, high social position, and thorough acquaintance with the character, temper, habits of thought and motives of action of the people of New Orleans, ought to have great and determining weight with me, a stranger among you, called upon to act promptly under the best light I may in matters affecting the administration of justice. In addition, your well-known and fully appreciated unswerving attachment to the government of the United States, renders it certain that nothing but the best interests of the country could have influenced your opinion.

"Of the justice which calls for the death of these men I can have no doubt. The mercy it would be to others, in like cases tempted to offend, to have the terrible example of the punishment to which these misguided men are sentenced, is the only matter left for discussion.

"Upon this question you who have suffered for the Union, who have stood by it in evil and in good report—you who have lived and are hereafter to live in this city as your home, when all are gathered again under the flag which has been so foully outraged, and to whose wrongs these men's lives are forfeit—you who, I have heard, exerted your talents to save the lives of Union men in the hour of their peril, ought to have a determining weight when your opinions have been deliberately formed. You ask for these men's lives. You shall have them. You say that the clemency of the government is best for the cause we all have at heart. Be it so. You are likely to be better informed upon this than I am. I have no wish to do anything but that which will show the men of Louisiana how great a good they were tempted to throw away when they were led to raise their hands against the constitution and laws of the United States.

"If this example of mercy is lost upon those in the same situation, swift justice can overtake others in like manner offending."

The men were reprieved, and consigned to Ship Island "during the pleasure of the president of the United States." This was on the fourth of June. Mumford was to die on the seventh.

The scaffold was erected in front of the Mint, near the scene of his crime. To the last minute General Butler was earnestly implored to spare him. The venerable Dr. Mercer, a man of eighty honorable years, once the familiar friend and frequent host of Henry Clay, a gentleman of boundless generosity and benevolence, the patron of all that redeemed New Orleans, came to head-quarters an hour before the execution, to ask for Mumford's life.

"Give me this man's life, General," said he, while the tears rolled down his aged cheeks. "It is but a scratch of your pen."

"True," replied the general. "But a scratch of my pen could burn New Orleans. I could as soon do the one act as the other. I think one would be as wrong as the other."

In truth, the reprieve of the six had rendered the saving of Mumford impossible. That act of mercy, like all the rest of General Butler's acts in New Orleans, was utterly misinterpreted by the people, who attributed it to weakness and cowardice. It was, and is, the conviction of the best informed officers and Union citizens then in New Orleans, that upon the question of hanging or sparing Mumford depended the final suppression or the continued turbulence of the mob of the city. Mumford hanged, the mob was subdued. Mumford spared, the mob remained to be quelled by final grape and canister. There was absolutely needed for the peaceful government of the city, a *certainty* that General Butler dared hang a rebel.

Mumford met his doom with the composure with which bad men usually die. He said that "the offense for which he was condemned was committed under excitement, and he did not consider he was suffering justly. He conjured all who heard him to act justly to all men; to rear their children properly; and when they met death they would meet it firmly. He was prepared to die; and as he had never wronged any one, he hoped to receive mercy."

"The unconscious is the alone complete," says the German poet. It is only good people who, on the approach of death, are dismayed and ashamed at reviewing their lives—comparing what might have been with what has been.

An immense concourse beheld the execution. The turbulent spirits of New Orleans drew the proper inferences from the scene. Every one concerned in the administration of justice in the city felt a certain confidence, before unfelt, in their ability to rule the city without violence. Every soldier felt safer; and the friends of the Union had an assurance that, at length, they were really on the stronger side. Order *reigned* in Warsaw.

The name of Mumford, if we may believe Confederate newspapers, was immediately added to the "roll" of martyrs to the cause of liberty. The fugitive governor of Louisiana, from some safe retreat up the river, fulminated a proclamation about this time, in which he commented upon the death of Mumford in the style of eloquence familiar to the readers of De Bow's Review—a curious mixture of Patrick Henry and Bedlam.

"The loss of New Orleans," said he, "and the opening of the Mississippi, which will soon follow, have greatly increased our danger, and deprived us of many resources for defense. With less means, we have more to do than before. Every weapon we have, and all that our skillful mechanics can make, will be needed. Let every citizen be an armed sentinel, to give warning of any approach of the insolent foe. Let all our river banks swarm with armed patriots, to teach the hated invader that the rifle will be his only welcome on his errands of plunder and destruction. Wherever he dares to raise the hated emblem of tyranny, tear it down, and rend it in tatters.

"The noble heroism of the patriot Mumford, has placed his name high on the list of our martyred sons. When the federal navy reached New Orleans, a squad of marines was sent on shore, who hoisted their flag on the Mint. The city was not occupied by the United States troops, nor had they reached there. The place was not in their possession. William B. Mumford pulled down the detested symbol with his own hands, and for that was condemned to be hung by General Butler after his arrival. Brought in full view of the scaffold, his murderers hoped to appall his heroic soul, by the exhibition of the implements of ignominious death. With the evidence of their determination to consummate their brutal purpose before his eyes, they offered him life on the condition that he would abjure his country, and swear allegiance to her foe. He spurned the offer. Scorning to stain his soul with such foul dishonor, he met his fate courageously, and has transmitted to his countrymen a fresh example of what men will do and dare when under the inspiration of fervid patriotism. I shall not forget the outrage of his murder, nor shall it pass unatoned.

"I am not introducing any new regulations for the conduct of our citizens, but am only placing before them those that every nation at war recognizes as necessary and proper to be enforced. It is needless, therefore, to say that they will not be relaxed. On the contrary, I am but awaiting the assistance and presence of the general appointed to the department, to inaugurate the most effectual method for their enforcement. It is well to repeat them:

"Trading with the enemy is prohibited under all circumstances.

"Traveling to and from New Orleans and other places occupied by the enemy is forbidden. All passengers will be arrested.

"Citizens going to those places, and returning with the enemy's usual passport, will be arrested.

"Conscripts or militia-men, having in possession such passports, and seeking to shun duty, under the pretext of a parole, shall be treated as public enemies. No such papers will be held as sufficient excuse for inaction by any citizen.

"The utmost vigilance must be used by officers and citizens in the detection of spies and salaried informers, and their apprehension promptly effected.

"Tories must suffer the fate that every betrayer of his country deserves.

"Confederate notes shall be received and used as the currency of the country.

"River steamboats must, in no case, be permitted to be captured. Burn them when they can not be saved.

"Provisions may be conveyed to New Orleans only in charge of officers, and under the precautionary regulations governing communication between belligerents.

"The loss of New Orleans, bitter humiliation as it was to Louisianians, has not created despondency, nor shaken our abiding faith in our success. Not to the eye of the enthusiastic patriot alone, who might be expected to color events with his hopes, but to the more impassioned gaze of the statesman that success was certain from the beginning.. It is only the timid, the unreflecting, and the property owner, who thinks more of his possessions than his country, that will succumb to the depressing influences of disaster. The great heart of the people has swelled with more intense aspirations for the cause the more it seemed to totter. Their confidence is well founded. The possession by the enemy of our seaboard and main water-courses ought to have been foreseen by us. His overwhelming naval force necessarily accomplished the same results attained by the British with the same force in their war of subjugation. The final result will be the same," etc., etc.

CHAPTER XX.

GENERAL BUTLER AND THE FOREIGN CONSULS.

"WHATEVER else may be said of business in New Orleans," remarked the humorous *Delta*, "one thing is certain, consuls are lower."

Consuls were very high indeed during the first few weeks of the occupation of the city. Their position in New Orleans had been one of first-rate importance during the rebellion; for it was chiefly through the foreign capitalists of the city that the Confederacy had been supplied with arms and munitions of war, and it had been the congenial office of the consuls to afford them aid and protection in that lucrative business. They forgot that they were only consuls. They forgot the United States. Often communicating directly with the cabinet ministers of their countries, always flattered and made much of by the supporters of the rebellion, expecting with the most perfect confidence the triumph of secession, representing powers every one of which desired or counted upon its success, they assumed the tone of embassadors; they courted the power which they assumed would finally rule in New Orleans, and held in contempt or aversion the one to which they were accredited.

These gentlemen gave General Butler more trouble, caused him more hard work, than any other class in New Orleans. They opposed every measure of his which could be supposed to bear upon any man of foreign origin. Mr. Seward was overrun with their protests, complaints and petitions. If the secretary of the treasury approved the commander of the Department of the Gulf as the cheapest of generals, the secretary of state found him much the most troublesome. The correspondence relating to this single subject would fill two or three volumes as large as this.

A collision between the foreign consuls and General Butler almost necessarily involved a difference between General Butler and Mr. Seward. The two men are moral antipodes. Mr. Seward has too little, General Butler has *enough*, of the spirit of warfare. Mr. Seward, by the constitution of his mind and the habits of thirty years, is a conciliator, one who shrinks from the final ordeal, who is reluctant to face the last consequences, skillful to postpone, explain away, and "make things pleasant." General Butler, on the contrary, rejoices in a clear issue, goes straight to the point, uses language that bears but one meaning, and "takes the responsibility" as naturally as he takes his breakfast. Mr. Seward so dreaded the approach of the war, that he was more than willing to make concessions which would pass the final, the inevitable conflict over to the next generation. General Butler picked up the glove with a feeling akin to exultation, and adopted war as the business of the country and his own, desiring no pause till the controversy was settled absolutely and for ever. Mr. Seward regarded the southern oligarchy as erring fellow-citizens, who could be won back to their allegiance. General Butler regarded them as traitors, utterly incapable of conversion, who could be rendered harmless only by being made powerless. Mr. Seward, as the head of the foreign department, felt that all his duties were subordinate to the one cardinal, central object of his policy, the maintenance of peace with foreign nations while the rebellion showed front. General Butler, always breasting the foremost wave of the rebellion, could not be very sensitive to the gentle murmurs of Mr.

Seward's reception-room. The men were subject to two opposite, antagonistic magnetisms. General Butler was John Heenan pegging away at Sayers, thinking of nothing but getting in fair blows. Mr. Seward was the distressed bottle-holder who wanted Heenan to win, but thought Sayers too good a fellow to be smashed.

Hence we find that when the foreign ministers brought their complaints to the department of state, Mr. Seward generally, and at once, took it for granted that General Butler was wrong. He could do no other way, without insincerity. The men are so essentially antagonistic, that no really characteristic act of either could fail to excite in the other an instinctive disapproval.

Similar remarks apply to Mr. Reverdy Johnson, of Maryland, the eminent and very able lawyer who was sent by Mr. Seward to New Orleans to investigate the consular imbroglio. In the Charleston Convention of 1860, he said that "under almost any conceivable circumstances, Maryland will acknowledge her rights as a southern state, and will vote with the people of the South." He spoke then from his heart. If, in 1862, he thought secession a mistake and a crime, in all other particulars he was in accord with his southern friends. His heart and mind, his friends and habits, were southern. In New Orleans he associated almost exclusively with secessionists—who felt, who avowed, who boasted that he was their friend. Granting that he had the most honorable intentions (I am sure he had no other), it was not in human nature that he should judge justly between General Butler and the rebels of New Orleans. Nor can we doubt that he was sent to New Orleans, and knew that he was sent, to comply with the demands of foreign powers, if it could be done without concessions too palpably humiliating.

Here is the point: every one knows the difference that *may* exist between a law case as presented in the law papers, and the known facts of the case. A merchant, for example, finds it convenient to "make over" his property to a friend. The *papers* show that he has not a dollar in the world, while the *fact* is, that he possesses a quarter of a million. Every one in the court may know the fact; yet the papers carry the day. A bank may find it advantageous to seem to possess no coin. Any lawyer can suggest a mode by which this can be done, and a judge in ordinary times might be obliged to decide in accordance with the documents. What General Butler would have liked was a commissioner who would have sought out the hidden fact, not one who was content with the paper case. But Mr. Seward was chiefly concerned to keep the peace with foreign powers, to deprive them not merely of all cause of complaint, but of all pretext. Far be it from me to presume to say that he was wrong. "One at a time" is a good rule, when a nation has a war on its hands. His course may have been justified by necessity.

It is impossible to detail here all the points of collision between General Butler and the foreign consuls. The more important cases were the following:

Case of the British Guard.

The British Guard consisted of fifty or sixty Englishmen, old residents of New Orleans, many of them men of large property and extensive business. On returning to their armory, late in the evening, after the disbanding of the Foreign Legion, they had held a formal meeting, at which it was voted to send their arms, accouterments, and uniforms to the camp of General Beauregard. On learning this, a few days after the occupation of the city, General Butler sent for Captain Burrows, the commander of the company, who confessed the fact. The general then directed him to order his company to leave New Orleans within twenty-four hours; and declared his intention to arrest and confine in Fort Jackson any who should fail to obey the order. The violation of the law of neutrality had been clear and indefensible. These men had enjoyed for many years the protection of the United States government, under which they acquired wealth and distinction, and then embraced the first opportunity that had offered to give material aid to its enemies. Captain Burrows could only object that part of the company had been absent from the meeting, and it would be unfair to punish the innocent with the guilty. General Butler assented, and ordered those of the company who had not participated in the offense, to appear before him with their arms and uniforms, the rest to obey the previous order.

The acting British consul, Mr. George Coppell, hastened to interpose. He could not deny that the act charged against his countrymen was a violation of the law; but he said they had done it with "no idea of wrong or harm." He enlarged upon the inconvenience it would be to those highly respectable gentlemen to leave the city, where their affairs were extensive and important. In fact, it would not be even "possible" for some of them to leave; and if General Butler should persist, it would be the duty of the consul to solemnly protest against the "verbal order of questionable legality, the enforcement of which would infringe the rights of British subjects residing in New Orleans."

The general replied by recounting the facts with the exactness of a lawyer. "These people," he added, "thought it of consequence that Beauregard should have sixty more uniforms and rifles. I think it of the same consequence that he should have sixty more of these faithless men, who may fill them if they choose. I intend this order to be strictly enforced. I am content for the present to suffer open enemies to remain in the city of their nativity; but law-defying and treacherous alien enemies shall not. I welcome all neutrals and foreigners who have kept aloof from these troubles which have been brought upon the city, and will, to the extent of my power, protect them and their property. They shall have the same hospitable and just treatment they have always received at the hands of the United States government. They will see, however, for themselves, that it is for the interest of all to have the unworthy among them rooted out; because the acts of such bring suspicion upon all. All the facts above set forth can easily be substantiated, and indeed, are all evasively admitted in your note by the very apology made for them. That apology says, that these men, when they took this action—sent these arms and munitions of war to Beauregard—'did it with no idea of wrong or harm.' I do not understand this. Can it be that such men, of age to enroll themselves as a military body, did not know that it was wrong to supply the enemies of the United States with arms? If so, I think they should be absent from the city long enough to learn so much international law; or do you mean to say, knowing their social proclivities, and the lateness of the hour when the vote was taken, therefore they were not responsible? There is another difficulty, however, in those people taking any protection under the British flag. The company received a charter or commission, or some form of rebel authorization from the governor of Louisiana, and one of them, whom I have under arrest, accompanied him to the rebel camp. There is still another difficulty. I am informed and believe that a majority of them have made declarations of their intentions to become citizens of the United States, and of the supposed Confederate States, and have taken the proper and improper oaths of allegiance to effect that purpose."

The order was executed. Every member of the company (for none of them could produce his arms or uniform) fled from the city, except the captain and one other. These two found themselves prisoners at Fort Jackson. Mr. Coppell related the case to Lord Lyons, who laid it before Mr. Seward. The secretary of state admitted the illegality of the act committed by the British Guard; but, in effect, recommended Captain Burrows and his friend to the mercy of the commanding general, and advised their release. Accordingly, after several weeks' detention, they were set at liberty.

General Butler, justly offended at the tone and substance of Mr. Coppell's remonstrance, intimated to that gentleman that, though he signed himself "Her Britannic Majesty's Acting Consul," he had exhibited no proof of his right to that honorable designation. "The respect," said General Butler, "which I feel for that government leads me to err, if at all, upon the side of recognition of your claims, and those of its officers; but I take leave to call your attention to the fact that you subscribed yourself 'Her Britannic Majesty's Acting Consul,' and that I have received no official information of any right you may have so to act, except your acts alone, and pardon me if I err in saying, that your acts in that capacity, which have come to my knowledge, have not been of such character as to induce the belief on my part, that you rightfully represent that noble government."

It happened that Mr. Coppell could not produce the regular documents. As he continued to interfere with General Butler's measures, and that too, in the style of a resident unfriendly minister, the general had the pleasure of refusing to recognize him, and he remained without official character until he could procure from Washington the necessary proofs of his appointment.

Case of Charles Heidsieck.

This individual, it appears, was the head of the great French house of dealers in Heidsieck champagne. He was a native and citizen of France, but had come to the southern states to look after his delinquent creditors, and had resided, for some time, at Mobile. He entered his name upon the books of the Dick Keys and the Natchez, steamboats permitted by General Butler to convey provisions to New Orleans, as bar-tender; made five trips in that disguise, and brought to and from Mobile a very large quantity of letters, several of which, containing treasonable information, were sent to Washington by General Butler. As Heidsieck was departing for Fort Jackson, he called on his consul for help. "I have the honor," he wrote, "to ask you to see what you have to do for me in this matter, having come and left this city under a flag of truce." What the consul concluded he had to do for him we shall see in a moment. After several months' imprisonment at Fort Jackson and Fort Pickens, he was released by orders from Washington. He then forwarded to the government a memorial, in the French manner, asking *reparation* for his detention. This impudent claim from a man who had only escaped the ignominious death of a spy by the clemency of the government, elicited from General Butler an amusing narrative of the case, which the evidence before me at this moment proves to be true in every particular.

"Let us," remarks the general, "in the light of the facts, examine Heidsieck's claims and pretensions. Of a very respectable social position, he claims to have engaged as a bar-tender on the steamer 'Dick Keys,' whose former bar-tender was conveniently sick, for the purpose and object of getting his letters from the consulate at New Orleans, and for the purpose of making money by the sale of his wines on board the boat during her trips. Now, a bar-tender at the South is one of the most menial employments, and is usually, on board steamers, intrusted to a negro steward. Is it likely that Heidsieck, without a controlling motive, would make one voyage from Mobile to New Orleans in that capacity? Is not a gentleman *disguised* when he takes upon himself such an employment? Is it an answer to say, that his full name was on the shipping articles, and by that he was to be recognized when 'bar-tender' was, as he admits, affixed to it? If we had found the name of 'Augustus Cæsar,' which might have been the name of the former black bar-tender whose place Heidsieck took, upon the shipping articles, should we have looked for and expected to find the Roman emperor?

"The motive for undertaking this menial occupation, as Heidsieck alleges, was to get his letters from the consulate. Why not send for them? If the military authorities would not let them go with his messenger, then he had no right to come in disguise and fetch them. But admit, for the sake of the argument, that his desire to get his correspondence was a sufficient motive for Heidsieck to take one such trip as bar-tender, why make five during a space of more than *two months?*

"To this he answers that the profits of the sales of his wines as bar-tender on board the boat, were not to be despised. But he admits that the boat could and did carry no passengers. To whom then was the wine to be sold, as he says that the boat was kept under strict surveillance. * * * Besides which, he admits that he spent his time between trips in the city of New Orleans. Indeed, what need of a bar-tender on board of that boat at all, especially one who was to be paid by the sale of wine? Is it possible that the crew of a small steamboat at the South drink enough of even so poor a wine as 'Heidsieck's champagne,' as to make it profitable for a gentleman to spend his time selling it as a menial? Again, if the bar-tender of the steamer 'Dick Keys' was sick, and the captain was willing to make such a bargain for such a bar-tender, how is it that when the 'Dick Keys' went out of the employment of carrying flour between Mobile and New Orleans, that the 'Natchez' which was employed in her stead, should also have a sick bar-tender and a captain who should be willing to make so remarkable a contract, as to give passage, board, and lodging where the cost of living was extremely heavy, to gentlemen to sell liquor to his own crew, as he could have no other customers? Still farther, after these boats were stopped by the United States authorities, because of the corrupt intelligence conveyed by them, Heidsieck was again found going to New Orleans, under the pretense of carrying dispatches to the French consul there, he having no business whatever in the city. Why not send the dispatches by Mr. Greenwood, the city agent? He was kind enough to take Heidsieck, dispatches and all, upon his schooner gratis; would he not have taken the dispatches alone?

"The facts with regard to Heidsieck may be stated in a word. I learned that intelligence was being conveyed to New Orleans and Mobile for the rebels. I believed the city agent to be trustworthy. There was no channel except the employés of the boat, no passengers being allowed. I caused an inquiry to be made, and found Heidsieck on board in disguise, and that he spent all his time, between trips, in this city. Before I had the facts reported to me, he had gone to Mobile with the last trip of the steamer. It may be assumed I was glad to see him, when he returned, in his true character of 'bearer of dispatches.' I arrested him as a spy—I confined him as a spy—I should have tried him as a spy, and hanged him upon conviction as a spy, if I had not been interfered with by the government at Washington.

"He had, when arrested, a canvas wrapper, of the size of a peck measure, firmly bound up with cords, covering letters from the French, Swiss, Spanish, Prussian, and Belgian consuls, also a great number of letters to private persons, mostly rebels, or worse, intermeddling foreigners, containing contraband intelligence. A portion of these letters were forwarded to the honorable secretary of state, in December last, by me. To show the utter falsity of Heidsieck's narrative, let me advert to his statement, that he stole away a paper which, he says, 'I recognized as the envelope of my dispatches; the envelope, by the folds, to which the remnant of the seals still adhered, which could alone give to M. De Mejan the correct idea of the bulk of the dispatches.' It will be recollected that it has already been stated by me that the letters were inclosed in a canvas wrapper, tied up with cord, which Heidsieck, in his memorial, represents me as being engaged for some minutes in 'cutting and breaking.' How then could any paper show the size of the package? I sent Heidsieck to Fort Jackson, which was, at that time, the only military prison in my department, and where confinements were usually made. Immediately after his arrest, the French consul notified me that he had referred the matter to his minister at Washington, and I accordingly sent my dispatch to the secretary of state, and rested in taking measures for the trial until I received instructions from the government.

"A number of French residents of New Orleans, however, petitioned me as an act of grace to release Heidsieck, and allow him to go to Europe, to remain during the war. I finally consented, and gave orders for his release upon that condition, as an act of clemency. For this order his friends were very grateful, and so expressed themselves both by letter and in person. This parole was declined by Heidsieck, although I supposed the application had been made by his consent and his procurement. Perhaps, however, this refusal may be explained by the fact stated in his memorial, that the French consul, two days afterward, started for Washington 'on my account.'

"It will be seen, in all points, Heidsieck claims that all suspicion should be diverted from himself as to his neutrality, because he was acting in concert with the Count Mejan, the French consul at New Orleans; but it will not escape recollection that M. Mejan's own propriety of conduct and neutrality has, by subsequent revelations, been shown to have been worse than doubtful—the repository of almost a half million of specie loaned by the Bank of New Orleans to the Confederate government, for the purpose of purchasing army clothing, and receiving a commission for his agency. Count Mejan has been, very properly, recalled by his government, and can hardly, by his character, cover the suspected acts of Heidsieck traveling between rebel cities in the guise of a bar-tender.

"Heidsieck was removed, with the other prisoners, to Fort Pickens, in August, because I was informed of a threatened attack by the rebels upon Fort Jackson, and I did not deem it proper that prisoners should either be exposed to the hazard of combat, or embarrass the defenders of the fort by their presence.

"Heidsieck's complaint as to his treatment during his confinement must be unfounded, because there was never any restriction, save in the matter of intoxicating liquors, upon prisoners and their friends furnishing any and everything desired by them for comfort or convenience; and his own memorial does not claim that any representations by him, or any other prisoner, were ever made to me on the subject, as indeed there were not.

"His complaint, that he was obliged to 'cook for his own mess,' will hardly excite much sympathy. I am unable to see the hardship to one who has, by his own confession, turned bar-keeper for a living, cooking his own food.

"His complaint that he could not write to his wife, because the officer, admitted by him to be 'a perfect gentleman,' who was to examine his letter, was too young to be trusted with the delicate revelations of a husband to his wife, who was three thousand miles away, is too absurd for comment.

"I received the order from the commanding general of the army, to release Heidsieck upon his giving his parole not to visit the Confederate States, which was transmitted in the usual course of business, and he accepted the condition, which only differed from the one offered by me in this, that by mine he was to go to Europe.

"He now desires reparation for his confinement. Let Heidsieck be ordered back into confinement; let a court-martial of impartial officers at New Orleans be ordered to try him as a spy, with a competent judge advocate; and if he is acquitted, I pledge myself to the extent of my private means, to make good to him all he has suffered, provided his government will agree, that if found guilty, he shall be hanged, as he ought to be, without any intervention on its part.

"If Heidsieck had not been taken out of my hands by the action of my government, I should have ordered him before a court for trial, and I believe he would have suffered for his crimes against the country that had given him the protection of its laws."

So much for Charles Heidsieck, bar-tender and dealer in champagne. We come now to an affair that made more noise in the world.

Seizure of $800,000 in Silver.

To justify the seizure of this mass of coin, it is not necessary to prove that it constituted part of the cash capital of the Confederate government, or that it was secreted for the purpose of defrauding the creditors of the Citizens' Bank, from the vaults of which it was so suddenly removed before the occupation of the city. It is only necessary to show that there existed strong grounds of suspicion with regard to it. The silver was not confiscated, it was merely seized and held for adjudication. The rebel government, at the beginning of the war, had not been content merely to seize and hold the coin in the mint and sub-treasury of the United States; but had appropriated the same to its own purposes. The subjects of that government had not merely postponed the payment of the two or three hundred millions which they owed northern merchants and manufacturers; but had first repudiated the debts, and then proceeded to place it for ever beyond their power to pay them; to say nothing of the universal confiscation of property in the South which belonged to northern men. This silver, on the contrary, was seized and detained, merely that the extremely suspicious circumstances of its concealment might be investigated.

Let me remark, first, that the mysterious transfer of the silver, in the quiet of a Sunday morning, from the Citizens' Bank to the Dutch consulate, was condemned, at the time of the transfer, by the *True Delta*, a secession paper; and condemned on grounds shown, in 1863, to be just. "If we are correctly informed," said the *True Delta* of April 26th, "the coin which has taken wings from the Citizens' Bank is transferred to Dutch hands to discharge indebtedness in Holland not yet for some time due, and for which the bank advancing the specie is no more responsible than is any other living institution in this place. Were it otherwise, however, were the debt its own, we can not see the propriety at a time like this, to deplete its vaults to anticipate a debt, or to pay a foreign creditor preferentially." It thus appears that the transaction, though imperfectly understood, made upon the honest mind of John Maginnis, editor of the *True Delta*, precisely the same impression that it made upon General Butler.

A few days after the landing of the troops, a negro informed

Lieutenant Kinsman that an immense number of kegs of silver had been taken to the store of a Frenchman named Conturié, a liquor dealer, and secreted in a large vault; in testimony whereof the negro produced a Bible in which he had made some hieroglyphic entry of the fact, with a view to its being communicated to the Union general when he should arrive. Farther inquiry substantiating the negro's story, General Butler sent Captain Shipley of the Thirtieth Massachusetts, with a file of six or eight soldiers, to examine the office of M. Conturié, who proved to be the consul of the Netherlands. At two in the afternoon of May 10th, Captain Shipley presented himself at the consulate. It appeared to be an insurance office, though the consular flag of the Netherlands was flying over the door. M. Conturié was found, and Captain Shipley, with marked courtesy, informed him of the object of his visit, adding, that he was ordered to prevent the departure of person or property from the building. M. Conturié, with needless vehemence, and in a style that savored of the dramatic, said:

"I am the consul of the Netherlands. This is the office of my consulate. I protest against any such violation of it."

He solemnly declared, and many times declared, that the part of the building occupied by him contained nothing but the property belonging or appertaining to the consulate, or to himself as an individual. He positively refused to allow the vault or the office to be searched. After some farther conversation with Captain Shipley, he wrote a note to the Count Mejan, consul-general of France, which he requested might be sent to that personage, as he wished to consult with him. Very naturally; for the Count Mejan was more deeply involved in the secretion of coin than M. Conturié. Captain Shipley promised to send the note to the French consul, provided it was approved at head-quarters. To head-quarters he accordingly repaired, leaving Conturié a prisoner in his consulate.

The general decided that M. Conturié's note should not be forwarded to the French consul, whom the affair did in no way concern. Captain Shipley reappeared at the Dutch consulate, communicated his intention to search the premises, and demanded of Conturié the key of his vault. The consul refused to deliver it.

"Then I shall be obliged to force the door," said the captain.

"With regard to that, you will do as you please," said Conturié, who again protested against the violation of his office and flag.

As Captain Shipley had not the means of forcing the vault, he was again compelled to return to head-quarters. As he turned to go, the consul said:

"Sir, am I to understand that my consular office is taken possession of, and myself am arrested by you; and that, too, by order of Major-General Butler?"

"Yes, sir," replied Captain Shipley.

General Butler, upon receiving the captain's report, sent him back to the consulate, accompanied by Lieutenant Kinsman, of his staff, an officer peculiarly well fitted for extracting a key from a contumacious consul—a gentleman perfectly capable of the *suaviter in modo*, but equally versed in the *fortiter in re*. To the consul, Lieutenant Kinsman politely said:

"Sir, I wish to look into your vault?"

The consul replied: "It contains only my private effects, and the property of the consulate."

Lieutenant Kinsman: "Sir, I wish to look into your vault. Give me the key."

Mr. Conturié: "I will not."

Lieutenant Kinsman to officers: "Search the office. Break open, if need be, the doors of the vault."

Mr. Conturié, rising: "I, Amedie Conturié, Consul of the Netherlands, protest against any occupation or search of my office; and this I do in the name of my government. The name of my consulate is over the door, and my flag floats over my head. If I cede, it is to force alone."

The search began. Conturié then said, it would be of no use to search the office, for the key of the vault was upon his own person.

Lieutenant Kinsman to officers: "Search this man."

Captain Shipley and Lieutenant Whitcomb, approached "this man" to obey the order.

Lieutenant Kinsman: "Search the fellow thoroughly. Strip him. Take off his coat, his stockings. Search even the soles of his shoes."

M. Conturié: "You call me fellow! That word is never applied to a gentleman, far less to a foreign consul, acting in his consular capacity, as I am now. I ask you to remember that you used that word."

Lieutenant Kinsman: "Certainly; fellow is the name I applied to you. I don't care, if you are the consul of Jerusalem; I am going to look into your vault."

One of the officers took a key from the coat-pocket of the consul, which proved not to be the one required. Conturié then made a slight movement, which plainly said, that the pocket to look into, was a certain one in his pantaloons. The silent hint was taken. The key was found. The vault was opened; and, lo! a cord and a half of kegs of silver coin, marked "Hope & Co." The kegs were one hundred and sixty in number, each containing five thousand Mexican dollars. Many other articles were found in the vault—tin boxes, containing bonds of the cities of New Orleans and Mobile, the consul's exequatur and other papers belonging to him. Certain dies, bank-plates, and engraving tools of the Citizens' Bank, were also discovered. A subsequent search brought to light plates of the Confederate treasury notes, and some of the paper upon which the notes were usually printed. Such were the articles which the veracious Conturié declared were the property of his consulate and of himself.

The consul was released early in the evening. The next day, the silver, three wagon loads, and all the other articles found in the vault, were removed to the Mint, and the office was vacated by the troops. The Confederate plates were forwarded to Washington, where they now are; the rest of the property was held, subject to the disposal of the government.

M. Conturié immediately drew up a narrative of what had occurred, suppressing his declarations, so emphatic, so oft repeated, that the vault contained nothing but his own and consular property, and complaining bitterly of Lieutenant Kinsman's strong language and stronger measures. This he sent to General Butler, who thus replied:

"Your communication of the 10th instant is received. The nature of the property found concealed beneath your consular flag—the specie, dies, and plates of the Citizens' Bank of New Orleans—under a claim that it was private property, which claim is now admitted to be groundless, shows you have merited, so far as I can judge, the treatment you have received, even if a little rough. Having prostituted your flag to a base purpose, you could not hope to have it respected so debased."

May 12th.—Every consul in New Orleans, except the Mexican, to the number of nineteen, joined in protesting against "the indignity," "the severe ill-usage," and the "imprisonment for several hours," to which the sacred person of M. Conturié had been subjected.

General Butler replied:

"MESSRS.: I have the protest which you have thought it proper to make in regard to the action of my officers toward the consul of the Netherlands, which action I approve and sustain. I am grieved that, without investigation of the facts, you, Messrs., should have thought it your duty to take action in the matter. The fact will appear to be, and easily to be demonstrated at the proper time, that the flag of the Netherlands was made to cover and conceal property of an incorporated company of Louisiana, secreted under it from the operation of the laws of the United States. That the supposed fact that the consul had under the flag only the property of Hope & Co., citizens of the Netherlands, is untrue. He had other property which could not by law be his property, or the property of Hope & Co.; of this I have abundant proof in my own hands. No person can excel me in the respect which I shall pay to the flags of all nations, and to the consulate authority, even while I do not recognize many claims made under them; but I wish it most distinctly understood that, in order to be respected, the consul, his office, and the use of his flag, must each and all be respectable."

M. Conturié's next step was, of course, to submit the case to Mr. Van Limburg, the minister of the Netherlands at Washington, who, in turn, laid it before Mr. Seward, with all the exaggerations of Conturié's own narrative. Mr. Van Limburg is a very respectable and most learned gentleman. It is pleasing to notice with what joyful alacrity he embraced the opportunity of writing long and erudite dispatches, such as has rarely fallen to the lot of a minister of the Netherlands residing at Washington. The ponderous dispatches with which this worthy gentleman kept Mr. Seward busy during the summer of 1862, are they not attached to the president's message, from page 625 to page 652? They are there, with all their Latin quotations considerately translated. "Justicia, regnorum fundamentum (justice is the foundation of kingdoms)." To describe these dispatches it is only necessary to say, that they are precisely such as Dominie Samson would have written, had he been minister of the Netherlands in the year 1862, at the city of Washington.

Mr. Seward, in reply to Mr. Van Limburg's first dispatch, said, that he thought the consul had done wrong, but not so wrong as to justify the roughness of Lieutenant Kinsman. "It appears," said the secretary of state, "*beyond dispute*, that the person of the consul was unnecessarily and rudely searched; that certain papers, which incontestably were archives of the consulate, were seized and removed, and that they are still withheld from him; and that he was not only denied the privilege of conferring with a friendly colleague, but was addressed in very discourteous and disrespectful language. In these proceedings the military agents assumed functions which belonged exclusively to the department of state, acting under the direction of the president. Their conduct was a violation of the law of nations, and of the comity due from this country to a friendly foreign state. The government disapproves of these proceedings, and also the sanction which was given to them by Major-General Butler, and expresses its regret that the misconduct thus censured has occurred."

This is a curious passage. It appears to say, that only the secretary of state, acting under the authority of the president, has the right to put his hand into a consul's pocket, and take out a key. Lieutenant Kinsman, one day in Washington, asked Mr. Seward what *was* the next thing to do after Conturié refused to give up the key? The secretary did not answer the question. It certainly was a puzzler.

Mr. Seward farther informed Mr. Van Limburg, that the president had appointed a military governor of Louisiana, General Shepley, "who has been instructed to pay due respect to all consular rights and privileges, and a commissioner will at once proceed to New Orleans to investigate the transaction which has been detailed, and take evidence concerning the title of the specie, and bonds, and other property in question, with a view to a disposition of the same, according to international law and justice. You are invited to designate any proper person to join such commissioner, and attend his investigations. This government holds itself responsible for the money and the bonds in question, to deliver them up to the consul, or to Hope & Co., if they shall appear to belong to them. The consular commission and exequatur, together with all the private papers, will be immediately returned to M. Conturié, and he will be allowed to resume, and, for the present, exercise his official functions. Should the facts, when ascertained, justify a representation to you of misconduct on his part, it will in due time be made, with the confidence that the subject will receive just consideration by a government with which the United States have lived in amity for so many years."

Mr. Van Limburg declined joining in the investigation. The United States, he said, must investigate the actions of its servants. For *him* to take part in it, would be to acknowledge that General Butler's conduct was possibly right. Besides, no seals had been placed upon the kegs and boxes, and these contained the very evidence of the consul's innocence. "It is for Major-General Butler to prove what he alleges. *Ei incumbit probatio qui dicit, non qui negat* (the burden of the proof lies upon him who asserts, not upon him who denies), says the Pandects. It is not for me, it is not for our consul, to prove that he is innocent. *Prima facie* the money delivered by the 'Citizen's Bank' to the agent of the house of Hope & Co., to be transmitted to that house, or to be deposited with the consul of the Netherlands, is a legitimate money legitimately transferred. I could not, without having received the orders of the government of the king, participate in any manner in an investigation which would tend to *investigate* that which I could not put in doubt—the good faith of the agent of the house of Hope & Co., the moral impossibility that that honorable house should lend itself to any culpable underplot, the good faith of the consul of the Netherlands. *Quilibet præsumiter justus donec probitur contrarium* (every one is to be presumed honest until the contrary is proven), saith the ancient universal rule of justice." If any charge is made against the consul, we will investigate that. And if General Butler is guilty of the acts charged by Conturié, we expect his—in fact—removal. Meantime, what is the status of M. Conturié? Is he consul, or is he not?

Mr. Seward had informed the minister, that M. Conturié would be "allowed" to resume his functions at once, before the affair had been investigated. The minister demanded that he should be "*invited*" to do so. Mr. Seward replied: "I have no objection to your writing to the consul that it is the president's *expectation* that he will resume and continue in the discharge of his official functions until there shall be farther occasion for him to relinquish them." The minister rejoined:—"I regret, sir, not to be able to accept that formula without submitting it to the judgment of the government of the king." The minister more than carried his point; for we find Mr. Seward writing to him, soon after, that, "*simultaneously with the appointment of Mr. Johnson as commissioner*, Major-General Butler was relieved of his functions as military governor of New Orleans, and Brigadier-General Shepley was appointed military governor of that city; the military authorities were at the same time directed *to invite* M. Conturié to resume his consular functions."

True, the appointment of a military governor was a mere diplomatic fiction, which did not in the slightest degree affect General Butler's position or power. In the view of the world, however, he was both censured and degraded; and that too, upon the extravagant, unsupported testimony of a foreign consul, whose conduct the secretary of state himself had censured. The public was not informed, as General Butler was informed by a member of the cabinet, that General Shepley was selected for the military governorship, because he was supposed to be the most acceptable officer to General Butler, who had already made him the military governor of the city.

To those who believe that the first duty of a government is to stand by its faithful servants, this mode of "backing" General Butler in his difficult position, will not commend itself. Whether General Butler's course had been right or wrong, was a question upon which there could have been two opinions; and Mr. Reverdy Johnson was sent to New Orleans to ascertain which of those opinions was correct. There could be but one opinion respecting the conduct of the consul of the Netherlands, who had lent the protection of his flag to property designed to support the credit of the armed foes of the power to which he was accredited. I can not conceive what there was in the position of the Dutch minister, or of the power he represented, to justify this unquestioning haste to concede everything which they thought proper to demand.

The commissioner selected to go to New Orleans, and investigate the consular imbroglio, arrived early in June, and was ready to begin his inquiries on the tenth. General Butler received Mr. Johnson with every courtesy, invited him to reside at head-quarters, and did all that in him lay to facilitate his investigations. Mr. Johnson was equally polite, though he declined the general's invitation with regard to his residence. He spent six weeks in investigating the several cases of collision, between General Butler and the consuls.

It appeared that on the 24th of February, 1862, the Citizens' Bank of New Orleans had conceived the idea of suddenly getting rid of a great part of its coin. With regard to the eight hundred thousand dollars deposited in the vault of M. Conturié, the following resolutions were shown to Mr. Johnson on the books of the bank:

"*Whereas*, the present rate of exchange on Europe would entail a ruinous loss in this bank for such sums as are due semi-annually in Amsterdam for the interest on the state bonds.

"*Be it therefore resolved*, That the President be and is hereby authorized to make a special deposit of eight hundred thousand dollars ($800,000) in Mexican dollars in the hands of Messrs. Hope & Co., of Amsterdam, Holland, agents of the bond-holders in Europe, through their authorized agent, Edmund J. Forstall, Esq., for the purpose of providing for the interest on said bonds.

"*Be it further resolved*, That such portions of the above sum as may be required from time to time to pay the interest accruing on the state bonds shall be so applied by Messrs. Hope & Co., provided, however, that the bank shall have the option of redeeming an equivalent amount in coin by approved sterling exchange to the satisfaction of the agents of Messrs. Hope & Co.; and provided farther, that in the event of the blockade of this port not being raised in time to allow of the shipment of the said coin, then the said Edmund J. Forstall will arrange with Messrs. Hope & Co. for the necessary advances to protect the credit of the state and of the bank until such time as the coin can go forward to liquidate said debt; but no commission shall be allowed for such shipment of coin or any other expenses, except those actually incurred; and on the resumption of specie payment by this bank this trust to cease and the balance of coin to be returned to the bank."

The papers farther showed, that on the 12th of April, the agent of Messrs. Hope & Co., "with a view to their better security in such times of excitement, deemed it his duty to withdraw the said sum of eight hundred thousand dollars, already marked and prepared for shipment, say, one hundred and sixty kegs, Hope & Co., containing five thousand dollars each, and to place the same under the protection of the consul of the Netherlands, Amadie Conturié, Esq., for which he held his receipt."

It also appeared, that two days after the removal of this large sum, the bank sold other coin amounting to seven hundred and sixteen thousand one hundred and ninety-six dollars, to the French bankers, Messrs. Dupasseur & Co., which they paid for in drafts upon bankers in Paris and Havre. This coin was deposited in the French consulate, where it was seized by General Butler, and where, for the moment, we will leave it.

Now, what did these strange transactions mean? The paper case was plain enough, and Mr. Johnson thought it his duty to decide according to the papers, and give up all the coin, and all the articles found with it, except the plates of the Confederate treasury notes. But the decision, though it satisfied the secretary of state, does not even appease the curiosity of a disinterested reader. Surely there was ground for suspicion here. The attempted transfer of so large an amount of coin to Europe, from the chief city of the rebel government, at a time when all legitimate commerce had ceased, was certainly a matter demanding the attention of the commanding general.

Mr. Forstall, the New Orleans agent of Hope & Co., in a letter to that eminent house, written three days after the seizure of the coin, gives a history of the affair:

"NEW ORLEANS, *May* 13, 1862.

"GENTLEMEN:—On 1st March last I wrote Messrs. Baring Brothers & Co. as follows:

"'Should there be a necessity, I shall place under the protection of the respective consuls all bonds and papers belonging to you, Messrs. Hope & Co., and other friends. I shall try and protect the cash assets of the two banks whose capitals have been furnished by Europe.'

"The great apprehension at that time, in the event of the fall of New Orleans, was not the action of the federal government, which, until then, on similar events, had left private property undisturbed, but the destruction of property and sacking of the banks by the rabble out of a mixed population of nearly two hundred thousand, pending the consequent delays of an abrupt and violent change of government; and the event proved that such apprehension was not idle, for after the destruction and robbery of an immense amount of property on our wharves and some of our front stores and warehouses, a general plunder of the city would have taken place by the rabble after the retreat of the Confederate troops, but for the armed interference, night and day, of the French and foreign brigades for nearly six days, when the federal troops took charge of the city with a sufficient force to maintain order.

"The position of the Citizens' Bank on the 24th February last, as per inclosed report of the board of currency, was as follows:

CASH RESPONSIBILITIES.

"Circulation,..	$2,084,380
"Individual deposits, returnable in gold to depositors up to September 16, 1861, when the banks were ordered by the government of the Confederacy to suspend specie payment, say about..	1,200,000
"Deposits in Confederate notes, and returnable in Confederates on hand..	4,354,755
"Total..	$5,554,755

CASH ASSETS.

"Gold and silver..	$4,025,932

"The bond-holders you represent yet hold bonds of the Citizens' Bank for $4,430,666.66. Deeply impressed with the danger threatening New Orleans after the fall of the Tennessee forts, and of the disastrous consequences that might follow its capture, with so heavy an amount of gold and silver centering in the vaults of our banks, and a rabble which for a time, however short, might be uncontrollable, and considering the interest of your bond-holders in as much danger as that of the stockholders, I deemed it my duty to call upon Mr. Denegre, so far back as the middle of February last, urging him to prepare for the worst, and then used every exertion to induce the president to dispose of his coin at once in the following manner, to wit:

"1st. To pay in full the circulation of the bank, amounting on 24th February last to about..	$2,084,380
"2d. To pay the depositors up to the 16th September last, when the bank suspended specie payment, and who had left their deposits, which Mr. Denegre said would require about	1,200,000
	$3,284,380

"This would have reduced the cash assets of the bank to about $800,000 in silver, without any responsibility save to the holders of the bonds, which, as things have turned out, would have been a most enviable position, with its large and well-protected 'portefeuille,' including a very large surplus, and its valuable banking privileges unimpaired, ready for active operations on the reopening of trade. Unfortunately, this course did not meet with the views of Mr. Denegre, but finding that he had coin on hand to meet the circulation and deposits of the bank, and a surplus of about $800,000 in silver, he proposed to place in my hands, on your account, for the purpose of meeting the interest on the bonds as maturing, the said sum of $800,000, which, he said, would otherwise remain dormant until a resumption of business, whilst, so used, it would sustain the credit of the bank in Europe, by showing that, even if the war lasted another year, and under all the difficulties of the present times, it had the means of paying the interest on its bonds as maturing, and had provided for the same in kind. Of course, consultation with you was out of the question, and I had to refer to your power of attorney, at the time when you considered the interest of the bond-holders you represent jeoparded, to guide me in the present instance; and, after mature consideration, I came to the conclusion that it was my duty to accept the deposit in your behalf, tendered by the Citizens' Bank, as advised in my letter of the 1st April last, copy of which is inclosed.

"And now allow me to refer you to the inclosed copy of a letter which I addressed Major-General Butler on the 11th instant, and which was handed him personally by my friend, Rendal Hunt, Esq., at 10 o'clock A. M. It contained a plain statement of facts, and a demand for the $800,000 forcibly taken from the vaults of the consul of the Netherlands. I have no answer as yet, and I may be arrested at any moment, as he said he could see fraud in every part of the document. We continue under the rule of martial law.

"It may be well to remark here that when M. Conturié learned that the French consul could not accommodate him, he hired the old vaults of the Orleans Bank, on Canal street, and the same square as the Citizens' Bank, the front being occupied by an insurance company, whose president used the front vault for his papers and books. When the money was brought, Mr. Denegre, who was laboring under the idea of a run upon the banks by the rabble, having received an anonymous letter to that effect, fancying, it appears, that the best hiding-place for the steel-plates of the bank was those same vaults, sent them there, attaching no other importance to this matter than that of protecting these plates, which, had they fallen in bad hands, might have given a good deal of trouble to the bank and public, and caused heavy losses. These plates, for $5 and $10, I believe, engraved and prepared before the secession, are in accordance with the charter of the Citizens' Bank and under the authority of the state of Louisiana. This is the property, I understand, alluded to by General Butler in his answer to the protest of the foreign consuls, and which no consul should have covered. Really and truly, I do not believe M. Conturié knew anything about it. As for my part, I did not. In the whole of this matter M. Conturié has shown all the energy and dignity that could be desired from the representative of a nation. I am, respectfully,

"EDM. J. FORSTALL.

"Messrs. HOPE & Co., Amsterdam."

It thus appears that the solicitude professed by the bank for the interests of Hope & Co., *was not shared by the agent of Hope & Co.*, who strongly advised another disposition of the silver, and accepted it with reluctance and doubt. It also appears that the office claimed by Conturié as the consulate of the Netherlands, was nothing but a vault, hired by him for the sole purpose of hiding the coin. Mr. Forstall's letter farther shows, that the explanation of the transfer of the coin, which Mr. Johnson read upon the books of the bank, was a fiction.

I believe this is all the light I am able to throw upon the transaction. One more fact, however, should be stated. It was not true, as the *True Delta* intimated, that the Citizens' Bank had no particular interest in sustaining the credit of the state bonds. Those bonds bore the indorsement of the bank, and constituted the basis of its capital. The explanation given by the editor of the *True Delta*, of the transfer of the coin, may, however, be the correct one. The Citizens' Bank, probably, deemed it more important to have a powerful friend in Europe than to secure its creditors at home. If this is the true view, then justice and patriotism appear to have required that the silver should have been replaced in the vault of the bank, not restored to the agent of Hope & Co. The money having been consigned to Europe, the bank has since gone into liquidation.

In the same spirit, Mr. Johnson decided upon the coin deposited with the French consul by the same bank.

"The bank," he says in his report, "in addition to the deposit of $800,000 with the agent of Messrs. Hope & Co., needed other credits in Europe. Their principal business was the dealing in foreign exchange, and, to enable them to do this, it was necessary to have a large credit abroad. To effect this object they made this negotiation with Messrs. Dupasseur & Co., known to be perfectly responsible merchants of New Orleans, to wit: to purchase from them bills at certain rates on Paris for the amount of $716,196, and to pay for the same in coin. The bills were not to be accepted until the drawees were advised of the shipment of the coin by Dupasseur & Co. The bills were drawn, delivered to the bank, and the coin handed over to Count Mejan, the French consul, to be retained until shipped. They were remitted by the bank to their correspondents abroad for acceptance, but have not been accepted because the coin has not been sent on.

"Things remained in this condition when Major-General Butler requested the consul to retain the coin, which he has ever since done.

"On these facts the only question is, have the United States a right to the fund? That the transaction was one of perfect good faith is evident from the depositions referred to. It was a mere business matter, in which the parties had a clear right to engage. That the bank at the time owned the coin was not denied. Nor was it questioned that the agreement was entered into and was being carried out when the major-general intervened. The United States can have no interest in the coin, except upon the ground of forfeiture, and for that there was not at the time, nor is there now, the slightest pretense. If it be alleged, as a matter of suspicion (the proof is all the other way), that the purpose of the bank was to place so much of its funds beyond the control of the United States, that, if true, would be no cause of forfeiture, there being no law, state or congressional, to prohibit it. If it be alleged, that the purpose was to place the fund in Europe for the advantage of the rebels, the answer is, there is not only no proof of the fact, but the proof actually before me wholly conflicts with it."

This is Mr. Johnson's explanation of a transaction which, to inexperienced minds, certainly wears the appearance of being fictitious, or worse. Perhaps some light may be thrown upon it by the relation of a later affair in which the consul of France was engaged.

Detection and Removal of the French Consul.

In September, 1862, Mr. Sandford, our minister at Brussels, wrote home that the Confederate agents in Europe were seriously embarrassed by the non-arrival of a large amount of coin from New Orleans. Notes had been renewed; purveyors of cloth could not be paid; and Confederate affairs generally were at a dead lock. "But," he added, "assurances are now given that the money is in the hands of the French consul, and would be shortly received."

A copy of this interesting letter was forwarded to General Butler, with directions to investigate. General Butler has a knack at investigating, and he performed this pleasing duty with an energy, skill, promptitude, and success rarely equaled. His report upon the subject was so irresistibly conclusive, that the French government felt compelled to recall a too assiduous, an imprudently faithful servant. I can not do the reader a better service than by transcribing this report. The supporting documents must necessarily be omitted, but to show their nature, I retain General Butler's references to them.

"HEAD-QUARTERS, DEPARTMENT OF THE GULF,
"NEW ORLEANS, *Nov.* 13, 1862.

"To Hon. EDWIN M. STANTON, Secretary of War:

"SIR:—I received the communication of the war department inclosing a copy of a letter from the state department, directing my attention to the statement made by Mr. Sandford, our minister resident at Brussels, a copy of which I inclose for the better understanding of the present communication. In obedience to its directions I set about making inquiries through my secret police, and finding it a matter of very grave import as affecting the relations of the French consul here, I undertook a personal examination of the subject. The facts as substantiated by the documentary and other testimony, hereto appended, are substantially these:

"The firm of Ed. Gautherin & Co., composed of Ed. Gautherin and Alfred and Jules Lemore, doing business in New Orleans, was also concerned in a house at Havre, S. A. Lemore & Co. Jules and Alfred Lemore, the partners in New Orleans, were also partners in that house. Gautherin & Co. were at first employed in buying tobacco for the French government, afterward they were concerned in shipping cotton in joint account. They represent themselves to be agents of Baron Villers, the contractor for French army clothing,

"On the 29th day of July, 1861, as will appear from the copy of a contract with the Confederate government, herewith inclosed, and marked X, the original of which is in my possession, Gautherin & Co. agreed to furnish the Confederates with a large amount of cloths for uniforms, which are the cloths spoken of in the communication of Mr. Sandford. About the first of April, of this year, a cargo of the goods was shipped to Havana, and from thence to Matamoras, under charge of the senior partner of the house of Edward Gautherin & Co., now in Europe.

"That cloth was smuggled across to Brownsville, and delivered to Captain Shankey, quartermaster and agent of the Confederate government. The original invoice and receipt are hereto annexed, marked E and F. Between the 14th and the 24th of April, the day the fleet passed the forts, Mr. J. B. D. De Bow, produce loan-agent of the Confederate States, made application to the 'Bank of New Orleans' for a loan of four hundred and five thousand dollars in coin without interest, as will appear by the communication hereto annexed, marked C. This proposition was acceded to by the bank, upon a pledge, made by Payne, Huntington & Co., the junior partner of which firm was president of the bank, of cotton to be delivered on the plantations in Louisiana and Mississippi. The contract is hereto annexed, and marked D.

"This transaction *was not entered into in good faith*, as is confessed by the testimony of the acting president, Mr. Davis, taken from his own lips, in short hand, a copy of which is hereto annexed, marked O.

"But the transaction was *a contrivance by which the specie might be got out of the bank.* Specie to this amount was placed in the hands of the French consul with his full knowledge of the intent of the transaction, and a receipt was given by him to hold it in trust for the Bank of New Orleans. At the same time, a pretended sale of the remainder of the specie in bank, amounting to four hundred thousand dollars for sterling, was made by the bank, and that sum was also placed in the hands of the French consul.* These two sums, amounting to eight hundred thousand dollars, made substantially the whole specie capital of the bank. This is shown by the confession of the only director of the bank who has not run away into the Confederacy, Mr. Harroll, a copy of whose statement is hereto annexed, marked R.

"Matters stood in this condition at the time the city of New Orleans was taken possession of by us. Upon my assurance to the bank, that if they would return their specie, they should be protected, the pretended sale for sterling exchange was annulled, and the French consul sent back the money, and the bank received into its vaults four hundred thousand dollars.

"In regard to the four hundred and five thousand dollars, the French consul became uneasy, and moved upon the bank to get at his receipt given to the Bank of New Orleans, and gave a new receipt, running directly to Gautherin & Co.

"At this point of time, I ordered all the specie in the hands of the French consul to be sequestered and held until affairs could be investigated.

"Reverdy Johnson, on commission of the state department, came down here, and without investigation, and without knowing anything of the transactions, and without even inquiring of me about them, made such representations to the department of state, that I was ordered to release the French consul from his promise not to deliver up any specie held in his hands without informing me, which order I obeyed.

"In the mean time, Gautherin & Co. had succeeded in delivering their goods to the Confederate States agents, and called upon the bank to get their money, which had been deposited in the hands of the French consul.

* I need hardly call the reader's attention to the similarity of this "contrivance" for getting rid of specie to that employed by the Citizens' Bank.

This delivery had not been completed at Brownsville until 22d June; and some time in the last of July, the bank, through its officers, gave up its receipts, which were destroyed, and took a receipt which was dated back to the 16th of April, directly from Gautherin & Co., so that the French consul's name would not appear in the transaction.

"These facts are established by the testimony of Mr. Belly, the cashier of the bank, which is written out and signed, and sworn to by him, a copy of which is annexed, marked O P. The money was sent on board the Spanish man-of-war Blasco de Garay, which left this port in September last, and has now returned, and has been carried to Havana, and thence shipped to New York. All this has been done with the knowledge and consent of the consul of France.

"You will see by the letter of Mr. Sandford the difficulties which the Confederates had of getting more goods, on account of the non-payment of the first bill. Another cargo is now in Havana, not to be delivered, of course, until the first is paid for. By this wrongful, illegal, and inimical interference of the French consul, aided by the Spanish ship-of-war, the money has gone forward, so that the holders of the goods will be ready to ship the remainder for the benefit of the Confederate army. A more flagrant violation of international law and national courtesy on the part of a consular agent, can not be imagined.

"Before I proceeded upon the investigation, not knowing the extent to which the French consul was implicated, I called upon him, and after showing him a letter from the commanding general of the army, in which I was directed to cultivate the most friendly relations with him, I read him a letter from our minister at Brussels, and told him I should desire his friendly aid in making the investigation, and then asked him if he knew anything of the transaction spoken of in the letter of Mr. Sandford, or if any money had been deposited with him for any such purpose. *He in the most emphatic manner assured me that he knew nothing of any such transaction.* He only knew that there was a French house of the name of Gautherin & Co. in New Orleans, and declared that no money had ever been deposited with him for any such purpose. I then informed him that it would become my duty to arrest and question Alfred and Jules Lemore, the resident partners of the French house. I did so, and they denied all such transaction, or refused to answer, lest they should 'criminate themselves.' But, in the mean time, I had possessed myself of their books and papers, and found two accounts, translations of which I inclose, marked B A, which show the whole transaction; and which also show that one Kossuth, a clerk of the French consul, whose name appears in the account, received $528.92 as a fee for keeping the money within the French consulate; that *a douceur was given to Madame Mejan for the purpose of 'carrying out the affair well;'* that a lawyer was paid to deal with the consul in this matter; and these papers, with the testimony of the president, director and cashier of the bank, put the guilt of Count Mejan beyond question. I beg leave to call your attention to this extraordinary amount of expenses ($19,939.40).

"I need not suggest to the department that it is its duty at once and peremptorily to revoke the *exequatur* of Count Mejan. He has connived at the delivery of army clothing of the Confederate army, since the occupation of New Orleans by the federal forces; he has taken away gold from the bank, nearly half a million of its specie, to aid the Confederates; acts which could not have been done without his aid, and that of the Spanish ship-of-war Blasco de Garay.

"I leave the consul to the government at Washington. I will take care sufficiently to punish the other alien enemies and domestic traitors concerned in this business whom I have here.

"Upon examination of the parties, I found that a box containing all the papers relating to the transaction, which were not kept with the commercial papers of the house of Gautherin & Co., was deposited with the French consul. I wrote to him, very politely, to have it delivered to me for the purpose of justice. I have again written him more peremptorily, and he has refused to do so, still concealing the proofs of guilt. If produced, I believe it will show him to be one of the five parties concerned in the illegal traffic mentioned in the account of expenses; and however that may be, he now covers the criminal as he lately concealed the booty, which he, his wife and his clerk so largely shared.

"I beg leave here to call the attention of the department to these transactions, as showing that I was clearly right when I ordered the specie deposits in the hands of Count Mejan to be sequestered. His flag has been made to cover all manner of illegal and hostile transactions, and the booty arising therefrom. I am glad that my action here has been vindicated to the world, and that the government of the United States will be able to demand of the French government a recall of its hostile agent.

"I have the honor to be,

"Very respectfully, your obedient servant,

"BENJ. F. BUTLER, *Major-General commanding.*"

This it is to "investigate" an affair. I know not which most to admire, the vigor and tact displayed in procuring the evidence, or the clearness with which the results of the inquiry are stated.

General Butler alludes several times to the bill of "charges and expenses" found in the books of Gautherin & Co. It is an extremely curious document. The following are the items:

"June 29. By payment to Ed. Gautherin and Jules Lemore to go to Richmond, $481.

"July 20. By remittance to them at Richmond, $450. French consul loan, $50.

"March 1. Expenses of E. Gautherin & Co. and Jules Lemore for passage from New Orleans to New York and Havre, $700.

"May 27. Voyage of Ch. Privelland to Richmond and back, $543. Maintain to Richmond, five weeks, $475.50. Expenses of L. Grotairs at Antwerp, $9.98. Consul fees and certificates, $36.20.

"August 10. *Present to Madame Mejan (wife of French consul), to close the affair well*, $153. Colonel Lemat, *as a bribe for the affair to start well*, $2,500. V. Pritert, for the bill of Alexander, according to the agreement of the five interested parties, $5,000. Kossuth (clerk of French consul), one-eighth per cent. of $405,000, deposited in consulate, $528.20. *Payment to Fuelle for getting the receipt*, $500. Robert (lawyer), for proceedings with authorities and consul, $500.

"August 31. Ch. Briolland, expenses to Matamoras, $3,790. Jules Lemore, expenses from January 1, to September 1, 1862, $1,089.71. Payment of cabs and transport of nine boxes of gold, $60. Expenses of telegraph and postage, $150. Insurance on gold in consulate, six months, one-half per cent. on $405,000, $2,025. River insurance on Blasco de Garay, one-eighth per cent. on $250,000, $312.50. Marine insurance, from here to New York, on specie, $585.26. E. Gautherin, expenses paid in sum, $4,058.50. Ferran & Duprerris, Havana, as a memorandum, $4,058.50."

Total, $19,939.40 ! !

So much for the French consul. I can not resist the impression that the same methods of investigation, applied to other cases, would have yielded results strikingly similar.

Seizure of 3,205 *Hogsheads of Sugar.*

This sugar was seized on the ground that it was designed as a support to the credit of the Confederate government in Europe, and that the ostensible owner was only an agent of a company of European merchants, formed chiefly for that purpose. Three of the foreign consuls objected to the seizure, averring that the sugar had been bought for purposes "strictly mercantile," and requesting its restoration; and if this were done, they expressed a willingness to "waive all past proceedings," and let the matter rest. General Butler made a spirited reply to their communication:

"HEAD-QUARTERS, DEPARTMENT OF THE GULF,
"NEW ORLEANS, *June* 12, 1862.

"GENTLEMEN:—In the matter of the sugars in possession of Mr. Covas, who is the only party known to the United States authorities, I have examined with care the statement you have sent me. I had information, the sources of which you will not expect me to disclose, that Mr. Covas had been engaged in buying Confederate notes, giving for them sterling exchange, thus transferring abroad the credit of the states in the rebellion, and enabling these bills of credit to be converted into bullion to be used there, as it has been, for the purpose of purchasing arms and munitions of war. That Mr. Covas was one of, and the agent of, an association or company of Greek merchants residing here, in London, and in Havana, who had set apart a large fund for this enterprise. That these Confederate notes, so purchased by Mr. Covas, had been used in the purchase of sugars and cotton, of which the sugars in question, in value almost two hundred thousand dollars, are a part.

"I directed Mr. Covas to hold these sugars until this matter could be investigated.

"I am satisfied of the substantial truth of this information. Mr. Covas' own books, will show the important facts that he sold sterling exchange for Confederate treasury notes, and then bought these sugars with the notes.

"Now this is claimed to be 'strictly mercantile.'

"It will not be denied that the sugars were intended for a foreign market.

"But the government of the United States had said, that with the port of New Orleans there should be no 'strictly mercantile' transactions.

"It would not be contended for a moment, that the exchanging of specie for Confederate treasury notes, and sending the specie to Europe, to enable the rebels to buy arms and munitions of war there, were not a breach of the blockade, as well as a violation of the neutrality laws and the proclamation of their majesties, the queen of Great Britain and the emperor of France. What distinguishes the two cases, save that drawing the sterling bills is a more safe and convenient way of eluding the laws, than sending bullion in specie, and thus assisting the rebellion in the point of its utmost need?

"It will be claimed, that to assist the rebellion was not the motive.

"Granted '*causa argumenti.*'

"It was done from the desire of gain, as doubtless all the violations of neutrality have been done by aliens during this war—a motive which is not sanctifying to acts by a foreigner, which, if done by a subject, would be treason, or a high misdemeanor.

"My proclamation of May 1 assured respect to all persons and property that were respectable. It was not an amnesty to murderers, thieves, and criminals of deeper dye or less heinousness, nor a mantle to cover the property of those aiders of the rebellion, whether citizens or aliens, whom I might find here. If numbers of the foreign residents here have been engaged in aiding the rebellion, either directly or indirectly, from a spirit of gain, and they now find themselves objects of watchful supervision by the authorities of the United States, they will console themselves with the reflection, that they are only getting the 'bitter with the sweet.' Nay, more, if honest and quiet foreign citizens find themselves the objects of suspicion to, and even their honest acts subjects of investigation by the authorities of the United States, to their inconvenience, they will, upon reflection, blame only the over-rapacious and greedy of their own fellow-citizens, who have, by their aid to rebellion, brought distrust and suspicion over all. Wishing to treat you, gentlemen, with every respect, I have set forth at length, some of the reasons which have prompted my action. There is one phrase in your letter which I do not understand, and can not permit to pass without calling attention to it. You say, 'the undersigned are disposed to waive all past proceedings,' etc.

"What 'proceedings' have you, or either of you, to 'waive,' if you do feel disposed so to do? What right have you in the matter? What authority is vested in you by the laws of nations, or of this country, which gives you the power to use such language to the representative of the United States, in a quasi official communication?

"Commercial agents merely of a subordinate class, consuls, have no power to waive or condone any proceedings, past or present, of the government under whose protection they are permitted to reside so long as they behave well. If I have committed any wrong to Mr. Covas, you have no power to 'waive' or pardon the penalty, or prevent his having redress. If he has committed any wrong to the United States, you have still less power to shield him from punishment.

"I take leave to suggest, as a possible explanation of this sentence, that you have been so long dealing with a rebel Confederation, which has been supplicating you to make such representations to the governments whose subjects you are, as would induce your sovereigns to aid it in its traitorous designs, that you have become rusty in the language proper to be used in representing the claims of your fellow-citizens to the consideration of a great and powerful government, entitled to equal respect with your own.

"In order to prevent all misconception, and that for the future you gentlemen may know exactly the position upon which I act in regard to foreigners resident here, permit me to explain to you, that I think a foreign resident here has not one right more than an American citizen, but at least one right less; *i. e.*, that of meddling or interfering, by discussion, vote, or otherwise, with the affairs of the government.

"I have the honor to subscribe myself your obedient servant,

"B. F. BUTLER,

"*Major-General Commanding.*

"Messrs. GEORGE COPPELL, claiming to be H. B. M. Acting Consul; A. MEJAN, French Consul; M. W. BENACHI, Greek Consul."

The matter was referred to Mr. Reverdy Johnson. He decided in favor of the claimants, and the sugar was consequently restored. He found the transactions to have been strictly mercantile. "There is not," he reported, "a scintilla of evidence that they ever belonged to such an association, if there was one (of which, however, there is no proof), but, on the contrary, their conduct in negotiating their bills, as exhibited in the many depositions annexed, is absolutely inconsistent with such a connection. The seizure by the major-general was evidently made under a misapprehension. His conduct in this particular, as in those of the eight hundred thousand dollars and seven hundred and sixteen thousand one hundred and ninety-six dollars, is to be referred to the patriotic zeal which governs him, to the circumstances encircling his command at the time so well calculated to awaken suspicion, and to an ardent desire to punish, to the extent of his supposed power, all who had contributed, or were contributing, to the aid of a rebellion, the most unjustifiable and wicked that insane or bad men were ever engaged in."

In giving up the sugar, General Butler politely congratulated the owners that, owing to the rapid enhancement of the value of the article, in consequence of the opening of the port, its detention would prove a great gain to them.

Case of Kennedy & Co.

Steamboat-hunting was a favorite pastime with the Union soldiers during the first weeks of their occupation of the city. The rebels had burnt a large number of their steamboats, but many had been hidden in bayous and swamps supposed to be impenetrable to the unaccustomed Yankee. The men had rare adventures in hunting this valuable game, some of which may hereafter be related. On board one of the steamers found, named the Fox, captured by General McMillan, a mail-bag was discovered, the contents of which brought several of the people of New Orleans into trouble—Messrs. Kennedy & Co., cotton merchants, among the number.

General Butler briefly relates the case: "Kennedy & Co. were merchants doing business in New Orleans, the members of which firm were citizens of the United States. They shipped cotton (bought at Vicksburg and brought to New Orleans) from a bayou on the coast, whence steamers were accustomed to run the blockade to Havana, in defiance of the law and the president's proclamation, and under the farther agreement with the Confederate authorties here, that a given per cent. of the value of their cargoes should be returned in arms and munitions of war for the use of the rebels.

"Without such an agreement no cotton could be shipped from New Orleans, and this was publicly known; and the fact of knowledge that a permit for the vessel to ship cotton could only be got on such terms was not denied at the hearing.

"The cotton was sold in Havana, and the net proceeds invested in a draft (first, second, and third of exchange) dated April 30th, 1862, payable to the London agent of the house of Kennedy & Co., and the first and second sent forward to London, and the third, with account sales and vouchers, forwarded to the firm here through an illicit mail on board the steamer 'Fox,' likewise engaged in carrying unlawful merchandise and an illicit mail between Havana and the rebel states.

"The third of exchange and papers were captured by the army of the United States, on the 10th day of May, on board the 'Fox,' *flagrante delictu*, surrounded by the rebel arms and munitions, concealed in a bayou leading out of Barataria bay, attempting to land her contraband mails and scarcely less destructive arms and munitions to be sent through the bayous and swamps to the enemy.

"During all this time, P. H. Kennedy & Co. have not accepted the amnesty proffered by the proclamation of the commanding general, but preferred to remain within its terms rebels and enemies.

"Upon this state of facts, the commanding general called upon Kennedy & Co. to pay the amount of the net proceeds of the cotton (the third of exchange of the draft), which, with the documents relating to this unlawful transaction he had captured, as a proper forfeiture to the government under the facts above stated; which was done."

General Butler voluntarily submitted this case to the judgment of Mr. Johnson, who decided against the forfeiture, on the following grounds:

1. That there was no capture of the property or its representative while actually running the blockade.

2. That there was no personal delection in Kennedy & Co. in the acts done by them, which could render them subject to forfeiture.

3. That the blockade being raised by the proclamation of the president before the capture of the draft, all delection on account of the transaction was purged.

These points he argued precisely as he would have argued them had the rebellion been a legitimate war between two foreign nations; quoting such authorities as Vattel, Grotius, Puffendorf, and Wheaton, who wrote on international law. General Butler yielded to the decision, and paid back the money ($8,641); but he could not refrain from reviewing Mr. Johnson's argument. Addressing Mr. Johnson himself, he remarked that, "as applied to this transaction, the citations and arguments derived from elementary writers upon the law of nations, are of no value. This is not the case of a resident subject of a foreign state attempting to elude the vigilance of a blockade by a foreign power of a port of a third nation. The rule that the successful running of the blockade, or a subsequent raising of the blockade purges the transaction so far as punishment for personal delection is concerned, is too familiar to need citation, at least by a lawyer to a lawyer. It would be desirable to see some citations to show that there was no personal delection in the transaction under consideration.

"A traitorous commercial house directly engage in the treasonable work of aiding a rebellion against the government, by entering into a trade the direct effect of which is to furnish the rebels with arms and munitions. To do this they intentionally violate the revenue laws, the postal laws of their country, as well as the laws prohibiting trade with foreign countries from this port, and are caught in the act, and fined only the amount of the proceeds of their illegal and treasonable transaction.

"Their lives, by every law, were forfeit to the country of their allegiance.

"The representative of that country takes a comparatively small fine from them and a commissioner of that same country refunds it because of its impropriety.

"Grotius, Puffendorf, Vattel, and Wheaton will be searched, it is believed, in vain, for a precedent for such action. Why cite international law to govern a transaction between the rebellious traitor and his own government? Around the state of Louisiana the government had placed the impassable barrier of law, covering each and every subject, saying to him, from that state no cotton should be shipped and no arms imported, and there no mails or letters should be delivered.

"To warn off foreigners, to prevent bad men of our own citizens violating that law, the government had placed ships. Now, whatever may be the law relating to the intruding foreigner, can it be said for a moment that the fact that a traitor has successfully eluded the vigilance of the government, that that very success purges the crime, which might never have been criminal but for that success.

"The fine will be restored, because *stare decisus*, but the guilty party ought to be and will be punished.

"A course of treatment of rebels which should have such results, would not only be 'rose-water,' but diluted 'rose-water.'

"The other reason given for the decision that the blockade had been raised, is a mistake in point of fact, both in the date and the place of capture. The capture was not made of a vessel running into the port of New Orleans when the blockade was raised, but from one of those lagoons where, in former times, Lafitte the pirate carried on a hardly more atrocious business.

"Something was said at the hearing that this money was intended by Kennedy & Co. for northern creditors.

"Sending it to England does not seem the best evidence of that intention.

"But, of course, no such consideration could enter into the decision. I have reviewed this decision at some length, because it seems to me that it offers a premium for treasonable acts to traitors in the Confederate States. It says, in substance, 'Violate the laws of the United States as well as you can, send abroad all the produce of the Confederate States you can, to be converted into arms for the rebellion; you only take the risk of losing *in transitu;* and as the profits are four-fold you can afford to do so. But it is solemnly decided that in all this there is no '*personal delection*,' for which you can or ought to be punished even by a fine, and if you are, the fine shall be returned.' "

Mr. Johnson replied to this review in a voluminous and ably written argument, which was handed to General Butler three hours before its author sailed for the North. There was, therefore, no opportunity for reply. The chief point of Mr. Johnson's new argument was, that there was no evidence that Kennedy & Co. had agreed to invest any portion of the proceeds of the cotton in arms and munitions of war. They denied that they had either engaged to do this, or had done it. This defense, since by Confederate law no cotton could be exported on any other terms, was equivalent to saying that Kennedy & Co. had been faithless to both governments, and were liable to two actions for treason instead of one.

Case of Avendano Brothers.

The capture of the steamer Fox led to the discovery of the complicity of this firm also with the rebellion. The case was so clear and aggravated, that the house never thought of complaining of General Butler's conduct with regard to it, until the decisions of Mr. Reverdy Johnson gave them hopes of a successful appeal to the government at Washington. General Butler being called upon for a statement of the facts, gave them with such cogency as to silence the Spanish minister.

"The house of Avendano Brothers," he wrote, in October, "has been established in New Orleans so long that its members have become an integral part of the population, in interest, in feeling, and in social ties. Before the breaking out of this rebellion, its members never thought of seeking the protection of Spain. But since this rebellion all has changed, and now the Spanish consul claims that persons thirty years of age, born of Spanish parents, who have lived here from their birth, and their ancestors before them, are still Spanish subjects, and is issuing certificates of nationality accordingly; so that this city has become almost entirely depopulated as to citizens, except of free persons of color, who singularly claim protection of our government where so little has been heretofore afforded them.

"The house of Avendano Brothers has been largely engaged in running cotton through the blockade, and importing arms and munitions of war.

"No cotton was allowed by the Confederates to be shipped unless arms and munitions of war were returned in the proportion of one-half. Avendano Brothers shipped largely under this permission, and have been engaged in breaking every law of neutrality and national hospitality that can be well conceived.

"Somewhere about the 10th of May I captured the Confederate steamer Fox, which had been seized by the Confederates from her Union owners and turned into their service, and employed in running the blockade (she made three trips thus). She had on board a cargo of arms, powder, lead, quicksilver, acids for telegraphic purposes, chloroform and morphine for medical stores, to the amount of $300,000 or thereabouts—all of the greatest necessity to the rebels, and had run into the Bayou La Fourche, in the west bank of the Mississippi, from which bayou she might, if she thought proper, run to Vicksburg.

"She had besides the invoices, letters of advice, bills of lading, bills of exchange, and the evidences of the transactions of many of the mercantile houses of New Orleans.

"The letters of advice, bills of lading, and invoices show the nature of the transaction between these parties and their correspondents at Havana. The bills of exchange were products of the shipments of cotton, less the proportion invested in contraband goods. Among them were the bills of exchange payable to the house of Avendano Brothers, the first having been forwarded by some other conveyance, but still unpaid, and these bills of exchange were for one-half the proceeds of the cargo shipped, the other half being invested in munitions of war.

"This vessel also carried a mail, containing amongst other things, the official correspondence between the rebel commissioner Rost, which I forwarded to the state department, and the rebel ordnance office in Europe, relating to his movements there, which I forwarded to the war department, as well as other important letters which developed the nature of the business being carried on between this port and the miscalled neutral ports—Havana and Nassau. Upon personal examination, I had no doubt that the house of Avendano was largely interested in, or the consignees of the major part of the cargo of the 'Fox;' and in order to put a stop to this traffic, which could still be carried on through the fifty-three openings in the Gulf of Mexico from Louisiana, I called upon the house of Avendano; and upon personal examination they did not deny the part they had taken in the traffic.

"I required them, therefore, having captured in bulk one-half the fruits of their illegal traffic, and having captured the other half thereof in the shape of a bill of exchange, to pay over the other half, being the bills of exchange. This they did, and received the bills of exchange and papers, regarding that as a light punishment for their crimes.

"Because of other transactions which have come to my knowledge, the senior partner has escaped to Havana, but the house is still carrying on business here, and are the consignees of the steamer 'Cardenas,' which has been the cause of so many breaches of our quarantine laws and so many complaints of the Spanish minister.

"Avendano sent a rebel lawyer, who had refused to renew his oath of allegiance to the United States, to me to make some representations of the matter and to argue certain legal questions. In answer to some suggestions as to the amount of fine, I told him that Avendano might think himself well off if he lost no more of the profits of his infernal trade.

"This, it will be observed, was about the 19th of May, and no complaints are made of it for three months, until emboldened by the success of the complaints to the commission here, which has done more to strengthen the hand of secession than any other occurrence of the south-west since my advent in New Orleans, and the commissioner of which commission, as I am now ready to prove, acted as the paid attorney of rebels in making claims against the United States from retainers taken because of his acting here in his official capacity.

"This commission, I say, emboldened these new complaints of my action by mercantile pirates and marauders, who supplied arms and powder to traitors, and who are only saved from the consequences of treason because they have not given their allegiance to the country that had given them protection and enabled them to accumulate fortunes; advantages they believed their own governments could not give them, and so preferred to live under ours, but not to assume their proper obligations.

"They should have been *hanged;* they were only *fined.*

"His excellency, the Spanish minister, seems to think that running the blockade carries its own punishment with it; but this is not a case of running a blockade merely, but is the case of an importer of arms, of an army contractor for the rebel government; and this draft, which the house of Avendano has paid, and the money used for the support of the troops of the United States in this department, is only one-half the proceeds of a single adventure of the house of Avendano in breaking the laws and aiding the rebellion—the other half being returned to the Confederates in arms and munitions of war.

"I aver to the secretary of war, upon my official responsibility, that without aid furnished by foreign mercantile houses in New Orleans, Mobile, Savannah and Charleston, as I am convinced by the most irrefragable evidence, this rebellion would have wholly failed to arm and supply itself. And the most active agents, and most efficient supporters have been the same quasi foreign houses, mostly Jews and their correspondents, principally in Havana and Nassau; who all deserve to receive at the hands of this government what is due to the Jew Benjamin, Slidell, Mallory or Floyd. Only the strong repressive measures which have been fearlessly and energetically taken in this department, have prevented the supply from still going on here as it does at Charleston in South Carolina.

"Tempted by the immense profits, waging the war in order to realize those profits, these foreign adventurers have done everything they could to sustain the war, and to inflame the passions of the people against the United States; and their reiterated complaints of my conduct, and the howl in Europe and elsewhere set up by them at my every act, have been simply the result of the disappointment of those who desire that some action may be taken by the government which would reopen to them a most profitable trade, which I have closed by the measures of which complaint has been made, and as to which the honorable secretary of state has been pleased to say redress will be made if I fail to justify my acts.

"I have stated the grounds upon which my action proceeded, and the purpose for which it was taken. Of course, to do this work could be of no personal advantage to myself and only entailed great and severe labor.

"It was dictated by a sense of duty, and upon full and thorough examination I have failed to see any reason why it should not be persevered in. But I respectfully submit that it adds not a little to the already overtasking labor of this department, to be continually called upon, months after, to reinvestigate and report upon acts which were within the scope of my jurisdiction in the fair exercise of the discretion of a military commander, and for which I should be called to account, not by a letter of a foreign consular agent on the ex parte statement of a Spanish smuggler, but by the commander-in-chief of the army, or the president of the United States, to whom I am as ready to account for my every action, as I am to my country and my God."

This is strong language. The documents before me justify it. They show beyond all doubt that the rebels in New Orleans, both native and foreign, were only deterred from ministering to the rebellion by the fact which General Butler never allowed them to forget, that in New Orleans the United States was Master.

English and Spanish Men-of-War at New Orleans.

The officers and crews of foreign vessels-of-war that chanced to visit New Orleans in the summer and autumn of 1862, took pains to show that they were in accord with the secession consuls and the disloyal citizens. New Orleans was a good place to learn that in this great quarrel there are arrayed against the United States the entire baseness, and a great part ot the ignorance, of the human race. Every one in the world is against us, who is willing to live upon the unrequited, or upon the ill-requited labor of others.

The British ship-of-war Rinaldo was in port during the early days of July. The humor of the officers and crew of this ship may best be shown from the matter-of-fact report of Mr. James Duane, lieutenant of police:—"Having learned on Thursday evening that a large crowd of turbulent citizens was collected on the levee opposite the steamer Rinaldo, and that on board that vessel certain parties were engaged in singing the 'Bonnie Blue Flag,' and crying 'Down with the Stars and Stripes,' and that the crowd were responding by cheers for Jeff. Davis, the Southern Confederacy, &c.; and, apprehending a riot, I detailed my entire force, and accompanied them myself to the levee, where I arrived about eight o'clock P. M., and found a crowd of nearly two thousand men, women, and children. From the ship I distinctly heard the singing of the 'Bonnie Blue Flag,' cheers for Jeff. Davis; cries of 'Down with the Stars and Stripes,' and 'Up with the Flag of the Single Star.' The response by the crowd was not general, but confined to an occasional voice, and as fast as it occurred I arrested the party so responding. The same conduct occurred on Friday night, to my personal knowledge.

"From my officers, and citizens residing in the neighborhood, I have received information that the same proceedings took place on the Wednesday evening preceding the above, and, in addition, that on that evening a secession flag was flying on board the Rinaldo for a short time, and that a smaller flag of the Confederacy was flying from the boats that conveyed visitors to and from the vessel and the levee. On Saturday evening, the same demonstrations were repeated, with the exception of the display of secession flags. And, furthermore, on the same evening, between eight and nine o'clock, one of my officers saw an officer of the Rinaldo, in uniform, accompanied by a man who claimed to belong to that vessel, and a tall negro. The officer was intoxicated, and was singing, the 'Bonnie Blue Flag.' My officer stepped up to him and told him he must not sing that song. The British officer replied that 'he would sing what he damn pleased.' They then went on down the levee and got into their ship's boat, and as soon as they were out of the reach of the police officer, called out 'God damn the Yankee sons of——, one Englishman can whip ten of them,' and again sung the 'Bonnie Blue Flag,' all joining in the song."

Word was brought to General Butler, on the 3d of July, that the captain of the Rinaldo had promised his secession friends to hoist the rebel flag on his ship on the morning of the fourth. The general, I am told, avowed to a confidential member of his staff, his solemn and deliberate resolve, if the flag was officially displayed, to open fire upon the ship with artillery. The hoisting of the flag, he considered, would be more than an insult to the United States; it would constitute the ship a rebel vessel, and, as such, she was to be fired upon, the very instant a Union gun could be brought to bear upon her. The report proved to be false.

Still more outrageous was the conduct of the Spanish man-of-war. It was in a Spanish vessel, as we have seen, that the French consul shipped his $405,000. Other Spanish vessels-of-war carried away passengers, treasure, plate, papers, which were justly liable to seizure. "The deck of the Blasco de Garay," wrote General Butler in October, "was literally crowded with passengers, selected with so little discrimination, that my detective officers found on board, as a passenger, an escaped convict of the penitentiary, who was in full flight from a most brutal murder, with his booty robbed from his victim with him." On other Spanish ships several persons deeply implicated in the rebellion, guilty of hostile acts after the capture of the city, effected their escape to Havana, with large amounts of treasure. Hence the claim of General Butler to search departing vessels-of-war, and hence a ream of complaints and protests from Spanish officers.

The Quarantine Imbroglio.

It is not generally known at the North, that, in the worst years, the mortality from yellow fever in New Orleans exceeds that from any epidemic that has ever raged in a civilized community. It is worse than the modern cholera, worse than the small-pox before inoculation, worse than the ancient plague. A competent and entirely trustworthy writer gives the facts of the yellow fever season of 1853, the most fatal year ever known:

"Commencing on the 1st of August, with one hundred and six deaths by yellow fever, one hundred and forty-two by all diseases, the number increased daily, until for the first week, ending on the 7th, they amounted to nine hundred and nine deaths by yellow fever, one thousand one hundred and eighty-six of all diseases. The next week showed a continued increase: one thousand two hundred and eighty-eight yellow fever, one thousand five hundred and twenty-six of all diseases. This was believed to be the maximum. There had been nothing to equal it in the history of any previous epidemics, and no one believed it could be exceeded. But the next week gave a mournful refutation of these predictions and calculations; for that ever memorable week, the total deaths were one thousand five hundred and seventy-five, of yellow fever one thousand three hundred and forty-six. But the next week commenced more gloomily still. The deaths on the 22d of August were two hundred and eighty-three of all diseases, two hundred and thirty-nine of yellow fever. This proved to be the maximum mortality of the season. From this it began slowly to decrease. The month of August exhibited a grand total of five thousand one hundred and twenty-two deaths by yellow fever, and nearly seven thousand deaths of all diseases. Slowly the disease continued to decrease, only for the want of victims, until on the 6th of September (at which time these notes are transcribed), when it reached sixty-five deaths by yellow fever, and ninety-five deaths of all diseases. Looking back from this point, we find that the whole number of deaths by yellow fever, from its first appearance on the 28th of May, were seven thousand one hundred and eighty-nine—deaths from all diseases nine thousand nine hundred and forty-one. But there are three hundred and forty-four deaths the cause of which is not stated in the burial certificates. At least three fourths of these may be set down to the yellow fever column—which would add two hundred and fifty more, and make the deaths by yellow fever seven thousand four hundred and thirty-nine.

"But do these figures include all the deaths? Alas! no. Hundreds have been buried of whom no note was taken, no record kept. Hundreds have died away from the city, in attempting to fly from it. Every steamer up the river contributed its share to the hecatombs of victims of the pestilence. Nor do these returns include those who have died in the suburbs, in the towns of Algiers and Jefferson City, in the villages of Gretna and Carrollton. But even these figures, deficient as they are, need no additions to swell them into proofs that the most destructive plague of modern times has just wreaked its vengeance upon New Orleans. Estimating the total deaths at eight thousand for three months, we have ten per cent. of the whole population of New Orleans. At this rate it would only require two years and four months to depopulate the city.

"But only the unacclimated are liable to the disease, and so we must exclude the old resident acclimated population, which, with slaves, and free colored persons, embrace at least two-thirds of the summer population of New Orleans. This would reduce the number liable to yellow fever below thirty thousand. Of that number one-fourth have died in three months. There is scarcely any parallel to this mortality. The great Plague of London, in 1665, destroyed one out of every thirteen, and one-third of its population. That of New Orleans, in 1853, destroyed one out of every ten of its total population, and one out of every four of those susceptible of the disease. This exceeds the mortality in Philadelphia, in 1798, when it was estimated that one out of every six died."*

These are terrible figures. The year 1853, was, however, an exceptional year. New Orleans has often escaped the yellow fever for years in succession. Its visitations were frequent enough to make it an ever present terror during the summer months, and to reduce the summer population of the city to a comparatively small number of unacclimated persons. The city had *never* escaped it in such circumstances as existed in 1862; had never escaped it when the fever raged in the neighboring ports of Havana and Nassau; had never escaped it when the city was filled with persons unaccustomed to the climate. The rebels were, therefore, justified in anticipating, with perfect confidence, that the season of 1862 would present the same scenes of horror and devastation as those of 1853.

No language can overstate the terrors of such a visitation. "Funeral processions," says the writer just quoted, "crowded every street. No vehicles could be seen except doctors' cabs and coaches, passing to and from the cemeteries, and hearses, often solitary, taking their way toward those gloomy destinations. The hum of trade was hushed. The levee was a desert. The streets, wont to shine with fashion and beauty, were silent. The tombs—the home of the dead—were the only places where there was life,

* *Harper's Magazine*, November, 1853.

where crowds assembled, where the incessant rumbling of carriages, the trampling of feet, the murmur of voices, and all the signs of active, stirring life could be heard and seen.

"To realize the full horror and virulence of the pestilence, you must go into the crowded localities of the laboring classes, into those miserable shanties which are the disgrace of the city, where the poor immigrant class cluster together in filth, sleeping a half-dozen in one room, without ventilation, and having access to filthy, wet yards, which have never been filled up, and when it rains are converted into green puddles—fit abodes for frogs and sources of poisonous malaria. Here you will find scenes of woe, misery, and death, which will haunt your memory in all time to come. Here you will see the dead and the dying, the sick and the convalescent, in one and the same bed. Here you will see the living babe sucking death from the yellow breast of its dead mother. Here father, mother, and child die in one another's arms. Here you will find whole families swept off in a few hours, so that none are left to mourn or to procure the rites of burial. Offensive odors frequently drew neighbors to such awful spectacles. Corpses would thus proclaim their existence, and enforce the observances due them. What a terrible disease! Terrible in its insidious character, in its treachery, in the quiet serpent-like manner in which it gradually winds its folds around its victim, beguiles him by its deceptive wiles; cheats his judgment and senses, and then consigns him to grim death. Not like the plague, with its red spot, its maddening fever, its wild delirium and stupor—not like the cholera, in violent spasms and prostrating pains, is the approach of the *vomito*. It assumes the guise of the most ordinary disease which flesh is heir to—a cold, a slight chill, a headache, a slight fever, and, after a while, pains in the back. Surely there is nothing in these! 'I won't lay by for them,' says the misguided victim; the poor laborer can not afford to do so. Instead of going to bed, sending for a nurse and doctor, taking a mustard-bath and a cathartic, he remains at his post until it is too late. He has reached the crisis of the disease before he is aware of its existence. The chances are thus against him. The fever mounts up rapidly, and the poison pervades his whole system. He tosses and rolls on his bed, and raves in agony. Thus he continues for thirty-six hours. Then the fever breaks, gradually it passes off—joy and hope begin to dawn upon him. He is through now. 'Am I not better, Doctor?' 'You are doing well, but must be very quiet.' Doing well! How does the learned gentleman know? Can he see into his stomach, and perceive there collecting the dark brown liquid which marks the dissolution that is going on? The fever suddenly returns, but now the paroxysm is more brief. Again the patient is quiet, but not so hopeful as before. He is weak, prostrate, and bloodless, but he has no fever; his pulse is regular, sound, and healthy, and his skin moist. 'He will get well,' says the casual observer. The doctor shakes his head ominously. After a while, drops of blood are seen collecting about his lips. Blood comes from his gums—that is a bad sign, but such cases frequently occur. Soon he has a hiccough. That is worse than the bleeding at the gums: then follows the ejection of a dark brown liquid which he throws up in large quantities; and this in nine hundred and ninety-nine cases out of a thousand is the signal that the doctor's function is at an end, and the undertaker's is to commence. In a few hours the coffin will receive its tenant, and mother earth her customary tribute."

Dr. McCormick, who was in the city during those fearful weeks, has assured me that this picture is not overcharged.

It was such an evil as this that General Butler set himself to ward from the city which he had been called to govern and protect. His success was most remarkable. The yellow fever raged at Nassau, at Havana, and at other neighboring ports, but New Orleans escaped. Twenty thousand unacclimated persons, strangers, northerners, were in Louisiana, but not one of them had the fever. On the contrary, the men of his command enjoyed an extraordinary exemption from all mortal disease. They suffered little from the continuous heat, less from violent maladies.

There was, indeed, one moment of danger, and of great alarm at head-quarters. Dr. McCormick, late in the season, when the danger was supposed to be nearly over, came into the general's office one morning, and reported that a case of yellow fever of the worst type had been landed in the city. It was even so. The rigor of the quarantine had been once relaxed, and this was the alarming result. The affair was kept as secret as possible. The house in which the man lay was cleared of all inmates save himself and one acclimated attendant. The block of which the house was part was walled around by sentinels. No living creature was permitted to enter or leave it. In five days the man died. Every article in his room was burnt or buried. His attendant was quarantined. The house, the block, the quarter of the city, was fumigated, cleansed, and whitewashed. Every precaution which the skill of the doctors could devise and the authority of the general enforce was employed. No one caught the disease. This single case, brought from Nassau, was all the yellow fever known in New Orleans during the season of 1862.

It is of the highest importance to the future of Louisiana that the means employed by General Butler to preserve the health of the city should be known. Sanitary science, as the reader is aware, was a familiar subject with him before he began his military career. His researches led him to adopt the theory that the yellow fever is indigenous in no region where there is frost every winter. There is frost every winter in every part of the United States. He, therefore, concluded that the yellow fever is not a disease native to our soil, but is always brought from a tropical port. The gulf coasts generate, it is true, the malaria which serves as a medium for the most calamitous *spread* of the disease; but the deadly poison which issues in the yellow fever is brought from abroad. The magazine is ready, but the foreign spark is indispensable. He relied chiefly, therefore, upon a quarantine; and this he enforced with such rigorous impartiality, that the state department was inundated with complaints, reclamations, and protests, and the ear of the public was assailed with charges of favoritism and corruption. But he never relaxed his clutch upon the throat of the Mississippi. "My orders," he wrote on one occasion, "are imperative and distinct to my health-officers, to subject *all* vessels coming from infected ports to such a quarantine as shall insure safety from disease. Whether one day or one hundred is necessary for the purpose, it will be done. It will be done if it is necessary to take the vessel to pieces to do it, so long as the United States has the physical power to enforce it. I have submitted to the judgment of my very competent surgeon at the quarantine the question of the length of time and the action to be taken to insure safety. I have by no order interfered with his discretion. If he thinks ten days sufficient in a given case, be it so; if forty in another, be it so; if one hundred in another, it shall be so."

And so it was, as the volumes of documents unanswerably show.

The consular complaints had at length the usual fortunate effect of extorting from General Butler one of those clear and interesting statements of fact, of which the reader has already been favored with several specimens. In this masterly paper, he gives a history of his expedients for keeping away the yellow fever, and replies to the numberless accusations of partiality, which had been, and still are brought against him. It was the case of the Cardenas, a Spanish ship, plying between Havana and New Orleans, which he was requested by the secretary of war to elucidate, and which called forth the following important narrative:

"When New Orleans was captured," wrote the general, October 1st, "it was found in the utmost possible filthy condition, because of the troublesome times. The contractors upon all the streets and canals had utterly neglected to comply with their contracts for cleaning and purifying the streets, and the filth was indescribable.

"In view of this most alarming sanitary condition of the city, and the approach of the epidemic season, after consultation with the most eminent local physicians, who would give advice (some refusing to give any opinion with the apparent hope that the pestilence would do what their rebel arms could not, drive us out), and acting with the advice of my medical staff, I took the most energetic measures to purify the city itself from the possibility of engendering disease. Believing at the same time that the yellow fever was no more indigenous to New Orleans than the sugar cane, but must be imparted or propagated as that is by cuttings, and that a firmly administered quarantine, guided by science and honesty of purpose, discriminating as regards cargoes and cleanliness of ships, would effectually keep out the scourge of the city, the prayed for ally of the rebellion, I ordered quarantine to be enforced with these discriminations, not 'a procrustean period of quarantine to all.' A vessel loaded with hides and wool, the absorbants of the malaria, with a filthy hold reeking with dead and putrid organic matter, loaded at an infected port with infected hands, sown thick with the seeds of disease, only waiting for time and the warm sun to develop them into a plague, was not put on an equality as to time with a steamer for passengers, kept clean and sweet as a mercantile necessity to procure business, laden with flour, tight casks of salted provisions and round shot and shell, which would not be likely either to absorb or generate contagion.

"Again, the length of time in which a ship and cargo had been exposed to the danger of contagion had much to do with the quarantine. A ship belonging to an infected port, loaded there with the product or the manufacture of that port, her crew acclimated and therefore indifferent to sanitary regulations and appliances, required to be kept under quarantine longer, to watch the probable development of disease, and to await the operation of purification, than a vessel loaded at a northern port, where the frost insured health in this regard, and which had merely touched at a port afflicted with yellow fever, and held communication with the shore under the restriction imposed by the fears of unacclimated officers and crew.

"These and kindred considerations which will readily suggest themselves to your mind, were the controlling guide to the very intelligent medical officers who were in charge at quarantine, as they were to my own mind upon the necessity and length of detention. We determined, however, to err, if at all, upon the safe side, remembering ever the far greater importance of the lives of a large city and an army committed to our charge, than the possible damage to any commercial adventure from detention.

"I need not assure you, sir, that the question of 'nationality' never entered into our thought in the exercise of our judgment and power, except in one possible relation.

"We could not help looking with a little less care to, and holding under advisement a little less time, a vessel of a nation proverbial for the neatness of their ships, as compared with one which enjoyed an unenviable reputation the other way. With these theories, and upon these bases, have the quarantine and health laws been administered at New Orleans, up to the first day of October.

"I can point with a reasonably justified pride to the results as an explanation and a vindication of my acts and administration in this particular. Pardon me, if I add, that I claim for this triumph of science, integrity, firmness, and skill of my medical staff, by which thousands of lives have been saved, and by far the most dreaded foe driven from the city of New Orleans, as much credit, as if by the disposition of my troops we had won a victory over the less deadly but hardly less implacable enemy in a conflict of arms.

"Up to this date, there has been no malignant, or epidemical, or virulent fevers or diseases in New Orleans, and its mortality returns show it to be *the most healthy city in the United States*. In one regiment, the Thirteenth Connecticut, a thousand strong, quartered in the Custom-House since the 15th of May, but one man was lost during the months of July and August.

"His excellency, Mr. Tarsara, the Spanish minister, is most grievously misinformed when he says to the secretary of state, that the salubrity of New Orleans is no better than that of the island of Cuba.

"Our quarantine has been more perfect than the blockade. We have had serious cases of fever at the quarantine, only seventy-five miles from us, and but a *single one* at New Orleans, and this one at once justifies and illustrates our sanitary laws.

"The United States steamship 'Ida,' having only touched at Nassau, and no disease having been reported as existing there at the time of her departure, was permitted to pass up by the health-officer after fumigation and other precautions. The day after her arrival in the city, one of her passengers on shore was taken sick and on the sixth day died; an unmistakable case of malignant yellow fever. The most strenuous measures were taken to isolate the disease. Everything that touched or was about the diseased man was buried; acclimated persons only were allowed to do the last sad offices. The house in which he died was most thoroughly purified, and by the blessing of 'Him who holdeth all things in the hollow of his hand,' the pestilence was stayed.

"The steamer was ordered at once below, where she is undergoing quarantine. Even while I write this, the English consul reports the British brig 'Volunteer' to me at the mouth of the river, out of provisions, her officers and crew, including the captain, dead or sick with fever, and prays for assistance; and a telegraphic message sends from the quarantine my health-officer on board with medical supplies and other aid.

"I have thus given to the department a full explanation of the complaints involved in my administration of the quarantine laws. Upon the other branches of the inquiry relative to the Spanish steamer 'Cardenas,' I am most happy to report:

"As to the Spanish 'Cardenas,' let me observe, that she did not come to me in such manner as to demand the highest degree of courtesy or respect. The 'Cardenas' left Havana on the 31st of May, after epidemic yellow fever had made its appearance, bringing many passengers, a large portion of whom were rebels who had been in Havana buying arms and munitions of war for the Confederates, having on board to bring her up the river two pilots who had successfully conducted vessels through the blockade.

"She ran past the forts without stopping, which was permitted because she was mistaken for the U. S. steamer 'Connecticut,' then hourly expected, which mistake caused the 'Connecticut' to be fired at when she made her appearance, and attempted to go by without reporting.

"The 'Cardenas' then loitered up the river till near night, and without coming up to the usual place of landing, or reporting to the harbor-master, came alongside a wharf some three miles below the usual places of steamboat landing, and put on shore all her passengers without passports being examined, or any report to any person, so that many obnoxious persons escaped into the city, and the provost-marshal has never been able to ascertain the character of all her passengers.

"Will it be pretended that any captain of a Spanish steamer is so ignorant as not to know that such conduct is in the highest degree improper in landing passengers at a military post.

"Mr. Tarsara says well, 'that no difficulty was made about landing the passengers from the steamer.' True, because they and their baggage were surreptitiously landed miles below the usual landing-place, without the knowledge of any person friendly to the United States, but evidently with the knowledge of the secessionists, because the captain says, in his protest, that 'crowds invaded the vessel as soon as she made the wharf.'

"She was ordered back to quarantine; but many frivolous excuses and delays were interposed by her officers until a most peremptory order, accompanied by a threat, was given, which she obeyed.

"After a proper quarantine, the 'Cardenas' came up—not of thirty days, but one precisely such as was thought sufficient. I do not understand Mr. Tarsara's notions about reciprocity in quarantine. He seems to insist that if we require a long quarantine at New Orleans, the governor-general of Cuba will require an equally long one at Havana. But what need of quarantines at all against epidemic yellow fever in its most virulent form? What possible reciprocity of quarantine could there be between Iceland and Vera Cruz? I have endeavored to make quarantine a sensible, not a useless regulation.

"It is complained, however, that the U. S. steamship 'Roanoke' suffered a shorter detention at quarantine than the 'Cardenas,' and that she sailed from Havana on the day after.

"This is an uncandid way of stating the fact. The 'Roanoke' sailed from New York, went into the harbor at Havana, stayed there less than twenty-four hours, and held little or no communication with the shore. Her captain reported her at the quarantine station as direct from New York.

"Was there any reason for so long a quarantine for her as for a vessel loaded at Havana?

"When the 'Roanoke' was about to sail for New York on her return from New Orleans, a large number of Spanish persons were desirous of taking passage in her for Havana, and engaged passage accordingly. Upon application to the Spanish consul for a bill of health, as the purser of the 'Roanoke' informed me, the consul or vice-consul told him that as 'I had quarantined the 'Cardenas,' the consul would not give the 'Roanoke' a bill of health, but would report that New Orleans was afflicted with epidemic fever unless I would permit the 'Cardenas' to come up, and if so a clean bill of health would be given.'

"The effect of and motive for this conduct was obvious. If the 'Roanoke' went to Havana and carried her passengers, she would take away this business from the 'Cardenas.' If she carried such a bill of health as to put her in quarantine at Havana, no New York passengers would sail in her, so that she must lose one or the other lot of passengers.

"This seemed to me so unjust that I sent for the consul for an explanation. I understood his explanations to be exactly what the purser of the 'Roanoke' informed me had been given him.

"It is proper here to remark that I have since been assured by the Spanish consul, for whom I really entertain high respect, that this conversation was misunderstood by all parties, neither understanding the other's language.

"I told the consul at that interview, that any retaliation upon the 'Roanoke' for any supposed wrong done by me to the 'Cardenas' ought not to be, and could not be permitted; 'that if he slandered the health of the city of New Orleans, by giving any report that epidemic yellow fever existed here, when he knew it not to be the fact, preventing trade and commerce coming to this port by such false report, that I would certainly send him out of the city to Havana, and report his conduct to the captain-general, as the nearest Spanish authority;' and, in that event, this I would most assuredly have done. I told him, that the bill of health of the 'Roanoke' must be such as was required by the laws and his instructions, precisely as if nothing had been done to the 'Cardenas.'

"To this (as he was interpreted to me to say) the consul replied, that he would not give a clean bill of health to the 'Roanoke,' because it was now past the first of June, and whatever might be the health of the city in fact, he must report it unhealthy. Farther, that if I still held the 'Cardenas' under quarantine, he would write to the captain-general of Cuba, not to send any more vessels here.

"To that I replied, that he should give my compliments to the captain-general, and say that, until the yellow fever season was over, he could do me and the city no greater favor than to prevent vessels from coming here.

"I then put in writing, and handed the consul my claim, that he should give a bill of health to the Roanoke required by the laws and regulations of his government, regardless of my treatment of the 'Cardenas.'

"The interview here ended. The bill of health, however, which was given to the Roanoke, was such (although the city was perfectly healthy) that her officers did not dare to sail to Havana, lest they should be held to quarantine there, in a city where the small-pox and yellow fever were both raging. She was in consequence obliged to discharge her Havana passengers, and pay back the passage money.

"I take leave here to observe upon a remark of Mr. Tarsara, the Spanish minister, 'that I had not the authority to send out of my lines the Spanish consul,' for so gross a dereliction of duty: in the first place, that I should have done it, if the occasion had called; and that secondly, I know of no law, national or municipal, that requires the commander of a captured city, occupied as a military post, to keep any person in it, consul or other, who is deliberately working to render the place untenable, by keeping away supplies of provisions from it through false reports.

"I wish, however, again to repeat, that subsequent conversations, through a more intelligent interpreter in his understanding of English, has convinced me that the consul's remarks were misinterpreted and mistaken by me, as mine were by him. These subsequent explanations have, I believe, established the most cordial relations between us. I have also learned that I have done Mr. Callijon an injustice in another respect, in supposing him, as I was informed, to be a Spanish merchant. Such I am now convinced is not the case; but that he is a soldier, who has won honorable distinction in the wars of his country.

"In Mr. Tarsara's letter of complaint, it is alleged that I have permitted the French brigantine 'Marie Felicia,' and the English schooner 'Virginia Antoinette,' and other vessels, to come up without the same length of quarantine as the 'Cardenas.' These facts, it is said, will convict me of capricious discrimination against Spain in favor of other European nations. There is no reason given why I should be possessed of feelings which would lead me thus to discriminate. Indeed, if I permitted my indignation and sense of wrong as regards the manner in which my government has been treated by other nations to influence my official action, I assure you Spain would not be the nation toward which these feelings would most actively operate. On the contrary, I have felt that the conduct of Spain has been most friendly, especially taking in view the wrong done her by some of the citizens of the United States in the invasion of Cuba. No rebel privateers have fitted out from her ports. I have not known that any of her islands have been made arsenals and naval dépôts for the Confederacy, and I have yet to be informed of any discrimination made by her between our armed vessels and those of the enemy. I have ventured to say thus much because, in weighing one's acts, motives are specially to be looked at.

"Perhaps, however, the two cases of the 'Marie Felicia' and the 'Virginia Antoinette' deserve a word of comment, as they illustrate the animus with which our quarantine has been conducted.

"The 'Marie' having an acclimated crew, having been loaded at Havre, and only touched at Havana without landing, was detained only long enough to examine her present condition as to health, presuming that she contained no latent disease or malaria which develops itself by time. The 'Virginia' having only touched at Havana, was without passengers, and laden wholly with loose salt, a powerful disinfectant itself. One might as well quarantine a barrel of chloride of lime. And yet permitting this schooner to come up after twenty days' absence from the infected port, is brought forward as evidence of a 'capricious discrimination against the Spanish government.'

"Mr. Tarsara, in his communication of the 28th of June, wishes the secretary to require me 'to treat the consuls of foreign nations with more consideration; and that I must refrain from expressions which are not suited to give security to trade or maintain friendly relations between the authorities of the Island and those of the United States.'

"It will be seen by examination of the letter of the commander of the 'Blasco de Garay,' hereto annexed, under date of August 13th, that he complains that my acts do not come up to my professions of friendship and the courtesies of my language. I have, therefore, appended all of the more important of my correspondence with the Spanish authorities here, so that the department may see whether, either in the manner or matter of that correspondence, there is anything which should be a *casus belli* between two otherwise friendly nations.

"That I answered somewhat sharply the letter of the captain of the 'Blasco de Garay,' who seized the occasion in replying to a note, wherein I offered him assistance and courtesy, to read me a lecture on my duties, I admit. I thought, and still think, I was justified in so doing.

"A nation may be friendly and its consul quite the reverse, as witness the late Prussian consul, who is now a general in the rebel army, for which he recruited a battalion of his countrymen.

"When, therefore, I find a consul aiding the rebels, I must treat him as a rebel; and the exceptions are very few indeed among the consuls here. Bound up with the rebels by marriage and social relations, most of the consular offices are only asylums where rebels are harbored and rebellion fostered.

"Before I close this report, which pressure of public duties more urgent has delayed till the departure of the mail on the 6th of October, allow me to repeat that, with the blessing of God, to whom our most devout thanks are daily due for His goodness, the fell scourge, the yellow fever, has been kept from my command and the city of New Orleans till now, when all danger is past, by the firm administration of sanitary and quarantine regulations, in spite of complaints and difficulties; and if my acts need it, I point to the results as an unanswerable vindication."

Here, I believe, we may take leave of the consuls for a while. As time wore on, they came to understand the altered conditions of their tenure of office. They learned that there really was in the world such a power as the United States. They changed their opinion, too, of the man who represented that power in New Orleans; and during the latter half of General Butler's administration, his intercourse with them was generally of the most friendly and agreeable character.

CHAPTER XXI.

EFFORTS TOWARD RESTORATION.

To revive the business of New Orleans and cause its stagnant life to flow again in its ordinary channels, was among the first endeavors of General Butler after reducing the city to order and providing for its subsistence. It was necessary, at first, to compel the opening of retail stores, by the threat of a fine of a hundred dollars a day for keeping them closed. Mechanics refused to work for the United States. Certain repairs upon the light steamers, essential to the supply of the troops, could only be got done by the threat of Fort Jackson. One burly contractor was imprisoned and kept upon bread and water till he consented to undertake a piece of work of urgent necessity. The cabmen and draymen, as we have seen, required to be cajoled or impressed. This state of feeling, however, soon passed away. It was half affectation, half terror—the men only needed such a show of compulsion as would serve them as an excuse to their comrades. The ordinary business of the city soon went on as it had before the capture. The railroads were set running as far as the Union lines extended.

"Will it pay to run it?" the general would ask.

"Yes."

"Then go ahead."

So the people trafficked, and rode, and passed their days as they had been wont to do while under the sway of Mayor Monroe, General Lovell, and Mr. Soulé. Perfect order generally prevailed. The general walked and rode about the city with a single attendant, by day and by night. A child could have carried a purse in its hand from Carrollton to Chalmette without risk of molestation.

The commerce of the city could not be revived before the opening the port. In one of his earliest dispatches, General Butler advised that measure, as well as a general amnesty for all past political offenses. The planters, however, were distrustful, and feared to place their sugar within reach of the Union authorities.

To remove their apprehensions, the following general order was issued:

"New Orleans, *May* 4, 1862.

"The commanding general of the department having been informed that rebellious, lying and desperate men have represented, and are now representing, to the honest planters and good people of the state of Louisiana, that the United States government, by its forces, have come here to confiscate and destroy their crops of cotton and sugar, it is hereby ordered to be made known, by publication in all the newspapers of this city, that all cargoes of cotton and sugar shall receive the safe conduct of the forces of the United States, and the boats bringing them from beyond the lines of the United States forces, may be allowed to return in safety, after a reasonable delay, if their owners so desire; provided, they bring no passengers except the owners and managers of said boat, and of the property so conveyed, and no other merchandise except provisions, of which such boats are requested to bring a full supply, for the benefit of the poor of this city."

In anticipation of the opening of the port to northern trade, and in order to convince the holders of produce that New Orleans was already a safe market, the general determined, at once, to commence the purchase and exportation of sugar on government account. What merchants would call a "brilliant operation" was the result of his endeavors. Lying at the levee he had a large fleet of transports, which, by the terms of their charters, he was bound to send home in ballast. There is no ballast to be had in New Orleans at any time, and none nearer than the white sand of Ship Island, five days' sail and thirty hours' steam from the city. There was sugar enough on the levee to ballast all the vessels, at an immense saving to the government, to say nothing of the profit to be realized in the sale of the sugar at the North. He determined to buy enough sugar for the purpose.

To show the wisdom of this measure, take the case of the steamer Mississippi, hired at the rate of fifteen hundred dollars a day. "She must have," explained the general, "two hundred and fifty tons of ballast. To go to Ship Island and have sand brought alongside in small boats, will take at least ten days; to discharge the same and haul it away, will take four more. Thus, it will cost the government twenty-one thousand dollars to ballast and discharge the ship with sand, to say nothing of the cost of taking the sand away, or the average delays of getting it, if it storms at Ship Island. Now, if I can get some merchant to ship four hundred hogsheads of sugar in the Mississippi as ballast, which can be received in two days almost at the wharf where she lies, and discharged in two more, the government will save fifteen thousand dollars by the difference, even if it gets nothing for freight. But, by employing a party to get the ballast, see to its shipment, and take charge of the business, as a ship's broker, and agreeing to let him have all he can get over a given sum—say five dollars per hogshead for his trouble and expenses of lading—the government in the case given will save two thousand dollars more—four hundred hogsheads, at five dollars—say, in all, seventeen thousand dollars."

It was difficult to start the affair from want of money. The government had no money then in New Orleans, and the general had none. By the pledge of the whole of his private fortune ($150,000), he borrowed of Jacob Barker, the well-known banker, one hundred thousand dollars in gold, and with this sum at command, he proceeded to purchase. Merchants were also permitted to send forward sugar as ballast, on paying to the government a moderate freight. The details of this transaction were ably arranged by the general's brother, a shrewd and experienced man of business, who was allowed a commission for his trouble. The affair succeeded to admiration. The ships were all ballasted with sugar. The government took the sugar bought by the general's own money, and repaid him the amount expended; the whole advantage of the operation accruing to the United States. The sole result to General Butler was a great deal of trouble, and, at a later period, a great deal of calumny. The owners of some of the transports conceived the idea that the freight should be paid to them, or at least a part of it. General Butler opposed their claims, and the dispute was protracted through several months. The captains of the vessels, I am told, still rest under the impression that in some mysterious way the general gained an immense sum by this export of sugar. Mr. Chase knows better. *He*, if no one else, was abundantly satisfied with the transaction.

Having touched upon the subject of the calumnies so assiduously circulated with regard to the administration of General Butler in New Orleans, it may, perhaps, be as well to add here the little that remains to be said on that edifying subject.

First, let me adduce another little operation which has been construed to his disadvantage. I refer to a small quantity of cotton sent home from Ship Island by General Butler, which chanced to arrive a short time before the papers that explained the transaction.

"This cotton," wrote General Butler to the quartermaster-general, "was captured by the navy on board a small schooner, which it would have been unsafe to send to sea. I needed the schooner as a lighter, and took her from the navy. What should be done with the cotton? A transport was going home empty—it would cost the United States nothing to transport it. To whom should I send it? To my quartermaster at Boston? But I supposed him on the way here. Owing to the delays of the expedition, I found all the quartermaster's men and artisans on the island, whose services were indispensable, almost in a state of mutiny for want of pay. There was not a dollar of government funds on the island. I had seventy-five dollars of my own. The sutler had money he would lend on my draft on my private banker. I borrowed on such draft about four thousand dollars, quite equal to the value of the cotton as I received it, and with the money I paid the government debts to the laborers, so that their wives and children would not starve. In order that my draft should be paid, I sent the cotton to my correspondent at Boston, with directions to sell it, pay the draft out of the proceeds, and hold the rest, if any, subject to my order; so that, upon the account stated, I might settle with the government. What was done? The government seized the cotton without a word of explanation to me, kept it until it had depreciated ten per cent., and allowed my draft to be dishonored; and it had to be paid out of the little fund I left at home for the support of my children in my absence."

Subsequent explanations completely satisfied the government, and the money was refunded.

As these two transactions were the only ones of a commercial nature in which General Butler engaged while commanding the Department of the Gulf, and the only ones, I believe, in which he was ever concerned, the reader now has before him the entire basis of the huge superstructure of calumny raised by the malign persistence of rebels and their allies. Both of these transactions were solely designed to aid the work in hand, to remove unexpected obstacles, to anticipate measures which the government must instantly have ordered had it been near the scene of action.

But, as Mr. Toodles remarks, and repeats, "he had a brother."

It is true, he *had* a brother. He *has* a brother, alive and flourishing at this moment in New York, enjoying, I trust, the fortune gained by him in New Orleans during General Butler's administration.

When the port was opened in June, the condition of affairs was such that no man in business, with either capital or credit at command, could fail to make money with almost unexampled rapidity. Turpentine in New Orleans was a drug at three dollars; in New York, it was in demand at thirty-eight. Sugar in New Orleans was worth three cents a pound; in New York, six. Flour, in New York, six dollars a barrel; New Orleans, twenty-four. Dry goods in New York were selling at rates not greatly in advance of prices before the war; in New Orleans, every article in the trade was scarce and dear. The rates of exchange were such as to afford an additional profit of fifteen per cent. on all transactions between the two ports. In such a state of affairs, the most useful class of persons are those whom ignorance and envy stigmatize as speculators. It is they who quickly restore the commercial equilibrium, who raise the value of commodities in one port and reduce it in the other, who give New York sugar and turpentine which are useless in New Orleans, and supply New Orleans with the means of procuring commodities essential to comfort and health. The general's brother was one of the lucky men who chanced to be in business at New Orleans at the critical moment. An able man of business, with an experience of thirty years, with considerable capital and more credit, he engaged in this lucrative commerce with all the means and credit he could command. His gains were large; not as large as those of some other men; but large enough to satisfy a reasonable ambition. He neither had nor needed any advantages which were not enjoyed by other merchants. The anomalous state of things was his sufficient opportunity. A merchant of half his talent could not have failed to increase his capital with a rapidity altogether exceptional. Later in the year, came the confiscations of rebel property, with frequent sales at auction of valuable commodities. Of this business, too, he had an ample share—just the share his means and talents entitled him to. No more and no less.

It is impossible to prove a negative. Any one can make a vague charge of corruption, but no man can demonstrate it to be false. I can, therefore, only say, with reference to these intangible accusa

18

tions, that I have now spent the greater part of a year surrounded by the papers, printed and manuscript, relating to General Butler's administration of the Department of the Gulf; I have become, by repeated perusal, as familiar with those papers as a lawyer does with the documents of his greatest case; I have conversed almost daily with the gentlemen of stainless name and lineage who were in the closest intimacy with him during the whole period of his administration, such as the heroic, lamented Strong, beau-ideal of gentleman and soldier, such as Major Bell, another name for uprightness; I have listened attentively to all who had a tale to tell against General Butler, and have read the articles adverse to him that have appeared in the papers, and tried, in all ways, to get hold of some one charge definite enough for investigation; and the result of all this conversation and inquiry has been to produce in my mind the utmost possible completeness of conviction that General Butler's administration was as pure as it was able. Everywhere in his dispatches I find truth and candor—no suppression, no half-truths, nothing designed to convey an impression at variance with the truth. I find that men loved him in proportion to their own loyalty and truth. I find his enemies, both there and here, to be enemies of their country and of human rights. All the testimony, including especially that of his foes, points to one conclusion—that he was a wise, humane, and honest ruler of a most perverse generation.

Corruption there was in New Orleans, as one notorious individual can testify, who found himself in the penitentiary one day, sentenced to twenty-one years at hard labor for peculating the property of the government. Power was abused in New Orleans, as power always is by whomsoever it is wielded. But it was not abused with the knowledge or consent of the commanding general, nor were the evil-doers shielded by him from the just penalty either of crime or of error. His rule in Louisiana was greatly just and greatly wise. It was the harsh conflict of two antagonistic civilizations, both imperfect, one fatally so. It was the sudden setting up of the rule of justice in a community which had almost lost the tradition of a just rule. It was a bringing of the inflation, the arrogance, the meanness, and the falsehood engendered by slavery, to the test of Yankee common sense and Yankee common law. From such a conflict there must needs arise a great outcry. Somebody must be hurt. Every creature that is hurt, cries out in the language natural to it. The natural language of an "original secessionist," damaged in a conflict with justice and good sense, and, at the same time, deprived of bowie-knife and pistol, is calumny of the man by whom that justice and good sense are brought to bear upon his pretensions. Falsehood is the element in which those unhappy people live, move, and have their being.

Every honest man who served under General Butler at New Orleans, and was in a position to observe his conduct, would, I believe, most heartily subscribe to the language employed by Colonel S. H. Stafford (1st La. N. G.), when refuting one of the vague, incoherent slanders to which I have referred. Colonel Stafford was deputy provost-marshal of New Orleans, but acted independently of his chief, and communicated directly with the general. "In all my intercourse with General Butler," he writes, "which, in my position, was to a great extent confidential, I am bound to say, that I never saw anything that was not upright, faithful, and honest; and had he been corrupt, I believe I would have seen the signs of it. I am proud to have served under him, and devoutly wish he was still my commander. I believe that any man that ever served under him, who does not feel the same, is influenced in his feeling and opinion by what he may himself have suffered under the infliction of some just condemnation."

But to resume. In one particular, General Butler's designs with regard to the commerce of New Orleans were baffled. He could not get cotton in any considerable quantity, although it was a constant object of his endeavors. The reason, as given him by well-informed Louisianians, was this: About one-half of the planters had burned their cotton, and these men would not permit their less enthusiastic neighbors to reap the advantage of their prudence. A little cotton was procured from Mobile, by exchanging one bale of cotton for one sack of salt, and a little more was brought from Texas by special arrangement. It can not be said, however, that the world's supply of this commodity was much increased by the capture of New Orleans. Perhaps, two or three thousand bales may have been procured in all.

The currency of New Orleans was in a condition deplorably chaotic. Omnibus tickets, car tickets, shinplasters and Confederate notes, the last named depreciated seventy per cent. by the fall of the city, were the chief medium of exchange. The coin had been removed from the vaults of the banks to a place within the Confederate lines, except that part of it which was deposited in the consulates. In compliance with the entreaties of Mr. Soulé, and with the obvious necessities of the situation, General Butler had permitted the temporary circulation of Confederate notes; but as this concession was known to be but temporary, it did not materially enhance the value of that spurious currency. The banks had been growing rich upon the traffic in Confederate paper, bought at a discount, paid out at par. When most other investments were unproductive, bank shares had yielded large dividends. Until September, 1861, as many readers remember, the banks of New Orleans had held aloof from the practical support of the Confederacy, had refused to suspend specie payments, and had transacted only a legitimate business. At that time, however, a threat of "harsh measures" from the Richmond government gave to some of the banks the pretext which they coveted for abandoning the honest course, and the rest were compelled to follow the bad example. Thenceforward, business in Louisiana was done in Confederate notes, and the paper of the banks was little seen in circulation. The consequences of the sudden depreciation of those notes may be readily imagined. As the offer of the city to redeem the notes was not fulfilled, they remained almost the sole medium of exchange in the hands of the people.

Such a state of things obviously demanded the prompt interference of the commanding general. The series of bold, original and masterly measures by which General Butler, in the course of a few weeks, gave to New Orleans a currency as sound and convenient as that of New York and Boston, merits the reader's particular attention.

There was one redeeming fact in the financial condition of the city to serve as a fulcrum to the general's lever. Most of the banks (all of them but three) were solvent and strong. True, their coin was gone, but it was not supposed to be lost. Granting the coin to be safe, the banks were able to redeem their circulation, and safely afford the city the currency it needed. It required all the general's intimate knowledge of banking, and all the force of his will, to bring the banks to perform this duty; but after a struggle against manifest destiny, they all submitted.

The banks, I may premise, were anxious respecting the safety of their coin. After a conference with the general on the subject, an important favor was asked him in writing by two gentlemen representing the banking interest. "We understood you to say," wrote these gentlemen, May 13th, "that you were disposed to reaffirm the declaration made in your first proclamation, that private property of all kinds should be respected. You added that if the treasure withdrawn by the banks should be restored to their vaults, you would not only abstain from interference, but that you would give it safe conduct, and use all your power individually, as well as of the forces of the United States under your command, for its protection; that the question as to the proper time of the resumption of specie payments should be left entirely to the judgment and discretion of the banks themselves, with the understanding on your part and ours that the coin should be held in good faith for the protection of the bill-holders and depositors. On their part the banks promised to act with scrupulous good faith to carry out their understanding with you; that is, to restore a sound currency as soon as possible, and to provide for the resumption of regular business as soon as the exigencies of our trade require it. You are aware that a large portion of the coin of the banks is beyond their control, and that we can only promise to use our best exertions for its return. Should we fail, we will immediately advise you of the fact. In the mean time, we request of you the favor to give us the authority to bring back the treasure within your lines, with the safe conduct of the same from that point to this city."

The general's reply was as follows:

"HEAD-QUARTERS, DEPARTMENT OF THE GULF,
"NEW ORLEANS, *May* 14, 1862.

"MESSIEURS:—I have given very careful consideration to the matter of the communication handed me through you from the banks of the city. With a slight variation, to which I call your attention, you were correct in your understanding of the interview had by me with the banks. Specie or bullion in coin or ingots, is entitled to the same protection as other property under the same uses, and will be so protected by the United States forces under my command.

"If, therefore, the banks bring back their specie which they have so unadvisedly carried away, it shall have safe conduct through my lines, and be fully protected here so long as it is used in good faith to make good the obligations of the banks to their creditors by bills and deposit.

"Now, as in the present disturbed state of the public mind, specie, if paid out, would be at once hoarded, I am content to leave the time of redemption of their bills to the good judgment of the banks themselves, governed in it by the analogy of the laws of the state and the fullest good faith. Indeed, the exercise of that on both sides relieves every difficulty, and ends at once all negotiations.

"In order that there may be no misunderstanding, it must be observed that I by no means mean to pledge myself that the banks, like other persons, shall not return to the United States authorities all the property of the United States which they may have received. I come to retake, repossess, and occupy, all and singular, the property of the United States of whatever name and nature. Farther than that I shall not go, save upon the most urgent military necessity, under which right every citizen holds all his possessions. But as any claim which the United States may have against the banks can easily be enforced against the personal as well as the property of the corporations, such claims need not enter into this discussion in such form. Therefore, as in good faith safe conducts may be needed for agents of banks to go and return with the property, and for no other purpose whatever, such safe conducts will be granted for a limited but reasonable period of time.

"Personal illness has caused the slight delay which has attended this reply. I have the honor to be, your most obedient servant,

"(Signed), BENJ. F. BUTLER, *Major-General Commanding.*

"Messieurs WILLIAM N. MERCER, J. M. LEPAYRE, *Committee.*"

No safe conducts were required for the treasure. Memminger, the secretary of the rebel treasury, refused to give it up. "The coin of the banks of New Orleans," he wrote, July 6th, "was seized by the government to prevent it falling into the hands of the public enemy. It has been deposited in a place of security, under charge of the government; and it is not intended to interfere with the rights of property in the banks farther than to insure its safe custody. They may proceed to conduct their business in the Confederate States upon this deposit, just as though it were in their own vaults."

The banks then endeavored to get both governments to consent to their sending the coin to Europe during the war; and General Butler rather favored the scheme, provided a European *government* would take it in charge. The plan failed, however, to gain approval; and the general consented to permit the banks to do business upon the basis of the absent coin, "just as though it was in their own vaults." Unless he had done this, his whole scheme of reforming the currency must have failed.

General Butler's first financial measure was to suppress the Confederate notes. At the beginning of the third week of the occupation of the city, the following general order appeared:—

"NEW ORLEANS, *May* 16, 1862.

"I. It is hereby ordered that neither the city of New Orleans, nor the banks thereof, exchange their notes, bills, or obligations for Confederate notes, bills, or bonds, nor issue any bill, note, or obligation payable in Confederate notes.

"II. On the 27th day of May inst., all circulation of, or trade in, Confederate notes and bills will cease within this department; and all sales or transfers of property made on or after that day, in consideration of such notes or bills, directly or indirectly, will be void, and the property confiscated to the United States, one-fourth thereof to go to the informer."

Great was the agitation in bank parties upon the day this order was promulgated. At once the question arose, Who is to bear the loss, the banks or the public? The banks had no doubts upon the subject. The newspapers of the next morning contained a long string of short advertisements, which agreeably diversified the usual uniformity of the advertising columns. The following may serve as specimens:

"All parties having deposits of Confederate notes with us are hereby notified to withdraw them prior to the 27th inst. Such balances as may not be withdrawn will be considered at the risk of the owners, and held subject to their order."

"JUDSON & Co., corner of Camp and Canal streets."

"BANKING HOUSE OF SAM'L SMITH & Co.,
"NEW ORLEANS, *May* 19, 1862.

"All persons having deposited Confederate notes in this banking-house are notified to withdraw them before the 27th inst. Such balances as may not then be withdrawn will be considered at the risk of the owners."

"SAM'L SMITH & Co."

"BANK OF AMERICA,
"NEW ORLEANS, *May* 19, 1862.

"All persons having deposits of Confederate notes in this bank are notified to withdraw them by the 25th inst. Such balances as may not then be withdrawn will be considered at the risk of the owners.

"C. CAVAROC, *Cashier pro tem.*"

"MERCHANTS' BANK,
"NEW ORLEANS, *May* 19, 1862.

"This bank is prepared to pay balances in Confederate notes, which must be drawn before the 27th inst.

"WM. S. MOUNT, *Cashier.*"

"UNION BANK OF LOUISIANA,
"NEW ORLEANS, *May* 17, 1862.

"NOTICE.—All persons having deposits of Confederate notes in this bank are notified to withdraw them prior to the 27th inst. Such balances as may not be withdrawn will be considered at the risk of the owners.

"GEO. A. FRERET, *Cashier.*"

The banks, therefore, were resolved to throw the entire mass of the Confederate currency upon the impoverished people. They had introduced that currency, grown rich upon it, received it at par; and now, when it was nearly worthless, they designed to escape the entire loss of the depreciation. Every one outside of the banks was in consternation. The people knew not what to do. If they withdrew their deposits, they would receive sundry pieces of valueless printed paper. If they did not, the deposits were "at their own risk"—a phrase of fearful import at such a time. What rendered the course of the banks the more exasperating was the fact, that a great and wealthy corporation, professing an entire faith in the ultimate triumph of the Confederacy, could afford to hold Confederate paper, while a poor trader in New Orleans would be ruined by the suspension of his little capital.

The anger of General Butler was kindled. *He*, the "enemy," was striving night and day to save the people of New Orleans from starvation, and restore the business of the city to life. *They*, the fellow-citizens of those people, thought only of saving their ill-gotten wealth. In the course of the day upon which the bank advertisements appeared, he penned his famous General Order No. 30, which was published in the papers of the following morning:

"NEW ORLEANS, *May* 19, 1862.

"It is represented to the commanding general that great distress, privation, suffering, hunger and even starvation has been brought upon the people of New Orleans and vicinage by the course taken by the banks and dealers in currency.

"He has been urged to take measures to provide, as far as may be, for the relief of the citizens, so that the loss may fall, in part, at least, on those who have caused and ought to bear it.

"The general sees with regret that the banks and bankers causelessly suspended specie payments in September last, in contravention of the laws of the state and of the United States. Having done so, they introduced Confederate notes as currency, which they bought at a discount, in place of their own bills, receiving them on deposit, paying them out for their discounts, and collecting their customers' notes and drafts in them as money, sometimes even against their will, thus giving these notes credit and a wide general circulation, so that they were substituted in the hands of the middling men, the poor and unwary, as currency, in place of that provided by the constitution and laws of the country, or of any valuable equivalent.

"The banks and bankers now endeavor to take advantage of the re-establishment of the authority of the United States here, to throw the depreciation and loss from this worthless stuff of their creation and fostering upon their creditors, depositors and bill-holders.

"They refuse to receive these bills while they pay them over their counters.

"They require their depositors to take them.

"They change the obligation of contracts by stamping their bills, 'redeemable in Confederate notes.'

"They have invested the savings of labor and the pittance of the widow in this paper.

"They sent away or hid their specie, so that the people could have nothing but these notes, which they now depreciate—with which to buy bread.

"All other property has become nearly valueless from the calamities of this iniquitous and unjust war begun by rebellious guns, turned on the flag of our prosperous and happy country floating over Fort Sumter. Saved from the general ruin by the system of financiering, bank stocks alone are now selling at great premiums in the market, while the stockholders have received large dividends.

"To equalize, as far as may be, this general loss; to have it fall, at least in part, where it ought to lie; to enable the people of this city and vicinage to have a currency which shall at least be a semblance to that which the wisdom of the constitution provides for all citizens of the United States, it is therefore

"*Ordered:* 1. That the several incorporated banks pay out no more Confederate notes to their depositors or creditors, but that all deposits be paid in the bills of the bank, United States treasury notes, gold or silver.

"II. That all private bankers, receiving deposits, pay out to their depositors only the current bills of city banks, or United States treasury notes, gold or silver.

"III. That the savings banks pay to their depositors or creditors only gold, silver, or United States treasury notes, current bills of city banks, or their own bills, to an amount not exceeding one-third of their deposits, and of denomination not less than one dollar, which they are authorized to issue and for the redemption of which their assets shall be held liable.

"IV. The incorporated banks are authorized to issue bills of a less denomination than five dollars, but not less than one dollar, anything in their charters to the contrary notwithstanding, and are authorized to receive Confederate notes for any of their bills until the 27th day of May inst.

"V. That all persons and firms having issued small notes or 'shinplasters,' so called, are required to redeem them on presentation at their places of business, between the hours of 9. A. M. and 3 P. M., either in gold, silver, United States treasury notes, or current bills of city banks, under penalty of confiscation of their property and sale thereof, for the purpose of redemption of the notes so issued, or imprisonment for a term of hard labor.

"VI. Private bankers may issue notes of denominations not less than one nor more than ten dollars, to two-thirds of the amount of specie which they show to a commissioner appointed from these head-quarters, in their vaults, actually kept there for the purpose of redemption of such notes."

So the game of the banks was "blocked." The relief afforded to the people by the publication of this order was such, that, as a secessionist remarked to one of the general's staff, it was equivalent to a reinforcement of twenty thousand men to the Union army. Union men in New Orleans say, that nothing but the continual bad news from General McClellan's army in the peninsula prevented this measure from causing an open and general manifestation of Union feeling among the respectable traders of the city. But the impression could not be removed from the minds of the people, while such intelligence kept coming, that the stay of the army would be but short; and every man feared to commit himself to a course that would invite the vengeance of the returning Confederates.

All the banks submitted in silence, except one—the Bank of Louisiana. I think I must afford space for the following curious correspondence that passed between that institution and General Butler:

THE BANK TO GENERAL BUTLER.

"No. 148 Canal Street, *May* 21, 1862.

"Sir:—The Board of Directors of the Bank of Louisiana held a special meeting this morning, in order to take into consideration your Order No. 30. The meeting was full, with the exception of a single member; for all were impressed with the gravity of the question about to be submitted.

"The result of their deliberation was the adoption of certain resolutions, which I have now the honor to submit to you.

"At the same time I was instructed to make a few observations in explanation of their course, and especially to disclaim and disavow the justice of any imputation affecting their rectitude, integrity or honor. As a proof of their confidence in their disinterestedness, they invite the most searching examination of all their books, including the minutes of their proceedings, and of every act of their administration, even their private accounts with the bank, by any competent person whom you may select for that purpose; and they are willing to abide the result, either as officials or as individuals.

"In the discharge of their difficult and delicate duties, knowing and feeling that their intentions were pure and upright, they have an abiding confidence of their exculpation from the influence of all sordid or selfish motives.

"If required, I will wait on you and afford every explanation in my power.

"I have the honor, &c., &c.,

"W. Newton Mercer, President *pro tem.*

"Major-General Butler, *U. S. A.*, *&c.*

"Note.—Of the capital stock of the bank—28,000 shares—the directors own about one-tenth. To the bank they owe nothing."

RESOLUTIONS OF THE DIRECTORS.

"Bank of Louisiana, *May* 21, 1862.

"As this bank is unable to comply with the conditions, and act under the restrictions imposed upon it by Order No. 30, issued by General Butler, and as imputations have been cast upon the conduct and characters of its directors,

"*Therefore, Resolved, unanimously*, That General Butler be invited to appoint some competent person, in whom he has confidence, to examine thoroughly the condition of this bank since its suspension of specie payments, as well as the action of its directors since the 1st day of September last.

"That the cashier be instructed to give to General Butler's agent, if one be appointed, every facility for such an examination of all its books, papers, vaults, desks and drawers, and to afford him every information touching the administration of this bank during the period already mentioned, together with an inspection of the private accounts of the directors.

"That, in the mean time, till General Butler's final determination be ascertained, the operations of the bank must necessarily be suspended, as it has in its possession none of its own issue and only a very small amount of coin.

"I certify that the action above mentioned was held this morning by the Bank of Louisiana.

"W. NEWTON MERCER, President *pro tem.*

"NEW ORLEANS, *May* 21, 1862."

GENERAL BUTLER TO THE BANK.

HEAD-QUARTERS, DEPARTMENT OF THE GULF,
"NEW ORLEANS, *May* 22, 1862.

"W. NEWTON MERCER, ESQ., President of the Bank of Louisiana:

"SIR:—I have received your communication, covering the unanimous action of the directors of the Bank of Louisiana. To their request, that I would appoint a commission to examine the affairs of the bank, I can not accede. With the mismanagement, or the contrary of the bank, I have nothing to do, except so far as either affects the interest of the United States.

"The assigned reason for the call for this examination, that 'the integrity and good faith of the directors have been impugned,' will not move me, if it refer to General Order No. 30, which speaks of acts and facts, not motives.

"Your note says, that the directors own but one-tenth of the capital stock of the bank. Without consulting the owners of the other nine-tenths—nearly three millions of dollars—this one-tenth took this immense wealth from its legal place of deposit, and sent it flying over the country in company with fugitive property burners, among the masses of a disorganized, retreating, and starving army, whence it is more than likely never to return. Again; the time it would take to make an investigation, which would show the good management, to say nothing of the purity of motive of such a transaction, can not be spared by any officer of my command. *Ex uno disce omnes.*

"The directors of the bank of Louisiana have all seen General Order No. 30, and have acted upon it as a corporation. So your note shows.

"They will now advise themselves whether they will act in accordance with its requirements upon their corporate and individual peril, and inform me, within six hours after the receipt of this, of their determination.

"I havethe honor to be, respectfully, your obedient servant,

"B. F. BUTLER."

THE BANK TO GENERAL BUTLER.

"BANK OF LOUISIANA,
"NEW ORLEANS, *May* 22, 1862.

"To Major-General B. F. BUTLER, Commanding Department of the Gulf:—

"SIR:—I have received your communication of this day in answer to my letter accompanying the proceedings of the directors of this bank.

"The board of directors were immediately summoned to a special meeting; and as you leave no alternative but compliance with your mandate, they will conform to Order No. 30.

"Respectfully, your obedient servant,
"W. NEWTON MERCER, President *pro tem.*"

The bank, however, was still disposed to be contumacious. Mr. Durand had deposited in the bank Confederate notes, when Confederate notes were *money;* he demanded the amount of his deposit in something that was money *then*—the notes of the bank, for example. The bank, "to make a case," refused, and Mr. Durand brought suit in the provost court, where Major Bell decided in his favor, and ordered the bank to comply with his demand. The bank appealed from this decision to the general commanding, who sustained the judgment of the court. Law papers are not generally considered to be very entertaining; but General Butler's decision in this case will be found an exception to the rule:

"HEAD-QUARTERS, DEPARTMENT OF THE GULF,
"NEW ORLEANS, LA., *June*, 1862.

"In the matter of the appeal of W. N. Mercer, president, and Auguste Montreuil, cashier, of the Bank of Louisiana, defendants, from the judgment of the provost court, upon the complaint of A. Durand, complainant.

"This is an application by the defendants representing the bank, made to the general commanding, asking him to revise and set aside the judgment of the provost court, made in favor of the plaintiff, Durand.

"It is based upon the legal theory, that over all matters within garrison, camp, and perhaps geographical military department, wherein martial law has been declared, the power of the commanding general is absolute; and that, looking at him as the representative of the martial power of the government here, all applications for redress must be made when any wrong is supposed to have been done.

"This view being sound, so far as I can see, I have, with the best thought possible under the circumstances, re-examined the case and the reasons assigned for the appeal.

"Error is claimed on two grounds: first, that the provost court had no jurisdiction of the cause; and second, that the judgment was not in accordance with the law which should govern its decision.

"The argument assumes that law to be General Order No. 30, and does not dispute the authority which made or the effect of that order, but contents itself with endeavoring to construe the order.

"The objection to the jurisdiction of the court is put upon two grounds: first, that the provost court has not jurisdiction of the subject-matter; second, that the proper parties were not before it, so as to enable it to act with regard to the rights of those who were not summoned in the case.

"It is said that this question, being one of a right of property, can not be entertained by a court which only acts to punish the infractions of military orders and police regulations.

"A technical answer to this objection, which is in the nature of a plea to the jurisdiction, would be that it does not appear that this plea was put in till after the hearing upon the merits. It is a familiar rule that a party shall not be allowed to go into court and have a hearing on his case, take the chances of a decision in his favor, and then, if adverse, repudiate the court before which he has appeared, and to whose judgment he has submitted his cause. This rule has been held very strictly, both as to jurisdiction over the subject-matter and the parties. But in a court where no technical rules are allowed to work injustice, a technical answer is not sufficient.

"Of what, then, do the defendants complain? The bank says the court has made an order which takes away the property of the bank, and gives it to another, and that the court has no power so to act. But is that so? Is it not the commanding general's order which does that of which complaint is made? The bank nowhere complains that the general has not the power to make such an order, if in his judgment it become a military necessity, and that some order on the subject-matter was so, is shown by the fact that the first question put to him, upon entering the city, was—what currency would be provided for the people, to save them from starvation and bread-riots? It has passed into history that he permitted a vicious currency as a medium of circulation for the purpose of meeting this exigency.

"Again, it will be remembered that the bank now claims that it is exempted from the effects of this order, because, by order of another military commander in September last (there was no civil law for it), it was obliged to suspend specie payment, against its will, and substitute Confederate notes for its daily currency, instead of its own bills. This order was submitted to, if not with joy, at least not under protest, so far as I am informed.

"The order, as well as the law of the land, then, is that the bank shall pay its depositors in gold, silver coin, and United States treasury notes, or its own bills. A citizen complains that this order of the commanding general has not been obeyed, to his prejudice.

"For what, then, is a provost court, in military phrase, constituted? Confessedly, to inquire into, determine, and punish the infraction of military orders.

"To do this, the court must act in *rem* as well as in *personam*. A familiar example would be, if the commanding general orders all arms to be given up, and some citizen neglects or refuses to obey, would it not be within the jurisdiction of a provost court, although its judgment should act upon a right of property involving millions of dollars' worth of muskets?

"If the act brought before the court, therefore, is alleged to be an infraction of a military order, it is determinable in a military court. Again, it is said that the court has not jurisdiction because the stockholders of the bank were not summoned in and made parties, and that their rights and interests will be affected by the decision. This is all true. But did the learned counsel for the bank ever hear of a suit against a bank, in any court, where the stockholders were summoned in, unless it was sought to charge them individually, which is not the case here? A corporation acts through its authorized agents, and is bound by their acts, and is to be charged upon notice to them. This objection of want of sufficient power in the president and directors of the Bank of Louisiana to pay the deposit of Mr. Durand in their own bills, which is only changing the form of indebtedness from a depositor to a bill-holder, under the order of the provost court, without the consent of their stockholders, would provoke a smile in a less serious discussion, when we remember that this same board of directors, without asking leave of their stockholders, against law and right, put three million dollars of its bullion out of their hands and out of the state, whence they will probably never see it again.

"I am of opinion that these objections to the jurisdiction of the court are untenable.

"The other objection, as to the merits of the decision, can, it seems to me, be disposed of in a word. If the order is a proper one, it must be obeyed. Its propriety can not be discussed by me. It is admitted that Durand is a depositor in the bank of what the bank chose to take as money—treated as money—credited to him as money—nay, forced upon the community as money. He has not been paid his deposit. The bank should pay him in specie. The decision, following the letter of the order, is that the bank may give him their own bills instead of money. Of that decision the bank has no cause to complain. Durand is now the creditor of the bank as a depositor. The decision makes him their creditor as a bill-holder. In equity they have nothing to complain of—*he* may have, because he does not get his gold, to which by the laws of banking, laws of the state and the United States, he is entitled.

"He does not seek to reverse the decision. Let it stand.

"BENJ. F. BUTLER, *Major-General Commanding*."

Confederate notes disappeared from circulation. Bank-notes and green-backs took their place. A few weeks later, the omnibus tickets and shinplasters were replaced by small notes issued by Governor Shepley and the city government. Thus, the currency of the city was completely restored.

General Butler required from the banks a monthly report of their transactions and their condition. Two of them, which he ascertained to be hopelessly insolvent, he ordered to be closed and to go into liquidation. Another, which was weak, he caused to be strengthened. His later intercourse with the officers of the banks was more amicable than at first. They were surprised to find that a major-general of volunteers was as much at home in their own province as if he had spent his life in a banking-house.

An anecdote from the *Delta* will serve to show how the general's order secured the rights of enemies as well as friends:

"Among the rebel prisoners taken the other day was an officer, whom we shall call Captain Johnson. He, before going to the war, had deposited three hundred dollars in the Bank of Commerce. Upon his return to the city upon parole, he called at the bank to inquire about his funds. After much fumbling, it was admitted that he had deposited the sum named.

"'Well,' said he, 'I want it.'

* * "Thereupon he was reminded that he had made his deposit in Confederate notes.

"'Very true,' he replied, 'but at that time Confederate notes were current and valuable.'

"'Oh,' muttered the banker, 'I must give it to you in the currency in which you deposited.'

"'But,' said the captain, 'Confederate notes are worthless now.'

"The banker was firm, and the captain retired. He called the next day and renewed his demand for his money. He was told, as before, that he must take Confederate notes.

"'I suppose I must,' observed the Confederate captain.

"The banker paused, and then inquired: 'But what can you do with Confederate notes? They are worthless here, and it is against the law to pass them.'

"'That's just what I have been telling you,' said the captain; "but since you will not give me anything else, I presume I had better take Confederate notes.'

"'Yes, yes, yes, yes,' nervously spluttered the banker; 'but what can you do with Confederate notes?'

"'Well,' replied Johnson, 'I will tell you squarely what I will do. I will take them to General Butler and try to get gold for them.'

"Upon this, the banker counted out three hundred dollars in United States treasury notes, and Captain Johnson retired."

Some stern retributory measures remained to be enforced against the banks of New Orleans. The following general order was issued early in June:

"NEW ORLEANS, *June* 6, 1862.

"Any person who has in his possession, or subject to his control, any property of any kind or description whatever, of the so-called Confederate States, or who has secreted or concealed, or aided in the concealment of such property, who shall not, within three days from the publication of this order, give full information of the same, in writing, at the head-quarters of the military commandant, in the Custom-House, to the assistant military commandant, Godfrey Weitzel, shall be liable to imprisonment and to have his property confiscated."

This order, being interpreted, signified (among other things), that whatever sums of money might be standing upon the books of the banks in the name of the rebel government, were now the property of the United States; which property the banks would please prepare to surrender. The order was promptly obeyed. That this measure may be completely understood, I will present here the response of one of the banks to the order, and the general's characteristic reply to the same.

THE CITIZENS' BANK TO GENERAL BUTLER.

"CITIZENS' BANK OF LOUISIANA,
"NEW ORLEANS, *June* 11, 1862.

"Major-General B. F. BUTLER, commanding at New Orleans:

"GENERAL:—In obedience to your General Order No. 40, I beg to inform you that on the first of May last, there was to the credit of the treasurer of the Confederate States in this bank the sum of $219,090.94; and also on special account the farther sum of $12,465; and this bank holding a larger amount in the notes of the Confederate treasury, an equivalent amount in said treasury notes has been set aside, and is now held by the bank, to offset the above stated amount, and which notes I will return as the property of the Confederate States under your order.

"Also, one small tin box, marked 'Conf. States District Court.'

"The following named parties have also to their credit on deposit these sums, viz:

J. M. Huger, Confederate States Receiver,			....	$106,812.60
G. W. Ward,	"	"	"	72,084.90
J. C. Manning,	"	"	"	1,120.00
Major M. L. Smith,	"	"	"	16,026.52
Major Macklin,	"	"	"	6,814.57
Major Reichard,	"	"	"	476.30

"As the deposits by the receivers were made in this bank by virtue of an order of the Confederate court, in accordance with the act of congress, they were to that extent compulsory on the receivers as well as on the banks. To have refused to comply with the mandate of that court, might have brought both parties into conflict with the constituted authorities for the time being.

"All the above-mentioned deposits were made in the currency of the Confederate government by its appointed officers.

"Had the bank resumed specie payment or become bankrupt in the mean time, those depositors would have had no claim to the coin or to a *pro rata* distribution of the other assets of the bank. They could only have claimed the currency deposited by them, and hence it may be classed in reality as *special deposits* of Confederate funds, payable in same, in accordance with the contracts and understanding at the time. Under these circumstances, the bank appeals to General Butler's sense of equity and justice to allow these deposits to be paid to whom it may concern in the same currency in which they were received.

"Some time during the month of November last, an order of sequestration was issued to the marshals of the Confederate States to take charge of the assets of the Bank of Kentucky, then held by this Bank in the usual course of business.

"The assets have never been removed from the bank, yet still are nominally beyond its control.

"I therefore respectfully request from the commanding general an order to refund to the Kentucky bank, the owners of said assets, that the accounts may be made out accordingly and a due return forwarded to them.

"The banks were informed of the seizure of their assets at the time, and one of them, the Bank of Kentucky, had a resident agent here at that time.

"With great respect,

"Your obedient servant,

"JAMES D. DENEGRE, *President.*"

GENERAL BUTLER TO THE CITIZENS' BANK.

"HEAD-QUARTERS, DEPARTMENT OF THE GULF,
"NEW ORLEANS, *June 13th*, 1862.

"The return of the Citizens' Bank of New Orleans to General Order No. 40, has been carefully examined, and the various claims set up by the bank to the funds in its hands weighed.

"The report finds that there is to the credit of the Confederate States $219,090.94.

"This of course is due *in presenti* from the bank. The bank claims that it holds an equal amount of Confederate treasury notes, and desires to set off these notes against the amount so due and payable.

"This can not be permitted. Many answers might be suggested to the claim. One or two are sufficient.

"Confederate States treasury notes are not due till six months after the conclusion of a treaty of peace between the Confederate States and the United States. When that time comes it will be in season to set off such claims. Again: The United States being entitled to the credits due the Confederate States in the bank, that amount must be paid in money or valuable property.

"I can not recognize the Confederate notes as either money or property. The bank having done so by receiving them, issuing their banking upon them, loaning upon them, thus giving them credit to the injury of the United States, is estopped to deny their value.

"The 'tin box' belonging to an officer of the supposed Confederate States, being a special deposit, will be handed over (to me) in bulk, whether its contents are more or less valuable.

"The bank is responsible only for safe custody. The several deposits of the officers of the supposed Confederate States were received in the usual course of business; were, doubtless, some of them, perhaps largely, received in Confederate notes; but, for the reason above stated, can only be paid to the United States in its own constitutional currency. These are in no sense of language 'special deposits.'

"They were held in general account, went into the funds of the bank, were paid out in the discounts of the bank, and if called upon to-day for the identical notes put into the bank, which is the only idea of a special deposit, the bank would be utterly unable to produce them.

"As well might my private banker, with whom I have deposited my neighbor's check or draft as money, which has been received as money, and paid out as money, months afterward, when my neighbor has become bankrupt, buy up *other* of his checks and drafts at discount, and pay them to me instead of money, upon the ground that I had made a *special deposit*.

"The respectability of the source from which the claim of the bank proceeds alone saves it from ridicule.

"The United States can in no form recognize any of the sequestrations or confiscations of the supposed Confederate States; therefore, the account with the Bank of Kentucky will be made up, and all its property will be paid over and delivered, as if such atttempted confiscation had never been made.

"The result is, therefore, upon the showing of the bank by its return, that there is due and payable to the Confederate States, and therefore, now to be paid to the United States, the sums following:—

Confederate States treasurer's account	$219,090.94
" " special accounts	12,465.00
Deposits by officers	
J. M. Huger, receiver	106,812.60
G. M. Ward "	72,084.90
J. C. Manning "	1,120.00
	$411,573.44
M. L. Smith '	16,026.52
S. Macklin "	6,814.57
Reichard "	497.30
Total	$434,911.83

"This is the legal result to which the mind must arrive in this discussion.

"But there are other considerations which may apply to the first item of the account.

"Only the notes of the Confederate States were deposited by the treasurer in the bank, and, by the order of the ruling authority then here, the bank was obliged to receive them.

"In equity and good conscience, the Confederate States could call for nothing more than they had compelled the bank to take.

"The United States succeed to the rights of the Confederate States, and should only take that which the Confederate States ought to take.

"But the United States, not taking or recognizing Confederate notes, can only leave them with the bank, to be held by it hereafter in special deposit, as so much worthless paper.

"Therefore, I must direct all the items but the first to be paid to my order for the United States, in gold, silver, or United States treasury notes at once. The first item of $219,090.94, I will refer to the home government for adjudication; and, in the mean time, the bank must hold, as a special deposit, the amount of Confederate treasury notes above mentioned, and a like amount of bullion to await the decision.

"BENJAMIN F. BUTLER,

"*Major-General Commanding.*"

A few days after, General Butler had the pleasure of sending to Mr. Chase the sum of $245,760, the amount of Confederate funds given up by the several banks. "This," remarked the general, "will make a fund upon which those whose property has been confiscated may have claim." The "home government" took its time over the item of $219,090.94. The matter had not been decided when General Butler left the Department.

Another act of justice remained to be done by the banks and other dividend-paying corporations of New Orleans. Witness the following order:

"New Orleans, *July* 9, 1862.

"All dividends, interests, coupons, stock-certificates, and accruing interest, due any or payable by any incorporated or joint-stock company, to any citizen of the United States; and any notes, dues, claims, and accounts of any such citizen, due from any such company, or any private person or company within this department, which have heretofore been retained under any supposed order, authority, act of sequestration, garnishee process, or in any way emanating under the supposed Confederate States, or the state of Louisiana, since the fraudulent ordinance of secession, are hereby ordered to be paid and delivered respectively to the lawful owners thereof, or their duly authorized agents."

This order restored to many citizens of the northern states a portion of their annual income which they had long ago given up as lost. Nor was this all. The mercantile debts were extracted from such of the debtors as had not squandered all their property. The papers before me show that there was an active business done, at this time, in compelling the payment of sums due to northern creditors. The ingenious devices of the repudiators to avoid or postpone the agony of disgorging, were numerous and sometimes successful. The usual issue of the struggle, however, was a short, sharp order from the general: Pay instanter, or be sold up! The individual, I observe, who repudiated a debt of $20,000 to General Anderson, of Fort Sumter celebrity, was one of those upon whose property General Butler laid his retributive hand.

Direct efforts were systematically made, during the whole period of General Butler's rule, to promote Union feeling. Union clubs were encouraged. The "Union Ladies' Association" for clothing the children of volunteers, held frequent meetings. The fourth of

July was celebrated with all possible *eclat.* There were numerous flag-raisings. Union meetings were often held, addressed by the orators both of the army and of the city. The general caused to be cut deep into the granite base of the statue of General Jackson, the motto originally designed to adorn it:

"THE UNION—IT MUST AND SHALL BE PRESERVED."

Much good was done by these efforts. Seed was sown which might have borne glorious fruit when the success of the Union arms had given the Union men of the city an assurance of safety.

New Orleans, during the administration of General Butler, possessed, for the first time in its history, a court of justice in which it was *possible* for justice to be done. A code of law which excludes from the witness-box the very class who are the most likely to be the witnesses of crime, and against whom the greatest number of crimes are committed, banishes justice from the land in which it exists. One of Major Bell's first decisions in the provost court placed white men and black men upon an equality before the law. A hunker democrat did this glorious thing! A negro was called to the witness-stand.

"I object," said the counsel for the prisoner; "by the laws of Louisiana a negro can not testify against a white man."

"Has Louisiana gone out of the Union?" asked Major Bell, with that imperturbable gravity of his, that veils his keen sense of humor.

"Yes," said the lawyer.

"Well, then," said the judge, "she took her laws with her. LET THE MAN BE SWORN!"

Immortal words! From that moment dates the renovation of Louisiana!

Again. Henry Dominique, a free man of color, was arrested for not having free papers. The prisoner could only protest that he was a free man. The court decided, that every man must be presumed to be free until the contrary was shown. Dominique was discharged.

Major Bell's court was among the lions of the town. During a considerable part of General Butler's stay, he administered all the justice that was done in New Orleans, according to the forms of a court. He decided all cases, from a street broil to questions of constitutional law, from petty larency to high treason, from matrimonial squabbles to suits for divorce. He would dispose of fifteen cases in thirty minutes. An hour was a long trial. He was pestered, at first, with malicious suits, to avenge injuries committed before the capture of the city—a kind of case that sometimes resulted in penalties to both parties; oftener in a prompt dismissal of both from the court. Suits of the most frivolous character were brought before him. One morning, two women presented themselves, each to prefer a complaint against the other.

"Stand there," said he to one of them. "Stand there," to the other. "Now both speak at once, and talk for five minutes."

Two torrents of vituperation poured from the two mouths. The judge kept his eye upon his watch, and at the end of the time, said:

"Now, both of you go home and behave yourselves."

The women departed with evident satisfaction; they had relieved their minds.

Some of the cases demanded an intimate knowledge of local law. For example: Major Bell observed a colored woman hanging about his office for several successive days, in evident distress of mind. He asked her, one day, what she wanted. She said that all her goods had been seized by her landlord for rent, though she had paid the rent and had his receipt. It was another tenant of the same house, she said, who was delinquent, and had moved away in the night, leaving her goods liable to seizure. The landlord being summoned, admitted the truth of the woman's story, and pointed out the old statute which gave landlords the right to seize *any* property in his house for unpaid rent. Major Bell read this astonishing statute, and was compelled to admit that the landlord had the law on his side. He remonstrated with him, however, and pointed out the cruel injustice which he had committed in seizing the property of an honest woman. The man was surly, and said that all he wanted was the law. The law gave him the goods and he meant to keep them. Major Bell was posed. He scratched his wise-looking head. Suddenly, he had an idea.

"Are you a free woman?" he asked the complainant.

"No," said she, "I belong to ——."

"Sir," said the judge to the landlord, "another statute requires the written consent of the owner before a tenement can be let to a slave. Produce it."

The man had forgotten this statute. He could not produce the document.

"Take your choice," said Major Bell; "either give back the woman's property or pay the fine."

The man preferred to restore the goods, and the poor washer-woman was saved from ruin.

"Master," said she, with the eloquence of perfect gratitude, "if you get the yellow fever, send for me, and I'll come and take care of you."

Among the many able men who surrounded General Butler, no one labored more assiduously or more effectively in the service of the people of New Orleans than Major Bell. He had to ransack all books and all the by-ways of his memory for law and precedent to guide him in his novel situation. French law, Spanish law, admiralty law, the slave code, state law, municipal law, common law, were all laid under contribution; and when these failed to meet the case, he drew upon the ample resources of his own common sense. I should add, that during his midsummer absence from the city, his seat was worthily filled by Lieutenant-Colonel Kinsman, the Lieutenant Kinsman of previous pages. Both of these officers were much indebted to the local and legal knowledge of the clerk of the provost court, Mr. Samuel F. Glenn, formerly a member of the bar of New Orleans.

A government needs a government organ. During the month of May, several of the newspapers of New Orleans were suspended by orders from head-quarters. They published the most extravagant rumors of federal disasters, and closed their columns against the true intelligence. Their comments hovered upon the verge of treason, and, not unfrequently, passed beyond the verge. A sudden order to suspend would bring them to a sense of the anomalous situation; they would promise submission; and were generally allowed to resume publication in a day or two.*

* "HEAD-QUARTERS, DEPARTMENT OF THE GULF,
"NEW ORLEANS, *Sept. 5th*, 1862.

"It having been made to appear that the suppression of the '*Estafette du Sud*,' French newspaper, will work distress among the employés of the office who are faultless, and the proprietors having assured the United States authorities that nothing shall be published that is offensive or inimical, or in any way reflecting upon the United States or its authorities,--the publication, upon this pledge, is permitted to be resumed at the instance of the acting French consul, M. Fauconnett.

"By order of MAJOR-GENERAL BUTLER.

"A. F. PUFFER, *Lieutenant and A. D. C.*"

One of these newspapers, the *Delta*, noted for the virulence of its treason, was otherwise treated. The office was seized, and permanently held. Two officers, experienced in the conduct of newspapers, Captain John Clark, of Boston, and Lieutenant-Colonel E. M. Brown, of the Eighth Vermont, were detailed to edit the paper in the interest of the United States. The first number of the regenerated *Delta* appeared on the 24th of May, 1862, and it continued under the same direction until the 8th of February, 1863. It was conducted with very great ability and spirit. Besides the labor of the editors, it had the advantage of occasional contributions from Major Bell and other officers; the commanding general himself frequently giving it the aid of his suggestions. Several ladies of New Orleans contributed. One of them, Mrs. Taylor, who adopted the signature of "Nellie," wrote many lively satirical sketches, which greatly amused the readers of the paper, besides calling forth the exertions of other ladies of similar character. In one feature the *Delta* differed strikingly from the ordinary newspapers of the South. Your true southerner, your "original secessionist," is a very serious personage. Vanity of the intenser sort is a serious foible; proud ignorance is serious; cruelty is serious; one-idea is serious. There is no joke in your true southerner; and as a consequence, his newspaper is generally a grave and heavy thing, enlivened only by vituperation and ferocity. The sport-impulse comes of an excess of strength. The man of true humor is so much the master of his subject that he can play with it, as the strong man of the circus plays with cannon-balls. The regenerated *Delta* was one of the most humorous of newspapers. Almost every issue had its good joke, and a great many of its jocular paragraphs were exceedingly happy hits.

Allusion has been made to the secession songs and secession sentiments taught to the children of the public schools. The schools were dismissed for the summer vacation two weeks earlier than usual, and during the interval the school system was reorganized on the model of that of Boston. A bureau of education and a superintendent of public schools were appointed—good Union men, all. The old teachers were dismissed, and a corps, true to their country, selected in their stead. School-books tainted with treason and pro-slavery were banished, and were replaced by such as are used in northern schools—Union song-books not being forgotten. The new system worked well, and continues, to this day, to diffuse sound knowledge and correct sentiments among the people of New Orleans.

Such were some of the measures of the commanding general, designed to restore Louisiana to a degree of its former prosperity and good feeling. They were as successful as the circumstances of the time permitted. The levee showed some signs of commercial activity. The money distributed by the army gave life to the retail trade. The poorer classes were won back to a love for the power which protected and sustained them. The original secessionists were, are, and will ever be, there and everywhere, the bitter foes of the United States; but, among those who had reluctantly accepted secession because they supposed it inevitable, the general and the Union gained hosts of friends, who remain to this day, in spite of much discouragement, loyal to the government.

CHAPTER XXII.

THE EFFECT IN NEW ORLEANS OF OUR LOSSES IN VIRGINIA.

THE Union army in the Department of the Gulf consisted of about fourteen thousand men, and the disasters in Virginia, which increased a hundred-fold the difficulty of holding New Orleans, forbade the re-enforcement of that army. Ship Island, Fort Jackson, Fort St. Philip, Baton Rouge, posts upon the lakes and elsewhere, required strong garrisons, which reduced the effective men in and near the city to a number inadequate to a successful defense of the place against such an attack as might be expected. General Butler was perfectly aware that the recovery of the city was an object which the rebels had distinctly proposed to themselves. It was the real aim of all that series of movements of which the attack upon Baton Rouge, by Breckinridge, was the most conspicuous. The general's excellent spy system brought him this information, and most of his own measures were more or less influenced by it.

One powerful iron-clad ram could have cleared the river in an hour of the Union fleet. That done, the city might have fallen before the well-concerted attack of a force such as the rebels were known to be able to assemble. They could not have held the city long; but they might have taken it, and held it long enough to do infinite mischief; or they might have necessitated its destruction.

The temper of the secessionists in New Orleans was the worst possible. Liars are generally credulous. At least, they are easily made to believe *lies*, though they find it so difficult to receive the truth. The news from Virginia would have sufficed to neutralize, for a time, the general's best measures, even if it had come without exaggerations. But news from Virginia uniformly came first through rebel sources by telegraph, while the truth arrived only after a long sea voyage. To show the effect of this inflammatory intelligence, take one incident as related by an officer of General Butler's staff:

"As a result of this continuous report of national defeats before Richmond, St. Charles street, near the hotel, was yesterday (July 10th) the scene of violence and threatening trouble. A young woman dressed in white and of handsome personal appearance, about 10 o'clock, passed by the hotel, wearing a secession badge. She finally insulted one of our soldiers, and was arrested by a policeman, who attempted to take her to the mayor's office. As a matter of course, there was instantly a scene of confusion, as she had selected the time when she would find the most obnoxious secessionists parading the vicinity. Upon reaching the building next to the Bank of Orleans, she theatrically appealed to the crowd for protection, and the next moment the policeman was knocked down, and a shot was fired out of the store, and wounded the soldier assisting the civil officer. Thereupon a hundred persons, returned soldiers of Beauregard's army, cried murder, and one of the national officers at the same moment fired at the assassin who wounded the soldier. In the confusion the murderers escaped, but the woman, together with some of her most prominent sympathizers, were conveyed before General Shepley at the City Hall. Upon being brought into the presence of General Shepley, she commenced the utterance of threats and abuse, and, further, took out of her bosom innumerable bits of paper, on which were written insulting epithets, addressed to the United States authorities, and one by one thrust them into General Shepley's hand. After some few questions she was put into a carriage and conveyed to General Butler's head-quarters, where she was recognized as the mistress of a gambler and murderer, now, by General Butler's orders, confined at Fort Jackson, but nominally passing as the wife of one John H. Larue."

There was every reason to believe that this was a concerted scene between the woman and the crowd. General Butler sent for her husband, who, on being asked his occupation, replied that he "played cards for a living." The general disposed of the case thus:

"John H. Larue, being by his own confession a vagrant, a person without visible means of support, and one who gets his living by playing cards, is committed to the parish prison until farther orders. Anna Larue, his wife, having been found in the public streets, wearing a Confederate flag upon her person, in order to incite a riot, which act has already resulted in a breach of the peace, and danger to the life of a soldier of the United Sates, is sent to Ship Island till farther orders. She is to be kept separate and apart from the other women confined there."

The hideous events attending the funeral of Lieutenant De Kay, of General Williams's staff, showed the true quality of the "original secessionists;" showed, at once, their cowardice, their meanness, and their ferocity; and proved the necessity for those strong measures by which the secessionists of the city were deprived of their power to co-operate with their friends beyond the Union lines.

Lieutenant De Kay, summoned from his studies in Europe by the peril of his country, was on board a gun-boat descending the Mississippi, when it was fired into by guerillas. He received twelve buck-shots in his body. He lingered a month in New Orleans, enduring his sufferings with heroic cheerfulness, content to die for his country. He expired on the 27th of June, mourned by the whole army. General Butler was at Baton Rouge on the day of the funeral, and his absence emboldened the baser rebels, who seized the opportunity to insult the funeral cortege with laughter and opprobrious outcries. Women again appeared in the streets wearing Confederate colors. The notorious Mrs. Philips, formerly a member of Mr. Buchanan's boudoir cabinet, banished from Washington as an ally of traitors, saluted the procession with ostentatious laughter from the balcony of her house. Many other women took pains to exhibit their exultation. A bookseller placed in the window of his store a skeleton labeled "Chickahominy." Another miscreant exhibited, in a club-room and elsewhere, a cross which he said was made of a Yankee's bone. When the procession arrived at the church, the galleries were found filled with a rabble of filthy scoundrels, the "dregs of the city," whose demeanor was in keeping with that of their instigators out-of-doors. No minister appeared to conduct the last ceremonies. Dr. Leacock, the pastor of the church, a weak, vacillating man, had promised to officiate, but had been induced to break his promise by the persuasions of members of his church; and other arrangements for the ceremony had to be hastily made amid the sneers and exultation of the crowd.

The scenes of that afternoon were so profoundly disgusting, so exasperating to the long-suffering troops, that, probably, no other body of men ever assembled in arms would have had the self-control to bear them in silence.* They *did* bear them in silence. Not a resentful word, still less a resentful act escaped them. It probably occurred to most of the troops that General Butler was expected home on the following day; and to him they knew they could safely commit the vindication of outraged decency.

The general, meanwhile, had been enjoying a pleasant excursion

* The following, from the pen of Lieutenant (now General) Godfrey Weitzel, appeared in the *Delta* the next morning:

"To THE EDITOR OF THE DELTA.—This afternoon the funeral of De Kay was held. A young officer of the United States army was buried, who, in every respect, was the peer of any young man in the South. We who knew, loved and admired him. He was fatally wounded a month ago while defending a cause in which he took the sword as honestly, with as high toned feelings of duty, as any man now fighting for the South. He left his studies in Europe to espouse this cause, because he honestly and sincerely believed it to be his duty. He was wounded, but how? From behind a bush, with buck-shot fired from a gun, probably by a man who would not have dared to meet him openly. He lingers a month. Not a word of complaint or reproach passed his lip. Always happy and cheerful even unto his last moment. We requested yesterday the use of a house of God, in which to show to his mortal remains our respect. It is granted, but how? After moving through collections of street cars, crowded with ladies wearing secession badges, and passively smiling and cheerful crowds studiously collected to insult the dead, we arrived at the house of the Lord. We find it thrown open like a stable, as if by military compulsion. We enter, and find the galleries and the most prominent places occupied by a rabble and negroes—a collection such as never defiled a church before.

"Gentlemen and ladies of New Orleans and of the South, there was no chivalry in this.

"G. WEITZEL, *Lieutenant U. S. Engineers.*

"NEW ORLEANS, *June* 28, 1862."

up the river, and was returning well pleased with what he had seen and heard at the capital of the state. "I have been agreeably disappointed," he wrote to the secretary of war, "in the feeling at Baton Rouge. There is a longing for the restoration of the old state of things under the Union, which is gratifying. I had a visit from a dozen or more of the gentlemen of Baton Rouge, and vicinity, representing some five or six millions of property, and had conversation with them upon the new system of partisan rangers just now inaugurated, *i. e.*, guerilla warfare. They deprecated it, and will do everything possible to discountenance it. They offered to take the oath of allegiance if required, but assured me they thought they could do more good by abstaining from that oath for the present, because it would be impossible for them to have communication with these partisans if they took the oath and it should be publicly known."

"I brought before me some of the most violent of the rebels, and, after calling their attention to the present state of things, I proposed to them the oath of allegiance, and after consideration over night, two of them, Mr. Benjamin, brother of the rebel secretary of war, and Byam, the mayor of the city, took the oath. I brought away with me, and now have under arrest, five of those who had used threats toward the men who had shown themselves favorable to the Union.

"Upon full reflection and observation, I find the condition of public sentiment to be this: The planters and men of property are now tired of the war; are well disposed toward the Union; only fearing lest their negroes should not be let alone; would be quite happy to have the Union restored in all things.

"The operative classes of white men, of all trades, are, as a rule, in favor of the Union.

"In fact, the rebellion was at first inaugurated for the purpose of establishing a landed aristocracy, as against the poor and middling whites, who had shown some disposition to assert their equality with the planter, and had begun to express themselves through organizations, on the basis of the Masonic Order, of which the South is full, and of which that ritual is the pattern."

Returning from these encouraging scenes, he was called upon to deal with the savages of New Orleans. Mrs. Philips, and the exhibitors of the skeleton and the cross, were brought before him.

The manner in which he disposed of their cases can best be shown by presenting three special orders, issued on the day after his return:

"NEW ORLEANS, *June* 30, 1862.

"Mrs. Philips, wife of Philip Philips, having been once imprisoned for her traitorous proclivities and acts at Washington, and released by the clemency of the government, and having been found training her children to spit upon officers of the United States at New Orleans, for which act of one of those children both her husband and herself apologized and were again forgiven, is now found on the balcony of her house during the passage of the funeral procession of Lieutenant De Kay, laughing and mocking at his remains; and, upon being inquired of by the commanding general if this fact were so, contemptuously replies, 'I was in good spirits that day.'

"*It is, therefore, ordered*, That she be not regarded and treated as a common woman of whom no officer or soldier is bound to take notice, but as an uncommon, bad, and dangerous woman, stirring up strife and inciting to riot.

"And that, therefore, she be confined at Ship Island, in the state of Mississippi, within proper limits there, till farther orders; and that she be allowed one female servant and no more if she so choose. That one of the houses for hospital purposes be assigned her as quarters; and a soldier's ration each day be served out to her, with the means of cooking the same; and that no verbal or written communication be allowed with her except through this office; and that she be kept in close confinement until removed to Ship Island."

"NEW ORLEANS, *June* 30, 1862.

"Fidel Keller has been found exhibiting a human skeleton in his bookstore window, in a public place in this city, labeled 'Chickahominy,' in large letters, meaning and intending that the bones should be taken by the populace to be the bones of a United States soldier slain in that battle, in order to bring the authority of the United States and our army into contempt, and for that purpose had stated to the passers-by that the bones were those of a Yankee soldier; whereas, in truth and fact, they were the bones purchased some weeks before of the Mexican consul, to whom they were pledged by a medical student.

"*It is, therefore, ordered*, That for this desecration of the dead, he be confined at Ship Island for two years at hard labor, and that he be allowed to communicate with no person on the island except Mrs. Philips, who has been sent there for a like offense. Any written message may be sent by him through these head-quarters.

"Upon this order being read to him, the said Keller requested that so much of it as associated him with 'that woman' might be recalled, which request was therefore reduced to writing by him as follows:

"'NEW ORLEANS, *June* 30, 1862.

"'Mr. Keller desires that that part of the sentence which refers to the communication with Mrs. Philips be stricken out, as he does not wish to have communication with the said Mrs. Philips.

"'F. KELLER.

"'*Witness*, D. WATERS.'

"Said request seeming to the commanding general reasonable, so much of said order is revoked, and the remainder will be executed."*

"NEW ORLEANS, *June* 30, 1862.

"John W. Andrews exhibited a cross, the emblem of the suffering of our blessed Saviour, fashioned for a personal ornament, which he said was made from the bones of a Yankee soldier, and having shown this too, without rebuke, in the Louisiana Club, which claims to be composed of chivalric gentlemen,

"*It is, therefore, ordered*, That for this desecration of the dead, he be confined at hard labor for two years on the fortifications of Ship Island, and that he be allowed no verbal or written communication to or with any one, except through these head-quarters."

Mrs. Philips, I may add, was released after several weeks detention.† She went to Mobile, where she received an ovation from the leaders of society, and was the subject of laudatory paragraphs in the newspapers. She had the grace, however, to deny having intended to insult the remains of Lieutenant De Kay. She said that she really was in high spirits that day, and that her ill-timed merriment was not provoked by the passage of the funeral procession.

*The explanation of Keller's curious request is this: There was another Mrs. Philips in New Orleans, notorious as a keeper of a house of ill-fame. The prisoner having only heard of this Mrs. Philips, had the decency to desire to be kept apart from her, fearing, as he said, the effect upon the feelings of his wife if he should be associated with such a woman. The general was not aware of the cause of his scruples at the time.

†"HEAD-QUARTERS, DEPARTMENT OF THE GULF,
"NEW ORLEANS, LA., *September* 14, 1862.

"*Ordered*:—The Commanding General having learned that the farther imprisonment of Mrs. Philips may result in injury to the wholly innocent, directs her to be released, if she chooses to give her parole, that in nothing she will give aid, comfort, or information to the enemies of the United States.

"By order of MAJOR-GENERAL BUTLER.

"A. A. FULLER, *Lieut. and A. D. C.*"

A trifling circumstance, of a ludicrous nature, may serve to show something of the disposition of the people—just as we learn the feelings of a family from the prattle of the children. Among a batch of captured letters was found one from a certain Edward Wright, a resident of New Orleans, to a lady in Secessia, full of the most ridiculous lies. He told his correspondent that the Yankee officers were the most craven creatures on earth. One of them, he said, had insulted a lady in the streets, which Wright perceiving, he had slapped the officer's face and kicked him, and then offered to meet him in the field; but the officer gave some "rigmarole excuse" and declined. For this, he continued, he was taken before Picayune Butler, and came near being sent to Fort Jackson.

General Butler caused the writer of this epistle to be brought before him, when the following conversation occurred between them:—

"What is your name?"

"Edward Wright."

"Have I ever had the pleasure of seeing you before?"

"Not that I know of."

"Have you ever been before an officer of the United States charged with any offense?"

"No, sir."

"Have you ever had any difficulty or misunderstanding with an officer of the United States in the streets or elsewhere?"

"Never, sir."

"Have you any complaint to make of the conduct of any of my officers or men?"

"None, sir."

"Have you ever observed any misconduct on their part, since we arrived in the city?

"Never, sir."

The general now produced the letter, and handed it to the prisoner.

"Did you write that letter?"

"It looks like my handwriting."

"Did you write the letter?"

"Yes; I wrote it."

"Is not the story of your slapping and kicking the officer, an unmitigated and malicious lie, designed to bring the army of the United States into contempt?"

"Well, sir, it isn't true, I admit."

The general then dictated a sentence like this, which was written at the bottom of the letter: "I, Edward Wright, acknowledge that this letter is basely and abominably false, and that I wrote it for the purpose of bringing the army of the United States into contempt."

"Sign that, sir."

"I won't. I am a British subject, and claim the protection of the British consul."

"Sign it, sir."

"General Butler, you may put every ball of that pistol through my brain, but I will never sign that paper."

"Captain Davis, make out an order to the provost-marshal, to hang this man at daybreak to-morrow. In the mean time, let him have any priest he chooses to send for. Gentlemen, I am going to dinner."

Before the general had reached his quarters, an orderly came running up.

"General, he has signed."

"Well, keep him in the guard-house all night, and let him go in the morning."

A conspiracy to assassinate General Butler was detected early in June. The proofs were sufficient to warrant the arrest of four abandoned characters. The general, content with the discovery and frustration of the plot, forbore to prosecute the men, and agreed to pardon the ringleader on condition of his leaving the city. The general did this in compliance with the entreaties of his aged father, who had fought under General Jackson, in the war of 1812, and had remained true to his country.

These incidents may suffice to show the disposition of the secessionists of New Orleans, inflamed by the news from Virginia, increased in number by the partial dissolution of Beauregard's army, and encouraged to expect an attempt to drive the Union army from the soil of Louisiana.

Hence the justification of those measures, about to be related, which reduced the secession party in New Orleans to a state of "subjugation," the most complete. Before entering upon those measures, it will be proper to show that not the rebels only felt the weight of General Butler's iron hand. Offenses committed by adherents of the Union against the people of the city, were visited with punishment as prompt and rigorous as any which were perpetrated against the country and the flag.

It was in connection with the searches for concealed property of the Confederate government, under the general order of June 6th, that the tragical events occurred to which I allude, and which were among the most notable of General Butler's administration. No one was allowed to enter a house for the purpose of searching, without a written order from General Butler, General Shepley, or Colonel French. For several days the searches proceeded quietly enough, without exciting remark. But about the middle of June, complaints came pouring into head-quarters of parties entering houses for the ostensible purpose of searching for Confederate arms, who carried off valuable private property, such as money and jewels. The detection of these villains was remarkably prompt.

On the 12th of June, at noon, a complaint was brought to General Butler of a most audacious and flagrant outrage of this kind. A cab drove up to a house in Toulouse street, from which issued two men, who entered the house and presented to the inmates an order to search for arms, signed, apparently, by General Butler. Two men remained in the cab while the search proceeded. The two who entered the house, and rummaged its closets and drawers, behaved to the family with great politeness, expressing their regret at having been ordered upon so unpleasant a duty, and declaring their desire to perform that duty with as little inconvenience to the inmates of the house as possible. Upon retiring, they were so good as to leave a certificate to this effect:

"J. William Henry, First-Lieutenant of the Eighteenth Massachusetts volunteers, has searched the premises No. 93 Toulouse street, and find, to the best of my judgment, that all the people who live there are loyal. Please examine no more.

"J. William Henry."

After the departure of these urbane and considerate gentlemen, the lady of the house found that they had carried with them eighteen hundred and eighty dollars, a gold watch, and a breastpin. Another sum of over eight thousand dollars they had overlooked.

There was but one clue to the discovery of these men. They had ridden to the house in cab No. 50, which had remained before the door during the search, and in which the searchers had departed. The driver of cab No. 50, who was immediately brought before the general, was required to relate the history of his doings during the previous night. In the course of the afternoon, the coffee-house to which he had last conveyed his passengers, was surrounded, and every man in it was brought before the general. There were four of them. General Butler never forgets a face that he has once seen. After looking at the men a moment, he asked one of them:

"Where have I seen you?"

"In Boston."

"Where in Boston?"

"In the Municipal Court."

"For what offense were you tried before that court?"

"Burglary."

"Did you join any regiment?"

"Yes."

"Which?"

"The Thirtieth Massachusetts."

"Why are you not with your regiment?"

"I was discharged."

"What for?"

"Disease."

"Well, *you* ought to be hanged any how, for you have robbed before, and been convicted."

"Don't do it, general, and I'll tell you all about it."

"Well, make a clean breast of it, then."

The man confessed. He said that he was one of an organized gang, who had been entering houses for several nights and plundering. The particular offense committed in Toulouse street was brought home, on the spot, to two others of the arrested men, who confessed their guilt. A considerable part of the stolen money was recovered and restored. Three more of the gang were arrested by Colonel Stafford's detectives on the following day. General Butler disposed of these flagrant cases in the two special orders following:

"NEW ORLEANS, *June* 13, 1862.

"William M. Clary, late second officer of the United States steam transport Saxon, and Stanislaus Roy, of New Orleans, on the night of the 11th of June inst., having forged a pretended authority of the major-general commanding, being armed, in company with other evil disposed persons, under false names, and in a pretended uniform of the soldiers of the United States, entered the house of a peaceable citizen, No. 93 Toulouse street, about the hour of eleven o'clock in the night time, and there, in a pretended search for arms and treasonable correspondence, by virtue of such forged authority, plundered said house and stole therefrom eighteen hundred and eighty-five dollars in current bank-notes, one gold watch and chain, and one bosom pin.

"This outrage was reported to the commanding general at twelve o'clock A. M. on the 12th of June instant, and by his order Clary and Roy were detected and arrested on the same day, and brought before the commanding general at one o'clock of this day, and where it appeared by incontrovertible evidence that the facts above stated were true, and all material parts thereof were voluntarily confessed by Clary and Roy.

"It farther appeared that Clary and Roy had before this occasion visited other houses of peaceable citizens in the night time, for like purposes and under like false pretenses.

"'Brass knuckles,' burglars' keys, and a portion of the stolen property and other property stolen from other parties, were found upon the person of Roy, and in his lodgings.

"Whereupon, after a full hearing of the defense of said Clary and Roy, and due consideration of the evidence, it was ordered by the commanding general that Wm. M. Clary and Stanislaus Roy, for their offenses, be punished by being hanged by the neck until they are dead, and this sentence be executed upon them and each of them, between the hours of eight o'clock A. M. and twelve M. on Monday, the 16th of June inst., at or near the parish prison, in the city of New Orleans.

"The provost-marshal will cause said sentence to be executed, and for so doing this order will be sufficient warrant."

"NEW ORLEANS, *June* 15, 1862.

"Theodore Lieb, of New Orleans, George William Crage, late first officer of the ship City of New York, and Frank Newton, late private of the Thirteenth regiment Connecticut volunteers, having, upon their own confession and clear proof, after a full hearing, been convicted of being members of a gang of thieves, consisting of seven or more, of which William M. Clary and Stanislaus Roy, mentioned in Special Order No. 98, and now under sentence of death, were principals, bound together by an oath or obligation, engaged by means of a forged authority and false uniforms, in robbing the houses of divers peaceable citizens of their moneys, watches, jewelry and valuables, under pretense of searching for arms and articles of war, must suffer the proper penalty.

"At least eight houses, as appears by their confession, were plundered by three or more of the gang, while others were watching without, at various times, and a large amount of property carried off, a large portion of which has since been recovered.

"The heinousness of this offense, heightened by the contempt and disgrace brought upon the uniform, authority and flag of the United States by their fraudulent acts, in making it cover their nefarious practices, renders them peculiarly the subjects of prompt and condign punishment.

"It is therefore ordered that George William Crage and Frank Newton (for the offenses aforesaid) be hanged by the neck until they and each of them be dead, and that this sentence be executed upon them at or near the parish prison, in the city of New Orleans, on Monday, the 16th day of June instant, between the hours of six A. M. and twelve M., under the direction of the provost-marshal; and for so doing this shall be sufficient warrant.

"Theodore Lieb, being a youth of eighteen years only, in consideration of his tender years, has his punishment commuted to confinement at hard labor on the fortifications at Ship Island, or the nearest military post, during the pleasure of the president of the United States."

Thus, the crime was committed on the 11th, detected on the 12th, two of the criminals were tried on the 13th, two more on the 15th, and the whole ordered to be executed on the 16th. The man whose confession led to the conviction of the offenders was sentenced to five years' imprisonment at hard labor. Two or three other less guilty participants were sentenced to six months at Ship Island with ball and chain.

Those who observed the mingled nonchalance and severity of General Butler's demeanor during those four days, may naturally have concluded that it cost him no great exertion of will to hang these criminals. In reality, it caused him the severest internal conflict of his whole life. During the excitement of the detection and trial, there was, indeed, no room for any emotions but disgust at the crime and exultation at his success in discovering the perpetrators. It was far different on the Sunday preceding the day of execution, when the men lay at his mercy in prison, when the wives of two of them came imploring for mercy, when the distant families of the other two were brought to his knowledge, and when the softer hearted of his own military family pleaded for a commutation of the sentence. Mrs. Butler was at the North for the summer. Alone that night, the general paced his room, considering and reconsidering the case. He could not find a door of escape for these men. He had executed a citizen of New Orleans for an offense against the flag of his country; how could he pardon a crime committed by Union men against the citizens of New Orleans, a crime involving several distinct offenses of the deepest dye? His duty was clear, but he could not sleep. He paced his room till the dawn of day.

The men were executed in the morning; all but one of them confessing their guilt. To one of the families thus left destitute, the general gave a sewing-machine, by which they were enabled to earn a subsistence.

The effect of this prompt and rigorous justice was most salutary upon the minds of both parties in New Orleans; and its effect would have been as manifest as it was real, but for the disturbing influence of the terrible tidings from Virginia; in the presence of which the wisdom of an archangel would have failed to give confidence to the loyal people of Louisiana, or win to the Union cause any considerable number of the party for secession.

CHAPTER XXIII.

THE SHEEP AND THE GOATS.

We may now proceed to consider the iron-handed measures of the commanding general, which were designed to isolate the secessionists, and render them innoxious.

Crowds were forbidden to assemble, and public meetings, unless expressly authorized. The police were ordered to disperse all street-gatherings of a greater number of persons than three.

In the sixth week of the occupation of the city, General Butler began the long series of measures, by which the sheep were separated from the goats; by which the attitude of every inhabitant of

New Orleans toward the government of the United States was ascertained and recorded. The people might be politically divided thus: Union men; rebels; foreigners friendly to the United States; foreigners sympathizing with the Confederates; soldiers from Beauregard's army inclined to submission; soldiers from Beauregard's army not inclined to submission. These soldiers, who numbered several thousands, were required to come forward and define their position, and either take the oath of allegiance, or surrender themselves prisoners of war; in which latter case, they would be admitted to parole until regularly exchanged, or if they preferred it, remain in confinement. In this way, the name, standing, residence, and political sympathies of this concourse of men were placed on record, and the general was enabled to know where they were to be found, and what he had to expect from them in time of danger.

His next step was to decree, that no authority of any kind should be exercised in New Orleans by traitors, and that no favors should be granted to traitors by the United States, except the mere protection from personal violence secured by the police. The following general order was designed to secure these objects:

"New Orleans, *June* 10, 1862.

"General Order No. 41.

"The constitution and laws of the United States require that all military, civil, judicial, executive and legislative officers of the United States, and of the several states, shall take an oath to support the constitution and laws. If a person desires to serve the United States, or to receive special profit from a protection from the United States, he should take upon himself the corresponding obligations. This oath will not be, as it has never been, forced upon any. It is too sacred an obligation, too exalted in its tenure, and brings with it too many benefits and privileges, to be profaned by unwilling lip service. It enables its recipient to say, 'I am an American citizen,' the highest title known, save that of him who can say with St. Paul, 'I was free born,' and have never renounced that freedom.

"Judges, justices, sheriffs, attorneys, notaries, and all officers of the law whatever, and all persons who have ever been, or who have ever claimed to be, citizens of the United States in this department, who therefore exercise any office, hold any place of trust or calling whatever which calls for the doing of any legal act whatever, or for the doing of any act, judicial or administrative, which shall or may affect any other person than the actor, must take and subscribe the following oath: 'I do solemnly swear (or affirm) that I will bear true faith and allegiance to the United States of America, and will support the constitution thereof.' All acts, doings, deeds, instruments, records or certificates, certified or attested by, and transactions done, performed, or made by any of the persons above described, from and after the 15th day of June inst., who shall not have taken and subscribed such oath, are void and of no effect.

"It having become necessary, in the judgment of the commanding general, as a 'public exigency,' to distinguish those who are well disposed toward the government of the United States, from those who still hold allegiance to the Confederate States, and ample time having been given to all citizens for reflection upon this subject, and full protection to person and property of every law-abiding citizen having been afforded, according to the terms of the proclamation of May 1st:

"*Be it further ordered*, That all persons ever heretofore citizens of the United States, asking or receiving any favor, protection, privilege, passport, or to have money paid them, property, or other valuable thing whatever delivered to them, or any benefit of the power of the United States extended to them, except protection from personal violence, must take and subscribe the oath above specified, before their request can be heard, or any act done in their favor by any officer of the United States within this department. And for this purpose all persons shall be deemed to have been citizens of the United States who shall have been residents therein for the space of five years and upward, and if foreign born, shall not have claimed and received a protection of their government, duly signed and registered by the proper officer, more than sixty days previous to the publication of this order.

"It having come to the knowledge of the commanding general that many persons resident within this department have heretofore been aiding rebellion by furnishing arms and munitions of war, running the blockade, giving information, concealing property, and abetting by other ways, the so-called Confederate States, in violation of the laws of neutrality imposed upon them by their sovereigns, as well as the laws of the United States, and that a less number are still so engaged; it is therefore ordered, that all foreigners claiming any of the privileges of an American citizen, or protection or favor from the government of the United States (except protection from personal violence), shall previously take and subscribe an oath in the form following:

"I, —— ——, do solemnly swear, or affirm, that so long as my government remains at peace with the United States, I will do no act, or consent that any be done, or conceal any that has been or is about to be done, that shall be done, that shall aid or comfort any of the enemies or opposers of the United States whatever.

"(Signed), —— ——

"Subject of ——."

"At the City Hall, at the provost court, at the provost-marshal's office, and at the several police stations, books will be opened, and a proper officer will be present to administer the proper oaths to any person desiring to take the same, and to witness the subscription of the same by the party taking it. Such officer will furnish to each person so taking and subscribing, a certificate in form following:

"DEPARTMENT OF THE GULF, New Orleans, —— 1862.

"—— —— has taken and subscribed the oath required by General Order No. 41, for a —— of ——

"(Signed), —— ——."

General orders issued at New Orleans usually produced considerable stir among the parties interested; but none of them caused so much excitement and such universal alarm as this. If the citizens were astounded, the foreigners were puzzled. No one was OBLIGED to take the oath; but what would happen to those who did not take it? The office-holders, however, could entertain no doubts respecting their fate, and all of them who adhered still to the Richmond government at once resigned their places. The residue of the city government was dissolved, and the military commandant reigned alone over New Orleans. One of the city officials, I observe from divers documents, made a parting dive into the city treasury, but he was caught in the act, and compelled to let go his booty.

General Shepley issued the following order relative to the government of the city:

"HEAD-QUARTERS MILITARY COMMANDANT,
"NEW ORLEANS, CITY HALL, *June* 27, 1862.

"The legislative power of the city of New Orleans has heretofore been vested by law, in a board of aldermen and a board of assistant aldermen, who together formed the common council of the city. This power is now suspended. The seats of the aldermen and assistant aldermen have all been vacated; one class of them by the expiration of their term of office, and the remainder by their neglect to take the oath of allegiance to the United States, as required by General Order No. 41 of the commanding general of this department.

"Believing that the inconvenience incident to a temporary suspension of legislative power will be slight compared with the evils which have heretofore been consequent on excessive and frequently corrupt legislation, these vacancies will not be filled until such time as there shall be a sufficient number of the citizens of New Orleans loyal to their country and their constitution to entitle them to resume the right of self-government.

"So much of the executive power of the city as has heretofore been vested in the mayor, will, for the present, be exercised by the military commandant of New Orleans.

"A 'bureau of finance' is hereby constituted, composed of a board of three persons, one of whom shall be the chairman of the board, to be appointed by the military commandant, with such clerks as may from time to time be found necessary, and may be appointed by the chairman of the board, subject to the approval of the military commandant. The duties of said bureau shall be the same as those which—under the act approved March 20, 1856, and under other laws constituting the charter of said city of New Orleans, and under the ordinances of the city now in force—have been attributed to the several committees on finance, fire, police, judiciary, claims, education, and health, in the board of aldermen and in the board of assistant aldermen of the common council of New Orleans. The offices of said bureau shall be in the City Hall.

"A 'bureau of streets and landings,' consisting of three persons, one of whom shall be chairman, is hereby constituted. The duties of said bureau shall be the same which, under the charters, laws and ordinances of the city of New Orleans, have been appropriated to the several committees on streets and landings, workhouses and prisons, and house of refuge, in the board of aldermen and board of assistant aldermen. The office of said bureau shall be in the City Hall, and the chairman shall appoint, subject to the approval of the military commandant, the necessary clerks, whose compensation will be fixed by the bureau, subject to the same approval.

"The following named persons will constitute the bureau of finance: E. H. Durell, chairman; D. S. Dewees, Stoddart Howell.

"The following named persons will constitute the bureau of streets and landings: Julian Neville, chairman; Edward Ames, Benjamin Campbell.

"By order. G. F. SHEPLEY,
"*Military Commandant of New Orleans.*

"Approved and ordered. B. F. BUTLER,
"*Major-General Commanding Department of the Gulf.*"

The consuls, as usual, had something to say to the general upon the new topic. "If General Butler rides up Canal street," said the *Delta*, "the consuls are sure to come in a body, and 'protest' that he did not ride *down*. If he smokes a pipe in the morning, he is sure to have a deputation in the evening, asking why he did not smoke a cigar. If he drinks coffee, they will send some rude messenger with a note asking, in the name of some tottering dynasty, why he did not drink tea." The consuls did not gain much glory in this new contest with the general.

THE CONSULS TO GENERAL BUTLER.

"NEW ORLEANS, *June* —, 1862.

"To Major-General B. F. BUTLER, Commanding Department of the Gulf:

"GENERAL:—The undersigned, foreign consuls, accredited to the United States, have the honor to represent that General Order No. 41, under date of 10th instant, contains certain clauses against which they deem it their duty to protest, not only in order to comply with their obligations as representatives of their respective governments, now at peace and in friendly relations with the United States, but also to protect, by all possible means, such of their fellow-citizens as may be morally or materially injured by the execution of an order which they consider as contrary both to that justice which they have a right to expect at the hands of the government of the United States, and to the laws of nations.

"The 'Order' contains two oaths: one, applicable both to the native born and to such foreigners as have not claimed and received a protection from their government, &c.; the second applicable, it would seem, to such foreigners as may have claimed and received the above protection: thus, unnaturalized foreigners are divided into two categories, a distinction which the undersigned can not admit.

"The 'Order' says that the required 'oath will not be, as it has never been, forced upon any;' that 'it is too sacred an obligation, too exalted in its tenure, and brings with it too many benefits and privileges, to be profaned by unwilling lip-service;' that 'all persons shall be deemed to have been citizens of the United States who shall have been resident therein for the space of five years and upward, and, if foreign born, shall not have claimed and received a protection of their government, duly signed and registered by the proper officer, more than sixty days previous to the publication of this order.'

"Whence it follows that foreigners are placed on the same footing with the native born and naturalized citizens, and in the alternative either of being deprived of their means of existence or forced implicitly to take the required oath, if they wish to ask and do receive 'any favor, protection, privilege, passport, or to have money paid them, property or other valuable thing whatever delivered to them, or any benefit of the power of the United States extended to them, except protection from personal violence.'

"Now, of course, when a foreigner does not wish to submit to the laws of the country of which he is a resident, he is invariably and everywhere at liberty to leave that country. But here he does not even enjoy that privilege; for to leave he must procure a passport, to obtain which he must take an oath that he is unwilling to take; and yet that oath 'is so sacred and so exalted in its tenure that it must not be profaned by unwilling lip-service.'

"It is true that the 'Order' excepts those foreigners who claimed and received the protection of their government more than sixty days previous to its publication; but this exception is merely nominal, because the very great majority of foreigners never had any cause hitherto, in this country, to ask, and therefore to receive, 'a protection of their government.' Besides, this exception implies an interference with the interior administration of foreign governments—an act contrary to the laws of nations. Whether the foreign residents have or have not complied with the laws and edicts of their own governments is a matter between them and their consuls, and the undersigned deny the right of any foreign power to meddle with, and still less to enforce, the laws of their respective countries, as far as their fellow-citizens are concerned. When a consul extends the high protection of his government to such of his countrymen as are neither naturalized nor charged with any breach of the laws of the country in which they reside, he is to be supported by a friendly government; for it is a law in all civilized countries, that if foreigners must submit to the laws of the country in which they reside, they, and *a fortiori* their consuls, must, in exchange of that respect for those laws, receive due protection, that protection, in fact, which the foreigners have invariably enjoyed in this country up to the present time. Now, foreigners are deprived of that protection unless they become citizens of the United States; and this is done without a warning and in opposition to the laws of the United States concerning the mode in which foreigners may become citizens of this country. The undersigned must remark that a just law can have no retroactive action, and can be enforced only from the day of its promulgation, while the order requires that acts should have been done, the necessity of which was unforeseen, especially in this country.

"The required oath is contrary not only to the rights, duty and dignity of foreigners, who are all 'free born,' but also to the dignity of the government of the United States, and even to the spirit of the order itself.

"1. Because it virtually forces a certain class of foreigners, in order to save their property, to swear 'true faith and allegiance' to the United States, and thereby to 'renounce and abjure' that true faith and allegiance which they owe to their own country only, while naturalization is and can be but an act of free will; and because it is disgraceful for any 'free man' to do, through motives of material interest, those moral acts which are repugnant to his conscience.

"If the order merely required the English oath of 'allegiance,' it might be argued, according to the definition given by Blackstone (I., p. 370), that said oath signifies only the submission of foreigners to the police laws of the country in which they reside; but the oath, as worded in the 'order, is a virtual act of naturalization. A citizen of the United States might take the oath, although Art. 6 of the Federal Constitution and the act of

Congress of June 1, 1789, do not require as much. But no consideration can compel a foreigner to take such an oath.

"2. Because, if according to the order the 'highest title known was really that of an American citizen,' it would be the very reason why it should be sought after and not imposed upon the unwilling, whether openly or impliedly.

"3. Because, while the order advocates the 'neutrality imposed upon foreigners by their sovereigns,' it virtually tends to violate that neutrality, not by forcing them openly to take up arms and bravely shed their blood in defense even of a cause that is not their own, but by enjoining upon them, if they wish to redeem their property, to descend to the level of spies and denunciators for the benefit of the United States.

"The undersigned will close by remarking that their countrymen, since the beginning of this war, have been neutral. As such they can not be considered and treated as a conquered population. The conquered may be submitted to exceptional laws; but neutral foreigners have a right to be treated as they have always been by the government of the United States.

"We have the honor to be, General, your most obedient servants,

"Juan Callejon, Consul de España.
"Ch. Mejan, French Consul.
"Jos. Deynoodt, Consul of Belgium.
"M. W. Benachi, Greek Consul.
"Joseph Lanata, Consul of Italy.
"B. Teryaghi, Vice-Consul.
"Ad. Piaget, Swiss Consul."

A little bird whispered in the ear of General Butler that the author of this letter was Mr. George Coppell, whose papers had not yet arrived, and whose signature, therefore, did not appear.

GENERAL BUTLER TO THE CONSULS.

"Head-quarters, Department of the Gulf,
"New Orleans, La., *June* 16, 1862.

"Gentlemen:—Your protest against General Order No. 41 has been received.

"It appears more like a labored argument, in which the imagination has been drawn on for the facts to support it. Were it not that some of the idiomatic expressions of the document show that it was composed by some one born in the English tongue, I should have supposed that many of the misconceptions of the purport of the order, which appear in the protest, arose from an imperfect acquaintance with the peculiarities of our language.

"As it is, I am obliged to believe that the faithlessness of the Englishman who transmitted the order to you and wrote the protest, will account for the misapprehensions under which you labor in regard to its terms.

"The order prescribes—

"1. A form of oath to be taken by those who claim to be citizens of the United States, and those only who desire to hold office, civil or military, under the laws of the United States, or who desire some act to be done in their favor by the officers of the United States in this department, other than protection from personal violence, which is afforded to all.

"With that oath, of course, the alien has nothing to do.

"But there is a large class of foreign born persons here who, by their acts, have lost their nationalities.

"Familiar examples of that class are those subjects of France who, in contravention of the '*Code Civile*,' have, without authorization by the emperor, joined themselves to a military organization of a foreign state (*s'affilierait à une corporation militaire étrangère*), or received military commissions (*fonctions publiques, conférées par un gouvernement étranger*) from the governor thereof, or who have left France without intention of returning (*sans esprit de retour*), or, as in the case of the Greek consul, have taken the office of opener and examiner of letters in the post-office of the Confederate States, or the Prussian consul, who is still leading a recruited body of his countrymen in the rebel army.

"As many of such aliens had been naturalized, and many of the bad men among them had concealed the fact of their naturalization, it became necessary, in order to meet the case of these bad men, to prescribe some rule by which those foreign born who might not be entitled to the protection of their several governments, or had heretofore become naturalized citizens of the United States, might be distinguished from those foreigners who were still to be treated as neutrals.

"This rule must be a comprehensive one and one easily to be understood, because it was for the guidance of subordinate officers, who should be called upon to administer the proper oath.

"Therefore, it was provided that all who had resided here five years—a length of time which would seem to be sufficient evidence that they had not the intention of returning (*esprit de retour*), and who should not have, in that time, claimed certificate of nationality, called commonly a 'protection' of their government, should, for this purpose, be deemed *prima facie*, of course, American citizens, and should, if they desired any favor or protection of the government, save from violence, take the oath of allegiance. But it is complained that the order farther provides that they must have received that 'protection' sixty days previous to the date of the order so as to have the 'protection' avail them.

"The reason of this limitation was that, as some of the consuls had gone to the rebel army, and some of the consuls had been aiding the rebellion here, and as 'protections' had been given by some of the consuls to those who were not entitled to them, for the purpose of enabling the holders to evade the blockade, it was necessary to make some limitations to secure good faith.

"Indeed, gentlemen, you will remember that all rules and regulations are made to restrain bad men, and not the good.

"For instance, if I allowed the 'protections' given now to avail for this purpose, that Prussian consul might give them to the whole of his militia company that live to get back; and they might come, claiming to be neutrals, as did that British Guard who sent their arms and equipments to Beauregard.

"The naturalization laws of the United States were in abeyance for want of United States courts here. Their provisions permitted all foreigners who had resided here five years and not claimed protection of their government, who felt disposed to avail themselves of them, to become entitled to the high privileges of an American citizen, which so many foreigners value so greatly that they leave their own prosperous, peaceful, and happy countries to come and live here, even although allowed to enjoy those privileges in a limited degree only. So greatly do they compliment us upon our laws that they prefer to, and insist upon, stopping here, even at the risk of being exposed to the chances of our intestine war, which chances they seem willing to take, in preference to living in peace at home, under laws enacted by their own sovereigns. But it is said that, unless foreigners take the oath of allegiance, they will not be allowed a 'passport.'

"This is an entire mistake, and probably comes from confounding a 'pass' through my lines, which I grant or withhold for military reasons, with a 'passport,' which must be given a foreigner by his own government.

"The order refuses all 'passports' to American citizens who do not take the oath of allegiance; but it nowhere meddles with the 'passports' of foreigners, with which I have nothing to do.

"There is nothing compulsory about this order.

"If a foreigner desires the privileges which the military government of this department accords to American citizens, let him take the oath of allegiance; but that does not naturalize him. If he does not wish to do so, but chooses to be an honest neutral, then let him not take the oath of allegiance, but the other oath set forth in the order.

"If he chooses to do neither, but simply to remain here with protection from personal violence, a privilege he has not enjoyed in this city for many years until now, let him be quiet, live on, keep away from his consul, and be happy. For honest alien neutrals another oath was provided, which, in my judgment, contains nothing but what an honest and honorable neutral will do and maintain, and, of course, only that which he will promise to do.

"But it is said that this oath compels every 'foreigner to descend to the level of spies and denunciators for the benefit of the United States.'

"There is no possible just construction of language which will give any such interpretation to the order. This mistake arises from a misconception of the meaning of the word 'conceal,' so false, so gross, so unjust and illiterate, that in the Englishman who penned the protest sent to me it must have been intentional, but an error into which those not born and reared in the idioms of our language might easily have fallen.

"The oath requires him who takes it not to 'conceal' any wrong that has been, or is about to be done, in aid or comfort of the enemies of the United States.

"It has been read and translated to you as if it required you to reveal all such acts. 'Conceal' is a verb active in our language; 'concealment' is an act done, not a thing suffered by, the 'concealers.'

"Let me illustrate this difference of meaning:

"If I am passing about and see a thief picking the pocket of my neighbor, and I say nothing about it unless called upon by a proper tribunal, that is not 'concealment' of the theft; but if I throw my cloak over the thief to screen him from the police-officer while he does it, I then 'conceal' the theft. Again, if I know that my neighbor is about to join the rebel army, and I go about my usual business, I do not 'conceal' the fact; but if, upon being inquired of by the proper authority as to where my neighbor is about to go, I say that he is going to sea, I then 'conceal' his acts and intentions.

"Now, if any citizen or foreigner means to 'conceal' rebellious or traitorous acts against the United States, in the sense above given, it will be much more for his personal comfort that he gets out of this department at once.

"Indeed, gentlemen, if any subject of a foreign state does not like our laws, or the administration of them, he has an immediate, effectual, and appropriate remedy in his own hands, alike pleasant to him and to us; and that is, not to annoy his consul with complaints of those laws or the administration of them, or his consul wearying the authorities with verbose protests, but simply to go home—'stay not on the order of his going, but go at once.' Such a person came here without our invitation; he will be parted with without our regrets.

"But he must not have committed crimes against our laws, and then expect to be allowed to go home to escape the punishment of those crimes.

"I must beg, gentlemen, that no more argumentative protests against my orders be sent to me by you as a body. If any consul has anything to offer for my consideration, he will easily learn the proper mode of presenting it. It is no part of your duties or your rights.

"I have, gentlemen, the honor to be your obedient servant,

"BENJ. F. BUTLER, *Major-General Commanding.*

"Messrs. CH. MEJAN, French Consul; JUAN CALLEJON, Consul de Espana; JOS. DEYNOODT, Consul of Belgium; M. W. BENACHI, Greek Consul; JOSEPH LANATA, Consul of Italy; B. TERYAGHI, Vice-Consul; AD. PIAGET, Swiss Consul."

Mr. Coppell had a word to say in his own name:

MR. COPPELL TO GENERAL BUTLER.

"BRITISH CONSULATE,
"NEW ORLEANS, LA., *June* 14, 1862.

"SIR:—I beg to inform you that great doubt exists in the minds of British subjects, who, under the provisions of your Order No. 41, are called upon to subscribe the oaths therein set forth, as to the consequences of compliance with the behests of that order.

"I would therefore respectfully request that you will inform me whether the oath prescribed in the first instance is intended, or, in your understanding, can be construed to affect the natural allegiance they owe to the government of their nativity.

"Objections have also been very generally urged against the oath prescribed to duly registered aliens, on the ground that it imposes on them (in words, at least) the office of spy, and forces them to acts inconsistent with the ordinary obligations of probity, honor and neutrality.

"Hoping that I may receive such explanations as may obviate the difficulties suggested, I have the honor to be, sir, your obedient servant,

"GEORGE COPPELL,
"*Her Britannic Majesty's Acting Consul.*"

REPLY FROM HEAD-QUARTERS.

"HEAD-QUARTERS, DEPARTMENT OF THE GULF,
"NEW ORLEANS, LA., *June* 14, 1862.

"SIR:—I am directed by the major-general commanding to inform you that no answer is to be given to the note of George Coppell, Esq., of this date, until his credentials and pretensions are recognized by his own government and the government of the United States. All attempts at official action on Mr. Coppell's part must cease. His credentials have been sought for, but not exhibited. I have the honor to be

"Your obedient servant,
"P. HAGGERTY,
"*Captain and Assistant Adjutant-General.*"

Mr. Coppell, however, received another answer. To complete the discomfiture of the consuls, General Butler employed one of his very happiest expedients—a measure at once so just and so witty, as to extort grim laughter and sulky approval from the sourest rebels. The following general order appeared three days after the date of the general's reply to the consuls:

"NEW ORLEANS, *June* 19, 1862.

"GENERAL ORDER NO. 42.

"The commanding general has received information that certain of the foreign residents in this department, notwithstanding the explanations of the terms of the oath prescribed in General Order No. 41, contained in his reply to the foreign consuls, have still scruples about taking that oath.

"Anxious to relieve the consciences of all who honestly entertain doubts upon this matter, and not to embarrass any, especially neutrals, by his necessary military orders, the commanding general hereby revises General Order No. 41, so far as to permit any foreign subject, at his election, to take and subscribe the following oath, instead of the oath as set forth:

"I, —— ——, do solemnly swear that I will, to the best of my ability, support, protect, and defend the constitution of the United States. So help me God!

"[Traduction.]

"Je, —— ——, jure solennellement, autant qu'il sera en moi, de soutenir, de maintenir, et de défendre la constitution des Etats-Unis. Que Dieu me soit en aide!

"The general is sure that no foreign subject can object to this oath, as it is in the very words of the oath taken by every officer of the European brigade, prescribed more than a year ago in 'Les règlements de la Légion Française, formée à la Nouvelle Orléans, le 26 d'Avril, 1861,' as will be seen by the extract below (page 22), and claimed as an act of the strictest neutrality by the officers taking it, and, for more than a year, has passed by all the foreign consuls—so far as he is informed—without protest.

"Serment que doivent prêter tous les officiers de la 'Légion Française.'

"STATE OF LOUISIANA, PARISH OF ORLEANS.

"I, —— ——, do solemnly swear that I will, to the best of ability, discharge the duties of —— —— of the French Legion, and that I will support, protect, and defend the constitution of the state and of the Confederate States. So help me God!

"Sworn to and subscribed before me.

"[Traduction.]

"ETAT DE LA LOUISIANE, PAROISSE D'ORLEANS.

"Je, —— ——, jure solennellement de remplir, autant qu'il sera en moi, les devoirs de —— —— de la Légion Française, et je promets de soutenir, de maintenir et de défendre la constitution de l'Etat et celle des Etats Confedérés. Que Dieu me soit en aide!

"Assermenté et signé devant moi."

I think this must be pronounced the neatest hit of the kind on record.

The oath-taking, meanwhile, went vigorously on. On the 7th of August, Colonel French had the pleasure of reporting that the oath prescribed to citizens had been taken by 11,723 persons; the foreign neutrals' oath, by 2,499 persons; and that 4,933 privates and 211 officers of the Confederate army had given the required parole.

This was the more gratifying from the fact, that the social influence of the city was all employed against the taking of the oath. Ladies refused to receive gentlemen who were known to have taken it. Gentlemen were notified to leave their boarding-houses who had thus avowed their attachment to the Union. Books were kept, by noted secessionists, in which the names of such were recorded for future vengeance. Men who were accused of having taken the oath thought it necessary, in some instances, to resent the charge as a calumny.* Others who had recently taken it,

* A perfectly well-informed officer related the following incidents:

"Holt's drinking-saloon was one of the most fashionable in the city. The proprietor, the son of the famous New York hotel-keeper of that name, kept fast horses, a fashionable private residence, and received his income by the hundred dollars a day. In an evil hour secession seized upon the land, and Holt was induced to issue shinplasters. His reputation for wealth and business profits made them popular, and inducements were held out for immense issues. Gradually, however, business fell off, and Holt, when General Butler ordered that personal paper money should be redeemed by bank-notes, found it impossible to comply with the proclamation, and this inability was increased by the fact that he had taken the oath of allegiance, and his regular customers refused, therefore, to be comforted at his house. The finale was that Holt was sold out, and his establishment, repainted and restocked, opened under the auspices of one John Hawkins. To give the place the due amount of *éclat*, Captain Clark, of the *Delta*, knowing that it was against the law for any one to sell liquor in the city, unless by a person who had taken the oath of allegiance and obtained a license, caused it to be published that at last our citizens were blessed with a 'Union drinking-saloon,' and at the same time invited all persons who loved the stars and stripes to patronize this new establishment.

"This flattering notice fell upon John Hawkins as a thunderbolt; he frantically rushed over to the newspaper office and protested that he was a rebel, and that he relied upon his secession friends for patronage; he declared that he was a ruined man unless something was done to immediately purge his fair fame of any taint of loyalty to his native land. Captain Clark, who fully appreciated the unfortunate publican's feelings, and with the spirit and liberality of a chivalrous editor, offered his columns for an explanation, which offer resulted in the publication of the following card:

"'HAWKINS HOUSE.

"'*To the Editor of the New Orleans Delta:*

"'The editorial statement in your journal of this morning, to the effect that I have taken the oath of allegiance, is a fabrication. JOHN HAWKINS.

"'NEW ORLEANS, *July* 17, 1862.'

"Secessia was delighted; John's friends crowded his precincts all day, and drank to John's health, *and at John's expense.* The dawn of the following morning promised a brilliant future; but, alas! Deputy provost-marshal Colonel Stafford, whose business it is to see that public drinking-house keepers *have* taken the oath of allegiance, sent after Mr. Hawkins, and asked him what right he had to keep a shop open without a license, and farther inquired if John did not boasted that they had done so only to secure the temporary advantages attached to the act, and avowed their readiness to take as many oaths as Picayune Butler thought it necessary to impose; as no faith was to be kept with Yankees. All these things were noted by General Butler, who "bided his time."

Another of the general's precautionary measures, was the disarming of New Orleans. The city was full of arms. Nearly every house, of any pretensions, contained some, and nearly every well-dressed man carried a weapon of some kind. At first, the general had no intention of depriving private persons of their arms, since he had assured the public, in his proclamation, that private property should be respected. Under the general order, commanding the disclosure and surrender of Confederate property, a considerable quantity of arms and munitions of war were seized; but the most virulent of the rebels were still allowed the inestimable privilege of carrying a pocketful of revolvers, and a bowie-knife parallel to the back bone. The event which led to the universal disarming of the city was this: In August, on the bloody field of Baton Rouge, were found dead and wounded *citizens* of Baton Rouge, wearing still their usual arms, who, on the very evening before the attack, had mingled familiarly with the officers of the Union army, and who, on the approach of Breckinridge, had hastened to join his troops, and to engage in the conflict. Lieutenant Weitzel reported this significant fact to General Butler, who immediately determined to compel the surrender of every private weapon in New Orleans. The requisite orders were issued; arms in great quantities were brought in and safely deposited; for all of which receipts were given.

The French consul objected, of course. His protest had only the effect of adding one more to General Butler's amusing consular letters.

THE FRENCH CONSUL TO LIEUTENANT WEITZEL.

"FRENCH CONSULATE AT NEW ORLEANS,
"NEW ORLEANS, *August* 12, 1862.

"SIR:—The new order of the day, which has been published this morning, and by which you require that all and whatever arms which may be

know that he could not get a license unless he took oath to be a good citizen under the national government. This interference on the part of General Butler and his subordinates with the unalienable rights of Secessia has, of course, thrown a new brand of discord into the community, and the fearful catastrophe seems impending, that will compel the habitués of the fashionable drinking-saloons to have the slow poison dealt out by loyal citizens."

in the possession of the people of this city, must be delivered up, has caused the most serious alarm among the French subjects of New Orleans.

"Foreigners, sir, and particularly Frenchmen, have, notwithstanding the accusations brought against some of them by certain persons, sacrificed everything to maintain, during the actual conflict, the neutrality imposed upon them.

"When arms were delivered them by the municipal authorities, they only used them to maintain order and defend personal property; and those arms have since been almost all returned.

"And it now appears, according to the tenor of your order of to-day, that French subjects, as well as citizens, are required to surrender their personal arms, which could only be used in self-defense.

"For some time past, unmistakable signs have manifested themselves among the servile population of the city and surrounding country, of their intention to break the bonds which bind them to their masters, and many persons apprehend an actual revolt.

"It is these signs, this prospect of finding ourselves completely unarmed, in the presence of a population from which the greatest excesses are feared, that we are above all things justly alarmed; for the result of such a state of things would fall on all alike who were left without the means of self-defense.

"It is not denied that the protection of the United States government would be extended to them in such an event, but that protection could not be effective at all times and in all places, nor provide against those internal enemies, whose unrestrained language and manners are constantly increasing, and who are but partially kept in subjection by the conviction that their masters are armed.

"I submit to you, sir, these observations, with the request that you take them into consideration.

"Please accept, sir, the assurance of my high esteem.

"The Consul of France,

"COUNT MEJAN.

"Lieutenant WEITZEL, *U. S. Engineers, and Assistant Military Commandant of New Orleans.*"

GENERAL BUTLER TO THE FRENCH CONSUL.

"HEAD-QUARTERS, DEPARTMENT OF THE GULF,

"NEW ORLEANS, *August* 14, 1862.

"SIR:—Your official note to Lieutenant Weitzel has been forwarded to me.

"I see no just cause of complaint against the order requiring the arms of private citizens to be given up. It is the usual course pursued in cities similarly situated to this, even without any exterior force in the neighborhood.

"You will observe that it will not do to trust to mere professions of neutrality. I trust most of your countrymen are in good faith *neutral;* but it is unfortunately true that some of them are not. This causes the good, of necessity, to suffer for the acts of the bad.

"I take leave to call your attention to the fact, that the United States forces gave every immunity to Monsieur Bonnegrass, who claimed to be the French consul at Baton Rouge; allowed him to keep his arms, and relied upon his neutrality; but his son was taken prisoner on the battle-field in arms against us.

"You will also do me the favor to remember that very few of the French subjects here have taken the oath of neutrality, which was offered to, but not required of them, by my Order No. 41, although all the officers of the French Legion had, with your knowledge and assent, taken the oath to support the constitution of the Confederate States. Thus you see I have no guarantee for the good faith of bad men.

"I do not understand how it is that arms are altered in their effectiveness by being 'personal property,' nor do I see how arms which will serve for personal defense ('qui ne peuvent servir que pour leur défense personnelle'), can not be as effectually used for offensive warfare.

"Of the disquiet of which you say there are signs manifesting themselves among the black population, from a desire to break their bonds, ('certaines dispositions à rompre les liens qui les attachent à leurs maîtres'), I have been a not inattentive observer, without wonder, because it would seem natural, when their masters had set them the example of rebellion against constituted authorities, that the negroes, being an imitative race, should do likewise.

"But surely the representative of the emperor, who does not tolerate slavery in France, does not desire his countrymen to be armed for the purpose of preventing the negroes from breaking their bonds.

"Let me assure you that the protection of the United States against violence, either by negroes or white men, whether citizens or foreign, will continue to be as perfect as it has been since our advent here; and far more so, manifesting itself at all moments and everywhere ('tous les instants et partout'), than any improvised citizens' organization can be.

"Whenever the inhabitants of this city will, by a public and united act, show both their loyalty and neutrality, I shall be glad of their aid to keep the peace, and indeed to restore the city to them. Till that time, however, I must require the arms of all the inhabitants, white and black, to be under my control. I have the honor to be, your obedient servant,

"BENJ. F. BUTLER, *Major-General Commanding.*

"To Count MEJAN, *French Consul.*"

To secure the surrender of arms still secreted, the following stringent general order was issued:

"New Orleans, *August* 16, 1862.

"*Ordered*, That after Tuesday, 19th inst., there be paid for information leading to the discovery of weapons not held under a written permit from the United States authorities, but retained and concealed by the keepers thereof, the sums following:

For each serviceable gun, musket or rifle	$ 10
" revolver	7
" pistol	5
" sabre or officer's sword	5
" dirk, dagger, bowie-knife or sword-cane	3

"Said arms to be confiscated, and the keeper so concealing them to be punished by imprisonment.

"The crime being an overt act of rebellion against the authority of the United States, whether by a citizen or an alien, works a forfeiture of the property of the offender, and, therefore, every slave giving information that shall discover the concealed arms of his or her master, shall be held to be emancipated.

"II. As the United States authorities have disarmed the inhabitants of the parish of Orleans, and as some fearful citizens seem to think it necessary that they should have arms to protect themselves from violence, *it is ordered*,

"That hereafter, the offenses of robbery by violence or aggravated assault that ought to be replied by the use of deadly weapons, burglaries, rapes and murders, whether committed by blacks or whites, will be, on conviction, punished by death."

Union men, known and tried, were permitted to keep their arms. To one or two old soldiers of the war of 1812, the privilege was accorded of retaining the weapons once honorably borne in the service of their country. Many weapons were, doubtless, still secreted; but, for all purposes of co-operation with an attacking force, New Orleans was disarmed. The whole number of surrendered weapons was about six thousand.

CHAPTER XXIV.

THE CONFISCATION ACT.

THE act of Congress confiscating the property of rebellious citizens was approved July 17th.

Before the passage of the act, General Butler had taken the liberty to "sequester" the estates of those two notorious traitors, General Twiggs and John Slidell, both of whom possessed large property in New Orleans. These estates he held for the adjudication of the government, and, in the mean time, selected the spacious mansion of General Twiggs for his own residence and that of a portion of his staff. Among the papers found in this house were certain letters which tended to show that Twiggs had sought the command in Texas with a view to the betrayal of his trust, a crime only once paralleled in the history of the country. Twiggs fled from New Orleans on the approach of the fleet, conscious that such turpitude as his could not fail to meet its just retribution. He died soon after, but not before he had heard that the flag of his betrayed country floated over his residence as the head-quarters of the army of occupation.

Three swords, presented to him for his gallantry in Mexico, one by Congress, one by the state of Georgia, his native state, one by Augusta, his native city, were left behind in the custody of a young lady, and fell into the hands of General Butler. The young lady claimed them as her own. She said that General Twiggs had given them to her on new-year's day, with a box of family silver, alleging as a reason for this strange gift the recent death of a beloved niece to whom he had previously bequeathed them. Three facts were elicited which induced the general to set aside her claim. One was, that Twiggs had brought the articles to the young lady's residence, not on new-year's day, but at the moment of his flight from the city. Another was, that she had never mentioned so extraordinary a present to any member of her family—as appeared on the separate examination of each. Another was, that General Twiggs had left with the articles the document following: "I

20*

leave my swords to Miss Rowena Florence, and box of silver. New Orleans, April 25, 1862. D. E. TWIGGS:" which was hastily written in the carriage at the door.

General Butler ventured to disbelieve Miss Rowena Florence, and sent the swords to the president of the United States. He suggested that the one presented by congress should be given to some officer distinguished in the war; that the one given by the state of Georgia, should be deposited at the military academy at West Point, with a suitable inscription, as a warning to the cadets; and that the third should be placed in the patent office as a memento of the folly of such an "invention" as secession. In forwarding the swords to congress, the president remarked, that if either of them were presented to an officer of the army, "General Butler is entitled to the first consideration."

The sword voted by Kentucky to General Zachary Taylor, was rescued by General Butler from disloyal hands in New Orleans. He sent it to the son of the late president—Brigadier-General Joseph Taylor of the Union army.

The confiscation act, it will be remembered, divided rebels into two classes. The property of one class was to be confiscated at once, or as soon as it fell into the possession of the United States; the property of the other class was to be confiscated after sixty days' warning. The first class consisted of all military and naval officers commanding rebels in arms; the president, vice president, judges, members of congress, cabinet ministers, foreign emissaries, and other agents of the Confederate States; the governors and judges of seceded states; in short, all who hold office under the Confederate government, or under the government of a seceded state, as well as citizens of loyal states who gave aid and comfort to the rebellion. The second class included the great mass of the privates in the Confederate army and navy, and all unofficial abettors of the rebellion. The property of these last was to be declared confiscated sixty days after the date of the president's proclamation warning them to lay down their arms and return to their allegiance. As this proclamation was issued on the 25th of July, the days of grace expired on the 23d of September.

With this explanation, the reader will understand the object of the following general order, and will be able to imagine its effect upon the secessionists of New Orleans:

"NEW ORLEANS, *Sept.* 13, 1862.

"As in the course of ten days it may become necessary to distinguish the disloyal from the loyal citizens and honest neutral foreigners residing in this department:

"*It is ordered*, That each neutral foreigner, resident in this department, shall present himself, with the evidence of his nationality, to the nearest provost-marshal for registration of himself and his family.

"This registration shall include the following particulars:

"The country of birth.

"The length of time the person has resided within the United States.

"The names of his family.

"The present place of residence, by street, number or other description.

"The occupation.

"The date of protection or certificate of nationality, which shall be indorsed by the passport-clerk, 'registered,' with date of register.

"All false or simulated claims of foreign allegiance, by native or naturalized citizens, will be severely punished."

This premonition of coming retribution called attention anew to the clause of the confiscation act which declared all conveyances of property made after the expiration of the sixty days to be void. Instantly there began such a universal transferring of property as no city had ever before seen. Property was given away; property was sold for next to nothing; all the known expedients for getting rid of property were employed; until it seemed probable that by the 23d of September, not a rebel in New Orleans would be found to possess anything whatever, and the entire wealth of the city would be held by that portion of the people who had taken the oath of allegiance, or by parties at a great distance, and inaccessible, or by minors and women. General Butler determined to use his autocratic authority to put a stop to these fictitious transfers. The following general order accomplished this purpose.

"NEW ORLEANS, *Sept.* 1862.

"I. All transfers of property, or rights of property, real, mixed, personal or incorporeal, except necessary food, medicine and clothing, either by way of sale, gift, pledge, payment, lease or loan, by an inhabitant of this department, who has not returned to his or her allegiance to the United States (having once been a citizen thereof), are forbidden and void, and the person transferring and the person receiving shall be punished by fine or imprisonment, or both.

"II. All registers of the transfer of certificates of stock or shares in any incorporated or joint-stock company or association, in which any inhabitant of this department, who has not returned to his or her allegiance to the United States (having once been a citizen thereof), has any interest, are forbidden, and the clerk or other officer making or recording the transfer will be held equally guilty with the transferrer."

And more. Some wise men of New Orleans, foreseeing the evil, had long ago reduced themselves to fictitious beggary. The decisions of Mr. Reverdy Johnson, sustained by the government, had given rise to the impression that papers made out in the forms of law, would be permitted to nullify an act of Congress, as well as set at naught the decrees of General Butler. Many men of wealth had acted upon this impression, "making over" valuable estates to others, for considerations that were ridiculously small. General Butler seized and "sequestered" some property thus transferred, holding it for the government to decide upon the legality of such proceedings. One noted case of this kind he selected as a test, and submitted it to the secretary of state. The dispatch in which the particulars were detailed, shall be presented here, for the light it throws upon the state of things in New Orleans and the peculiar difficulties of General Butler's position. It is fair to *guess* that this dispatch had something to do with General Butler's recall from the Department of the Gulf,—a measure which was not suggested by the president.

GENERAL BUTLER TO MR. SEWARD.

"HEAD-QUARTERS, DEPARTMENT OF THE GULF,
"NEW ORLEANS, *September* 19, 1862.

"Hon. WILLIAM H. SEWARD, Secretary of State:

"SIR:—I have the honor to report to you the following facts:

"C. McDonald Fago, a British subject, resident many years in New Orleans, is about to make claim to the property of Wright & Allen in New Orleans, which has been taken possession of by the United States authorities here under the following state of facts:

"Wright & Allen are cotton-brokers, who claim to have property outside of New Orleans of two millions of dollars. They are most rabid rebels, and were of those who published a card advising the planters not to send forward their crop of cotton for the purpose of inducing foreign intervention.

"Soon after we came to New Orleans, they mortgaged their real estate here, consisting of a house, for $60,000, to planters in the state of Arkansas, and then sold the equity, together with their furniture, for $5,000 to Mr. Fago; paying about four thousand five hundred dollars per annum interest on the property, and to receive nothing. His only payment, however, was by his own note in twelve months, which was sent to their friend, the planter in Arkansas.

"Wright & Allen were then openly boasting that they would not take the oath of allegiance to the United States, and were encouraging others to refuse and stand by secession. In order to divest themselves of the last vestige of visible property upon which the confiscation act could take effect, having given to the widow of their deceased partner, an Irish woman, a note or notes for three thousand five hundred dollars, they then sell her their plate for that amount, and then have it shipped under another name to Liverpool.

"A large number of others are following their example; and, indeed, all the property of New Orleans is changing hands into those of foreigners and women, to avoid the consequences of the confiscation act.

"Believing all this to be deplorable, I have resolved to make this a test case, and have seized this property, and intend to hold it where it is until the matter can be submitted to the courts.

"Mr. Fago has sent to Washington to have this property given up as a test case. If the course of authority here is interfered with in this case, it will be next to impossible to maintain order in this city. This Mr. Fago has first had a large amount of sugar, belonging to an aid of Governor Moore, given up to him by the decision of Reverdy Johnson. Emboldened by this experiment he proposes to try once more. If successful, I should prefer that the government would get some one else to hold New Orleans instead of myself. Indeed, sir, I beg leave to add, that another such commissioner as Mr. Johnson sent to New Orleans would render the city untenable. The town itself got into such a state while Mr. Johnson was here, that he confessed to me that he could hardly sleep from nervousness from fear of a rising, and hurried away, hardly completing his work, as soon as he heard Baton Rouge was about to be attacked.

"The result of his mission here has caused it to be understood that I am not supported by the government; that I am soon to be relieved; that all my acts are to be overhauled, and that a rebel may do anything he pleases in the city, as the worst may be a few days' imprisonment, when my successor will come and he will be released.

"To such an extent has this thing gone, that inmates of the parish prison, sent there for grand larceny, robbery, &c., in humble imitation of the foreign consuls, have agreed together to send an agent to Washington to ask for a commissioner to investigate charges made by these thieves against the provost-marshal, by whose vigilance they were detected.

"Alexander the coppersmith, by his cry, 'Great is Diana of the Ephesians' ('the institution of slavery is in danger'), did me much harm in Louisiana, from the effects of which I am just recovering; and the only fear I now have is, that if the last accounts are true, Mr. Johnson will have so much more nervous apprehension for his personal safety in Baltimore than he had in New Orleans, that he will want to come back here, now the yellow fever season is over, as to a place of security.*

"I have done myself the honor to make this detail of the case at length to the state department, so that all the facts are before it upon which I act. The inferences from those facts must, from the nature of testimony, be left to my judgment until the courts can act authoritatively in the matter.

"Another reason why I have detailed the facts is, that in the reports of Mr. Johnson furnished to the consuls to be read here, every fact is repressed which would form a shadow of justification for my acts, and ex parte affidavits of parties accused by me of fraudulent transfers of large amounts of property are the sole basis of the report.

"True, by that report more than three-quarters of a million of specie is placed in the hands of one Forstall, a rebel, a leading member of the 'Southern Independent Association,' a league wherein each member bound himself by a horrid and impious oath 'to resist unto death itself all attempts to restore the Union.' A confrere of Pierre Soulé in the committee of the city which destroyed more than ten millions of property by fire, to prevent its coming into the hands of the United States authorities, when the fleet passed the forts.

"I beg of you, sir, to consider that I mention the characteristics of this report not in any tone of complaint of the state department. If it is necessary to suppress facts, to impugn the motives and disown the acts of a commanding officer of the army in the field, or to publish to those plotting the destruction of the republic, that he has had control of public affairs in New Orleans taken from him and transferred to a subordinate, because of the harshness of his administration, as was done in the dispatch to the minister of the Netherlands, even if the fact is not true, I bow to the mandate of 'state necessity' without a murmur. I have made larger sacrifices than this for my country, and am prepared for still greater, if need be, but I only wish to make them when they will be useful, and therefore have painted the effect of the commission, report, and dispatch upon a turbulent, rebellious, uneasy, excitable, vindictive, brutalized, half foreign population, maddened by exaggerated reports of the actions of their fellows, the fall of the national capital, the invasion of the North, and excited to insubordination by the double hope, that either by the success of the arms of their brethren, or the interference of the national executive in their behalf, they shall soon be released from the only government which has ever held the city in quiet order, or unplundering peace. Awaiting instructions,

"I have the honor to be your obedient servant,

"BENJAMIN F. BUTLER, *Major-General Commanding.*"

* The rebel army was then in Maryland.

This letter clearly marks the point of divergence between the two modes of dealing with the rebellion. As the reports of Mr. Johnston and the correspondence of Mr. Seward with Mr. Van Limburgh have been published, it is but fair that this dispatch should be also printed. Whether the confiscation act was a politic or an impolitic measure is a question upon which honest and patriotic men may differ—do differ. But the act having been passed and approved, there can be no doubt that the duty of commanding generals was to give it *real* effect—not allow the government to be defrauded by the hasty manufacture of fictitious legal papers.

General Butler continued his preparations for enforcing the confiscation act. The day after the expiration of the sixty days' grace, the following general order was issued:

"NEW ORLEANS, *September* 24, 1862.

"All persons, male or female, within this department, of the age of eighteen years and upward, who have ever been citizens of the United States, and have not renewed their allegiance before this date to the United States, or who now hold or pretend any allegiance or sympathy with the so-called Confederate States, are ordered to report themselves, on or before the first day of October next, to the nearest provost-marshal, with a descriptive list of all their property and rights of property, both real, personal and mixed, made out and signed by themselves respectively, with the same particularity as for taxation. They shall also report their place of residence by number, street, or other proper description, and their occupation, which registry shall be signed by themselves, and each shall receive a certificate from the marshal of registration as claiming to be an enemy of the United States.

"Any persons, of those described in this order, neglecting so to register themselves, shall be subject to fine, or imprisonment at hard labor, or both, and all his or her property confiscated, by order, as punishment for such neglect.

"On the first day of October next, every householder shall return to the provost-marshal nearest him, a list of each inmate in his or her house, of the age of eighteen years or upward, which list shall contain the following particulars: The name, sex, age and occupation of each inmate, whether a registered alien, one who has taken the oath of allegiance to the United States, a registered enemy of the United States, or one who has neglected to register himself or herself, either as an alien, a loyal citizen, or a registered enemy. All householders neglecting to make such returns, or making a false return, shall be punished by fine, or imprisonment with hard labor, or both.

"Each policeman will, within his beat, be held responsible that every householder failing to make such return, within three days from the first of October, is reported to the provost-marshal; and five dollars for such neglect, for every day in which it is not reported, will be deducted from such policeman's pay, and he shall be dismissed. And a like sum for conviction of any householder not making his or her return shall be paid to the policeman reporting such householder.

"Every person who shall, in good faith, renew his or her allegiance to the United States previous to the first day of October next, and shall remain truly loyal, will be recommended to the president for pardon of his or her previous offenses."

This order led to a *run* on the oath offices. It was "understood" among the secessionists that an oath given to Yankees for the purpose of retaining property was a mere form of words not binding upon the consciences of the chivalric sons of the South. A very large number of persons, it is thought, acted upon this opinion; for while the offices appointed for receiving the oaths were thronged and surrounded by eager multitudes of oath-takers, the number of "registered enemies" was less than four thousand. "People," said the *Delta*, "who take the oath of allegiance, and afterward say, with a sneer, 'it did not go farther than there' (pointing to their throat), should bear in mind that if it is *kept* in that position, and they conduct themselves accordingly, there is great danger of its *choking* them some fine morning."

Before General Butler left the department, sixty thousand of its inhabitants had taken the oath of allegiance to the government of the United States.

The rebel General Jeff. Thompson, who was in command near the Union lines, contrived to get in a word on this subject:

"PONCHATOULA, LA., *September* 28th,
"Sunday, 8 o'clock A. M.

"Major-General B. F. BUTLER, U. S. A., New Orleans, La.:

"[Per Underground Telegraph.]

"GENERAL:—We thank you for General Order No. 76. It will answer us for a precedent at New Orleans, St. Louis, Louisville, Baltimore, Washington, each of which we will have in a few days. We were undetermined how to act. Please 'pile it on.'

"Yours respectfully, JEFFERSON THOMPSON,
"*Brigadier-General S. C., commanding Southern Line.*"

If the general could regard this epistle as a joke, there were other correspondents whose communications caused him real distress. The venerable and benevolent Dr. Mercer, for example, a gentleman for whom General Butler, in common with the whole army, entertained the most sincere respect, addressed him upon the subject of General Order No. 76.

"You have probably inferred, from our various conversations, that I have not taken an oath of allegiance to the Confederate States, nor have been a member of any society or public body in New Orleans, or elsewhere in the confederacy; and that since your arrival here, I have maintained a strict neutrality. In pursuance of your Order No. 76, I will make a faithful return, substantially, if not minutely accurate, of all my property here, except about $3,000, the greater part of which is in gold, that I have reserved for an emergency. I mention this to you now to avoid misapprehension. Your order referred to exempts only those who have taken the oath of allegiance; but I can not think you intend to include those in my situation as claiming to be 'enemies of the United States.' Such an interpretation is, in my opinion, at variance with the act of congress, as well as with the proclamation of President Lincoln."

General Butler replied:

"In my judgment, there can be no such thing as neutrality by a citizen of the United States in this contest for the life of the government. As an officer, I can not recognize such neutrality. 'He that is not for us is against us.'

"All good citizens are called upon to lend their influence to the United States; all that do not do so, are the enemies of the United States; the line is to be distinctly and broadly drawn. Every citizen must find himself on one side or the other of that line, and can claim no other position than that of a friend or an enemy of the United States.

"While I am sorry to be obliged to differ from you in your construction of the act of congress and the proclamation of the president, I cannot permit any reservation of property from the list, or exemption of persons from the requirement of Order No. 76. It may be, and, I trust, is quite true, that by no act of yours have you rendered yourself liable to the confiscation of your property under the act and proclamation; but that is for the military or other courts (to decide). You, however, will advise yourself, with your usual care and caution, what may be the effect, now that you are solemnly called upon to declare yourself in favor of the government, of contumaciously refusing to renew your allegiance to it, thereby inducing, from your example, others of your fellow-citizens to remain in the same opposition. I am glad to acknowledge your long and upright life as a man, your former services as an officer of the government, and the high respect I entertain for your personal character and moral worth; but I am dealing with your duty as a citizen of the United States. All these noble qualities, as well as your high social condition, render your example all the more influential and pernicious; and, I grieve to add, in my opinion, more dangerous to the interests of the United States than if, a younger man, you had shouldered your musket and marched to the field in the army of rebellion."

Dr. Mercer was, therefore, compelled to choose a position on one side or the other of the "broad line." He did not take the oath of allegiance, but preferred to enroll himself among the registered enemies of his country. After the departure of General Butler, he escaped to New York, where he has since resided.

General Butler proceeded in the work recommended by Jeff. Thompson, of "piling it on," taking the material from the "piles" of the friends and comrades of that humorous officer. Another of his raking general orders appeared in October, which sensibly reduced the income of many conspicuous abettors of the rebellion.

"New Orleans, *October* 17, 1862.

"All persons holding powers of attorney or letters of authorization from, or who are merely acting for, or tenants of, or intrusted with any moneys, goods, wares, property or merchandise, real, personal or mixed, of any person now in the service of the so-called Confederate States, or any person not known by such agent, tenant or trustee to be a loyal citizen of the United States, or a *bona fide* neutral subject of a foreign government, will retain in their own hand, until farther orders, all such moneys, goods, wares, merchandise and property, and make an accurate return of the same to David C. G. Field, Esq., the financial clerk of this department, upon oath, on or before the first day of November next. Every such agent, tenant or trustee failing to make true return, or shall pay over or deliver any such moneys, goods, wares, merchandise and property to, or for the use, directly or indirectly, of any person not known by him to be a loyal citizen of the United States, without an order from these head-quarters, will be held personally responsible for the amount so neglected to be returned, paid over or delivered. All rents due or to become due by tenants of property belonging to persons not known to be loyal citizens of the United States, will be paid as they become due, to D. C. G. Field, Esq., financial clerk of the department."

To complete the reader's knowledge of this subject, it is only necessary to add that, early in December, all registered enemies who desired to leave New Orleans, not to return, were permitted to do so. Several hundreds availed themselves of this permission, much to the relief of the party for the Union.

It was these stern and rigorously executed measures which completed the subjugation of the secessionists of New Orleans, and deprived them of all power to co-operate with treason beyond the Union lines. It was these measures which alone could have prepared the way for the sincere return of Louisiana to the Union, the first requisite to which was the suppression of the small party which had traitorously taken the state out of the Union. To complete the regeneration of the state, it was necessary to foster the self-respect, protect the interests, maintain the rights, and raise in the scale of civilization that vast majority of the people of Louisiana, white and black, bond and free, whose interests and the interests of the United States are identical. This great and difficult work General Butler was permitted only to begin. The backwoodsman was called from his fields when the forests had been cleared, the swamps drained, the noxious creatures driven away, and all the rough, wild work done. There would have been a harvest in the following year, if the same energetic and fertile mind had continued to wield the resources of the land.

CHAPTER XXV.

MORE OF THE IRON HAND.

Certain of the Episcopal clergy of New Orleans felt the rigor of General Butler's rule. The clergy of New Orleans were secessionists, of course. Any Christian minister capable of voluntarily living in the South during the last twenty years, or any one who was permitted to live there, must have been a person prepared to forsake all and follow slavery. This was the condition of their exercising the clerical office in the cotton kingdom, and when the time came they complied with that condition.

One " eminent divine" of New Orleans, it is said, was heard to remark, that strong as was his belief in special providential dispensations, that faith would receive a severe, perhaps a fatal shock, if the yellow fever did not become epidemic in New Orleans that summer.

When the confiscation act was about to be enforced, General Butler had a controversy with Dr. Leacock, the Episcopal clergyman who promised to read the burial service over Lieutenant De Kay, and broke his promise. This gentleman was of English birth, but had long resided in New Orleans, and, I believe, had become a citizen of the United States; at least, he expressly disclaimed the protection of British law. Dr. Leacock, it appears, now desired exemption from the decrees which tended to separate the friends from the enemies of the Union, and which denied all favor and privileges to those who openly adhered to the Confederate cause. He claimed to be a friend of the Union—in fact, a Union man. Still, he was not prepared to take the oath of allegiance. Now, this man, in November, 1860, had preached a sermon in favor of secession, which so exactly chimed in with the feelings of the secessionists, that four editions of it were printed and sold, to the number of 30,000 copies. The sermon was the usual silly tirade against "the abolitionists," "the savage fanatics of the North," the deadly enemies of a noble southern chivalry. It contained, also, the regulation paragraphs upon John Brown and his "band of assassins," and the "infidel preachers" who had "stimulated" them to fall upon a poor, innocent, unsuspecting, persecuted, patient, long-suffering southern people. The concluding paragraph of this sermon was the following:

"Now, in justice to myself, I must be permitted to make a remark before I close. But a few weeks ago I counseled you, from this place, to avoid all precipitate action; but at the same time to take determined action—such action only as you thought you could take with the conscious support of reason and religion. I give that counsel still. But I am one of you. I feel as a southerner. Southern honor is my honor—southern degradation is my degradation. Let no man mistake my meaning or call my words idle. As a southerner, then, I will speak, and I give it as my firm and unhesitating belief, that nothing is now left us but secession. I do not like the word, but it is the only one to express my meaning. We do not secede—our enemies have seceded. We are on the constitution—our enemies are not on the constitution; and our language should be, if you will not go with us, we will not go with you. You may form for yourselves a constitution; but we will administer among ourselves the constitution which our fathers have left us. This should be our language and solemn determination. Such action our honor demands; such action will save the Union, if anything can. We have yet friends left us in the North, but they can not act for us till we have acted for ourselves; and it would be as pusillanimous in us to desert our friends as to cower before our enemies. To advance, is to secure our rights; to recede, is to lay our fortunes, our honor, our liberty, under the feet of our enemies. I know that the consequences of such a course, unless guided by discretion, are perilous. But, peril our fortunes, peril our lives, come what will, let us never peril our liberty and our honor. I am willing, at the call of my honor and my liberty, to die a freeman; but I'll never, no, never, live a slave; and the alternative now presented by our enemies is secession or slavery. Let it be liberty or death!"

General Butler ventured to adduce this sermon as evidence of its author's enmity to the Union. Dr. Leacock's reply revealed an astounding moral obliquity.

DR. LEACOCK TO GENERAL BUTLER.

"*September* 26, 1862.

"Major-General BUTLER:

"SIR:—I have not the sermon in manuscript to which, in your note of yesterday, you refer. It was taken down during its delivery by a reporter unknown to me, but, being called away from the church before it was concluded, he requested the manuscript, that he might not, as he said, give a wrong report of my views. It was given, but never returned. I send, however, a printed copy of it with this remark: that the last section, which I have circumscribed in pencil, was not delivered from the pulpit, as my whole congregation can testify; and that the publisher was immediately required by me, in the presence of several gentlemen, to state this fact, that it might be omitted in any future publication.

"There is no man that desires more heartily than myself the restoration of this Union, as it was before the present controversy arose. In evidence of this fact, I send you another sermon, which was delivered a few weeks after the one in print; and as you will find great difficulty in reading it, I will transcribe the closing paragraph, to which I desire to refer you, as expressive of what I felt then, and of what I feel now.

"'The destruction of our Union! Oh, there is not a spot on the civilized globe that would not lament the destruction of our Union. The wail with which the fathers in Egypt pierced the air on the death of their first-born, is ready to burst forth from our bosoms if this dire event should happen. I speak for myself. There are those among us who may be indifferent to it. But the nations around us will consider it a world-wide misfortune. The discontented and aspiring, the exile and the adventurer, all seek its borders, and are at once elevated in the scale of being—enjoying a freer air, a fresher nature. It is the land of the aspirations and dreams of the poor and oppressed of other countries. Even tyrants who hate it, would not see it fall, because they know not how soon they may have to fly to it for refuge. Let the fanatics of the North consider this, and know that they owe it to the world, as well as to the South, to heal the wounds they have inflicted, and restore harmony and happiness to our country.

"'The Union, the Union destroyed! Our hearts can scarcely bear the thought, much more the weight of such a visitation. Yet where is the man to arrest its downward progress? North, south, east, west, where is the man? There is none to answer; there is none to be found. Then, Lord, we come to Thee. Save us, we perish! Say to the troubled spirits of men, be still, that there may be a calm—a calm for deliberate, just, devout consideration to heal the wounds that have been inflicted, and to restore peace and brotherly love to our Union, the Union which has been bequeathed us, the Union of equal rights and equal protection. O Lord, save this Union!'

"These are still my feelings—I have never held any other—I have never avowed any other. And I mention this with the *alone intention* that I should not be misunderstood. I desire to be known as I am. My position demands that I should speak what I believe to be the truth. I have done this, and I leave all consequences with God. Please return me the manuscript.

"I am, sir, respectfully,

"W. T. Leacock."

General Butler, not desiring farther correspondence with this reverend person, caused Captain Puffer to ask him whether he had published any recantation or disavowal of the secession paragraph of his sermon, or whether any one else had done so for him. He replied: "I do not know. I only know that I requested the reporter, both in person and by letter, to omit the last paragraph, because I did not give utterance to it." It thus appeared that this Union man had stood by and seen tens of thousands of copies of a sermon advising the dismemberment of the Union, and had enjoyed the popularity attached to the utterance of such advice, without deeming it worth while to inform the public that the passage had never been delivered, and did not express his mature opinion. Those who can believe in such Unionism may also be able to believe that the sermon quoted in the doctor's letter was delivered *after* the published one, which *every man in his congregation must have read.*

On the day upon which he had replied to Captain Puffer's question, he sought to re-open a correspondence directly with General Butler. Something was in the mind of this tender-conscienced priest. He now became the accuser of General Butler, and warned him of the error of his ways.

DR. LEACOCK TO GENERAL BUTLER.

"*September* 29, 1862.

"Major-General BUTLER, &c., &c., &c.:

"MY DEAR SIR:—I desire to speak affectionately, but candidly, to you, and I beseech you to hear me patiently.

"General Butler, 'You are eating up God's people, as it were bread.' You have possessed them with such fear, that they are rushing, innocent and weak women, most unwarrantably, guiltless and timid men, most ingloriously, are rushing to their destruction, through fear of being deprived of their substance or of their personal liberty.

"You are playing a dangerous game with public morals—you are committing desperate havoc with the consciences of God's people. Thousands have perjured themselves—thousands are rushing to perjure themselves in the sight of Almighty God, by bringing themselves under oath to do what they intend not to do, what they will not do, and what you know they neither intend to do nor will do. All this you have seen, and yet you have not raised your voice to check the ruinous deception practiced on the community by your organ, the *Delta.*

"The law under which you act does not call for this universal wickedness; but if it did, you should not, as a man professing Christianity, obey it, because obedience to human law ceases where transgression to the Divine law is involved; and who will not say the Divine law is not transgressed, is not openly defied, and that by you, when God is set at naught by numbers only to avoid the terrors of your will. I say your will, not the will of the law, for the law is more merciful than you; it exacts of armed offenders only what you exact indiscriminately of all. You elevate your will above the law for people to bow down and obey; and in their obedience they deny God, and rush into the arms of Satan—and whose is the sin?

"My dear General Butler, I beseech you in God's name to pause and consider your course. I know you desire to serve your country; but in your efforts to serve your country you must not forget that you are a man, and, therefore, should deal mercifully with your fellow-man, as you would have God to deal mercifully with you; we are nowhere commanded to love our country, but we are everywhere commanded to love our fellow-men; and, therefore, in dealing with our fellow-men in connection with our country, you should not deal with such undue severity, nor place him in a condition to risk his salvation for the glorification of saying, or of hearing it said, that you have done good to your country—and where is the good? not one in ten, that has taken the oath, are you willing to trust.

"It is with pain and grief that I say all this; but I must be true to my God, and my conscience; when I see my people rushing thus headlong to destruction, I must speak; though all hell stared me in the face, I must speak—silence is my destruction; for hear the word of the Lord—'Son of man, I have made thee a watchman over the house of Israel; therefore hear the word at my mouth, and give them warning from me. When I say unto the wicked, Thou shalt surely die, and thou givest him not warning, nor speakest to warn the wicked from his wicked way to save his life, the same wicked man shall die in his iniquity; but his blood will I require at thine hand.'

"General Butler—God has given you great talents—few are blessed with such—and my prayer to God is, that you may use those talents to his glory; but to do this, you must take a very different course to that which you are now pursuing. I pray you, pardon the liberty I have taken; but I have great sympathy for you, and I can not restrain this evidence of my love for your soul.

"May God give you grace to see your error, and to sustain you in the proper discharge of your arduous and manifold duties.

"I am, my dear sir, with great sincerity, your obedient servant,

"W. T. LEACOCK."

No answer, I believe, was made to this communication. A few days after, an event occurred which brought General Butler into such direct collision with the Episcopal clergy, that New Orleans was not considered by the general large enough to contain both parties in the controversy.

On a Sunday morning, early in October, Major Strong entered the office of the general in plain clothes, and said:

"I havn't been able to go to church since we came to New Orleans. This morning I am going."

He crossed the street, and took a front seat in the Episcopal church of Dr. Goodrich, opposite the mansion of General Twiggs. He joined in the exercises with the earnestness which was natural to his devout mind, until the clergyman reached that part of the service where the prayer for the president of the United States occurs. That prayer was omitted, and the minister invited the congregation to spend a few moments in silent prayer. The young officer had not previously heard of this mode of evading, at once, the requirements of the church, and the orders of the commanding general. He rose in his place and said:

"Stop, sir. It is my duty to bring these exercises to a close. I came here for the purpose, and the sole purpose, of worshiping God; but inasmuch as your minister has seen fit to omit invoking a blessing, as our church service requires, upon the president of the United States, I propose to close the services. This house will be shut within ten minutes."

The clergyman, astounded, began to remonstrate.

"This is no time for discussion, sir," said the major.

The minister was speechless and indignant. The ladies flashed wrath upon the officer, who stood motionless with folded arms. The men scowled at him. The minister soon pronounced the benediction, the congregation dispersed, and Major Strong retired to report the circumstances at head-quarters.

This brought the matter to a crisis. General Butler sent for the Episcopal clergymen, Dr. Leacock, Dr. Goodrich, Dr. Fulton, and others, who were all accustomed to omit the prayer for the president, and pray in silence for the triumph of treason. The general patiently and courteously argued the point with them at great length, quoting Bible, rubrics and history with his wonted fluency. They replied that, in omitting the prayer, they were only obeying the orders of the Right Reverend Major-General Polk, their ecclesiastical superior. The general denied the authority of that military prelate to change the liturgy, and contended that the omission of the prayer, in the peculiar circumstances of the time and place, was an overt act of treason. Obedience to the powers that *be*, he said, was the peculiar aim and boast of the Episcopal church; and no one could doubt that the dominant power in New Orleans was the president of the United States. And even granting that the president was a usurper, that would be only one reason more for praying for him. The Union forces had not come to New Orleans for a temporary purpose; they meant to stay. There was no power on the continent or off the continent that could expel them. This praying for Davis must stop at some time; why not now? Besides, the clergy of the Episcopal church had taken upon themselves the most solemn vows to obey the canons and rubrics of the church, and their omission of part of the liturgy was of the nature of perjury.

"But, General," said Dr. Leacock, "your insisting upon the taking of the oath of allegiance is causing half of my church-members to perjure themselves."

"Well," replied the general, "if that is the result of your nine years' preaching; if your people will commit perjury so freely, the sooner you leave your pulpit the better."

After further conversation, Dr. Leacock asked:

"Well, General, are you going to shut up the churches?"

"No, sir, I am more likely to shut up the ministers."

The clergymen showing no disposition to yield, General Butler ended the interview by stating his ultimatum: "Read the prayer for the president, omit the silent act of devotion, or leave New Orleans prisoners of state for Fort Lafayette."

After consultation with one another and with their people, after endless vacillation on the part of Dr. Leacock, three of the clergymen, Dr. Leacock, Dr. Goodrich and Mr. Fulton, decided *not* to read the prayer for the president. Captain Puffer was detailed to conduct them to New York, and they sailed in the next transport. On the voyage, Captain Puffer informs me, Dr. Goodrich, a benevolent, venerable man, read prayers to the returning troops, and did not omit the prayer for the president. He ministered to the sick and dying, and won the sincere regard of all on board. Three weeks after their arrival, all the state prisoners were released, and they returned to New Orleans. General Banks demanded the oath of allegiance as a condition of their landing. They declined the condition, and returned to New York.

General Strong chanced to meet Dr. Goodrich, one day, at the St. Nicholas Hotel. They looked at each other for a moment in some embarrassment, neither knowing what were the feelings of the other. A smile overspread the benevolent countenance of the doctor. General Strong offered his hand, which Dr. Goodrich accepted, and the two men laughed heartily at the odd encounter.

"You did that well," said the clergyman, "since you had made up your mind to do it; but why didn't you come to me privately and give me notice?"

General Strong explained the circumstances, and they continued to converse amicably.

On the Sunday after the departure of the clergymen from New Orleans, their churches were open as usual, but the exercises were conducted by chaplains of the Union army, who read the service without abridgment. Not many of the auditors were of the secessionist persuasion. Church going, however, became a more frequent practice among officers and men after this purging of the pulpits, and, consequently, the places of the absent members were not all vacant.

The pass-office at head-quarters presented the most distressing illustrations of the iron-handed rule to which Louisiana was necessarily subjected. Within the Union lines there was comparative plenty; beyond them there was desolation and want. Food, clothing and medicines were to be had in New Orleans by all who could pay for them; and to such as could not they were given. Across the lakes, and above the camp of General Phelps, at Carrollton, and in the region lying on the western side of the river, food was scarce in the extreme, clothing was scarcer, and the stock of medicines had long been exhausted. There were parents in the city who had starving children or sick children in the enemy's country, only a few miles distant. There were people in New Orleans whose aged parents, just beyond the lines, were suffering for the necessaries of life. There were others whose near relations, people of substance and respectability, were going half naked, or were dying for want of medicines. On the other hand, there were hundreds of secessionists in the city, whose constant aim, whose sole employment was, to devise means of smuggling supplies across the lines to the camps of rebel soldiery.

The pressure, therefore, upon the commanding general for passes to go beyond the Union lines, was great and continuous. There were a hundred applications a day. Women came to head-quarters imploring permission to take a little clothing, medicine and food to their perishing children, calling all the saints to witness the truth of their story and the honesty of their intentions. A large majority of the applicants were women, who assailed the tender hearts of the general and his staff with tears, entreaties and protestations.

During the first weeks, General Butler himself heard the applicants, and decided upon their claims. But as this business involved a great deal of questioning, cross-questioning and examination of papers, he was compelled, at length, to establish a member of his staff in an outer office at head-quarters, whose duty it was to sift from the mass of suitors the few whose story seemed credible and to warrant the indulgence of a pass. These were reported to the general, who then decided upon their application. Captain A. F. Puffer, of Boston, was the officer selected for this duty. When he left the city to conduct the three clergymen northward, his place was filled by Lieutenant Frederick Martin, of New York. These young officers held a post which severely taxed their patience, their firmness and their sagacity. I might add their integrity, also, if the integrity of an honorable soldier could ever be severely tried. "I was so often offered money for a pass," said Captain Puffer, "that, at last, I ceased to be indignant, and would merely say to the orderly in attendance, as a matter of business, 'Show this woman out.' He was once offered three thousand dollars for a pass, the money to be paid before it was procured.

From the first, nine in ten of the applications were refused. Every one at head-quarters was aware that the indulgence was almost certain to be abused in some instances, and that the only safe course was to make the lines impassable. But many of the cases were so movingly piteous, the agony of the applicants seemed so real and so great, that it was not in human nature to shut the door inexorably upon them. Every possible precaution was taken to prevent the conveyance of contraband articles, or articles in contraband quantities. Every box and package was minutely examined; every departing boat was searched. A list was required of everything allowed to be taken, and the applicant pledged his honor that he would take nothing else, nor apply the articles to any but the specified use.

It soon appeared, however, that nearly every pass that was granted was abused. It soon appeared that a secessionist considered it no more dishonorable to lie to a Union officer than Jews once deemed it a sin to lie to a Christian. Here would come a woman, having the appearance and manners of a lady, begging with tears and sobs for permission to convey to her starving children across the lake just one barrel of flour, that they might have at least the means of sustaining life. She would bring friends and papers in great numbers to testify to the truth of her story. After many days, the pass would be granted; and the detective officer, upon probing the barrel with a probe of extra length, would find a pound or two of quinine in the middle. A trunk of clothes would be found to have a false bottom stuffed with contraband articles. A barrel of potatoes would serve to hide some thousands of percussion-caps. Letters, too, giving contraband information, were frequently discovered concealed in the boats.

Every detection, of course, increased the stringency of the pass-office. In August, the rebels began to seize boats that ventured within their lines, with a view to collect a flotilla for operations against the city. Then, at length, was adopted the inflexible rule, that no passes should be granted. The adoption of the rule, however, did not lessen the number of applicants, nor diminish their importunity. "I was plied," says Captain Puffer, "with every conceivable story of heart-rending woe and misery, which the general, in consequence of the fact that in almost every instance where he had yielded to such importunities, his confidence had been abused by the carrying of supplies and information to the rebel army, had ordered me invariably to refuse. Ordinarily, I succeeded in steeling my heart against these urgent entreaties; but occasionally some story, peculiarly harrowing in its details, seemed to demand a special effort in behalf of the applicant, and I would go to the general, and, in the desperation of my cause, exclaim:

"General, you must see some of these people. I know, if you would only hear their stories, you would give them passes."

"You are entirely correct, captain," he would reply. "I am sure I should; and that is precisely why I want you to see them for me."

"And with this very doubtful satisfaction I would return to my desk, convinced that sensibility in a man who was allowed no discretion in its exercise, was an entirely useless attribute, and that in future, I would set my face as a flint against every appeal to my feelings."*

Two incidents of the pass-office, related to me by Lieutenant Martin, will place this matter distinctly before the reader's mind.

One Mrs. L. haunted the office for three weeks, pleading with tears for her starving children, to whom she wished to convey a little food. She had shown some kindness to Union troops on one occasion, when they were passing her house, and this was remembered in her favor. A pass was given her to go to St. Johns and return. Something led a detective officer to examine her boat with unusual thoroughness. He found that "false hips" had been built out upon her sides, which were filled with commodities outrageously contraband. The woman had deceived every one. Her simulation of a mother's agony and tears, sustained, too, for three weeks, was so perfect, that no one could doubt the reality of her emotions. Yet she was a professional smuggler.

Some weeks later, a lady applied to Lieutenant Martin for a similar permit. Her children, too, were starving, almost within sight of their mother; and, alas! this was a genuine case. Her children *were* starving. She was a lady in every sense of the word, and she convinced the lieutenant of the perfect truth of her story at the first interview. But he could only inform her, that no passes were then issued, and that any application to the general on her behalf would be useless. She came every day for a month, always hoping for a relaxation of the rule. At length, the young officer was so deeply moved by her distress, that he promised to disobey orders so far as to lay her case before the general, and she might come the next day to learn the result. She came. Lieutenant Martin had the anguish of telling her that her application was necessarily refused, as her boat was certain to be seized if she crossed the lake. She turned pale as death, and fell senseless to the floor. She was carried to the nearest physician. In half an hour she revived—a raving maniac. She has never known a gleam of reason to this day.

* *Atlantic Monthly*, July, 1863.

CHAPTER XXVI.

THE NEGRO QUESTION—FIRST DIFFICULTIES.

LOUISIANA has a population of about six hundred thousand. Before the war, there was a slight excess of whites over slaves, but when the Union troops landed at New Orleans, there was one slave in the state to every white person. Many of the parishes contain twice as many slaves as whites; some, three times as many; a few, four times as many; one has nine hundred white inhabitants to nearly nine thousand slaves. The marching of a Union column into one of those sugar parishes, was like thrusting a walking-stick into an ant-hill—the negroes swarmed about the troops, every soldier's gun and knapsack carried by a black man, exulting in the service. For, in some way, this great multitude of bondmen had derived the impression that part of the errand of these troops was to set them free.

The population of New Orleans was about one hundred and fifty thousand, of whom eighteen thousand were slaves and ten thousand free colored. The class last named is the result of that universal licentiousness which exists, necessarily, in every community where the number of slaves is large. In New Orleans, that licentiousness was systematized, and partook, in some degree, of the character of matrimony. The connections formed with the quadroons and octoroons were often permanent enough for the rearing of large families, some of whom obtained their freedom from the affection of their father-master, and received the education he would have bestowed upon legitimate offspring. The class of free colored, therefore, includes a considerable number of wealthy, instructed, able, and estimable persons. They have been styled by competent observers, the richest class in New Orleans; many having inherited large estates, and many carrying on lucrative business. One of them entertained General Butler at a banquet of seven courses, served on silver.

The secret, darling desire of this class is to rank as human beings in their native city; or, as the giver of the grand banquet expressed it, "No matter where I fight; I only wish to spend what I have, and fight as long as I can, if only my boy may stand in the street equal to a white boy when the war is over."

It is difficult for an inhabitant of the North to know how far such men as he were from the likelihood of ever enjoying the equality he craved. There was at the North a general, mild prejudice against color, before the late riots in New York expelled the last vestige of it from the heart of every decent human being. But, at the South, the prejudice is so complete that the people are not aware of its existence; they fondle and pet their favorite slaves, and let their children play with black children as with dogs and cats. The slightest taint of black blood in the superbest man, in the loveliest woman, one all radiant with golden curls and a blonde complexion, perfect in manners and abounding in the best fruits of culture, suffices to damn them to an eternal exclusion from the companionship of the people with whom they would naturally associate. The most striking illustration of the intensity of this abhorrence of African blood is the well-known fact, that a white wife in New Orleans is not generally jealous of her husband's slave mistress; and is frequently capable of consoling herself by the reflection that the *other* family, in the next street, are worth a hundred dollars each on the day of their birth, and increase in value a hundred dollars a year during the first fifteen years of their lives. She does not recognize in the mother of those children a being that could, in any sense of the word, be a rival of a woman in whose veins flowed no African blood that was discoverable. The slave mistress, also, relieved the sickly white wife of the burden of childbearing. This is southern prejudice against color. The prejudice that prevailed at the North, before the recent scenes revealed to every one its hellish nature, was base enough, and was strongest in the basest; but it was a trivial matter compared with the unconscious completeness of aversion that is observable in the true southerner—the "original secessionist."

There were a great many loose negroes about New Orleans when the troops landed, slaves of masters in the rebel army left to shift for themselves. A still larger number hired their time from their masters, and demonstrated that they *could* take care of themselves, besides contributing from sixty cents to a dollar and a half a day to the maintenance of another family.

"These colored girls," said a new-comer one day to a Union officer, "whom I see selling bouquets, nuts, oranges, cakes, candies, and small wares, on the street corners, must save a great deal of money."

"These people," was the reply, "are merely the agents of their white masters and mistresses, who grow their flowers and oranges, make the bouquets, pies and candies, and send their slaves to sell them in the streets. If she is an apple or a violet short, the balance is struck on her back. Many of the people of New Orleans live, and have lived for years, in this way."

It is obvious to the most unreflecting person, that the negro question at New Orleans could not be disposed of, as at Fortress Monroe, by an epigram. Fortress Monroe was a Union island in a secession sea. The number of slaves in the vicinity was not great; only nine hundred in all found their way to Freedom Fort; and every laborer who came in was one laborer lost to the rebel batteries. The duty of the commanding general was clear the moment the "epigram" occurred to his mind. But, in Louisiana, any considerable disturbance of the relations of labor to capital would have been a revolution far more revolutionary than any merely political change ever was. Suppose, for example, that all slaves coming into a Union camp had been received and maintained, as they were at the fortress. General Butler would have had upon his hands, in a month, in addition to the thirty thousand destitute whites, not less than fifty thousand blacks, for whom he would have had to provide food, shelter, clothing and employment; while the plantations from which the city was supplied with daily food would have lain waste. The Fortress Monroe experience was, evidently, of no avail in dealing with the negro question at New Orleans.

The instructions given by General McClellan to General Butler were silent on this most perplexing subject. General Butler, however, *had* instructions with regard to it. On leaving Washington he was verbally informed by the president, that the government was not yet prepared to announce a negro policy. They were anxiously considering the subject, and hoped, ere long, to arrive at conclusions. Meanwhile, he must "get along" with the negro question the best way he could; endeavor to avoid raising insoluble problems and sharply defined issues; and try to manage so that neither abolitionists nor "conservatives" would find in his acts occasions for clamor. This, however, only for a short time. The moment the administration were prepared to announce a general policy with regard to the negroes, all generals commanding departments would be notified, and required to pursue the same system.

This sounded reasonably enough at Washington. It wore a very different aspect when it had to be applied to the state of things in Louisiana.

The difficulty began on the day after the landing of the troops, and became every day more formidable. Some negroes came into the St. Charles hotel, penetrated to the quarters of staff-officers, and gave information which proved to be reliable. Great numbers soon flocked into the Custom-House, pervading the numberless apartments and passages of that extensive edifice, all testifying the most fervent good-will toward the Union troops, all asking to be allowed to serve them. Wherever there was a Union post, negroes made their appearance—at Fort St. Philip, Fort Jackson, Carrollton, Algiers, Baton Rouge, and elsewhere.

A new article of war forbade the return of these fugitives to their masters. What was to be done with them? Their labor in the city was not wanted; there was a superabundance of white laborers. If they were entertained and encouraged, what was to prevent an overwhelming irruption of blacks into every post? The whole negro population was in such a ferment, that only a slight misstep on the part of the commanding general would have sufficed to reduce society to chaos.

In these circumstances, the wise, the great, the splendid thing to do, was to declare all the slaves in Louisiana free, and put them all upon wages, leaving questions of compensation to loyal masters to be settled afterward. General Butler was capable of writing a general order that would have achieved this sublime revolution with speedy advantage to every white and every black in the state. It was possible, it was feasible. It was, of all conceivable solutions of the problem, the most easy, the most simple, the most expeditious, the least costly, the least dangerous. But even if the general had not been restrained by instructions, this course was excluded even from consideration by the arrival of news, on the 9th of May, that General Hunter's proclamation of freedom to the slaves of South Carolina had been revoked by the president.

He was, therefore, shut up to this one course: To preserve, for the present, the *status in quo*, minus as much of the cruelty and wrong of it as it might be in the power of the Union officers to prevent. To use Mr. Lincoln's expression, he was obliged "to run the machine as he found it," with such slight and temporary repairs and modifications as could be hastily made. This was the policy adopted. It was never announced, but it was the principle acted upon.

Hence the negroes were not encouraged to come in to the Union posts. As many as were required for public and private service were employed, each officer being allowed one as a servant. Several were assigned to the hospitals. General Butler himself was served by "General Twiggs's William." After some days had elapsed, negroes were no longer harbored in the Custom-House, and orders were issued that no more should be admitted within the Union lines, or into the Union camps.

But negroes, as we have seen, were placed on an equality with white men before the law, and allowed to testify against a white man in court. The whipping-houses were quietly abolished, and the jailers notified that no more human beings must be brought to the jails to be whipped. One of these jailers ventured to advertise, a few weeks after the capture of the city, that the "law of Louisiana for the correction of slaves would be enforced as heretofore." The attention of the general was called to this announcement, and Colonel Stafford was ordered to inquire into it. It was found that one slave had been brought in and whipped that morning; but there the fell business stopped. Whatever cruelty was committed in New Orleans upon the slaves, was done in secret; no traffic in torture was allowed; and every slave who asked redress for cruelties inflicted, and could give reasonable proof of the truth of his story, *had* redress—had it promptly and fully. Major Bell judged such cases as he would have judged similar ones in Boston. General Butler never refused a black man admittance to his presence by day or by night, and never failed to do him justice when justice was possible. The orders were, that whoever else might be excluded from head-quarters, no negro should ever be. One consequence was, that the general had a spy in every house, behind every rebel's chair as he sat at table. Another consequence was, that every slave in New Orleans had, at all times, a protector from cruelty in the commanding general.

The mere diminution of the slaves' awful revenue of torture was an unspeakable boon to them. Those hunkers used to hug the delusion, in the old party contests, that kindness was the rule and cruelty the rare exception, in the treatment of the slaves. As if despotism could be sustained by anything but cruelty! They found that cruelty was the rule, and that such exceptional kindness as is shown to favorite slaves, greatly increases the sum-total of their lifetime's misery. Slavery is all cruelty.* It was much to only lessen the vast, the incalculable, the inconceivable amount of agony inflicted by the lash alone. Probably one whipping of thirty-nine lashes with the infernal cowhide inflicts more anguish than a respectable Massachusetts hunker has to endure during his whole life. What an instantaneous change of sentiment on present political issues would occur, all over the country, if thirty-nine arguments of that nature were addressed to the devotees of slavery who, whatever may be the metal of their heads, are not copper-backed.

Some planters who had not the means of supporting their slaves, or of employing them profitably, obliged them to go within the Union lines, trusting to reclaim them in better times. This practice was stopped by declaring all such slaves emancipated, and giving them free papers. Several slaves were also emancipated who had been treated with extreme cruelty by their masters. The "star car" system was abolished. Colored people were formerly allowed to ride only in the street cars that were marked with a black star. General Butler required the admission of decent colored people into all the public vehicles. Some of the police regulations with regard to the slaves were still enforced; the rule requiring them to be at home by nine o'clock in the evening, for example.

* Dr. Wesley Humphrey writes from Corinth, Mississippi, May 25, 1863:

"I have been selected as the surgeon of the regiment of African descent, now forming here (not all black by any means), and during the past week had occasion to examine about seven hundred men in a *nude state*, preparatory to their being mustered into the United States service, and I then saw evidences of abuse and maltreatment perfectly horrifying to relate, and must be *seen* to fully understand the abuse to which they have been subjected. I think I am safe in saying that at *least one-half* of that number bore evidence of having been severely *whipped* and maltreated in various ways; some were *stabbed* with a knife; others shot through the limbs; some pounded with clubs, until their bones were broken. One man told me he had received for a trifling offense two thousand lashes; and, upon examination, I found seventy-five scars on his back and limbs, that rose above the skin the size of your finger, saying nothing of the smaller ones. Others had the cords of their legs cut (hamstrings, as they call them), to prevent their running off; and some were shot in resenting such insults. These were witnessed by the colonel, J M. Alexander, lieutenant-colonel, major, &c., of the regiment."

Such were some of the measures by which General Butler strove to "get along" with this hideous anomaly, while the president was feeling his way to a general policy, and waiting for the ripening of public opinion. General Butler, like the president himself, stood between two fires. One set of Unionists in New Orleans kept saying to him, as I read in their letters, now before me:

Return all fugitives to their masters; show, by word and deed, that your sole object is the restoration of the old state of things; and Louisiana will return to the Union "in a month."

Another party said: "No; the original secessionists are incurable; destroy their power by abolishing slavery; crush that insolent faction utterly; and Louisiana will hoist the old flag with enthusiasm."

He could do neither of these things. An article of war forbade the first; the revocation of General Hunter's proclamation forbade the second. His struggle, meanwhile, to "get along" with a difficulty that would not wait for the tardy action of the government, brought him into painful and lamentable collision with General Phelps, which resulted in the country's losing the services of that noble soldier.

CHAPTER XXVII.

GENERAL BUTLER AND GENERAL PHELPS.

General Phelps was in command at Carrollton, seven miles above the city, the post of honor in the defensive *cordon* around New Orleans. "I found myself," he remarks, "in the midst of a slave region, where the institution existed in all its pride and gloom, and where its victims needed no inducement from me to seek the protection of our flag—that flag, which now, after a long interval, gleamed once more amid the darkling scene, like the effusion of morning light. Fugitives began to throng to our lines in large numbers. Some came loaded with chains and barbarous irons; some bleeding with bird-shot wounds; many had been deeply scored with lashes, and all complained of the extinction of their moral rights. They had originally come chiefly from Maryland, Virginia, and North Carolina, and were generally religious persons, who had been accustomed to better treatment than that which they experienced there."

General Butler was aware of this influx of fugitives; but, in obedience to the temporary policy enjoined upon him by the government, he took no notice of the fact. The vehement desire of General Phelps was, not merely to welcome and harbor the fugitives, but form them into military companies and drill them into serviceable soldiers. He was grieved, therefore, when, on the 12th of May, General Butler requested him to place his able-bodied negroes under the direction of two planters of the vicinity, that they might be employed in closing a break in the levee above Carrollton, which threatened a disastrous inundation. "You will see," wrote General Butler, "the need of giving them every aid in your power to save and protect the levee, even to returning their own negroes and adding others, if need be, to their force. This is outside of the question of returning negroes. You should send your own soldiers, let alone allowing the men who are protecting us all from the Mississippi to have the workmen who are accustomed to this service."

General Phelps did not "see" the need of sending back his fugitives. A positive order settled the question on the 23d of May: "In view of the disaster which might occur to us, in case a crevasse should occur above our lines, I have concluded to send a force of one hundred laborers, in charge of a guard, to attend to raising and guarding the levee above your lines. You will also place every able-bodied contraband within your camp in charge of Captain Page, the officer of this guard, to assist in this work." This was better, thought General Phelps, than consigning the negroes to the custody and direction of their former masters. The order was obeyed, of course.

Meanwhile, General Butler was besieged with complaints of the harboring of fugitives in General Phelps's camp. All the complainants professed to be Union men; some of them were such; and most of them were the producers of vegetables for the New Orleans market. Besides, the harboring of the negroes involved the necessity of their maintenance, and invited the entire negro population to fly to the refuge of Union posts. It seemed to General Butler necessary to check the irruption before it became unmanageable. The following order was therefore issued:

"NEW ORLEANS, *May* 23, 1862.

"GENERAL:—You will cause all unemployed persons, black and white, to be excluded from your lines.

"You will not permit either black or white persons to pass your lines, not officers and soldiers or belonging to the navy of the United States, without a pass from these head-quarters, except they are brought in under guard as captured persons, with information, and those to be examined and detained as prisoners of war, if they have been in arms against the United States, or dismissed and sent away at once, as the case may be. This does not apply to boats passing up the river without landing within the lines.

"Provision dealers and marketmen are to be allowed to pass in with provisions and their wares, but not to remain over night.

"Persons having had their permanent residence within your lines before the occupation of our troops, are not to be considered unemployed persons.

"Your officers have reported a large number of servants. Every officer so reported employing servants will have the allowance for servants deducted from his pay-roll.

"Respectfully, your obedient servant,

"B. F. BUTLER.

"Brig.-Gen. PHELPS, *Commanding Camp Parapet.*"

General Phelps was struck with horror at this command. The fugitives, however, were removed to a point just above the lines, where they found partial shelter, and lived on the bounty of the soldiers, who generously shared with them their rations. An event occurred on the 12th of June, which brought on the crisis. On the morning of that day the negroes numbered seventy-five; but, within the next twenty-four hours, the number was doubled.

"The first installment," reported Major Peck, the officer of the day, "were *sent* by a man named La Blanche, from the other side of the river, on the night of the 13th, he giving them their choice, according to their statement, of leaving before sundown, or receiving fifty lashes each. Many of them desire to return to their master, but are prevented by fear of harsh treatment. They are of all ages and physical conditions—a number of infants in arms, many young children, robust men and women, and a large number of lame, old, and infirm of both sexes. The rest of them came in singly and in small parties from various points up the river within a hundred miles. They brought with them boxes, bedding and luggage of all sorts, which lie strewn upon the levee and the open spaces around the picket. The women and children, and some feeble ones who needed shelter, were permitted to occupy a deserted house just outside the lines. They are quite destitute of provisions, many having eaten nothing for days, except what our soldiers have given them from their own rations. In accordance with orders already issued, the guard was instructed to permit none of them to enter the lines. As each 'officer of the day' will be called upon successively to deal with the matter, I take the liberty to suggest whether some farther regulation in reference to these unfortunate persons is not necessary to enable him to do his duty intelligently, as well as for the very apparent additional reasons, that the congregation of such large numbers in our immediate vicinity affords inviting opportunity for mischief to ourselves, and also, that unless supplied with the means of sustaining life by the benevolence of the military authorities, or of the citizens (which is scarcely supposable), they must shortly be reduced to suffering and starvation, in the very sight of the overflowing store-houses of the government."

General Phelps could endure this state of things no longer. He now wrote a paper on the subject for the president's own eye, which is one of the most pathetic, eloquent, and convincing pieces of composition which the war has produced; a paper which anticipated, by many months, both the policy of the government, and the march of public opinion. Public opinion has now come up to it. The policy of the government is now the policy recommended by it. It will *now* be read with profound approval and hearty admiration, mad as it seemed to many only sixteen months ago:

"Camp Parapet, near Carrollton, La., *June* 16, 1862.

"Capt. R. S. Davis, Acting Assistant Adjutant-General, New Orleans, La.:

"Sir:—I inclose herewith, for the information of the major-general commanding the department, a report of Major Peck, officer of the day, concerning a large number of negroes, of both sexes and all ages, who are lying near our pickets, with bag and baggage, as if they had already commenced an exodus. Many of these negroes have been sent away from one of the neighboring sugar plantations by their owner, a Mr. Babilliard La

Blanche, who tells them, I am informed, that 'the Yankees are king here now, and that they must go to their king for food and shelter.'

"They are of that four millions of our colored subjects who have no king or chief, nor in fact any government that can secure to them the simplest natural rights. They can not even be entered into treaty stipulations with and deported to the east, as our Indian tribes have been to the west. They have no right to the mediation of a justice of the peace or jury between them and chains and lashes. They have no right to wages for their labor; no right to the Sabbath; no right to the institution of marriage; no right to letters or to self-defense. A small class of owners, rendered unfeeling, and even unconscious and unreflecting by habit, and a large part of them ignorant and vicious, stand between them and their government, destroying its sovereignty. This government has not the power even to regulate the number of lashes that its subjects may receive. It can not say that they shall receive thirty-nine instead of forty. To a large and growing class of its subjects it can secure neither justice, moderation, nor the advantages of Christian religion; and if it can not protect *all* its subjects, it can protect none, either black or white.

"It is nearly a hundred years since our people first declared to the nations of the world that all men are born free; and still we have not made our declaration good. Highly revolutionary measures have since then been adopted by the admission of Missouri and the annexation of Texas in favor of slavery by the barest majorities of votes, while the highly conservative vote of two-thirds has at length been attained against slavery, and still slavery exists—even, moreover, although two-thirds of the blood in the veins of our slaves is fast becoming from our own race. If we wait for a larger vote, or until our slaves' blood becomes more consanguined still with our own, the danger of a violent revolution, over which we can have no control, must become more imminent every day. By a course of undecided action, determined by no policy but the vague will of a war-distracted people, we run the risk of precipitating that very revolutionary violence which we seem seeking to avoid.

"Let us regard for a moment the elements of such a revolution.

"Many of the slaves here have been sold away from the border states as a punishment, being too refractory to be dealt with there in the face of the civilization of the North. They come here with the knowledge of the Christian religion, with its germs planted and expanding, as it were, in the dark, rich soil of their African nature, with a feeling of relationship with the families from which they came, and with a sense of unmerited banishment as culprits, all which tends to bring upon them a greater severity of treatment and a corresponding disinclination 'to receive punishment.' They are far superior beings to their ancestors, who were brought from Africa two generations ago, and who occasionally rebelled against comparatively less severe punishment than is inflicted now. While rising in the scale of Christian beings, their treatment is being rendered more severe than ever. The whip, the chains, the stocks, and imprisonment are no mere fancies here; they are used to any extent to which the imagination of civilized man may reach. Many of them are as intelligent as their masters, and far more moral, for while the slave appeals to the moral law as his vindication, clinging to it as to the very horns of the altar of his safety and his hope, the master seldom hesitates to wrest him from it with violence and contempt. The slave, it is true, bears no resentment; he asks for no punishment for his master; he simply claims justice for himself; and it is this feature of his condition that promises more terror to the retribution when it comes. Even now the whites stand accursed by their oppression of humanity, being subject to a degree of confusion, chaos, and enslavement to error and wrong, which northern society could not credit or comprehend.

"Added to the four millions of the colored race whose disaffection is increasing even more rapidly than their number, there are at least four millions more of the white race whose growing miseries will naturally seek companionship with those of the blacks. This latter portion of southern society has its representatives, who swing from the scaffold with the same desperate coolness, though from a directly different cause, as that which was manifested by John Brown. The traitor Mumford, who swung the other day for trampling on the national flag, had been rendered placid and indifferent in his desperation by a government that either could not or would not secure to its subjects the blessings of liberty which that flag imports. The South cries for justice from the government as well as the North, though in a proud and resentful spirit; and in what manner is that justice to be obtained? Is it to be secured by that wretched resource of a set of profligate politicians, called 'reconstruction?' No, it is to be obtained by the abolition of slavery, and by no other course.

"It is vain to deny that the slave system of labor is giving shape to the government of the society where it exists, and that that government is not republican, either in form or spirit. It was through this system that the leading conspirators have sought to fasten upon the people an aristocracy or a despotism; and it is not sufficient that they should be merely defeated in their object, and the country be rid of their rebellion; for by our constitution we are imperatively obliged to sustain the state against the ambition of unprincipled leaders, and secure to them the republican form of government. We have positive duties to perform, and should hence adopt and pursue a positive, decided policy. We have services to render to certain states which they can not perform for themselves. We are in an emergency which the framers of the constitution might easily have foreseen, and for which they have amply provided.

"It is clear that the public good requires slavery to be abolished; but in what manner is it to be done? The mere quiet operation of congressional law can not deal with slavery as in its former status before the war, because the spirit of law is right reason, and there is no reason in slavery. A system so unreasonable as slavery can not be regulated by reason. We can hardly expect the several states to adopt laws or measures against their own immediate interests. We have seen that they will rather find arguments for crime than seek measures for abolishing or modifying slavery. But there is one principle which is fully recognized as a necessity in conditions like ours, and that is that the public safety is the supreme law of the state, and that amid the clash of arms the laws of peace are silent. It is then for our president, the commander-in-chief of our armies, to declare the abolition of slavery, leaving it to the wisdom of congress to adopt measures to meet the consequences. This is the usual course pursued by a general or by a military power. That power gives orders affecting complicated interests and millions of property, leaving it to the other functions of government to adjust and regulate the effects produced. Let the president abolish slavery, and it would be an easy matter for congress, through a well regulated system of apprenticeship, to adopt safe measures for effecting a gradual transition from slavery to freedom.

"The existing system of labor in Louisiana is unsuited to the age; and by the intrusion of the national forces it seems falling to pieces. It is a system of mutual jealousy and suspicion between the master and the man—a system of violence, immorality and vice. The fugitive negro tells us that our presence renders his condition worse with his master than it was before, and that we offer no alleviation in return. The system is impolitic, because it offers but one stimulant to labor and effort, viz.: the lash, when another, viz.: money, might be added with good effect. Fear, and the other low and bad qualities of the slave, are appealed to, but never the good. The relation, therefore, between capital and labor, which ought to be generous and confiding, is darkling, suspicious, unkindly, full of reproachful threats, and without concord or peace. This condition of things renders the interests of society a prey to politicians. Politics cease to be practical or useful.

"The questions that ought to have been discussed in the late extraordinary convention of Louisiana, are: *First*, What ought the state of Louisiana to do to adapt her ancient system of labor to the present advanced spirit of the age? And *Second*, How can the state be assisted by the general government in effecting the change? But instead of this, the only question before that body was how to vindicate slavery by flogging the Yankees!

"Compromises hereafter are not to be made with politicians, but with sturdy labor and the right to work. The interests of workingmen resent political trifling. Our political education, shaped almost entirely to the interest of slavery, has been false and vicious in the extreme, and it must be corrected with as much suddenness, almost, as that with which Salem witchcraft came to its end. The only question that remains to decide is how the change shall take place.

"We are not without examples and precedents in the history of the past. The enfranchisement of the people of Europe has been, and is still going on, through the instrumentality of military service; and by this means our slaves might be raised in the scale of civilization and prepared for freedom. Fifty regiments might be raised among them at once, which could be employed in this climate to preserve order, and thus prevent the necessity of retrenching our liberties, as we should do by a large army exclusively of whites. For it is evident that a considerable army of whites would give stringency to our government, while an army, partly of blacks, would naturally operate in favor of freedom and against those influences which at present most endanger our liberties. At the end of five years they could be sent to Africa, and their places filled with new enlistments.

"There is no practical evidence against the effects of immediate abolition, even if there is not in its favor. I have witnessed the sudden abolition of flogging at will in the army, and of legalized flogging in the navy, against the prejudice-warped judgments of both, and, from the beneficial effects there, I have nothing to fear from the immediate abolition of slavery. I fear, rather, the violent consequences from a continuance of the evil. But should such an act devastate the whole state of Louisiana, and render the whole soil here but the mere passage-way of the fruits of the enterprise and industry of the Northwest, it would be better for the country at large than it is now as the seat of disaffection and rebellion.

"When it is remembered that not a word is found in our constitution sanctioning the buying and selling of human beings, a shameless act which renders our country the disgrace of Christendom, and worse, in this respect, even than Africa herself, we should have less dread of seeing the degrading traffic stopped at once and for ever. Half wages are already virtually paid for slave labor in the system of tasks which, in an unwilling spirit of compromise, most of the slave states have already been compelled to adopt. At the end of five years of apprenticeship, or of fifteen at farthest, full wages could be paid to the enfranchised negro race, to the double advantage of both master and man. This is just; for we now hold the slaves of Louisiana by the same tenure that the state can alone claim them, viz.: by the original right of conquest. We have so far conquered them that a proclamation setting them free, coupled with offers of protection, would devastate every plantation in the state.

"In conclusion, I may state that Mr. La Blanche is, as I am informed, a descendant from one of the oldest families of Louisiana. He is wealthy and a man of standing, and his act in sending away his negroes to our lines, with their clothes and furniture, appears to indicate the convictions of his own mind as to the proper logical consequences and deductions that should follow from the present relative status of the two contending parties. He seems to be convinced that the proper result of the conflict is the manumission of the slave, and he may be safely regarded in this respect as a representative man of the state. I so regard him myself, and thus do I interpret his action, although my camp now contains some of the highest symbols of secessionism, which have been taken by a party of the Seventh Vermont volunteers from his residence.

"Meantime his slaves, old and young, little ones and all, are suffering from exposure and uncertainty as to their future condition. Driven away by their master, with threats of violence if they return, and with no decided welcome or reception from us, what is to be their lot? Considerations of humanity are pressing for an immediate solution of their difficulties; and they are but a small portion of their race who have sought, and are still seeking, our pickets and our military stations, declaring that they can not and will not any longer serve their masters, and that all they want is work and protection from us. In such a state of things, the question occurs as to my own action in the case. I can not return them to their masters, who not unfrequently come in search of them, for I am, fortunately, prohibited by an article of war from doing that, even if my own nature did not revolt at it. I can not receive them, for I have neither work, shelter, nor the means or plan of transporting them to Hayti, or of making suitable arrangements with their masters until they can be provided for.

"It is evident that some plan, some policy, or some system is necessary on the part of the government, without which the agent can do nothing, and all his efforts are rendered useless and of no effect. This is no new condition in which I find myself; it is my experience during the some twenty-five years of my public life as a military officer of the government. The new article of war recently adopted by congress, rendering it criminal in an officer of the army to return fugitives from injustice, is the first support that I have ever felt from the government in contending against those slave influences which are opposed to its character and to its interests. But the mere refusal to return fugitives does not now meet the case. A public agent in the present emergency must be invested with wider and more positive powers than this, or his services will prove as valueless to the country as they are unsatisfactory to himself.

"Desiring this communication to be laid before the president, and leaving my commission at his disposal,

"I have the honor to remain, sir,

"Very respectfully, your obedient servant,

"J. W. PHELPS, *Brigadier-General.*"

General Butler received this communication just as a mail steamer was about to sail for New York. He detained the steamer while he wrote the following just and considerate dispatch, a copy of which was courteously sent to General Phelps:

"New Orleans, La., *June* 18, 1862.

"Hon. E. M. Stanton, Secretary of War:

"Sir:—Since my last dispatch was written, I have received the accompanying report from General Phelps.

"It is not my duty to enter into a discussion of the questions which it presents.

"I desire, however, to state the information of Mr. La Blanche, given me by his friends and neighbors, and also gathered from *Jack* La Blanche, his slave, who seems to be the leader of this party of negroes. Mr. La Blanche I have not seen. He, however, claims to be loyal, and to have taken no part in the war, but to have lived quietly on his plantation, some twelve miles above New Orleans, on the opposite side of the river. He has a son in the secession army, whose uniform and equipments, &c., are the symbols of secession of which General Phelps speaks. Mr. La Blanche's house was searched by the order of General Phelps, for arms and contraband of war, and his neighbors say that his negroes were told that they were free if they would come to the general's camp.

"That thereupon the negroes, under the lead of Jack, determined to leave, and for that purpose crowded into a small boat which, from overloading, was in danger of swamping.

"La Blanche then told his negroes that if they were determined to go, they would be drowned, and he would hire them a large boat to put them across the river, and that they might have their furniture if they would go and leave his plantation and crop to ruin.

"They decided to go, and La Blanche did all a man could to make that going safe.

"The account of General Phelps is the negro side of the story; that above given is the story of Mr. La Blanche's neighbors, some of whom I know to be loyal men.

"An order against negroes being allowed in camp is the reason they are outside.

"Mr. La Blanche is represented to be a humane man, and did not consent to the 'exodus' of his negroes.

"General Phelps, I believe, intends making this a test case for the policy of the government. I wish it might be so, for the difference of our action upon this subject is a source of trouble. I respect his honest sincerity of opinion, but I am a soldier, bound to carry out the wishes of my government so long as I hold its commission, and I understand that policy to be the one I am pursuing. I do not feel at liberty to pursue any other. If the policy of the government is nearly that I sketched in my report upon this subject and that which I have ordered in this department, then the services of General Phelps are worse than useless here. If the views set forth in his report are to obtain, then he is invaluable, for his whole soul is in it, and he is a good soldier of large experience, and no braver man lives. I beg to leave the whole question with the president, with perhaps the needless assurance that his wishes shall be loyally followed, were they not in accordance with my own, as I have now no right to have any upon the subject.

"I write in haste, as the steamer Mississippi is awaiting this dispatch.

"Awaiting the earliest possible instructions, I have the honor to be,

"Your most obedient servant,

"B. F. BUTLER, *Major-General Commanding.*"

A month or more passed. The negroes remained in the vicinity of Camp Parapet. "I awaited an answer from Washington," says General Phelps, "for about six weeks, when, as a great many negroes had in the mean time thronged to my camp, and no answer came, I was left to the inference that silence gives consent, and proceeded therefore to take such decided measures as appeared best calculated, to me, to dispose of the difficulty."

In other words, General Phelps determined to act as if the government had given just the answer which he desired. He accordingly sent to head-quarters the following requisition:

"CAMP PARAPET, LA., *July* 30, 1862.

"Captain R. S. DAVIS, A. A. A. General, New Orleans, La.:

"SIR:—I inclose herewith requisitions for arms, accouterments, clothing, camp and garrison equipage, &c., for three regiments of Africans, which I propose to raise for the defense of this point. The location is swampy and unhealthy, and our men are dying at the rate of two or three a day.

"The southern loyalists are willing, as I understand, to furnish their share of the tax for the support of the war; but they should also furnish their quota of men, which they have not thus far done. An opportunity now offers of supplying the deficiency; and it is not safe to neglect opportunities in war. I think that, with the proper facilities, I could raise the three regiments proposed in a short time. Without holding out any inducements, or offering any reward, I have now upward of three hundred Africans organized into five companies, who are all willing and ready to show their devotion to our cause in any way that it may be put to the test. They are willing to submit to anything rather than to slavery.

"Society in the South seems to be on the point of dissolution; and the best way of preventing the African from becoming instrumental in a general state of anarchy, is to enlist him in the cause of the Republic. If we reject his services, any petty military chieftain, by offering him freedom, can have them for the purpose of robbery and plunder. It is for the interests of the South, as well as of the North, that the African should be permitted to offer his block for the temple of freedom. Sentiments unworthy of the man of the present day—worthy only of another Cain—could alone prevent such an offer from being accepted.

"I would recommend that the cadet graduates of the present year should be sent to South Carolina and this point to organize and discipline our African levies, and that the more promising non-commissioned officers and privates of the army be appointed as company officers to command them. Prompt and energetic efforts in this direction would probably accomplish more toward a speedy termination of the war, and an early restoration of peace and unity, than any other course which could be adopted.

"I have the honor to remain, sir, very respectfully, your obedient servant,

"J. W. PHELPS, *Brigadier-General.*"

About this time, arrived at New Orleans the intelligence that congress had passed an act authorizing officers commanding departments and posts, to employ as many negro laborers as the public service required. General Butler hailed the act with delight, since it afforded a promise of an arrangement with General Phelps. He caused the following answer to be given to the requisition:

"NEW ORLEANS, *July* 31, 1862.

"GENERAL:—The general commanding wishes you to employ the contrabands in and about your camp in cutting down all the trees, &c., between your lines and the lake, and in forming abatis, according to the plan agreed upon between you and Lieutenant Weitzel when he visited you some time since. What wood is not needed by you is much needed in this city. For this purpose I have ordered the quartermaster to furnish you with axes, and tents for the contrabands to be quartered in.

"I am, sir, very respectfully, your obedient servant,

"By order of Major-General BUTLER.

"R. S. DAVIS, *Capt. and A. A. A. G.*

"To Brigadier-General J. W. PHELPS, Camp Parapet."

It was of no avail. In his reply to this communication, General Phelps, I can not but think, put himself signally in the wrong.

"CAMP PARAPET, LA., *July* 31, 1862.

"Captain R. S. DAVIS, A. A. A. General, New Orleans, La.:

"SIR:—The communication from your office of this date, signed, 'By order of Major-General Butler,' directing me to employ the 'contrabands' in and about my camp in cutting down all the trees between my lines and the lake, etc., has just been received.

"In reply, I must state that while I am willing to prepare African regiments for the defense of the government against its assailants, I am not willing to become the mere slave-driver which you propose, having no qualifications in that way. I am, therefore, under the necessity of tendering the resignation of my commission as an officer of the army of the United States, and respectfully request a leave of absence until it is accepted, in accordance with paragraph 29, page 12, of the general regulations.

"While I am writing, at half-past eight o'clock P. M., a colored man is brought in by one of the pickets who has just been wounded in the side by a charge of shot, which he says was fired at him by one of a party of three slave-hunters or guerillas, a mile or more from our line of sentinels. As it is some distance from the camp to the lake, the party of wood-choppers which you have directed will probably need a considerable force to guard them against similar attacks.

"I have the honor to be, sir, very respectfully, your obedient servant,

"J. W. PHELPS, *Brigadier-General.*"

General Butler thus replied:

"NEW ORLEANS, *August* 2, 1862.

"GENERAL:—I was somewhat surprised to receive your resignation for the reasons stated.

"When you were put in command at Camp Parapet, I sent Lieutenant Weitzel, my chief engineer, to make a reconnoissance of the lines of Carrollton, and I understand it was agreed between you and the engineer that a removal of the wood between Lake Pontchartrain and the right of your intrenchment was a necessary military precaution. The work could not be done at that time because of the stage of water and the want of men. But now both water and men concur. You have five hundred Africans organized into companies, you write me. This work they are fitted to do. It must either be done by them or my soldiers, now drilled and disciplined. You have said the location is unhealthy for the soldier, it is not to the negro; is it not best that these unemployed Africans should do this labor? My attention is specially called to this matter at the present time, because there are reports of demonstrations to be made on your lines by the rebels, and in my judgment it is a matter of necessary precaution thus to clear the right of your line, so that you can receive the proper aid from the gun-boats

22

on the lake, besides preventing the enemy from having cover. To do this the negroes ought to be employed; and in so employing them I see no evidence of 'slave-driving' or employing you as a 'slave-driver.'

"The soldiers of the Army of the Potomac did this very thing last summer in front of Arlington Hights: are the negroes any better than they?

"Because of an order to do this necessary thing to protect your front, threatened by the enemy, you tender your resignation and ask immediate leave of absence. I assure you I did not expect this, either from your courage, your patriotism, or your good sense. To resign in the face of an enemy has not been the highest plaudit to a soldier, especially when the reason assigned is that he is ordered to do that which a recent act of congress has specially authorized a military commander to do, *i. e.*, employ the Africans to do the necessary work about a camp or upon a fortification.

"General, your resignation will not be accepted by me, leave of absence will not be granted, and you will see to it that my orders, thus necessary for the defense of the city, are faithfully and diligently executed, upon the responsibility that a soldier in the field owes to his superior. I will see that all proper requisitions for the food, shelter, and clothing of these negroes so at work are at once filled by the proper departments. You will also send out a proper guard to protect the laborers against the guerilla force, if any, that may be in the neighborhood.

"I am your obedient servant,

"BENJ. F. BUTLER, *Major-General Commanding.*

"Brigadier-General J. W. PHELPS, *commanding at Camp Parapet.*"

On the same day, General Butler wrote again to General Phelps:

"NEW ORLEANS, *August* 2, 1862.

"GENERAL:—By the act of congress, as I understand it, the president of the United States alone has the authority to employ Africans in arms as a part of the military forces of the United States.

"Every law up to this time raising volunteer or militia forces has been opposed to their employment. The president has not as yet indicated his purpose to employ the Africans in arms.

"The arms, clothing, and camp equipage which I have here for the Louisiana volunteers, is, by the letter of the secretary of war, expressly limited to white soldiers, so that I have no authority to divert them, however much I may desire so to do.

"I do not think you are empowered to organize into companies negroes, and drill them as a military organization, as I am not surprised, but unexpectedly informed you have done. I can not sanction this course of action as at present advised, specially when we have need of the services of the blacks, who are being sheltered upon the outskirts of your camp, as you will see by the orders for their employment sent you by the assistant adjutant-general.

"I will send your application to the president, but in the mean time you must desist from the formation of any negro military organization.

"I am your obedient servant,

"BENJ. F. BUTLER, *Major-General Commanding.*

"Brigadier-General PHELPS, *commanding forces at Camp Parapet.*"

With these official letters General Butler sent a private one, in which he gave utterance to his sincere appreciation of General Phelps's abilities, patriotism and humanity, and implored him not to persist in a course which must place him in an attitude of hostility to the commander of the department. "A more delicate, generous, or considerate letter I never read," says Captain Puffer, who wrote it from the general's dictation.

General Phelps was immovable. He at once replied to the two official letters:

"CAMP PARAPET, LA., *August* 2, 1862.

"Major-General B. F. BUTLER, commanding the Department of the Gulf:

"SIR:—Two communications from you of this date have this moment been received. One of them refers to the raising of volunteers or militia forces, stating that I 'must desist from the formation of any negro military organization,' and the other declaring, in a spirit contrary to all usage of military service, and to all the rights and liberties of a citizen of a free government, that my resignation will not be accepted by you; that a leave of absence until its acceptance by the president will not be granted me; and that I must see to it that your orders, which I could not obey without becoming a slave myself, are 'faithfully and diligently executed.'

"It can be of but little consequence to me as to what kind of slavery I am to be subjected, whether to African slavery or to that which you thus so offensively propose for me, giving me an order wholly opposed to my convictions of right as well as of the higher scale of public necessities in the case, and insisting upon my complying with it *faithfully* and *diligently*, allowing me no room to escape with my convictions or my principles at any sacrifice that I may make. I can not submit to either kind of slavery, and can not, therefore, for a double reason, comply with your order of the 31st of July; in complying with which I should submit to both kinds—both to African slavery and to that to which you resort in its defense.

"Desirous to the last of saving the public interests involved, I appeal to your sense of justice to reconsider your decision, and make the most to the cause out of the sacrifice which I offer, by granting the quiet, proper, and customary action upon my resignation. By refusing my request, you would subject me to great inconvenience, without, as far as I can see, any advantage either to yourself or to the service.

"With the view of securing myself a tardy justice in the case, being remote from the capital, where the transmission of the mails is remarkably irregular and uncertain, and in order to give you every assurance that my resignation is tendered in strict compliance with paragraph 29 of the regulations, to be 'unconditional and immediate,' I herewith inclose a copy for the adjutant-general of the army, which I desire may be forwarded to him to lay before the president for as early action in the case as his excellency may be pleased to accord. And as my position, sufficiently unpleasant already, promises to become much more so still by the course of action which I am sorry to find that you deem it proper to pursue, I urgently request his excellency, by a speedy acceptance of my commission, to liberate me from that sense of suffocation, from that darkling sense of bondage and enthrallment which, it appears to me, like the snake around the muscles and sinews of Laocoon, is entangling and deadening the energies of the government and country, when a decisive act might cut the coils and liberate us from their baneful and fascinating influence for ever.

"In conclusion of this communication, and I should also hope of my services in this department, I deem it my duty to state, lest it might not otherwise come to your notice, that several parties of the free colored men of New Orleans have recently come to consult me on the propriety of raising one or two regiments of volunteers from their class of the population for the defense of the government and good order, and that I have recommended them to propose the measure to you, having no power to act upon it myself.

"I am, sir, very respectfully,
"Your obedient servant,
"J. W. PHELPS, *Brigadier-General.*

"P. S. Monday, *August* 4.—The negroes increase rapidly. There are doubtless now six hundred able-bodied men in camp. These, added to those who are suffering uselessly in the prisons and jails of New Orleans and vicinity, and feeding from the general stock of provisions, would make a good regiment of one thousand men, who might contribute as much to the preservation of law and good order as a regiment of Caucasians, and probably much more. Now a mere burden, they might become a benificent element of governmental power.

"J. W. P."

General Butler remained firm to his purpose.

"NEW ORLEANS, *August* 4, 1862.

"GENERAL:—Your communication of to-day has been received. I had forwarded your resignation on the day it was received, to the president of the United States, so that there will be no occasion of forwarding a duplicate. I am not at liberty to accept your resignation. I can not consistently with my duty and the orders of the war department grant you a leave of absence till it is accepted by the president, for want of officers to supply your place.

"I see nothing unusual, nor do I intend anything so, in the refusal to accept the resignation of an officer, where his place can not be at the present moment supplied.

"I pray you to understand that there was nothing intended to be offensive to you in either the matter or manner of my communication. In directing you to cease military organization of the negroes, I do but carry out the law of congress as I understand it; and in doing which I have no choice. I can see neither African nor other slavery in the commander of the post clearing from the front of his line, by means of able-bodied men under his control, the trees and underbrush, which would afford cover and shelter to his enemies in case of attack, especially where the very measure, as a precautionary one, was advised by yourself; and while in deference to your age and experience as a soldier, and the appreciation I have of your many good qualities of heart, I have withdrawn and do withdraw anything you may find offensive in my communication; still I must request a categorical answer to this question: Will you or will you not employ a proper portion of the negroes now within your lines in cutting down the trees which afford cover to the enemy in the front and right of your line?

"I pray you to observe, that if there is anything of wrong in this order, that wrong is mine, for you have sufficiently protested against it. You are not responsible for it more than the hand that executes it; it can offend neither your political nor moral sense.

"With sentiments of the utmost kindness and respect, I am your obedient servant,

"B. F. BUTLER, *Major-General Commanding.*

"Brigadier-General J. W. PHELPS, *commanding at Carrollton.*"

General Phelps would not give the "categorical answer" required. Instead of that, he favored the president with an unanswerable argument in favor of employing the negroes as soldiers.

"CAMP PARAPET, LA., *August* 5, 1862.

"Major-General BENJAMIN F. BUTLER, commanding the Department of the Gulf, New Orleans, Louisiana:

"SIR:—I have the honor to acknowledge the receipt of your communication of yesterday, proposing a question for a categorical answer, which came to hand at a quarter before one o'clock P. M. to-day.

"To propose a question, either specific or abstract, of obedience to orders, after I had tendered my resignation immediate and unconditional, seems to me hardly compatible with the 'sentiments of kindness' that you express. If I am to be detained here against my wishes because my place can not at present be supplied, then, at least, I ought not to be troubled with unnecessary issues between my sense of obedience to orders, and my convictions and principles. I am willing to fill a place temporarily, and perform the routinary duties of my profession until the acceptance of my resignation; but as I am left wholly destitute of the proper power and authority to meet the urgent and practical questions that come up every day for solution, it would seem to me idle to comply with merely one measure among many, especially when we have work enough already for our negroes to do, and when the order proposed, if extended to other obstructions as well as trees, would occasion a great amount of unnecessary labor and destruction.

"My dear sir, it is not a question of obedience to orders between us. I fully appreciate the difficulties of your position, and the varied abilities, patriotism and untiring diligence which you have shown in meeting them; and it is with great reluctance and regret that I have to trouble you with anything of my own; but at a crisis in our national affairs so important as this, I should not be doing my duty either to the country or to the government—I should mislead them both, were I to remain quietly at my post, with the semblance, but without the power of fulfilling the duties incumbent upon it. I should endanger and complicate public interests in this way, rather than serve them.

"The distance of this station from the capital of the country; the irregularity and studied uncertainty of the mails; the uncongenial character of Latin laws and education, and slave labor to democratic institutions; the speculating character of the people habituated to conspiratorial associations, idle combinations and fraudulent collusions; all these and many other elements of disorder and opposition to legitimate authority, Lilliputian as they are when viewed by themselves, seem threatening to entangle the feeble, hesitating and undecided action of the government, and render its great and beneficent power of no avail. As it is, we seem to be in a foreign country rather than in the United States, not so much from the character of the people as from the want of action of the government upon it.

"You ask me whether I will obey a certain order or not. With perfect respect and deference for yourself and your position, I beg leave to be permitted in return to submit the following propositions to his excellency the president of the United States, as those under which I could alone consent to serve.

"1st. The people purchased a large region of country called Louisiana, which, at the time of purchase, embraced a very considerable portion of the south-west, and they have a right to this territory for the purposes designed by their constitution, viz.: to secure the blessings of liberty to themselves and their posterity.

"2d. The people are temporarily withheld from a full, perfect and peaceable possession of this territory, by a few ambitious leaders and their deluded partisans.

"3d. Every state of the Union is bound to furnish her share of taxes and her quota of men for the suppression of *domestic insurrection;* and the quota of men of the slave states should be based upon the total number of whites, and three-fifths of all other persons in those states.

"4th. Society here is on the verge of dissolution; and it is the true policy of the government to seize upon the chief elements of disorder and anarchy, and employ them in favor of law and order. The African, ignorant and benighted, yet newly awakened to liberty, threatens to be a fearful element of ruin and disaster; and the best way to prevent it, is to arm and organize him on the side of the government.

"5th. The slave states have already gone through the chief suffering incident to a state of revolution; and to return them to their former condition would be as impolitic as it would be cruel and impossible.

"6th. The system of labor in the South is ripe for and demands a change; and a transition from forced to paid labor is of easy and necessary accomplishment.

"7th. Military art and science, the most potent, and perhaps the only rudimentary element of civilizing power which has not yet been taught to the African during his bondage in America, is essential for extending the colony of Liberia, and opening up to civilization the cane and cotton lands of Africa.

"Inclosing herewith a report of Major Peck, which discloses the condition of things on the borders of Lake Pontchartrain, I have the honor to remain, with sentiments of high esteem,

"Very respectfully, your obedient servant,

"J. W. PHELPS, *Brigadier-General.*"

Here the correspondence rested for a month; when another collision occurred between the generals. Three slaves from the New Orleans gas works ran away and found refuge at Camp Parapet. Colonel French ordered them to be returned. General Phelps objected on two grounds; 1. An article of war forbade the return of fugitive slaves; 2. The men had been inhumanly punished. General Butler, however, peremptorily ordered them to be given up. "They belong," said he, "to the gas-works, which are now under military authority, and we need them for public service. A proper investigation, whether they have been improperly or inhumanly punished or not, shall be made."

The resignation of General Phelps was accepted by the government. He received notification of the fact on the 8th of September, and immediately prepared to return to his farm in Vermont. All of his command loved him, from the drummer-boys to the colonels, whether they approved or disapproved his course on the negro question. He was such a commander as soldiers love; firm, gentle, courteous; gentlest and most courteous to the lowliest; with a vein of quaint humor that relieved the severity of military rule, and supplied the camp-gossips with anecdotes. His officers gathered about him, before his departure, to say farewell. He was touched with the compliment, for he had been accustomed, for twenty years, to live among his comrades in a lonely minority of one; respected, it is true, and beloved, but beloved rather as a noble lunatic than as a wise and noble man.

"Gentlemen," said he, in his fine, simple manner, "I wish, earnestly, that I were able to reply to you—that I had been gifted with the faculty or practiced in the habit of public speaking—so that I might make some fitting answer to the kind words which you have addressed to me; so that I might express my gratitude for the feelings which prompt you to come here. This is the greatest compliment I ever received in my life. Indeed, this is the only compliment of the kind I ever received. Lieutenant-Colonel Lall traced out to you, in more flattering colors than the subject deserved, my military career, and you observed that it has almost all been on the frontier, or at small military posts, where I would naturally not come in contact with large social gatherings, so that I have never been exposed, even had I deserved it, to receive compliments like this which you offer me. Therefore it is that I now wish, for the first time, that I possessed the gift of utterance; and I assure you that I desire it solely because I am extremely grateful for this expression of your regard.

"So far as the motives which prompted me to the step which I have taken are concerned, I do not see any reason to regret it. My heart tells me that, under the circumstances, I did right in resigning my commission. But I do regret exceedingly that its first consequence will be to separate me from your society. I am truly sorry to part with you. I was greatly struck—I was most favorably impressed—with your appearance, and bearing, and expression, when you arrived to re-enforce me at Ship Island. I was touched when I thought I saw in your looks that you felt your true position; that you realized that you had left your business and homes to fight in an extraordinarily just and holy war; that your souls were full of the motives which ought to move men who enter into a conflict for country and liberty. As I watched our division review there, I was more than ever impressed with this appearance of moral nobleness. I had seen armies before, but never such an army as that; never an army which knew it had come out to fight for the highest principles of right, for the good of humanity, and for nothing else.

"And here, in Louisiana, I have seen you growing up to be true soldiers. You have borne, worthily, sickness and exposure. You have carried your comrades every day to the grave, and yet you have not been discouraged, but have been patient, and cheerful, and assiduous in your duties. As I have watched this, I have learned to value and esteem you; and, therefore, I am all the more grateful for the good-will which you show me.

"Yet, I must not believe that this kind feeling has been aroused solely by what I am personally. It must come chiefly from the fact that you look upon me as in some measure the exponent of a great and just cause. It is because you sympathize more or less with me in my hatred of slavery. Perhaps some of you are not yet of my opinion. Perhaps the past has still a strong hold upon your sentiments. But I firmly believe—yes, I have a happy confidence—that, before another year is finished, your hearts will all be where mine is on this question. And let me tell you that this faith is no small consolation for the trial of leaving you.

"And now, with earnest wishes for your welfare, and aspirations for the success of the great cause for which you are here, I bid you good-by."

When, at length, the government had arrived at a negro policy, and was arming slaves, the president offered General Phelps a major-general's commission. He replied, it is said, that he would willingly accept the commission if it were dated back to the day of his resignation, so as to carry with it an approval of his course at Camp Parapet. This was declined, and General Phelps remains in retirement. I suppose the president felt that an indorsement of

General Phelps's conduct would imply a censure of General Butler, whose conduct every candid person, I think, must admit, was just, forbearing, magnanimous.

We can not but regret that General Phelps could not have sympathized in some degree with the painful necessities of General Butler's position, and endeavored for a while to "get along" with the negro difficulty at Camp Parapet, as General Butler was striving to do at New Orleans. We should remember, however, that General Phelps had been waiting and longing for twenty-five years, and he could not foresee that, in six months more, the government would be as eager as himself in arming the slaves against their oppressors.

CHAPTER XXVIII.

GENERAL BUTLER ARMS THE FREE COLORED MEN, AND FINDS WORK FOR THE FUGITIVE SLAVES.

General Phelps might have seen the dawn of a brighter day, even before his departure. General Butler himself could wait no longer for the tardy action of the government. Denied re-enforcements from the North, he had determined to "call on Africa" to assist him in defending New Orleans from threatened attack. The spirited assault upon Baton Rouge on the fifth of August, though it was so gallantly repulsed by General Williams and his command, was a warning not to be disregarded. All the summer, General Butler had been asking for re-enforcements, pointing to the growing strength of Vicksburg, the rising batteries at the new rebel post of Port Hudson, the inviting condition of Mobile, the menacing camps near New Orleans, the virulence of the secessionists in the city. The uniform answer from the war department was: We can not spare you one man; we will send you men when we have them to send. You must hold New Orleans by all means and at all hazards.

So the general called on Africa. Not upon the slaves, but

upon the free colored men of the city, whom General Jackson had enrolled in 1814, and Governor Moore in 1861. He sent for several of the most influential of this class, and conversed freely with them upon his project. He asked them why they had accepted service under the Confederate government, which was set up for the distinctly avowed purpose of holding in eternal slavery their brethren and kindred. They answered, that they had not dared to refuse; that they had hoped, by serving the Confederates, to advance a little nearer to equality with whites; that they longed to throw the weight of their class into the scale of the Union, and only asked an opportunity to show their devotion to the cause with which their own dearest hopes were identified. The general took them at their word. The proper orders were issued. Enlistment offices were opened. Colored men were commissioned. Of the first colored regiment, all the field officers were white men, and all the line officers colored. Of the second, the colonel and lieutenant-colonel alone were white men, and all the rest colored. For the third, the officers were selected without the slightest regard to color; the best men that offered were taken, white or yellow. The two batteries of artillery were officered wholly by white men, for the simple reason that no colored men acquainted with artillery presented themselves as candidates for the commissions.

The free colored men of New Orleans flew to arms. One of the regiments of a thousand men was completed in fourteen days. In a very few weeks, General Butler had his three regiments of infantry and two batteries of artillery enrolled, equipped, officered, drilled, and ready for service. Better soldiers never shouldered arms. They were zealous, attentive, obedient, and intelligent. No men in the Union army had such a stake in the contest as they. Few understood it as well as they. The best blood of the South flowed in their veins, and a great deal of it; for "the darkest of them," said General Butler, "were about of the complexion of the late Mr. Webster." At Port Hudson, in the summer of 1863, these fine regiments, though shamefully despoiled of the colored officers to whom General Butler gave commissions, demonstrated to the whole army that witnessed their exploits, and to the whole country that read of them, their right to rank with the soldiers of the Union as brothers in arms.

This bold measure of General Butler—bold a year ago—was not

achieved without opposition. Public opinion, in New Orleans, was thus divided in regard to arming the free colored men: nearly every Union man in the city favored it; every secessionist opposed it. Many of the Union officers had not yet traveled far enough away from old hunkerism to approve the measure, but a large minority of them warmly seconded their general. There was but one breach of the peace in the city in connection with the colored troops. A party of them were stoned by some low Frenchmen, who, it appears, received, at the hands of the assailed soldiers, prompt and condign punishment. Need I say, that the French consul complained to General Butler? The general set the consul right as to the facts of the case, and, at the same time, asked him "to warn his countrymen against the prejudices they may have imbibed, the same as were lately mine, against my colored soldiers, because their race is of the same hue and blood as those of your celebrated compatriot and author, Alexander Dumas, who, I believe, is treated with the utmost respect in Paris." In fact, a majority of these colored soldiers are whiter men than Dumas.

In November, the colored regiments were employed in the field, in an expedition upon the western bank of the river. They were not engaged in actual conflict with the enemy, but their conduct, on all occasions, was most exemplary and soldier-like. Their presence in a region where there were ten slaves to one white man, was thought by General Weitzel to tend to provoke an insurrection. He was in so much dread of such an event, that he asked General Butler to relieve him of the command. The general replied in his usual exhaustive manner.

"You say," wrote General Butler, "that in these organizations you have no confidence. As your reading must have made you aware, General Jackson entertained a different opinion upon that subject. It was arranged between the commanding general and yourself, that the colored regiments should be employed in guarding the railroad. You don't complain, in your report, that they either failed in this duty, or that they have acted otherwise than correctly and obediently to the commands of their officers, or that they have committed any outrage or pillage upon the inhabitants. The general was aware of your opinion, that colored men will not fight. You have failed to show, by the conduct of these free men, so far, anything to sustain that opinion. And the general can not see why you should decline the command, especially as you express a willingness to go forward to meet the only organized enemy with your brigade alone, without farther support. The commanding general can not see how the fact that they are guarding your line of communication by railroad, can weaken your defense. He must, therefore, look to the other reasons stated by you, for an explanation of your declining the command.

"You say that since the arrival of the negro regiment you have seen symptoms of a servile insurrection. But, as the only regiment that arrived there got there as soon as your own command, of course the appearance of such symptoms is since their arrival.

"Have you not mistaken the cause? Is it the arrival of a negro regiment, or is it the arrival of United States troops, carrying by the act of congress freedom to this servile race? Did you expect to march into that country, drained, as you say it is, by conscription of all its able-bodied white men, without leaving the negroes free to show symptoms of servile insurrection? Does not this state of things arise from the very fact of war itself? You are in a country where now the negroes outnumber the whites ten to one, and these whites are in rebellion against the government, or in terror seeking its protection. Upon reflection, can you doubt that the same state of things would have arisen without the presence of a colored regiment? Did you not see symptoms of the same things upon the plantations here upon our arrival, although under much less favorable circumstances for revolt?

"You say that the prospect of such an insurrection is heart-rending, and that you can not be responsible for it. The responsibility rests upon those who have begun and carried out this war, and who have stopped at no barbarity, at no act of outrage, upon the citizens and soldiers of the United States. You have forwarded me the records of a pretended court-martial, showing that seven men of one of your regiments, who enlisted here in the Eighth Vermont, who had surrendered themselves prisoners of war, were in cold blood murdered, and, as certain information shows me, required to dig their own graves! You are asked if this is not an occurrence as heart-rending as a prospective servile insurrection.

"The question is now to be met, whether, in a hostile, rebellious part of the state, where this very murder has been committed by the militia, you are to stop in the operations of the field to put down servile insurrection, because the men and women are terror-stricken? When ever was it heard before that a victorious general, in an unsurrendered province, stopped in his course for the purpose of preventing the rebellious inhabitants of that province from destroying each other, or refuse to take command of a conquered province lest he should be made responsible for their self-destruction?

"As a military question, perhaps, the more terror-stricken the inhabitants are that are left in your rear, the more safe will be your lines of communication. You say there have appeared before your eyes the very facts, in terror-stricken women and children and men, which you had before contemplated in theory. Grant it. But is not the remedy to be found in the surrender of the neighbors, fathers, brothers, and sons of the terror-stricken women and children, who are now in arms against the government within twenty miles of you? And when that is done, and you have no longer to fear from these organized forces, and they have returned peaceably to their homes, you will be able to use the full power of your troops to insure your safety from the so much feared (by them, not by you) servile insurrection.

"If you desire, you can send a flag of truce to the commander of these forces, embracing these views, and placing upon him the responsibility which belongs to him. Even that course will not remove it from you, for upon you it has never rested. Say to them, that if all armed opposition to the authority of the United States shall cease in Louisiana, on the west bank of the river, you are authorized by the commanding general to say, that the same protection against negro or other violence will be afforded that part of Louisiana that has been in the part already in the possession of the United States. If that is refused, whatever may ensue is upon them, and not upon you or upon the United States. You will have done all that is required of a brave, humane man, to avert from these deluded people the horrible consequences of their insane war upon the government. * * * *

"Consider this case. General Bragg is at liberty to ravage the houses of our brethren of Kentucky because the Union army of Louisiana are protecting his wife and his home against his negroes. Without that protection he would have to come back to take care of his wife, his home and his negroes. It is understood that Mrs.

Bragg is one of the terrified women of whom you speak in your report.

"This subject is not for the first time under the consideration of the commanding general. When in command of the Department of Annapolis, in May, 1861, he was asked to protect a community against the consequences of a servile insurrection. He replied, that when that community laid down its arms, and called upon him for protection, he would give it, because from that moment between them and him war would cease. The same principle initiated there will govern his and your actions now; and you will afford such protection as soon as the community through its organized rulers shall ask it.

"* * * * In the mean time, these colored regiments of free men, raised by the authority of the president, and approved by him as the commander-in-chief of the army, must be commanded by the officers of the army of the United States, like any other regiment."

General Butler, however, while continuing General Weitzel in command, contrived to gratify him by placing the colored troops under another officer, one who believed in them. General Weitzel, in acknowledging this complaisance, remarked that if the colored troops, in action, proved only half as trustworthy as General Butler thought them, the rebellion would most certainly be crushed.

General Weitzel has since had an opportunity of witnessing the conduct of colored troops in battle. If he was not convinced by General Butler's reasoning, he must have been convinced by what he saw of the conduct of these very colored regiments at Port Hudson, where he himself gave such a glorious example of prudence and gallantry. I may add, that the country owes the promotion of this accomplished officer from the rank of lieutenant of engineers to that of brigadier-general of volunteers, to the discernment of General Butler, who twice urged it upon the war department. The heroic Strong was another of General Butler's recommendations to the same rank. Few men would have ventured to ask such sudden advancement for officers not thirty-two years of age. Fort Wagner and Port Hudson justified their almost unprecedented promotion.

As the season advanced, the negro question did not diminish in difficulty. The number of fugitives constantly increased, until, in the city alone, there were ten thousand, many of whom were women and children, and all of whom were dependent upon the government for support. There were great numbers at Fort Jackson, Fort St. Philip and Camp Parapet. Many plantations had been abandoned by their owners, and the negroes remained in their huts idle and destitute. The conquests of General Weitzel greatly added to the number of abandoned and confiscated plantations, and set free thousands of slaves. From the starving country bordering on the lakes whole families of whites were continually coming to the city, sometimes bringing their slaves with them, sometimes leaving them behind to wander off to the nearest post. Society, as General Phelps had remarked, seemed on the point of dissolution, and General Butler saw before him a prospect of having a countless host of white and black looking to him for daily bread.

He determined, in October, to take the responsibility of working the abandoned plantations on behalf of the United States, their rightful owner, and of employing upon them his fugitive and emancipated slaves at fair wages. The first of his special orders relating to this matter has an historical interest and value :

"NEW ORLEANS, *October* 20, 1862.

"SPECIAL ORDER, No. 441.

"It appearing to the commanding general, that the sugar plantations of Brown and McMannus have been abandoned by their late owners, who are in the rebellion, are now running to waste, and the valuable crops will be lost, as well to the late owners as to the United States, if they are not wrought; and as large numbers of negroes have come and are coming within the lines of the army, who need employment, it is ordered:

"That Charles A. Weed, Esq., take charge of such plantations, and such others as may be abandoned along the river, between the city and Fort Jackson, and gather and make these crops for the benefit of the United States, keeping an exact and accurate account of the expenses of such.

"That Mr. Weed's requisition for labor be answered by the several commanders of camps for labor; or, in the scarcity of contrabands, that Mr. Weed may employ white laborers at one dollar each per day, or each ten hours' labor.

"That for any stores or necessaries for such work, the quartermaster's or commissary's department will answer Mr. Weed's approved requisitions.

"That said Weed shall be paid such rate of compensation as may be agreed on; and that all receipts of whatever nature from such plantations, be accurately accounted for by him; and that for this purpose Mr. Weed shall be considered in the military service of the United States.

"By command of Major-General BUTLER.

"GEORGE C. STRONG, *A. A. G.*"

But this was not all. Among the papers relating to the negroes of Louisiana, there is a document still more interesting. It contains the plan devised by the commanding general for enabling the loyal planters to give a trial to the system of free labor:

"NEW ORLEANS, LA., *October* 18, 1862.

"Memorandum of an agreement, entered into between the planters, loyal citizens of the United States, in the parishes of 'St. Bernard' and 'Plaquemines,' in the state of Louisiana, and the civil and military authorities of the United States in said state.

"Whereas, many of the persons held to service and labor have left their masters and claimants, and have come to the city of New Orleans, and to the camps of the army of the gulf, and are claiming to be emancipated and free;

"And whereas, these men and women are in a destitute condition;

"And whereas, it is clearly the duty, by law, as well as in humanity, of the United States to provide them with food and clothing, and to employ them in some useful occupation;

"And whereas, it is necessary that the crop of cane and cereals now growing and approaching maturity in said parishes shall be preserved, and the levees repaired and strengthened against floods;

"And whereas, the planters claim that these persons are still held to service and labor, and of right ought to labor for their masters, and that the ruin of their crops and plantations will happen if deprived of such services;

"And whereas, these conflicting rights and claims can not immediately be determined by any tribunals now existing in the state of Louisiana:

"In order, therefore, to preserve the rights of all parties, as well those of the planters as of the persons claimed as held to service and labor, and claiming their freedom, and those of the United States; and to preserve the crops and property of loyal citizens of the United States; and to provide profitable employment at the rate of compensation fixed by act of congress for those persons who have come within the lines of the army of the United States,

"It is agreed and determined, that the United States will employ all the persons heretofore held to labor on the several plantations in the parishes of St. Bernard and Plaquemines belonging to loyal citizens as they have heretofore been employed, and as nearly as may be under the charge of the loyal planters and overseers of said parishes and other necessary direction.

"The United States will authorize or provide suitable guards and patrols to preserve order and prevent crime in the said parishes.

"The planters shall pay for the services of each able-bodied male person ten (10) dollars per month, three (3) of which may be expended for necessary clothing; and for each woman —— (—) dollars; and for each child above the age of ten (10) years, and under the age of sixteen (16) years, the sum of —— (—) dollars; all the persons above the age of sixteen years being considered as men and women for the purpose of labor.

"Planters shall furnish suitable and proper food for each of these laborers, and take care of them, and furnish proper medicines in case of sickness.

"The planters shall also suitably provide for all the persons incapacitated by sickness or age from labor, bearing the relation of parent, child or wife, of the laborer so laboring for him.

"Ten hours a day shall be a day's labor; and any extra hours during which the laborer may be called by the necessities of the occasion to work, shall be returned as so much toward another day's labor. Twenty-six days, of ten hours each, shall make a month's labor. It shall be the duty of the overseer to keep a true and exact account of the time of labor of each person, and any wrong or inaccuracy therein, shall forfeit a month's pay to the person so wronged.

"No cruel or corporal punishment shall be inflicted by any one upon the person so laboring, or upon his or her relatives; but any insubordination or refusal to perform suitable labor, or other crime or offense, shall be at once reported to the provost-marshal for the district, and punishment suitable for the offense shall be inflicted under his orders, preferably imprisonment in darkness on bread and water.

"This agreement to continue at the pleasure of the United States.

"If any planter of the parishes of St. Bernard or Plaquemines refuses to enter into this agreement or remains a disloyal citizen, the persons claimed to be held to service by him may hire themselves to any loyal planter, or the United States may elect to carry on his plantation by their own agents, and other persons than those thus claimed may be hired by any planter at his election.

"It is expressly understood and agreed that this arrangement shall not be held to affect, after its termination, the legal rights of either master or slave; but that the question of freedom or slavery is to be determined by considerations wholly outside of the provisions of this contract, provided always, that the abuse by any master or overseer of any persons laboring under the provisions of this contract, shall, after trial and adjudication by the military or other courts, emancipate the person so abused."

And, now, what were the results of the experiment? We have explicit information on this point.

Among those who heard of the startling innovation, none listened to the tale with deeper interest than the president of the United States. Mr. Chase read to him one of General Butler's private letters upon the subject, and the president then wrote a note to the general, asking detailed information. The president was also curious to know something respecting the election of members of congress in Louisiana, then about to take place. General Butler replied in a letter, which the citizens of free Louisiana will consider historically important:

"Our experiment," wrote the general, November 28th, 1862, "in attempting the cultivation of sugar by free labor, I am happy to report, is succeeding admirably. I am informed by the government agent who has charge, that upon one of the plantations, where sugar is being made by the negroes who had escaped therefrom into our lines, and have been sent back under wages, that with the same negroes and the same machinery, by free labor, a hogshead and a half more of sugar has been made in a day than was ever before made in the same time on the plantation under slave labor.

"Your friend, Colonel Shaffer, has had put up, to be forwarded to you, a barrel of the first sugar ever made by free black labor in Louisiana; and the fact that it will have no flavor of the degrading whip, will not, I know, render it less sweet to your taste. The planters seem to have been struck with a sort of judicial blindness, and some of them so deluded have abandoned their crops rather than work them with free labor. I offered them, as a basis, a contract, a copy of which is inclosed for your information. It was rejected by many of them, because they would not relinquish the right to use the whip, although I have provided a punishment for the refractory, by means of the provost-marshal, as you will see—imprisonment in darkness, on bread and water. I did not feel that I had a right, by the military power of the United States, to send back to be scourged, at the will of their former and, in some cases, infuriated masters, those black men who had fled to me for protection; while I had no doubt of my right to employ them under the charge of whomsoever I might choose, to work for the benefit of themselves and the government. I have, therefore, caused the negroes to be informed that they should have the same rights as to freedom, if so the law was, on the plantation as if they were in camp; and they have, in a great majority of instances, gone willingly to work, and work with a will. They were, at first, a little averse to going back, lest they should lose some rights which would come to them in camp; but, upon our assurances, are quite content.

"I think this scheme can be carried out without loss to the government, and I hope with profit enough to enable us to support, for six months longer, the starving whites and blacks here,—a somewhat herculean task.

"We are feeding now daily, in the city of New Orleans, more than thirty-two thousand whites, seventeen thousand of whom are British-born subjects, and mostly claiming British protection; and only about two thousand of whom are American citizens, the rest being of the several nationalities who are represented here from all parts of the globe.

"Besides these, we have some ten thousand negroes to feed, besides those at work on the plantations, principally women and children. All this has, thus far, been done without any draft upon the treasury, although how much longer we can go on, is a problem of which I am not anxiously seeking the solution. * * *

"The operations of General Weitzel, in the Lafourche country, the richest sugar planting part of Louisiana, have opened to us a very large number of slaves, all of whom, under the act, are free; and large crops of sugar, as well those already made, as those in process of being made. * * * All this portion of the country are rapidly returning to their allegiance, and the elections are being organized for Wednesday next, and I doubt not a large vote will be thrown.

"I bound Dr. Cotman not to be one of the candidates in the field. He had voluntarily signed the ordinance of secession as one of the convention which passed it, and had sat for his portrait in the cartoon which was intended to render those signers immortal, and which was published and exhibited here in imitation of the picture of *our* signers of the declaration of independence; and as the doctor had never, by any public act, testified his abnegation of that act of signing, I thought it would be best that the government should not be put to the scandal of having a person so situated elected, although the doctor may be a good Union man now. So I very strongly advised him against the candidature. It looked too much like Aaron Burr's attempt to run for a seat in parliament, after he went to England to avoid his complication in the Mexican affairs and his combat with Hamilton. It is but fair to say that Doctor Cotman, after some urging, concluded to withdraw his name from the canvass. Two unconditional Union men will be elected. I fear however, we shall lose Mr. Bouligny. He was imprudent enough to run for the office of justice of peace under the secessionists, and although I believe him always to have been a good Union man, and to have sought that office for personal reasons only, yet that fact tells against him. However, Mr. Flanders will be elected in his district, and a more reliable or better Union man can not be found.

"But to return to our negroes. I find this difficulty in prospect: Many of the planters here, while professing loyalty, and I doubt not feeling it, if the 'institution' can be spared to them, have agreed together not to make any provision this autumn for another crop of sugar next season, hoping thereby to throw upon us this winter an immense number of blacks, without employment and without any means of support for the future; the planters themselves living upon what they made from this crop. Thus, no provision being made for the crop either of corn, potatoes or cereals, the government will be obliged to come to their terms for the future employment of the negroes, or to be at enormous expenses to support them.

"We shall have to meet this as best we may. Of course, we are not responsible for what may be done outside of our lines, but here I shall make what provisions I can for the future, as well for the cereal and root crop as the cane. We shall endeavor to get a stock of cane laid down on all the plantations worked by government, and to preserve seed corn and potatoes to meet this contingency.

"I shall send out my third regiment of Native Guards (colored), and set them to work preserving the cane and roots for a crop next year.

"It can not be supposed that this great change in a social and political system can be made without a shock; and I am only surprised that the possibility opens up to me that it can be made at all. Certain it is, and I speak the almost universal sentiment and opinion of my officers, that *slavery is doomed!* I have no doubt of it; and with every prejudice and early teaching against the result to which my mind has been irresistibly brought by my experience here, I am now convinced:

"1st. That labor can be done in this state by whites, and more economically than by blacks and slaves.

"2d. That black labor can be as well governed, used, and made as profitable in a state of freedom as in slavery.

"3d. That while it would have been better could this emancipation of the slaves be gradual, yet it is quite feasible even under this great change, as a governmental proposition, to organize, control and work the negro with profit and safety to the white; but this can be best done under military supervision."

"Slavery is doomed!" So says General Rosecrans, also. So says the reticent and modest General Grant. So says, I believe, every officer who has served in the heart of a slave state. We shall see, in a moment, by what means the true nature of slavery was brought home to the mind of General Butler, so that he not only foresaw, but exulted in the downfall of the "institution."

The *perfect* behavior of the black men in their new character of free laborers has been often remarked. A whole book full of testimony on this point could be adduced. If it be objected, that General Butler had too short an experience of his system to be able to judge its results, we can point to the testimony of men now in Louisiana, who have observed the working of the free-labor system for more than a year. One highly intelligent gentleman has recently written from New Orleans:

"No one has properly noticed how well the slaves in the South have maintained their difficult position. From the commencement up to this time they have in no instance called upon their heads the indignation of their masters by any impudent expression or untimely outbreak. Whenever our forces have afforded them an opportunity to break their bonds, they have done it promptly and efficiently; but they have, with rare prudence, not involved themselves in difficulties which would be fruitless of substantial good to their interests. This conduct on their part, it seems to me, exhibits a large amount of intellectual ability; for they have had the intelligence, while thoroughly understanding the nature of the revolution going on around them, of heartily sympathizing with the enemy; yet they have been secretive enough to keep their real opinions in their own hearts until the proper time came to give them utterance. I know of no people who, under the circumstances, could have acted better or wiser."*

* *New York Times*, October, 1863.

The following general order, which explains itself, as most of General Butler's orders do, is part of the history of his dealing with the negro question in New Orleans:

"NEW ORLEANS, *November* 21, 1862.

"A commission, to consist of Colonel T. W. Cahill, commanding United States forces in New Orleans and Algiers; Colonel H. C. Deming, acting mayor of New Orleans; E. H. Durell, chairman bureau of finance of New Orleans, is hereby appointed to determine the amount due as jail expenses from the United States, on account of negroes already released from the police jail, to be employed by the government.

"Hereafter, no negro slave will be confined in that jail, unless such expenses are prepaid, the slave to be released when the money is exhausted.

"It is also ordered, that a list of the reputed owners of slaves now in the police jail be published, and that all slaves whose jail fees are not paid within ten days after such publication, be discharged. This is the course taken in all countries with debtors confined by creditors; and slaves have not such commercial value in New Orleans as to justify their being held and fed by the city, relying upon any supposed lien upon the slave."

This order set free a considerable number of slaves left in jail for safe keeping, by officers serving in the rebel armies. It also limited one of the worst abuses of the system.

The president's proclamation of freedom, which took effect January 1st, 1863, suggested to General Butler's fertile genius a measure which, it is greatly to be deplored, he had not time to carry out before his sudden recall. The proclamation, it will be remembered, exempted from emancipation certain parishes of Louisiana, which were already in the possession of the United States. It was well known to General Butler that a large proportion of the slaves in those parishes belonged to foreign-born "neutrals," whose sympathy with secession had given him so much trouble. It occurred to him to inquire whether, by French law, those Frenchmen could hold slaves in a foreign country. Consulting with a French jurist on the subject, he received from him the following statement respecting the law of the French empire. The information which it contains may become valuable, ere long, to commanders of departments in the south-west.

GENERAL COLLECTION OF JURISPRUDENCE.—SUPPLEMENT.—VOLUME FIRST.

Slavery.—Slave.

"No. 40. 1*st*. In 1848, upon the advent of the republic, one of the first acts of the provisional government was to institute a commission, ordered to prepare the act of emancipation of the slaves in the colonies of the French republic. March 4th, 1848.

"2*d*. A short time afterward, the decree of April 27th, 1848, was rendered, which abolished slavery in all the French colonies and possessions.

"3*d*. Article 8, of this decree, accorded a delay of three years to all French citizens, established in foreign countries, to set free or alienate the slaves belonging to them. A law of February 11th, 1851, fixed the delay at ten years.

"5*th*. Later, the article 6th of the constitution of November 4th, 1848, proclaimed that 'slavery could not exist upon any French soil.'

"6*th*. At last the terms of article 4th of the Senatus-Consulte of May 3d, 1854, were: 'slavery can never be reëstablished in the French colonies.'

"However, in proclaiming the freedom of slaves, the decree of April 27th, 1848, granted that an indemnity should be accorded to planters, and the 'national assembly' should arrange the quota (article 5th). This was the object of the law of April 30th, 1849.

"*The indemnity has been accorded.*

"Therefore, the provisional government has, by two energetical acts, resolutely decided the question of the emacipation of the slaves.

"The first is the emancipation in the short time of two months; this is article 1st, of the decree of April 27th, 1848.

"The second is explained in article 8th of the same decree.

"This article reads as follows:

"'In future, even in foreign countries, it is forbidden to any Frenchman to possess, purchase, or sell slaves, and to participate directly or indirectly in any traffic or emolument of that kind. Any infraction of these provisions will entail the loss of French citizenship.

"'Nevertheless, those Frenchmen who find themselves affected by these prohibitions, at the time of the promulgation of the present decree, will be allowed a delay of three years to conform to it. Those who shall become possessors of slaves in foreign countries by heritage, gift or marriage, must, under the same penalty, either free or alienate them within the same period, calculating from the day when their possession will have commenced.'

"Law modifying paragraph 2d of article 8th, decree of April 22d, 1848, relative to proprietors of slaves.

"(Bull: Official, No. 5,627.)

"(May 28, 1858), promulgated June 5th. Article 1st, paragraph 2d, of article 8th, of the decree of April 27, 1848, is modified as follows:

"'The present article is not applicable to proprietors of slaves, whose possession is anterior to the decree of April 27th, 1848, whether resulting from succession, donation during life, or testamentary, or from matrimonial agreements.'"

It thus appeared, that no French citizen in Louisiana could lawfully own a slave. English law forbade the owning of slaves by British subjects in any part of the world, under heavy penalties. The confiscation act emancipated the slaves of rebels. So that, while the proclamation of January 1st appeared to retain in servitude eighty-seven thousand slaves in Louisiana, General Butler deemed it feasible, by enforcing the laws of France and England, and by the complete execution of the confiscation act, to give freedom to nearly the whole number of these eighty-seven thousand slaves. Probably not more than seven thousand of the eighty-seven thousand were the property of loyal citizens. The rest were free by the laws of France, England, or the United States. While he was considering the best means of bringing those laws to bear in "extending the area of freedom," the coming of his successor was announced by rebel telegraph, straight from the recesses of the French legation at the city of Washington. I should add, that the British consul, Mr. Coppell, who now appeared to be on friendly terms with the commanding general, entered warmly into the half-formed scheme.

I shall take leave of this subject by relating several anecdotes illustrative of the practical working of slavery in Louisiana, and of the manner in which the system presented itself there to the hunker mind. Most of these stories I had the pleasure of hearing General Butler himself relate.

CHAPTER XXIX.

REPRESENTATIVE NEGRO ANECDOTES.

Specimen of the Provost Court Slave Cases.

JOHN MONTAMAL, a free man of color, married a colored woman, who was a slave. Both were light mulattoes. From the savings of a small business, he bought his wife for six hundred dollars, so that he stood to her in the relation of proprietor as well as husband, and his children were his slaves. Their only surviving child, when the Union troops arrived, was an intelligent girl eleven years old, who had been sent to school and had been received into the Catholic church. The father falling into misfortune owing to the troubled times, in an evil hour mortgaged his daughter to his creditors, trusting to be able to redeem her in time to prevent her from being sold. The continuance of the war frustrated his plans ; the mortgage was foreclosed; the child was sold at auction by the sheriff. In this sad extremity, he came before the provost court, and asked the restoration of his daughter. The case was ably argued by counsel. Colonel Kinsman, who was then filling the place of provost judge, decided that the girl was free, and gave her back to her parents. This decision was manifestly contrary to the laws of Louisiana, which would have doomed the girl to slavery. But Colonel Kinsman agreed with his predecessor, Major Bell, that when Louisiana went out of the Union she took her black laws with her.

This is the mere outline of the story, which, fully related, would furnish the material for an Uncle Tom novel. Readers can understand it who have imagination enough to apply the situation to a favorite child, sister, niece, or ward of their own.

Specimen Letter from a Slave to the Commanding General.

"NEW ORLEANS, *June* 18*th*, 1862.

"GENERAL BUTLER—DEAR SIR :—

I am reputed the natural son of one Thomas Thornhill, an aristocratic cotton merchant of this city, an officer in the rebel army, recently killed in one of the battles in Virginia.

"My mother, my sister and myself are claimed as slaves by George Hawthorne, of this city, who has been a soldier in the rebel army from its first organization, and is now in that army near Richmond. Our wages are used for his benefit.

"He has given a power of attorney to one J. A. Banorres, his *mistress* in this city, to sell, hire, or dispose of us at her pleasure. We were not slaves for life, but to serve his lifetime by the will of his mother.

"Will your honor save us from perpetual slavery?

"Respectfully,

"Your humble servant,

"VIRGINIUS THORNHILL."

Cases of this kind were uniformly investigated. If the slave established his legal right to freedom, he was declared free.

General Butler on the Fugitive Slave Question.

Visitor.—"General, I wish you would give me an order to search for my negro."

"Have you lost your horse?"

"No, sir."

"Have you lost your mule?"

"No, sir."

"Well, sir, if you had lost your horse or your mule, would you come and ask me to neglect my duty to the government, for the purpose of assisting you to catch them?"

"Of course not."

"Then why should you expect me to employ myself in hunting after any other article of your property?" [*Exit Visitor.*

Two Masters.

"The first negro met by our soldiers at Baton Rouge was an old house servant. The picket brought down his gun, and stopped old Uncle Ned short in his effort to retreat. Then there followed this conversation, the negro standing, meantime, with his eyes sticking out of his head, and his face on a broad grin of astonishment and fear:

"*Soldier.*—Where's your master?"

"*Uncle Ned.*—Dun no, master."

"*Soldier.*—Tell me where is your master?"

"*Uncle Ned.*—'Pon my soul, dun no, master."

"*Soldier*—(affecting great sternness).—Look here, if you don't tell me where your master is, I'll blow your brains out!"

"*Uncle Ned*—(getting more than ever scared).—By golly, dis nigger is in a bad fix. If he tells whar Massa Charles Cassell is, Massa Charles, if he catch em, will whip dis nigger to def; if he don't tell, den you soger will blow his brains out. Dis nigger is in a bad fix, sartin."*

Convicts' Children.

In the state prison at Baton Rouge were found several children born in prison of female colored convicts. By the laws of Louisiana, these children were the property of the state, doomed to be sold as slaves to the highest bidder. The new superintendent, Moses Bates, applied to the general for orders with regard to them. "I certainly can not sanction," wrote General Butler, "any laws of the state of Louisiana, which enslaved any children of female convicts, born in the state prison. Their place of birth is certainly not their fault. You are, therefore, to take such care of them as would be done with other destitute children. If these children were born of female convict slaves, possibly the master might have some claim, but I do not see how the state can have any."

An Anecdote which the late Rioters and their friends will regard as a Good Joke.

General Butler had a dandy regiment in New Orleans—one a little nicer in uniform and personal habits than any other; and so ably commanded, that it had not lost a man by disease since leaving New England. One day, the colonel of this fine regiment came to head-quarters, wearing the expression of a man who had some

* Correspondence of the *New York Times.*

thing exceedingly pleasant to communicate. It was just before the fourth of July.

"General," said he, "two young ladies have been to me,—beautiful girls,—who say they have made a set of colors for the regiment, which they wish to present on the fourth of July."

"But is their father willing?" asked the general, well knowing what it must cost two young ladies of New Orleans, at that early time, to range themselves so conspicuously on the side of the Union.

"Oh, yes," replied the colonel; "their father gave them the money, and will attend at the ceremony. But have you any objection?"

"Not the least, if their father is willing."

"Will you ride out and review the regiment on the occasion?"

"With pleasure."

So, in the cool twilight of the evening of the fourth, the general, in his best uniform, with chapeau and feathers, worn then for the first time in New Orleans, reviewed the regiment, amid a concourse of spectators. One of the young ladies made a pretty presentation, to which the gallant colonel handsomely replied. The general made a brief address. It was a gay and joyful scene: everything passed off with the highest *éclat*, and was chronicled with all the due editorial flourish in the *Delta*.

Two days after, the young ladies addressed a note to the regiment, of which the following is a copy:

"NEW ORLEANS, *July* 5, 1862.

"GENTLEMEN:—We congratulate and thank you all for the manner in which you have received our flag. We did not expect such a reception. We offered the flag to you as a gift from our hearts, as a reward to your noble conduct. Be assured, gentlemen, that that day will be always present in our minds, and that we will never forget that we gave it to the bravest of the brave; but if ever danger threatens your heads, rally under that banner, call again your courage to defend it, as you have promised, and remember that those from whom you received it will help you by their prayers to win the palms of victory and triumph over your enemies.

"We tender our thanks to General Butler for lending his presence to the occasion, and for his courtesies to us. May he continue his noble work, and ere long may we behold the Union victorious over his foes and reunited throughout our great and glorious country. Very respectfully."

A few days later, an officer of the regiment came into the office of the commanding general, his countenance not clad in smiles. He looked like a man who had seen a ghost, or like one who had suddenly heard of some entirely crushing calamity.

"General," he gasped, "we have been sold. THEY WERE NEGROES!"

"What! Those lovely blondes, with blue eyes, and light hair? Impossible!"

"General, it's as true as there's a heaven above us. The whole town is laughing at us."

"Well," said the general, "there's no harm done. Say nothing about it. I suppose we must keep it out of the papers, and hush it up as well as we can."

They did not quite succeed in keeping it out of the papers, for one of the "foreign neutrals" of the city sent an account of the affair to the *Courrier des Etats Unis*, in New York, with the inevitable French decorations.

Comment suppressed.

The story of Jeff, now a Lowell Barber.

A young lawyer of New Orleans came one day to head-quarters with a petition.

"General," said he, "you have a favorite body-servant of mine, a mulatto man, named Jeff. One of your surgeons has him at the hospital. I am used to the fellow—he is a great favorite—had him ten years—can't do without him. Let me have him, and I will give you another man as good for your purpose as he is."

The general referred him to Surgeon Smith, who had the man. If the surgeon was willing, and Jeff was willing, the general had no objection. With a note to this effect from the general to the surgeon, the lawyer departed.

Soon after, surgeon Smith came hurrying to head-quarters with a very different version of the story. Jeff, he said, was no body-servant, but a barber, who had hired his time from his master at forty dollars a month. "He shaved me in his shop when we landed," added the doctor. "Every one in New Orleans knows him as a barber here, established for many years. His master only wants his forty dollars a month."

These facts being established, General Butler expressed himself upon the subject to the owner of this barber, in what Mr. Dickens styles "the English language." Jeff remained at the hospital.

A few days after, word was brought to the general, that Jeff, bearing free papers as a servant of the United States, had been seized in the streets, had been overpowered after a desperate fight, thrust into a carriage, and driven off to Foster's slave pen.

"Bring Foster here."

Foster was brought. He said that Jeff had remained at his pen only for an hour, and had then been carried off, he knew not where. The general notified him that the business of slave-pen keeping was obsolete in New Orleans, and warned him against attempting to continue it. The detective force was ordered to produce Jeff at their very earliest convenience. No trace of him, however, could be discovered that day, nor during the night.

The next morning, the captain of a gun-boat, stationed below the city, reported that a man had swam off to his vessel at daybreak, in irons, calling himself Jeff, who said that he has been kidnapped in New Orleans, and taken to a plantation, where a blacksmith had ironed him, and he had been chained in a garret all night, from which he had escaped by the aid of a file. Jeff himself soon arrived, and related his adventures. It was his master, he said, who had seized, carried off, and chained him.

For this offense the master was tried and sentenced to two years in the parish prison.

After these events, Jeff was made much of by the officers of the hospital; was trusted, at length, with the keys of the store-closets; which trust he variously abused, often getting drunk upon the hospital liquors. Hence, after many reformations and relapses, Jeff found himself an inmate of the same parish prison in which his master was confined.

It now occurred to the legal mind of the master that Jeff, being a prisoner, could no longer be considered under the protection or in the service of the United States. He ventured, therefore, to sell his barber. When Jeff's term of imprisonment had expired, the general received information that he had vanished again, and could nowhere be found. He sent for the master.

"Take your choice," said the general: "Produce Jeff, or live on bread and water till you do."

Bread and water did not agree with the luxurious constitution of a man accustomed to live upon the wages of a barber. Finding himself growing thin upon that austere diet, he soon gave the information desired, and Jeff was again restored to freedom. The purchaser was condemned to thirty days' imprisonment for buying a free man.

Jeff, being then removed from temptation, behaved so well that General Butler took him into his own service; in which he was at the time of the general's return home. Knowing well what would befall Jeff if he were left to the tender mercies of his master, he brought him to the North, where he is established in his old occupation.

Curious Entry.

The patriotic ex-hunkers who edited the loyal *Delta*, upon looking over the old books of the concern, found this entry in one of them:

"Whipping Wade, two dollars." Wade was the respectable porter of the establishment.

A colored Soldier in trouble.

Soon after the colored regiments had been raised, a provost officer, who augured the worst results from the arming of negroes, came to head-quarters with a story that was strongly confirmatory of his forebodings. One of the negro soldiers, he said, had killed his former master with a bayonet.

"I'm afraid it will never do, general," said he, "this arming of the blacks. I have always said so, and here is the proof of it."

Soon after, came a long letter from the British consul, detailing the case; Mr. Montgomery, the wounded man, being a British subject. "It appears," wrote Mr. Coppell, "that the colored man, John Andrew, a dark mulatto, twenty-two years of age, formerly owned by Mrs. Montgomery, was in the city on Saturday and Sunday last on furlough; that he called twice at Mr. Montgomery's house; that when there the second time, Montgomery saw him, and told him not to come there again; whereupon, Andrew drew the bayonet at his side, rushed upon Mr. Montgomery, and stabbed him in the left breast, at the same time using abusive and obscene language, and threatening that if Montgomery approached him he would kill him. Fortunately, the wound is not a serious one, and, soon after the occurrence, Mr. Montgomery was able to take steps to have Andrew arrested. Colonel French kindly allowed an officer to accompany Mr. Montgomery to the Opelousas railroad station this morning, but he was unable to find Andrew in the crowd. Unable to give definite information of the company or regiment to which John Andrew belongs, beyond that already stated, and that on the 13th ult. he dated an insulting letter to Mrs. Montgomery from Lafourche Crossing, I feel convinced that you will deem the crime one that will call forth such exertions as will lead to his speedy arrest and punishment."

The case looked black enough for poor John Andrew. Alas! for him, if such a complaint had been entered against him in the good old days when a dark mulatto had no rights which an Englishman of any complexion was bound to respect.

John Andrew was summoned to head-quarters. He came, accompanied by his captain, who gave him the highest character. Such had been the excellent conduct of the man since he had enlisted, and such was his capacity and intelligence, that though he could not read, he had been made a corporal. Mr. Montgomery was present, and told his story. Mr. Coppell was there to support his countryman.

"Now, Andrew," said the general, "state exactly what occurred. Tell me the truth, and all the truth."

"I will, general," said he. "I went to the camp and joined the regiment. When I had been away two weeks, I came back to see my sister, who is cook in master's house. I saw master as I passed, sitting at the front door. As I was talking with my sister at the back gate, I heard the front door slam, and thinking master was coming, and not wishing to get my sister into trouble, I walked away. I heard him calling me, but I kept on, as though I had not heard him. I walked on," said Andrew with flashing eyes, and the mien of a prince, "because no man has a right to stop a United States soldier, except his officer. 'Stop, or I'll blow your brains out,' said master. I turned, and saw that he had a revolver aimed at me. I drew my bayonet, and made one pass at him. He then turned and went into the house, and I walked away."

This was Andrew's story.

"Now, Mr. Montgomery," said the general, "tell us precisely what part of the man's story is *not* true."

"Well," said he, "I was sitting at my front door, reading the paper, and heard Andrew talking to my cook. I took a pistol to drive him away."

"But why take a pistol, and why drive him away?" asked the general. "As a British subject you can hold no slave."

"I did not want him there," said this lying coward, "talking with my cook. He had sent my wife an insulting letter."

"What was the letter? Produce it."

The letter, which Andrew had got one of his comrades to write for him, proved to be one of the most friendly and respectful character. It began thus: "Dear Mistress: I take my pen in hand to let you know that I am well, and hope you are the same. I was sorry to part from you," etc., etc. There was not a word in it which was not respectful or affectionate.

Witnesses of the affray confirmed the truth of Andrew's story.

"My judgment is," said the general to the consul, "that Andrew served him right. I see nothing to blame in his conduct, except that he did not strike hard enough; and if your friend wishes anything more done in connection with this case, we'll try *him* on a charge of assault with intent to kill."

Montgomery expressed no desire for farther proceedings, and the case was dismissed. Andrew returned to his regiment in triumph.

Anecdote showing the Good Disposition of the Emancipated Negroes, and the perfect safety of Immediate Abolition.

Major Strong received from an officer commanding an expedition, the following letter early in November:

"In still farther confirmation of what I wrote you, in my dispatch of this morning, relative to servile insurrection, I have the honor to inform you, that, on the plantation of Mr. David Pugh, a short distance above here, the negroes, who had returned under the terms fixed upon by Major-General Butler, without provocation or cause of any kind, refused, this morning, to work, and assaulted the overseer and Mr. Pugh, injuring them severely; also a gentleman who came to the assistance of Mr. Pugh. Upon the plantation, also, of Mr. W. J. Miner, on the Terrebonne road, about sixteen miles from here, an outbreak has already occurred, and the entire community thereabout are in hourly expectation and terror of a general rising."

Investigation ensued, which established the facts that follow:

Senator Pugh's negroes, when the Union troops possessed the Lafourche country, were among those who came pouring into the Union camp, and who had returned to their work under a promise of protection in all their rights, and a fair share of the proceeds of their labor. One morning, when the negroes were assembled as usual, to go to the field, one of them left the line and ran toward his cabin.

"Come back," shouted the overseer, in the old, brutal tone of command.

"I'm only going after my coat," said the man.

He went to his cabin, got his coat, and rejoined the gang before it started.

The next morning, when the negroes were again drawn up, before going to their work, Pugh himself came on the ground, when the overseer said to him, pointing out the negro:

"There's the damned rascal who was impudent to me yesterday morning."

Pugh, forgetting that old things had passed away in Lafourche, began to belabor the negro over the head with his walking stick. The negro, who had a better memory, resisted, and defended himself. The overseer came to the assistance of his employer. The other negroes joined in the fray, and, in a very few seconds, the two white men found themselves flat on the ground, each held down by half a dozen stout negroes.

What any other gang of laboring men, except negroes, would have done *next* in such circumstances, we all know; the savage Pugh and his lying overseer would have received the punishment due to their insolence and brutality. These negroes, unmoved by the memory of a thousand wrongs, carefully bound the two prostrate men, hand and foot; made two litters; placed them gently upon the litters; and, conveying them in silence to the nearest Union camp, laid them down before the tent of the commanding officer, and waited patiently there, cap in hand, to relate the occurrences which justified their novel proceedings. The most rigorous examination of both parties only proved that the negroes had told their story with religious exactness. The general justified and applauded the course they had taken, and gave them the protection needed in the circumstances.

Forbearance less meritorious than that shown by these poor negroes has been styled sublime, and no one has questioned the propriety of the epithet,

The kind of man that could once be elected a Judge in New Orleans.

John G. Cocks is his name—COCKS, JOHN G. He is the individual, to whom allusion has before been made in these pages, whose property General Butler seized in behalf of Major Anderson. At the beginning of the rebellion this Cocks, *Judge* Cocks, published in the New Orleans *Picayune* an impudent letter to Major Anderson.

A PROPOSITION TO MAJOR ANDERSON.

"NEW ORLEANS, *May* 16, 1861.

"Major ROBT. ANDERSON, late of Fort Sumter, S. C.:

"SIR:—You hold my three notes for $4,500 each, with about $1,000 accumulated interest, all due in the month of March, 1862, which notes were given in part payment of twenty-nine negroes, purchased of you in March, 1860. As I consider *fair play a jewel*, I take this method to notify you that I will not pay these notes; but, as I neither seek nor wish an advantage, I desire that you return me the notes and the money paid you, and the negroes shall be subject to your order, which you will find much improved by kind treatment since they came into my possession.

"I feel justified in giving you, and the public, this notice, as I do not consider it *fair play* that I should be held to pay for the very property you so opportunely dispossessed yourself of, and now seek to destroy both their value and usefulness to me. I ask no more than to cancel the sale, restore to you your property, and let each assume his original position; then your present efforts may be considered less selfish, because at your expense, and not mine.

"JOHN G. COCKS."

General Butler, in pursuance of his system of redressing the wrongs of Union men, seized the large estates of Judge Cocks, and held them for the future liquidation of Major Anderson's claim. Cocks justly thinking that New Orleans, under the rule of General Butler, was no fit place for him to reside in, vanished soon after into the congenial shades of Secessia.

A few days after his departure, a young woman sought an interview with Mrs. Butler, to whom many women came at that time, to relate their wrongs. So many women, indeed, resorted to her for that purpose, that at length it was found necessary to close that door to the commanding general's attention. The young woman who came to her on this occasion was a *perfect* blonde, her hair of a light shade of brown, her eyes "a clear, honest gray," her complexion remarkably pure and delicate, her bearing modest and refined, her language that of an educated woman. It has been often remarked that the women of the South, who have been made the victims of a master's brutal lust, escape moral contamination. Their souls remain chaste. This woman, so fair to look upon, so engaging in her demeanor, so refined in her address, was a slave, the slave of Judge Cocks. She told her incredible story—incredible until superabundant testimony compelled the most incredulous to believe.

She said that Judge Cocks was her father as well as her master. At an early age she had been sent to school at New York, the school of the Mechanics' Institute, in Broadway. When she was fifteen years of age, her father came to New York, took her from school to his hotel, and compelled her to live with him as his mistress. She became the mother of a child, of whom her master was father and grandfather.

"I am now twenty-one," said she, "and I am the mother of a boy five years old, who is my father's son."

Cocks took her home with him to New Orleans, where he continued to live with her for awhile; then ordered her to marry a favorite *protégé*. She refused. He had her horsewhipped in the streets, and continued a systematic torture till she consented. When she had been married for some time, the *protégé* (a man so nearly white, that he was employed as chief clerk in a wholesale house) discovered the shameless cheat that had been put upon him, and abandoned his wife. Then the master took her again to his incestuous bed, and gave her a deed of manumission, which he afterward took from her and destroyed.

"And now," she added, "he has gone off, and left me and my children without any means of support."

Mrs. Butler, amazed and confounded at this tale of horror, procured her an interview with the general, to whom the story was repeated. He spoke kindly to her, but told her frankly that he could not believe her story.

"It is too much," said he, "to believe on the testimony of one witness. Does any one else know of these things?"

"Yes," she replied: "everybody in New Orleans knows them."

"I will have the case investigated," said the general. "Come again in three days."

General Shepley undertook the investigation. He found that the woman's story was as true as it was notorious. The facts were completely substantiated. General Butler gave her her freedom, and assigned her an allowance from her father's estate; and, some time after, Captain Puffer, during his short tenure of power as deputy provost-marshal, gave her one of the best of her father's houses to live in, by letting apartments in which she added to her income.

It is now a year since the outline of this story was first published to the world, but no attempt has been made, from any quarter, to controvert any part of it.

Story of an old Gentleman who thought a Man could do what he liked with his own Servant.

A lieutenant searched a certain house in New Orleans, in which confederate arms were reported to be concealed. Arms and tents were found stowed in the garret, which were removed to that grand repository of contraband articles, the Custom-House. A gentleman of venerable aspect, with long white hair and a form bent with premature old age, was the occupant of the house from which the arms and tents were taken.

In the twilight of an evening soon after the search, the most fearful screams were heard proceeding from the yard of the house, as if a human being was suffering there the utmost that a mortal can endure of agony. A sentinel, who was pacing his beat near by, ran into the yard, where he beheld a hideous spectacle. A young mulatto girl was stretched upon the ground on her face, her feet tied to a stake, her hands held by a black man, her back uncovered, from neck to heels. The venerable old gentleman with the flowing white hair was *seated* in an arm-chair by the side of the girl, at a distance convenient for his purpose. He held in his hand a powerful horse-whip, with which he was lashing the delicate and sensitive flesh of the young girl. Her back was covered with blood. Every stroke of the infernal instrument of torture tore up her flesh in long dark ridges. The soldier, aghast at the sight, rushed to the guard-house, and reported what he had seen to his sergeant, and the sergeant ran to head-quarters and told the general. General Butler sent him flying back to stop the old miscreant, and ordered him to bring the torturer and his victim to head-quarters the next morning.

The sergeant hurried back and rescued the girl from the lash.

About nine the same evening, the sergeant came again to head-quarters, breathless, reporting that they were torturing the girl again, as the most heart-rending shrieks were heard coming from an upper room of the house. General Butler ordered him to arrest all the inmates of the house, and keep them in the guard-house all night, and bring them before him in the morning. On returning to the house, the sergeant found that the second outcry was caused by washing the lacerated back of the poor girl with strong brine. They do this at the South on the pretense that it causes the wounds of the lash to heal more quickly and with less pain. The real object is to make them heal without such scars as would lessen the value of the slave at the auction block. It is said really to have that effect; and the operation has the farther charm of being more exquisitely painful than the punishment itself; since the flooding of the back with brine revives the dull sensitiveness of the nerves, calls back the dead agony to life, renews, in one instant, the anguish of each several stroke, and that anguish intensified. The whole extent of the sufferer's back is one biting, burning, piercing, maddening pain.

In the morning, the hoary wretch and his tortured slave were brought to the general's office. The upper part of her dress was opened. It was a hideous and horrible sight.

"What have you to say, sir?" said General Butler to the old man.

He said the girl had given information respecting the arms and tents in his garret, and she was going to run away.

"It is false, sir," said the general, "so far as the information is concerned. We had our information from another source. What was the cause of the second outcry?"

The old man said he did not know. The general asked the girl. She said it was master washing her with brine.

"Is this so?" asked the general.

"Yes."

"You *damned* old rascal! What could tempt you to treat a human being so?"

"She is my servant, and I suppose I may do what I like with her. I washed her to relieve her from pain."

"To *relieve* her? Well, sir, I shall commit you to Fort Jackson."

"General, I am a native of South Carolina; my health is infirm. It will kill me."

"I can't help that. And see that you behave well, or you shall have precisely the same punishment that you have given this poor girl, and to relieve your pain, you shall be washed down with brine."

The old native of South Carolina went to Fort Jackson, where, I am happy to be able to state, he died in a month. General Butler gave the girl her freedom, and assigned her a sum of money sufficient to set her up in some little business, such as colored girls carry on in New Orleans.

A "respectable Merchant" and his Slave Daughter.

One Sunday morning, while General Butler was seated at the breakfast table, Major Strong, a gentleman who was not given to undue emotion, rushed into the room, pale with rage and horror.

"General," he exclaimed, "there is the most damnable thing out here!"

The general followed him to the office. There he found the staff assembled, standing round a woman, gazing upon her with flashing eyes, their countenances betraying mingled pity and fury. The servants of the house were crowding about the doors of the room. The woman who was the object of so much attention, was nearly white, aged about twenty-seven. Her face showed, at the first glance, that she was one of those unfortunate creatures whom *some* savages regard with a kind of religious awe, and whom civilized beings are accustomed to consider peculiarly entitled to tenderness and forbearance. She was simple-minded. Not absolutely an idiot, but imbecile, vacant, half silly.

"Look here, General," said Major Strong, as he opened the dress of this poor creature.

Her back was cut to pieces with the infernal cowhide. It was all black and red—red where the infernal instrument of torture had broken the skin, black where it had not. To convey an idea of its appearance, General Strong used to say that it resembled a very rare beefsteak, with the black marks of the gridiron across it.

No one ever saw General Butler so profoundly moved as he was while gazing upon this pitiable spectacle.

"Who did this?" he asked the girl.

"Master," she replied.

"Who is your master?"

"Mr. Landry."

Landry was a respectable merchant living near head-quarters, not unknown to the members of the staff.

"What did he do it for?" asked the general.

"I went out after the clothes from the wash," said she, "and I stayed out late. When I came home, master kicked me and said he would teach me to run away."

"Orderly, go to Landry's house and bring him before me."

In a few minutes, Landry entered the office—a spare, tall, gentlemanlike person of fifty-five.

"Mr. Landry," said the general, "this is infamous. The girl is evidently simple. It is the awfulest spectacle I ever beheld in my life."

At this moment Major Strong whispered in the general's ear a piece of information which caused him to compare the faces of the master and the slave. The resemblance between them was striking.

"Is this woman your daughter?" asked the general.

"There are reports to that effect," said Landry.

The insolent nonchalance of the man, as he replied to the last question, so inflamed the rage of all who witnessed it, that it needed but a wink from the general to set a dozen infuriated men at his throat. The general merely said,

"I am answered, sir."

The general, for once, seemed deprived of his power to judge with promptness. "He remained for some time," says an eye-witness, "apparently lost in abstraction. I shall never forget the singular expression on his face.

"I had been accustomed to see him in a storm of passion at any instance of oppression or flagrant injustice; but on this occasion he was too deeply affected to obtain relief in the usual way.

"His whole air was one of dejection, almost listlessness; his indignation too intense, and his anger too stern, to find expression even in his countenance.

"Never have I seen that peculiar look but on three or four occasions similar to the one I am narrating, when I knew he was pondering upon the baleful curse that had cast its withering blight upon all around, until the manhood and humanity were crushed out of the people, and outrages such as the above were looked upon with complacency, and the perpetrators treated as respected and worthy citizens,—and that he was realizing the great truth, that, however man might endeavor to guide this war to the advantage of a favorite idea or sagacious policy, the Almighty was directing it surely and steadily for the purification of our country from this greatest of national sins.

"After sitting in the mood which I have described, the general again turned to the prisoner, and said, in a quiet, subdued tone of voice:

"'Mr. Landry, I dare not trust myself to decide to-day what punishment would be meet for your offense, for I am in that state of mind that I fear I might exceed the strict demands of justice. I shall, therefore, place you under guard for the present, until I conclude upon your sentence.'"*

The next morning, came troops of Landry's friends to tell the general what an honorable, what a "high-toned," what an *amiable* gentleman Mr. Landry was, and how highly he was respected by all who knew him. They said that he had had his losses; the war had half ruined him; his friends had observed that he had been *irritable* of late, poor man; and no doubt, he had struck his daughter harder than he intended. His wife and his *other* children came

* *Atlantic Monthly*, July, 1863.

to plead for him. A legal gentleman appeared, also, to do what was possible for him in the way of argument.

General Butler decided the case thus: Landry should give his daughter her freedom, and settle upon her a thousand dollars.

Being in mortal terror of Fort Jackson, he gladly complied with these terms. The poor girl went forth that day a free woman, and a trustee was appointed to administer her little fortune and see that no farther harm befell her.

It was a light penalty for such a crime. I wish the general had treated the case *à la* Wellington—rung for three poles and a rope, and had the wretch hanged, that Sunday morning, in the nearest public square. God and man would have applauded the deed, and there would have been no more woman-whipping in New Orleans while the flag of the United States floated over the Custom-House.

I close this chapter of horrors. Each of these anecdotes illustrates one phase of the accursed thing, and all of them tend to show what has been already remarked, that the worst consequences of slavery fall upon the white race. It is better to be murdered than to be a murderer. It is better to be the victim of cruelty than to be capable of inflicting it. Mrs. Kemble judges rightly, when she says, in her recent noble and well-timed work, that it were far preferable to be a slave upon a Georgian rice plantation than to be the lord of one, with all that weight of crime upon the soul which slavery *necessitates*, and to become so completely depraved as to be able to contemplate so much suffering and iniquity with stolid indifference.

These scenes sank deeply into the hunker mind. General Butler, as he himself remarks, is not a man of the cast of character which we call humanitarian. A person of very great executive force never is, for nature does not bestow all her good gifts upon any individual. To his own circle of friends he would be more than generous; he makes their cause his own; he is faithful to them unto death, and after death. He was not satisfied to get for Major Strong a commission as brigadier-general, nor satisfied to come two hundred miles to attend his funeral; but he took care of his fame also, writing with his own hand the history of his career for the press, and correcting errors and supplying omissions in the eulogies penned by others. Still, he is not, in the modern sense of the term, a "philanthropist." He loves men more than he loves man. But a woman's bleeding back, the master's brutal insensibility, the absolute destruction in the character of slave-owners of all that redeems human nature, such as sense of truth, pity for the helpless, regard for the sanctities of domestic life; the flighty inferiority of their minds, their stupid improvidence, their incurable wrong-headedness and wrong-heartedness, their childish vanity and shameful ignorance, their boastful emptiness and contempt for all people and nations more enlightened than themselves; these things appealed to him, these things he marked and inwardly digested. Impatient as he had previously been at the slow progress of the war, he now became more reconciled to it, because he saw that every month of its continuance made the doom of slavery more certain and more speedy. He was now perfectly aware that the United States could never realize General Washington's modest aspiration, that it might become "a respectable nation," much less a great and glorious one, nor even a nation homogeneous enough to be truly powerful, until slavery had ceased to exist in every part of it.

Those who lived on intimate relations with the general, remarked his growing abhorrence of slavery. During the first weeks of the occupation of the city, he was occasionally capable, in the hurry of indorsing a peck of letters, of spelling negro with two g's. Not so in the later months. Not so when he had seen the torn and bleeding and blackened backs of fair and delicate women. Not so when he had reviewed his noble colored regiments. Not so when he had learned that the negroes of the South were among the heaven-destined means of restoring the integrity, the power, and the splendor of his country. Not so when he had learned how the oppression of the negroes had extinguished in the white race almost every trait of character which redeems and sanctifies human nature.

"God Almighty himself is doing it," he would say, when talking on this subject. "No man's hand can stay it. It is no other than the omnipotent God who has taken this mode of destroying slavery. We are but the instruments in his hands. We could not prevent it if we would. And let us strive as we might, the judicial blindness of the rebels would do the work of God without our aid, and in spite of all our endeavors against it."

AMEN!

CHAPTER XXX.

MILITARY OPERATIONS.

General McClellan's orders to the commander of the department of the gulf directed him, first, and before all other objects, to hold New Orleans. To that everything was to be sacrificed. Next, he was to seize and hold all the approaches to the city, above and below, on the east and on the west, which included the seizure of all the railroads and railroad property in the vicinity. He was farther directed to co-operate with the navy in an attack upon Mobile, and, if possible, to threaten Pensacola and Galveston. General McClellan added that it was the design of the government to send re-enforcements sufficient for the accomplishment of all these purposes, as well as more detailed instructions. Circumstances prevented the sending of re-enforcements, as we have seen. Nor were particular orders respecting military movements forwarded, except that the attack upon Mobile should be postponed until the completion of some of the monitors. Whatever General Butler accomplished in his department was done by the force he brought with him, and the regiments which he raised in New Orleans.

All the objects of the expedition named in the orders of the commander-in-chief were accomplished except two. One of these was the reduction of Mobile, which was countermanded. The other was the opening of the Mississippi, above Baton Rouge, which was attempted, but found impossible without a very large increase of force. Let us dispose of that matter first.

Attempt to Open the Mississippi.

The troops were no sooner posted around the city than General Butler began to prepare an expedition to ascend the river, to occupy Baton Rouge, and reconnoiter Vicksburg, which was then looming up as the most formidable obstacle which the enemy had yet interposed to the free navigation of the Mississippi. Port Hudson had not then been fortified. Later in the year General Butler had the pain and mortification of seeing the batteries of Port Hudson rising and strengthening daily, he powerless to prevent it. He gave early warning respecting this new position to the government. Two monitors and five thousand men, he said, could take the place in October, 1862, which a whole fleet and a large army might not be able to reduce six months later. The requisite force could not be sent in time, and it cost many thousands of precious lives to invest it in the summer of 1863. The peninsular losses paralyzed the powers of the government at the points most remote from the scene of those tremendous disasters, and nowhere was their baleful influence more manifest than in the southwest.

To procure river steamboats for transporting the troops was the first difficulty. The rebels had wisely burned all the steamboats at the levee of the city, except one or two small ones. It was known, however, that many boats had been hidden away in the bayous of the Delta; and hence the steamboat hunting to which allusion has before been made. Parties of troops went peering and floundering through the wooded swamps of the adjacent country in search of these hidden vessels. The gun-boats of the navy cruised for the same purpose along the borders of the lakes, and pushed up the tortuous streams that empty into them. Several steamers were obtained in this way, which the unwilling or timid mechanics of New Orleans were compelled to repair.

The most noted of these steamboat hunts was one achieved by Colonel Kinsman, the general's volunteer aid, serving then without pay or rank. Certain information was obtained that two of the largest steamboats belonging to New Orleans had been taken across Lake Pontchartrain, and stowed away somewhere in one of its tributary rivers. The naval vessels had sought for them in vain for several days. It occurred to the Yankee intelligence of Colonel Kinsman that the boats must have been taken higher up one of those streams than a gun-boat could navigate, and that the way to find them was to penetrate the country northward for several miles, and then sweep around the lake from one river to another, near the head of possible steamboat navigation. He won from the general a reluctant consent to this perilous enterprise. A steamboat landed him and a hundred men on the southern shore of Lake Pontchartrain. They marched northward through a dense forest, for two or three days; then turned to the east, exploring all the streams, aided only by the compass and an occasional friendly negro. No traces of steamboats were discovered. The heat was intense in those dense and lofty woods, and the men were becoming exhausted. One day, when the troops were resting, Colonel Kinsman went alone on the line of march, and came at length to the Pearl river, a stream that looked capable of harboring a steamboat. The men were brought up, and the exploration began.

At last they had caught the true scent. A steamboat of the largest size was discovered on the opposite side of the river, without a guard. A small boat floated alongside of her, and ere long a man appeared on deck. This was the critical moment; for the man could have applied the match, set the vessel on fire, and easily escaped into the forest. Colonel Kinsman took a musket from the hands of a soldier, and ordered the man to bring that small boat across the river. He obeyed. In ten minutes more Colonel Kinsman and half a dozen of his men were on board examining the prize. The boiler was empty; the "packing" of the engine was gone; parts of the machinery were displaced, and others were wanting. But, of course, among a hundred Yankees there is always at least one man who knows all about steam-engines. The needed man was there. Under his directions the troops worked with the energy of successful hunters; the packing was supplied; the machinery was put in order; fuel was collected. The most laborious part of the preparations was the filling of the boiler by means of pails. Hour after hour the men dipped, and carried, and hoisted, wondering at the slow progress of the work. But in twelve hours after boarding the vessel the engineer announced that she was ready to move.

Colonel Kinsman, meanwhile, with a small party, and an impressed but very willing negro guide, had been looking for the other steamboat. A remark made by this negro, when he was out of his master's hearing, greatly amused the troops:

"Master said you was whipped every time; but you comed nearer and nearer, and here you be."

The grinning exultation of the man, as he said these words, was in the highest degree comic. The troops were ready to drop with heat and fatigue, but they found strength to make the woods resound with laughter at this black man's epitome of the war. Colonel Kinsman found the second steamer, but she was far inferior to the first, and was so securely lodged, that he feared the alarm would call down upon him a rescuing party if he should attempt to bring away both. So he returned to the larger vessel, and all the troops slept on board without disturbance.

The greatest difficulty remained to be overcome, to navigate so large a boat down a river so rapid, narrow and crooked as the Pearl. None of the party had ever commanded or steered a steamboat; none of them had ever seen the Pearl river before yesterday. But were they not Yankees? Colonel Kinsman assumed the command. The boat was cast off, and away she rushed down the swift stream. They had but about twenty miles to go, and it took them all day to accomplish the distance. The boat grounded oftener than once a mile; sometimes both ends were fast at the same time; sometimes she seemed involved in the mud and trees beyond extrication; sometimes she was turned completely around and went stern foremost for a while. The yielding nature of the soil saved her from destruction; and, toward the close of the day, she made her way to the lake, and hove in sight of a gun-boat which had been employed for a week in searching for this very vessel. The naval officers could scarcely hide their chagrin at being outdone on their own element by a party of raw recruits. Moreover, if *they* had taken the vessel, there would have been forty thousand dollars of prize-money to be distributed among them.

Colonel Kinsman and his party were welcomed at New Orleans as men returned from the grave. General Butler renamed the boat the Kinsman. She did good service for many months, and met, at length, the fate of steamboats in war time; she sank to the bottom of the river pierced by sixty cannon balls.

A few steamers being thus obtained, General Williams and his brigade, convoyed by a naval force under Captain Farragut, went up the river to Baton Rouge, of which they took peaceable possession. Captain Farragut, General Williams and General Weitzel surveyed the bluffs upon which Vicksburg stands. They found the town too high to be reached by guns fired from the river, and too powerfully garrisoned and fortified to be carried by assault with less than ten thousand men. Army and navy were, therefore, obliged to confess, that with the forces then in the department, Vicksburg was an obstacle in the way of the free navigation of the river which could not be overcome.

This opinion being communicated to General Butler, he devoted the spare hours of a week to the study of the position. Maps, plans, measurements, natives of the town, engineer officers, and even works on geology were duly examined. The conception of the celebrated cut-off was the result of his inquiries and cogitations. It was a truly ingenious and most plausible scheme. Such a canal cut across almost any other bend of the river would have answered the purpose intended. But nature had concealed under the soft surface of that particular piece of land, a bed of tough clay, which baffled the project of diverting the course of the river. It happened, also, that the force of the stream at that point tends to the opposite shore, and could not be persuaded to co-operate effectually with the labors of the canal-cutters. Consequently the Father of Waters kept to his ancient bed, and Vicksburg remained a river town. For a long time General Butler lived in hopes of sending Vicksburg a few miles into the interior, and opening the Mississippi to commerce; but nature had taken her precautions, and he could not prevail.

Governing the Troops.

When the yellow fever season was approaching, the alarm among the officers of the army was such, that it amounted at times to something like panic. The general was overwhelmed with requests for leaves of absence; and when it was found that these were only granted in extreme cases, the resigning fever broke out and raged with dangerous violence. The manner in which the general met this new difficulty, which threatened to deprive him of indispensable officers, was characteristic and effectual. Take one scene as a specimen of those which were daily enacted at headquarters during the month of June.

Enter, a bluff rosy lieutenant, the picture of robust health, bearing in his hand a doctor's certificate, which declared that the lieutenant could not live thirty days longer in such a climate as that of Louisiana. The general looked at the man in some amazement.

"You see, General," said the lieutenant, "that the surgeon of my regiment says, I can't live thirty days in New Orleans."

"Do *you* think so?" asked the general, looking him steadily in the face.

"Well, General," replied the officer, with a manifest abatement of confidence in his cause, "I shouldn't wonder if the surgeon is right."

"I propose to try the experiment," said the general. "*I* think you'll live. But if I should prove wrong, I'll ask the surgeon's pardon. If he is wrong, he shall apologize to me."

The officer laughed and retired. He enjoyed perfect health all the summer; with the additional felicity of much bantering on his unsuccessful attempt to deprive the department of a lieutenant.

With regard to the resignations, General Butler, at once, took the ground, that to resign in such circumstances was precisely as infamous as to resign in presence of the enemy. The yellow fever *was* the enemy, and the only enemy that was really formidable to the troops stationed in and around the city. Nevertheless, a few resignations were promptly accepted; but so accepted as to serve as a warning to other officers not to avail themselves of that mode of escape. On the letter of a surgeon, who resigned for the alleged reason that his private affairs demanded his presence at home, the following words were written by the general:

"This application will be forwarded to the secretary of war, with this indorsement: 'A surgeon who would make his private and domestic affairs an excuse for leaving his regiment, and exposing his fellow-citizens to the want of medical attendance at this season of the year—knowing that his place could not be supplied for months—deserves to be cashiered for cowardice or neglect of duty. —B. F. B.'"

This indorsement was inserted in the *Delta* forthwith. There were not many resignations afterward—none of surgeons. I notice, however, a few more of those terrible "indorsements." Here is another, which was written on the letter of an officer, who assigned as a reason for resigning, that he was "incompetent."

"This officer has now been nine months in the service. If, in this time, he has just learned his incompetency, there must be something wrong in his mental or moral capacity. I believe the latter, and, therefore, he is dismissed the service, subject to the approval of the president. If incompetent, he has done the United States no service, but much harm, and is entitled to no pay."

Another:

"Any officer who makes 'business affairs' a reason for quitting the service at this juncture, has dishonored himself, and should be dishonorably discharged, as is done in the case of Captain ——."

Another:

"Captain ——'s resignation is accepted, but he is dishonorably discharged from the service. If his medical certificate is true, that he has been suffering for five years under the disease because of which he now leaves the service, without its yielding to medical skill, it was both immoral and dishonorable to have taken the commission."

There are indorsements of another character upon some of the applications for leave of absence; as witness this, upon the back of an application for a short leave from Lieutenant-Colonel Keith, of the Twenty-first Indiana.

"Granted. Colonel Keith's services to the government have been most valuable. His gallantry and courage are honorably mentioned."

General Butler's care of the health of the troops during the hot season was assiduous and wisely directed. Familiar with sanitary science, he was able to give explicit and effectual orders on the subject, as well as sound advice to the surgeons. The men were required to wear their woolen clothes during the summer; to bathe frequently; to avoid sleeping in the open air; to keep their camps religiously clean; to abstain from stimulating food and drink; to avoid needless fatigue and exposure to the sun.

Observe the four orders that follow, particularly the last paragraph of the second:

"New Orleans, *June* 3, 1862.

"I. The laundresses of companies are not permitted to come into the quarters of the men. They must be kept in their own quarters, and the clothing sent to them and sent for.

"II. Any officer who permits a woman, black or white, not his wife, in his quarters, or the quarters of his company, will be dismissed the service."

"New Orleans, *September* 19, 1862.

"I. It having been made to appear to the commanding general, that upon marches and expeditions, soldiers of the United States army have entered houses, and taken therefrom private property, and appropriated the same to their own use;

"It is therefore ordered, that a copy of General Order No. 107, current series, from the war department, be distributed to every commissioned officer of this command, and that the same be read, together with this order, to each company in this department three several times at different company roll-calls.

"II. It is farther ordered, that all complaints that private property has been taken from peaceable citizens, in contravention of said General Order No. 107, be submitted to a board of survey, and that *the amount of damage determined shall be deducted from the pay of the officers commanding the troops committing the outrage—in proportion to their rank.*"

"NEW ORLEANS, *November* 11, 1862.

"I. Any commissioned officer who is found drinking intoxicating liquors in any public drinking-place or other public house within this department, will be recommended to the president for dismissal from the service.

"II. All police-officers are ordered to report in writing to these headquarters all instances of the violation of this order, which may come under their notice."

"NEW ORLEANS, *July* 8, 1862.

"The acting sutler of the Twenty-sixth regiment of Massachusetts volunteers will be sent home by the first boat as a steerage passenger to New York; in the mean time, to be kept in close confinement.

"He has been engaged in selling liquors to the soldiers, and speculating upon the flour belonging to the United States.

"The provost-marshal will see to the execution of this order.

"By order of Major-General BUTLER,

"R. S. DAVIES, *Captain and A. A. A. G.*"

Another special order may be quoted in this connection: "First Lieutenant T. L. Lynch, quartermaster of Third regiment of Native Guards (colored), is hereby reduced to his former position as private in the Fifteenth Maine volunteers, for drunkenness in the streets, and in a public dance-house. Quartermaster Sergeant Henry C. Wright, Ninth Connecticut Volunteers, is hereby appointed first lieutenant of the Third Native Guards, *vice* Lynch, reduced to the ranks."

Discipline thus administered produces but one result. "The demeanor of our soldiers in New Orleans," remarks one disinterested observer, "entitles them to the highest encomiums. A more quiet, orderly, respectable set of private soldiers no army ever contained. Instances of rowdyism and intoxication are extremely rare, and those few which do occur are promptly and severely punished by deprivation of pay and imprisonment. Most of the troops here are of New England origin, and certainly they do credit to the land of their birth." Nor can we be surprised to read in the *Delta*, that after one pay day, three hundred thousand dollars were sent home in small packages, besides a very large sum under the allotment system.

The general himself noticed the behavior of the troops in a special order of June 14th:

"Soldiers! Your behavior in New Orleans has been admirable! Withstanding the temptations of a great city, to present such discipline and efficiency is the highest exhibition of soldierly qualities. You have done more than win a great battle; you have conquered yourselves. You have convinced the people of New Orleans that you are worthy of the flag you bear in triumph! He is more of a coward who yields to his own weakness, than he who surrenders to an enemy! Go on, as you have begun, true to your New England training and her religious influences, showing the men and women of the South that where our bayonets are, there are peace, quiet, liberty, safety, and order under the law!"

The devotion of officers and men to a general who took their part so well against *all* enemies, was remarkable. Many affecting proofs of this devotion could be adduced, but the growing bulk of my manuscript warns me to omit details that are not essential. I will transcribe one paragraph from a letter written by a father upon hearing that his son, a fine young officer, had fallen at his post:

"Now that all is over, let me say that Henry loved you, General; not with the selfish attachment of the recipient and expectant of favors, but with the devotion that one manly heart feels for another. He would have died for you, as he would for me, or for his mother. I am nothing worth now, if I ever was; but, to the end of my days, few or many, and sorrowful they must be, I shall remember your kindness to my poor boy with the deepest gratitude."

General Butler's Mode of Dealing with Guerillas.

Before noticing the important military events of the campaign, we should consider one of the commanding general's negative merits. He did not conquer more country than he could hold. The reason of this caution in an officer so enterprising and so prolific of ideas, was stated by himself in an early dispatch to the war department.

"In the present temper of the country here," wrote Gen. Butler, June 1st, "it is cruel to take possession of any point unless we continue to hold it with an armed force; because, when we take possession of any place those well disposed will show us kindness and good wishes; the moment we leave, a few ruffians come in and maltreat every person who has not scowled at the Yankees. Therefore it is, that I have been very chary of possessing myself of various small points which could easily be taken. * * * * What I would recommend is, that I be allowed to raise here, or have sent me, a force large enough to hold, by armed occupation, every place of the slightest importance, with a supporting force that could not be overcome, *and the country made to pay the expense of such occupation.* A few months under that regime would reduce the people to order, and assure the Union men that they are not to be given up to rapine and murder in a few days, by the retirement of our troops. In their present frame of mind, under the pressure of the orders of Gen. Lovell and the Confederate government—to burn all the cotton and sugar—such burning will take place in advance of my march, wherever I may move, entailing great destruction of property upon its innocent owners, who, with tears in their eyes, have entreated me not to advance into certain sections of the country lest their property should be burned!

"As an instance of recklessness of troops in arms, take the following: The river has been unusually high, and a crevasse opened at certain points would do an immensity of damage. A party of forty rebels surprised the train on the Opelousas railroad, ran down to within thirteen miles of the city on the opposite side of the river, and there deliberately cut the levee in six different places. If their design had been carried out, they would have drowned out every plantation between New Orleans and Fort Jackson, seventy miles, but not injured the United States; all this was done, because the planters were supposed to favor us. Prompt measures were taken by me to prevent the injury before it became irreparable, which proved successful."

For these reasons, the active operations of the army were confined, at first, to sudden incursions into the enemy's country, either for the purpose of rescuing Union men, who were threatened by their neighbors with destruction, or of breaking up camps and roving gangs of guerillas. The guerillas were numerous, enterprising, and wholly devoid of every kind of scruple. They made war precisely in the spirit and in the manner of the band of murderers who recently butchered the unresisting business men of Lawrence. At that time, too, an act of congress restrained the commanders of departments from retaliation upon these miscreants. "It is useless," wrote General Butler, "to tell me to try them, send the record to Washington, and then to shoot them if the record is approved. Events travel altogether too rapidly for that. In the mean time, they hang every Union man they catch, and by their proclamations, they threaten to hang every man who has my pass. All this, while they are prating in their papers, and by the message of Davis, about carrying on a civilized warfare."

The first dash into the inhabited country was made by Colonel Kinsman, who went fifty miles or more up the Opelousas railroad, to bring away the families of some Union men who had fled to the city, asking protection. He crossed the river to Algiers, and took possession of the dépôt and cars. He inquired of the bystanders where the engineers were to be found. "There goes one," a man replied. Colonel Kinsman hailed him, and he approached. A conversation ensued, which showed something of the quality of the more demonstrative secesh. Indeed, I allude to Colonel Kinsman's excursion, only for the purpose of introducing this model of a secessionist engineer to the admiration of his countrymen.

"Are you an engineer?" asked Colonel Kinsman.

"Yes."

"Do you run on this road?"

"Yes."

"How long have you been on the road?"

"Six years."

"I want you to run a train of cars for me?"

"I won't run a train for any damned Yankee."

"Yes, you will."

"No, I won't."

"You will, and without the slightest accident, too."

"I'll die first."

"Precisely. You have stated the exact alternative. The first thing that goes wrong, you're a dead man. So march along with us."

The man obeyed. Upon getting out of hearing of his townsmen, he appeared more pliant, and the conversation was resumed.

"What is your name?"

"Pierce."

"Pierce? why that is a Yankee name. Where were you born?"

"*In Boston.*"

"Are you married?"

"Yes."

"Where was your wife born?"

"At East Cambridge."

"How long have you been in the South?"

"About six years."

"And *you* are the man who wouldn't run a train for a damned Yankee! You are, indeed, a damned Yankee. Go home, and see that you are promptly on hand to-morrow morning."

He was promptly on hand in the morning, ready to run the train for his condemned countrymen. But as competent engineers were found among the troops, it was thought best not to risk the success of the expedition by trusting the renegade, and the objects of the party were accomplished without his aid. The train ran through the Lafourche district, the garden of Louisiana, the inhabitants of which Colonel Kinsman found to be fierce, uncompromising foes of the United States. At the city of Lafourche he met the leading men of the district, face to face, at the court-house.

"We are united as one man against you," said the spokesman of the party.

"I care not," responded Colonel Kinsman, "how united you are, or against what you are united; I have only this to say to you, that if one more Union man is harmed in Lafourche, the town will be burned to the last shed."

They could not disguise their astonishment at the spectacle of a hundred Union troops penetrating a region so populous with enemies. It was something they had not in the least expected. They were destined, however, to become extremely familiar with the dingy blue of the federal uniform.

The case of this Yankee engineer was very far from being the only instance of the kind. As a rule, the *loudest* secessionists in Louisiana were people of northern birth and education. Several of the female teachers in the public schools in New Orleans, who were among the most zealous in teaching their pupils to chant the songs of Secessia, and to insult the soldiers of the Union in the streets, were found to be natives of New England. The fact shows how exquisitely adapted the system of slavery is to evoke the latent baseness of the weak, the vain, and the unregenerate. It is, also, another proof that renegades are necessarily more zealous than the hereditary adherents of a bad cause.

The dash of Colonel John C. Keith, of the Twenty-first Indiana, into the same Lafourche, was a most brilliant little affair. He gave a lesson to guerillas which Lafourche will never forget. He gave a hint to guerilla hunters which, when it is universally *taken*, will soon extinguish the last of those savages.

In the course of the famous hunt after the steamer Fox, by Colonel M'Millan, a party of four sick soldiers had been sent back through the Lafourche country. A gang of guerillas, inhabitants of the district, lay in ambush near the road, fired into the wagons in which the sick men lay, killed two of them and wounded two. The bodies of the murdered men were stripped, then kicked and clubbed until they had lost almost all resemblance to human bodies, and, finally, thrown by some negroes into a hole two feet deep, dug in the very public square of the town of Houma. The mound of earth heaped over them was conspicuous to all residents and travelers. One of the wounded men, after almost incredible adventures, escaped. The other was thrown into a filthy calaboose at Houma with a negro convict.

General Butler sent Colonel Keith, with four companies of his regiment, and two pieces of Massachusetts artillery, to convey to the people of Houma *his* sense of the moral quality of their acts. He ordered Colonel Keith to use his best endeavors to arrest the perpetrators; to hang them if found; to arrest the abettors of the butchery; and to confiscate or destroy the property of every man who, in any way, before or after the deed, had been a participator in the crime.

Colonel Keith was the very man for this duty. Seldom, in the annals of warfare, do we find an account of a piece of work better done. On arriving in the vicinity of the town, he arrested every man that could be found. Having reached Houma, he discovered that most of the inhabitants had fled, but all the men that remained he seized and securely held. He compelled the leading residents of the place to provide suitable coffins for the murdered soldiers, to disinter them with their own hands, to place them in the coffins, and to dig graves for them in the principal church-yard. The bodies were then borne to the Catholic church, where Lieutenant Rose read over them the burial service, in the presence of the whole command. They were buried with the usual salute, and suitable inscriptions were placed over their graves.

This pious duty being performed, Colonel Keith demanded of his prisoners a complete list of the names of the men who had participated in the ambush and abused the bodies of the two soldiers.

They refused. He then gave them formal, written notice, that, unless within the next forty-eight hours the names were disclosed, he would burn and utterly destroy the town of Houma, lay waste all the plantations in the vicinity, and confiscate all the movable property to the United States.

The prisoners being left to their reflections, soon came to terms. They sent for Colonel Keith, gave up the names of the murderers, and furnished information as to the direction of their flight. Then ensued, for several days and nights, such a scouring of the country for the fugitives as Lafourche had never known before. They were traced from plantation to plantation, from the open country to the forest, through the forest to the bayou. The pursuers found the planters haughty and defiant. Several of them boasted that they had harbored the fugitives and helped them to escape, and refused to reveal the direction they had taken. There were five of these gentlemen. Colonel Keith swiftly doomed them to the penalty of participators after the fact. Their houses, barns, shops and stables were burned; their horses, mules and cattle driven away; their persons seized and conveyed to New Orleans.

The ringleaders of the ambush contrived to elude the pursuit; but several of the less guilty participants were arrested. Before leaving Houma, Colonel Keith caused the jail into which the wounded soldier had been thrown, to be leveled to the ground by battering-rams. He hoisted the flag of the United States upon the court-house, and announced to the assembled people that its removal would be the signal of his return to burn the town. He made a requisition upon the authorities for a sum of money to defray part of the expenses of the expedition. Finally, he heaped burning coals upon the sore heads of the residents of Houma by distributing among the suffering poor of the town a considerable quantity of provisions, and leaving behind him for their benefit a drove of confiscated cattle.

That is General Butler's idea of guerilla hunting. The highest praise that can be bestowed upon Colonel Keith's conduct was that vouchsafed by a rebel critic, who remarked that Keith was little better than Butler himself. The reader now knows one of the reasons why Colonel Keith's application for leave of absence was so agreeably indorsed by his chief.

The command of the lakes gave the Union forces an advantage over the guerillas which was frequently used with effect. There was a troublesome crew of guerillas near Manchac pass, at the beginning of June, who plundered the neighboring plantations. Colonel Kimball, of the Twelfth Maine, landed four companies of his regiment in the vicinity, and pounced upon the position, driving out the rebel troops and capturing all their camp equipage, artillery, and colors, as well as a general officer, with his valise full of Confederate recruiting money.

New Orleans threatened.

The attention of the commanding general, in July, was drawn to more important affairs than these. Rebel troops were concentrating at various points in menacing proximity to Baton Rouge and New Orleans. Breckinridge, the general's some time political chief, now appeared in the field as his principal military adversary. The rebel ram Arkansas was reported by Captain Porter to be "above water," and capable of doing mischief. The spies of the general continually reported movements of rebel troops, and everything betokened that the project of expelling the "ruthless invaders" was about to be attempted. The preliminary stroke was to fall upon Baton Rouge, which was to be assailed by Breckinridge on land, and by the ram Arkansas from the river. The attack was made on the 5th of August. The country well remembers how gallantly it was repulsed in one of the best contested actions of the war, and how the ram Arkansas ran aground, and was shot to pieces and blown up by the Union gun-boats. I need not detail the story of that memorable day; but there were some circumstances attending the battle not generally known, which may be profitably noted by military men.

The papers before me show how extremely difficult it is for commanding generals to procure information trustworthy enough to base operations upon. Both generals were deceived on this occasion. General Butler, though no man ever had a better spy system than he, or paid more liberally for intelligence, was misled by his spies into supposing that the attack had been deferred; and he wrote to General Williams to that effect, only two days before the battle, exhorting him, however, not to relax his vigilance. General Breckinridge, on the contrary, was deceived by intelligence that was perfectly true. The secessionists of Baton Rouge, who mingled daily with the Union troops, told Breckinridge, and told him truly, that more than one-half of the troops were on the sick-list. They told him, and it was a fact, that one regiment, six hundred strong, only mustered one hundred and fifty on dress parade, and that other regiments were in a similar condition. But they did not tell him that those patriotic troops, debilitated by the summer heats, and too sick to appear on the parade-ground, were well enough to fight a battle for their country. They did not tell him that that very regiment, which could only muster a hundred and fifty men at dress parade, would turn out more than five hundred on the day of battle. He expected to meet skeleton regiments of skeleton soldiers; he met regiments with full ranks, stanch and steady. His friends told him where the sick regiments were to be posted, and he directed his main attack against that part of the field. It is said that the reason why he threw away his sword, in a paroxysm of disgust, was not the loss of the battle, but a conviction that he had been deceived and betrayed by the people of Baton Rouge. His sword was found on the field with his name engraved on the hilt.

The death of General Williams, on this bloody day, was a grievous loss to the department and the country. He was not a popular officer, except in the hour of danger. The rigor of his discipline would not have lessened the good-will of his command toward him, for soldiers love a strict disciplinarian. Soldiers, indeed, will never *long* love an officer who is not inflexible in his administration of military law. But the manner of this heroic man was sometimes ungracious; and, perhaps, he allowed his keen sense of the defects of the volunteer system to be too manifest. But on the day of battle only his great qualities were remembered, and every soldier felt that what General Williams ordered to be done was, infallibly, the movement which the moment required. Toward the close of the engagement, he came up to a regiment which had lost every field officer, and a large number of the company officers.

"We have no officers, General," said some of the men.

"Forward! my brave Indianians," he cried: "I will lead you myself."

At that instant, a ball pierced his breast, and he fell never to rise again.

The manner in which General Butler commemorated the conduct of his victorious troops merits the attention of readers. A general order was dedicated to the memory of General Williams:

"NEW ORLEANS, *August* 7, 1862.

"The commanding general announces to the army of the gulf the sad event of the death of Brigadier-General Thomas Williams, commanding Second brigade, in camp at Baton Rouge.

"The victorious achievement—the repulse of the division of Major-General Breckinridge, by the troops led on by General Williams, and the destruction of the mail-clad Arkansas, by Captain Porter, of the navy—is made sorrowful by the fall of our brave, gallant and successful fellow-soldier.

"General Williams graduated at West Point in 1837; at once joined the Fourth artillery in Florida, where he served with distinction; was thrice breveted for gallant and meritorious services in Mexico, as a member of General Scott's staff. His life was that of a soldier devoted to his country's service. His country mourns in sympathy with his wife and children, now that country's care and precious charge.

"We, his companions in arms, who had learned to love him, weep the true friend, the gallant gentleman, the brave soldier, the accomplished officer, the pure patriot and victorious hero, and the devoted Christian. All, and more, went out when Williams died. By a singular felicity, the manner of his death illustrated each of these generous qualities.

"The chivalric American gentleman, he gave up the vantage of the cover of the houses of the city—forming his lines in the open field—lest the women and children of his enemies should be hurt in the fight!

"A good general, he made his dispositions and prepared for battle at the break of day, when he met his foe!

"A brave soldier, he received his death-shot leading his men!

"A patriot hero, he was fighting the battle of his country, and died as went up the cheer of victory!

"A Christian, he sleeps in the hope of a blessed Redeemer!

"His virtues we can not exceed—his example we may emulate; and, mourning his death, we pray, 'may our last end be like his.'

"The customary tribute of mourning will be worn by the officers in the department."

The funeral was celebrated in New Orleans, with all the pomp and solemnity which the resources of the department permitted. General Butler noticed, as he passed the British consulate, that the flag of the consulate was not lowered as the procession moved by. He sent to know why the customary tribute of respect had been omitted. Mr. Coppell explained the omission satisfactorily; he was absent from his office, and was not aware that the funeral was to take place that day.

Another general order was issued a day or two after the funeral, which gave a characteristic summary of the fight.

"NEW ORLEANS, *August* 9, 1862.

"Soldiers of the Army of the Gulf:

"Your successes have heretofore been substantially bloodless.

"Taking and holding the most important strategic and commercial positions with the aid of the gallant navy, by the wisdom of your combinations and the moral power of your arms, it has been left for the last few days to baptize you in blood.

"The Spanish conqueror of Mexico won imperishable renown by landing in that country and burning his transport ships, to cut off all hope of retreat. You, more wise and economical, but with equal providence against retreat, sent yours home.

"Organized to operate on the sea-coast, you advanced your outposts to Baton Rouge, the capital of the state of Louisiana, more than two hundred and fifty miles into the interior.

"Attacked there by a division of our rebel enemies, under command of a major-general recreant to loyal Kentucky, whom some of us would have honored before his apostasy, of doubly superior numbers, you have repulsed in the open field his myrmidons, who took advantage of your sickness, from the malaria of the marshes of Vicksburg, to make a cowardly attack.

"The brigade at Baton Rouge has routed the enemy.

"He has lost three brigadier-generals, killed, wounded and prisoners; many colonels and field officers. He has more than a thousand killed and wounded.

"You have captured three pieces of artillery, six caissons, two stand of colors, and a large number of prisoners.

"You have buried his dead on the field of battle, and are caring for his wounded. You have convinced him that you are never so sick as not to fight your enemy if he desires the contest.

"You have shown him that if he can not take an outpost after weeks of preparation, what would be his fate with the main body. If your general should say he was proud of you, it would only be to praise himself; but he will say, he is proud to be one of you.

"In this battle, the northeast and the northwest mingled their blood on the field—as they had long ago joined their hearts—in the support of the Union.

"Michigan stood by Maine, Massachusetts supported Indiana, Wisconsin aided Vermont, while Connecticut, represented by the sons of the ever green shamrock, fought as their fathers did at the Boyne Water.

"While we mourn the loss of many brave comrades, we, who were absent, envy them the privilege of dying upon the battle-field for our country, under the starry folds of her victorious flag.

"The colors and guidons of the several corps engaged in the contest will have inscribed on them—'BATON ROUGE.'

"To complete the victory, the iron-clad steamer Arkansas, the last naval hope of the rebellion, hardly awaited the gallant attack of the Essex, but followed the example of her sisters, the Merrimac, the Manassas, and the Louisiana, by her own destruction."

There was yet another general order relating to the battle of Baton Rouge, which, long as it is, I can not condense, and can not endure the thought of omitting—so honorable is it to the heart of him who penned it, and so honorable to the brave men whose good conduct it chronicles.

"NEW ORLEANS, *August* 25, 186[illegible].

"The commanding general has carefully revised the official reports of the action of August 5th, at Baton Rouge, to collect the evidence of the gallant deeds and meritorious services of those engaged in that brilliant victory.

"The name of the lamented and gallant General Williams has already passed into history.

"Colonel Roberts, of the Seventh Vermont volunteers, fell mortally wounded, while rallying his men. He was worthy of a better disciplined regiment and a better fate.

"Glorious as it is to die for one's country, yet his regiment gave him the inexpressible pain of seeing it break in confusion when not pressed by the enemy, and refuse to march to the aid of the outnumbered and almost overwhelmed Indianians.

"The Seventh Vermont regiment, by a fatal mistake, had already fired into the same regiment they had refused to support, killing and wounding several.

"The commanding general, therefore, excepts the Seventh Vermont from General Order No. 57, and will not permit their colors to be inscribed with a name which could bring to its officers and men no proud thought.

"It is farther ordered, that the colors of that regiment be not borne by them until such time as they shall have earned the right to them, and the earliest opportunity will be given this regiment to show whether they are worthy descendants of those who fought beside Allen, and with Stark at Bennington.

"The men of the Ninth Connecticut, who were detailed to man Nim's battery, deserve special commendation.

"The Fourteenth Maine volunteers have credit for their gallant conduct throughout the day.

"Colonel Nickerson deserves well of his country, not more for his daring and cool courage displayed on the field when his horse was killed from under him, but for his skill, energy and perseverance in bringing his men in such a state of discipline as to enable them to execute most difficult maneuvers, under fire, with steadiness and efficiency. His regiment behaved admirably.

"Nim's battery, Second Massachusetts, under command of Lieutenant Trull, its captain being confined by sickness; Everett's battery, Sixth Massachusetts, under command of Lieutenant Carruth, who fought his battery admirably; Manning's battery, Fourth Massachusetts, and a section of a battery taken by the Twenty-first Indiana from the enemy, and attached to that regiment, under command of Lieutenant Brown, are honorably mentioned for the efficiency and skill with which they were served. The heaps of dead and dying within their range attested the fatal accuracy of their fire.

"The Sixth Michigan fought rather by detachments than as a regiment, but deserves the fullest commendation for the gallant behavior of its officers and men. Companies A, B, and F, under command of Captain Cordin, receive special mention for the coolness and courage with which they supported and retook Brown's battery, routing the Fourth Louisiana, and capturing their colors, which the regiment has leave to send to its native state.

"Colonel Dudley, Thirtieth Massachusetts volunteers, has credit for the conduct of the right wing under his command. The Thirtieth Massachusetts was promptly brought into action by Major Whittemore, and held its position with steadiness and success.

"To the Twenty-first Indiana a high meed of praise is awarded. 'Honor to whom honor is due.' Deprived of the services of their brave colonel, suffering under wounds previously received, who essayed twice to join his regiment in the fight, but fell from his horse from weakness. With every field officer wounded and borne from the field, its adjutant, the gallant Latham, killed, seeing their general fall, while uttering his last known words on earth, 'Indianians, your field officers are all killed—I will lead you,' still this brave corps fought on without a thought of defeat. Lieutenant-Colonel Keith was everywhere, cheering on his men and directing their movements, and even after his very severe wound, gave them advice and assistance. Major Hayes, while sustaining the very charge of the enemy, wounded early in the action, showed himself worthy of his regiment.

"The Ninth Connecticut and Fourth Wisconsin regiments, being posted in reserve, were not brought into action, but held their position. Colonel T. W. Cahill, Ninth Connecticut, on whom the command devolved by the death of the lamented Williams, prosecuted the engagement to its ultimate glorious success, and made all proper disposition for a farther attack.

"Magee's cavalry (Massachusetts), by their unwearied exertions on picket and outpost duty, contributed largely to our success, and deserve favorable mention.

"The patriotic courage of the following officers and privates, who left the hospitals to fight, is specially commended:

"Captain H. C. Wells, company A, Thirtieth Massachusetts;

"Captain Eugene Kelty, company I, Thirtieth Massachusetts;

"First Lieutenant C. A. R. Dimon, adjutant Thirtieth Massachusetts;

"Second Lieutenant Fred. M. Norcross, company G, Thirtieth Massachusetts;

"Third Lieutenant Wm. B. Allyn, Sixth Massachusetts battery;

"Second Lieutenant Taylor, Fourth Massachusetts battery;

"Sergeant Cheever, Ninth Connecticut;

"Private Tyler, Ninth Connecticut.

"The following have honorable mention:

"Lieutenant H. H. Elliot, A. A. A. G. to General Williams, for his coolness and intrepidity in action, and the promptness with which he fulfilled his duties;

"Lieutenant J. F. Tenney, quartermaster of Thirtieth Massachusetts, who fell severely wounded while acting aid to General Williams;

"Lieutenant W. G. Howe, of company A, Thirtieth Massachusetts, acting aid to Colonel Dudley, dangerously wounded in five places before he quit the field;

"Lieutenant C. A. R. Dimon, adjutant Thirtieth Massachusetts, acting aid to Colonel Dudley, behaved most gallantly;

"Lieutenant Fred. M. Norcross, Thirtieth Massachusetts, acting aid to Colonel Dudley, for daring courage in the field;

"Alfred T. Holt, assistant surgeon Thirtieth Massachusetts, for humane courage, taking on his back, under a hot fire, the wounded soldiers as they fell;

"Lieutenant G. F. Whitcomb, Thirtieth Massachusetts, gallantly dashing into the smoke of the enemy's musketry, bringing off a caisson left by Manning's battery;

"The gallant officer and admirable soldier, Captain Eugene Kelty, of company I, Thirtieth Massachusetts, who was ordered to deploy his brave and active company of Zouaves as skirmishers on the right, and in the performance of this duty fell bravely at their head;

"Lieutenant W. H. Gardner, company K, Thirtieth Massachusetts, who fell wounded severely, but entreated not to be taken from the field until the battle should be ended;

"Color Sergeant Brooks, company C, Thirtieth Massachusetts, and Color Corporal Rogers, company K, Thirtieth Massachusetts, who lost his left arm. Both behaved admirably during the entire engagement;

"Private McKinzie, company B, Thirtieth Massachusetts, who, though wounded, with a bullet still in his body, remained on duty throughout the engagement, and is now at his post;

"First Sergeant John Haley, company E, Thirtieth Massachusetts, commanded his company bravely and well, in the necessary absence of his line officers;

"Captain James Grimsly, company B, Twenty-first Indiana, who commanded the regiment after Colonel Keith was wounded, for his gallant behavior in following up the battle to its complete success;

"Adjutant Matthew A. Latham, Twenty-first Indiana, instantly killed while in the act of waving his sword and urging on the men to deeds of valor;

"Lieutenant Chas. D. Seeley, Orderly Sergeant John A. Bovington, Corporal Isaac Knight, and private Henry T. Batchelor, all of company A, Twenty-first Indiana, who were killed instantly, while bravely contesting the ground with the enemy;

"Captain Noblett, Twenty-first Indiana, detailing men from his company to assist in working the guns in the Sixth Massachusetts battery, after the gunners were disabled, for his supporting Lieutenant Carruth and his battery;

"Lieutenant Brown of the Twenty-first Indiana, commanding a battery, improvised from his regiment, for the efficient manner in which he handled the guns. He deserves promotion to a battery;

"Captain Chas. E. Clarke, acting colonel Sixth Michigan regiment, prevented the enemy from flanking our right, bringing his command at the critical moment to the support of Nim's battery;

"Lieutenant Howell, company F, Sixth Michigan, and Lieutenant A. J. Ralph, acting adjutant, for intrepidity;

"Captain Spitzer, Sixth Michigan, in command of the company of pickets who handsomely held in check the enemy's advance;

"The fearless conduct of Lieutenant Howell, company F, and Sergeant Thayer, company A, Sixth Michigan regiment, after they were wounded, in supporting Lieutenant Brown's battery; Lieutenant Russey, company A, for his coolness and daring;

"Captain Soule and Lieutenant Fasset, company I, Sixth Michigan, as skirmishers, were wounded; deserve special notice for the steadiness of their command, which lost heavily in killed and wounded. First Sergeant B. Stoddard, company I; Captain Smith, company A; Lieutenant Chessman, company B; Captain Davies Bacon, company K, provost judge;

"Major Bickmore and Adjutant J. H. Metcalf, of the Fourteenth Maine, wounded while nobly discharging their duty;

"Captain French, company K, Fourteenth Maine, who was terribly wounded while leading on his men to one of the finest charges of the battle. It is sorrowful indeed to add that by the accident to the steamer Whiteman he was drowned.

"Second Sergeant J. N. Seavy, company C;

"Corporal Edminster, company D;

"Second Sergeant Snow, company D;

"Private A. Blackman, company F;

"Private Preble, company F;

"All of the Fourteenth Maine, and are commended for rare bravery.

"Acting Ordnance Sergeant Long;

"Quartermaster Sergeant Gardner, and

"Commissary Sergeant Jackman;

"All of the Fourteenth Maine, and all of whom borrowed guns and entered the ranks at the commencement of the action.

"Captain Chas. H. Manning, Fourth Massachusetts battery, who fought his battery admirably, and established his reputation as a commander.

"John Donaghue, Fourth Massachusetts battery, who brought off from the camp of the Seventh Vermont regiment their colors at the time of their retreat.

"Private John R. Duffee, Fourth Massachusetts battery; private Ralph O. Rowley, of Magee's cavalry, who together went into the field, hitched horses unto a battery wagon of the Sixth Massachusetts battery, and brought it off under the fire of the enemy;

"Lieutenant Wm. B. Allyn, who had two horses shot under him; Lieutenant Frank Bruce, Orderly Sergeant Baker, Sergeant Wachter, Corporal Wood and private George Andrews, all of the Sixth Massachusetts battery, for especial bravery, gallantry, and good conduct;

"Sergeant Cheever and privates Tyler, Shields and Clogston, of the Ninth Connecticut, for the skill and bravery with which they worked one of their guns;

"Captain S. W. Sawyer, of company H, Ninth Connecticut, for his daring reconnoissance on the morning of the 9th, during which he found and secured three of the enemy's caissons, filled with ammunition."

The paragraphs reflecting upon the conduct of the Seventh Vermont led to an investigation of its behavior in the battle, which resulted in the vindication of the regiment. General Butler published an order, which corrected the error into which the first reports of the action had led him, and restored the regiment to all its honors.

The repulse at Baton Rouge changed the plans of the rebel leaders; but did not induce them to give up their main design. General Butler himself had no fear for the safety of New Orleans. He fully expected an attack, however, and disposed his forces to meet it, even withdrawing the troops from Baton Rouge, and leaving it to the custody of the gun-boats. But the Confederate leaders, before the month of September was ended, abandoned their scheme. The Union army in New Orleans had been recruited by white and colored troops, and at whatever point the enemy "felt" the Union lines, they found them unyielding to the touch.

More of the Guerilla Warfare.

The absurd guerilla warfare, however, was never intermitted. I call it absurd, because while it was fomented by the Confederate government, and encouraged by its non-combatant partisans, it was more destructive of rebel property than injurious to the United States. It is melancholy to read the reports of officers who commanded parties sent against the bandits who were ravaging Louisiana. Major F. H. Peck, of the Twelfth Connecticut, who spent a week in the early part of August, in guerilla hunting on the shores of Lake Pontchartrain, found everywhere the traces of indiscriminate plunder and destruction.

Ascending the Pearl river, he says, "We found the people in great destitution, and beset by plunderers on every side." Again, at Pass Christian: "We found the place deserted by nearly all its population, who, as from other towns we visited, are daily flying by boat-loads to avoid impressment into the Confederate service. They are destitute of the necessaries of life." "At Shields's Bow, outrages too gross for description have been recently perpetrated by guerillas, who find apologists among the most prominent citizens of the place." "At Louisburgh all the docks and buildings were burned by a party of guerillas two weeks since. It will cost many thousand dollars to rebuild them." "Madisonville was deserted, and nearly every public and private building closed." "In many places flour had not been seen for months." "We met large numbers flying to the protection of the federal army, and at each place visited by us, without exception, we were besought by men and women for passage to New Orleans. At several places we were asked to leave troops for protection against their professed friends." "Authorized and commissioned as the guerillas are, they are actuated by no motive but plunder; they fight only from ambuscade, and war indiscriminately upon friend and foe."

So it was in Spain, when the Spanish people asked Marshal Soult for protection against their own guerillas. Mexico tells the same story. So it is now in Tennessee, Kentucky, Missouri, and Virginia. The world will never know what the people of the South have suffered, and are suffering, from bandits bearing the authorization of the rebel government, and carrying the ugly flag of organized treason.

Through this starving land streamed incessantly droves of cattle from Texas for the rebel armies. There is one ferry upon the Mississippi over which, it is computed, two hundred thousand Texan cattle were carried during the first eighteen months of the war. A few days after Major Peck's return, Colonel S. Thomas, of the Eighth Vermont dashed northward, with a force of cavalry and artillery, and captured a drove of fifteen hundred cattle from Texas, and brought them all safely within the Union lines.

One of these raids into the enemy's country I will relate with a little more detail. It was the most daring little enterprise of the campaign, and well illustrated the splendid valor of the officer who commanded it, the late General George C. Strong. I little thought, when I heard him tell the story in his gay and sprightly manner, a few days before his departure for Charleston, that before the tale could get into print, his eyes would be closed for ever. He died as he wished to die, and as he meant to die. "I shall not die by disease," he said to a friend, who spoke to him upon his health, about the time of this exploit in Louisiana. In war, the more valuable a life is, the more likely it is to be lost, and never was a life more lavishly risked than his.

General Jeff. Thompson, who commanded the rebel forces near the shores of Lake Pontchartrain, is an officer of a humorous turn of mind. He had written some saucy notes to General Butler, during the summer, one of which has been given in a previous chapter. He was, also, the animating spirit of the predatory warfare which devastated the country in the vicinity of his camp, and commanded part of the forces designed to invest New Orleans. Major Strong learned from the Union spies that the head-quarters of this merry chieftain were at the village of Ponchatoula, where he had but two companies of infantry, and no cannon, the main camp being nine miles to the north of it. At Ponchatoula, also, were dépôts of supplies, a post-office, and a telegraph-office, the sudden seizure of which might disclose valuable information. The village was six miles from the Tangipaho river, a navigable stream. Major Strong conceived the project of ascending this river in a steamboat, landing a force soon after midnight, surprising the village at daybreak, capturing the general, the letters and the dispatches, destroying the supplies, and beating a hasty retreat to the steamer before the alarm could reach the main body of the enemy.

At four in the afternoon of September 13, three companies of the Twelfth Maine, under Captain Thornton, Captain Farrington, and Captain Winter, and one company of the Twenty-sixth Massachusetts, under Captain Pickering, embarked on board the Ceres. At eleven in the evening the steamer reached the mouth of the Tangipaho, and grounded on the bar. When, after a severe struggle, this obstacle had been overcome, the boat pushed up the narrow, winding river four miles; when it was one o'clock—too late for the contemplated surprise. Major Strong determined to wait till the next night, and returned to the mouth of the river. To prevent the sending of intelligence to the enemy, he directed Lieutenant Martin to collect and bring in every small boat on the Tangipaho.

Lieutenant Martin, a very young officer, fresh from a comfortable home in New York, who had volunteered to serve as aid to the commander of the party, had a view of the horrors of war in performing this duty, which he will never forget, if he should live to be a lieutenant-general. The shores of the river, in the dim light of the morning, presented to his view nothing but desolation. Many of the houses were deserted, and every garden and field lay waste. Gaunt, yellow, silent figures stood looking at the passing boat, images of despair. The people there had been small farmers, market-gardeners, fishermen, and shell-diggers; all of them being absolutely dependent upon the market of New Orleans, from which they had been cut off for four months. Roving bands of guerillas and the march of regiments had robbed them of the last pig, the last chicken, the last egg, and even of their half-grown vegetables. In all that region there was nothing to eat but corn on the cob, and of that only a few pecks in each house. Lieutenant Martin was hailed from one of the houses:

"There's a child dying here. For God's sake send a doctor ashore to save it!"

The nature of the duty he was upon forbade delay; but, as he was returning, an hour later, with his fleet of boats, he stopped at the house. The corpse of a girl, ten years old, wasted to a skeleton, lay upon a bed in the cabin. Wasted as she was, it was evident that she had been a pretty, refined-looking girl.

"Of what did she die?"

"We had nothing to give her but corn and fresh fish. We had no medicine. She could not eat what we had. She starved for want of proper food. That's what she died of."

It was an awful scene—the white skeleton upon the bed; the sullen, hungry, despairing family standing silently around; the bare, comfortless room; the utter devastation without.

The young officer was obliged to tell them that he must have their boat.

"If you do," said one of them, "we shall *all* starve, for we live on fish, and without a boat we can get no fish."

The boat had to be taken, but it was returned within twenty-four hours; and, in the mean time, Lieutenant Martin sent them a week's provisions. They seemed relieved when he left them, fearing to be "compromised" by his presence. On slighter grounds than the chance visit of a Union officer, the guerillas had burned houses and heaped every kind of outrage upon the heads of helpless and unoffending people. Terror evidently possessed every mind. One man on the Tangipaho, of whom some slight service was requested, replied to Major Strong:

"I'll do it, if you will agree to take me away with you. If you leave me here, I'm a dead man before your steamboat is out of sight."

The Ceres could not ascend the river to the point proposed. Major Strong then steamed to Manchac bridge, the terminus of a railroad that led to Ponchatoula, ten miles distant. He had resolved, rather than return to New Orleans defeated, to march along this railroad, and fall upon the place in open day. With two companies only, those of Captain Thornton and Captain Farrington, numbering one hundred and twelve men, he started soon after sunrise. It was one of the hottest days of a Louisiana summer, without a breath of wind to temper the blistering rays of the sun. The path lay through a wooded swamp, and the railroad being laid upon trestle-work, the march was difficult and laborious in the extreme. Those huge lumbermen of Maine sank under the blazing heat. Four were sun-struck. Many fell through the trestles, and had to be hoisted out of the swamp by their comrades. They saw but one human being on the way. As they were sweltering slowly and silently along, the grinning face of a negro emerged from the bushes in the swamp. He waved his old hat above his head, and shouted,

"Hurrah! I always said the Yankees would come—and here you is!"

They were more than four hours in marching the ten miles. About eleven o'clock they began to see signs of the village. Another negro here darted from behind a car that was standing on the track:

"Don't go no furder, master," said he to the major, "they've got cannon—they'll kill you all *shore*."

The party pushed on. They soon descried a locomotive slowly backing toward the village, the engineer striving to get up steam. A dozen muskets were fired at him. He did not fall, but continued to recede with increasing velocity, and backed through the village, and beyond the village toward Camp Moore, screaming the alarm. There was no time to be lost. Major Strong ranged a file of men across the railroad, to hide the smallness of his force, while he formed his troops. They advanced at the double-quick, which soon became a full run, and so rushed into the village. The negro was right—the enemy *had* cannon. A blast of canister greeted the panting troops, and laid Captain Thornton low, with three balls in his body and four more through his clothes. Most of this canister, however, went crashing through a house in which many women had taken refuge, who came screaming into the street, and ran wildly about between the two hostile bodies. Major Strong halted his men, and made new dispositions with most admirable coolness. One company he moved to the right, the other to the left; and both, from partial cover or from advantageous ground, poured a steady fire into the ranks of the foe. For a few minutes the action was exceedingly sharp. Of Major Strong's 112 men, 33 were killed or wounded. Twice the enemy fled and rallied. But, within fifteen minutes from the moment when the Union column entered the place, the rebel force, three hundred in number and six pieces of artillery, abandoned the village in hopeless confusion.

But the bird had flown. Jeff. Thompson had left the evening before. His sword, his spurs, his bridle, his papers, were seized. These only—not his clothing and personal effects. The post-office and telegraph-office were searched. A large quantity of old U. S. postage stamps, and a considerable number of letters and dispatches were found and brought away. Twenty car loads of supplies were burnt. The telegraphic instruments were broken to pieces.

As there were some thousands of rebel troops within nine miles of Ponchatoula, and a locomotive had carried the alarm thither, Major Strong was compelled to deny himself the pleasure of a long stay in the village. The weary tramp on the tressel-work was resumed. Several of the severely wounded were left behind—Capt. Thornton among them. The gallant Captain was exchanged a few days after; he recovered from his wounds, and returned to his regiment. Before the troops had gone two miles from the village, down came a train of platform cars, with a howitzer upon each of them and men to work it. But Major Strong, who had anticipated a movement of that nature, had removed some rails from the track, and caused them to be carried along with the troops. The howitzers, therefore, played upon the slowly retiring column from a distance which rendered their fire ineffectual.

It was terrible, that march back to the steamboat. The men were exhausted to the degree that they begged and implored to be left behind. One young officer, deaf to the word of command and to the voice of entreaty, Major Strong could only rouse from the last stupor of fatigue by violently kicking him as he lay across the track. Nothing saved the command from destruction but a drenching shower, which put new life into them all, and enabled them to drag their weary limbs to the boat before dark.

General Butler characterized this incursion as "one of the most daring and successful exploits of the war, equal in dash, spirit, and cool courage, to anything attempted on either side. Major Strong and his officers and men deserve great credit. It may have been a little too daring, perhaps rash, but that has not been an epidemic fault with our officers."

No man who went with this expedition was surprised at the promotion of Major Strong to the rank of brigadier-general: still less at his splendid heroism in Charleston harbor. He was expressly formed to lead a forlorn hope upon an enterprise that was only one remove from the impossible. Like Winthrop, and so many other gallant spirits, he had given his life to his country long before the moment when the gift was accepted.

Conquest of Lafourche.

When the enemy had ceased to threaten New Orleans and its outposts, General Butler deemed it prudent to extend the area of conquest by reannexing the Lafourche district to the United States. A brigade of infantry, with the requisite artillery, and a body of cavalry, under an able and enterprising officer, Captain Perkins, was placed under the command of General Weitzel for this purpose. General Weitzel penetrated this wealthy and populous region in the last week of October. A series of rapid marches, one spirited action, and a number of minor combats, placed him in complete and permanent possession of the country in four days.

It was here that the negro question presented itself so appallingly to the mind of the commander of the invading force. "What shall I do about the negroes?" he wrote to head-quarters October 29th. "You can form no idea of the vicinity of my camp, nor can you form an idea of the appearance of my brigade as it marched down the bayou. My train was larger than an army train for 25,000 men. Every soldier had a negro marching in the flanks, carrying his knapsack. Plantation carts, filled with negro women and children, with their effects; and of course compelled to pillage for their subsistence, as I have no rations to issue to them. I have a great many more negroes in my camp now than I have whites. * * These negroes are a perfect nuisance."

And the next morning a party of General Weitzel's troops captured four hundred wagon loads of negroes, which the enemy were attempting to carry with them in their retreat. There were in the whole district about 6,000 slaves, all of whom were in a ferment, and for the moment useless; especially in the neighborhood whence almost the whole white population had fled.

For several days it could be truly said of Lafourche that chaos had come again. But General Butler's abandoned plantation system was soon in operation, and restored the community to a tolerable degree of order and safety. The standing cane was gathered; the sugar-mills were set going; the negroes were merrily working at ten dollars a month; and the United States was reaping some of the advantage of their labor. A considerable number of the negroes, freed by the confiscation act, found the way into their regiments of "Native Guards," a procedure that was not pleasing in the sight of General Weitzel.

By the conquest of Lafourche, an immense amount of property liable to confiscation fell into the hands of the commanding general. The people who remained on the plantations, made haste to endeavor to save their property by making fictitious transfers. Some of the officers of the invading force, finding large quantities of sugar lying about loose, which the owners were only too glad to sell at any price, caught the fever of speculation, and bought sugar to the extent of their means. General Butler visited the principal camp of occupation, and soon learned what was going on. Feeling that the whole army was in danger of demoralization if this speculation in sugar, and in commodities more portable, was allowed to continue, he determined to apply a sweeping remedy. He devised a scheme, which not only stopped this irregular speculation, but poured the whole of the proceeds of the forfeited property into the public treasury. He *sequestered* the entire district, and all that it contained, subject to the final adjudication of a commission of officers. The following general order unfolds his scheme. As none of General Butler's acts in Louisiana has caused, or is causing, so much outcry as this, the reader should read this order with particular attention. The order was executed to the letter:

"New Orleans, *November* 9, 1862.

"The commanding general being informed, and believing, that the district west of the Mississippi river, lately taken possession of by the United

States troops, is most largely occupied by persons disloyal to the United States, and whose property has become liable to confiscation under the acts of congress and the proclamation of the president, and that sales and transfers of said property are being made for the purpose of depriving the government of the same, has determined, in order to secure the rights of all persons as well as those of the government, and for the purpose of enabling the crops now growing to be taken care of and secured, and the unemployed laborers to be set at work, and provision made for payment of their labor

"To order, as follows:

"I. That all the property within the district to be known as the 'District of Lafourche' be and hereby is sequestered, and all sales or transfers are forbidden, and will be held invalid.

"II. The district of Lafourche will comprise all the territory in the state of Louisiana lying west of the Mississippi river, except the parishes of Plaquemines and Jefferson.

"III. That Major Joseph M. Bell, provost judge, president, Lieutenant-Colonel J. B. Kinsman, A. D. C., Captain Fuller (75th N. Y. Vols.), provost-marshal of the district, be a commission to take possession of the property in said district, to make an accurate inventory of the same, and gather up and collect all such personal property, and turn over to the proper officers, upon their receipts, such of said property as may be required for the use of the United States army; to collect together all the other personal property, and bring the same to New Orleans and cause it to be sold at public auction to the highest bidders, and after deducting the necessary expenses of care, collection, and transportation, to hold the proceeds thereof subject to the just claims of loyal citizens and those neutral foreigners who in good faith shall appear to be the owners of the same.

"IV. Every loyal citizen or neutral foreigner who shall be found in actual possession and ownership of any property in said district, not having acquired the same by any title since the 18th day of September last, may have his property returned or delivered to him without sale, upon establishing his condition to the judgment of the commission.

"V. All sales made by any person not a loyal citizen or foreign neutral, since the 18th day of September, shall be held void; and all sales whatever made with the intent to deprive the government of its rights of confiscation, will be held void, at what time soever made.

"VI. The commission is authorized to employ in working the plantation of any person who has remained quietly at his home, whether he be loyal or disloyal, the negroes who may be found in said district, or who have, or may hereafter claim the protection of the United States, upon the terms set forth in a memorandum of a contract heretofore offered to the planters of the parishes of Plaquemines and St. Bernard, or white labor may be employed at the election of the commission.

"VII. The commissioners will cause to be purchased such supplies as may be necessary, and convey them to such convenient dépôts as to supply the planters in the making of the crop; which supplies will be charged against the crop manufactured, and shall constitute a lien thereon.

"VIII. The commissioners are authorized to work for the account of the United States such plantations as are deserted by their owners, or are held by disloyal owners, as may seem to them expedient, for the purpose of saving the crops.

"IX. Any persons who have not been actually in arms against the United States since the occupation of New Orleans by its forces, and who shall remain peaceably upon their plantations, affording no aid or comfort to the enemies of the United States, and who shall return to their allegiance, and who shall, by all reasonable methods, aid the United States when called upon, may be empowered by the commission to work their own plantations, to make their own crop, and to retain possession of their own property, except such as is necessary for the military uses of the United States. And to all such persons the commission are authorized to furnish means of transportation for their crops and supplies, at just and equitable prices.

"X. The commissioners are empowered and authorized to hear, determine, and definitely report upon all questions of the loyalty, disloyalty, or neutrality of the various claimants of property within said district; and farther, to report such persons as in their judgment ought to be recommended by the commanding general to the president for amnesty and pardon, so that they may have their property returned; to the end that all persons that are loyal may suffer as little injury as possible, and that all persons who have been heretofore disloyal, may have opportunity now to prove their loyalty and to return to their allegiance, and save their property from confiscation, if such shall be the determination of the government of the United States."

For six weeks the commissioners were employed in applying the confiscation act to the property in Lafourche, in establishing the loose negroes upon the abandoned lands, and in restoring to Union men their temporarily sequestered estates.

The chief labor of the commission devolved upon Colonel Kinsman, as his associates had already their hands full of occupation. When the people came crowding about him professing loyalty to the Union, he reminded them that he had had the pleasure of visiting Lafourche in the month of May, when he had been informed that the inhabitants of Lafourche were united as one man against the United States. He gave them to understand that the taking of the oath of allegiance, at the last moment, by men who had given a thousand proofs of their complicity with treason, was not enough to secure their property from confiscation. The strict observance of this rule added, in the course of time, about a million dollars to the revenue of the United States, and deprived a large number of rebels of the means of doing harm. Colonel Kinsman had a most difficult duty to perform; one that tasked equally his sagacity and his firmness; and one that he shrank from undertaking. He acquitted himself well. He executed the order and the law with care and fidelity, and won the approval of all disinterested persons who had the means of judging his conduct. Some of the military speculators in sugar grumbled at the rigor of decisions which deprived them of anticipated gain, and all the victims of the confiscation act abhorred the officer who executed it. But the friends of the Union observed with admiration his tact and patience in investigating, and the impartial justice of his awards. A corrupt man in his situation could have made a fortune with absolute security against detection. He forbore even to buy a hogshead of confiscated sugar, which he would have liked to send as a present to his New England home, lest he should give a pretext for the tongue of slander.

Every dollar's worth of confiscated property was sold at New Orleans at public auction, of which previous notice was publicly given. No man had the slightest advantage over another in purchasing, and the entire proceeds of the sales were paid into the public treasury.

Every secessionist in Louisiana will tell you to-day, that this pure and faithful officer retired from Lafourche a millionaire. They will also assure you that the rest of the proceeds of the confiscated property were divided between General Butler and his brother. They really believe that the general sent at least two millions away for investment during the eight months of his administration.

I was myself informed by a gentleman fresh from New Orleans, who had spent several weeks in the society of that city, that General Butler had invested immense sums in New York lots. So he had been told in New Orleans; all secessionists in New Orleans believed it. "Corner lots," he particularly mentioned as objects of the general's ambition. As the two millions may not all have been expended, gentlemen having desirable corner lots to dispose of may, perhaps, find a purchaser somewhere in Lowell.

Such were the principal military operations in the department of the gulf. If they were less splendid than those of other fields, if they were not all that the circumstances invited and required, it can be truly said that they were all that the force at the disposal of the commanding general permitted. What could be prudently attempted was handsomely done. In November General Butler, if he had dared to leave New Orleans inadequately defended for ten days, would have nipped Port Hudson in the bud. He dared not, with the force at his command, risk the tempting enterprise. And when, after months of waiting and beseeching for re-enforcements, re-enforcements arrived, they came provided with a major-general.

Much of the success of General Butler in his department was owing to the fact that he contrived, in spite of opposing influences in Massachusetts, to take with him many officers of his own selection—men whom he understood, and who were peculiarly adapted to render *him* efficient service. Several of these officers served long without commission and without pay. They were afterward commissioned by a stroke of General Butler's legal legerdemain. They were appointed to positions on the staff of some other major-general, not of Massachusetts, and then "assigned" to the staff of General Butler.

The general, however, was most ably assisted by the officers of his command, generally. Perhaps, I may say, without impropriety, that among those to whom he feels peculiarly indebted are the following officers:

General Strong, now in glory; Major Bell, General Weitzel, Captain Peter Haggerty, General Williams, now with General Strong; Dr. McCormick, Colonel Shaffer, Captain John Clark, Colonel J. W. Turner, Colonel Lall, of the Eighth New Hampshire; Captain Thorne, of the Twelfth Maine; Colonel Kennebec, of the same; Colonel McMillan, of the Twenty-first Indiana, now brigadier-general; Colonel Keith, Lieutenant-Colonel Kinsman, Captain Perkins, of the Massachusetts cavalry; Colonel Deming, of the Twelfth Connecticut; Colonel Birge, of the Thirteenth Connecticut; General Shepley, Colonel Thomas, of the Eighth Vermont; Captain R. S. Davis, Captain Kensel, chief of artillery; Captain John F. Appleton, Colonel Payne, of the Second Louisiana; Lieutenant-Colonel Everett, Major W. O. Fiske.

Many others, doubtless. But these are, certainly, *among* those whom General Butler would like to have with him if he had another New Orleans to take and tame.

CHAPTER XXXI.

ROUTINE OF A DAY IN NEW ORLEANS.

A Major-General commanding, as modern warfare is conducted, is in danger of becoming the slave of the desk. He carries a sword in obedience to custom, but the instrument that he is most familiar with is that one, which, 'eminent tragedians' say, is mightier than the sword. The quantity of writing required for the business of a division stationed in a quiet district is very great. But in such a department as that of the Gulf in 1862, a general must manage well, or he will find himself reduced to the condition of the 'sole editor and proprietor' of a daily newspaper. His life will resolve itself into a vain struggle to keep down his pile of unanswered letters. General Butler employed seven clerks at head-quarters; he had, also, the assistance of the younger members of his staff; but, with all this force of writers to assist him, he wrote or dictated more hours in the twenty-four than professional writers usually do.

Let us see how the day went in New Orleans.

From eight to nine in the morning, General Butler usually received ladies at his residence, who desired to avoid the publicity of the office at the Custom-House, or who had communications to make of a confidential nature. At nine, he went, in some state, to his public office. On his appearance at the front door, the guard, drawn up before the house, saluted, and the general entered his carriage, two orderlies being mounted on the box. The same ceremonial was observed when he entered the Custom-House. The six mounted orderlies, employed in conveying messages and orders, were drawn up before the principal entrance, and saluted the general. On his way to his own apartment, he had to pass through the court-room in which Major Bell was dispensing justice to the people of New Orleans. The major remarked the good effect it had upon the spectators to see the commander of the department remove his cap, as he entered the court-room, and bow to the presiding judge. On reaching his office, the general would find from one hundred to two hundred people, in and around the adjoining rooms, waiting to see him.

The office was a large room, furnished with little more than a long table and a few chairs. In one corner, behind the table, sat, unobserved, a short-hand reporter, who, at a signal from the general, would take down the examination of an applicant or an informer. The general began business by placing his pistol upon the table, within easy reach. After the detection of two or three plots to assassinate him, one of the aids caused a little shelf to be made under the table for the pistol, while another pistol, unloaded, lay upon the table, which any gentleman, disposed to attempt the game of assassination, was at liberty to snatch.

That single loaded pistol, carried in a pocket or laid upon a shelf, was General Butler's sole precaution against assassination in a community of whom a majority would have treated his murderer as a patriotic hero, and rewarded him with honor and with wealth. But that precaution sufficed. Chance gave him the reputation of being a dead shot, and every man who observed his movements could infer that his handling of his pistol would be quick and dexterous. He was riding along one day, with a numerous retinue, where some orange trees, loaded with fruit, hung over a wall. As he rode by, he took out his pistol, and aiming it at a twig which sustained three fine oranges, severed the twig, and brought the game rolling on the ground. It was a chance shot, which, probably, he could not have equaled in ten trials. But it answered the purpose of giving the impression that he was the best shot in New Orleans. Yet, it was surprising that no one attempted his assassination. He went everywhere with one attendant, or with none. His apparent carelessness was a daily invitation to the assassin.

Another member of the staff, of a mischievous turn, had exercised his talents in printing, in large letters, the following sentence, legible to all visitors, on the wall of the room:

"THERE IS NO DIFFERENCE BETWEEN A HE AND A SHE ADDER IN THEIR VENOM."

Mrs. Philips, and other ladies of a similar disposition, would glare at the legend indignantly, as though this simple statement of a fact in natural history had some special reference to *them*.

There was another little contrivance, which I believe was an achievement of the general's own genius. Some of his Creole visitors, and some of the Israelitish money-changers who came to him, were addicted to the use of garlic—a fact which did not render a close confidential interview with them so desirable as a conference from a point more remote. Consequently, the chair provided for the use of such persons was tied by the leg to the leg of the table, so that it could not be drawn very near the one occupied by the general. The anxious petitioner, not observing the cord, was likely to open the conference by throwing the chair over. Others, who succeeded in seating themselves without this embarrassing catastrophe, found all their attempts to edge up confidentially to the general's ear unavailing. This invention saved the general from the fumes of garlic, and compelled the visitor to speak loud enough for the reporter to hear him.

The general being seated in his chair behind the table, with his artillery in position, heads of departments were first admitted, such as the medical director and the chief of police. Their reports having been received and acted upon, the chiefs of the Relief Commission and the Labor Commission entered and reported. Next to them such persons as consuls and bank directors. The first hour of the morning was usually consumed in conference with these and other important official individuals. Then the public were admitted, thirty at a time, who stood in a semi-circle before the table. The general would begin at one end of the line, and ask:

"What do you want?"

They wanted everything that creature ever wanted: a pass to go beyond the lines; an order on the relief committee for food; protection against a hard landlord; a permit to search for a slave; aid to recover a debt; the arbitration of a dispute; payment of a claim against the government; the restoration of forfeited property; the suppression of a nuisance; employment in the public offices; a gift of money; information on points of law; protection against a cruel master. Others came to give information, or to wreak an inexpensive revenge by denouncing a private foe as a public enemy. The general devoted an average of twenty seconds to the consideration of each. A few, short, sharp, incisive questions, and then the decision, clear as yes or no could make it. And the decision once pronounced, there was not another syllable to be said. Every one got, at least, *an answer*, and the answer was generally right. Under the fire of General Butler's cross-questioning, the subterfuges and evasions of the unskillful rebels melted rapidly away, and the truth stood out clear and unmistakable. Sometimes, when a man had been detected in a falsehood, he would try again.

"Well, General, I own it was a lie, but *now* I am going to tell the truth."

It happened, not unfrequently, that the general would overturn, by an adroit question or two, the second version of the tale, and the man would essay a third time, calling all the saints to witness that now, at last, the pure truth should be told, and then immediately coin a new series of falsehoods, to be instantly detected by the general. Scenes of this kind occurred so often, that it became a by-word at head-quarters: "Now I am going to tell you the truth."

At eleven o'clock, the door being closed to miscellaneous applicants, the letters of the day were placed upon the table opened, to the number of eighty or a hundred. The general read over each, and disposed of most of them by writing a word or two on the back, "yes," "no," "granted," "refused;" in accordance with which the answer was prepared by clerk or secretary. Others were reserved for consideration or for answer by the general's own hand. Military business was next in order, which brought him to the hungry hour of one. After luncheon, the writing of reports and letters occupied the time till half-past four. Then home to dinner. From half-past five till dark, the general was on horseback, reviewing a regiment here, visiting an outpost there, thus uniting duty with recreation. Then home to his private office, where he wrote or dictated letters till ten. The last tired scribe being then dismissed, the general retired to the only apartment into which no visitor ever entered, where, at a little desk in a corner, he wrote the papers and dispatches which were of most importance, or which were designed only for the eye of the person addressed.

Even this constant devotion to the business of his position could not prevent an accumulation of unanswered letters. Frequently he was obliged to ply the pen all day Sunday, in order to reduce the mountain of papers, and begin the week with a clear conscience and a clean table. The business, however, was all *done*. No letter but received its due attention. Letters from home asking information respecting soldiers who had suddenly ceased to write to their friends were invariably answered, and the fullest accounts given which could be procured. A decent application for an autograph was not neglected; for the general kept a supply of the article on hand, ready folded, enveloped, and stamped.

"Why not?" he said one day to Major Strong, who laughed at this business-like proceeding. "If I can gratify a person, by writing my name, why should not I do it? At the same time, why should not I do it with the least trouble to myself?"*

Thus the days passed. A trip up the river to Baton Rouge, or down the river to the forts, a ride to Carrollton, or a brigade review, varied the uniformity of the general's life. But most of his days were employed in the manner just described. "For hours," writes one, "he sits and patiently listens to complaints, and suggests punishments or redress. Returning to his hotel, he partakes of a simple meal, retires to his room, to be again besieged by crowds of officers and orderlies, charged with reports, or waiting orders. Late at night, I have seen the gas gleaming from his room (the door open by the necessity of getting some air in this suffocating climate), and the general buried in the labor of his extensive military correspondence."†

It was not General Butler's office alone which was besieged by crowds of anxious people. Colonel French, General Shepley, Col. Stafford, Dr. McCormick, were only less busy than he, in answering the arguments, and supplying the wants of the people. The intelligent writer just quoted attended, at the City Hall, the headquarters of Governor Shepley, and noted the cases disposed of by him in one morning. The catalogue will interest the reader:

"General G. F. Shepley," he remarks, "the least observant of people would point out as a man of more than ordinary character. His figure is as straight as an Indian's, his eye—a light blue—is remarkably expressive; the hair sweeps in a broad, bold dash away from his square forehead, and his moustache and imperial are perfect. With his sword at his side, and standing up listening to the numerous people who call on him, I have rarely seen a more soldierly-looking man.

* N.B. The supply is now said to be exhausted, the demand having exceeded the resources of the market.

† Correspondence of the *New York Times*.

"The first thing brought to the general's notice by the attendant clerks was a petition from the sheriff of New Orleans for the relief of certain prisoners. A tall, shrewish woman, now entered and asked for an order to make a tenant pay rent. Next came a woman, child in arms, detailing her sufferings, her husband having been impressed into the Confederate service. An old and very respectable gentleman desired a pass for a family of a mother, six children, and four servants, to Baton Rouge. A committee appeared, desiring work on the streets for poor men who had been in rebel service; petition instantly granted, if the parties named would take the oath of allegiance. A gentleman appears, who wishes to get an order to repair a building occupied by United States troops as a hospital; he was waved out with impatience. Merchants now crowd in with all sorts of questions regarding business matters. An officer of the navy obtrudes his gold-laced cuff, and places a letter on the table from Commodore Porter; it is opened, read, and answer dictated, in a moment. A man now presents himself, and says his negro, who had been absent several days, said he was forcibly retained in the national lines; General Shepley rises from his seat, his eyes flash; he replies, mildly but positively, that he don't believe the negro's story, and demands a responsible white man for a witness, the complainant leaving precipitately. Old gentleman in an undertone asks a favor; it is granted, and old gentleman goes off delighted. An old lady in black now comes in, with a little negro girl following in the rear, carrying her work-bag. Old lady seats herself on the lounge, and the little negro girl crouches on the carpet at her feet. General Shepley gets up and speaks to old lady; she says nothing, pouts at the contraband, and gets some answer that is satisfactory—for exit old lady, little negro, and work-bag.

"A delegation of merchants now appear, who have some conversation about the currency. A city official makes a report about cleaning the streets. A Maine skipper comes in—his eyes enlarged, and his face on a broad grin. General Shepley is from his town; but something more, the Maine skipper has found his vessel over at Algiers, that was taken from him some months before by the privateers; he gets an order to take possession of his vessel, and announces that he has more sugar offered him for New York than he can put in his newly gained prize. Meantime, two handsome young ladies in gay colors have been quietly watching the proceedings through their half-drawn-aside veils, never deigning to come forward to make their requests. The General approaches them, and a most animated conversation in an undertone, so far as they are concerned, ensues. The general listens very attentively, evidently becomes interested, and grants the request. Now he goes to the ladylike personage in black. It is clear she is a widow; and the way she rolled her large, speaking, dark creole eyes up into the face of the general, was well calculated to make an impression on the 'governor' if he had been born even farther north than Maine. The lady next pointed out her sons, and asked a favor. She wanted to get out of the city, and would the general be so kind as to give her a pass to go beyond the federal lines?

"A committee is now announced. It is headed by the president of the Union association, and is composed of its prominent members. They present a petition to the general, requesting certain municipal reforms. The next person introduced was a highly respectable and wealthy planter, who had never yielded to the pressure of secession, or never concealed his sentiments, though daily persecuted, and often threatened with imprisonment or assassination. He represented the sufferings in the 'interior parishes' as fearful, the evils of starvation and suffering occasioned by the rebellion being aggravated by the high water that had flowed in from the river, the levee law being entirely disregarded by the landed proprietors.

"For five long hours the audiences continue, and only end to enable the general to resume new duties at his military head-quarters at the custom-house."

The general life of the city had resumed something of its wonted careless gayety and business bustle. The morning markets of New Orleans were bright once more with red bandannas, and noisy with the many-tongued chatter of the hucksters—Creole, French, German, Spanish, and English. "I suppose," remarks a spirited writer,* "that nowhere since the dispersion of the builders of Babel, could be heard such polyglot vociferations as proceed from the sidewalk peddlers in the French market at New Orleans. On one side, the gesticulative Gaul rolls his r's with absolutely canine emphasis in the utterance of his native language, or gallicizes the English

* Mr. Thomas Butler Gunn, the able correspondent of the *New York Tribune*.

appellation of the most popular of vegetables into 'pa-ta-ta—s!' or informs you that the price of a bird or fish is 'two bit! two bit—you no like him, you no hab him!' On another, the German vociferates with as harmonious an effect as might be produced by the simultaneous shaking up of pebbles in a quart pot, and the filing of a hand-saw; while on a third and fourth, the Creole, Sicilian, and Dego rival each other in vocal discord. Fancy all this, and throw in any amount of obstreperous, broad-mouthed, gleeful negro laughter, and you have some approximation toward the sounds audible at the time and locality I have undertaken to describe."

The far-famed rotunda of the St. Charles hotel again resounded with the noise of multitudinous conversation; but its lofty dome echoed not back the sound of the auctioneer's hammer, that doomed the pampered house-slave to the horrors of a Red River plantation, or consigned a beautiful quadroon to the arms of a lucky gambler. The levee still looked bare and deserted to those who had known it in former years; but there was some life there. A few vessels were loading or discharging. The ferry-boats were plying on the river. The scream of the steam-whistle was heard, and steamboats were "up" for Carrollton, Baton Rouge, or Fort Jackson. In the stream lay at anchor a few representatives of the immortal fleet, the arrival of which, in the last days of April, ushered in a new era of the history of Louisiana.

CHAPTER XXXII.

RECALL.

THERE had been rumors all the summer that General Butler was about to be recalled from the Department of the Gulf. In August, he alluded to these rumors in one of his letters to General Halleck, and said, that if the government meant to remove him, it was only fair for his successor to come at once, and take part of the yellow fever season. General Halleck replied, September 14, that these rumors were "without foundation." Mr. Stanton had written approvingly of his course. Mr. Chase and Mr. Blair expressed very cordial approval of it. The president, in October, wrote to the general in a friendly and confidential manner. It was only the secretary of state who appeared to dread that total suppression of the enemies of the United States in Louisiana, which it was General Butler's aim to effect. But it was not supposed that his policy would carry him so far as to deprive his country of the services of the man who, wherever he had been employed, had shown so much ability, and who had just achieved the ablest and the noblest piece of impromptu statesmanship the modern world has seen.

General Butler was going on in the usual tenor of his way. His favorite scheme, as the winter drew near, was the roofing of the custom-house, the citadel of New Orleans. The government had expended millions upon that edifice, and its marble walls had been completed, but it stood exposed to the weather, and was rapidly depreciating. The estimates of competent engineer officers showed that it could be covered for about forty thousand dollars with a roof of wood, which would last thirty or forty years, save the costly structure from decay, and render the upper stories inhabitable. He procured part of the necessary timber by seizing a large quantity which was the property of those notorious 'foreign neutrals,' Gautherin and Co., and which, he was prepared to show, had been bought by the Confederate government. In executing the work, he intended to employ a large number of the men who were daily fed by the bounty of the government. The operation was about to be begun, when the order for his recall arrived. It would have been done in three months from the revenues of the department. The Custom-House is still without a roof.

Another project engaged his attention toward the close of the year. He received information that a speculative firm in Havana had imported from Europe a large quantity of arms, which they hoped to sell to the Confederate government. He sent an officer to Havana to examine these arms, procure samples, and endeavor to get the refusal of them for three months, so as to gain time for the war department to effect the purchase of the arms for the United States. Captain Hill, the officer employed on this errand, had obtained a refusal of the arms for several weeks, when the change of commanders took place, and the affair was dropped. Captain Hill reports, that no citizen of the United States, supposed to have a public commission, was safe at that time in Havana. He was subjected to every kind of annoyance, and was warned by friendly Cubans not to be in the streets alone after dark. The town swarmed with rebel emissaries and rebel sympathizers, affording another proof that, in this quarrel, we are alone against the benighted men, and classes of men, who are interested in retarding the progress of civilization. The day after the departure of Captain Hill from New Orleans, the report was current in the city that he had been sent by General Butler to the North, with two millions in gold, the spoils of Lafourche, to deposit in some place of safety against the coming day of wrath. He carried, in fact, just two thousand dollars in gold, to defray his expenses in Havana.

New Orleans elected two members of congress in December, Mr. Benjamin F. Flanders, and Mr. Michael Hahn, both unconditional Union men. Mr. Flanders received 2,370 votes out of 2,543; Mr. Hahn received 2,581, which was a majority of 144 over all competitors. The canvass was spirited, and no restriction was placed upon the voting, except to exclude all who had not taken the oath of allegiance. At this election, the number of Union votes exceeded, by one thousand, the whole number of votes cast in the city for secession.

It could be truly said in December, that there was in New Orleans, after seven months of General Butler's government, a numerous party for the Union, probably a majority of the whole number of voters. The men of wealth were secessionists, almost to a man. The gamblers and ruffians were on the same side. The lowest class of whites exhibited the same impious antipathy to the negroes, and the same leaning toward their oppressors, that we observe in the corresponding class in two or three northern cities. But, among the respectable mechanics and smaller traders, there was a great host who were either committed to the side of the Union, or were only deterred from committing themselves by a fear that, after all, the city was destined to fall again under the dominion of the Confederates. The Union meetings were attended by enthusiastic crowds, and the eloquence of a Deming, a Durant, a Hamilton, was greeted with the same applause that it elicits at the North. When General Butler appeared in public he was greeted with cheers not less hearty nor less unanimous than he has since been accustomed to receive nearer home. Late in November he made a public visit to the theater. When he entered the house the audience rose and gave him cheer upon cheer, just as in New York or Boston.

The Union party, too, was a growing power. Union men now felt that they were on the side of the strongest. They knew that no man could be anything or effect anything, or enjoy anything in Louisiana, who was not on the side of his country. For Union men there were offices, employments, privileges, favors, honors, everything which a government can bestow. For rebels there was mere protection against personal violence—mere toleration of their presence; and that only so long as they remained perfectly submissive and quiescent. It has been truly remarked, that of the three powers of a community—the government, the rich and the multitude—any two can always overcome the third. In New Orleans the government and the multitude were forming daily a closer union; and the wealthy faction, who had ruined the state, were becoming daily more isolated and more powerless.

Meanwhile, the general was urging upon the war department the necessity of a larger force, that he might employ the cool season in reducing Port Hudson and extending the area of conquest in other directions. He entreated his old friend Senator Wilson to use his influence at the war department in his behalf. The senator's reply is curious, when we consider that at the time of the interview which it records General Butler's successor in the Department of the Gulf had been appointed twenty-three days. "Your note," said Senator Wilson, "was placed in my hand to-day (Dec. 2), and I at once called upon the secretary of war, and pressed the importance of increasing your force. He agreed with me and promised to do what he could to aid you. He expressed his confidence in you and his approval of your vigor and ability. This was gratifying to me, but I should have been more pleased to have had him order an addition to your force, so that you might have a larger field of action. I will press the matter all I can."

Early in December it became well known in New Orleans that the government was preparing, in the ports of the North, one of those imposing expeditions of which so many have sailed on mysterious errands during the war. Texas was supposed to be its object. Texas, I believe, *was* its ultimate object.

In the absence of official information, and supposing his own services approved by the government, General Butler was left to infer that General Banks was to hold an independent command in the Department of the Gulf. He feared a conflict of authority. Nor could he regard with complacency the coming of another major-general to reap the laurels of the field, while he himself, after having done the painful and odious part of the work, was left still to battle only with the sullen, unarmed secessionists of New Orleans. Not to embarrass the government, he wrote to the president an unofficial letter on the subject.

"I see by the papers," he writes, November 29th, "that General Banks is about being sent into this department with troops, upon an independent expedition and command. This seems to imply a want of confidence in the commander of this department, perhaps deserved, but still painful. In my judgment, it will be prejudicial to the public service to attempt any expedition into Texas without making New Orleans a base of supplies and co-operation. To do this there must be but one head, and one department.

"I do not propose to argue the question here; still farther is it from my purpose to suggest even that there may not be a better head than the one now in the department. I beg leave to call your attention, that since I came into the field, the day after your first proclamation, I have ever been in the frontier line of the rebellion —Annapolis, when Washington was threatened; Relay House, when Harper's Ferry was being evacuated; Baltimore, Fort Monroe, Newport News, Hatteras, Ship Island, and New Orleans. It is not for me to say with what meed of success. But I have a right to say that I have lived at this station exposed, at once, to the pestilence and the assassin, for eight months, awaiting re-enforcements which the government could not give until now. And now they are to be given to another. I have never complained. I do not now complain. I have done as well as I could everything which the government asked me to do. I have eaten that which was set before me, asking no questions.

"It is safe for any person to come to New Orleans and stay. It has been demonstrated that the quarantine can keep away the fever. The assassins are overawed or punished.

"Why, then, am I left here when another is sent into the field in this department? If it is because of my disqualification for the service, in which I have as long an experience as any general in the United States army now in the service (being the senior in rank),

I pray you say so; and so far from being even aggrieved, I will return to my home, consoled by the reflection, that I have at least done my duty as far as endeavor and application go. I am only desirous of not being kept where I am not needed or desired, and I will relieve the administration of all embarrassment. Pray do me the favor to reflect that I am not asking for the command of any other person; but, simply, that unless the government service require it, that my own, which, I have a right to say, has not been the least successful of the war, shall not be taken from me in such a manner as to leave me all the burden without any of the results.

"Permit me also to say, that toward General Banks, who is selected to be the leader of the Texas expedition, I have none but the kindest feelings, he having been my personal friend for years, and still being so.

"Writing about my personal affairs, which I have never done before, I hardly know how to express myself; but what I mean is this: If the commander-in-chief find me incompetent (unfaithful I know he can not), let me be removed, and be allowed to meet the issue before him and my country; but, as I never do anything by indirection myself, all I ask of the president, as a just man, is that the same course may be taken toward me.

"Allow me to repeat again, sir, what I have before said—although the determination may cause my recall—*put the department which includes Louisiana and Texas under one head, and it will be best for the service.* I pray you, sir, not to misunderstand me. I have given up something for my country, and can give up more. And this command is a small matter in comparison, in my mind, to my own self-respect, or to the good of the service.

"I do not seek to embarrass the government by any action of mine, or in regard to myself. Far from it. I could even take myself away rather than to do any thing which would weaken, by one ounce, the strength with which the administration should strangle this rebellion."

It was too late. When this letter was written, the fate of the writer had been decided for twenty days. The answer to it came by rebel telegraph to the outlying camps of the enemy, and was brought in by the Union spies ten days, or more, before General Banks himself knew his destination. It came in the form of a positive statement that General Banks was coming to New Orleans to supersede General Butler. The higher circles of secessionists were so certain of the fact that bets were made, in the principal club of the city, of a hundred dollars to ten, that General Butler would be recalled before the end of the year. It now appears, that the French government was first notified of the intended change. The news, probably, came direct, either from the state department or from the French legation. From whatever source it was derived, the rebels knew it before it had been whispered about Washington. Jefferson Davis knew it before General Banks, though Davis was at Jackson, in Mississippi, and General Banks was at Washington.

General Butler submitted to the inevitable stroke with the best possible grace. He had had practice in submission. Had he not been recalled from Baltimore for doing his duty too well? Had he not been recalled from Fortress Monroe at the moment it had become possible to reap the fruit of his most able and arduous labors?

He gave General Banks a cordial and brilliant reception. At Fort Jackson, the arriving general, much to his surprise, was saluted by the number of guns which, by regulation, announce the presence of the commander of the department. At the levee of New Orleans, General Butler provided carriages, escort, and a saluting battery, and detailed members of his staff to superintend the arrangements for the honorable entertainment of his successor. General Banks arrived on Sunday evening, December 14, and immediately drove to General Butler's residence, where he was received with every honor. He had a little billet to deliver, which explained the object of his presence in Louisiana with a brevity more than Roman:

"War Department, Adjutant-General's Office,
" Washington, *November* 9, 1862.

"General Order No. 184.

" By direction of the president of the United States, Major-General Banks is assigned to the command of the Department of the Gulf, including the state of Texas. By order of the secretary of war,

" E. D. Thomas, *Assistant Adjutant-General.*

" H. W. Halleck, *General-in-Chief.*"

On Tuesday, the sixteenth, the two generals met at head-quarters, where General Butler formally surrendered the command of the department. Each general introduced his staff to the staff of the other. General Butler pronounced an eulogium upon the character and career of his successor, and ordered his staff to extend to him and to his officers every facility in their power for acquiring the requisite information relating to the department. The *Delta*, in chronicling the interview, bestowed due commendation upon the retiring general, but commended General Banks to the people and to the army with equal warmth. The *Delta* of the same day, published the last general order of the retiring commander:

"HEAD-QUARTERS, DEPARTMENT OF THE GULF,
"NEW ORLEANS, *December* 15, 1862.

GENERAL ORDER No. 106.

"Soldiers of the Army of the Gulf:

"Relieved from farther duties in this department by direction of the president, under date of November 9, 1862, I take leave of you by this final order, it being impossible to visit your scattered outposts, covering hundreds of miles of the frontier of a larger territory than some of the kingdoms of Europe.

"I greet you, my brave comrades, and say farewell!

"This word, endeared as you are by a community of privations, hardships, dangers, victories, successes, military and civil, is the only sorrowful thought I have.

"You have deserved well of your country. Without a murmur you sustained an encampment on a sand bar, so desolate that banishment to it, with every care and comfort possible, has been the most dreaded punishment inflicted upon your bitterest and most insulting enemies.

"You had so little transportation, that but a handful could advance to compel submission by the queen city of the rebellion, whilst others waded breast-deep in the marshes which surround St. Philip, and forced the surrender of a fort deemed impregnable to land attack by the most skillful engineers of your country and her enemy.

"At your occupation, order, law, quiet, and peace sprang to this city, filled with the bravos of all nations, where for a score of years, during the profoundest peace, human life was scarcely safe at noonday.

"By your discipline you illustrated the best traits of the American soldier, and enchained the admiration of those that came to scoff.

"Landing with a military chest containing but seventy-five dollars, from the hoards of a rebel government you have given to your country's treasury nearly a half million of dollars, and so supplied yourselves with the needs of your service that your expedition has cost your government less by *four-fifths than any other.*

"You have fed the starving poor, the wives and children of your enemies, so converting enemies into friends, that they have sent their representatives to your congress, by a vote greater than your entire numbers, from districts in which, when you entered, you were tauntingly told that there was 'no one to raise your flag.'

"By your practical philanthropy you have won the confidence of the 'oppressed race' and the slave. Hailing you as deliverers, they are ready to aid you as willing servants, faithful laborers, or, using the tactics taught them by your enemies, to fight with you in the field.

"By steady attention to the laws of health, you have stayed the pestilence, and, humble instruments in the hands of God, you have demonstrated the necessity that His creatures should obey His laws, and, reaping His blessing in this most unhealthy climate, you have preserved your ranks fuller than those of any other battalions of the same length of service.

"You have met double numbers of the enemy, and defeated him in the open field; but I need not farther enlarge upon this topic. You were sent here to do that.

"I commend you to your commander. You are worthy of his love.

"Farewell, my comrades! again farewell!

"BENJ. F. BUTLER,
"*Major-General Commanding.*"

The general immediately prepared for his departure. As he had received no directions as to his future course, he presumed that the place for him to retire to was his own home at Lowell. "Having received no further orders," he wrote to the president, "either to report to the commander-in-chief, or otherwise, I have taken the liberty to suppose that I was permitted to return home, my services being no longer needed here. I have given Major-General Banks all the information in my power, and more than he has asked, in relation to the affairs of this department."

The general's farewell order to his troops called forth many pleasing proofs of the strength of their attachment to a commander who, on all occasions, had made their cause his own. Among the letters of those last days I find one which, I trust, may be printed without impropriety:

"LAKEPORT, *December* 15, 1862.

"Major-General B. F. BUTLER:

"SIR:—Last summer you had occasion to reprimand an officer for an unintentional neglect of duty. Your manner and your words sunk deep into his memory; and he always wished some opportunity might present itself when he could evidence by his actions his full appreciation of your delicate reproval. I am that officer; and, in part, the wished-for opportunity came when I was ordered here. I have tried to do my duty, and feel that I have done it, because my general, for whose command I raised my company, who never forgets to censure or to reward, has not reproved me.

"For your kindness to the soldiers you will ever be held in loving remembrance; your past services will be remembered by the country, and be rewarded.

"Now that you are to leave us, there can be no want of delicacy in my thus expressing my feelings. I say, good fortune attend you. Good-by, General; God bless you!

"I remain, with great regard, yours ever to command,

"JOHN F. APPLETON, *Captain commanding at Lakeport.*"

On the twenty-third, there was a public leave-taking, when a great number of officers and citizens gathered round the general to bid him farewell. For two hours, a continuous procession of his friends passed by where he stood, and shook him by the hand. General Banks and his officers were among them. Admiral Farragut was there, with many officers of the fleet.

It seemed good to the general to say a word of farewell to the people of New Orleans. Amid the hurry and bustle of his departure, he found time to produce a Farewell Address, so grand in its truth, wisdom, and simplicity, that it must ever be regarded as one of the noblest utterances of the time, or of any time:

FAREWELL ADDRESS.

"CITIZENS OF NEW ORLEANS:—It may not be inappropriate, as it is not inopportune in occasion, that there should be addressed to you a few words at parting, by one whose name is to be hereafter indissolubly connected with your city.

"I shall speak in no bitterness, because I am not conscious of a single personal animosity. Commanding the Army of the Gulf, I found you captured, but not surrendered; conquered, but not orderly; relieved from the presence of an army, but incapable of taking care of yourselves. I restored order, punished crime, opened commerce, brought provisions to your starving people, reformed your currency, and gave you quiet protection, such as you had not enjoyed for many years.

"While doing this, my soldiers were subjected to obloquy, reproach, and insult.

"And now, speaking to you, who know the truth, I here declare that whoever has quietly remained about his business, affording neither aid nor comfort to the enemies of the United States, has never been interfered with by the soldiers of the United States.

"The men who had assumed to govern you and to defend your city in arms having fled, some of your women flouted at the presence of those who came to protect them. By a simple order (No. 28), I called upon every soldier of this army to treat the women of New Orleans as gentlemen should deal with the sex, with such effect that I now call upon the just-minded ladies of New Orleans to say whether they have ever enjoyed so complete protection and calm quiet for themselves and their families as since the advent of the United States troops.

"The enemies of my country, unrepentant and implacable, I have treated with merited severity. I hold that rebellion is treason, and that treason persisted in is *death*, and any punishment short of that due a traitor gives so much clear gain to him from the clemency of the government. Upon this thesis have I administered the authority of the United States, because of which I am not unconscious of complaint. I do not feel that I have erred in too much harshness, for that harshness has ever been exhibited to disloyal enemies to my country, and not to loyal friends. To be sure, I might have regaled you with the amenities of British civilization, and yet been within the supposed rules of civilized warfare. You might have been smoked to death in caverns, as were the Covenanters of Scotland by the command of a general of the royal house of England; or roasted, like the inhabitants of Algiers during the French campaign; your wives and daughters might have been given over to the ravisher, as were the unfortunate dames of Spain in the Peninsular war; or you might have been scalped and tomahawked as our mothers were at Wyoming by the savage allies of Great Britain in our own Revolution; your property could have been turned over to indiscriminate 'loot,' like the palace of the Emperor of China; works of art which adorned your buildings might have been sent away, like the paintings of the Vatican; your sons might have been blown from the mouths of cannon, like the Sepoys at Delhi; and yet all this would have been within the rules of civilized warfare as practiced by the most polished and the most hypocritical nations of Europe. For such acts the records of the doings of some of the inhabitants of your city toward the friends of the Union, before my coming, were a sufficient provocative and justification.

"But I have not so conducted. On the contrary, the worst punishment inflicted, except for criminal acts punishable by every law, has been banishment with labor to a barren island, where I encamped my own soldiers before marching here.

"It is true, I have levied upon the wealthy rebels, and paid out nearly half a million of dollars to feed 40,000 of the starving poor of all nations assembled here, made so by this war.

"I saw that this rebellion was a war of the aristocrats against the middling men—of the rich against the poor; a war of the land-owner against the laborer; that it was a struggle for the retention of power in the hands of the few against the many; and I found no conclusion to it, save in the subjugation of the few and the disinthrallment of the many. I, therefore, felt no hesitation in taking the substance of the wealthy, who had caused the war, to feed the innocent poor, who had suffered by the war. And I shall now leave you with the proud consciousness that I carry with me the blessings of the humble and loyal, under the roof of the cottage and in the cabin of the slave, and so am quite content to incur the sneers of the *salon*, or the curses of the rich.

"I found you trembling at the terrors of servile insurrection. All danger of this I have prevented by so treating the slave that he had no cause to rebel.

"I found the dungeon, the chain, and the lash your only means of enforcing obedience in your servants. I leave them peaceful, laborious, controlled by the laws of kindness and justice.

"I have demonstrated that the pestilence can be kept from your borders.

"I have added a million of dollars to your wealth in the form of new land from the batture of the Mississippi.

"I have cleansed and improved your streets, canals, and public squares, and opened new avenues to unoccupied land.

"I have given you freedom of elections greater than you have ever enjoyed before.

"I have caused justice to be administered so impartially that your own advocates have unanimously complimented the judges of my appointment.*

"You have seen, therefore, the benefit of the laws and justice of the government against which you have rebelled.

"Why, then, will you not all return to your allegiance to that government,—not with lip-service, but with the heart?

"I conjure you, if you desire ever to see renewed prosperity, giving business to your streets and wharves—if you hope to see your city become again the mart of the western world, fed by its rivers for more than three thousand miles, draining the commerce of a country greater than the mind of man hath ever conceived—return to your allegiance.

"If you desire to leave to your children the inheritance you received from your fathers—a stable constitutional government; if you desire that they should in the future be a portion of the greatest empire the sun ever shone upon—return to your allegiance.

"There is but one thing that stands in the way.

"There is but one thing that at this hour stands between you and the government—and that is slavery.

"The institution, cursed of God, which has taken its last refuge here, in His providence will be rooted out as the tares from the wheat, although the wheat be torn up with it.

* Upon the retirement of Major Bell from the bench of the provost court, the lawyers and others who had attended it presented to the major a valuable cane, accompanying the gift with expressions of esteem and gratitude, far more precious than any gift could be.

"I have given much thought to this subject.

"I came among you, by teachings, by habit of mind, by political position, by social affinity, inclined to sustain your domestic laws, if by possibility they might be with safety to the Union.

"Months of experience and of observation have forced the conviction that the existence of slavery is incompatible with the safety either of yourselves or of the Union. As the system has gradually grown to its present huge dimensions, it were best if it could be gradually removed; but it is better, far better, that it should be taken out at once, than that it should longer vitiate the social, political and family relations of your country. I am speaking with no philanthropic views as regards the slave, but simply of the effect of slavery on the master. See for yourselves.

"Look around you and say whether this saddening, deadening influence has not all but destroyed the very framework of your society.

"I am speaking the farewell words of one who has shown his devotion to his country at the peril of his life and fortune, who in these words can have neither hope nor interest, save the good of those whom he addresses; and let me here repeat, with all the solemnity of an appeal to Heaven to bear me witness, that such are the views forced upon me by experience.

"Come, then, to the unconditional support of the government. Take into your own hands your own institutions; remodel them according to the laws of nations and of God, and thus attain that great prosperity assured to you by geographical position, only a portion of which was heretofore yours."

"BENJAMIN F. BUTLER.

"NEW ORLEANS, *Dec. 24th*, 1862."

Where is there a nobler piece than this? Where one more exactly true? Where one more irrefragably wise? Happy the land which, at a crisis of public danger, can summon from the walks of private life a man capable, first, of doing these things, and then of recording them in a strain of such severe and grand simplicity. So

Cæsar might have written, when Cæsar was a patriot. So Napoleon, had Napoleon been the citizen of a free country. But they did not. The situation was unique, and the piece stands alone, above and beyond all the writings of the great soldiers of the world.

Peıhaps I may be pardoned for mentioning the effect which its perusal produced upon one individual, the reader's most humble and most devoted servant and scribe. He had been for three years absorbed in writing, or preparing to write, a complete biography of the greatest of all Yankees, Benjamin Franklin. Upon reading this farewell address, he was drawn irresistibly to the conclusion that he must discontinue that fascinating employment for a time, and endeavor to inform his fellow-citizens how it had come to pass, that a hunker democrat, the Breckinridge candidate for the governorship of Massachusetts, a voter for Jefferson Davis in the Charleston convention, had become capable, in the course of two years, of writing General Butler's farewell address to the people of New Orleans.

Another review of General Butler's administration has seen the light. It was written by Jefferson Davis, who was so considerate as to defer its publication until he had every reason to suppose that the general was on his way home. It was, in fact, published in Richmond the day before General Butler left New Orleans, so that he never saw it until his arrival at New York. As every one of the short sentences in General Butler's address is the simplest statement of a fact, so each of the paragraphs of Jefferson Davis's proclamation which relates to General Butler's conduct is the distinct utterance of a lie.

A PROCLAMATION.

BY THE PRESIDENT OF THE CONFEDERATE STATES.

"WHEREAS, a communication was addressed on the 6th day of July last, 1862, by General Robert E. Lee, acting under the instructions of the secretary of war of the Confederate States of America, to General H. W. Halleck, commander-in-chief of the United States army, informing the latter that a report had reached this government that Wm. B. Mumford, a citizen of the Confederate States, had been executed by the United States authorities at New Orleans for having pulled down the United States flag in that city before its occupation by the United States forces, and calling for a statement of the facts, with a view of retaliation if such an outrage had really been committed under the sanction of the authorities of the United States;

"And whereas (no answer having been received to said letter), another letter was, on the 2d of August last, 1862, addressed by General Lee, under my instructions, to General Halleck, renewing the inquiries in relation to the execution of the said Mumford, with the information that, in the event of not receiving a reply within fifteen days, it would be assumed that the fact was true, and was sanctioned by the government of the United States;

"And whereas, an answer, dated on the 7th of August last, 1862, was addressed to General Lee by General H. W. Halleck, the said general-in-chief of the armies of the United States, alleging sufficient cause for failure to make early reply to said letter of the 6th of July, asserting that 'no authentic information had been received in relation to the execution of Mumford; but measures will be immediately taken to ascertain the facts of the alleged execution,' and promising that General Lee should be duly informed thereof;

"And whereas, on the 26th of November last, 1862, another letter was addressed, under my instructions, by Robert Ould, Confederate agent for the exchange of prisoners, under the cartel between the two governments, to Lieutenant-Colonel W. H. Ludlow, agent of the United States under said cartel, informing him that the explanation promised in the said letter of General Halleck, of 7th of August last, had not yet been received, and that if no answer was sent to the government within fifteen days from the delivery of this last communication, it would be considered that an answer is declined;

"And whereas, by a letter dated on the 3d day of the present month of December, the said Lieutenant-Colonel Ludlow apprised the said Robert Ould that the above recited communication of the 19th of November had been received and forwarded to the secretary of war of the United States; and whereas, this last delay of fifteen days allowed for answer has elapsed, and no answer has been received;

"And whereas, in addition to the tacit admission resulting from the above refusal to answer, I have received evidence fully establishing the truth of the fact that the said William B. Mumford, a citizen of the Confederacy, was actually and publicly executed, in cold blood, by hanging, after the occupation of the city of New Orleans by the forces under General Benjamin F. Butler, when said Mumford was an unresisting and non-combatant captive, and for no offense even alleged to have been committed by him subsequent to the date of the capture of the said city;

"And whereas, the silence of the government of the United States, and its maintaining of said Butler in high office under its authority for many months after his commission of an act that can be viewed in no other light than as a deliberate murder, as well as of numerous other outrages and atrocities hereafter to be mentioned, afford evidence too conclusive that the said government sanctions the conduct of the said Butler, and is determined that he shall remain unpunished for these crimes;

"Now, therefore, I, Jefferson Davis, President of the Confederate States of America, and in their name, do pronounce and declare the said Benjamin F. Butler to be a felon, deserving of capital punishment. I do order that he shall no longer be considered or treated simply as a public enemy of the Confederate States of America, but as an outlaw and common enemy of mankind, and that, in the event of his capture, the officer in command of the capturing force do cause him to be immediately executed by hanging.

"And I do farther order that no commissioned officer of the United States, taken captive, shall be released on parole, before exchanged, until the said Butler shall have met with due punishment for his crimes.

"And whereas, the hostilities waged against this Confederacy by the forces of the United States, under the command of said Benjamin F. Butler, have borne no resemblance to such warfare as is alone permissible by the rules of international law or the usages of civilization, but have been characterized by repeated atrocities and outrages, among the large number of which the following may be cited as examples:

"Peaceful and aged citizens, unresisting captives and non-combatants, have been confined at hard labor, with hard chains attached to their limbs, and are still so held, in dungeons and fortresses.

"Others have been submitted to a like degrading punishment for selling medicines to the sick soldiers of the Confederacy.

"The soldiers of the United States have been invited and encouraged in general orders to insult and outrage the wives, the mothers, and the sisters of our citizens.

"Helpless women have been torn from their homes, and subjected to solitary confinement, some in fortresses and prisons, and one especially on an island of barren sand, under a tropical sun; have been fed with loathsome rations that have been condemned as unfit for soldiers, and have been exposed to the vilest insults.

"Prisoners of war, who surrendered to the naval forces of the United States, on agreement that they should be released on parole, have been seized and kept in close confinement.

"Repeated pretexts have been sought or invented for plundering the inhabitants of a captured city, by fines levied and collected under threats of imprisoning recusants at hard labor with ball and chain. The entire population of New Orleans have been forced to elect between starvation by the confiscation of all their property and taking an oath against conscience to bear allegiance to the invader of their country.

"Egress from the city has been refused to those whose fortitude withstood the test, and even to lone and aged women, and to helpless children;

and, after being ejected from their homes and robbed of their property, they have been left to starve in the streets or subsist on charity.

"The slaves have been driven from the plantations in the neighborhood of New Orleans until their owners would consent to share their crops with the commanding general, his brother, Andrew J. Butler, and other officers; and when such consent had been extorted, the slaves have been restored to the plantations, and there compelled to work under the bayonets of the guards of United States soldiers. Where that partnership was refused, armed expeditions have been sent to the plantations to rob them of everything that was susceptible of removal.

"And even slaves, too aged or infirm for work, have, in spite of their entreaties, been forced from the homes provided by their owners, and driven to wander helpless on the highway.

"By a recent General Order No. 91, the entire property in that part of Louisiana west of the Mississippi river has been sequestrated for confiscation, and officers have been assigned to duty, with orders to gather up and collect the personal property, and turn over to the proper officers, upon their receipts, such of said property as may be required for the use of the United States army; to collect together all the other personal property and bring the same to New Orleans, and cause it to be sold at public auction to highest bidders—an order which, if executed, condemns to punishment, by starvation, at least a quarter of a million of human beings, of all ages, sexes, and conditions, and of which the execution, although forbidden to military officers by the orders of President Lincoln, is in accordance with the confiscation law of our enemies, which he has effected to be enforced through the agency of civil officials.

"And, finally, the African slaves have not only been incited to insurrection by every license and encouragement, but numbers of them have actually been armed for a servile war—a war in its nature far exceeding the horrors and most merciless atrocities of savages.

"And whereas, the officers under command of the said Butler have been, in many instances, active and zealous agents in the commission of these crimes, and no instance is known of the refusal of any one of them to participate in the outrages above narrated;

"And whereas, the president of the United States has, by public and official declarations, signified not only his approval of the effort to excite servile war within the Confederacy, but his intention to give aid and encouragement thereto, if these independent states shall continue to refuse submission to a foreign power after the 1st day of January next, and has thus made known that all appeal to the law of nations, the dictates of reason, and the instincts of humanity would be addressed in vain to our enemies, and that they can be deterred from the commission of these crimes only by the terrors of just retribution;

"Now, therefore, I, Jefferson Davis, president of the Confederate States of America, and acting by their authority, appealing to the Divine Judge in attestation that their conduct is not guided by the passion of revenge, but that they reluctantly yield to the solemn duty of redressing, by necessary severity, crimes of which their citizens are the victims, do issue this my proclamation, and, by virtue of my authority as commander-in-chief of the armies of the Confederate States, do order—

"*First*—That all commissioned officers in the command of said Benjamin F. Butler be declared not entitled to be considered as soldiers engaged in honorable warfare, but as robbers and criminals, deserving death; and that they and each of them be, whenever captured, reserved for execution.

"*Second*—That the private soldiers and non-commissioned officers in the army of said Butler be considered as only the instruments used for the commission of crimes perpetrated by his orders, and not as free agents; that they, therefore, be treated when captured as prisoners of war, with kindness and humanity, and be sent home on the usual parole that they will in no manner aid or serve the United States in any capacity during the continuance of this war, unless duly exchanged.

"*Third*—That all negro slaves captured in arms be at once delivered over to the executive authorities of the respective states to which they belong, to be dealt with according to the law of said states.

"*Fourth*—That the like orders be issued in all cases with respect to the commissioned officers of the United States when found serving in company with said slaves in insurrection against the authorities of the different states of this Confederacy.

"In testimony whereof, I have signed these presents, and caused the seal of the Confederate States of America to be affixed thereto, at the city of Richmond, on the 23d day of December, in the year of our Lord one thousand eight hundred and sixty-two.

"JEFFERSON DAVIS.

"By the President.

"J. P. BENJAMIN, *Secretary of State.*"

All unconscious of this fulmination, General Butler engaged passage in an unarmed transport. On the morning of his departure, December 24th, the levee was crowded with a concourse of people extremely different in their demeanor and their feelings from the angry and tumultuous throng which howled defiance at him when he landed on the first of May. He spent his last hour with Admiral Farragut on board the flag-ship Hartford, endeared to both of them by glorious recollections. "Admiral Farragut is one of the men I love," the general frequently remarks. He had given the admiral a salute when the news came of his promotion to his present nobly-won rank in the naval service, and the admiral, in acknowledging the honor done him, had promised to return the compliment, with "interest," on the first opportunity. So, amid the thunder of the Hartford's great guns, mingling with that of a battery on shore, and the cheers of a great crowd of soldiers and citizens, the general and his family waved farewell to New Orleans.

On the voyage home, he passed within six hours sail of the Alabama—a fact which derives some interest from such paragraphs as the following:

"TEN THOUSAND DOLLARS REWARD!—$10,000!—President Davis having proclaimed Benjamin F. Butler, of Massachusetts, to be a felon, deserving of capital punishment, for the deliberate murder of Wm. B. Mumford, a citizen of the Confederate States at New Orleans; and having ordered that the said Benjamin F. Butler be considered or treated as an outlaw and common enemy of mankind, and that, in the event of his capture, the officer in command of the capturing force do cause him to be immediately executed by hanging, the undersigned hereby offers a reward of ten thousand dollars ($10,000) for the capture and delivery of the said Benjamin F. Butler, dead or alive, to any proper Confederate authority.

"RICHARD YEADON.

"CHARLESTON, S. C., *January* 1."

"A daughter of South Carolina writes to the Charleston *Courier* from Darlington District:

"'I propose to spin the thread to make the cord to execute the order of our noble president, Davis, when old Butler is caught, and my daughter asks that she may be allowed to adjust it around his neck.'"

After the departure of General Butler from New Orleans, his successor gave a fair trial to the policy of conciliation. Its failure was immediate, complete, and undeniable. "These southern people," remarks an English writer who went to New Orleans with General Banks, "with their oriental civilization and institution, cherish something of the eastern impression that kindness and conciliation imply weakness, originating in a fear of inflicting punishment. They hated Butler and feared him; now the more foolish sort hope for a certain amount of impunity to the treason yet latent among them." General Banks was obliged to abandon the attempt to win the enemies of his country by soft words and lenient measures. The testimony of notorious and unquestionable facts has shown the country, that, in so far as General Banks has adopted the policy of his predecessor, his administration of the Department of the Gulf has been successful, and that, in so far as he has essentially departed from that policy, his administration has been a failure. I had collected a great deal of evidence on this point, but as every witness tells the same story, and the facts are familiar to most of us, I will not increase the magnitude of this too portly volume by detailing it. The Iron Hand, and that alone, till slavery is everywhere abolished, will keep down the insolent and remorseless faction who have brought such woful and wide-spread ruin upon the southern states. Slavery dead, the bitterness of that faction is as harmless as a cooing dove. Jefferson Davis, representing *free* Mississippi, would be obnoxious in the senate itself. To kill slavery is to extract the poison from the fangs of all those deadly foes of their country and their kind. Till that is done, there is no safety but in the iron rule.

CHAPTER XXXIII.

AT HOME.

And why was he recalled from the Department of the Gulf? It was natural that the general himself should feel some curiosity upon this subject. His curiosity has not been gratified.

Upon reaching New York, he found a letter from the president, requesting his presence at Washington. He was received by all the members of the government with the cordiality and consideration due to his eminent services. He asked the president the reason of his recall, and the president referred him to the secretary of state and the secretary of war, who, he said, had recommended the measure. The general then turned to Mr. Stanton. Mr. Stanton replied, that the reason was one which did not imply, on the part of the government, any want of confidence in his honor as a man, or in his ability as a commander.

"Well," said the general, "you have now told me what I was *not* recalled for. I now ask you to tell me what I *was* recalled for."

"You and I," answered Mr. Stanton, laughing, "are both lawyers, and it is of no use you're filing a bill of discovery upon *me*, for I sha'n't tell you."

And that is all the explanation which the government has vouchsafed to him. We are justified, however, in concluding, that he was recalled for the purpose of conciliating the French government, which had expressed disapproval of his course toward the "foreign neutrals" of Louisiana.

The question then occurs: Has the French government been conciliated? Has the policy of conciliation been successful? Has it done any good to deprive the country of the services of one of its ablest administrators? The recent scenes in the harbor of Brest appear to answer the question.

General Butler's claim to be the senior major-general chanced to become a subject of conversation at the White House on this occasion. Without having bestowed much thought upon the matter, he had innocently taken it for granted that a major-general, who had won his rank and received his commission several weeks before any other major-general had been appointed, must necessarily be the senior major-general. "The president," as he afterward remarked in the formal statement of his claim, requested by the secretary of war, "has power to do many things; but it has been said that even 'an act of parliament could not make one's uncle his aunt.' How then can the president make a junior officer a senior officer in the same grade? I grant that the president can put the junior in command of the senior, but it took an act of congress to enable the president to do that. But there is no act of congress which has or can settle seniority of rank otherwise than as the almanac, taking note of the lapse of time, has settled it."

The president said that he knew nothing about the dates of the several commissions.

"I only know," said he, "that I gave you your commission the first of anybody."

The board of officers, to whom the question was referred, decided that the president was not bound by the almanac in dating commissions, and *could* make a junior senior if he pleased. Consequently, General McClellan, General Fremont, General Dix, and General Banks, all of whom were appointed many weeks after General Butler, take rank before him. This is a small matter, hardly worth mentioning. It is merely one instance more of the systematic snubbing with which one of the very few men of first-rate executive ability in the public service has been rewarded.

In conversing with the president upon the negro question, the general said that if it was considered necessary to abolitionize the whole army, it was only necessary to give each corps a turn of service in the extreme south, where, as General Phelps remarked, the institution exists "in all its pride and gloom."

It is worthy of note, that the only members of the diplomatic corps at Washington, who called upon the general, were the Russian minister and the representative of the free city of Bremen. The friends and the foes of the United States, also the "neutral" powers, appear to have an instinctive perception of the fact, that General Butler is the Union Cause incarnate.

The people, I need not say, gave the returning general a reception that left no doubt in his mind that his labors in the southwest were understood and appreciated by his fellow-citizens. Baltimore, Washington, New York, Boston, Lowell, Philadelphia, Harrisburgh, and Portland, have each received him with every circumstance which could enhance the dignity or the *éclat* of an honorable welcome.

Or, to use the language of the *Richmond Examiner*:

"After inflicting innumerable tortures upon an innocent and unarmed people; after outraging the sensibilities of civilized humanity by his brutal treatment of women and children; after placing bayonets in the hands of slaves; after peculation the most prodigious, and lies the most infamous, he returns, reeking with crime, to his own people, and they receive him with acclamations of joy in a manner that befits him and becomes themselves. Nothing is out of keeping; his whole career and its rewards are strictly artistic in conception and in execution. He was a thief. A sword that he had stolen from a woman—the niece of the brave Twiggs—was presented to him as a reward of valor. He had violated the laws of God and man. The law-makers of the United States voted him thanks, and the preachers of the Yankee gospel of blood came to him and worshiped him. He had broken into the safes and strong boxes of merchants. The New York Chamber of Commerce gave him a dinner. He had insulted women. Things in female attire lavished harlot smiles upon him. He was a murderer, and a nation of assassins have deified him. He is at this time the representative man of a people lost to all shame, to all humanity, all honor, all virtue, all manhood. Cowards by nature, thieves upon principle, and assassins at heart, it would be marvelous, indeed, if the people of the North refused to render homage to Benjamin Butler—the beastliest, bloodiest poltroon and pickpocket the world ever saw."

Or, to borrow the words of the New York *World:*

"The warm applause with which he was greeted by a great public assembly in this Christian city, is a phenomenon as shocking to a cultivated moral sense as the mode of propagating religion in ages when the rack and the stake were approved means of grace. This discreditable applause is a new testimony to the barbarizing effects of civil war. It exemplifies the rude logic of violent passions, which, assuming a sacred end for its premises, infers that any means are justifiable for its attainment."

Or we might quote the comments of the *London Times*, since there is the most perfect accord on this subject between rebels, peace democrats and foreign neutrals.

Perhaps, however, the reader may incline to the opinion of the hundred merchants of New York, as expressed in their letter inviting the general to a public dinner:

"They share with you the conviction that there is no middle or neutral ground between loyalty and treason; that traitors against the government forfeit all rights of protection and of property; that those who persist in armed rebellion, or aid it less openly but not less effectively, must be put down and kept down by the strong hand of power and by the use of all rightful means, and that so far as may be, the sufferings of the poor and misguided, caused by the rebellion, should be visited upon the authors of their calamities. We have seen, with approbation, that in applying these principles, amidst the peculiar difficulties and embarrassments incident to your administration in your recent command, you have had the sagacity to devise, the will to execute, and the courage to enforce the measures which they demanded, and we rejoice at the success which has vindicated the wisdom and the justice of your offi cial course. In thus congratulating you upon these results, we believe that we express the feeling of all those who most earnestly desire the speedy restoration of the Union in its full integrity and power."

The public dinner was declined. "I too well know," replied the general, "the revulsion of feeling with which the soldier in the field, occupying the trenches, pacing the sentinel's weary path in the blazing heat, or watching from his cold bivouac the stars shut out by the drenching cloud, hears of feasting and merry-making at home by those who ought to bear his hardships with him, and the bitterness with which he speaks of those who, thus engaged, are wearing his uniform. Upon the scorching sand, and under the brain-trying sun of the gulf coast, I have too much shared that feeling to add one pang, however slight, to the discomfort which my fellow-soldiers suffer, doing the duties of the camp and field, by my own act, while separated momentarily from them by the exigencies of the public service."

Not the less did the city of New York respond to the sentiments of the merchants' letter. The scene at the Academy of Music, on the evening of the 2d of April, 1863, when General Butler advanced to the front of the stage, will never be forgotten by the youngest person who witnessed it. The house was crowded to the remotest standing-place of the amphitheater. The immense stage was filled with the citizens of whom New York is proudest. When the general appeared, the audience sprang to their feet, and gave, not three cheers, nor three times three and one cheer more, but a unanimous, long-sustained roar of cheers, with a universal waving of hats and handkerchiefs. Several minutes elapsed before silence was restored. General Butler spoke for two hours, interrupted at every other sentence with enthusiastic applause. At Boston, in old Faneuil Hall, he could not escape from the crowd till he had shaken three thousand hands.

Since the return of General Butler to the North, he has, on all occasions, public and private, given to the administration a most hearty and unwavering support. A man less magnanimous, or less patriotic, would have been tempted to, at least, a silent resentment at the censure of his conduct implied in his sudden and unexplained recall, and the repeated refusal of the government to comply with the desire expressed on so many occasions for his employment in the cabinet and in the field. On the contrary, he has used the whole of his influence in sustaining the government.

"The present government," he said, in his speech of April 2d, at New York, "was not the government of my choice. I did not vote for it, nor for any part of it; but it is the government of my country; it is the only organ by which I can exert the force of the country to protect its integrity; and as long as I believe that government to be honestly administered, I will throw a mantle over any mistakes that I may think it has made, and support it heartily, with hand and purse, so help me God! I have no loyalty to any man or men. My loyalty is to the government; and it makes no difference to me who the people have chosen to administer the government. So long as the choice has been constitutionally made, and the persons so chosen hold their places and powers, I am a traitor and a false man if I falter in my support. This is what I understand to be loyalty to a government."

Perhaps a few sentences and paragraphs from General Butler's recent speeches may be in place here, to indicate his present opinions upon the momentous issues upon which the people are called, from time to time, to express their judgment.

SLAVERY.

"I think I may say that the principal members of my staff, and the prominent officers of my regiments, without any exception, went out to New Orleans hunker democrats of the hunkerest sort; for it was but natural that I should draw around me those whose views were similar to my own; and every individual of the number has come to precisely the same belief on the question of slavery, as I put forth in my farewell address to the people of New Orleans. This change came about from seeing what all of them saw, day by day. In this war the entire property of the South is against us, because almost the entire property of the South is bound up in that institution. This is a well-known fact, probably; but I did not become fully aware of it until I had spent some time in New Orleans. The South has $163,000,000 of taxable property in slaves, and $163,000,000 in all other kinds of property. And this was the cause why the merchants of New Orleans had not remained loyal. They found themselves ruined—all their property being loaned upon planters' notes, and mortgages upon plantations and slaves, all of which property is now worthless. Again I learned, what I did not know before, that this is not a rebellion against *us*, but simply a rebellion to perpetuate power in the hands of a few slave-holders. At first

I did not believe that slavery was the cause of the rebellion, but attributed it to Davis, Slidell, and others, who had brought it about to make political triumphs by which to regain their former ascendency. The rebellion is against the humble and poorer classes; and there were in the South large numbers of secret societies dealing in cabalistic signs, organized for the purpose of perpetuating the power of the rich over the poor. It was feared that these common people would come into power, and that three or four hundred thousand men could not hold out against eight millions. The first movement of these men was to make land the basis of political power, and that was not enough, for land could not be owned by many persons. Then they annexed land to slaves, and divided the property into movable and immovable.

"I am not generally accused of being a humanitarian—at least, not by my southern friends. When I saw the utter demoralization of the people, resulting from slavery, it struck me that it was an institution which should be thrust out of the Union. I had, on reading Mrs. Stowe's book—Uncle Tom's Cabin—believed it to be an overdrawn, highly-wrought picture of southern life; but I have seen with my own eyes, and heard with my own ears, many things which go beyond her book, as much as her book does beyond an ordinary school-girl's novel. * * * * *

"Yes, no right-minded man could be sent to New Orleans without returning an unconditional anti-slavery man, even though the roof of the houses were not taken off, and the full extent of the corruption exposed.

"The war can only be successfully prosecuted by the destruction of slavery, which was made the corner-stone of the confederacy. This is the second time in the history of the world that a rebellion of property-holders against the lower classes and against the government was ever carried on. The Hungarian rebellion was one of that kind, and that failed, as must every rebellion of men of property against government and against the rights of the many. One of the greatest arguments which I can find against slavery is the demoralizing influences it exerts upon the lower white classes, who were brought into secession by the hundred because they ignorantly supposed that great wrong was to be done them by the Lincoln government, as they termed it, if the North succeeded. Therefore, if you meet an old hunker democrat, and send him for sixty days to New Orleans, and he comes back a hunker still, he is merely incorrigible. There is one thing about the president's edict of emancipation to which I would call attention. In Louisiana he had excepted from freedom about eighty-seven thousand slaves. These comprise all the negroes held in the Lafourche district, who have been emancipated already for some time under the law which frees slaves taken in rebellious territory by our armies. Others of these negroes had been freed by the proclamation of September, which declared all slaves to be free whose owners should be in arms on the first of January. The slaves of Frenchmen were free because the *Code Civile* expressly prohibits a Frenchman from holding slaves, and, by the 7th and 8th Victoria, every Englishman holding slaves subjects himself to a penalty of $500 for each. Now, take the negroes of secessionists, Frenchmen and Englishmen out of the eighty-seven thousand, and the number is reduced to an infinitesimal portion of those excepted. This fact came to my knowledge from having required every inhabitant in the city to register his nationality. After all these names had been fairly registered, I explained these laws to the English and French consuls, and thus replied to demands which had been made by English and French residents of Louisiana upon the government for slaves alleged to have been seized."*

THE WAR DEBT.

"A question has been a thousand times asked me since I arrived home, how is this great war debt to be paid? That speaks to the material interests. How can we ever be able to pay this war debt? Who can pay it? Who shall pay it? Shall we tax the coming generations? Shall we overtax ourselves? For one—and I speak as a citizen to citizens—I think I can see clearly a way in which this great expense can be paid by those who ought to pay it, and be borne by those who ought to bear it. Let us bring the South into subjection to the Union. We have offered them equality. If they choose it, let them have it. But, at all events, they must come under the power of the Union. And when once this war is closed by that subjugation, if you please, if necessary, then the increased productions of the great staples of the South, cotton and tobacco—with which we ought, and can, and shall supply the world—this increased production, by the immigration of white men into the South, where labor shall be honorable as it is here, will pay the debt. With the millions of hogsheads of the one, and the millions of bales of the other, and with a proper internal tax, which shall be paid by England and France, who have largely caused this mischief, this debt will be paid. Without stopping to be didactic or to discuss principles here, let us examine this matter for a moment. They are willing to pay fifty and sixty cents a pound for cotton; the past has demonstrated that even by the uneconomical use of slave labor, it can be profitably raised—ay, profitably beyond all conception of agricultural profit here—at ten cents a pound. A simple impost of ten cents a pound, which will increase it to twenty cents only, will pay the interest of a war debt double what it is to-day. And that cotton can be more profitably raised under free labor than under slave labor, no man who has examined the subject doubts. By the imposition of this tax those men who fitted out the Alabama and sent her forth to prey upon our commerce, will be

* Speech at Fifth Avenue Hotel, New York, *Jan.* 8, 1863.

compelled by the laws of trade and the laws of nations to pay for the mischief they have done. So that when we look around in this country, which has just begun to put forth her strength, because no country has ever come to her full strength until her institutions have proved themselves strong enough to govern the country against the will, even the voluntary will of the people—when this government, which has now demonstrated itself to be the strongest government in the world, puts forth her strength as to men, and when this country of ours, richer and more abundant in its harvests and in its productions than any other country on earth, puts forth her riches, we have a strength in men, we have an amount in money, to battle the world for liberty, and for the freedom to do, in the borders of the United States and on the continent of America, that which God, when he sent us forth as a missionary nation, intended we should do. So, allow me to return your words of congratulation and your words of welcome, with words of good cheer. Be of good cheer! God gave us this continent to civilize and to free, as an example to the nations of the earth; and if He has struck us in His wrath, because we have halted in our work, let us begin again and go on, not doubting that we shall have His blessing to the end. Be, therefore, I say, of good cheer; there can be no doubt of this issue. We feel the struggle; we feel what it costs to carry on this war. Go with me to Louisiana—go with me to the South, and you shall see what it costs our enemies to carry on this war; and you will have no doubt, as I have none, of the result of this unhappy strife, out of which the nation shall come stronger, better, purified, North and South—better than ever before."*

NO DANGER FROM THE ARMY.

"There never has been any division of sentiment in the army itself. They have always been for the Union unconditionally, for the government and the laws at any and all times. And who are this army? Are they men different from us? Not at all. I see some here that have come back from the army, and are now waiting to recover their health to go back and join that army. Are they to be any different on the banks of the Potomac or in the marshes of Louisiana, or struggling with the turbid current of the Mississippi than they are here? Are our sons, our brothers, to have different thoughts and different feelings from us, simply because to-day they wear blue and to-morrow they wear black, or to-day they wear black and to-morrow they wear blue? Not at all. They are from us, they are of us, they are with us. The same love of liberty, ay, and you will pardon me for saying it, a little more love for the Union, have caused them to go out than has actuated those who have stayed behind. The same desire to

* Speech at Boston, *Jan.* 13, 1863.

see the constitution restored has sent them out that animates us, the same love of good government, the same faith in this great experiment of freedom and free government that actuates us actuates them, and there need be no trouble, it seems to me, in the mind of any man upon the question of what is the army to do. There need be no fears. I have seen men, too, good, virtuous, candid, upright, patriotic men, who seem to feel this great increase of the army to be somewhat dangerous to our liberties. Is the army to take away their own liberties? is the army to destroy their own country? is the army to do anything that patriotic men won't do? Oh, no; they answer with universal accord upon that subject. Then where is the danger men see? Why, in the olden time, at the head of large armies, some ambitious man, some ambitious military leader, gets the control of the army and destroys the liberty of the country; but the difficulty is, the examples of nations in the old world are by no means analogies for this. No general of the old world ever commanded such an army; no general of the old world ever had such a country; no general of the old world ever had such a government to fight for, to fight with, to fight under, or will have ever and for ever; and no general of the old world, no general thus far on the face of the earth ever was in a country, where, by elevating his country first, last, and all the time, he might more surely elevate himself. But we do not depend upon either the patriotism, or the ability, or the prudence, or the courage of any one man; we depend upon the courage, the patriotism, and the intelligence of this half million of men in the army who know that the place to regulate government affairs is in the ballot-box, and who, as long as they can get matters regulated, and can have fair play through the ballot-box, will go home and be much more ready to use the ballot-box than the cartridge-box.

"Therefore, I say to you, sir, let no man have fear on this subject. There are no better friends of free institutions, there are no more intelligent, no truer men and citizens at home and in peace than in the army of the United States."*

RECONSTRUCTION.

"I am not for the Union as it was. I have the honor to say, as a democrat, and an Andrew Jackson democrat, I am not for the Union to be again as it was. Understand me, I was for the Union as it was, because I saw, or thought I saw, the troubles in the future which have burst upon us; but having undergone those troubles, having spent all this blood and this treasure, I do not mean to go back again and be cheek to jole, as I was before with South Carolina, if I can help it. Mark me now; let no man misunderstand me; and I repeat, lest I may be misunderstood (for there are none so difficult to understand as those that don't want to)—mark me

* Speech at Boston, *April*, 1863.

again, I say, I do not mean to give up a single inch of the soil of South Carolina. If I had been living at that time, and had the position, the will, and the ability, I would have dealt with South Carolina as Jackson did, and kept her in the Union at all hazards; but now she has gone out, and I will take care that when she comes in again she will come in better behaved; that she shall no longer be the fire-brand of the Union, ay, that she shall enjoy what her people never yet enjoyed, the blessings of a republican form of government. And, therefore, in that view I am not for the reconstruction of the Union as it was. I have spent treasure and blood enough upon it, in conjunction with my fellow-citizens, to make it a little better, and I think we can have a better Union. It was good enough if it had been let alone. The old house was good enough for me, but the South pulled it down, and I propose, when we build it up, to build it up with all the modern improvements. Another one of the logical sequences, it seems to me, that follow inexorably, and is not to be shunned, from the proposition that we are dealing with alien enemies, what is our duty with regard to the confiscation of their property? And that would seem to me to be very easy of settlement under the constitution, and without any discussion, if my first proposition is right. Hasn't it been held from the beginning of the world down to this day, from the time the Israelites took possession of the land of Canaan, which they got from alien enemies, hasn't it been held that the whole of the property of those alien enemies belongs to the conqueror, and that it has been at his mercy and his clemency what should be done with it? And for one, I would take it and give to the loyal man, who was loyal from the heart, at the South, enough to make him as well as he was before, and I would take the balance of it and distribute it among the volunteer soldiers who have gone forth in the service of their country; and so far as I know them, if we should settle South Carolina with them, in the course of a few years I should be quite willing to receive her back into the Union."*

ARMING THE NEGROES.

"If these men are alien enemies, is there any objection that you know of, and if so state it, to our arming one portion of that foreign country against the other, while they are fighting us? Suppose we were at war with England, who here would get up in New York and say we must not arm the Irish, lest they should hurt some Englishman? Well, at one time, not very far gone, all those Englishmen were our grandfathers' brothers. Either they or we erred; but we are now separate nations, arising out of the contest. So again I say, if you will look carefully you will see that there can be no objection for another reason. There is no law, either of war or of international law, or law of governmental action that I know of, which prevents

* Speech at New York, *April* 2, 1863.

a country arming any portion of its citizens or its subjects for the defense of that portion, or of any other, and they become (if they do not take part with those rebels) simply our citizens, residing upon our territory, which at the present hour is usurped by our enemies. At this moment, and in the waning hour, I do not propose to discuss, more than to hint at these various subjects. But there is one question that I have been so often asked, that I want to make an answer to, once for all, and when I have answered it to everybody, nobody will ask me again, and that is this (and most frequently am I asked that question by my old democratic friends): 'Why, General Butler, what is your experience? Will the negroes fight?' To that I have to answer, that upon that subject I have no personal experience. I left the Department of the Gulf before they were fairly brought into action; but they did fight under Jackson at Chalmette. More than that, I will bring in some other man to answer that question. Let Napoleon III. answer it, who has hired them to do what the veterans of the Crimea can not do—to whip the Mexicans. I will answer it in another form. Let the veterans of Napoleon the First, under his brother-in-law, Le Clerc, who were whipped out of St. Domingo by them, tell whether they will fight or not. I will ask you to remember it in another form still. What has been the demoralizing effect upon them as a race by their contact with the white man, I know not; but I can not forget that they and their fathers would not have been slaves except they were captives of war in their own countries, in hand to hand fights among the several chiefs, and were sold into slavery because they were captives in war. They would fight at some time, and if you want to know any more about it, I can only advise you to try them."*

THE QUESTION BEFORE US.

"No Union man wants to abrogate the old constitution. It is good enough. The only question is, how can we take back an absconding member of the firm under the old articles of agreement." †

It has been mentioned in a previous chapter that, at the time of the seizure of Mason and Slidell, General Butler was of opinion that they ought not to be given up. It is proper to record here, that his more mature opinion, as expressed in his speech of April 2d, 1863, is that "we acted wisely at that time in not getting into serious trouble with England." At the same time, he avowed the conviction that the United States ought not to continue to hold friendly relations with a power in practical alliance with the rebel

* Speech at New York, *April* 2, 1863.

† Speech at Harrisburgh, *September*, 1863.

government. He advised a declaration of non-intercourse with England.

"England told us what to do when we took Mason and Slidell, and she thought there was a likelihood to be a war. She stopped exportation of those articles which she thought we wanted, and which she had allowed to be exported before. Let us do the same thing. Let us proclaim non-intercourse, so that no ounce of food from the United States shall ever by any accident get into an Englishman's mouth until this rebellion ceases. I say again, let us proclaim non-intercourse, so that no ounce of food shall by any accident get into an Englishman's mouth until these piracies are stopped. That we have a right to do; and when we ever do do it, my word for it, they will find out where these vessels are going to, and they will write to the Emperor of China."

CHAPTER XXXV.

SUMMARY.

The speciality of General Butler is this: He is a great achiever. He is the victorious kind of man. He is that combination of qualities and powers which is most potent in bringing things to pass. Upon reviewing his life, we find that he has been signally successful in the undertakings which have seriously tasked his powers.

A good example of his ready adaptation of means to ends, has just been related to me by one of his legal friends. A wealthy corporation in New England refused to pay for a bridge, on the ground that the contractor had been a few days behind the stipulated time in completing it. General Butler was retained on behalf of the contractor. Aware that he really had no case, though the delay in finishing the bridge was abundantly excusable, he brought the cause to the bar of public opinion. In other words, he *told the story* to every man and group of men whom chance threw in his way. He caused endless paragraphs upon the subject to be inserted in the newspapers. The bridge was justly commended as a most admirable piece of work, and remarks were appended upon the soullessness of a corporation, which could avail itself of the letter of a contract to deprive a fellow-citizen of the reward of his labors. In a word, he enlisted the feelings and the judgment of the whole community on the side of the contractor, and thus shamed the corporation into a compromise. You may call this, if you please, an illegitimate mode of proceeding for a learned advocate. It remains true, nevertheless, that the plan adopted answered the end proposed, and that the end proposed was justice.

It may be profitable to inquire what is the secret of General Butler's success.

Brains. That is a great part of the secret. This man has understood the matter. He has been able to grasp the situation at all times, and to know what the situation required at all times. From the hour when he shook hands with Jefferson Davis, in December, 1860, to the present moment, he has never been groping in the dark, or feeling his way to a policy. And his opinion, generally scouted at the moment, has always been justified by the progress of events. He was right in getting Massachusetts ready to march. He took the right road to Washington. He was right in regarding Fortress Monroe as the base against Richmond. The flash of inspiration which pronounced the negroes contraband of war, was right. Each step in the progress of his mind upon the negro question was right at the time and in the circumstances. That single suggestion of a board to decide upon the fitness of officers, was worth all he has received from the government. His order, making officers pay for the pillage committed by their men, was another masterly stroke. Better still, perhaps, it would be to make the whole regiment responsible—privates as well as officers. At New Orleans, he was magnificently right, both in theory and in practice. Every day brought forth some new proof of the fertility of his mind—of his genius for governing. That policy of isolating, crippling, and destroying the malignants, and of raising in the scale of being the laboring multitude, white, black, or yellow, is the only policy which can ever make the country A NATION, homogeneous, united, powerful and free. No man has, no man can, point out another path to permanent reconstruction. To dethrone the false king, Minority, and to crown in his stead the true king, Majority—that was the scheme attempted in Louisiana. But one thing is wanting to its complete success—the total abolition of slavery, which constitutes the power of the ruling faction, and keeps in heathenish bondage every poor man in the South, whatever his color.

General Butler, on the other hand, is no dreamer or theorizer. Dreamers and theorizers are good and helpful; but he is not one of them. His forte is to devise expedients to meet a new state of things, or to effect a special purpose. He is singularly happy in framing a measure, on the spur of the moment, which precisely answers the end proposed, and works good in many directions not specially contemplated. His plan for feeding the poor of New Orleans, for example, besides effecting the main purpose of saving thousands from starvation, brought home to the authors of their ruin a part of the ill-consequences of their conduct, and chimed in with his general policy of suppressing one class and raising another.

Brains are the great secret. He is endowed with a large, healthy, active, instructed, experienced brain—Heaven's best gift, and the medium through which all other good gifts are given.

Courage, will, firmness, nerve—call it what you will—General Butler has it. He has not been called to face the leaden rain and iron hail of battle; but he has exhibited on every occasion the courage which the occasion required. He has shown a singular insensibility to the phantoms which play so important a part in war. He has shown the courage to go forward and meet the imaginary danger, as well as the real. He has the courage of opinion—so rare in a republic where public men all want the favor of the many. He dares accept the remote consequences of a policy. He dares to take the responsibility. He dares to incur obloquy. He dares to tell the truth, and all the truth. I venture to declare, that in the many thousand pages of his writings as an officer of the government, there is not one intentional misstatement or unfair suppression. Falsehood is the natural resort of timidity. A brave man does not lie, and need not.

Honesty. With opportunities of irregular gain, such as no other man has had since the days of Warren Hastings, his hands are spotless. He could have made a safe half million by a wink; and, if he had done so, he would have come home with a peculiar and marked reputation for integrity; because then he would have had an interest to create such a reputation, and could not have indulged the noble carelessness with regard to his good name which

27

is the privilege of a man strong in conscious rectitude. The fact that so able a man is accused of corruption, is itself a kind of proof of his honesty.

Humor. The happy word is part of the art of governing. There is apt to be a fund of humor in *good* victorious men, which enables them to get the laugh of mankind on their side. Would Lord Palmerston ever have been premier of England without his jokes, or Mr. Lincoln president of the United States unless he had first overspread acres of prairie mass-meetings with a grin? The point, humor and vivacity of General Butler's utterances have been an element of his success in the service of his country.

Faith. "After our return to the North," says one of the general's staff, "an ex-mayor of Chicago was introduced to the general at the St. Nicholas Hotel in New York. It was just at a time when our cause looked very gloomy. The mayor was evidently much depressed by the indications of national misfortune, and in a tone of great despondency asked the general—

"'Do you believe we shall ever get through this war successfully?'

"'Yes, sir,' the general answered, very decidedly.

"'Well, but how?' asked the mayor.

"'God knows, I don't; but I know He does, so I am satisfied,' the general replied.* I have often heard him reply thus to anxious questioners.

"'We ought to *march* through,' he once said; 'but we shan't; I'm afraid we shall only *tumble* through. No matter; we shall get through somehow.'"

Humanity. The papers relating to our general's military career teem with evidence that he is a kind, considerate man. He governed his soldiers strictly, but always so as to promote their best interests. He was lenient and forgiving toward offenses of inadvertence, or such as betrayed only a weakness or infirmity of nature. He was generous to the poor. He was solicitous to bestow honor where it was due. He was ingenious in devising ways of procuring promotion to deserving officers. He sympathized with the anxiety of parents for their sons in the army, and assuaged many a bleeding heart by the kind thoughtfulness with which ill news was broken to them.

Courtesy. The etiquette of his position was most punctiliously

* *Atlantic Monthly*, July, 1863.

observed; not more so toward admirals and general officers than boy lieutenants and private soldiers. To the enemies of his country he could be a roaring lion or a growling bear. The men of his command and the loyal citizens of his department enjoyed the satisfaction of knowing that their general was a gentleman. No littleness toward other commanders; only gratitude and admiration for the Farraguts, the Grants, the Rosecranses, the Meades, and all the other heroes of the war. Consideration, too, for the many able and well-intentioned men who have been less successful.

Patriotism. No man should be praised for loving his country, any more than for loving his mother. If the country is lost, we are all lost. If the country is disgraced, we all hang our heads in shame. To love one's country is a part of our natural and proper self-love. But if there is one man who has gone along more entirely than he with his country in this great struggle to preserve its life; if there is one man who has taken the great cause more deeply to heart, or striven with a purer aim to do his part in the mighty and holy work, he must, indeed, be the very model of a pure and burning patriot. Let none of us, however, claim for himself or for another any pre-eminence in patriotism. In this alone we are all agreed, that if it takes as long to restore the country as it took the Spaniards to expel the Moors from Spain (800 years), the work is to be done. If the treasury is bankrupt, no matter, it is to be done. If we have to make twenty truces, still it is to be done. If we pause, it will be only to renew the strife as soon as we have taken breath.

Brains without courage may be a delusion and a snare. To have courage without brains is to be a human bull-dog. Brains and valor without experience in human affairs, without knowledge of the world and mankind, will often lead a man far astray. Brains, valor and experience united, still require the honest heart, the lofty aim. And even all these are ineffective in times like these, unless there is also an enormous capacity for labor. But when a man presents himself to view who possesses a fertile genius, courage, knowledge, experience, patriotism and honesty, with a soundness of bodily constitution that gives him the complete use of all his powers, a country must be rich indeed in able men, if it can afford, at a time of public danger, to dispense with his services.

APPENDIX.

GENERAL M. JEFF. THOMPSON.

The following correspondence has recently passed between General Butler and General Jeff. Thompson of the Confederate army, now a prisoner of war. General Thompson was long General Butler's principal adversary in Louisiana, as he was in command of the largest Confederate force in the vicinity of New Orleans. General Butler having been kind enough to send me the letters, as a matter of curiosity, I have taken the liberty to consider them part of the documents relating to the Department of the Gulf. The correspondence tends to show that, when the war is over, the people of the North and the people of the South will be astonished to find what excellent and cordial friends they are, after thirty years of alienation.

GENERAL THOMPSON TO GENERAL BUTLER.

"Depôt of Prisoners,
"Johnson's Island, near Sandusky, Ohio,
"*September* 28, 1863.

"Major-General B. F. Butler, U. S. A., Washington, D. C.:

"General:—About this time last year, the fortunes of war placed in my hands a Captain Thornton of your command, wounded and a prisoner of war. You will remember that I sent Captain Thornton on parole back to New Orleans, in your yacht. I promised Captain Thornton that, if I was ever captured, I would notify him of my whereabouts, that he might return the favors which *he thought* I extended to him.

"I do not think that Captain Thornton is under any obligations to me, as I simply acted toward him as I have to all gentlemen who have been so unfortunate as to be captured by me; but, in conformity with my promise, I would like to let him know that I am here; and as I do not know his address, and understanding at the time that he was a *personal* friend of yours, I hope it will not be presuming to request you to forward him this letter, let me know his address, or otherwise let him know that I am at this prison, as may be most convenient or agreeable to yourself.

"Yours most respectfully,
"M. Jeff. Thompson, *Brigadier-General, M. S. G.*"

GENERAL BUTLER TO GENERAL THOMPSON.

"LOWELL, MASS., *October* 6, 1863.

"Brigadier-General M. JEFF. THOMPSON:

"GENERAL:—Your note addressed to me was received to-day. I will forward it to Captain Thornton, now on Brigadier-General Shepley's staff at New Orleans, as you request.

"I retain a lively sense of the courtesy and urbanity with which you conducted operations, when in command, opposed to me in Louisiana, and desire again, as before, to thank you for your kindness to Captain Thornton in sending him home wounded, by which kindness I have no doubt his life was saved.

"Although an outlaw, by the proclamation of those whom you serve, for acts which no one knows more surely than yourself were untruly reported and unjustly construed, I will endeavor to have your imprisonment lightened, or commuted, if possible.

"I have, therefore, taken the liberty to forward a copy of your communication to the war department, with a note, of which the inclosed shows the contents.

"Sympathizing with you that the fortune of war has made you a prisoner, yet you will pardon me when I add, that I am glad the enemies of my country are deprived of the services of so effective an officer.

"Respectfully, your obedient servant,

"BENJ. F. BUTLER."

GENERAL BUTLER TO THE OFFICER COMMANDING AT JOHNSON'S ISLAND.

"LOWELL, MASS., *October* 6, 1863.

"To the Officer Commanding Dépôt of Prisoners, at Johnson's Island, near Sandusky, Ohio:

"SIR:—Inclosed please find an unsealed note, to General M. Jeff. Thompson, now, as I am informed, a prisoner under your charge. If not inconsistent with the regulations of your dépôt, please deliver it. You will read it, if agreeable to you, and will learn therefrom, that General Thompson showed great kindness to wounded officers and soldiers that fell into his hands; and I beg leave to bespeak for him all the indulgence and liberty which can be shown him consistently with your discipline.

"Please inform me if General Thompson is destitute, so that he can not supply himself with any little comforts that would alleviate and accord with his situation.

"Most truly yours,

"BENJ. F. BUTLER."

GENERAL BUTLER TO THE SECRETARY OF WAR.

"LOWELL, MASS., *October* 6, 1863.

"Hon. E. M. STANTON, Secretary of War:

"SIR:—I have the honor to inclose a note, received from Brigadier-General M. Jeff. Thompson, whom I knew in command of the forces immediately opposed to me at Pontchatoula, on the northern side of Lake Pontchartrain, when I was in command in the Department of the Gulf. The original I have sent, as requested, to Captain Thornton, on Brigadier-General Geo. F. Shepley's staff.

"Captain Thornton, a most valuable, brave, and efficient officer, was grievously wounded, with at least seven bullet holes through his clothes and various parts of his body, in the attack on Pontchatoula in September of last year, under the command of the late lamented Major-General Strong, then my chief of staff. Captain Thornton was left in the hands of the enemy, and received of General Thompson every care and kindness, and, at my request, was sent to New Orleans upon his parole. This courteous consideration on the part of General Thompson, I have no doubt, enabled us, with the blessing of heaven, to save Captain Thornton's valuable life. General Thompson is now a prisoner at Johnson's Island, near Sandusky, Ohio. If not inconsistent with public service, I most earnestly ask that General Thompson may be released upon his parole.

"While I can testify to the uniform urbanity and courtesy with which all the operations of General Thompson were conducted, I am most decidedly of opinion that the kindness which he showed to Captain Thornton alone should entitle him to every possible consideration. That kindness was not alone given to the officers, but the wounded men spoke of his treatment with the utmost gratitude.

"I found him a troublesome enemy enough, but his humanity, which was in contrast with the conduct of General Taylor, leads me to ask this favor for him at the hands of the government.

"As I am not much in the habit of asking leniency for rebels, I trust the war department will take it as a guaranty that this is a proper case for the extension of every indulgence.

"I am, most respectfully, your obedient servant,

"BENJ. F. BUTLER, *Major-General U. S. Vols.*"

GENERAL THOMPSON TO GENERAL BUTLER.

"DEPÔT OF PRISONERS OF WAR,
"JOHNSON'S ISLAND, NEAR SANDUSKY, OHIO,
"*October* 12, 1863.

"Major-General B. F. BUTLER, U. S. Vols., Lowell, Mass.:

"GENERAL:—Your kind letter of the 6th inst. was received on the 10th, but a violent headache has prevented me from answering it until now.

"I am very much obliged to you for the interest you take in my welfare, and thank you for your unsolicited and flattering application to the United States war department in my behalf, and I am also grateful for the complimentary manner in which you speak of my conduct as an officer.

"Should the United States war department prefer to 'parole' me, I will cheerfully accept it, not so much for the *restricted liberty* that it will give, as for the purpose of showing to the people of both governments that the *stories* that have been told about my being a guerilla, etc., are false; and that, with all the eccentricities and peculiarities that have been imputed to me, I have not forgotten to be a gentleman; and also that Captain Thornton and various other officers, who are under the impression that they are under obligations to me for similar favors, may feel that their government has shown a disposition to reciprocate for them.

"You say that no one more surely than myself knows that the acts for which my government blames you were untruly reported and unjustly construed. What your intentions were when you issued the 'order' which brought so much censure upon yourself, I, of course, can not tell, but I can testify, and do with pleasure, that nearly all of the many persons who passed through my lines, to and from New Orleans, during the months of August and September, 1862, spoke favorably of the treatment they had received from you, and with all my inquiries, which were constant, I did not hear of one single instance of a lady being insulted by your command.

"Thanking you again for your kindness and compliments, and hoping that your government will soon conclude to 'let us alone,'

"I am, most respectfully, your obedient servant,

"M. JEFF. THOMPSON, *Brigadier-General, M. S. G.*"

The following letter from General Thompson to his sister, recently published in the newspapers, shows that General Butler's efforts in his behalf have not been fruitless.

INTERESTING FROM JEFF. TO HIS SISTER—WHAT HE SAYS ABOUT THINGS GENERALLY.

"JOHNSON'S ISLAND, NEAR SANDUSKY, OHIO,
"SUNDAY, *Oct.* 11, 1863.

"DEAR SISTER:—I know you will be astonished at an article which appeared in the St. Louis *Republican* of the 7th inst. about me, and in which the writer speaks of letters written by me to General Grant about Emma. Of course, everybody in St. Joseph will know how false this report is; but still I feel grieved that any man should exist who is mean enough to write such an article. All know that at the beginning of the war Emma was at the asylum, and that, as soon as I heard that she was well, I sent Colonel Chappell to Cairo, to endeavor to get her sent down to me, and that, as soon as permits were granted to any one, she came down to me. I simply remind you of these facts for fear some person who is not acquainted with me may believe the slander, and that you can show them the falsity.

"I am to be offered my parole, in consideration of the courtesy and kindness which I have universally shown to all my enemies, and I may accept it, not that I care about the 'restricted liberty' that it will give, but it will show to my friends and enemies (I mean personal) that the stories that have been told about me are false, and that I have always conducted myself, especially to those who were so unfortunate as to be taken prisoners (and more especially so when wounded), as a soldier and a gentleman. I can assure you, dear sister, that, when the truth shall be told, you will never hear anything of me of which you need be ashamed, although you will probably be often mortified by reports, anecdotes, and stories that may be told upon me. I have hung and shot my own men for disobeying me, and I will do it again; but the citizens where I have commanded have never been troubled by my troops or by my orders, and many Union men were and are in my district who can testify to this fact. You would be very proud to see some letters that I have received from prominent Union men and federal generals since I have been a prisoner. I am writing thus for fear I may not have time to write again before I leave, as, should the parole arrive and I accept it, I will immediately start to Richmond or to Canada.

* * * * * * *

"I have authority to draw on George D. Prentice, of Louisville, or Major-General Benj. F. Butler, for what money I want; but should I not accept the parole, I will prefer to trust to my old personal friendship for little dribs until I am exchanged.

"You will hear through the newspapers whether I go to Canada or the Confederacy; for I would be fearful to accept the parole for the United States, as I would quarrel with half the men I met.

"Farewell, dear sister; I may not have time to write again before I may again be on the war path, and then my life is always in danger. * * *

"Your affectionate brother,

"M. JEFF. THOMPSON."

INDEX.

www.ingramcontent.com/pod-product-compliance
Lightning Source LLC
LaVergne TN
LVHW021055110826
845150LV00001B/79